*Major Problems
in Atlantic History*

MAJOR PROBLEMS IN AMERICAN HISTORY SERIES

GENERAL EDITOR
THOMAS G. PATERSON

Major Problems
in Atlantic History

DOCUMENTS AND ESSAYS

EDITED BY

ALISON GAMES
GEORGETOWN UNIVERSITY

ADAM ROTHMAN
GEORGETOWN UNIVERSITY

HOUGHTON MIFFLIN COMPANY
Boston   New York

Publisher: Suzanne Jeans
Sponsoring Editor: Jeffrey Greene
Senior Marketing Manager: Katherine Bates
Senior Project Editor: Aileen Mason
Cover Design Manager: Anne S. Katzeff
New Title Project Manager: Susan Brooks-Peltier
Editorial Assistant: Paola Moll
Marketing Assistant: Lauren Bussard

Cover image: © The British Library Picture Library

Printed in the U.S.A.

Library of Congress Control Number: 2007938107

ISBN-10: 0-618-61114-2
ISBN-13: 978-0-618-61114-0

1 2 3 4 5 6 7 8 9-CRS-11 10 09 08 07

For our students

Contents

C H A P T E R   4
European Challenges to Iberian Hegemony
Page 93

C H A P T E R   5
The Columbian Exchange
Page 122

CHAPTER 6
Migrations
Page 156

CHAPTER 7
Atlantic Economies
Page 189

C H A P T E R   1 5
Legacies
Page 451

Preface

As a child in the African city of Djougou, Mahommah Gardo Baquaqua could never have imagined the twists and turns his life would take. Kidnapped and enslaved in the early 1840s, Baquaqua suffered the miseries of an Atlantic passage to Brazil. His owner, a sea captain, foolishly took him to New York City, where an abolitionist group called the New York Vigilance Society helped him to escape. Now free, Baquaqua continued his remarkable journey. He first moved to Haiti, the only country in the Americas governed by people of African descent. There he converted to Christianity, but the restless wanderer soon returned to New York to enroll in college. He became an abolitionist, traveled to Canada and Great Britain, and dreamed of returning to Africa. Baquaqua crossed political, linguistic, and religious borders. He lived on all four Atlantic continents. He encountered Islamic, Catholic, and Protestant cultures. He endured slavery and rejoiced in his freedom, but he discovered that freedom did not protect him from the racism forged by Atlantic slavery. His life was an odyssey of the Atlantic world.

Baquaqua is only one of the millions of people who have lived in that vast Atlantic zone of human activity stretching across Europe, Africa, and the Americas. This book investigates their history from the middle of the fifteenth century, when the people of the Atlantic world began to forge new connections, through the great transformations of the nineteenth century. As Baquaqua's journey suggests, we cannot understand the history of any one locale around or within the Atlantic without appreciating how that locale was connected to and transformed by people in other places around the Atlantic basin. Poised between national and world history, Atlantic history offers a style of inquiry that requires us to look across modern political borders to understand how the region developed as it did. Rather than explore the history of any single place, nation, or empire within the context of the Atlantic, this collection of essays and documents reveals multiple perspectives and tells a complex story of interaction over a period of four centuries. In other words, *Major Problems in Atlantic History* is not a book about the United States, or even all of North America, any more than it is a book about Europe, Africa, or South Africa, or about Brazil, Benin, or France. It is about an ensemble of people, nations, and empires.

Atlantic history is a relatively new field of study. Although historians have advanced Atlantic perspectives and interpretations for several decades, only in recent years has this scholarly approach emerged as a distinct field of inquiry, complete with a journal (*Atlantic Studies*) and a major book prize (the James A. Rawley Prize in Atlantic History, awarded annually by the American Historical Association). Those interested in joining the electronic community of scholars can subscribe to H-Atlantic (http://www.h-net.org/~atlantic/). Atlantic history has taken firmer hold in history departments at high schools and colleges, but until recently, no textbook has aided this enterprise. *Major Problems in Atlantic History* is the very first collection of primary sources and essays intended specifically for undergraduate classes in the subject. Whereas other books written for the college classroom look at particular regions (most notably colonial British America) in an Atlantic context, only *Major Problems in Atlantic History* encompasses the entire Atlantic world.

Atlantic history teachers appreciate that one of the great challenges of the field is to balance all constituent parts of the region for different historical periods and questions. Because we have struggled with precisely this problem in our own efforts to teach Atlantic history to college students, our goal has been to produce a volume that represents the entirety of the Atlantic world. To that end, we include documents translated from Nahuatl, Latin, Dutch, French, Portuguese, Polish, Spanish, and German. Some of the documents in this volume have never before been translated into English. The sources take us from Newfoundland to Natal, from Paris to Paramaribo, from Bermuda to Brazil. Our goal has been to depict the diverse experiences of the Atlantic world's inhabitants, whether European, African, American, colonial, free, enslaved, male, female, Christian, Muslim, animist, or Jew.

This book's organization follows both change over time and important themes. After a chapter that introduces students to the field of Atlantic history, our early chapters move chronologically (from roughly 1400 to 1650) to convey the origins of the Atlantic as a zone of interaction and to emphasize the historical context that shaped how Europeans, Africans, and Americans encountered each other in this period. Chapter 2 focuses on initial Portuguese forays in Africa, Chapter 3 on the experiences of the Spanish and Portuguese in the western Atlantic, and Chapter 4 on the challenges launched by northern Europeans to the newfound power of Spain in Europe. After this chronological examination of the creation of the Atlantic world, we retrace our steps in five thematic chapters, which take up crucial topics for understanding Atlantic history. Chapter 5 examines what the historian Alfred W. Crosby so memorably dubbed the "Columbian exchange," the movement of people, pathogens, plants, and animals that crossed the Atlantic in the wake of Christopher Columbus's voyage in 1492. Chapter 6 focuses on free and coerced migration, examining the experiences of Europeans and Africans in tandem for the period from 1570 to 1800. In Chapter 7, we look at Atlantic economies, with particular attention to some of the major commodities and crops of the Atlantic, including sugar and silver, and to the many different labor regimes that sustained them. Chapter 8 analyzes patterns of resistance against authority, ranging from piracy to rebellion. In Chapter 9, we turn to the new cultures that emerged as people from all different parts of the Atlantic came into contact with each other. Although the chapter concentrates on religion as a way to understand the complex process of cultural interactions in the Atlantic, we also explore ideas about sexuality, race, marriage, and identity as they developed in the Atlantic. We would like to draw special attention to the many essays and documents in this volume that highlight the presence of women and the power of gender in Atlantic history, vitally important issues in recent Atlantic scholarship. Although we have not devoted any single chapter to the history of women and gender, relevant essays and documents may be found throughout the volume.

With Chapters 10 through 14 we return to a chronological narrative of the long series of cataclysmic and connected events from the Seven Years' War in the middle of the eighteenth century to the end of slavery in the western Atlantic and the rise of transatlantic European migration. Chapter 10 addresses wars and reforms, primarily in the eighteenth century, that rocked and renovated Atlantic empires. Chapter 11 looks at the "age of revolution" that began in the 1760s and lasted intermittently for about seven decades. This chapter highlights the political ideas animating these movements and the political ruptures they provoked. Chapter 12 then investigates the social dimension of these revolutions and considers the strategies that different groups pursued in their quest for political inclusion and empowerment. Chapter 13 follows the protracted demise of slavery in the western Atlantic, and Chapter 14 shifts to the transformed migration patterns of the nineteenth and early twentieth centuries, when European migrants finally eclipsed Africans and newcomers from Asia journeyed into the Atlantic. Our final chapter tackles two modern legacies of Atlantic history, introducing students to debates over reparations for slavery and over the commemoration of Christopher Columbus.

Like other books in this series, *Major Problems in Atlantic History* contains documents and essays that engage students in important current debates in the field. Each chapter starts with an introduction that provides an overview of the problem under examination. Several primary documents follow, accompanied by essays written by historians who approach the problem from different perspectives. The documents and essays enable students to work like historians—sifting through different interpretations and grappling with enigmatic sources to reach their own conclusions. Headnotes introduce the documents and the essays, and a bibliography of further readings permits students to pursue topics that intrigue them. Full sources are provided for each item in the chapter.

A volume as wide-ranging as this one could never have been completed without the extraordinary generosity and support of colleagues in our own department and elsewhere. The Georgetown University Graduate School of Arts and Sciences awarded us two grants that enabled us to hire graduate research assistants and translators for this project. Shona Johnston and Okezi Otovo spent a summer tracking down primary sources, and their initiative and enterprise vastly improved this text. Okezi Otovo, Danny Noorlander, and Luis Granados translated documents from Spanish, Portuguese, and Dutch. Our colleagues and the staff in the cramped confines of the Georgetown Department of History allowed us to monopolize a file cabinet and tolerated the chaos of chapter assembly with patience and good humor. Our colleagues' generosity extended to the contents of this book. Henriette de Bruyn Kops helped us make sense of a collection of Dutch documents about Piet Heyn and provided the translation for *De Zilverfloot*. Bryan McCann translated the excerpts from the Brazilian constitution. John Tutino drew our attention to Don Francisco María Colombini y Camayori's poem about Our Lady of Pueblito. David J. Collins helped clarify the politics of central Europe. Tim Scarnecchia made helpful suggestions about African materials. The interlibrary loan office at Georgetown University's Lauinger Library tracked down every item we requested, however obscure, with remarkable efficiency. We would also like to thank the hundreds of students who have taken History 3 and who have provided helpful and frank feedback about some of the documents and essays included in this volume.

Colleagues at other institutions have been equally generous. Douglas R. Egerton (Le Moyne College) and Robert Paquette (Hamilton College) shared documents about Haitian recruitment of free blacks in the United States. Wim Klooster (Clark University) provided the text of a Dutch account of an attack on the Portuguese in Angola. And we thank the following colleagues for their thoughtful comments on our selection of essays and documents:

Juanita De Barros, McMaster University
Sally Hadden, Florida State University
Wim Klooster, Clark University
Wayne E. Lee, University of North Carolina
Sue Peabody, Washington State University, Vancouver
James H. Sweet, University of Wisconsin

Finally, we are grateful to Houghton Mifflin for its interest in this project and for its willingness to allow us to produce a volume for the *Major Problems* series that offers a different perspective on U.S. history. Terri Wise helped us shepherd this project through to completion.

A.G.
A.R.

Major Problems
in Atlantic History

CHAPTER
1

What Is

Atlantic History?

What is Atlantic history? In the broadest sense, Atlantic history encompasses the interactions among the people of Europe, Africa, and the Americas from the fifteenth century onward. From the era when Portuguese and Spanish explorers navigated down the coast of Africa and out to the Atlantic islands, the ocean ceased to be a barrier to the integration of the continents that ringed it, and instead became a watery highway linking them together. Since those early sallies into the ocean world, millions of human beings have traveled to and fro across the Atlantic, where their movements (and the things they carried) created more than a "New World" in the Americas, but new worlds throughout the Atlantic basin. The linked history of these new worlds, and the connections among them, their similarities and differences, and their evolution over time, comprises Atlantic history.

As a concept, Atlantic history has a relatively recent vintage. It has emerged from a variety of older historiographical fields, including scholarship in European imperial history, colonial American history, and the history of the transatlantic slave trade. For many historians, the Atlantic concept offers a way to break out of the — *Beyond the nation-State* intellectual prison of the nation-state, which has done so much to shape the way history has been studied and understood in the modern era. Thus, for instance, an Atlantic perspective makes it possible to see the colonial history of North America as something richer and more complex than a mere precursor to the United States. At the same time, it allows historians of the United States to situate the nation's history in the context of broader patterns that crisscrossed the whole Atlantic world in different degrees and with varying consequences.

Atlantic history is also part of world history, although historians argue over the precise intersections between the two. The Atlantic has been embedded in global *Empire,* processes of empire, trade, and migration from the beginning of European overseas *trade,* expansion. Columbus famously thought he was on the way to Asia when he stumbled *migration* into islands that become known as the "West Indies." That slave traders carried enslaved Africans across the Indian as well as the Atlantic oceans, and that much of the silver mined in Spanish America ended up in China is less well known. The density of linkages among Europe, Africa, and the Americas—epitomized by the transatlantic slave trade—justifies our thinking of Atlantic history as a coherent slice of

*world history worth studying in its own right, at least until the late nineteenth or
early twentieth century, when Atlantic history seems finally to dissolve into truly
global patterns of trade, migration, and warfare.*

*Atlantic history emphasizes connections and comparisons. Technologies of trans-
portation and communication have connected Europe, Africa, and the Americas in
increasingly efficient ways over time. People moved around, diseases spread, commodities circulated, and ideas proliferated—often in ways that crossed conventional
political boundaries. What were the causes and consequences of these Atlantic connections? Broad patterns of empire, colonization, migration, trade, religion, gender,
and warfare can be spotted, but so too can the extraordinary diversity of Atlantic
experiences. Thus the Atlantic world provides a rich field for comparative history.
Why did some prosper and others suffer? Why did one region develop in one way,
and another in a different way? Why did certain transformations and events happen
sooner or last longer in one place than another? These are some of the questions that
Atlantic historians interested in comparative issues might ask.*

*Potential
themes:
empire
colonization
migration
trade
religion
gender
warfare*

ESSAYS

We probably think that we know what the Atlantic is. We can look at any decent
atlas and the ocean emerges clearly, demarcated by geographers, bounded by four
continents, connected to various seas, and divided at two capes, one at the southern
tip of Africa and the other at the base of South America. These barriers distinguish
it from the earth's other great oceans, the Pacific and the Indian. When we speak of
Atlantic history, then, it might logically follow that such a history is set within this
clearly delineated geographic space. But the essays that follow suggest that there is
nothing natural or self-evident about either the ocean or what its history might entail.
Instead, Atlantic history has emerged from changing ideas about both geography
and history.

Before there could be an Atlantic history, there first had to be an Atlantic Ocean.
The geographer Martin Lewis sketches the emergence of the modern classification
of oceans. He insists that geographical characterizations, such as modern ocean
basins, derive not from objective natural features and scientific knowledge, but
rather from complex intellectual and political constructions. On the other hand, the
Atlantic Ocean did present formidable natural barriers to seafaring that had to be overcome before the era of Atlantic history could begin. The historian Alfred W. Crosby
shows that Iberian sailors' mastery of wind patterns in the Atlantic was crucial to the
early phase of European oceanic expansion. Iberian seafaring was no more technologically sophisticated than that of Muslims or Chinese. Instead, their advantage
in the Atlantic derived from experience. As they leapfrogged down the African
coast in ever-widening circles, they mastered the sea's complex winds and currents.
Columbus's eventual "discovery" of America (as the event has been described by
Europeans; the people who already inhabited the islands of the Caribbean knew
precisely where they were) rested on the mariners' prior understanding of the ocean.
Finally, in an essay that pairs optimism with caution, David Armitage analyzes the
emergence of the relatively new field of Atlantic history. Atlantic history, like the
history of oceans, has antecedents rooted in different fields of study and characterized by diverse approaches and methodologies. Armitage explores the origins of this
new geographic unit of historical analysis and sketches three different visions of
what Atlantic history might look like.

Inventing Oceans

MARTIN W. LEWIS

Global geography operates under a widespread assumption of naturalism. The continents and oceans that constitute the most basic divisions of the world are generally regarded—to the extent that they are considered at all—as nonproblematic features of the natural world, features that have been discovered rather than delimited by convention. A quick glance at a globe, however, reveals that the continental distinction between Asia and Europe is not discernable by physical criteria; closer investigation reveals that the differentiation of North and South America, the insistence that Australia forms a continent and not an island, and even, to some extent, the separation of Asia and North America are as much intellectual constructs as they are given features of the natural world.

The conventional nature of oceanic divisions is perhaps more obvious than that of continents, for the simple reason that all of the world's oceans, unlike all of the continents, are interconnected by broad passageways. Yet atlases, almanacs, encyclopedias, and other standard sources of geographical information invariably present an assuringly exact depiction of each ocean's areal extent. In *Goode's World Atlas*, for example, we are informed that the Pacific covers 63,800,000 square miles, as if it were an unambiguously bounded body that one could simply measure. Where the Pacific ends and the Indian or Atlantic Ocean begins—a far from obvious matter— is rarely addressed in such sources. Yet different geographical reference works evidently employ different boundaries, for they disagree profoundly about how large the Pacific actually is. The *World Almanac*'s Pacific, at a precise-sounding 64,186,300 square miles, is almost 400,000 square miles larger than that of *Goode's*, and that of the *Encyclopaedia Britannica*, with marginal seas included, is more than 5 million square miles larger still.

[handwritten margin note: Oceans as an intellectual Construct]

At one level, such ambiguity is of little account. Adding or subtracting a few million square miles from or to the Pacific is hardly a pressing matter. Most geographers would probably contend that such numbers are merely vague approximations anyway, reflecting somewhat arbitrary divisions of the boundless sea. And despite the discrepancy regarding the size of the Pacific, global agreement on maritime divisions is actually striking. The same oceans and seas, given the same names (albeit often in translation) and bounded, more or less, at the same places, are recognized across most of the globe. . . . The resulting global concord in geographical naming and bounding is tremendously useful, for it facilitates the exchange of information and aids the nascent movement to provide some form of international governance for the marine world.

But although it is useful to divide the seas into relatively well demarcated and internationally recognized units, such a maneuver is problematic to the extent that it disguises the conventional nature of their construction. The maritime realm can be, and has been, divided in different ways, yielding units that are nonetheless just as logically constituted—and just as faithful to the underlying patterns of the physical world—as

Source: Martin W. Lewis, "Dividing the Ocean Sea," *Geographical Review*, 89.2 (April 1999): 188–214. ✳
Reprinted with permission of American Geographical Society.

those presently on our maps. . . . The current taken-for-granted system of maritime spatial classification did not, in fact, emerge in broad outlines until the 1800s and did not assume its full-blown form until the twentieth century. In earlier times, especially during the eighteenth-century Enlightenment, radically different notions of sea space prevailed. By examining changes in the Western oceanic imagination, I seek to show not only that alternative views are possible but that such alternative visions can conceivably shed light on certain geographical patterns and processes that are obscured by our constricted and naturalistic assumptions about maritime space.

Three major variations in the conceptualization of sea space can be seen over the centuries. First is the manner in which the oceanic realm as a whole has been divided into its major constituent units, now called "oceans." Second is the changing way in which the hierarchy of oceanic divisions and subdivisions has been arrayed: Seas, for example, are now considered constituent units of the larger oceans, but this has not always been the case. Third is the matter of nomenclature, the changing names assigned to the (more or less) same bodies of water. Although naming is seemingly the least complex issue at hand, it can have significant political and ideological ramifications; the demise of the "Ethiopian Ocean" in the nineteenth century, for example, perhaps reflects the denigration of Africa that occurred with the rise of racist pseudoscience.

The conventional present-day schema of global geography, encompassing continental and oceanic constructs alike, is rooted in a specifically European worldview. During the colonial era, Western ideas about the division of the globe were forced on, and often eagerly borrowed by, other societies the world over, thereby largely extinguishing competing geographies. To examine the history of imagining the ocean, one must therefore begin with ancient Greek geography, even though Greek ideas on this score may ultimately have been rooted in Babylonian, Egyptian, and Phoenician concepts that are now largely lost. . . .

The Classical Tradition

The ancient Greek view of maritime geography was focused, not surprisingly, on the Mediterranean system—on Thalassa, the sea. The earliest recorded representations, most importantly that of Homer, pictured the Mediterranean as situated at the center of a circular world, a view that may be rooted in Babylonian conceptions. This circular world, in turn, was bounded by "Ocean," a flowing stream—the Ocean River—coursing around the Afroeurasian landmass. Mythologically, the Ocean River was ruled by, and named after, the titan Oceanus. Just as Oceanus was held to be the father of personified rivers (river gods) in the Greek world, so the primeval water of the Ocean River was considered the ultimate font of all terrestrial streams. In this view, the Mediterranean Sea was literally and figuratively a central place, whereas Ocean formed the potent and foreboding limit of the habitable world.

The mythological vision of a primordial Ocean River gradually yielded to a more mundane perspective. Although Hecataeus and the other philosophers of the sixth-century B.C. Ionian enlightenment subjected much of geography to formal analysis, their underlying concept of the maritime system remained relatively unchanged. Ocean was still conceived as a circumfluent stream coursing around an essentially circular "known world." . . .

. . . [M]ost classical geographers continued to posit an earth-encompassing Ocean. Different Greek and Roman scholars appended various names to this body of water and its several segments without challenging its essential unity. Many writers used the term "Atlantic" (derived from the titan Atlas) to refer to the entire Ocean Sea, whereas others called this water body the "Outer Sea," "Great Sea," or simply "Oceanus." . . .

In short, in the classical Mediterranean world a dominant oceanic model, predicated on a single sea encircling a limited ecumenical body of land, vied with a continental model, in which seas were separated from each other by extensions of dry land. These two views, in various permutations, were to coexist for centuries; the issue was not finally settled, in favor of a (modified) oceanic model, until the completion of the voyage of Ferdinand Magellan in the early 1500s. . . .

Medieval Constructs

. . . During the High Middle Ages, world maps grew far more intricate . . . sacrificing geometrical order for the portrayal of specific, if not always accurate, information. In most instances, however, they continued to depict the ocean as a narrow, encircling boundary of the inhabited world. . . .

This maritime boundary at the periphery of the terrestrial world, whatever its width might be, was not conceived as the edge of a flat earth, beyond which lay the void. As Jeffrey Burton Russell has shown, the flat-earth scenario was largely the invention of nineteenth-century Darwinists seeking to discredit the Christian worldview. Most medieval European thinkers fully accepted the sphericity of the earth, and most of those who did not were at least agnostic on the issue. But the ocean was still largely perceived as a barrier to, rather than as a potential conduit for, interregional communication. Some thinkers, following a tradition dating back to the ancient Greeks, averred that the ocean was far too shallow, too blocked by muddy shoals and seaweed thickets, to allow westward voyages that might eventually reach eastern Asia. Circumnavigation of the world island, moreover, was usually deemed impossible because of the hypothesized torridity of the equatorial zone and the frigidity of the Arctic. In the 1200s, however, a few bold thinkers, including Albertus Magnus and Roger Bacon, did suggest that the torrid zone might be surmountable. . . .

[Handwritten margin note: The world understood to be round, but the ocean as impassable]

The Oceans Mapped and Knit Together

The European voyages of exploration and plundering in the 1400s and 1500s necessitated a radically new vision of the world and its oceanic reaches. This period saw what J. H. Parry aptly calls the "discovery of the sea"—a discovery, in other words, "of continuous sea passages from ocean to ocean." Knowledge gained of the vast, interconnected, yet to some extent subdivided maritime expanse was as significant cosmographically as was the discovery of a fourth part of the terrestrial world.

After the voyage of Vasco da Gama, the Ptolemaic conception of an enclosed Indian Ocean could no longer be maintained. Still, several cosmographers associated with Iberian courts upheld a modified continental model of the world in which land bridges enclosed the seas, preventing global maritime communication. Lopo Homem, an official cartographer of the Portuguese government, for example, depicted America in 1519 as joined to the hypothesized great southern landmass that in turn was linked with eastern Asia, thus enclosing the Atlantic and Indian Oceans together in an isolated maritime realm. The voyage of Magellan, however, put a quick end to such speculation. Henceforth, the interconnectedness of the marine world was fully recognized. . . .

Over the course of the 1500s, cartographers increasingly distinguished discrete oceans on the map of the world. In Diego Ribero's map of 1529, for example, the South Atlantic Basin is labeled, as it generally would be over the next 300 years, the "Ethiopian Ocean." In Sebastian Cabot's map of 1544, the Pacific seems to appear as a distinct place. But it was not—nor would it often be until the 1800s—called "the Pacific." Although Magellan bestowed this name in the early 1500s, it was Balboa's term, the "Mar del Sur" (South Sea), that stuck—even though it originally referred only to the Bay of Panama. (One reason why this seemingly incongruous label continued to be employed was the fact that European mariners had to sail far to the south to enter its water.) Elsewhere, classical terms and concepts continued to be used where possible, even if they did not correspond to any visible marine divisions. Sebastian Cabot, for example, designated the central portion of the Indian Ocean as the "Mare Prasodum" (Green Sea), reserving the label "Indian Ocean" for areas farther to the north.

Although most sixteenth-century world maps show the familiar roster of oceanic place-names—some classical, others derived from recent feats of navigation—nomenclature remained far from fixed. A few cartographers used wildly divergent classification systems. In Pierre Descelier's map of 1553, for example, the South Atlantic becomes the "Southern Sea" and the Indian Ocean is called the "Eastern Indian Ocean" (Mer des Indes Orientales). But it is the North Atlantic in which Descelier's scheme is most unusual. Rather than viewing this expanse of sea as a distinct basin, Desceliers treats it as a series of oceanic strips or bands extending seaward from, and named in accordance with, segments of the European and American coasts. Thus one encounters, in midocean, not only the "Great Ocean Sea" but also the "Sea of France," the "Sea of Spain," and the "Sea of the Antilles."

Although Descelier's view of the Atlantic failed to gain acceptance, it does dramatically illustrate an important feature of early modern maritime nomenclature. He may have defied convention by extending land-based names across a major ocean basin, but it was common at the time to conceptualize certain "seas" or even "oceans" as segments of water situated off an eponymous area of land, rather than, as modern geography has it, distinct bodies of water partially separated from other waters by intervening lands. . . .

Enlightenment Reconceptualizations

In the late 1600s, new ways of imagining the ocean began to emerge. . . . In the 1700s, many, if not most, European cartographers had come to depict named oceans not as distinct basins but as stretches of water linking one basin to another. A possible precursor of this new system of maritime division was Jacques-Dominique Cassini's unusual map of 1696. . . .

[I]ts most significant conceptual innovation is its abandonment of discrete basins in favor of a novel and idiosyncratic mode of ocean classification. In the

Southern Hemisphere, Cassini adopted a modified zonal scheme, with a Southern Ocean at the Antarctic latitudes being flanked on its north by the "Ethiopian," Indian, and Pacific Oceans. Cassini's "Occidental" and "Ethiopian" Oceans, bearing no connection to any recognizable basins, appear to wrap themselves around the African and Asian landmasses. And a remarkable serpentine arc of water, stretching from the Caribbean through the North Atlantic and hence across the Arctic to Kamchatka, is labeled the "Sea of the North and the Northern Ocean."

Cassini's strange "Sea of the North and the Northern Ocean" does not, to my knowledge, appear in any other map. But the "ocean-arc" concept, in which oceanic designations are displaced from basin cores to skirt or wrap around landmasses, became a standard feature of Enlightenment cartography. . . .

A map showing ocean arcs looks strange to modern eyes. We are so accustomed to viewing ocean basins as given features of global geography that it seems almost perverse to delimit sea space in accordance with intervening lands. The "Ethiopian Ocean," for example, seemingly ignores hydrography altogether, taking not only its name but also its very form through reference to the adjacent landmass of Africa.

But the ocean-arc concept is not without its virtues. When considering oceans not as physical units but rather as spaces of human activity, ocean arcs can elucidate patterns obscured in the basin schema. In the eighteenth century, the Indian Ocean of our textbooks, stretching from Durban to Perth, did not compose any kind of meaningful interaction sphere. Yet the "Eastern Indian Ocean," an arc linking the Swahili coast to the South China Sea, did constitute a closely linked series of trading circuits. Similarly, one could argue that as Atlantic-based slave and plantation economies extended to Réunion and Mauritius, they effectively carved out an "Ethiopian Ocean" that did indeed stretch from the (modern) South Atlantic to the Mascarene Islands. Even a "Magellanic Sea" could be justified by the similar maritime conditions encountered by sailors on both sides of southern South America.

[margin note: Ocean arcs can show cultural & economic connections]

Late-Eighteenth- and Nineteenth-Century Imaginings

Ocean arcs were the most common means of portraying maritime space in the eighteenth century, but other schemes remained in use. . . . By the end of the century, moreover, a revivified basin view was clearly gaining ground.

One of the main sources of inspiration for the new basins perspective was the model of physical geography proposed in 1758 by Philippe Buache. Buache imagined a global framework of interconnected mountain ranges—both terrestrial and submarine—that formed a kind of global exoskeleton. These world-encompassing ridges divided the sea into three discrete basins: the Atlantic (which Buache simply called "the ocean"), the Indian, and the Pacific. Although Buache's imaginative depiction of global physical geography did not stand the test of time, his vision of discrete ocean basins was eventually to prevail.

By the late 1700s, perhaps under the influence of Buache, seemingly modern depictions of maritime space begin to appear in atlases. In Samuel Dunn's "Chart of the World" of 1774, for example, the Atlantic is still divided into separate northern and southern oceans (the north being the "Western or Atlantic Ocean" and the south the "Southern Ocean"), and the Pacific is separated into eastern (the "Great South Sea or Pacific Ocean") and western ("Eastern Ocean") basins. But all one would have to do to transform this into a modern-looking map would be to substitute the term "South Atlantic" for "Ethiopian" and remove the "Eastern Ocean" label. . . .

In the nineteenth century, the conceptualization of sea space emerged as a significant geographical issue, addressed by some of the finest geographical minds. Élisée Reclus, in 1872, argued that the Southern Ocean, rather than the Pacific, forms the dominant feature of the planet's maritime realm: "The southern Ocean alone— that mighty breadth of waters, in comparison with which all other oceans seem but mere arms of the sea—extends over nearly an entire hemisphere of our planet." In this view, the Atlantic, Pacific, and Indian Oceans are effectively immense embayments extending northward from the globe-girdling Southern Ocean. Such a position is evident in the *Oxford English Dictionary*: "But the Pacific, Indian, and Antarctic really form one great ocean, the 'South Sea'; of which the Atlantic and Arctic again form a smaller prolongation." . . .

Reclus's imagining of a massive Southern Ocean was based on the knowledge of the time. Before the existence of an Antarctic landmass had been established, one could reasonably imagine a vast, virtually hemispheric, Southern Ocean. Even today, one is struck by the scope and continuity of this "Southern Ocean" when viewing a globe from the Antarctic perspective. The world is much more commonly imagined, however, from the equatorial vantage point, if not from that of the Northern Hemisphere's midlatitudes, where the oceans do indeed appear to form separate basins. In the twentieth century, that perspective—emphasizing the "natural" separation of the sea into discrete oceans—again became dominant as the globalist vision of scholars like von Humboldt and Reclus waned.

The Modern View

The transition to the modern, English-language conception of maritime space required that oceans be fully differentiated from seas. The two terms—the first classical and learned, the second based on a Germanic root meaning "wetland"—had long been deployed more or less as synonyms. Indeed, they are still complexly intertwined: Although "oceans" are larger than "seas," the entire oceanic extent remains "the sea," as in "the high seas" or "sea level." This united water body was, until 1400, often called the "sea ocean," or "sea of ocean," and down to 1650 was commonly the "ocean sea." . . .

The major problem in the transition to the modern hydrographic view was gaining agreement on the number of oceans found on the globe. In the late 1800s, one could find, depending on which authors and cartographers one consulted, between one and seven oceans. Increasingly, however, scientifically minded geographers and oceanographers sought to standardize and simplify the list. In 1878, *Black's General Atlas of the World* joined the northern and southern sections of the Atlantic to create a unified ocean separating the Americas from Europe and Africa. Reuniting the North and South Pacific Oceans, it arrived at a five-ocean scheme (Atlantic, Pacific, Indian, Arctic, and Antarctic) that would prove popular. The suturing of the northern and southern portions of the Atlantic and Pacific Oceans, however, led some to question the status of the Indian Ocean. Ellen Churchill Semple, following Arnold Guyot and ultimately Carl Ritter, thus declared that the Indian Ocean was actually only a "half ocean," considering its limited extent in the Northern Hemisphere.

The five-ocean scheme failed to gain universal acceptance. . . . A four-ocean model (including the Arctic) remained common in geographical circles through the 1960s and beyond, and even the five-ocean model is not extinct. Indeed, the *Encyclopaedia Britannica* itself, as recently as 1963, anachronistically advanced a seven-ocean scheme. Meanwhile, not a few oceanographers continue to insist that any division of the singular Ocean has no scientific legitimacy. . . .

Conclusion

The *Encyclopaedia Britannica*'s claim that a three-ocean model has prevailed since the time of [Otto] Krümmel [in the late nineteenth century]—despite the conflicting evidence found in earlier editions of the same encyclopedia —is telling. The vision that it exemplifies is essentially positivistic, suggesting that large-scale geographical divisions are discovered through objective analysis rather than defined by convention. It also implies that the history of geographical ideas can be reduced to a simple narrative of progress, one in which better accounts replace the misinformed views of the past. . . .

As traced here, the Western conceptualization of the oceans may better be described as one of aimless wanderings. In this Foucauldian story line, different ways of dividing and labeling the sea come in and out of fashion, each successive view reflecting the epistemic environment of its time without adding any cumulative conceptual purchase. By this reading, our present system of hydrography, from the IHO's emphasis on unambiguous divisions to the popular press's enthusiasm for "Pacific Rim discourse," may be said to reflect the strategic interests of contemporary global capitalism.

Alternatively, one may tell the history of the imagining of the oceans as a story of conceptual decline. For those who favor a human-centered geography, the Enlightenment maps that depicted oceans within comprehensible frameworks of interaction may seem preferable to our current basin scheme. Others may favor the unitary perspective advocated by Reclus: When viewed from an Antarctic perspective, the map of the world quite literally shows the ocean as a singular, albeit deeply embayed, entity. Such a view may rhetorically appeal to those who advocate a "one-world" approach to global affairs, downplaying the distinctions among continents, civilizations, or even nation-states.

To be sure, it can be argued that the odd march from the River Ocean to the modern schema does represent a sort of progress, despite the many bizarre twists and dead ends along the way. Arbitrary though some of its boundaries may be, our modern view of oceanic divisions is at least founded upon an accurate picture of the distribution of lands and waters over the surface of the globe. Reclus stressed oceanic unity in the southern latitudes in part because he did not know about Antarctica. Or again, one could insist that the modern system represents progress on the grounds that a single set of conventions has been, by and large, accepted across the globe. Even the names of the major water bodies have been largely internationalized. In earlier times one could never be sure what a specific maritime designation referred to; terms wandered across large areas of the globe, and partial synonyms abounded. Today, one can consult the IHO to learn precisely where the conventional limits of the Atlantic Ocean, as well as all of its marginal seas, bays, and gulfs, are

[margin note: Our contemp. vision of the oceans reflects the strategic interests of global capitalism]

[margin note: history of the oceans keeps us think globally]

located. Although scholars and journalists obviously do not follow these boundaries religiously, they are certainly used to good effect by states and international agencies in political negotiations.

In the final analysis, perhaps it is pointless to ask whether our imaginings of the oceans have improved, declined, or merely changed. What is certain is that no standard textbook definitions can ever reveal "real" divisions across the undivided Ocean Sea. Dividing up sea space in a regular manner allows effective communication, but it does so by guiding our imaginations along certain preset pathways, pathways that reflect specific cultural and political outlooks.

Perhaps the most effective way to expose those outlooks is to experiment with novel modes of mapping. On standard equatorially based world maps, discrete ocean basins do indeed leap to the eye. But on polar-based projections—which are almost as rare today as they were in the time of Cassini—different patterns emerge. One of the best ways to see the world afresh—and to reveal a global sea—is simply to invert a globe. Whether or not such maneuvers can help us escape our habitual "Northern Hemispherism," they do at least offer a bracing lesson in the constructedness of our oceanic categories.

The Discovery of the Atlantic

ALFRED W. CROSBY

If the Old World expansionists were to be able to take full advantage of the global opportunities for ecological imperialism prefigured by the European successes in the islands of the eastern Atlantic, they would have to cross the seams of Pangaea—the oceans—in large numbers, along with their servant and parasite organisms. That great endeavor waited on five developments. One of the five was simply the emergence of a strong desire to undertake imperialistic adventures overseas—a prerequisite that may seem too obvious to bother mentioning, but not one we can omit, as the Chinese case, to which we shall refer presently, proves. The other four developments were technological in nature. Vessels were needed that were large enough, fast enough, and maneuverable enough to carry a worthwhile payload of freight and passengers across thousands of kilometers of ocean, past shoals, reefs, and menacing headlands, and back again in reasonable safety. Equipment and techniques were needed to find courses across oceans while out of sight of land for weeks, even months, on voyages far longer than any the Norse ever survived. Weaponry was needed that was portable enough to be carried on board ship and yet effective enough to intimidate the indigenes of the lands across the oceans. A source of energy was needed to drive the vessels across the oceans. Oars would not do: Neither freemen nor slaves could row without fresh water and plenty of calories, and a galley large enough to carry sufficient supplies for an oar-powered crossing of the Pacific would, paradoxically, be too large to row anywhere. Wind, of course, was the answer to this last requirement, but which winds, where, and when? The explorer who

Source: Alfred W. Crosby, "Winds," in *Ecological Imperialism: The Biological Expansion of Europe, 900–1900* (New York: Cambridge University Press, 1986), pp. 105–118. Reprinted with the permission of Cambridge University Press.

puts to sea in the faith that there will always be a wind to carry him where he listeth will find that the wind will carry him where *it* listeth. The births of the Neo-Europes had to wait for the sailors of Europe, who rarely ventured beyond the continental shelf, to become blue-water sailors.

To make short work of a long story that has been well told elsewhere by such historians as J. H. Parry and Samuel Eliot Morison, most of the foregoing requirements were met no later than the 1490s, the decade of the triumphs of Columbus and Da Gama. In many ways, they had been met three or four generations before. Chinese maritime technology was sufficiently advanced at the beginning of the fifteenth century for Cheng Ho, chief admiral and eunuch of the Ming emperor, to despatch to India and all the way to East Africa fleets of scores of vessels armed with multitudes of small cannon and manned by thousands of crewmen and passengers. It is this admiral, rather than, say, Bartholomeu Dias, who should be credited as the first great figure of the age of exploration. If political changes and cultural endogeny had not stifled the ambitions of Chinese sailors, then it is likely that history's greatest imperialists would have been Far Easterners, not Europeans.

But China chose to turn its back to the oceans, leaving history only two possibilities for the role of the greatest imperialists: the Muslims, led by their sailors, and the Europeans, led by theirs. (There were other expansionistic peoples, but none both as powerful and as experienced on the high seas.) As of 1400, the mariners of these two sets of prospective imperialists still lagged behind the Chinese, but their ships, though smaller than those of Cheng Ho, were seaworthy and adequate in size; some were fitted with cannon, and more soon would be, and their navigators had compasses and crude instruments with which to estimate speed and latitude. Neither the Muslims nor the Europeans could accurately judge longitude, but neither could anyone else until the invention of an accurate chronometer in the eighteenth century. Meanwhile, they made do with what they had and guessed about longitude— exactly as Columbus was to do in his time. Science made its great contributions to navigation after the fifteenth century.

The unsolved problem was the wind. It was not that they did not understand how to tap its force: Christian square sails and Muslim lateen sails, used in combination more and more frequently as the century went on, could have carried Magellan across the Pacific about as well in 1421 as in 1521. The problem was that in 1421 no one knew much about where and when the winds blew over the major oceans, with the exception of the Indian Ocean. The Indian Ocean was certainly vast enough to get lost in, but it was landlocked on three sides, and its winds were under the discipline of the monsoon, a seasonal weather system that could be comprehended from land. The lessons the Indian Ocean taught its indigenous sailors were only imperfectly applicable elsewhere, and that may have had something to do with their general inferiority to European sailors outside the waters of monsoon Asia. It is also true that the fifteenth century was one in which the attention of Muslims was fully engaged on land, or, if on water, then on that sea-of-the-lands-around-it, the Mediterranean. The very placement of the Indian Ocean discouraged curiosity. Beyond its known waters lay primitive peoples and more and more ocean. How different from the Atlantic: Beyond it lay Aztecs, Incas, and the lush Americas.

The history of the closing of the seams of Pangaea is a European story—not completely, of course; for the essential compass was Chinese, and the lateen sail that enabled ships to beat into the wind, a necessity for exploration of unfamiliar coasts, was Muslim—but the actual ships, owners, bankers, interested monarchs and noblemen, cartographers, mathematicians, navigators, astronomers, masters, mates, and common seamen were Europeans or their servants. They led humanity into its greatest adventure since the Neolithic. John H. Parry has called that adventure not "the discovery of America," for that was only one of its chapters; he has named it "the discovery of the sea," which is to say, the discovery of the where and when of the oceanic winds and the currents they drive before them.

When the sailors of the Mediterranean and Iberia first ventured into the pelagic waters beyond Gibraltar, they were familiar with only the winds of their home waters. They knew nothing whatever about those that glide and gust (spin, whirl? blow straight up?) beyond the continental shelf. These mariners did inherit—at many removes, because they were not, most of them, of a scholarly bent—what the savants of the ancient world and their latter-day disciplines had to say on the general nature of the world. There was a tradition, raised almost to the level of revealed truth by Aristotle, that climates and therefore a lot of other things would be found spread out in latitudinal strata from the North Pole to the equator, and then, in reverse order, to the South Pole. Hence, in 1492, Columbus was not surprised that the people of the Bahamas and Antilles were tawny, because that was the color of the Guanches, who lived in the same latitude. The theory was, of course, an oversimplification, and it led, for instance, to the false assumption that there would be an enormous southern continent, a *Terra australis incognita*, to balance the masses of land north of the equator, but the theory was not entirely wrong-headed. It is valid, generally speaking, and for many practical purposes, in regard to the winds of the Atlantic and Pacific—which is all the fifteenth- and sixteenth-century explorers, who crossed oceans as if playing blindman's buff, asked.

The winds of the Atlantic and Pacific flow in gigantic wind wheels. In each ocean north of the equator, one airy carousel revolves clockwise, and south of the equator another spins counterclockwise. The poleward edges of the carousels are the prevailing westerlies of the temperate zones, north and south. In the tropics, between the wind wheels, broad bands of moving air swing out and plunge obliquely toward a belt of low pressure steaming under the vertical equatorial sun. These are the famous trade winds, called such in English because of the obsolete meaning of "trade" as a course or track. The low-pressure belt is the detested doldrums, source of so many horror stories of thirst and starvation for those becalmed in their sweaty clasp. The whole vast system—westerlies, trades, doldrums, and all—rocks gigantically north and south with the seasons, cuing on the annual veering of the vertical sun back and forth between the Tropic of Cancer and Tropic of Capricorn. The latitudinal nature and rough predictability of the system (very rough, because local variations are legion, and every so often the whole system shuts down for a while) contain the key to sailing across the seams of Pangaea from Europe to new worlds.

The sailors of southern Europe who in their historical prime were to discover America, round the Cape of Good Hope, and circumnavigate the globe went to primary school in the Mediterranean and to secondary school in the next best thing to a closed sea: a large spread of open ocean with reasonably predictable winds and enough islands for the navigator to practice his skills without losing his life the first time he lost his bearings. This watery expanse the historian Pierre Chaunu has shrewdly called "the Mediterranean Atlantic." It is that wide wedge of the Atlantic west and south of the Iberian peninsula that has as its far boundary stones the archipelagos of the Canaries and the Azores and includes the Madeira group, and over which firm northerlies blow during the warmer months. Southerlies are rare any time, and the general flow of air commonly comes from the west only in the temperate Azorean latitudes. The Vivaldi brothers disappeared into the Mediterranean Atlantic in 1291, but the majority of those who followed survived. They familiarized themselves with these waters, and in doing so became blue-water sailors, true mariners—*marinheiros*, to use the most appropriate language, Portuguese. The key to understanding what they learned and how they learned it is the Canaries. It is that island group that tempted Portuguese sailors (plus Genoese, Majorcan, Spanish, and others, many sailing for the Portuguese) far out into the Atlantic and into their historic roles as Europe's first oceanic sailors after the Norse. The voyage to these islands down the trades was an easy one of a week or less, with the archipelago almost too wide and its peaks too high to miss. "In the Island of Teneriffe," said a Dutch traveler in the sixteenth century, "there is a hill called Pico de Terraira, which is thought to be the highest hill that ever was found, for it may easily be seene at the least threescore miles in the sea." And at the end of a voyage in this cozy patch of the Atlantic lay profit in the Canaries: animal skins, dyestuffs, and slaves.

Getting from Iberia to the Canaries was not the problem; getting back was the problem. In solving that puzzle, the sailors of Europe certainly sharpened and perhaps even invented some of the skills that enabled them to sail to America, to India, and around the world, and to bind up the seams of Pangaea. The course from Iberia to the Canaries is often about as straight as a sailor can sail, because usually both current and wind carry him to his destination, perhaps with not so much as a squall, if he has chosen the season rightly. Square sail, lateen sail, or perhaps, with luck, no sail at all will suffice; but to return by anything approximating the same route he must tack to and fro, to and fro, for many days, sliding backward every time the vessel comes about, and gaining little on the best reach, because the current is relentlessly contrary. If he sails conservatively, his only hope is to shave the coastline, taking full advantage of the shore winds that blow from the south and southwest during the hours immediately before and after dawn. Then, at midday, he must tack back toward the coast, praying to gain some northing, or at least not to lose any, before anchoring or before the shore winds pick up again. Much of the real hope for northing lies in the strength in the backs of his oarsmen, but where on that inhospitable coast is there food and water to keep them going? A good guess as to the fate of the Vivaldi brothers is that they sailed perhaps as far as the Canaries, perhaps farther, and then found their sails inadequate for the voyage back, and the task of rowing against the Canary Current too much for their thirsty rowers. Perhaps they died of deprivation and exhaustion, or perhaps, in attempting to finesse their way home by means of the shore winds, they were hit by a squall and, lacking sea room, were flung on the shoals of Morocco.

When faced with strong contrary winds, European sailors prior to the *marinheiros*—even the Norse—either gave up and went home or took down their sails until the wind changed, busying themselves with the housekeeping chores that always need doing on a vessel. There was no other way to buy a passage from a relentless headwind. The Europeans who sailed the Mediterranean Atlantic found a new way.

If they could not sail close enough to a contrary wind to gain against it, then they had to try "to sail around the wind," that is, steer as close to the wind as they could, holding their course for as long as it took to find a wind they could use to get them where they wanted to go. Sailors of the Mediterranean Atlantic pinned in the Canaries by the southward rush of air and water had to steer northwest into the open ocean and steadily sail farther and farther away from their last landfall, perhaps without gaining a centimeter toward home for many days, until they finally sailed far enough out of the tropics to tap the prevailing westerlies of the temperate zone. Then they could steer for home. They had to have faith in their knowledge of the winds, turn their backs to land, and become, possibly for weeks, creatures of the pelagic deeps. They had to become true *marinheiros*. The Portuguese, who perfected this strategy, called it the *volta do mar*, the returning by sea or the veering out and around by sea.

This alternating use of the trade winds on the outward leg, then the *volta* (the crabwise slide off to the northwest) to the zone of the westerlies, and then the swoop home with the westerlies as following winds—this pattern of voyaging and this pattern of prevailing winds made the gambles of Columbus, Da Gama, and Magellan acts of adventure, not acts of probable suicide. These sailors knew they could sail out on the trades and back on the westerlies, and with this faith, as the Jesuit José de Acosta put it, "men have indangered themselves to undertake strange Navigations, and to seeke out farre Countries unknowne."

It is doubtful that the sailors of the age of exploration thought about the *volta* in any sort of formal way. It is improbable that they learned the technique as a principle; they were, after all, not searching after laws of nature but simply groping out to sea for a favorable wind. But prevailing patterns of thought grew up to match the patterns of prevailing winds, and Iberian sailors used the *volta* as a template with which to plot their courses to Asia, to the Americas, and around the world.

In the fifteenth century, Portuguese navigators continued past the Canaries down the African coast, feeling their way along desert and then jungle shores, and learning the tricks of trading with the Africans for gold, pepper, and slaves. About 1460, they colonized the Cape Verde Islands and then sailed on farther, south and round the bulge of Africa. There they found themselves in dangerous and confusing waters. Near shore during the summer months they were hostages to the violent doings of the West African monsoon. The continent, baking under the vertical sun, sucks the relatively cool ocean air inland, and the prevailing winds back around to the southwest, carrying vessels toward a coast that is almost without harbors. If the *marinheiros* stood out to sea away from monsoon weather, they sailed right out of the zone of the northeast trades into the doldrums, where the superheated air rises vertically, producing calms alternating with dangerous storms. The worst large expanse of ocean in the world for thunderstorms lies off the coast of Africa from the Senegal River to the Congo River. Often it takes the longest to drift out of the doldrums not far south of the Cape Verdes. Columbus strayed into this buckle on the doldrums belt on his third voyage: "There the wind failed me and the heat grew so great that I was afraid my ships and crew would be burnt."

In the Atlantic off the southwest "corner" of the bulge of Africa, the *marinheiros* set courses and sails according to the season and the educated guess; but sail on they did, due east to the rich islands of Fernando Po and São Tomé, which the Portuguese came upon in the 1470s and soon transformed into new Madeiras staffed with black labor. East of these islands, the coast turned south again; the secret of the passage to India was not to be come by easily. King João II, who came to the throne in 1481, spurred the *marinheiros* forward, and soon they were at the estuary of the Congo River, but south of the mouth of the Congo they met new but oddly familiar obstacles: the Benguela Current, southern counterpart of the Canary Current, and the southeast trades, southern counterpart of the northeast trades.

In 1487, Bartholomeu Dias pushed south beyond the Congo along the coast of southwest Africa, today's Namibia, fighting the adverse current and wind. He was in the same dilemma as the first *marinheiros* a century before trying to sail back to Europe along the coast of Morocco. Somewhere south of the Orange River, the present border of the Union of South Africa, he ran into stormy weather, and there he made a sensible change in course, sensible for a *marinheiro*. He put out to sea, close-hauled, in search of sea room and a favorable wind. Perhaps he turned as simply as a sheep turns away from the rain, but more likely he turned southwest on the basis of the old tradition that God or the gods like symmetry: If there are trade winds off Morocco slanting from the northeast toward the equator, with westerlies prevailing to their north, and if there are trades off Namibia, slanting from the southeast toward the equator, then there must be westerlies beyond them, too. Perhaps Dias realized that the wind system of the South Atlantic is much like that of the North Atlantic and that the *volta* template, flipped upside down to match the upside-down conditions of the bottom half of the world, would work as well south of the Orange River as north of the Senegal River.

Dias ran into westerlies well south of the southern tip of Africa, and he ran with them east and north to the verge of the Indian Ocean. There, unrest among his crew turned him around somewhere in the vicinity of the Great Fish River and sent him back to Portugal. A nautical Moses, he had seen the Promised Ocean but was never to enter it. He brought home with him two precious bits of knowledge: one, there was a passage to the Indian Ocean from the Atlantic; two, the wind patterns of the South Atlantic were, according to his experience, very much like those of the North Atlantic, only upside-down.

For reasons we do not fully understand, the Portuguese paused for several years before capitalizing on Dias's findings. The next master of the *volta* to prove himself was not even Portuguese, but rather a Genoese mapmaker named Christopher Columbus working for the Spanish. Dias had turned the *volta* upside down; Columbus stretched it sideways.

Columbus, as every schoolchild knows, was interested in sailing west to Asia, believing that would be a shorter route than around Africa. His obvious course was due west from Spain to Cipangu (Japan), but he and every other *marinheiro* knew that the prevailing westerlies in those latitudes made that choice a foolish one. He dropped south to the Canaries, and in September of 1492 turned west with the trades blowing over his starboard quarter and filling the sails of his small fleet. At that season he was on the far northern edge of the trades, where the winds often are not dependable (on his other voyages to America he always dropped farther south before turning west), but 1492 was his lucky year, and he had a splendid voyage to the West Indies. His choice of a course to America was so nearly optimal for sailing craft that navigators, even those from ports in northern Europe, followed it, with a few adjustments such as those he later made himself, for generations. The English expedition that founded the Virginia colony 115 years later and the Dutch fleet that founded New Amsterdam two decades after that both sailed to America via the general vicinity of the Canaries. The Spanish called the warm and dependable trades *las brisas* and named the expanse of the Atlantic between the Canaries and Cape Verdes on one side and the West Indies on the other the *Golfo de Damas*, the Ladies' Gulf.

Columbus bowled down the trades to the Bahamas, to the Greater Antilles, and to immortality. Then he faced the old nagging question of the Mediterranean Atlantic: How to return home against the trades? Beat against them for the thousands of kilometers between Española and Spain? He started the return voyage by noodling about in the waters of Española for a few days, trying to find a crack in the relentless *brisas* to slip through—much like a man looking for a way through a thick hedge—and then did the only sensible thing. He resorted to the *volta do mar*, sidling northeast through the Sargasso Sea (where the weed was so thick his sailors worried it might hold them fast) to the latitudes of the westerlies, and then sailed east to the Azores and back to Spain.

Columbus himself did not quite believe in his own brilliance as a sage of the winds. When in 1496 he made his second trip back from the West Indies to Spain, he again tried to butt his way through the trades. Headwinds and horse-latitude calms reduced him and his crew to starvation rations and the thought of eating their Carib captives before they whistled up a fair wind. Since then, no one but a fool has bucked the North Atlantic trades. As an English scholar of the *marinheiros* said in the early seventeenth century: "For such is the statute of the windes, which all Shipping in that Sea must obey: they must goe one way and returne another."

The Varieties of Atlantic History

DAVID ARMITAGE

We are all Atlanticists now—or so it would seem from the explosion of interest in the Atlantic and the Atlantic world as subjects of study among historians of North and South America, the Caribbean, Africa and western Europe. The Atlantic is even beginning to shape the study of literature, economics, and sociology on topics as diverse as theatrical performance, the early history of globalization, and the sociology of race. However, no field seems to have taken an Atlantic perspective with more seriousness and enthusiasm than history. Indeed, Atlantic history has been called "one of the most important new historiographical developments of recent years." It is affecting the teaching of history at all levels, especially in the United States; it now has its own conferences, seminars and graduate programs; prizes are being awarded for the best books on it; even the first textbooks are being planned. Like the national histories it is designed to supplement and even replace, Atlantic history is becoming institutionalized. This might therefore be a good moment to ask just what Atlantic history is and where it is going, before it becomes entrenched and inflexible.

The attraction of Atlantic history lies, in part, in nature: after all, is not an ocean a natural fact? The Atlantic might seem to be one of the few historical categories

Source: David Armitage, "Three Concepts of Atlantic History," in *The British Atlantic World 1500–1800*, eds. Armitage and Braddick (London: Palgrave Macmillan 2002), pp. 11–27. Reproduced with permission of Palgrave Macmillan.

that has an inbuilt geography, unlike the histories of nation-states with their shifting borders and imperfect overlaps between political allegiances and geographical boundaries. Atlantic history also seems to have a reasonably clear chronology, beginning with its first crossing by Columbus in 1492 (though of course he went to his death largely in ignorance of the implications of his discovery) and ending, conventionally, with the age of revolutions in the late eighteenth and early nineteenth centuries. There is thus a distinguished pedigree for identifying Atlantic history with "early" modernity, before the onset of industrialization, mass democracy, the nation-state, and all the other classic defining features of full-fledged modernity, a condition whose origins both Adam Smith and Karl Marx associated with the European voyages of discovery and especially with 1492.

The Atlantic's geography should be considered flexible, for "oceans" are no less mythical than continents. The Atlantic was a European invention. It was the product of successive waves of navigation, exploration, settlement, administration, and imagination. It did not spring fully formed into European consciousness any more than "America" did, though it could certainly be found on maps—and hence in minds—two centuries before the full extent and outline of the Americas would be. It was a European invention not because Europeans were its only denizens, but because Europeans were the first to connect its four sides into a single entity, both as a system and as the representation of a discrete natural feature. The precise limits of the ocean were, of course, fluid: exactly where it ended was less clear than what it touched and what it connected as long as "the Ocean" was thought of as a single body of circulating water rather than as seven distinct seas. The chronology of Atlantic history should also be considered fluid. An Atlantic approach has already made inroads into nineteenth- and twentieth-century history. . . .

E. P. Thompson once remarked that whenever he saw a new god he felt the urge to blaspheme. . . .

If blasphemy is one response to the rise of Atlantic history, it is unlikely to provide good answers to these important questions. More profitable approaches can be found in genealogy—in the history of Atlantic history—and in anatomy—in the forms Atlantic history has taken and might yet take. . . .

The genealogical approach to Atlantic history exposes a white Atlantic with Cold War roots, a black Atlantic with post-Civil War origins in the United States, and a red Atlantic reaching back to the cosmopolitanism of Marx. Their radically different ancestries may, in themselves, have prevented any reconciliations between these different strains of Atlantic history until the advent of a supposedly post-ideological—that is, both post-Cold War and post-imperial—age. The emergence of multicolored Atlantic histories, and of histories of the Atlantic world that encompass more than just the anglophone north Atlantic, testifies to the success of cross-fertilization. Building on that success, I should like to turn to the anatomy of Atlantic history in order to propose a threefold typology of Atlantic history. Like all good trichotomies, this one is meant to be exhaustive but not exclusive: it should cover all conceivable forms of Atlantic history but does not preclude their combination. With that caveat in mind, then, let me offer these three concepts of Atlantic history:

1. *Circum*-Atlantic history—the transnational history of the Atlantic world.
2. *Trans*-Atlantic history—the international history of the Atlantic world.
3. *Cis*-Atlantic history—national or regional history within an Atlantic context.

My aim in what follows is to describe each approach, to account for its utility, and to suggest its relationship with the other two forms. I will pay particular attention to the third concept—cis-Atlantic history—both because it needs the most elucidation and because it may prove to be the most useful as a means of integrating national, regional, or local histories into the broader perspectives afforded by Atlantic history. I will also ask in conclusion what are the limitations of Atlantic history, both as an example of oceanic history and as a fashionable mode of historical inquiry in the English-speaking world.

1. Circum-Atlantic History

Circum-Atlantic history is the history of the Atlantic as a particular zone of exchange and interchange, circulation and transmission. It is therefore the history of the ocean as an arena distinct from any of the particular, narrower, oceanic zones that comprise it. It certainly encompasses the shores of the Atlantic, but does so only insofar as those shores form part of a larger oceanic history rather than a set of specific national or regional histories abutting onto the Atlantic. It is the history of the people who crossed the Atlantic, who lived on its shores and who participated in the communities it made possible, of their commerce and their ideas, as well as the diseases they carried, the flora they transplanted and the fauna they transported.

Circum-Atlantic history may be the most self-evident way to approach Atlantic history. However, of the three possible concepts of Atlantic history it is the one that has been least investigated. . . .

. . . Circum-Atlantic history . . . incorporates everything *around* the Atlantic basin, and it is mobile and connective, tracing circulations *about* the Atlantic world. There were, of course, many smaller zones of interchange around the fringes of the Atlantic basin, whether in West Africa, in western Europe, or around the Caribbean, which had possessed similar characteristics. Such lesser systems existed within more limited seafaring cultures which had developed their own identities and interdependence thousands of years before Columbus's voyages. The European achievement was to link these subzones together into a single Atlantic system. Within that system there was continuing interaction between the societies migrants had left and those they created together across the Atlantic: it is this achievement that allows us to say that the Atlantic was a European invention, while also acknowledging the contribution of non-European peoples to this development. In contrast, the Indian Ocean's subzones had been integrated long before the arrival of the Portuguese or other Europeans. Some commentators have seen the history of the early modern Atlantic as "a sort of precursor of globalisation at the turn of the twenty-first century." However, this overlooks the precocious integration of the Indian Ocean, not to mention that of the Mediterranean. . . .

Circum-Atlantic history is transnational history. Its conventional chronology begins in just the period usually associated with the rise of the state, that is, in the late fifteenth and early sixteenth centuries, but it ends just before the epoch of the nation-state, in the mid-nineteenth century. Empires and composite monarchies, not states, were the characteristic political units of this era. The history of the Atlantic world has often been told as the sum of the histories of those empires, but such a history could necessarily encompass only European perspectives on the Atlantic system. A truly circum-Atlantic history eludes the history of nation-states chronologically; it also overflows the boundaries of empires geographically, like the silver bullion that was drawn from the Spanish American empire into China, creating a link between the Atlantic world and the Asian trade that has been identified as the starting point for a truly global economy in the sixteenth century.

As the history of a zone, its products, and its inhabitants, circum-Atlantic history is therefore a classic example of a transnational oceanic history: classic, but not defining, because, unlike the Mediterranean of Fernand Braudel's account, it does not make up a single identifiable climatic and geological unit. As Braudel himself noted, "[t]he Atlantic, stretching from pole to pole, reflects the colours of all the earth's climates." It is thus too diverse in the range of climatic zones it straddles— from the Arctic to the Capes, and from the coastal regions of western Europe to the archipelago of the Caribbean—for geographical determinism to have any useful explanatory force. It resembles the Indian Ocean in that variety, as well as in the cultural and economic links gradually forged within it, but not insofar as those links long preceded the intervention of Europeans. And if the Indian Ocean was precocious, the Pacific was belated when judged by the standards of the Atlantic world. The Pacific also had expansive subzones which had been created by Polynesian seafaring cultures thousands of years before the entry of Europeans, but it, too, was ultimately a European creation, in the sense that it was Europeans who first saw it whole; it was also they who first distinguished it from its neighbor and tributary, the Atlantic. Yet, for all these significant differences, the oceanic histories of the Mediterranean, the Indian Ocean, the Atlantic, and the Pacific share one important defining characteristic: that as specifically *oceanic* histories (rather than maritime or imperial histories, for example) they join the land and the sea in a relationship which is "symbiotic, but asymmetric": that is, the two are interdependent, but the history of the ocean predominates and is not the only object of study, as it would be in a strictly maritime history. The national histories of territorial states or empires are only part of this history when an ocean creates long-distance connections between them. Like all such oceanic histories, then, circum-Atlantic history is *trans*national but not *inter*national. That is instead the province of what can be termed "*trans*-Atlantic" history.

2. Trans-Atlantic History

Trans-Atlantic history is the history of the Atlantic world told through comparisons. Circum-Atlantic history makes trans-Atlantic history possible. The circulatory system of the Atlantic created links between regions and peoples formerly kept distinct. This allows trans-Atlantic historians to draw meaningful—rather than merely arbitrary— comparisons between otherwise distinct histories. Unlike the "symbiotic, but asymmetric" relations of land and sea traced by Atlantic history as an oceanic history, trans-Atlantic history concentrates on the shores of the ocean, and assumes the existence of nations and states, as well as societies and economic formations (like plantations or cities), around the Atlantic rim. It can bring those different units into meaningful comparison because they already share some common features by virtue of being enmeshed within circum-Atlantic relationships. Their common Atlantic history defines, but does not determine, the nature of the connection between diverse entities; it may be excluded from comparison, as a common variable, but might itself become the object of study within a specifically circum-Atlantic history.

Trans-Atlantic history can be called international history for two reasons. The first is etymological and contextual; the second, comparative and conceptual. Both terms—"trans-Atlantic" and "international"—first made their way into the English language during the American War of Independence. . . .

Yet more than this common origin in the context of the American war identifies trans-Atlantic history with international history. Just as international history may be said to be the history of the relations between nations (or, in fact, states) within a larger political and economic system, so trans-Atlantic history joins states, nations, and regions within an oceanic system. Trans-Atlantic history is especially suited to the seventeenth- and eighteenth-century histories of the Atlantic world, when state-formation went hand-in-hand with empire-building to create a convergent process we might call "empire-state-building." And it is particularly useful as an approach to the histories of those Atlantic states most prone to exceptionalism in their history—for example, the United Kingdom and the United States—but whose common features can be excavated and displayed more readily within a transatlantic frame of comparison.

Trans-Atlantic history as comparative history has most often been conducted along a north–south axis within the Atlantic world. It has therefore been performed more often as an exercise in inter-*imperial* history than as one in international history. . . . However, the potential for comparative trans-Atlantic histories along an east–west axis remains largely unexplored. When it has been undertaken . . . it has usually been within an imperial framework, often explicitly divided between centers and peripheries.

Yet the units of analysis could be larger and the framework more generous. . . .

Comparison as an historical tool may most usefully reveal difference, but it depends for its viability on some initial similarity. A history within the context of empire, and a history of resistance to empire, provides an obvious point of comparison between the United States and the Latin American republics, though their divergent institutional origins and distinctive traditions of religion, governance, and inter-ethnic relations also reveal intractable differences. Such comparisons can help to define more precisely the historical features of segments of the Atlantic world but only within the context of that larger trans-Atlantic perspective. Such precision of definition, taken one stage further, and out of the context of comparison, is the aim of the third and final concept of Atlantic history, "*cis*-Atlantic history."

3. Cis-Atlantic History

"Cis-Atlantic" history studies particular places as unique locations within an Atlantic world and seeks to define that uniqueness as the result of the interaction between local particularity and a wider web of connections (and comparisons). The term "cis-Atlantic" may seem like a barbarous neologism but, like "trans-Atlantic" and "international," it was also a child of the late eighteenth century. The parentage belongs to Thomas Jefferson, and the barbarism, not to the coinage itself, but to the very condition against which Jefferson defined the term. That barbarism—along with feebleness and shrinkage—had been imputed to the fauna of the New World by European naturalists like the comte de Buffon. Jefferson, in his *Notes on the State of Virginia* (1785), had replied by adducing a wealth of information to rebut charges based (as he thought them) on mere ignorance and prejudice:

> I do not mean to deny that there are varieties in the race of man, distinguished by their powers both of body and mind. I believe there are, as I see to be the case in the races of other animals. I only mean to suggest a doubt, whether the bulk and faculties of animals depend on the side of the Atlantic on which their food happens to grow, or which furnishes the elements of which they are compounded? Whether nature has enlisted herself as a Cis or Trans-Atlantic partisan?

Jefferson thus used the term to mean "on this side of the Atlantic," to distinguish it from the trans-Atlantic world of Europe, a meaning he amplified politically when he told James Monroe in 1823 that it was in the interest of the United States "never to suffer Europe to inter-meddle with cis-Atlantic affairs." The term was thus both a badge of difference and a marker of a novel American perspective just as it was defined in relation to the Atlantic Ocean.

Cis-Atlantic history, in the more expansive sense proposed here, is the history of any particular place—a nation, a state, a region, even a specific institution—in relation to the wider Atlantic world. . . .

Cis-Atlantic history may overcome artificial, but nonetheless enduring, divisions between histories usually distinguished from each other as internal and external, domestic and foreign, or national and imperial. The rise of nationalist history in the nineteenth century coincided with the invention of extra-national histories, whether of diplomacy or of imperial expansion. The boundaries between such histories have, until recently, remained mostly impermeable until the rise of postwar multilateralism, decolonization, and the creation of transnational federations, along with separatist sentiment at the subnational level, together helped to dissolve some of those boundaries. Larger narratives of historical development may be harder to dislodge. For example, the processes implied by the labels "early modern" in European history and "colonial" in the histories of British or Spanish America are distinct from one another: "early modern" implied a movement toward modernity, while "colonial" denoted subordination within an empire that would precede independence and the acquisition of nationhood and statehood. Latin American history rarely, if ever, has the label "early modern" applied to it, and attempts to encourage the replacement of "colonial" with "early modern" in North American history have not been entirely successful. The incompatibility of such master-narratives has been especially debilitating in studies of the period called, variously, "early modern" and "colonial," not least because it has obscured the continuities between processes usually kept apart, such as state-formation within Europe and empire-building beyond it. Like the comparisons made possible by trans-Atlantic history, so cis-Atlantic history confronts such separations by insisting on commonalities and by studying the local effects of ocean movements.

Cis-Atlantic history, at this local level, can be most fruitfully applied to the very places most obviously transformed by their Atlantic connections: port towns and cities. For example, Bristol's economy moved from a fifteenth-century dependence on the wine trade to its seventeenth-century concentration on Atlantic staples. This involved not only a radical re-orientation from east to west, and from Europe to the

Americas, but also upheavals in the social order, in the disposition of cultural space, and in the distribution of power. Similar transformations can be traced in other settlements around the Atlantic basin, whether on the Atlantic coasts of Europe and Africa, in the cities of the Caribbean, or along the eastern seaboard of North America. For example, crossing points within the Atlantic world gained new significance when imperial rivalries increased and local polities took advantage of the competition for their allegiance, as among the Kuna Indians of the isthmus of Darién. Wherever local populations encountered or collided with outsiders (not always Europeans), "middle grounds" of negotiation and contest arose like this which would not have existed were it not for the circulation and competition created by the thickening of the connections within the Atlantic system. Likewise, new economies arose to meet novel demands, whether by the wholesale export of the plantation system from the Mediterranean to the Americas in the sixteenth and seventeenth centuries or, arising more organically, by gradual specialization like that among the wine-producers of Madeira in the eighteenth century who created their eponymous wines in direct response to various consumers' tastes. . . .

* * *

Braudel warned that "the historical Mediterranean seems to be a concept of infinite expansion" and wondered aloud: "But how far in space are we justified in extending it?" One might wonder the same about the Atlantic, and about Atlantic history. Circum-Atlantic history would seem to extend no further than the ocean's shores; as soon as we leave the circulatory system of the Atlantic itself, we enter a series of cis-Atlantic histories. Trans-Atlantic history combines such cis-Atlantic histories into units of comparison; the possibilities for combination are various, but not infinite, because adjacency to the Atlantic determines the possibility of comparison. Cis-Atlantic histories, though superficially the most precisely bounded, may in fact be those of greatest extension: such histories protrude deep into the continents of the circum-Atlantic rim, indeed as far as the goods, ideas, and people circulated within the Atlantic system penetrated. Cis-Atlantic histories of entirely land-locked regions would then be possible.

The three concepts of Atlantic history outlined here are not exclusive but rather reinforcing. Taken together, they offer the possibility of a three-dimensional history of the Atlantic world. A circum-Atlantic history would draw upon the fruits of various cis-Atlantic histories and generate comparisons between them. Trans-Atlantic history can link those cis-Atlantic histories because of the existence of a circum-Atlantic system. Cis-Atlantic history in turn feeds trans-Atlantic comparisons. Such a set of cross-fertilized histories might show that the Atlantic's is the only oceanic history to possess these three conceptual dimensions, because it may be the only one that can be construed as at once transnational, international, and national in scope. Global comparisons among different oceanic histories have barely been imagined yet, but they should be central to any future oceanic history.

Atlantic history has not yet suffered the death by a thousand textbooks that has befallen other fields. It has no agreed canon of problems, events, or processes. It follows no common method or practice. It has even begun productively to escape the early modern boundaries of *c.* 1492–1815 within which it has most usually been confined. Like the Atlantic itself, the field is fluid, in motion, and potentially boundless, depending on how it is defined; that is part of its appeal, but also one of its drawbacks. It is unlikely to replace traditional national histories and it will compete with other forms of transnational and international history. However, as a field that links national histories, facilitates comparisons between them, and opens up new areas of study or gives greater focus to better-established modes of inquiry, it surely presents more opportunities than disadvantages. Atlantic history—whether circum-Atlantic, trans-Atlantic, or cis-Atlantic—pushes historians towards methodological pluralism and expanded horizons. That is surely the most one can ask of any emergent field of study.

FURTHER READING

Bailyn, Bernard. *Atlantic History: Concepts and Contours.* Cambridge, MA: Harvard University Press, 2005.

Bentley, Jerry. "Seas and Ocean Basins as Frameworks of Historical Analysis," *Geographical Review* 89, no. 2 (April 1999): 215–224.

Braudel, Fernand. *The Mediterranean and the Mediterranean World in the Age of Philip II.* Translated by Sian Reynolds. New York: Harper & Row, 1973.

Butel, Paul. *The Atlantic.* Translated by Iain Hamilton Grant. New York: Routledge, 1999.

Cañizares-Esguerra, Jorge. "Some Caveats About the 'Atlantic' Paradigm." *History Compass.* www.history-compass.com.

Coclanis, Peter A. "*Drang Nach Osten*: Bernard Bailyn, the World-Island, and the Idea of American History," *Journal of World History* 13, No. 1 (Spring 2002): 169–182.

Curtin, Philip D. *The Rise and Fall of the Plantation Complex: Essays in Atlantic History.* New York: Cambridge University Press, 1990.

Egerton, Douglas R., Alison Games, Jane Landers, Kris Lane, and Donald R. Wright. *The Atlantic World: A History, 1400–1888.* Wheeling, IL: Harlan Davidson Inc., 2007.

Elliott, John Huxtable. *Empires of the Atlantic World: Britain and Spain in America, 1492–1830.* New Haven, CT: Yale University Press, 2006.

Emmer, Pieter C. et al. "Round Table Conference: The Nature of Atlantic History." *Itinerario* 23, no. 2 (1999): 48–173.

Gabaccia, Donna. "A Long Atlantic in a Wider World," *Atlantic Studies* [Great Britain] 1, no. 1 (2004): 1–27.

Games, Alison. "Atlantic History: Definitions, Challenges, and Opportunities," *American Historical Review* 111, no. 3 (June 2006): 741–757.

Gillis, John R. *Islands of the Mind: How the Human Imagination Created the Atlantic World.* New York: Palgrave Macmillan, 2004.

Gilroy, Paul. *The Black Atlantic: Modernity and Double Consciousness.* Cambridge, MA: Harvard University Press, 1993.

Lewis, Martin W., and Kären E. Wigen. *The Myth of Continents: A Critique of Metageography.* Berkeley, CA: University of California Press, 1997.

Meinig, D. W. *The Shaping of America: A Geographical Perspective on 500 Years of History.* Vol. 1, *Atlantic America, 1491–1800.* New Haven, CT: Yale University Press, 1986.

Roach, Joseph R. *Cities of the Dead: Circum-Atlantic Performance.* New York: Columbia University Press, 1996.

Rozwadowski, Helen M. *Fathoming the Ocean: The Discovery and Exploration of the Deep Sea.* Cambridge, MA: Belknap Press of Harvard University Press, 2005.

Sensbach, Jon F. *Rebecca's Revival: Creating Black Christianity in the Atlantic World.* Cambridge, MA: Harvard University Press, 2005.

Thornton, John Kelly, *Africa and Africans in the Making of the Atlantic World, 1400–1800.* New York: Cambridge University Press, 1998.

Thrower, Norman. *Maps and Civilization: Cartography in Culture and Society.* Rev. ed. Chicago: University of Chicago Press, 1996.

CHAPTER

2

Origins of the
Atlantic World

*After a false start by the Vikings in the medieval era, the Christian Iberian king-
doms of Castile, Aragon, and Portugal took the first step toward creating an enduring Atlantic world in the fifteenth century. Two principal motivations guided the
Iberians' activities. They dreamed of finding new sea-based routes to the gold fields
of western Africa and rich spice markets of Asia, circumventing the middlemen who
controlled existing land-based trade routes. They also hoped to crusade against the
western borders of the Islamic world, enlarging the dominions of Christianity. The
Iberian foray into the eastern Atlantic drew from knowledge and experience accumulated over centuries of seafaring, commerce, and cross-cultural interaction in the
Mediterranean, which linked southern Europe, north Africa, and the Near East.
Gradually, Spanish and Portuguese sailors pushed farther into the Atlantic Ocean,
stumbling into the Canaries, Madeiras, and Azores island chains and learning about
the ocean's winds and currents. Stimulated by the patronage of Prince Henry the
Navigator (1394–1460), Portuguese explorers ventured down Africa's Atlantic
coast, eventually rounding the Cape of Good Hope in 1497. These voyages brought
Iberian sailors, soldiers, merchants, and missionaries into direct contact with the
diverse people of sub-Saharan Africa and the Atlantic islands. Dynamics of disease,
trade, enslavement, religious conversion, colonization, and resistance that came to
define the Atlantic world after 1492 were set in motion well before Christopher
Columbus landed in Hispaniola. Indeed, Columbus's own motives and expectations
emerged from his maritime and mercantile experiences in the early Atlantic world
of the fifteenth century.*

DOCUMENTS

How did Europeans first make their way into the Atlantic world, and who did they
find there? Centuries before Columbus, the Vikings established settlements in the
western Atlantic, exploring Greenland in 982 and the North American continent
around 1000. Thorfinn Karlsefni set out around 1010 from Greenland on an expedition

to North America. Document 1 presents an excerpt from the Greenland Saga (c. 1380) describing the short-lived settlement at Vinland (in what today is Canada), where the Vikings marveled at the riches of the land and dreaded the hostility of the people they called "Skrellings."

In the fifteenth century, the Iberians struck out in a different direction from the Vikings, crossing into Africa and leapfrogging the islands of the eastern Atlantic. In part, the Spanish and Portuguese expansion extended the Christian "reconquest" of the Iberian peninsula. Document 2 comes from a body of laws compiled between 1251 and 1265 under the direction of Alfonso I of Castile and known as the Siete Partidas. These illustrate the treatment of Muslim and Jewish subjects before their forced conversions in the fifteenth century. In Document 3, Pope Eugene IV offers religious sanction for the Portuguese assault on the city of Ceuta in North Africa in 1436.

Portuguese contacts with Atlantic Africa were crucial to the early integration of the Atlantic world. In Document 4, the Portuguese chronicler Luis de Cadamosto narrates the events of an expedition to Gambia in 1455, which met with a hostile reception. Yet West Africa had much to offer European merchants and traders, as Leo Africanus suggests in Document 6, a description of the commercial culture in the Songhai Empire, located along the Niger River in the early sixteenth century. Compare and contrast the de Cadamosto and Africanus documents with Document 5, Christopher Columbus's account of his landfall in the Caribbean in 1492, which he mistook for the Indies. Columbus's impressions of the Taíno people owed much to his prior experiences with non-Europeans in the eastern Atlantic.

How did early Atlantic people think about the ocean? Document 7 pairs two different sets of myths. The first is a Taíno creation story recorded by Ramón Pané, a Hieronymite friar who traveled with Christopher Columbus's second voyage in 1493. He lived on Hispaniola for four years, and he worked diligently (if not always accurately) to record what he could about the Taínos' customs and beliefs. The second excerpt comes from the Jesuit José de Acosta (1539–1600), who lived and worked in the Caribbean, Peru, and New Spain. Acosta confidently fit the Americas into his Biblical view of the world and into the knowledge of the writers of classical antiquity.

1. The Vikings Explore North America, c. 1010

Of the Wineland Voyages of Thorfinn and His Companions.

That same summer a ship came from Norway to Greenland. The skipper's name was Thorfinn Karlsefni; he was a son of Thord Horsehead, and a grandson of Snorri, the son of Thord of Hofdi. Thorfin Karlsefni, who was a very wealthy man, passed the winter at Brattahlid with Leif Ericsson. He very soon set his heart upon Gudrid, and sought her hand in marriage; she referred him to Leif for her answer, and was subsequently betrothed to him, and their marriage was celebrated that same winter. A renewed discussion arose concerning a Wineland voyage, and the folk urged Karlsefni to make the venture, Gudrid joining with the others. He determined to undertake the voyage, and assembled a company of sixty men and five women, and entered into an

---

Source: Arthur Middleton Reeves, trans., "The Greenland Saga" in Rasmus Anderson, ed., *The Norse Discovery of America* (London: Norroena Society, 1907), pp. 92–96.

agreement with his shipmates that they should each share equally in all the spoils of the enterprise. They took with them all kinds of cattle, as it was their intention to settle the country, if they could. Karlsefni asked Leif for the house in Wineland, and he replied, that he would lend it but not give it. They sailed out to sea with the ship, and arrived safe and sound at Leifs-booths, and carried their hammocks ashore there. They were soon provided with an abundant and goodly supply of food, for a whale of good size and quality was driven ashore there, and they secured it, and flensed it, and had then no lack of provisions. The cattle were turned out upon the land, and the males soon became very restless and vicious; they had brought a bull with them. Karlsefni caused trees to be felled, and to be hewed into timbers, wherewith to load his ship, and the wood was placed upon a cliff to dry. They gathered somewhat of all of the valuable products of the land, grapes, and all kinds of game and fish, and other good things. In the summer succeeding the first winter, Skrellings were discovered. A great troop of men came forth from out the woods. The cattle were hard by, and the bull began to bellow and roar with a great noise, whereat the Skrellings were frightened, and ran away, with their packs wherein were grey furs, sables and all kinds of peltries. They fled towards Karlsefni's dwelling, and sought to effect an entrance into the house, but Karlsefni caused the doors to be defended [against them]. Neither [people] could understand the other's language. The Skrellings put down their bundles then, and loosed them, and offered their wares [for barter], and were especially anxious to exchange these for weapons, but Karlsefni forbade his men to sell their weapons, and taking counsel with himself, he bade the women carry out milk to the Skrellings, which they no sooner saw than they wanted to buy it, and nothing else. Now the outcome of the Skrelling's trading was, that they carried their wares away in their stomachs, while they left their packs and peltries behind with Karlsefni and his companions, and having accomplished this [exchange] they went away. Now it is to be told that Karlsefni caused a strong wooden palisade to be constructed and set up around the house. It was at this time that Gudrid, Karlsefni's wife, gave birth to a male child, and the boy was called Snorri. In the early part of the second winter the Skrellings came to them again, and these were now much more numerous than before, and brought with them the same wares as at first. Then said Karlsefni to the women: "Do ye carry out now the same food, which proved so profitable before, and nought else." When they saw this they cast their packs in over the palisade. Gudrid was sitting within, in the doorway, beside the cradle of her infant son, Snorri, when a shadow fell upon the door, and a woman in a black nam-kirtle entered. She was short in stature, and wore a fillet about her head; her hair was of a light chestnut colour, and she was pale of hue, and so big-eyed that never before had eyes so large been seen in a human skull. She went up to where Gudrid was seated, and said: "What is thy name?" "My name is Gudrid; but what is thy name?" "My name is Gudrid," says she. The housewife, Gudrid, motioned her with her hand to a seat beside her; but it so happened, that at that very instant Gudrid heard a great crash, whereupon the woman vanished, and at that same moment one of the Skrellings, who had tried to seize their weapons, was killed by one of Karlsefni's followers. At this the Skrellings fled precipitately, leaving their garments and wares behind them; and not a soul, save Gudrid alone, beheld this woman. "Now we must needs take counsel together," says Karlsefni, "for that I believe they will visit us a third time, in great numbers, and attack us. Let us now adopt this plan: ten of our number shall go out upon the cape, and show themselves there, while the remainder of our company shall go into the woods and hew a clearing for our cattle, when the troop approaches from the forest. We will also take our bull, and let him go in advance of us." The lay of the land was such that the proposed meeting-place had the lake upon the one side and the forest upon the other. Karlsefni's advice was now carried into execution. The Skrellings advanced to the spot which Karlsefni had selected for the encounter, and a battle was fought there, in which great numbers of the band of the Skrellings were slain. There was one man among the Skrellings, of a large size and fine bearing, whom Karlsefni concluded must be their chief. One of the Skrellings picked up an axe, and having looked at it for a time, he brandished it about one of his companions, and hewed at him, and on the instant the man fell dead. Thereupon the big man seized the axe and after examining it for a moment he hurled it as far as he could, out into the sea; then they fled helter-skelter into the woods, and thus their intercourse came to an end. Karlsefni and his party remained there throughout the winter, but in the spring Karlsefni announced that he was not minded to remain there longer, but would return to Greenland. They now made ready for the voyage, and carried away with them much booty in vines and grapes and peltries. They sailed out upon the high seas, and brought their ship safely to Ericsfirth, where they remained during the winter.

2. Castilian Law Incorporates Slaves and Others Before 1492

TITLE XXII. . . .

LAW I.

What Liberty Is, Who Can Give It, to Whom It Can Be Given, and in What Way.

Liberty is the power which every man has by nature to do what he wishes, except where the force or right of law or *fuero* does not prevent him. This liberty can be granted by a master to his slave, in church or out of it, before a judge or anywhere else, by will or without a will, or by a written instrument. He should, however, do this himself, and not by an attorney, except where he orders some of those in his direct line to do so. It is necessary when he frees a slave by a written instrument, or in the presence of his friends, to do so before five witnesses. When he desires to liberate him by will, the master granting such emancipation cannot do so unless he is fourteen years old. A master who wishes to liberate a slave in any other way by a written instrument, or before witnesses, or friends, cannot do so unless he is twenty years old; except where the person whom he desires to emancipate is his son or his daughter, whom he had by some female slave; or where said slave is his father, his mother, his brother, or his sister; or his master who gave him instruction; or his tutor or his nurse who brought him up; or his servant, either male or female; or where he had the same foster-mother

Source: Robert I. Burns, ed., *Las Siete Partidas* (Philadelphia: University of Pennsylvania Press, 2001), vol. 4, pp. 981, 982; vol. 5, pp. 1433–1436, 1438–1442.

as his servant; or where the said slave had rescued his master from death, or defended his good name; or where anyone desires to enfranchise one of his slaves, in order to appoint him his agent to attend to his business out of court, and the slave is at least seventeen years old; or where he enfranchises his female slave in order to marry her; but in this case he should swear that he enfranchises her for this purpose, and that he will marry her within six months. Where a master proves any of the aforesaid matters before a judge, if he is under twenty years of age and over seventeen, he has the right to enfranchise his slave, doing so always with the consent of his guardian. . . .

LAW IV.

A Female Slave Becomes Free When Her Master Places Her in a Brothel to Earn Money by Her.

When a man places his female slaves publicly in a brothel, or in any house, or in any other place whatsoever, in order that they may give themselves to men for money; we decree that on account of such depravity as this, which he orders them to commit, the master shall lose his slaves, and that they, for this reason, become free; and we order that those magistrates who represent Us in court, in the district where this takes place, shall protect said female slaves, so that the party who was their master can never afterwards reduce them to servitude, or have any rights whatever in them. . . .

TITLE XXIV. . . .

LAW II.

In What Way Jews Should Pass Their Lives Among Christians; What Things They Should Not Make Use of or Practice, According to Our Religion; and What Penalty Those Deserve Who Act Contrary to Its Ordinances.

Jews should pass their lives among Christians quietly and without disorder, practicing their own religious rites, and not speaking ill of the faith of Our Lord Jesus Christ, which Christians acknowledge. Moreover, a Jew should be very careful to avoid preaching to, or converting any Christian, to the end that he may become a Jew, by exalting his own belief and disparaging ours. Whoever violates this law shall be put to death and lose all his property. And because we have heard it said that in some places Jews celebrated, and still celebrate Good Friday, which commemorates the Passion of Our Lord Jesus Christ, by way of contempt; stealing children and fastening them to crosses, and making images of wax and crucifying them, when they cannot obtain children; we order that, hereafter, if in any part of our dominions anything like this is done, and can be proved, all persons who were present when the act was committed shall be seized, arrested and brought before the king; and after the king ascertains that they are guilty, he shall cause them to be put to death in a disgraceful manner, no matter how many there may be.

We also forbid any Jew to dare to leave his house or his quarter on Good Friday, but they must all remain shut up until Saturday morning; and if they violate this regulation, we decree that they shall not be entitled to reparation for any injury or dishonor inflicted upon them by Christians. . . .

LAW VII.

What Penalty a Christian Deserves Who Becomes a Jew.

Where a Christian is so unfortunate as to become a Jew, we order that he shall be put to death just as if he had become a heretic; and we decree that his property shall be disposed of in the same way that we stated should be done with that of heretics.

LAW VIII.

No Christian, Man or Woman Shall Live with a Jew.

We forbid any Jew to keep Christian men or women in his house, to be served by them; although he may have them to cultivate and take care of his lands, or protect him on the way when he is compelled to go to some dangerous place. Moreover, we forbid any Christian man or woman to invite a Jew or a Jewess, or to accept an invitation from them, to eat or drink together, or to drink any wine made by their hands. We also order that no Jews shall dare to bathe in company with Christians, and that no Christian shall take any medicine or cathartic made by a Jew; but he can take it by the advice of some intelligent person, only where it is made by a Christian, who knows and is familiar with its ingredients. . . .

TITLE XXV. . . .

LAW I.

Whence the Name of Moor Is Derived, How Many Kinds of the Latter There Are, and in What Way They Should Live Among Christians.

. . . We decree that Moors shall live among Christians in the same way that we mentioned in the preceding Title that Jews shall do, by observing their own law and not insulting ours. Moors, however, shall not have mosques in Christian towns, or make their sacrifices publicly in the presence of men. The mosques which they formerly possessed shall belong to the king; and he can give them to whomsoever he wishes. Although the Moors do not acknowledge a good religion, so long as they live among Christians with their assurance of security, their property shall not be stolen from them or taken by force; and we order that whoever violates this law shall pay a sum equal to double the value of what he took.

LAW II.

Christians Should Convert the Moors by Kind Words, and Not by Compulsion.

Christians should endeavor to convert the Moors by causing them to believe in our religion, and bring them into it by kind words and suitable discourses, and not by violence or compulsion; for if it should be the will of Our Lord to bring them into it and to make them believe by force, He can use compulsion against them if He so desires, since He has full power to do so; but He is not pleased with the service which men perform through fear, but with that which they do voluntarily and without coercion, and as He does not wish to restrain them or employ violence, we forbid anyone to do so for this purpose; and if the wish to become Christians should arise among them, we forbid anyone to refuse assent to it, or oppose it in any way whatsoever. Whoever violates this law shall receive the penalty we mentioned in the preceding Title, which treats of how Jews who interfere with, or kill those belonging to their religion who afterwards become Christians, shall be punished. . . .

LAW IV.

What Punishment a Christian Deserves Who Becomes a Moor.

Men sometimes become insane and lose their prudence and understanding, as, for instance, where unfortunate persons, and those who despair of everything, renounce the faith of Our Lord Jesus Christ, and become Moors; and there are some of them who are induced to do this through the desire to live according to their customs, or on account of the loss of relatives who have been killed or died; or because they have lost their property and become poor; or because of unlawful acts which they commit, dreading the punishment which they deserve on account of them; and when they are induced to do a thing of this kind for any of the reasons aforesaid, or others similar to them, they are guilty of very great wickedness and treason, for on account of no loss or affliction which may come upon them, nor for any profit, riches, good fortune, or pleasure which they may expect to obtain in this world, should they renounce the faith of Our Lord Jesus Christ by which they will be saved and have everlasting life.

Wherefore we order that all those who are guilty of this wickedness shall lose all their possessions, and have no right to any portion of them, but that all shall belong to their children (if they have any) who remain steadfast in our Faith and do not renounce it; and if they have no children, their property shall belong to their nearest relatives within the tenth degree, who remain steadfast in the belief of the Christians; and if they have neither children nor relatives, all their possessions shall be forfeited to the royal treasury; and, in addition to this, we order that if any person who has committed such an offense shall be found in any part of our dominions he shall be put to death. . . .

LAW IX.

Moors Who Come on a Mission from Other Kingdoms to the Court of the King Should, with Their Property, Be Safe and Secure.

Envoys frequently come from the land of the Moors and other countries to the Court of the King, and although they may come from the enemy's country and by his order, we consider it proper and we direct that every envoy who comes to our country, whether he be Christian, Moor, or Jew, shall come and go in safety and security through all our dominions, and we forbid anyone to do him violence, wrong, or harm, or to injure his property.

Moreover, we decree that although an envoy who visits our country may owe a debt to some man in our dominions, which was contracted before he came on the mission, he shall not be arrested or brought into court for it; but if he should not be willing to pay any debts which he contracted in our country after he came on the mission, suit can be brought against him for them, and he can be compelled to pay them by a judgment of court.

LAW X.

What Penalty a Moor and a Christian Woman Deserve Who Have Intercourse with One Another.

If a Moor has sexual intercourse with a Christian virgin, we order that he shall be stoned, and that she, for the first offense, shall lose half of her property, and that her father, mother, or grandfather, shall have it, and if she has no such relatives, that it shall belong to the king. For the second offense, she shall lose all her property, and the heirs aforesaid, if she has any, shall obtain it, and if she has none, the king shall be entitled to it, and she shall be put to death. We decree and order that the same rule shall apply to a widow who commits this crime. If a Moor has sexual intercourse with a Christian married woman, he shall be stoned to death, and she shall be placed in the power of her husband who may burn her to death, or release her, or do what he pleases with her. If a Moor has intercourse with a common woman who abandons herself to everyone, for the first offense, they shall be scourged together through the town, and for the second, they shall be put to death.

3. The Pope Supports Portugal's Conquest of Ceuta, 1436

Bull of Pope Eugene IV, September 8, 1436

Addressed to: High Bishops, Archbishops, Bishops, Administrators, Abbots, Rectors, and Other Prelates

The Pontiff affirms that, as Christ demonstrated the road to salvation, experiencing the suffering on the Cross, the mission of his ministers is to continue to demonstrate that same path. And, seeing that there are some men—Saracens and Agarites and other infidels—who continue to persecute the followers of God, justifies King Dom João in his initiative to attack the infidels in Africa, namely by taking the city of Ceuta by force. At present, it is for the legacy of these same purposes that the King Dom Duarte, with identical objectives, requests the assistance of Rome. Therefore, the Pope summons all other emperors, kings, dukes, marquis, princes, barons, counts, authorities, captains, masters, officials and communities in general to follow and to imitate the Portuguese monarch. Thus, the Pope advises the High Bishops, Archbishops, Bishops, Administrators, Abbots, Rectors and other Prelates, through means of sermons, preaching and other practices, to incite laymen as well as clergymen in their respective areas of jurisdiction to follow this example. And all who engage in this cause are granted plenary absolution for all their sins. And to the King Dom Duarte and his heirs claim possession of the lands, cities and castles that they subjugate, and all who participate in these missions are granted plenary absolution. And power is granted to all the dignitaries of the Church and to the priests, secular or regular clergy, to hear in confession those who will participate in these campaigns and absolve them of all their sins.

Source: José Manuel Garcia, *Documentação Henriquina* (Maia: Castoliva editora, lda., 1995), p. 163. Translated for this volume by Okezi Otovo.

4. A Portuguese Expedition Meets Resistance in Gambia, 1455

The next morning, about the third hour, with the wind favoring the tide, we fixed the sails of the vessels to navigate with our accompaniment and enter the river, in the name of God, with people waiting by the shoreline who were more benevolent than those of the almadias [a kind of canoe]. And thus, arriving at our accompanying vessels, and all following, we began to enter the river, with our caravel in front and one ship behind another following us, all along the banks.

After entering some four miles, I saw some almadias coming up behind us (I don't know where they came from) and rowing as fast as they could. We turned towards them but unsure of poisonous arrows (which I have heard that they use often), we covered our boats as well as we could and armed ourselves, taking our posts, in spite of being poorly armed. Soon, they approached us who were still and quiet, looking at the bow of my ship and dividing themselves into two lines, placing themselves in the middle. Counting those almadias, we think that there were 15, large as if they were good vessels. They stopped rowing and lifted their oars into the air, fixing their gaze on us, a marvelous sight. And examining them, we judged there to be at most 130 to 150 blacks that looked to have very good bodies, very black skin. All dressed in white cotton shirts and with white hats on their heads almost in a Teutonesque style, save for some species of bird on each side and a white feather in the middle of the hat—almost as if they meant to give the impression that they were men of war. The front of each almadia was black with a shield on the brace that seemed to be made of leather. And, they did not fire on us nor did we make any move against them, having seen two other vessels coming up behind and making their way towards them. The boats approached and got closer to them and without any salutation, they released their oars, and all began firing their arrows.

Upon seeing the assault, our boats discharged four cannons first. Hearing this, astonished and perplexed by the loud noise, the blacks released their arrows and some looking to one side and others to the other, they admired the stones of the cannons striking the water near them. And they spent some time looking at them. But without seeing anything else, they lost their fear of the noise and then after we had fired many shots, they picked up their arrows and began to fire again with great ardor, firing upon our boats. The soldiers began to aim at them with their cross-bows and the first to fire was a bastard son of that Genovese gentleman. He hit a black in the chest who fell dead in the almadia. Upon seeing this, they took their own arrows and considered the crossbows to be marvelous weapons. But even for this, they did not stop firing at the boats vigorously and those in the caravels back at them. In little time, many blacks were killed and two Christians, thanks to God that none were wounded.

Seeing the blacks shot and dead, almost all of the almadias in harmony turned to the stern of the small caravel and gave them a great battle, because they were few men and poorly armed. Seeing this, I furled the sails of the small boat and arriving

Source: Alvise Cá da Mosto (Luis de Cadamosto). *Navegações Luís de Cadamosto* (Lisbon: Instituto para a Alta Cultura, 1944), 65–68. Translated for this volume by Okezi Otovo.

at it, we guided it to the middle of the larger boats, firing cannons and crossbows. The blacks stood back and we fastened the three caravels with a rope, lowering an anchor and calmly the three were secure.

Then, we attempted to speak with these blacks through our interpreters but we made so much beckoning and screaming that one of the almadias fired at us. We had the interpreters ask them why we had offended them being that we are men of peace, who came to trade goods and who had had good relations and friendships with the blacks of the kingdom of Senegal. That we hoped to have equal relations with them if they approved and that we had come from countries far away to bring gifts to their king and senhor from our king of Portugal who hoped to have friendship and peace with him. And we asked them what country we were in, and who was the master of these lands, and what was the name of this river, and if they wanted to come to us in peace and amicably to take some of our goods and that we could take of theirs, little or nothing, when they approved until all were satisfied with everything.

Their response was that in the past they had some news of us and our way of trading with the blacks of Senegal who couldn't be anything other than bad men for wanting our friendship. But they were certain that we Christians eat human flesh and we buy blacks solely to eat them. For this reason, they did not want any type of friendship with us, but rather only to kill us all and afterwards present our goods to their master who they said was three days journey from here. And that that country was Gambia and that the river was very large—the name of which they told me but I do not remember.

In that moment, the wind rose and seeing us raise our sails before them, they noted this and escaped towards the land. And thus our war ended.

After this, the leaders who were in charge of the boats consulted among ourselves on whether we would go further up the river to 100 miles if we could and hopefully encounter better people. But our sailors who wished to return to their homes without experiencing more danger, all together began to shout, saying that they did not want to comply and that what they had already done on that voyage was enough.

Because of this, seeing the common will, we agreed to acquiesce to evade scandal as these are very willful and obstinate men. So much so that the next day we left there in the direction of Cape Verde to return to Portugal, in the name of God.

5. Columbus Arrives in the "Indies," October 11, 1492

Thursday, October 11th / He navigated to the west-south-west; they had a rougher sea than they had experienced during the whole voyage. They saw petrels and a green reed near the ship. Those in the caravel *Pinta* saw a cane and a stick, and they secured another small stick, carved, as it appeared with iron, and a piece of cane, and other vegetation which grows on land, and a small board. Those in the caravel *Niña* also saw other indications of land and a stick loaded with barnacles. At these signs, all

---

Source: *The Journal of Christopher Columbus*, trans. Cecil Jane (London: Anthony Bland, 1968), pp. 22–24. Reprinted with permission of the Hakluyt Society and David Higham Associates.

breathed again and rejoiced. . . . This land was first sighted by a sailor called Rodrigo de Triana, although the admiral, at ten o'clock in the night, being on the sterncastle, saw a light. It was, however, so obscured that he would not affirm that it was land, but called Pero Gutierrez, butler of the King's dais, and told him that there seemed to be a light, and that he should watch for it. He did so, and saw it. He said the same also to Rodrigo Sanchez de Segovia, whom the King and Queen had sent in the fleet as *veedor*, and he saw nothing since he was not in a position from which it could be seen. After the admiral had so spoken, it was seen once or twice, and it was like a small wax candle, which was raised and lowered. Few thought that this was an indication of land, but the admiral was certain that they were near land. Accordingly, when they had said the *Salve*, which all sailors are accustomed to say and chant in their manner, and when they had all been gathered together, the admiral asked and urged them to keep a good look out from the forecastle and to watch carefully for land, and to him who should say first that he saw land, he would give at once a silk doublet apart from the other rewards which the Sovereigns had promised, which were ten thousand maravedis annually to him who first sighted it. Two hours after midnight land appeared, at a distance of about two leagues from them. They took in all sail, remaining with the mainsail, which is the great sail without bonnets, and kept jogging, waiting for day, a Friday, on which they reached a small island of the Lucayos, which is called in the language of the Indians "Guanahaní." Immediately they saw naked people, and the admiral went ashore in the armed boat, and Martin Alonso Pinzón and Vicente Yañez, his brother, who was captain of the *Niña*. The admiral brought out the royal standard, and the captains went with two banners of the Green Cross, which the admiral flew on all the ships as a flag, with an F and a Y, and over each letter their crown, one being on one side of the ✖ and the other on the other. When they had landed, they saw very green trees and much water and fruit of various kinds. The admiral called the two captains and the others who had landed, and Rodrigo de Escobedo, secretary of the whole fleet, and Rodrigo Sanchez de Segovia, and said that they should bear witness and testimony how he, before them all, took possession of the island, as in fact he did, for the King and Queen, his Sovereigns, making the declarations which are required, as is contained more at length in the testimonies which were there made in writing. Soon many people of the island gathered there. What follows are the actual words of the admiral, in his book of his first voyage and discovery of these Indies.

"I," he says, "in order that they might feel great amity towards us, because I knew that they were a people to be delivered and converted to our holy faith rather by love than by force, gave to some among them some red caps and some glass beads, which they hung round their necks, and many other things of little value. At this they were greatly pleased and became so entirely our friends that it was a wonder to see. Afterwards they came swimming to the ships' boats, where we were, and brought us parrots and cotton thread in balls, and spears and many other things, and we exchanged for them other things, such as small glass beads and hawks' bells, which we gave to them. In fact, they took all and gave all, such as they had, with good will, but it seemed to me that they were a people very deficient in everything. They all go naked as their mothers bore them, and the women also, although I saw only one very young girl. And all those whom I did see were youths, so that I did not see one who was over thirty years of age; they were very well built, with very handsome bodies and very good faces. Their hair is coarse almost like the hairs of a horse's tail and short; they wear their hair down over their eyebrows, except for a few strands behind, which they wear long and never cut. Some of them are painted black, and they are the colour of the people of the Canaries, neither black nor white, and some of them are painted white and some red and some in any colour that they find. Some of them paint their faces, some their whole bodies, some only the eyes, and some only the nose. They do not bear arms or know them, for I showed to them swords and they took them by the blade and cut themselves through ignorance. They have no iron. Their spears are certain reeds, without iron, and some of these have a fish tooth at the end, while others are pointed in various ways. They are all generally fairly tall, good looking and well proportioned. I saw some who bore marks of wounds on their bodies, and I made signs to them to ask how this came about, and they indicated to me that people came from other islands, which are near, and wished to capture them, and they defended themselves. And I believed and still believe that they come here from the mainland to take them for slaves. They should be good servants and of quick intelligence, since I see that they very soon say all that is said to them, and I believe that they would easily be made Christians, for it appeared to me that they had no creed. Our Lord willing, at the time of my departure I will bring back six of them to Your Highnesses, that they may learn to talk. I saw no beast of any kind in this island, except parrots." All these are the words of the admiral.

6. Leo Africanus Describes a West African World of Trade, c. 1515

A Description of the Kingdome of Ghinea.

This kingdome called by the merchants of our nation Gheneoa, by the natural inhabitants thereof Genni, and by the Portugals and other people of Europe Ghinea, standeth in the midst betweene Gualata on the north, Tombuto on the east, and the kingdome of Melli on the south. In length it containeth almost five hundred miles, and extendeth two hundred and fiftie miles along the river of Niger, and bordereth upon the Ocean sea in the same place, where Niger falleth into the saide sea. This place exceedingly aboundeth with barlie, rice, cattell, fishes, and cotton: and their cotton they sell unto the merchants of Barbarie, for cloth of Europe, for brazen vessels, for armour, and other such commodities. Their coine is of gold without any stampe or inscription at all: they have certaine iron-money also, which they use about matters of small value, some peeces whereof weigh a pound, some halfe a pound, and some one quarter of a pound. In all this kingdome there is no fruite to be found but onely dates, which are brought hither either out of Gualata or Numidia. Heere is neither towne nor castle, but a certaine great village onely, wherein the prince of Ghinea, together with his priestes, doctors, merchants, and all the principall men of the region inhabite. The walles of their houses are built of chalke, and the roofes are covered with strawe: the inhabitants are clad in blacke or blew cotton, wherewith they cover their heads also: but the priests and doctors of their law go apparelled in white cotton. This region during the three moneths of Julie, August, and September, is yeerely environed with the overflowings of Niger in manner of an Island; all which time the

Source: John Leo [Leo Africanus], *A Geographical Historie of Africa*, translated by John Pory (London: George Bishop, 1600), pp. 284–290.

merchants of Tombuto conveigh their merchandize hither in certaine Canoas or narrow boats made of one tree, which they rowe all the day long, but at night they binde them to the shore, and lodge themselves upon the lande. This kingdome was subject in times past unto a certaine people of Libya, and became afterward tributarie unto king *Soni Heli*, after whom succeeded *Soni Heli Izchia*, who kept the prince of this region prisoner at Gago, where togither with a certaine nobleman, he miserably died.

Of the Kingdome of Melli.

This region extending it selfe almost three hundred miles along the side of a river which falleth into Niger, bordereth northward upon the region last described, southward upon certaine deserts and drie mountaines, westward upon huge woods and forrests stretching to the Ocean sea shore, and eastward upon the territories of Gago. In this kingdome there is a large and ample village containing to the number of six thousand or mo families, and called Melli, whereof the whole kingdome is so named. And here the king hath his place of residence. The region it selfe yeeldeth great abundance of corne, flesh, and cotton. Heere are many artificers and merchants in all places: and yet the king honorably entertaineth all strangers. The inhabitants are rich, and have plentie of wares. Heere are great store of temples, priests, and professours, which professours read their lectures onely in the temples, bicause they have no colleges at all. The people of this region excell all other Negros in witte, civilitie, and industry; and were the first that embraced the law of Mahumet, at the same time when the uncle of *Joseph* the king of Maroco was their prince, and the government remained for a while unto his posterity: at length *Izchia* subdued the prince of this region, and made him his tributarie, and so oppressed him with greevous exactions, that he was scarce able to maintaine his family.

Of the Kingdome of Tombuto.

This name was in our times (as some thinke) imposed upon this kingdome from the name of a certain towne so called, which (they say) king *Mense Suleiman* founded in the yeere of the Hegeira 610. And it is situate within twelve miles of a certaine branch of Niger, all the houses whereof are now changed into cottages built of chalke, and covered with thatch. Howbeit there is a most stately temple to be seene, the wals whereof are made of stone and lime, and a princely palace also built by a most excellent workeman of Granada. Here are many shops of artificers, and merchants, and especially of such as weave linnen and cotton cloth. And hither do the Barbarie-merchants bring cloth of Europe. All the women of this region except maidservants go with their faces covered, and sell all necessarie victuals. The inhabitants, & especially strangers there residing, are exceeding rich, insomuch, that the king that now is, married both his daughters unto two rich merchants. Here are many wels, containing most sweete water; and so often as the river Niger overfloweth, they conveigh the water thereof by certaine sluces into the towne. Corne, cattle, milke, and butter this region yeeldeth in great abundance: but salt is verie scarce heere; for it is brought hither by land from Tegaza, which is five hundred miles distant. When I my selfe was here, I saw one camels loade of salt sold for 80. ducates. The rich king of Tombuto hath many plates and scepters of gold, some whereof weigh 1300. poundes: and he keepes a magnificent and well furnished court. When he travelleth any whither he rideth upon a camell, which is lead by some of his noblemen; and so he doth likewise when hee goeth to warfar, and all his souldiers rise upon horses. Whosoever will speake unto this king must first fall downe before his feete, & then taking up earth must sprinkle it upon his owne head & shoulders: which custom is ordinarily observed by them that never saluted the king before, or come as ambassadors from other princes. He hath alwaies three thousand horsemen, and a great number of footmen that shoot poysoned arrowes, attending upon him. They have often skirmishes with those that refuse to pay tribute, and so many as they take, they sell unto the merchants of Tombuto. Here are verie few horses bred, and the merchants and courtiers keepe certaine little nags which they use to travell upon: but their best horses are brought out of Barbarie. And the king so soone as he heareth that any merchants are come to towne with horses, he commandeth a certaine number to be brought before him, and chusing the best horse for himselfe, he payeth a most liberall price for him. He so deadly hateth all Jewes, that he will not admit any into his citie: and whatsoever Barbarie merchants he understandeth to have any dealings with the Jewes, he presently causeth their goods to be confiscate. Here are great store of doctors, judges, priests, and other learned men, that are bountifully maintained at the kings cost and charges. And hither are brought divers manuscripts or written bookes out of Barbarie, which are sold for more money then any other merchandize. The coine of Tombuto is of gold without any stampe or superscription: but in matters of smal value they use certaine shels brought hither out of the kingdome of Persia, fower hundred of which shels are worth a ducate: and sixe peeces of their golden coine with two third parts weigh an ounce. The inhabitants are people of a gentle and cherefull disposition, and spend a great part of the night in singing and dancing through all the streets of the citie: they keepe great store of men and women-slaves, and their towne is much in danger of fire: at my second being there halfe the town almost was burnt in five howers space. Without the suburbs there are no gardens nor orchards at all. . . .

Of the Towne and Kingdome of Gago.

The great towne of Gago being unwalled also, is distant southward of Tombuto almost fower hundred miles, and enclineth somewhat to the southeast. The houses thereof are but meane, except those wherein the king and his courtiers remaine. Here are exceeding rich merchants: and hither continually resort great store of Negros which buy cloth here brought out of Barbarie and Europe. This towne aboundeth with corne and flesh, but is much destitute of wine, trees, and fruits. Howbeit here is plentie of melons, citrons, and rice: here are many welles also containing most sweete and holesome water. Here is likewise a certaine place where slaves are to be sold, especially upon such daies as the merchants use to assemble; and a yoong slave of fifteene yeeres age is sold for sixe ducates, and so are children sold also. The king of this region hath a certaine private palace wherein he maintaineth a great number of concubines and slaves, which are kept by eunuches: and for the guard of his owne person he keepeth a sufficient troupe of horsemen and footmen. Betweene the first gate of the palace and the inner part thereof, there is a place walled round about, wherein the king himselfe decideth all his subjects controversies: and albeit the king be in this function most diligent, and performeth all things thereto appertayning, yet

hath he about him his counsellors & other officers, as namely his secretaries, treas-
urers, factors, and auditors. It is a woonder to see what plentie of Merchandize is
dayly brought hither, and how costly and sumptuous all things be. Horses bought in
Europe for ten ducates, are here sold againe for fortie and sometimes for fiftie ducates
a piece. There is not any cloth of Europe so course, which will not here be sold for
fower ducates an elle, and it if be any thing fine they will give fifteene ducates for an
ell: and an ell of the scarlet of Venice or of Turkie-cloath is here worth thirtie ducates.
A sword is here valued at three or fower crownes, and so likewise are spurs, bridles,
with other like commodities, and spices also are sold at an high rate: but of al other
commodities salt is most extremelie deere. The residue of this kingdome containeth
nought but villages and hamlets inhabited by husbandmen and shepherds, who in
winter cover their bodies with beasts skins; but in sommer they goe all naked save
their privie members: and sometimes they weare upon their feet certaine shooes made
of camels leather. They are ignorant and rude people, and you shall scarce finde one
learned man in the space of an hundred miles. They are continually burthened with
grievous exactions, so that they have scarce any thing remaining to live upon.

7. Two Atlantic Inhabitants Explain the Origins of the Sea, 1490s and 1590

Taino Creation Myth

The Relation of Fray Ramón Concerning the Antiquities of the Indians, Which He, Knowing Their Language, Carefully Compiled by Order of the Admiral

I, Fray Ramón, a poor anchorite of the Order of St. Jerome, write by order of the illustrious Lord Admiral, viceroy, and governor of the islands and mainland of the Indies
what I have been able to learn concerning the beliefs and idolatry of the Indians, and
the manner in which they worship their gods. Of these matters I shall give an account
in the present treatise. . . .

I write only of the Indians of the island of Española, for I know nothing about
the other islands and have never seen them. These Indians also know whence they
came and where the sun and moon had their beginning, and how the sea was made,
and of the place to which the dead go. . . .

IX. *How the sea was made.* There was a man called Yaya, whose name they do
not know; his son was called Yayael, which means son of Yaya. This Yayael wishing
to kill his father, the latter banished him, and he was banished for four months; after
that his father killed him and put his bones in a calabash which he hung from the
ceiling of his hut, where it hung for some time. One day, wishing to see his son, Yaya
said to his wife, "I want to see our son Yayael." She was content and, taking the calabash, turned it over to see the bones of their son. Out of it came many large and
small fish. Perceiving that the bones had been changed into fish, they decided to eat
them. One day, when Yaya had gone to his maize fields, that were his inheritance,

Source: Benjamin Keen, ed., *The Life of the Admiral Christopher Columbus by His Son Ferdinand* (New Brunswick: Rutgers University Press, 1959), pp. 153, 156; José de Acosta, *Natural and Moral History of the Indies (1590)*, ed. by Jane E. Mangan (Durham: Duke University Press, 2002), pp. 27–29.

there came four sons of a woman named Itiba Tahuvava, all born at a single birth; for this woman having died in childbirth, they cut her open and took out these four sons. And the first one they took out was *caracaracol*, which means scabby, and his name was . . . ; the others had no name.

X. The four twin sons of Itiba Tahuvava, who died in childbirth, went together to get the calabash in which Yaya kept the bones of his son Yayael who had been changed into a fish; but none of them dared to get it except Dimivan Caracaracol, who took it down; and they all had their fill of fish. While they were eating, they heard Yaya coming back from his fields; and in their haste to hang the calabash up again they did not do it right, so that it fell to earth and broke. They say so much water came out of the calabash that it filled the whole earth, and with it came many fish. They say this was how the sea began. . . .

Acosta's Account of the Continents

. . . We know from Holy Writ that at the beginning of the world the waters were gathered together into one place and that thereupon the dry land appeared. And the same holy writings tell us that these gatherings of waters were called seas and, as there were many of them, there are of necessity many seas. And there is this diversity of seas not only in the Mediterranean, with one being called the Euxinian, another the Caspian, another the Erythraean or Red Sea, another the Persian, another that of Italy, and many more, but also the great ocean itself, which in Divine Writ is often called the abyss, though in truth it is one ocean but in many variations and manners. . . . I have observed, during my own travels by sea as well as what I have learned from the accounts of others, that the sea is never separated from the land for more than a thousand leagues and never surpasses that measure no matter how extensive the ocean. I do not mean that the Ocean Sea cannot be navigated for more than a thousand leagues; that would be a foolish statement because we know that the ships of Portugal sail for four thousand leagues and more, and it is possible to sail completely around the world, as we have seen in our own time, and of this there can be no doubt. But what I say and affirm is that, in the parts of the world that have already been discovered, no land is more distant in a straight line from the nearest continent or nearby islands than a thousand leagues at most, and so there is never a sea distance greater than that between land and land, measuring from the place where one land is closest to the next. . . . And because it has been observed, and is a fact, that wherever there are many large islands there will be a continent not far away, many persons, and I among them, believe that near those same Solomon Islands there is a large continent that corresponds to our America on the west and that continent may possibly extend as far to the south as does the Strait of Magellan. New Guinea is believed to be a continent, and some learned men place it very near the Solomon Islands. Thus, it is most reasonable to believe that a good part of the world still remains to be discovered, for already our people sail this Southern Sea to China and the Philippines, and in traveling from here to there they do not report the voyage to be longer than that from Spain to these Indies. But where one Ocean Sea continues and connects with the other—I mean the Southern Sea with that of the north—in the direction of the Antarctic pole we well know that it is through the famous Strait of Magellan, which lies at fifty-one degrees of latitude. If these two seas also continue and flow on the other side of the world, at the Arctic pole, it would be a wonderful thing, which many have sought, but as far as I know no one has discovered it, only by conjecture. Some have put forward, by I know not what signs, that there is another strait to the north similar to that of Magellan. For our purposes, we need only know for certain that there is land here in the south and that it is a land as large as all of Europe and Asia and even Africa, and that in the world's two poles there are lands and seas embracing each other. Since the ancients lacked experience of this, they could express doubt and issue contradictory statements.

◁ *E S S A Y S*

The essays in this chapter contrast the two major patterns of early Atlantic expansion and interaction in the fifteenth century. One pattern centered on trade and the other on the development of plantation colonies. As the Portuguese explorers and merchants ventured down the African coast, they established trading relationships with the African people and societies they encountered. In the first essay, David Northrup assesses the character of these Portuguese-African interactions, using Vasco da Gama's famous 1498 voyage as a starting point. Northrup argues that commercial exchange was the basis of the relationship from the very beginning, and he shows that African interests and values shaped these interactions in crucial ways. African merchants and consumers actively participated in the exchanges that took place, often from a position of relative strength. Although the Atlantic slave trade that emerged from these exchanges had devastating consequences for enslaved Africans, Northrup cautions against exaggerating its destructive effects on West African society as a whole.

A second pattern of expansion and interaction emerged in the Atlantic islands, where the Spanish and Portuguese established plantation colonies. Philip Curtin's essay tracks the migration of sugar planting from the eastern Mediterranean to the Atlantic islands of the Madeiras and São Tomé and finally to the Caribbean and Brazil in the late 1400s and 1500s. Sugar production on the Atlantic islands provided a crucial stepping-stone between the medieval Mediterranean world of sugar production and its modern Atlantic successor. Curtin argues that the sugar plantation complex changed as it moved. Sugar plantations became larger, more important to Europe, and more reliant on slave labor. Over time, sugar would become the most important agricultural commodity cultivated in the Americas and the engine of the Atlantic slave trade.

The Portuguese-African Encounter

DAVID NORTHRUP

In late May 1498, ten and a half months after leaving Lisbon, the Portuguese expedition led by Vasco da Gama reached the Indian port of Calicut, just a few weeks before Christopher Columbus first made contact with the American mainland while on his third trans-Atlantic voyage. As Daniel Boorstin has pointed out, Vasco da Gama's much longer and technically more difficult voyage had far greater immediate significance than the celebrated series of voyages by Columbus. The successful

Source: David Northrup, "Vasco da Gama and Africa: An Era of Mutual Discovery, 1497–1800," *Journal of World History* 1998 9(2): 189–191, 196–197, 199–202, 203–206, 207–210. Reprinted with permission of the University of Hawaii Press.

culmination of decades of systematic exploration, da Gama's expedition opened up a practical and highly profitable new all-water route around Africa to Asia, whereas Columbus's ill-conceived ventures failed to achieve their objective of finding a direct route across the Atlantic to the riches of the Indian Ocean trade.

The long-term consequences of da Gama's feat were also noteworthy. A. J. R. Russell-Wood suggests that da Gama launched "a new era as momentous as that heralded by the Columbus landfall in the Bahamas." Other historians contend that da Gama's voyage was actually of much greater importance historically than Columbus's "discovery" of the Americas, since, along with Pedro Álvares Cabral's discovery of Brazil in 1500 and Ferdinand Magellan's around-the-world expedition, it laid the foundation of global maritime trade. For this reason, Paul Kennedy applies the label "the Vasco da Gama Era" to the period of European hegemony that extended to World War I. However, just as some of the most exciting reflections occasioned by the five-hundredth anniversary of Columbus's first voyage examined its long-term significance from the perspectives of the indigenous inhabitants of the New World, so the quincentenary of 1498 should also be marked by a careful reevaluation of the significance of the Vasco da Gama era from the perspectives of the indigenous Africans, Asians, and Pacific Islanders.

This essay explores a small part of that agenda: the significance of the new relations resulting from da Gama's voyage for the peoples of sub-Saharan Africa. Africa had been the primary focus of Portugal's early decades of exploration and the first field where new commercial and cultural exchanges were developed. For a time, the contacts that earlier expeditions had established with coastal Atlantic Africans were eclipsed by the establishment of direct contacts with the Indian Ocean basin (including parts of eastern Africa). But the development of a new Atlantic economy that came fast on the colonization of the Americas soon restored western Africa's importance. Thus, African experiences illuminate many of the complex relationships launched by the Vasco da Gama era.

This essay suggests that, as was the case elsewhere in the world, the new commercial and cultural encounters in Africa were not simply the product of European initiatives but depended in fundamental ways on African actions and initiatives. . . .

First Contacts and Impressions

During the fifteenth century Portuguese expansion along the Atlantic coast of Africa had generally been peaceful and based on mutually beneficial commercial exchanges. Coastal Africans quickly appreciated that Portuguese ships could provide an attractive alternative to long overland routes to the north and saw that they opened new trading possibilities as well. For example, along the Gold Coast of West Africa, first visited by the Portuguese in 1471, African rulers and merchants responded positively to the representative of King João II of Portugal who arrived in 1482 seeking permission to erect a trading fort. The African ruler, whose name the Portuguese rendered as Caramansa (perhaps a corruption of Kwamin Ansa, i.e., King Ansa) gave the Portuguese permission to build a small trading fort but warned that, should they fail to be peaceful and honest traders, he and his people would simply move away, leaving the post bereft of food and trade. Originally called the castle of São Jorge da Mina, its name was soon corrupted to Elmina, this Arabic word for "the port" apparently having displaced the Portuguese name. As expected, both sides profited. The Portuguese crown was soon purchasing gold equal to a tenth of the world's production at the time, in return for which Africans received large quantities of goods brought by Portuguese ships from Asia, Europe, and other parts of Africa.

In 1486, the powerful kingdom of Benin in the Niger delta established commercial ties with the Portuguese. After consulting with the ambassador he had sent to Portugal to learn more about the homeland of these strangers, the *oba* (king) of Benin made overseas trade a royal monopoly, selling pepper and ivory that the Portuguese took back to Europe, as well as stone beads, textiles, and prisoners of war to be resold at Elmina. In return, Portuguese merchants provided Benin with copper and brass, fine textiles, glass beads, and a horse for use in the king's royal procession. As the demand for slaves grew in the early sixteenth century, the *oba* first raised the price of slaves and then restricted their sale. Contacts were also established in this period with the large kingdom of Kongo at the mouth of the Congo River in west-central Africa. Here too, both sides cooperated to establish commercial and cultural links that laid the basis for Portugal's most extensive sphere of influence in equatorial Atlantic Africa. . . .

Long-Term Consequences

In the decades and centuries that followed these early encounters, Africa felt the impact of a growing European and Middle Eastern involvement in the Indian Ocean, as well as the effects of a growing Atlantic trading system tied to Europe and the European colonies in the Americas. It is no longer possible to examine these centuries only in terms of European actions and perspectives. A generation of diligent research has made it clear that the agendas and outlooks of the African participants also shaped these interactions.

The revisionists' detailed examination of the inner workings of African societies shows that, with few exceptions, Africans remained in direct control of their communities and territories during these centuries. Still, there has been much debate about how determinant external relations were in indirectly shaping the course of the continent's history. At one extreme, Walter Rodney's *How Europe Underdeveloped Africa* seeks to locate in these early centuries the blame for the continent's modern economic woes. But Kenyan historian Bethwell Ogot cautions that too great an emphasis on "the gradual integration of Africa into the world capitalist economy dominated by Europe" in this period exaggerates the importance of external factors in African history and reinforces "racist ideas" of Africans "as hapless victims of world forces which they can neither comprehend nor control." Indeed, for Immanuel Wallerstein, the founder of the world-system approach, the incorporation of West Africa into "the capitalist world-economy" did not occur until after 1750, while eastern and southern Africa remained external to that system until a century later. . . .

Western Africa

Although contacts on the western side of the continent began more peacefully than in eastern Africa, the arrival of the Portuguese constituted a turning point of much greater long-term importance for Atlantic Africans. For Africans of the western coast, who had previously had little or no sustained contact with the outside world, in John Thornton's words, the arrival of the Portuguese mariners "opened up a new and virtually unprecedented chapter in human history." The commercial exchanges between Africans and Europeans grew rapidly over the next several centuries. David Eltis has calculated that the trade between western Africa and the Atlantic world reached a value of £8.2 million in the period 1681–90 and expanded nearly sixfold in value over the next century to £47.4 million. Such commercial expansion depended upon Africans developing ports of call, state and private trading companies, currencies of account, and other infrastructure mechanisms along a 5,000-kilometer expanse of the Atlantic coast. Great quantities of goods from Europe, Asia, and the Americas passed through the hands of coastal African middlemen deep into inland marketing networks.

Stereotypes of Africans as undiscriminating consumers who were easily tricked into accepting shoddy goods and worthless trifles are highly misleading. Although, as da Gama had discovered, bits of copper and iron might be accorded a high value by isolated populations in southern Africa, Africans in the major ports of western and west-central Africa became highly selective, even finicky in their preferences as the volume of their foreign trade grew. Lengthy guidebooks sought to keep European traders abreast of the changing tastes of African consumers at the many ports of call along the Atlantic seaboard.

Although most of the imports were consumables that did little to stimulate African economic development, the assortment of goods resembled what was imported by most other parts of the world in this period. Overall, about half the imports consisted of textiles in a great variety of colors, patterns, and weaves, with which Africans of both sexes wrapped their bodies, just as they did with locally made cloths. The operation of the global trading networks can be seen in the gradual replacement of European woolen and linen cloth with vast quantities and varieties of Indian textiles, until they in turn were displaced by English cottons during the industrial revolution. Other goods in great demand included firearms and stimulants. The Portuguese had tried to restrict the sale of weapons to Christian allies, but other Europeans were eager to serve African demand for hunting and military firearms. As production costs fell during the eighteenth century, sales soared. Though still a modest proportion of total imports, firearms and ammunition went from 7.5% by value in the 1680s to 14.6% in 1820. African demand for alcoholic drinks and tobacco also rose.

The bulk of the imports were of modest quality, used by persons of ordinary status, but certain items, such as expensive silks and brocades, were intended for the political and merchant elites, some of whom also developed a fondness for tailored European clothing, the fancier the better. British explorers in the Niger delta in the early 1830s were amused at the then well-established clothing preferences of local elites: "A soldier's jacket was the utmost of their wishes," which, when donned, elicited "loud yells of approbation" from their admiring subjects. Taste for European architecture also dates from this period (some Old Calabar chiefs even imported prefabricated iron houses in the nineteenth century), though the study of this subject before 1800 is still in its infancy.

Africans' demand for the imported goods was both discriminating enough to dispel notions of their gullibility and strong enough to demonstrate their enthusiasm for the opportunities offered by the new Atlantic economy. Yet the movement of the terms of the trade in Africans' favor as trade volume rose during the eighteenth century strongly suggests that Western demand for African exports was even stronger. From the time of the early Portuguese arrivals, western African exports had consisted of gold, ivory, dye woods, slaves, and other items. The expansion of plantation systems in the Americas drove upward both the volume and the price of slaves from Africa. Virtually all the growth in the eighteenth-century trade was attributable to the rising exports of slaves—whose value rose from about half of African exports in 1681–90 to 93% in 1781–90.

Thus any evaluation of the Vasco da Gama era in Africa must confront the facts and the emotions of the slave trade. This is no easy task, for the impact of the Atlantic slave trade in Africa is racked with controversy, and for good reasons. In the first place, the paucity of direct contemporaneous evidence of the trade's effects in inland Africa makes it impossible to measure many consequences with any precision. For another, the passionate moral crusades that the abolitionists launched have continued to shape most discussion of the subject. However justified such moral outrage may be, it is not a reliable yardstick for measuring historical change. Finally, there is the tendency, whether from ignorance or prejudice, to exaggerate the impact of external forces in shaping African history and to underestimate the resilience of African societies in the face of adverse circumstances. . . .

Modern historians of Africa do not consider the Atlantic slave trade as the central engine of African history. Although they are far from claiming that the Atlantic slave trade was "good for" Africa, they show that its consequences were not uniformly devastating, especially when differentiated by place, class, and time. Modern historians also give due considerations to the inner workings of African societies, not just to the external forces. While recognizing the myriad horrors that the slave trade imposed on its victims and the great (but unmeasurable) suffering in many parts of Africa brought about by the warfare, social conflict, and population loss engendered by foreign slave trades, modern scholarship has also identified several external and internal factors that mitigated the destructive effects of the slave trade in Africa.

The external factors relate very directly to the magnitude and complexity of sub-Saharan Africa's relationship to the Atlantic economy. First, the Atlantic slave trade was divided among a large number of coastal African ports and, over time, drew its victims from different parts of their hinterland, so that a single locale was usually not subjected to the destructive effects of the slave trade for long. Second, in contrast to the Americas, most of Africa remained free of European control. Aside from the small Dutch colony at Cape Town to serve the East Indian trade (which *imported* slaves mostly from the Indian Ocean territories) and the Portuguese slaving port of Luanda in Angola, Europeans generally limited their territorial holdings to small forts and trading enclaves along the coasts and were in turn limited by the strength of African states upon whose indulgence these outposts depended. Since the growing volume of trade functioned best under amicable relations, the general practice was to encourage good relations. Third, the scale of the Atlantic trade, for all its importance, was not so large as to dominate the inner workings of western Africa. Eltis calculates that the value of the Atlantic trade in western Africa in the mid-1780s averaged only £0.1 per capita per year, compared to £1.4 for the United States, £2.3 for Britain, and £5.7 for the British West Indies, though in many locales it was far more important than these averages suggest.

Several factors internal to the continent that mitigated the destructive effects of the Atlantic slave trade have also come to light from modern research on the structures and workings of African societies. First, while most slaves were the product of warfare, the testimony of African slave traders and correlations between wars and prices cast doubt on the once popular belief that obtaining slaves was the principal reason most wars took place. At the very least, a significant portion (perhaps most) of the wars in Africa of these centuries—like the far larger wars in early modern Europe—would have taken place for "reasons of state" even if the Atlantic slave trade had not existed. Second, in places like inland Angola where periodic famine was a significant source of the slave trade victims, the Atlantic exchanges also led to the accidental introduction from the Americas of high-yield, drought-resistant cassava and maize, whose cultivation appears to have lessened losses of life due to famine. Third, although some parts of western Africa probably experienced much greater population loss due to the export of slaves, a demographic model constructed by Patrick Manning, which has found general acceptance among historians, projects that losses would have averaged a bit over 10% for western Africa as a whole between 1680 and 1860. While this was tragic and substantial, Africa largely escaped the much greater epidemiological disasters that contact with European diseases inflicted on the Americas in the sixteenth century and on the Pacific Islands in the nineteenth. Since African population recovered rapidly once the Atlantic slave trade came to an end, long-term demographic consequences were slight—in contrast to the Americas, where the demographic consequences of the introduction of enslaved Africans constitute one of the most prominent long-term effects of this period.

The debates about the role of the Atlantic economy in Africa continue, but although historians differ about the details—many of which are incalculable—and the extent of its impact, it is clear that coastal and inland African elites entered into this new economy willingly, even enthusiastically, and generally from a position of strength. Participation carried with it high negative consequences, but those Africans whose desire for imported goods was the reason for their participation seem to have believed that the gains outweighed the losses. Class standing and other circumstances shaped such perspectives. Clearly victims of the enslavement, refugees, prisoners of war, kidnapping victims, and those trodden underfoot would have held quite different views.

Culture

Despite their obvious importance, the material aspects of the Vasco da Gama era are not the only features worth considering. Significant cultural changes also took place in African societies. As one historical survey points out, "to an impartial observer living in the year 1400 Africa would have seemed inevitably destined to join the world of Islam." However, the new contacts with Europe that directly challenged Muslim power in Ethiopia and on the Swahili coast also began to counter the Muslim world's cultural hegemony. As in the case of the commercial influences, the greatest period of cultural change would come in the nineteenth and twentieth centuries, but the pattern and direction of cultural change were set before 1800. Here too, one needs to beware of the tendency to presume that cultural change was largely destructive or otherwise negative. As Ian Campbell has persuasively argued in the case of Polynesia, cultural contact is generally nonviolent and mutually advantageous, a characterization that applies to Africa in this period.

One cultural area of major concern to the Portuguese was religion, which featured prominently in early African-Portuguese contacts. For their part, the Portuguese were intently interested in spreading their faith, whose adoption, as they were well aware, would also help stabilize commercial and military alliances. Many secular-minded modern historians are inclined to discount the sincerity of Portuguese religious motives; one English authority on Portuguese expansion speaks of "the way in which the Portuguese tried to hide policy behind a show of missionary zeal." Likewise, many modern historians of Africa, while accepting the genuineness of Africans' interest in firearms and other material goods, have been dismissive of the sincerity of their interest in spiritual imports.

Such modern skepticism may be misplaced. Although religious and secular motives were often mixed up in the historical record, Christian missions were an important policy goal of the Portuguese, not a front for other interests. For their part, African rulers were similarly capable of seeing religion, trade, and politics as a package, but this should not be taken to mean that their interest in Christianity was insincere. Non-Muslim African rulers were as eager to add to their spiritual arsenals as to increase their military ones, and indigenous African religions were far more open to new religious knowledge and practices than was contemporary Christianity or Islam.

The introduction of Christianity in Africa was often tied to the introduction of firearms, since the Portuguese refused to sell these weapons to non-Christians. Because both Africans and Portuguese believed that human events had natural as well as supernatural causes, neither side found it contradictory to combine new weaponry and new beliefs. This was vividly illustrated by the rulers of the large coastal kingdoms of Benin and Kongo, both of whom invited early missionaries to battle fronts, apparently to test the power of their religion to affect the outcome. As it happened, both battles ended in victory for the monarchs concerned, both of whom then opened their kingdoms to the missionaries. The experiment failed in Benin, whose rulers declined to admit more missionaries after 1538, but the rulers of the kingdom of Kongo adopted Christianity permanently, along with a commercial relationship based on a royal monopoly over the export of slaves. When the growing slave trade became disruptive, *Manikongo* Afonso I (r. 1506–c. 1540) appealed to "our brother," the king of Portugal, for help in stopping all trade "except wine and flour for the holy sacrament," a strong suggestion of the depth of his commitment to Christianity. . . .

The considerable efforts of the Portuguese over three centuries produced mixed results. Although in some states, such as Benin, rulers quickly abandoned their experiment with the new faith, in many other places the missionaries had more lasting success. By the early seventeenth century, according to the authoritative survey by Adrian Hastings, there was "a network of Catholic rulers spread all across Africa." Then the endeavor soured. Though Portuguese missionaries continued their efforts in Ethiopia through the seventeenth century, the Christian Ethiopian rulers ultimately refused to sever their ties to the patriarchate of Alexandria and affiliate with Rome. Almost everywhere else (except for the Soyo kingdom at the mouth of the Congo River), the fledgling African Christian communities declined rapidly during the seventeenth century, burdened by a missionary effort too closely under the control of Portugal and too closely tied to the rising Atlantic slave trade. By 1700, Hastings notes, the "likelihood of any enduring Catholic presence in black Africa of more than minuscule size had become extremely slight."

Nevertheless, the historical significance of these conversion efforts may be greater than it seems. John Thornton has made a highly suggestive case for Africans' importance in shaping the form of Christianity among slaves in the New World. He argues that the small number of enslaved Africans imported to the Americas who were already Christians (mostly from west-central Africa) were often used as catechists and that many other enslaved Africans who were not converts had acquired a sufficient knowledge of Christianity before crossing the Atlantic to influence the shape of Afro-Christian practice in the Americas. It is also worth remembering that African American settlers and missionaries were significant in the renewed efforts to spread Christianity in Africa after 1800.

A second arena of culture contact involved Africans' use of European languages. Beginning with their earliest voyages, the Portuguese had taken Africans back to Portugal to be taught Portuguese so that they might serve as interpreters on future diplomatic and trading missions. Until 1538 the monastery of St. Eloy in Lisbon functioned as a center for training African linguists as well as European missionaries to Africa. As overseas trade grew in western Africa, local inhabitants took the initiative in learning Portuguese and other European languages, a situation that recurred in western coastal India and Brazil. Although some Europeans learned African languages, no African language had sufficient currency along the Atlantic coast to become a lingua franca.

Portuguese remained the principal language of communication in western Africa well into the seventeenth century. Early northern European traders conversed with Africans in Portuguese, and the Danes and Dutch generally continued to do so. In the islands of Cape Verde, São Tomé, and Principe, as well as in coastal Angola, Mozambique and Guiné-Bissau the Portuguese language retains its influence, even if in a pidgin form, such as the Cape Verdean Kriolu. As French and English traders became more numerous in the coastal trade, Africans learned their languages so as to serve as interpreters and middlemen in the trade. Dutch also came into use around Cape Town and the Dutch outposts on the Gold Coast. Some coastal Africans became fluent in several European languages. In parts of West Africa frequented by the English, an English-based pidgin (incorporating some Portuguese words) was widely used by Africans of different languages as well. Some Africans could read and write pidgin English, and one prominent eighteenth-century trader of Old Calabar kept a diary in it.

For a time after 1696 the English Royal African Company ran a school on the Gold Coast to teach African boys standard English so that they might serve as interpreters, but it proved more efficient for the Company to send ambitious young Africans to study in Europe. In many parts of West Africa independent African merchants and rulers took the initiative in promoting Western education, making use of European trading vessels to dispatch their sons and daughters to Europe to improve their language skills, acquire literacy, and absorb other aspects of European culture. One scholar reports, "By the 1780s there were always at least 50 African schoolchildren, girls as well as boys, in Liverpool and the villages around" (plus others in Bristol), mostly from the Windward and Gold Coasts. At this time in Sierra Leone and other parts of the Windward Coast, there existed "an English speaking class of rulers, traders and middlemen, several of whom had been trained in Europe. They occasionally adopted certain European customs in dress and eating habits, and realized the importance of a good schooling for business [yet were] fully integrated into the fabric of native life with its secret societies and cults." A similar situation existed in the Niger delta area and in the neighboring trading towns of Old Calabar, where an English visitor at the end of the eighteenth century, when the slave trade was at its peak, noted that for some time many of the African traders had been able to write as well as speak English fluently, skills they polished during visits to England and through local schools established by the elites. Some Africans also went to study in France, but by the later part of the eighteenth century the French government, arguing that France had "a Negro problem," had banned the introduction of Africans for instruction or any other purpose.

Thus the Atlantic contacts provided the mechanism for the spread of Western belief, language, and learning in sub-Saharan Africa, much as the trans-Saharan, Red Sea, and Indian Ocean trades had long done for the spread of Islamic cultural influences. It is important to keep in mind that such cultural changes were generally additive and not substitutive—that is, they expanded a culture's range rather than displaced facets of it. As any modern study of cultural change in Africa can attest, "Westernization," like "Islamicization," has long been a complex process of interaction, not a process of one culture displacing another.

Finally, it is instructive to mention one other cultural consequence of the Vasco da Gama era: the establishment, by means of the slave trade, of large African populations in the Americas. By 1800 there were some 4.5 million persons entirely or partly of African descent in the Americas, a large number compared to a population of some 30 million in the regions of Africa their ancestors had been taken from. The Africanization of large parts of the Americas was significant by 1800, although African America would become increasingly molded by Western influences thereafter, particularly as the arrival of new slaves from Africa was brought to an end. Similarly, though to a lesser degree, the spread of Western Christianity, languages, and education would also spread rapidly in Africa after 1800, in part thanks to roots already in place, in part due to new influences.

Sugar Comes to the Atlantic Islands

PHILIP D. CURTIN

As the plantation complex moved out of the Mediterranean, bound for the Caribbean, it changed. First of all, the scale of operations in the Mediterranean was small, and the relative weight of the complex in the Mediterranean economy was also small. In addition, the Mediterranean slave trade of the Middle Ages mainly supplied service slaves destined to be soldiers, domestic servants, concubines, harem guards, and the like—occupations of particular trust or intimacy that were better done by strangers than by people from within the Mediterranean society. The Mediterranean

Source: Philip D. Curtin, *The Rise and Fall of the Plantation Complex: Essays in Atlantic History* (New York: Cambridge University Press, 1990), pp. 17–27. Reprinted with the permission of Cambridge University Press.

slave trade supplied a few plantation workers as well, but the Atlantic slave trade dealt mainly in agricultural labor. On Mediterranean plantations, many workers were slaves, but not all. In the later plantations at the height of the system, all were slaves. Indeed, most of the drivers and foremen in the sugar house—definitely management, even at a low level—were slaves as well.

The demography of the Mediterranean and Atlantic slave trades also appears to have been different. Deaths exceeded births on the West Indian plantations from the sixteenth century on, and the slave trade supplied the deficit. The migration of the slaves was not, therefore, a one-time event. The plantations needed a continuous supply of new labor, if only to remain the same size. Growth required still more. We know less about the demography of Mediterranean slavery, but from what is known about the epidemiology and environment, after the first generation a net natural decrease in plantation populations would not be expected. First-generation losses were the rule, because the Mediterranean slavers sold more women into service slavery and more men to the plantations. After the first generation, the number of men and women would have been more nearly equal.

The Atlantic Islands

Sugar grows best where heat and water are plentiful all year round. The Mediterranean is therefore less than ideal. Even the southern Mediterranean has a cool season in the winter and a dry season in the summer. With the European maritime revolution beginning in the fifteenth century, Europeans had easy access to the Atlantic islands, and some of them had a far better environment for sugar cultivation.

The climate of these islands varied enormously—from the Mediterranean type of southern Europe, to semidesert, to wet tropics. The Azores, for example, lay far out in the Atlantic due west of Portugal, with a climate much like that of mainland Portugal. They were uninhabited when Europeans first discovered them between 1427 and 1431. European settlers from Portugal followed during the next century, growing crops they had grown on the mainland—wheat, wine, and olives, not tropical staples like sugar. The Azores were therefore true colonies, not plantation colonies. They were to be stepping stones to later colonization of the New World, but not for the plantation complex. Their chief importance for the plantation complex was strategic, covering the return from the New World to Europe by way of the belt of prevailing westerly winds.

Farther to the south was Madeira, or the Madeiras, two habitable islands and a number of smaller islets. The largest, Madeira proper, was about thirty-four miles long by fourteen miles wide. The other island, Porto Santo, was tiny by comparison. Yet this insignificant island group became, for a time, the key center of European sugar production—and the crucial stepping-stone to carry the plantation regime from the Mediterranean to the New World. When Europeans first visited, perhaps in the fourteenth century, Madeira was completely uninhabited. It lay off the coast of Morocco in a similar climatic zone, but with a bit more rainfall because of its maritime setting and volcanic peaks. The final Portuguese exploration and settlement came after about 1420, coinciding with the maritime push down the African coast.

About 250 miles due south and closer to the African coast lay the Canary Islands, which also played a role in the westward movement of the sugar economy. Like

Madeira, the Canaries were volcanic islands, but higher, more rugged, with less flat land suitable for sugar. They were also drier, with less certainty of good rainfall. Sugar cultivation was possible, but conditions were far from ideal. The islands had been known to the Romans, but Europeans lost track of them during the Middle Ages, though Moroccans apparently visited from time to time. In the early fourteenth century, Western mariners rediscovered the islands—first the Portuguese, later the Spanish. For a time in the fourteenth century their control was hotly contested by the two Hispanic powers, but the Spanish finally made good their claim and the islands remained Spanish after 1480.

Still farther south, the Cape Verde Islands represent a further step in aridity. They lie straight west of the mouth of the Senegal River, at nearly the same latitude as the sahel that separates the Sahara desert from the savanna country of West Africa. The climate is much the same as that of coastal Senegal—ideal for tourism but far too dry for reliable sugarcane productions. The islands were uninhabited, though, when the Portuguese first discovered them in the late fifteenth century, and they made a convenient offshore base for trade with western Africa.

A final group of four islands lay still farther south, around the bulge of Africa in the Gulf of Guinea—São Tomé, Fernando Po, Principe, and Annobon. Europeans discovered all four of these volcanic peaks in 1471 and 1472, and the Portuguese crown claimed them a little later. Only Fernando Po and São Tomé, however, were important in the sixteenth century. Fernando Po had an existing African population, but São Tomé was uninhabited and provided a clean slate for a new sugar industry.

Thus, of the five island groups, the Gulf of Guinea islands were best for sugar but far from Europe. Madeira and the Canaries could support plantations, but they could also serve as true colonies with a European population—and in the long run that is what they became, after a plantation phase had come and gone. The Azores were ideal for true colonies, and the Cape Verdes were useful only as a base of trade with nearby Africa.

The whole set of island groups had a special attraction for Europeans in the fifteenth and sixteenth centuries. Europeans overseas were comparatively few, and whatever military strength they had depended on their maritime ability. Islands were safer and more easily dominated than equivalent spots on the mainland. Only Fernando Po and the Canaries had a native population, and the Canary Islanders died off rapidly on contact with European diseases. The Europeans were free to take over the land; all they needed was people to work it.

Colonial Institutions: The Canaries

As European colonization moved out into the Atlantic, the patterns of political and social control moved as well and changed in the process. The Atlantic islands in the fifteenth century thus came to be an intermediate step between the colonial institutions of the medieval Mediterranean and those of the Americas.

The Canary Islands, discovered in the 1320s—a full century before the major Portuguese explorations farther south—are a useful illustration. The native peoples were relatives of the Berbers of the nearby North African mainland. At the time of discovery, they had been cut off so long from the mainland that they were still in the Neolithic Age, lacking even the knowledge of metal working, which by that time had spread to the entire continent of Africa. Their isolation meant that they also lacked immunities from important European diseases. They began to die on their first contact with the Europeans, and they are now extinct.

Typical of many Atlantic voyages at this time and later, the sponsor was royal—King Denis of Portugal—but the personnel were Italians serving under Manuel Pessagno, who had been grand marshall of Genoa. Again typical of the times, Pessagno received a normal feudal charter over any lands he might discover, as well as some feudal grants in Portugal itself—presumably to cover his expenses in case he discovered nothing at all. Pessagno, in turn, recruited some twenty captains of galleys in Genoa. One of these captains discovered the Canary Islands between 1325 and 1339. The Portuguese began to establish settlements shortly afterward, but they were later driven away by superior Spanish power, and the islands became Spain's main stepping stone to the New World.

It is hardly surprising that a conquest this early in time followed medieval forms. It was, after all, contemporaneous with the last phases of the reconquest of peninsular Iberia and even a little earlier than the most active Genoese colonial efforts in the eastern Mediterranean. The legal forms were patterned exactly on those of the reconquest in Portugal. The military forms were patterned on those of the Genoese in the Levant at this same period—as might be expected, since the concessionaires were Italian.

Nor were the men who undertook the conquest and settlement feudal lords. They were merchants, ship masters, and capitalists, but happy enough to hold feudal concessions, if only to exploit them in their own capitalist way. Some of the later concessionaires were companies rather than individuals. Their apparent first intent was to set up something like the European manorial system, even though they themselves had no intention of settling down to enjoy their dominance over the countryside. They could hardly have envisaged, at this stage, the plantation regime that was to come, much less the ships of the trading post empires that were to pass on their way to the Indian Ocean or the cargoes of African slaves that would someday flow past them on the way north.

The capitalist element in this mixture of capitalism and feudalism was to become clearer a century or so later, when Europeans reached Madeira and the Gulf-of-Guinea islands. By the time explorers reached São Tomé, the possibility of using slaves from Africa on sugar estates was well known, though the legal titles were set in feudal forms. In 1500, the crown gave a certain Fernão de Mello a feudal grant to control São Tomé, and he proceeded to establish sugar plantations worked by African slaves.

The Westward Migration

São Tomé was the last of the Atlantic islands to be developed—the end product of the line of westward migration by sugar plantations that stretched back to the Levant, if not to India. The driving force was partly the expanding European demand for sugar, partly the technological change in sugar crushing, which made larger land holding units desirable, and partly the rise of Genoa in the Mediterranean, which shifted the emphasis from the eastern to the western basin. New sources of capital were also available in Genoa itself, but also in southern Germany, where the trans-Alpine trade had prospered during the fifteenth century. In the 1460s and later, the Grosse Ravens-burger Gesellschaft held extensive sugar estates near both Valencia and Malaga in southern Spain. The main agents, however, were the Genoese, whose long-standing contacts with Sicily made it easy for them to pass on the technology, first to southern Iberia and then out into the Atlantic.

Madeira was crucial; it was Portuguese and the natural stepping stone on the way to Brazil. Sugar planting came in 1455, thirty-five years after the place had first been settled. At that time, growing cane and processing it were still separate operations. Mills, with their large capital investment, were crucial, but most of the cane was grown by small cane farmers who sold to the mill. The capital was largely Genoese, though some was Portuguese. Technicians came from Sicily. In most ways, the move was typical of earlier westward steps of the Mediterranean plantation complex.

Economically, it was different. Madeira was out in the Atlantic, far from Genoa or Leghorn but relatively close to Antwerp, and direct shipping to Antwerp began in 1472. By 1480, Antwerp had seventy ships in the sugar trade of Madeira alone. Production rose from seventy-two metric tons in 1455 to 760 metric tons in 1493—and to 2,400 metric tons by 1570. Refineries and distribution networks for northern Europe were also based at Antwerp. By 1500 Madeira sugar dominated the northern European market, and it also sold in Genoa and even in Istanbul on the doorstep of earlier production centers in the Levant and Cyprus. The Canaries were a Spanish equivalent of Madeira, with Genoese enterprise and German capital, as in southern Spain itself.

The movement to São Tomé was a longer step. Here was an island off the coast of Africa far from Europe, but it had the advantages of a tropical climate, rich volcanic soils, and nearby sources of labor from the kingdoms of Kongo and Benin. Sugar production began to rise a little after 1500, reaching 2,250 metric tons by 1544 (nearly the same as that of Madeira), but that was the peak. The defense of the island became very expensive as Angolan slaves escaped into the mountains, set up a free African community, and raided sugar plantations. The Portuguese were not willing to invest heavily in the military defense of such a far-off place. Over the next decades, these raids, plus competition from still newer plantations in Brazil, drove the São Tomé sugar estates out of the market. The rebel states, moreover, were not conquered for another 300 years.

To the Americas

Once on the Atlantic islands, it was a small matter to carry the sugar industry across the ocean to the American colonies. But this further movement brought some changes. In the Mediterranean, the sugar industry had been international. Investment had come from all over Europe; individual estate owners were an international group who worked under various feudal or national authorities. Italian influence was strong, though political control was Spanish or Portuguese.

With the movement across the Atlantic, the sugar industry split into national sections—each jealously guarded from foreign influence, as Spain and Portugal both tried as much as possible to keep colonial shipping as a national monopoly. The northern European web of international commercial contacts weakened, though Flemish capital remained important in Brazil, as it had been in Madeira. The Hispanic powers in transatlantic trade adopted the militant relations that had characterized the Venetian–Genoese trade wars in the Mediterranean. The change reflected the rise of the national monarchies and the fact that Spain or Spain and Portugal together were at war with some combination of the Dutch, English, and French throughout the last third of the sixteenth century and into the seventeenth.

By the 1490s, Spain had its Atlantic extension to the Canaries. The Portuguese had theirs to Madeira. At the next stage, when the Portuguese moved on down the African coast to São Tomé, the Spanish sugar industry began to move on to the island of Hispaniola or Santo Domingo in the Caribbean. Columbus introduced sugarcane on his second voyage in 1493. Nothing came of it, and Columbus himself was still intent on the possibility of a trading post empire off the coast of Asia, where he still supposed Santo Domingo to be. In 1503, the Spanish reintroduced sugarcane with Canary Island technicians. This time, it failed for lack of labor. The local Arawak Indians had already begun to die off on contact with European diseases. In 1517, the Spanish tried again with men and machines from the Canaries. This time, it succeeded for a while, and sugar production rose steadily until it reached about 1,000 metric tons a little before 1570.

Then expansion stopped. A few new sugar plantations appeared in Jamaica, Puerto Rico, and coastal Mexico, but the essential problems remained. The demographic disaster in the tropical lowlands meant that the local sources of forced labor dried up. Portugal, not Spain, had the contacts on the African coast that would have made Africa a viable source. The Spanish government had more serious concerns in highland Peru and Mexico, with their well-publicized supplies of gold and silver. Neither Hispaniola nor São Tomé was to amount to much after the mid-sixteenth century.

Brazil was another matter, and it had several advantages. The voyage from Africa to Brazil took less than half the time of a voyage from Africa to the Caribbean. Portugal dominated—virtually monopolized—the Atlantic slave trade well into the seventeenth century, and, lacking the distraction of Peru and Mexico, the Portuguese were willing to put more resources into sugar planting. Yet in the much longer run, the western end of the island of Hispaniola was destined to become the French colony of Saint Domingue, the most prized of all sugar colonies in the eighteenth century.

The Portuguese success is clear enough from production and export figures, even allowing a wide margin for error. The Portuguese introduced sugar from Madeira to Brazil only in the mid-1540s. By 1560, production had reached about 2,500 metric tons (roughly the production of either Madeira or São Tomé at that time). By 1580, it had doubled once more to reach 5,000 tons. By 1600, it was up to 16,000 tons, and, by 1630, it was more than 20,000 tons. There it stabilized, between 20,000 and 30,000 tons a year during the rest of the seventeenth century. By the mid-seventeenth century, in short, Brazil had reached about ten times the production of the richest sugar colonies elsewhere, whereas the Caribbean as a whole hardly produced one-tenth as much sugar as Brazil.

These numbers are important, not for their own sake but because they help to put a brake on our normal expectations. Because Santo Domingo and Cuba later became big sugar centers, we half expect them to have been big at the beginning. Because São Tomé never developed, we—and most writers on Latin American history—forget that it ever rivaled the economic importance of Brazil.

◮ F U R T H E R   R E A D I N G

Barrett, James H. *Contact, Continuity, and Collapse: The Norse Colonization of the North Atlantic.* Turnhout, Belgium: Brepols, 2003.

Boxer, C. R. *The Portuguese Seaborne Empire, 1415–1825.* New York: A. A. Knopf, 1969.

Brooks, George E. *Landlords and Strangers: Ecology, Society, and Trade in Western Africa, 1000–1630.* Boulder, CO: Westview Press, 1993.

Crosby, Alfred W. *Ecological Imperialism: The Biological Expansion of Europe, 900–1900.* New York: Cambridge University Press, 2004.

Cunliffe, Barry W. *Facing the Ocean: The Atlantic and Its Peoples, 8000 BC–AD 1500.* New York: Oxford University Press, 2001.

Deagan, Kathleen, and José María Cruxent. *Columbus's Outposts Among the Taínos: Spain and America at La Isabela, 1493–1498.* New Haven, CT: Yale University Press, 2002.

Fernandez-Armesto, Felipe. *Before Columbus: Exploration and Colonization from the Mediterranean to the Atlantic, 1229–1492.* Philadelphia: University of Pennsylvania Press, 1987.

Kristjánsson, Jónas. *The First Settler of the New World: The Vinland Expedition of Thorfinn Karlsefni.* Reykjavik: University of Iceland Press, 2005.

Mann, Charles C. *1491: New Revelations of the Americas Before Columbus.* New York: Knopf, 2005.

Morison, Samuel Eliot. *Admiral of the Ocean Sea: A Life of Christopher Columbus.* Boston: Little, Brown and Co., 1942.

Newitt, M. D. D. *A History of Portuguese Overseas Expansion, 1400–1668.* London: Routledge, 2005.

Northrup, David. *Africa's Discovery of Europe: 1450 to 1850.* New York: Oxford University Press, 2002.

O'Callaghan, Joseph F. *Reconquest and Crusade in Medieval Spain.* Philadelphia: University of Pennsylvania Press, 2003.

Phillips, William D., and Carla Rahn Phillips. *The Worlds of Christopher Columbus.* New York: Cambridge University Press, 1992.

Reston, James, Jr. *Dogs of God: Columbus, the Inquisition, and the Defeat of the Moors.* New York: Doubleday, 2005.

Rouse, Irving. *The Tainos: Rise & Decline of the People Who Greeted Columbus.* New Haven, CT: Yale University Press, 1992.

Russell-Wood, A. J. R. *The Portuguese Empire, 1415–1808: A World on the Move.* Baltimore, MD: The Johns Hopkins University Press, 1998.

Sale, Kirkpatrick. *The Conquest of Paradise: Christopher Columbus and the Columbian Legacy.* New York: Knopf, 1990.

Thornton, John. *Africa and Africans in the Making of the Atlantic World, 1400–1680.* New York: Cambridge University Press, 1992.

Verlinden, Charles. *The Beginnings of Modern Colonization.* Translated by Yvonne Freccero. Ithaca, NY: Cornell University Press, 1970.

CHAPTER
3

Iberian Expansion

Spanish and Portuguese forays into the Atlantic Ocean eventually carried representatives of both nations to the shores of the Americas, where they encountered
remarkable and diverse civilizations, from the Mexican empire in Central America
to the Tupinambá people of the Brazilian Atlantic forest. The early meetings
between Europeans and Americans were filled with revelations and misunder-
standings, which often led to terrible violence. The consequences of these encounters were profound. While the indigenous population suffered a demographic
catastrophe, largely from diseases that spread faster than the Iberians themselves,
the Spanish and Portuguese extended their political power, economic organization,
and cultural influence over much of the Americas. They became the imperial masters
of the early Atlantic world.

From the sixteenth century, European chroniclers and historians have celebrated the epic feats of the Iberian conquistadors and missionaries who orches-
trated the conquest of the Americas. More recently, modern historians have taken
a different tack. Using methods drawn from archaeology, anthropology, and literature, they have tried to grasp the complex meaning of the Europeans' arrival
for the indigenous people of the Americas (misnamed "Indians" by Columbus—
an error that stuck). This has required a deeper appreciation of pre-Columbian
America and a puncturing of the assumptions of European cultural and racial
superiority that informed the work of earlier historians. This approach has
yielded not only a new understanding of the indigenous Americans' perspective,
but also new insights into the Iberians' values and actions in the early phases
of Atlantic history.

One lesson of this new history is that the "conquest" of the Americas should
not be exaggerated. Guns, germs, and steel (to use biohistorian Jared Diamond's
famous triad) had their limits. In many places, such as the Gulf Coast of North
America, indigenous people fought against Iberian encroachment with some success. Wherever indigenous people remained, the Spanish and Portuguese secured
their power only by taking their traditional norms and practices into account, and
by forging diverse alliances with them. Those Native Americans who survived epidemic disease and bloody warfare adjusted to their own new world in a variety of
ways ranging from persistent resistance against the Iberians to active collaboration
with them. Although both sides clung to tradition, neither the Europeans nor the
Americans were left unaffected by their engagement with the other.

△ D O C U M E N T S

Interpreting the dynamics and effects of Iberian expansion in the Americas is made more difficult by the fact that almost all the available documentary sources were written by Europeans, whose values and interests shaped their perception of indigenous societies. Historians must read these sources with a critical eye in order to grasp both the experiences of their European authors and the elusive "reality" of Indian life in the early colonial era. Document 1, a legal statement used by the Spanish to legitimate the conquest of indigenous people, was often read in Spanish to an uncomprehending audience and out of range of an enemy's weapons, thus often out of hearing. Yet Europeans did come face-to-face with indigenous society. Document 2 comes from the great Spanish conquistador Hernan Cortés's account of the people of the Yucatan coast and the great Mexica capital city of Tenochtitlan. In contrast, Document 3 tells the remarkable story of Hans Staden, a German gunner in the service of the Portuguese in Brazil, who was captured by hostile Tupi Indians. Cortés and Staden reveal the European fascination and horror with the Indians' ritual practices of human sacrifice and cannibalism.

Inevitably, Iberian conquest provoked controversy on both sides of the Atlantic. In Document 4, two Spaniards debate whether the Indians are natural slaves, while in Document 5, indigenous Mexica leaders protest the burdens of Spanish rule. Finally, the early colonial era also saw the rise of epic histories of conquest. In Document 6, the conquistador-turned-historian Bernal Diaz praises an Indian woman named Malintzin, whom the Spanish called Dona Marina or Malinche; she had served as an interpreter for Cortés and proved immensely useful to the Spanish during their conquest of Mexico. Document 7 offers a poetic celebration of Portuguese exploration in Africa. In the final document, the Spanish Catholic priest Diego Duran argues that the Native Americans were in fact one of the Lost Tribes of Israel, thus absorbing them into the sacred history of the Christian world.

1. A Spanish Jurist Explains the Legitimacy of Conquest, 1510

On the part of the King, Don Fernando, and of Doña Juana, his daughter, Queen of Castile and Leon, subduers of the barbarous nations, we their servants notify and make known to you, as best we can, that the Lord our God, Living and Eternal, created the Heaven and the Earth, and one man and one woman, of whom you and we, and all the men of the world, were and are descendants, and all those who come after us. But, on account of the multitude which has sprung from this man and woman in the five thousand years since the world was created, it was necessary that some men should go one way and some another, and that they should be divided into many kingdoms and provinces, for in one alone they could not be sustained.

Of all these nations God our Lord gave charge to one man, called St. Peter, that he should be Lord and Superior of all the men in the world, that all should obey him, and that he should be the head of the whole human race, wherever men should live, and under whatever law, sect, or belief they should be; and he gave him the world for his kingdom and jurisdiction.

Source: Arthur Helps, *The Spanish Conquest in America and Its Relation to the History of Slavery and to the Government of the Colonies*, v. 1 (London, 1900), pp. 264–267.

And he commanded him to place his seat in Rome, as the spot most fitting to rule the world from; but also he permitted him to have his seat in any other part of the world, and to judge and govern all Christians, Moors, Jews, Gentiles, and all other sects. This man was called Pope, as if to say, Admirable Great Father and Governor of men. The men who lived in that time obeyed that St. Peter, and took him for Lord, King, and Superior of the universe . . . so also they have regarded the others who after him have been elected to the pontificate, and so has it been continued even till now, and will continue till the end of the world.

One of these Pontiffs, who succeeded that St. Peter as Lord of the world, in the dignity and seat which I have before mentioned, made donation of these isles and Tierra-firme to the aforesaid King and Queen and to their successors, our lords, with all that there are in these territories, as is contained in certain writings which passed upon the subject as aforesaid, which you can see if you wish.

So their Highnesses are kings and lords of these islands and land of Tierra-firme by virtue of this donation: and some islands, and indeed almost all those to whom this has been notified, have received and served their Highnesses, as lords and kings, in the way that subjects ought to do, with good will, without any resistance, immediately, without delay, when they were informed of the aforesaid facts. And also they received and obeyed the priests whom their Highnesses sent to preach to them and to teach them our Holy Faith; and all these, of their own free will, without any reward or condition, have become Christians, and are so, and their Highnesses have joyfully and benignantly received them, and also have commanded them to be treated as their subjects and vassals; and you too are held and obliged to do the same. Wherefore, as best we can, we ask and require that you consider what we have said to you, and that you take the time that shall be necessary to understand and deliberate upon it, and that you acknowledge the Church as the Ruler and Superior of the whole world (*por Señora y Superiora del universo mundo*), and the high priest called Pope, and in his name the King and Queen Doña Juana our lords, in his place, as superiors and lords and kings of these islands and this Tierra-firme by virtue of the said donation, and that you consent and give place that these religious fathers should declare and preach to you the aforesaid.

If you do so, you will do well, and that which you are obliged to do to their Highnesses, and we in their name shall receive you in all love and charity, and shall leave you your wives, and your children, and your lands, free without servitude, that you may do with them and with yourselves freely that which you like and think best, and they shall not compel you to turn Christians, unless you yourselves, when informed of the truth, should wish to be converted to our Holy Catholic Faith, as almost all the inhabitants of the rest of the islands have done. And, besides this, their Highnesses award you many privileges and exemptions . . . and will grant you many benefits.

But, if you do not do this, and maliciously make delay in it, I certify to you that, with the help of God, we shall powerfully enter into your country, and shall make war against you in all ways and manners that we can, and shall subject you to the yoke and obedience of the Church and of their Highnesses; we shall take you and your wives and your children, and shall make slaves of them, and as such shall sell and dispose of them as their Highnesses may command; and we shall take away your goods, and shall do you all the mischief and damage that we can, as to vassals who do not obey, and refuse to receive their lord, and resist and contradict him; and we protest that the deaths and losses which shall accrue from this are your fault, and not that of their Highnesses, or ours, nor of these cavaliers who come with us. And that we have said this to you and made this Requisition, we request the notary here present to give us his testimony in writing, and we ask the rest who are present that they should be witnesses of this Requisition.

2. Cortés Marvels at a World of Wonders, 1518–1520

First Letter, July 10, 1519

The people who inhabit this land, from the island of Cozume[1] and the cape of Yucatan to the place where we are now, are of medium height and of well-proportioned bodies and features, save that in each province their customs are different; some pierce their ears and put very large and ugly objects into them; others pierce their nostrils down to the lip and put in them large round stones which look like mirrors; and others still split their lower lips as far as the gums and hang there some large stones or gold ornaments so heavy that they drag the lips down, giving a most deformed appearance. The clothes they wear are like large, highly colored yash-maks; the men cover their shameful parts, and on the top half of their bodies wear thin mantles which are decorated in a Moorish fashion. The common women wear highly colored mantles from the waist to the feet, and other which cover their breasts, leaving the rest uncovered. The women of rank wear skirts of very thin cotton, which are very loose-fitting and decorated and cut in the manner of a rochet. . . .

There are some large towns and well laid out. The houses in those parts where there is stone are of masonry and mortar and the rooms are small and low in the Moorish fashion. . . . Each of these chieftains has in front of the entrance to his house a very large courtyard and some two or three or four of them raised very high with steps up to them and all very well built. Likewise they have their shrines and temples with raised walks which run all around the outside and are very wide: there they keep the idols which they worship, some of stone, some of clay and some of wood, which they honor and serve with such customs and so many ceremonies that many sheets of paper would not suffice to give Your Royal Highnesses a true and detailed account of them all. And the temples where they are kept are the largest and the best and the finest built of all the buildings found in the towns; and they are much adorned with rich hanging cloths and featherwork and other fineries.

Each day before beginning any sort of work they burn incense in these temples and sometimes sacrifice their own persons, some cutting their tongues, others their ears, while there are some who stab their bodies with knives. All the blood which flows from them they offer to those idols, sprinkling it in all parts of the temple, or sometimes throwing it into the air or performing many other ceremonies, so that nothing is begun without sacrifice having first been made. They have a most horrid and abominable custom which truly ought to be punished and which until now we have seen in no other part, and this is that, whenever they wish to ask something of the idols, in order that their plea may find more acceptance, they take many girls and

Source: Hernan Cortés, *Letters from Mexico*, ed. and trans. Anthony Pagden (New Haven: Yale University Press, 1986), pp. 30–37, 101–108. Reprinted with permission of Yale University Press.

boys and even adults, and in the presence of the idols they open their chests while they are still alive and take out their hearts and entrails and burn them before the idols, offering the smoke as sacrifice. Some of us have seen this, and they say it is the most terrible and frightful thing they have ever witnessed.

This these Indians do so frequently that, as we have been informed, and, in part, have seen from our own experience during the short while we have been here, not one year passes in which they do not kill and sacrifice some fifty persons in each temple; and this is done and held as customary from the island of Cozumel to this land where we now have settled. Your Majesties may be most certain that, as this land seems to us to be very large, and to have many temples in it, not one year has passed, as far as we have been able to discover, in which three or four thousand souls have not been sacrificed in this manner. Let Your Royal Highnesses consider, therefore, whether they should not put an end to such evil practices, for certainly Our Lord God would be well pleased if by the hand of Your Royal Highnesses these people were initiated and instructed in our Holy Catholic Faith, and the devotion, trust and hope which they have in these their idols were transferred to the divine power of God; for it is certain that if they were to worship the true God with such fervor, faith and diligence, they would perform many miracles. And we believe that it is not without cause that Our Lord God has been pleased that these parts be discovered in the name of Your Royal Highnesses so that Your Majesties may gain much merit and reward in the sight of God by commanding that these barbarous people be instructed and by Your hands be brought to the True Faith. For, as far as we have been able to learn, we believe that had we interpreters and other people to explain to them the error of their ways and the nature of the True Faith, many of them, and perhaps even all, would soon renounce their false beliefs and come to the true knowledge of God; for they live in a more civilized and reasonable manner than any other people we have seen in these parts up to the present. . . .

. . . For in addition to those which we list above, of the children and men and women which they kill and offer in their sacrifices, we have been informed, and are most certain it is true, that they are all sodomites and practice that abominable sin. In all of which we entreat Your Majesties to provide as You judge most fitting to the service of God and Your Royal Highnesses and that we who are here in Your service be favored and rewarded. . . .

Second Letter, October 30, 1520

This great city of Temixtitan is built on the salt lake, and no matter by what road you travel there are two leagues from the main body of the city to the mainland. There are four artificial causeways leading to it, and each is as wide as two cavalry lances. The city itself is as big as Seville or Córdoba. The main streets are very wide and very straight; some of these are on the land, but the rest and all the smaller ones are half on land, half canals where they paddle their canoes. All the streets have openings in places so that the water may pass from one canal to another. Over all these openings, and some of them are very wide, there are bridges made of long and wide beams joined together very firmly and so well made that on some of them ten horsemen may ride abreast. . . .

This city has many squares where trading is done and markets are held continuously. There is also one square twice as big as that of Salamanca, with arcades all around, where more than sixty thousand people come each day to buy and sell, and where every kind of merchandise produced in these lands is found; provisions as well as ornaments of gold and silver, lead, brass, copper, tin, stones, shells, bones, and feathers. They also sell lime, hewn and unhewn stone, adobe bricks, tiles, and cut and uncut woods of various kinds. There is a street where they sell game and birds of every species found in this land: chickens, partridges and quails, wild ducks, flycatchers, widgeons, turtledoves, pigeons, cane birds, parrots, eagles and eagle owls, falcons, sparrow hawks and kestrels, and they sell the skins of some of these birds of prey with their feathers, heads and claws. They sell rabbits and hares, and stags and small gelded dogs which they breed for eating.

There are streets of herbalists where all the medicinal herbs and roots found in the land are sold. There are shops like apothecaries', where they sell ready-made medicines as well as liquid ointments and plasters. There are shops like barbers' where they have their hair washed and shaved, and shops where they sell food and drink. There are also men like porters to carry loads. There is much firewood and charcoal, earthenware braziers and mats of various kinds like mattresses for beds, and other, finer ones, for seats and for covering rooms and hallways. There is every sort of vegetable, especially onions, leeks, garlic, common cress and watercress, borage, sorrel, teasels and artichokes; and there are many sorts of fruit, among which are cherries and plums like those in Spain. . . .

Finally, besides those things which I have already mentioned, they sell in the market everything else to be found in this land, but they are so many and so varied that because of their great number and because I cannot remember many of them nor do I know what they are called I shall not mention them. . . .

There are, in all districts of this great city, many temples or houses for their idols. They are all very beautiful buildings, and in the important ones there are priests of their sect who live there permanently; and, in addition to the houses for the idols, they also have very good lodgings. All these priests dress in black and never comb their hair from the time they enter the priesthood until they leave; and all the sons of the persons of high rank, both the lords and honored citizens also, enter the priesthood and wear the habit from the age of seven or eight years until they are taken away to be married; this occurs more among the first-born sons, who are to inherit, than among the others. They abstain from eating things, and more at some times of the year than at others; and no woman is granted entry nor permitted inside these places of worship.

Amongst these temples there is one, the principal one, whose great size and magnificence no human tongue could describe, for it is so large that within the precincts, which are surrounded by a very high wall, a town of some five hundred inhabitants could easily be built. All round inside this wall there are very elegant quarters with very large rooms and corridors where their priests live. There are as many as forty towers, all of which are so high that in the case of the largest there are fifty steps leading up to the main part of it; and the most important of these towers is higher than that of the cathedral of Seville. They are so well constructed in both their stone and woodwork that there can be none better in any place, for all the stonework inside the chapels where they keep their idols is in high relief, with figures and little houses, and the woodwork is likewise of relief and painted with monsters and other figures and designs. All these towers are burial places of chiefs, and the chapels therein are each dedicated to the idol which he venerated. . . .

The most important of these idols, and the ones in whom they have most faith, I had taken from their places and thrown down the steps; and I had those chapels where they were cleaned, for they were full of the blood of sacrifices; and I had images of Our Lady and of other saints put there, which caused Mutezuma and the other natives some sorrow. First they asked me not to do it, for when the communities learnt of it they would rise against me, for they believed that those idols gave them all their worldly goods, and that if they were allowed to be ill treated, they would become angry and give them nothing and take the fruit from the earth leaving the people to die of hunger. I made them understand through the interpreters how deceived they were in placing their trust in those idols which they had made with their hands from unclean things. They must know that there was only one God, Lord of all things, who had created heaven and earth and all else and who made all of us; and He was without beginning or end, and they must adore and worship only Him, not any other creature or thing. And I told them all I knew about this to dissuade them from their idolatry and bring them to the knowledge of God our Saviour. All of them, especially Mutezuma, replied that they had already told me how they were not natives of this land, and that as it was many years since their forefathers had come here, they well knew that they might have erred somewhat in what they believed, for they had left their native land so long ago; and as I had only recently arrived from there, I would better know the things they should believe, and should explain to them and make them understand, for they would do as I said was best. Mutezuma and many of the chieftains of the city were with me until the idols were removed, the chapel cleaned and the images set up, and I urged them not to sacrifice living creatures to the idols, as they were accustomed, for, as well as being most abhorrent to God, Your Sacred Majesty's laws forbade it and ordered that he who kills shall be killed. And from then on they ceased to do it, and in all the time I stayed in that city I did not see a living creature killed or sacrificed. . . .

Every day, in all the markets and public places there are many workmen and craftsmen of every sort, waiting to be employed by the day. The people of this city are dressed with more elegance and are more courtly in their bearing than those of the other cities and provinces, and because Mutezuma and all those chieftains, his vassals, are always coming to the city, the people have more manners and politeness in all matters. Yet so as not to tire Your Highness with the description of the things of this city (although I would not complete it so briefly), I will say only that these people live almost like those in Spain, and in as much harmony and order as there, and considering that they are barbarous and so far from the knowledge of God and cut off from all civilized nations, it is truly remarkable to see what they have achieved in all things.

3. The Tupi Indians Capture a German Gunner, 1550

I had a savage man for a slave of the tribe called Carios who caught game for me, and it was my custom to make expeditions with him into the forest.

It fell out after a time that a Spaniard from Sancte Vincente came to me to the island of Sancte Maro, a distance of about five miles, and was with me in the fort where I lived, and with him came also a German called Heliodorus Hessus, son of the deceased Eobanus Hessus. He had been stationed in the island of Sancte Vincente

Source: Hans Staden, *The True History of His Captivity*, trans. and ed. by Malcolm Letts (Great Britain: Broadway Travellers, 1928), pp. 62–72.

in an Ingenio where they make sugar. This Ingenio belonged to a Genoese named Josepe Ornio, and Heliodorus was his clerk and manager. (Ingenio is used to designate the houses where sugar is made.) I had had dealings with this Heliodorus previously, for when I was shipwrecked with the Spaniards I found him in the Island of Sancte Vincente and he showed me much kindness. He came to see how I was situated, for he heard perchance that I was sick.

The day previously I had sent my slave into the forest to hunt for game, intending to go on the following day to fetch it so that we might have food, for in that country there is little to be had except what comes out of the wilderness.

As I was going through the forest I heard loud yells on either side of me, such as savages are accustomed to utter, and immediately a company of savages came running towards me, surrounding me on every side and shooting at me with their bows and arrows. Then I cried out: "Now may God preserve my soul." Scarcely had I uttered the words when they threw me to the ground and shot and stabbed at me. God be praised they only wounded me in the leg, but they tore my clothes from my body, one the jerkin, another the hat, a third the shirt, and so forth. Then they commenced to quarrel over me. One said he was the first to overtake me, another protested that it was he that caught me, while the rest smote me with their bows. At last two of them seized me and lifted me up, naked as I was, and taking me by the arms, some running in front and some behind, they carried me along with them through the forest at a great pace towards the sea where they had their canoes. As we approached the sea I saw the canoes about a stone's-throw away, which they had dragged out of the water and hidden behind the shrubs, and with the canoes were great multitudes of savages, all decked out with feathers according to their custom. When they saw me they rushed towards me, biting their arms and threatening me, and making gestures as if they would eat me. Then a king approached me carrying the club with which they kill their captives, who spoke saying that having captured me from the Perot, that is to say the Portuguese, they would now take vengeance on me for the death of their friends, and so carrying me to the canoes they beat me with their fists. Then they made haste to launch their canoes, for they feared that an alarm might be raised at Brikioka, as indeed was the case.

Before launching the canoes they bound my hands together, but since they were not all from the same place and no one wanted to go home empty-handed, they began to dispute with my two captors, saying that they had all been just as near to me when I was taken, and each one demanding a piece of me and clamouring to have me killed on the spot.

Then I stood and prayed, expecting every moment to be struck down. But at last the king, who desired to keep me, gave orders to carry me back alive so that their women might see me and make merry with me. For they intended to kill me "Kawewi Pepicke": that is, to prepare a drink and gather together for a feast at which they would eat me. At these words they desisted, but they bound four ropes round my neck, and I was forced to climb into a canoe, while they made fast the ends of the ropes to the boats and then pushed off and commenced the homeward journey. . . .

When we were about seven miles from Brikioka towards the country of the savages it was by the sun about four o'clock in the afternoon of the same day on which I was captured.

My captors passed by an island and ran the canoes ashore, intending to spend the night there, and they carried me from the canoe to the land. I could scarcely see, for I had been wounded in the face, nor could I walk on account of the wounds in my leg, but could only lie down on the sand. Then they stood round me and boasted that they would eat me.

So in mighty fear and terror I bethought me of matters which I had never dwelt upon before, and considered with myself how dark is the vale of sorrows in which we have our being. Then, weeping, I began in the bitterness of my heart to sing the Psalm: "Out of the depths have I cried unto thee." Whereupon the savages rejoiced and said: "See how he cries: now is he sorrowful indeed."

Then they considered and decided that the island was not a suitable place in which to spend the night, and they returned to the mainland where there were huts which they had erected previously, and it was night when we came there. The savages beached the canoes and lit a fire and afterwards took me to it. There I had to sleep in a net which they call in their tongue Inni. These nets are their beds and they make them fast to two posts above the ground, or if they are in the forest they tie them to two trees. So I lay there with the cord which I had about my neck tied high up in a tree, and they lay round about me all night and mocked me saying in their speech: *Schere inbau ende*, which is to say: "You are my bound beast."

Before daybreak we were once more on our way and rowed all day, so that by Vespers we were some two miles from the place where they intended to spend the night. Then great black clouds arose behind me which were terrible to see, and the savages laboured at the oars, striving to reach land and to escape the wind and darkness. But when they saw that their efforts were in vain they said to me: *Ne mungitta dee Tuppan do Quabe, amanasu y an dee Imme Ranni me sisse*, which is to say: "Speak with your God that we may escape the wind and rain." I kept silence, but prayed in my heart as the savages required of me: "O almighty God, Lord of heaven and earth, who from the beginning hast succoured those that call upon thee, now among the heathen show thy mercy to me that I may know that thou art with me, and establish thee among these savages who know thee not, that they may see that thou hast heard my prayer."

I lay bound in the canoe and could not turn myself to regard the sky, but the savages looked steadfastly behind them and commenced to say: *Oqua moa amanasu*, which means: "The great storm is departing." Then I raised myself as best I could and looked back and saw that the clouds were passing, and I praised God.

When we came to land they did with me as before and bound me to a tree, and lay about me all night telling me that we were approaching their country where we should arrive on the morrow about evening, at which I rejoiced not at all.

On the same day about Vesper time (reckoning by the sun) we came in sight of their dwellings after we had been journeying for three days. The place to which I had come was thirty miles distant from Brikioka where I had been captured.

When we were near the dwellings I saw that the place was a small village with seven huts, and it was called Uwattibi (Ubatúba). We landed on a beach close by the sea, and there were the women folk in a plantation of mandioca roots. They were going up and down gathering roots, and I was forced to call out to them and say: *A junesche been ermi vramme*, which means: "I your food have come."

As we landed, all the women, young and old, came running out of the huts, which were built on a hill, to stare at me. The men went into their huts with their bows and arrows, leaving me to the pleasure of the women who gathered round and went along with me, some in front and some behind, dancing and singing the songs they are wont to sing to their own people when they are about to eat them.

They then carried me to a kind of fort outside the huts called Ywara, which they defend against their enemies by means of great rails made like a garden fence. When I entered this enclosure the women fell upon me and beat me with their fists, plucking at my beard and crying out in their speech: *Sehe innamme pepikeae*, which is to say: "With this blow I avenge me of my friend, that one who was slain by your people."

After this they took me into the huts where I had to lie in a hammock while the women surrounded me and beat me and pulled at me on all sides, mocking me and offering to eat me. Meanwhile the men had assembled in a hut by themselves, drinking a drink which is known as Kawi, and having their gods, called Tammerka, about them, to whom they sang praises, since these gods, they said, had foretold my capture. I could hear this singing, but for half an hour none of the men came near me, and I was left with the women and children.

At this time I knew less of their customs than I knew later, and I thought to myself: now they are preparing to kill me. In a little time the two men who had captured me, namely Jeppipo Wasu and his brother, Alkindar Miri, came near and told me that they had presented me in friendship to their father's brother, Ipperu Wasu, who would keep me until I was ready to be eaten, when he would kill me and thus acquire a new name.

This Ipperu Wasu had captured a slave a year before, and had presented him in friendship to Alkindar Miri, who had slain him and gained a new name. This Alkindar Miri had then promised to present Ipperu Wasu with the first prisoner he caught. And I was that prisoner.

My two captors told me further that the women would lead me out Aprasse. This word I did not then understand, but it signifies a dance. Thus was I dragged from the huts by the rope which was still about my neck to the dancing place. All the women came running from the seven huts, and seized me while the men withdrew, some by the arms, some by the rope about my throat, which they pulled so tight that I could hardly breathe. So they carried me with them, for what purpose I knew not, and I could think only of our Saviour Jesus Christ, and of his innocent suffering at the hands of the Jews, whereat I was comforted and grew more patient. They brought me to the hut of their king, who was called Vratinge Wasu, which means the great white bird. In front of this hut was a heap of fresh earth, and they brought me to it and sat me there, holding me fast. I could not but think that they would slay me forthwith and began to look about me for the club Iwera Pemme which they use to kill their prisoners, and I asked whether I was now to die, but they told me "not yet." Upon this a woman approached carrying a piece of crystal fastened to a kind of ring and with it she scraped off my eyebrows and tried to scrape off my beard also, but I resisted, saying that I would die with my beard. Then they answered that they were not ready to kill me yet and left me my beard. But a few days later they cut it off with some scissors which the Frenchmen had given them.

4. Two Spaniards Debate the Conquest and the Nature of Americans, 1547–1553

Sepúlveda, 1547

You should remember that authority and power are not only of one kind but of several varieties, since in one way and with one kind of law the father commands his children, in another the husband commands his wife, in another the master commands his servants, in another the judge commands the citizens, in another the king commands the peoples and human beings confined to his authority. . . . Although each jurisdiction may appear different, they all go back to a single principle, as the wise men teach. That is, the perfect should command and rule over the imperfect, the excellent over its opposite. . . .

The man rules over the woman, the adult over the child, the father over his children. That is to say, the most powerful and most perfect rule over the weakest and most imperfect. This same relationship exists among men, there being some who by nature are masters and others who by nature are slaves. Those who surpass the rest in prudence and intelligence, although not in physical strength, are by nature the masters. On the other hand, those who are dim-witted and mentally lazy, although they may be physically strong enough to fulfill all the necessary tasks, are by nature slaves. It is just and useful that it be this way. We even see it sanctioned in divine law itself, for it is written in the Book of Proverbs: "He who is stupid will serve the wise man." And so it is with the barbarous and inhumane peoples [the Indians] who have no civil life and peaceful customs. It will always be just and in conformity with natural law that such people submit to the rule of more cultured and humane princes and nations. Thanks to their virtues and the practical wisdom of their laws, the latter can destroy barbarism and educate these [inferior] people to a more humane and virtuous life. And if the latter reject such rule, it can be imposed upon them by force of arms. Such a war will be just according to natural law. . . .

One may believe as certain and undeniable, since it is affirmed by the wisest authors, that it is just and natural that prudent, upright, and humane men should rule over those who are not. On this basis the Romans established their legitimate and just rule over many nations, according to St. Augustine in several passages of his work, *The City of God*, which St. Thomas [Aquinas] collected and cited in his work, *De regimine principum*. Such being the case, you can well understand . . . if you know the customs and nature of the two peoples, that with perfect right the Spaniards rule over these barbarians of the New World and the adjacent islands, who in wisdom, intelligence, virtue, and humanitas are as inferior to the Spaniards as infants to adults and women to men. There is as much difference between them as there is between cruel, wild peoples and the most merciful of peoples, between the most monstrously intemperate peoples and those who are temperate and moderate in their pleasures, that is to say, between apes and men. . . .

Source: John H. Parry, and Robert G. Keith, eds., *New Iberian World: A Documentary History of the Discovery and Settlement of Latin America to the Early 17th Century* (New York: Times Books: Hector & Rose, 1984), 1: 323–334.

Now compare these natural qualities of judgment, talent, magnanimity, temperance, humanity, and religion with those of these pitiful men [the Indians], in whom you will scarcely find any vestiges of humanness. These people possess neither science nor even an alphabet, nor do they preserve any monuments of their history except for some obscure and vague reminiscences depicted in certain paintings, nor do they have written laws, but barbarous institutions and customs. In regard to their virtues, how much restraint or gentleness are you to expect of men who are devoted to all kinds of intemperate acts and abominable lewdness, including the eating of human flesh? And you must realize that prior to the arrival of the Christians, they did not live in that peaceful kingdom of Saturn that the poets imagine, but on the contrary they made war against one another continually and fiercely, with such fury that victory was of no meaning if they did not satiate their monstrous hunger with the flesh of their enemies. . . .

Until now we have not mentioned their impious religion and their abominable sacrifices, in which they worship the Devil as God, to whom they thought of offering no better tribute than human hearts. . . . Interpreting their religion in an ignorant and barbarous manner, they sacrificed human victims by removing the hearts from the chests. They placed these hearts on their abominable altars. With this ritual they believed that they had appeased their gods. They also ate the flesh of the sacrificed men. . . .

War against these barbarians can be justified not only on the basis of their paganism but even more so because of their abominable licentiousness, their prodigious sacrifice of human victims, the extreme harm that they inflicted on innocent persons, their horrible banquets of human flesh, and the impious cult of their idols. . . . What is more appropriate and beneficial for these barbarians than to become subject to the rule of those whose wisdom, virtue, and religion have converted them from barbarians into civilized men (insofar as they are capable of becoming so), from being torpid and licentious to becoming upright and moral, from being impious servants of the Devil to becoming believers in the true God? They have already begun to receive the Christian religion, thanks to the prudent diligence of the Emperor Charles, an excellent and religious prince. They have already been provided with teachers learned in both the sciences and letters and, what is more important, with teachers of religion and good customs.

For numerous and grave reasons these barbarians are obligated to accept the rule of the Spaniards according to natural law. For them it ought to be even more advantageous than for the Spaniards, since virtue, humanity, and the true religion are more valuable than gold or silver. And if they refuse our rule, they may be compelled by force of arms to accept it. Such a war will be just according to natural law. . . . Such a war would be far more just than even the war that the Romans waged against all the nations of the world in order to force them to submit to their rule [for the following reasons]. The Christian religion is better and truer than the religion of the Romans. In addition, the genius, wisdom, humanity, fortitude, courage, and virtue of the Spaniards are as superior to those same qualities among those pitiful little men [the Indians] as were those of the Romans vis-à-vis the peoples whom they conquered. And the justice of this war becomes even more evident when you consider that the Sovereign Pontiff, who represents Christ, has authorized it. . . .

Las Casas, 1550s

Let us now speak about the unbelievers who live in kingdoms ruled by non-Christians, such as the Moors of Africa, the Turks, the Scythians, the Persians, and those with whom the present controversy is concerned, the Indians. Surely, no matter how despicable the crimes they may commit against God, or even against religion among themselves or within their territories, neither the Church nor Christian rulers can take cognizance of them or punish them for these. For there is no jurisdiction, which is the necessary basis for all juridical acts, especially for punishing a person. Therefore, in this case, the emperor, the prince, or the king has no jurisdiction but is the same as a private citizen, and whatever he does has no force. . . .

In this chapter and in those that follow we shall prove that unbelievers who have never embraced the faith of Christ and who are not Christian subjects cannot be punished by Christians, or even by the Church, for any crime at all, no matter how atrocious it may be.

This is proved, first, by the fact that unbelievers who have never accepted the faith of Christ are not actually subject to Christ and therefore not to the Church or its authority. . . .

Now God's word uproots idolatry and every other vice and softens the hearts of any nation, no matter how wild it may be, by its admirable power. For this reason his word will have a much greater effect upon the Indians than upon any other people, since the former have a docile character and are far more gentle, meek, and receptive than most peoples of the world in their well-known disposition to receive the faith. Experience has taught this, and for Christ's glory I candidly give to posterity what I have seen with my own eyes over a period of fifty years.

The Spaniards made an extremely bold entry into this New World, which was unheard of in past centuries. There, contrary to the intention of their ruler, they committed enormous and extraordinary crimes: they massacred uncounted thousands of persons, burned villages, drove away flocks, destroyed cities, and without cause or pretext of plausible cause did abominable and shameful things to a miserable people [. . .] fierce, rapacious, cruel, could they have a knowledge of the true God, to whose worship the religious were exhorting the Indians? Nevertheless, take note of the power of God's word and the docility of the Indians. Listen to the mercy of Christ, whose blessed name these very wicked men slandered by their crimes. The Indians embraced Christian truth very willingly, which true religious consider a great miracle. Yet some of the Indians persecuted the consecrated men and the religious monks who proclaimed the truth of the gospel to them. Alas, what if those gentle lambs should have the great Paul as their teacher, or someone who would seek to imitate Paul's virtues? How much and what [devout] service they would offer their Lord! How abundant would be the spiritual harvest, the fruit of divine exultation! If they do not spurn the gospel, which, unhappily, the preachers themselves sometimes disgrace by their way of life, what would happen if men who emulated the virtue of the Apostles were to go alone into those provinces whose inhabitants have embraced the faith of Christ, despite very bad examples and the crimes of enormous ferocity the Spaniards have committed against them?

Now whatever I say about the faith of the Indians I have seen with my own eyes, not only in one place or one nation but in very many. They honor the holy sacraments of the Catholic Church and receive them with a great indication of piety. If they cannot be helped by the sacraments because of a lack of priests, these sincere people grow pale, lament, grieve, and weep. Again, at the time of death you may see in them a wonderful concern about their salvation and their soul—a clear sign of eternal predestination that is characteristic of Christians. Would there be more among us who would be troubled with concerns of this type? Finally, with great solicitude they request the sacraments for themselves and their children. I shall speak at greater length about this in the second part of this apology. . . .

Finally, Sepúlveda claims that the Supreme Pontiff Alexander VI advised the kings of Castile to subjugate the Indians by war and that he condoned the war by which those peoples have been brought under our rule. This is absolutely false. The Pope granted the kings of Castile the right to set themselves over the Indian rulers whom they had converted to the faith of Christ and keep them as subjects under their protection and jurisdiction. But the Pope never commanded or permitted them to subjugate these rulers by war. For how would he permit something that conflicts with Christ's precept and instruction and produces hatred of the name of Christ in the hearts of unbelievers, and is utterly irreligious? For the will of a ruler is always judged to be in conformity with the law.

Now it is unlawful to force the Indians to the faith by war, or by the misfortunes of war to make them hate the Christian religion, by whose preaching they see so many regrettable evils inflicted on them. It is beyond belief, then, that the Vicar of Christ permitted war to be waged against them, since this is against all divine and human laws, and especially as it is his concern to spread the faith. Therefore we must believe that he wants what is just and in keeping with Christ's commands and example. And so this is what he ought to do.

Now Christ wanted his gospel to be preached with enticements, gentleness, and all meekness and pagans to be led to the truth not by armed forces but by holy examples, Christian conduct, and the word of God, so that no opportunity would be offered for blaspheming his sacred name or hating the true religion because of the conduct of the preachers. For this is nothing else than making the coming and passion of Christ useless, as long as the truth of the gospel is hated before it is either understood or heard or as long as innumerable human beings are slaughtered in a war waged on the grounds of preaching the gospel and spreading religion. We must think that the Pope wanted the gospel to be preached with Christian meekness. That this was the Pope's intention is proved by the fact that in his bull of concession he cites the petition of the Catholic Kings, which contains the statement that the Indians are a gentle people who have some knowledge of God and are such a people that if they were instructed in the faith, there would be hope that Christ's religion would be spread far and wide. Therefore it is unthinkable that the Pope believed that a people whom the petitioners called gentle had to be overcome by war. And so Sepúlveda's assertion that Pope Alexander exhorted the kings to subjugate those peoples by war is not true. . . .

The intention of the Pope, the plan the kings of Castile presented, and the command imposed on them to fulfill the enterprise are clear in the first and fifth points of the bull. This is why, in the fourth point, the Pope praises the Kings precisely because they wanted to seek new regions, unknown in former centuries, with the intention of spreading the Christian religion. In the bull's second point, where the Pope makes note of the meekness, sincerity, and simplicity of the Indians, as well as their capacity and receptiveness for God's word, he clearly implies the restriction that ought to be found in the third point; that is, that they subjugate (that is, dispose) them for the faith in a way in which one should subjugate a most civilized, sincere, naked, docile, decent, and peaceful people who are very ready to serve, that is, mildly, in a Christian and humane way. As a result, after they first know the true God through belief in the gospel, they may at last freely subject themselves to the king of Castile (from whom they have received such a benefit) as to their supreme prince and emperor, while the rights of their natural lords are retained. . . .

5. Mexica Nobles Protest the Burdens of Spanish Rule, 1556, 1560

To His Majesty [Don Philip, king of Spain], from the lords and principals [leaders] of the peoples of New Spain, May 11, 1556. . . .

Our very High and very Powerful King and Lord:

The lords and principals of the peoples of this New Spain, of Mexico and its surroundings, subjects and servants of Your Majesty, we kiss the royal feet of Your Majesty and with dutiful humility and respect we implore You and state that, given that we are in such great need of the protection and aid of Your Majesty, both for ourselves and for those whom we have in our charge, due to the many wrongs and damages that we receive from the Spaniards, because they are amongst us, and we amongst them, and because for the remedy of our necessities we are very much in need of a person who would be our defender, who would reside continuously in that royal court, to whom we could go with [our necessities], and give Your Majesty notice and true accounts of all of them, because we cannot, given the long distance there is from here to there, nor can we manifest them in writing, because they are so many and so great that it would be a great bother to Your Majesty, thus we ask and humbly beseech Your Majesty to appoint to us the bishop of Chiapas Don Fray Bartolomé de las Casas to take this charge of being our defender and that Your Majesty order him to accept; and if by chance said bishop were unable because of his death or sickness, we beseech Your Majesty in such a case to appoint to us one of the principal persons of your royal court of good will and very Christian to whom we can appeal with the things that would come up, because so many of them are of such a type that they require solely your royal presence, and from it only, after God, do we expect the remedy, because otherwise we will suffer daily so many needs and we are so aggrieved that soon we will be ended, since every day we are more consumed and finished, because they expel us from our lands and deprive us of our goods, beyond the many other labors and personal tributes that daily are increased for us.

Source: Miguel León-Portilla, ed., *The Broken Spears: The Aztec Account of the Conquest of Mexico* (Boston: Beacon Press, 1992), pp. 152–158.

May our Lord cause to prosper and keep the royal person and state of Our Majesty as we your subjects and servants desire. From this town of Tlacopan, where we are all assembled for this, the eleventh day of the month of May, the year one thousand five hundred fifty-six.

The loyal subjects and servants of your Royal Majesty, Don Esteban de Guzmán, judge of Mexico. Don Hernando Pimentel. Don Antonio Cortés. Don Juan of Coyoacan. Don Pedro de Moctezuma. Don Alonso of Iztapalapa. . . .

Letter to the Council of Huejotzingo to King Philip II, 1560 . . .

Our Lord sovereign, you the king don Felipe. . . .

[B]efore anyone told us of or made us acquainted with your fame and your story, . . . and before we were told or taught the glory and name of our Lord God, . . . when your servants the Spaniards reached us and your captain general don Hernando Cortés arrived, . . . our Lord God the ruler of heaven and possessor of earth . . . enlightened us so that we took you as our king to belong to you and become your people and your subjects; not a single town surpassed us here in New Spain in that first and earliest we threw ourselves toward you, we gave ourselves to you, and furthermore no one intimidated us, no one forced us into it, but truly God caused us to deserve that voluntarily we adhered to you so that we gladly received the newly arrived Spaniards who reached us here in New Spain. . . . We received them very gladly, we embraced them, we saluted them with many tears, though we were not acquainted with them, and our fathers and grandfathers also did not know them; but by the mercy of our Lord God we truly came to know them. Since they are our neighbors, therefore we loved them; nowhere did we attack them. Truly we fed them and served them; some arrived sick, so that we carried them in our arms and on our backs, and we served them in many other ways which we are not able to say here. Although the people who are called and named Tlaxcalans indeed helped, yet we strongly pressed them to give aid, and we admonished them not to make war; but though we so admonished them, they made war and fought for fifteen days. But we, when a Spaniard was afflicted, without fail at once we managed to reach him. . . . We do not lie in this, for all the conquerors know it well, those who have died and some now living.

And when they begin their conquest and war-making, then also we prepared ourselves well to aid them, for out came all of our war gear, our arms and provisions and all our equipment, and we not merely named someone, we went in person, we who rule, and we brought all our nobles and all of our vassals to aid the Spaniards. We helped not only in warfare, but we also gave them everything they needed; we fed and clothed them, and we would carry in our arms and on our backs those whom they wounded in war or who were very ill, and we did all the tasks in preparing for war. And so that they could fight the Mexica with boats, we worked hard; we gave them the wood and pitch with which the Spaniards made the boats. And when they conquered the Mexica and all belonging to them, we never abandoned them or left them behind in it. And when they went to conquer Michoacan, Jalisco, and Colhuacan, and there at Pánuco and there at Oaxaca and Tehuantepec and Guatemala, [we were] the only ones who went along while they conquered and made war here in New Spain until they finished the conquest; we never abandoned them, in no way did we prejudice their war-making, though some of us were destroyed in it [there was no one as deserving as we], for we did our duty very well. But as to those Tlaxcalans, several of their nobles were hanged for making war poorly; in many places they ran away, and often did badly in the war. In this we do not lie, for the conquerors know it well.

Our lord sovereign, we also say and declare before you that your fathers the twelve sons of St. Francis reached us, whom the very high priestly ruler the Holy Father sent and whom you sent, both taking pity on us so that they came to teach us the gospel, to teach us the holy Catholic faith and belief, to make us acquainted with the single deity God our Lord, and likewise God favored us and enlightened us, us of Huejotzingo, who dwell in your city, so that we gladly received them. When they entered the city of Huejotzingo, of our own free will we honored them and showed them esteem. When they embraced us so that we would abandon the wicked belief in many gods, we forthwith voluntarily left it; likewise they did us the good deed [of telling us] to destroy and burn the stones and wood that we worshiped as gods, and we did it; very willingly we destroyed, demolished, and burned the temples. Also when they gave us the holy gospel, the holy Catholic faith, with very good will and desire we received and grasped it; no one frightened us into it, no one forced us, but very willingly we seized it, and they gave us all the sacraments. Quietly and peacefully we arranged and ordered it among ourselves; no one, neither nobleman nor commoner, was ever tortured or burned for this, as was done on every hand here in New Spain. [The people of] many towns were forced and tortured, were hanged or burned, because they did not want to leave idolatry, and unwillingly they received the gospel and faith. Especially those Tlaxcalans pushed out and rejected the fathers, and would not receive the faith, for many of the high nobles were burned, and some hanged, for combating the advocacy and service of our Lord God. But we of Huejotzingo, we your poor vassals, we never did anything in your harm, always we served you in every command you sent or what at your command we were ordered. . . . Therefore now, in and through God, may you hear these our words, . . . so that you will exercise on us your rulership to console us and aid us in [this trouble] with which daily we weep and are sad. We are afflicted and sore pressed, and your town and city of Huejotzingo is as if it is about to disappear and be destroyed. Here is what is being done to us: now your stewards the royal officials and the prosecuting attorney Dr. Maldonado are assessing us a very great tribute to belong to you. The tribute we are to give is 14,800 pesos in money, and also all the bushels of maize.

Our lord sovereign, never has such happened to us in all the time since your servants and vassals the Spaniards came to us, for your servant don Hernando Cortés, late captain general, the Marqués del Valle, in all the time he lived here with us, always greatly cherished us and kept us happy; he never disturbed nor agitated us. Although we gave him tribute, he assigned it to us only with moderation; even though we gave him gold, it was only very little; no matter how much, no matter in what way, or if not very pure, he just received it gladly. He never reprimanded us or afflicted us, because it was evident to him and he understood well how very greatly we served and aided him. Also he told us many times that he would speak in our favor before you, that he would help us and inform you of all the ways in which we have aided and served you.

... But perhaps before you he forgot us. How then shall we speak? We did not reach you, we were not given audience before you. Who then will speak for us? Unfortunate are we. Therefore now we place ourselves before you, our sovereign lord. ...

Your poor vassals who bow down humbly to you from afar,

Don Leonardo Ramírez, governor. Don Mateo de la Corona, alcalde. ... Toribio de San [Cristó]bal Motolinía.

6. A Conquistador Praises Malinche, c. 1570

Doña Marina's Story

Before speaking of the great Montezuma, and of the famous city of Mexico and the Mexicans, I should like to give an account of Doña Marina, who had been a great lady and a *Cacique* over towns and vassals since her childhood.

Her father and mother were lords and *Caciques* of a town called Paynala, which had other towns subject to it, and lay about twenty-four miles from the town of Coatzacoalcos. Her father died while she was still very young, and her mother married another *Cacique*, a young man, to whom she bore a son. The mother and father seem to have been very fond of this son, for they agreed that he should succeed to the *Caciqueship* when they were dead. To avoid any impediment, they gave Doña Marina to some Indians from Xicalango, and this they did by night in order to be unobserved. They then spread the report that the child had died; and as the daughter of one of their Indian slaves happened to die at this time, they gave it out that this was their daughter the heiress.

The Indians of Xicalango gave the child to the people of Tabasco, and the Tabascans gave her to Cortes. I myself knew her mother and her half-brother, who was then a man and ruled the town jointly with his mother, since the old lady's second husband had died. After they became Christians, the mother was called Marta and the son Lazaro. All this I know very well, because in the year 1523, after the conquest of Mexico and the other provinces and at the time of Cristobal de Olid's revolt in Honduras, I passed through the place with Cortes, and the majority of its inhabitants accompanied him also. As Doña Marina had proved such an excellent person, and a good interpreter in all the wars of New Spain, Tlascala, and Mexico—as I shall relate hereafter—Cortes always took her with him. During this expedition she married a gentleman called Juan Jaramillo at the town of Orizaba. Doña Marina was a person of great importance, and was obeyed without question by all the Indians of New Spain. And while Cortes was in the town of Coatzacoalcos, he summoned all the *Caciques* of that province in order to address them on the subject of our holy religion, and the good way in which they had been treated; and Doña Marina's mother and her half-brother Lazaro were among those who came. Doña Marina had told me some time before that she belonged to this province, and that she was the mistress of vassals, and both Cortes and the interpreter Aguilar knew it well. Thus it was that mother, son, and daughter came together, and it was easy enough to see

Source: From *The Conquest of New Spain* by Bernal Díaz, translated with an introduction by J. M. Cohen. (Penguin Classics, 1963). Copyright © J. M. Cohen, 1963. Reprinted with permission of Penguin Group.

from the strong resemblance between them that Doña Marina and the old lady were related. Both she and her son were very much afraid of Doña Marina; they feared that she had sent for them to put them to death, and they wept.

When Doña Marina saw her mother and half-brother in tears, she comforted them, saying that they need have no fear. She told her mother that when they had handed her over to the men from Xicalango, they had not known what they were doing. She pardoned the old woman, and gave them many golden jewels and some clothes. Then she sent them back to their town, saying that God had been very gracious to her in freeing her from the worship of idols and making her a Christian, and giving her a son by her lord and master Cortes, also in marrying her to such a gentleman as her husband Juan Jaramillo. Even if they were to make her mistress of all the provinces of New Spain, she said, she would refuse the honour, for she would rather serve her husband and Cortes than anything else in the world. What I have related here I know for certain and swear to. The whole story seems very much like that of Joseph and his brethren in Egypt, when the Egyptians came into his power over the wheat.

To return to my subject, Doña Marina knew the language of Coatzacoalcos, which is that of Mexico, and she knew the Tabascan language also. This language is common to Tabasco and Yucatan, and Jeronimo de Aguilar spoke it also. These two understood one another well, and Aguilar translated into Castilian for Cortes.

This was the great beginning of our conquests, and thus, praise be to God, all things prospered with us. I have made a point of telling this story, because without Doña Marina we could not have understood the language of New Spain and Mexico.

7. An Epic Poet Celebrates Portuguese Exploration, 1572

Such words the noble ancient standing there
Cried out aloud, what time our wings we spread
To the serene and favorable air.
So from the harbor well-beloved we sped
And, as at sea it is the custom fair
When making sail, the welkin overhead
We rent with our "Fair Voyage." And the blast
Pushed, as his wont is, hard on every mast.

2

'Twas the season when the Eternal Light of Day
Through fierce Nemea's beast his course would run,
And this world, which with time consumes away,
Sickly and slow, through its sixth age went on,
Having counted, as the custom is to say,
Some fourteen hundred circles of the sun,
And ninety-seven, in which last, incomplete,
The sun wheeled, when to sea put forth the fleet.

Source: Luiz de Camoes, *The Lusiad*, trans. by Leonard Bacon (New York: The Hispanic Society of America, 1950), pp. 175–180. Reprinted by permission of The Hispanic Society of America, New York.

3

Little by little was exiled our sight
From hills of our own land that lay behind.
There was dear Tagus, there cool Cintra's height,
Toward which our eyes for a long while inclined.
But the spirit in the land of our delight
Stayed yet, for there abode what hurt the mind,
Until at length all vanished utterly,
And we saw nothing but the sky and sea.

4

Thus we went forth to break those oceans through,
Where none before had ever forced the way.
We saw the new isles and the climates new
 Henry the Great discovered in his day.
Mauretania's heights and cities full in view,
Lands over which Antaeus once held sway,
We had upon our left. On the right hand,
Although not certain, we might guess at land.

5

And we sailed by Madeira's island vast,
That from the giant forest takes its name,
The first of all we peopled in the past,
Known for the name rather than any fame.
But though it be of all this world the last,
Those Venus loves advance no nobler claim.
Were it hers, she would forget in little while
Cythera, Cnidus, Cyprus, Paphos' isle.

6

Now past Massylia's desert coast we go,
Where Azenegs put cattle out to hay.
Fresh water's taste that folk can never know,
Nor yet sufficiency of grass have they.
This is a land in which no fruit can grow,
Where iron in birds' gizzards wastes away.
The region knows extremest poverty,
Which Ethiopia parts from Barbary.

7

Our course beyond that limit did we hold,
The sun attains, who north his car would guide.
There also dwells that race, to whom of old
Clymene's son the hue of day denied.
There the black Senegal with current cold
That region of strange nations waters wide.
Cape Arsinarius' name no more is heard,
Which in our tongue today is called Cape Verde.

8

Past the Canary Islands on we bore,
The Fortunate Isles (for once so named were these),
And sailed amid the maids of Hesperus hoar,
Who hence were known as the Hesperides,
Regions to which our navies long before
Had come and looked on novel prodigies.
We made a port hard by, the wind being fair,
And went ashore to get provision there.

9

The isle we harbored in its name doth take
From that Saint James who was a soldier too.
And he it was who for the Spaniards' sake
Helped them brave slaughter on the Moor to do.
Thence, to sail over that enormous lake
Of the salt ocean, while the north wind blew,
We set our course, and left behind the ground
Where such a sweet refreshment we had found.

10

We circled Afric where it stretches wide
And, for us, ever to the east doth bear—
Jalofo's province, which the blacks divide
Among the various nations dwelling there,
Mandinga's greatest, whence we are supplied
So well with the rich metal shining fair.
There men drink Gambia's stream that winds and weaves,
And which the Atlantic huge at length receives.

11

Next past the Dorcades our course inclined,
The dwelling of those sisters anciently,
Who, though the three of them were wholly blind,
Yet used a single eye among the three.
Thou, and no other, whose locks crisply twined
Set fire to Neptune yonder in the sea,
Into the foulest of all things must turn,
And fill with vipers all the sands that burn.

12

With the sharp prow still southward headed right,
Into the greatest of all gulfs we drave,
Leaving behind Leone's saw-toothed height
And the Cape of Palms, for such the name we gave.
The giant stream is here, where still must smite,
On shores we know and hold, the roaring wave,
Likewise that island, whose name sanctified
Derives from him who touched his Savior's side.

13

Congo's vast kingdom is established there
(Erewhile by us brought to Christ's faith), wherethrough
Runs the long current of the crystal Zair,
A river which no ancient ever knew.
And from the Pole familiar of the Bear
At length in those vast oceans I withdrew,
For I had overpassed the burning bound,
Where the limit which divides the world is found.

14

We had discovered earlier in our way
A new star set in the new hemisphere,
Unknown to others, for, all ignorant, they
Of earlier times thereof heard nothing clear.
We saw those regions of less splendid ray,
Which, starless, not so beautiful appear,
Near the fixed Pole, where none yet comprehends
If other land begins or the sea ends.

15

Our course across those regions we had ta'en,
Through the which, passing twice, Apollo makes
A pair of winters and likewise summers twain,
What time from Pole to Pole his way he takes.
Through calamity and calm and hurricane,
Mad Eolus still over Ocean wakes,
We saw the Bears that Juno's wrath defied
Bathing themselves in Neptune's waters wide.

16

At length to tell the perils of the sea,
Things inconceivable to human wit,
The sudden bolt that crashes fearfully,
Lightnings whereby the flaming airs are lit,
Black squalls, and the night's dark intensity,
Bellow of thunders that creation split,
Were not less labor than erroneous choice,
Supposing that I had an iron voice.

17

But I beheld those things, which sailors rude,
Who long experience for their mistress own,
Count ever truth and perfect certitude,
Judging things by appearances alone.
But they with more intelligence endued,
Who see world mysteries, only to be known
By science or pure genius, reason still
Such things are false or else conceived of ill.

18

And I have clearly seen that living light,
A holy thing, as mariners consent,
In time of storm with wicked winds at height
And dark tornado making sad lament.
Nor was it less miraculous in our sight,
And surely 'tis a terrible event,
As in a pipe, the sea-mists to descry
Drawing up to Heaven Ocean's waters high.

19

I do not think that my sight cheated me,
For certainly I saw rise up in air
A smoke of fine and vaporous subtilty,
That whirled perpetual, as the wind might bear.
To the high pole rose the spout, as one might see,
And yet it was so tenuous and rare,
Discovery by the eye was scarce allowed.
It seemed the very substance of a cloud.

20

Little by little waxing, the thing grew
Till it was thicker than the mightiest mast.
Here it might thin or thicken out anew,
As it sucked up the sea with gulpings vast.
With the rolling wave it undulated too.
On its head a dense cloud darkened, overcast,
That swelled apace and still more ponderous showed,
For water it took up, a monstrous load.

21

As the red leech on the bullock's lip his fill
Sucks of strange blood, his hot thirst to abate
(For the ox, unthinking, at the fountain chill
Drank in the creature), and insatiate
The leech keeps at it and enlarges still,
Gorging itself, swelling, and growing great;
So the huge column, drawing up water, swelled,
Together with the black cloud it upheld.

22

But, after, having drunken its whole due,
It lifts the foot on the sea surface set,
And, raining out of Heaven, fades from view,
Making the ocean waters yet more wet,
To the waves the waves returning, that it drew,
Though it has robbed them of their salty whet.
Now let the men well skilled in letters see
How mighty nature's mysteries may be.

23

If old philosophers, who went to find
The secrets of so many lands afar,
Had witnessed, spreading sail to every wind,
As I have seen, the miracles that are,
What noble works they would have left behind!
What influences sweet of sign and star!
What qualities and what strange things uncouth!
And in good faith and everything pure truth!

8. A Priest Explains the Origins of the People of New Spain, 1581

Which Treats of the Possible Place of Origin of the Indians of These Indies, the Islands, and Mainland of This New Spain.

In order to provide a truthful and reliable account of the origin of these Indian nations, an origin so doubtful and obscure, we would need some divine revelation or assistance to reveal this origin to us and help us understand it. However, lacking that revelation we can only speculate and conjecture about these beginnings, basing ourselves on the evidence provided by these people, whose strange ways, conduct, and lowly actions are so like those of the Hebrews. Thus we can almost positively affirm that they are Jews and Hebrews, and I would not commit a great error if I were to state this as fact, considering their way of life, their ceremonies, their rites and superstitions, their omens and hypocrisies, so akin to and characteristic of those of the Jews; in no way do they seem to differ. The Holy Scriptures bear witness to this, and from them we draw proofs and reasons for holding this opinion to be true.

As proof thereof, we know that this newly arrived nation, latecomers from strange and remote regions, made a long and tedious journey, searching and finally taking possession of this land. They spent many months and years in coming to this place. The truth of this matter can be found by drawing on their traditions and paintings and by talking to their elders, some of whom are very old.

There are some people who tell fables about this subject. To wit, some say that the Indians were born of pools and springs; others that they were born of caves; still others, that they descended from the gods. All of this is clearly fabulous and shows that the natives themselves are ignorant of their origin and beginnings, inasmuch as they always profess to have come from strange lands. And I have found these things depicted in their painted manuscripts, where they portray great periods of hunger, thirst, and nakedness, with innumerable other afflictions that they suffered until they reached this land and settled it.

All of these things confirm my suspicions that these natives are part of the ten tribes of Israel that Shalmaneser, king of the Assyrians, captured and took to Assyria

Source: Fray Diego Durán, *The History of the Indies of New Spain*, ed. Doris Heyden (Norman: University of Oklahoma Press, 1994), chapter 1, pp. 3–5, 7–10.

in the time of Hoshea, king of Israel, and in the time of Ezekias, king of Jerusalem, as can be read in the fourth Book of Kings, chapter XVII. Here it is stated that Israel was taken from its own land to Assyria. And Ezra, in book four, chapter XIII, says about these people that they went to live in a remote and distant country that had never before been inhabited. There was a long and wearisome journey of a year and a half to reach the region of the Islands and the Mainland, to the west and beyond the seas, where today these people are found.

Other evidence found in the Holy Writ that can be cited to prove this idea is that God, in Hoshea, chapters I and II, and II up to XII, is said to have promised to multiply ten tribes of Israel, making them as numerous as sands of the sea. And the fact that they have taken possession of a large part of the world clearly and manifestly shows how great was this increase. But leaving [the biblical text] and coming to what the Spaniards saw in this country, one thing that amazed them was the large number of people they found here. This was remarked by [the Spaniards] who came early to this country, before the great plague of thirty-three years ago, when so many people died that not even a third of the Indians who lived here before the plague survived. And this does not include the innumerable men, women, and children killed by the Spaniards during the conquest a few years earlier. . . .

These people have traditions regarding a great man. They told me that after he had suffered many afflictions and persecutions from his countrymen he gathered the multitude of his followers and persuaded them to flee from that persecution to a land where they could live in peace. Having made himself leader of those people, he went to the seashore and moved the waters with a rod that he carried in his hand. Then the sea opened up and he and his followers went through. And his enemies, seeing this opening made, pursued him, but the waters returned to their place and the pursuers were never heard of again.

What clearer proof do we need that these people were Jews than their own reference to the flight from Egypt, wherein Moses moved the waters with his rod, the sea opened up, a path appeared, and after Pharaoh followed with his army God caused the sea to return to its place, with the result that all their enemies drowned in the deep? . . .

That I may leave nothing untold, I wish to cite the Holy Writ in defense of my opinion. I take my theme from the first chapter of Genesis, which states: "In the beginning God created the heaven and the earth." Just so an aged man from Cholula, about one hundred years old, began to describe their origins to me. This man, who because of his great age walked bent over toward the earth, was quite learned in their ancient traditions. When I begged him to enlighten me about some details I wished to put into this history, he asked me what I wanted him to tell. I realized I had found an old and learned person, so I answered, all that he knew about the history of his Indian nation from the beginning of the world. He responded: "Take pen and paper, because you will not be able to remember all that I shall tell you." And began thus:

In the beginning, before light or sun had been created, this world lay in darkness and shadows and was void of every living thing. It was all flat, without a hill or ravine, surrounded on all sides by water, without even a tree or any other created thing. And then, when the light and sun were born in the east, men of monstrous stature appeared and took possession of this country. These giants, desirous of seeing the birth of the sun and its setting, decided to go seek [dawn and dusk], and they separated into two groups. One band walked toward the west and the other toward the east. The latter walked until the sea cut off their route; from here they decided to return to the place from which they had set out, called Iztac Zolin Inemian.

Not having found a way to reach the sun but enamored of its light and beauty, they decided to build a tower so high that its summit would reach unto heaven. And gathering materials for this building, the giants found clay for bricks and an excellent mortar with which they began to build the tower very swiftly. When they had raised it as high as they could—and it seemed to reach to heaven—the Lord of the Heights became angry and said to the inhabitants of the heavens, "Have you seen that the men of the earth have built a proud and lofty tower in order to come up here, enamored as they are of the light of the sun and of its beauty? Come, let us confound them, for it is not right that these earthlings, made of flesh, mingle with us." Then swift as lightning those who dwell in the heavens came out from the four regions of the world and tore down the tower that had been constructed. And the giants, bewildered and filled with terror, separated and fled in all directions.

That is how an Indian relates the creation of the world, and I do not believe it necessary to call attention to the resemblance of this account to chapters I and II of Genesis. [The sixth and eleventh chapters] of that book deal with giants and the tower of Babel and how men, ambitious to reach heaven, moved only by the desire to praise their own name, built the tower and because of this were confounded by God. Therefore I am convinced and wish to convince others that those who tell this account heard it from their ancestors; and these natives belong, in my opinion, to the lineage of the chosen people of God for whom He worked great marvels. And so the knowledge of the paintings of the things told in the Bible and its mysteries have passed from hand to hand, from father to son. The people assign those events to this land, believing that they took place here, for they are ignorant of their own origins. . . .

Seeing that their stories are so like those found in the Holy Scriptures I cannot help but believe that [these Indians are the children of Israel].

As proof of this, in order to make it clear, I wish to mention the rites, idolatries, and superstitions these people had. They made sacrifices in the mountains, and under trees, in dark and gloomy caves, and in the caverns of the earth. They burned incense, killed their sons and daughters, sacrificed them, and offered them as victims to their gods. They sacrificed children, ate human flesh, killed prisoners and captives of war. All of these were also Hebrew rites practiced by those ten tribes of Israel, and all were carried out with the greatest ceremony and superstitions one can imagine.

What most forces me to believe that these Indians are of Hebrew descent is their strange insistence in clinging to their idolatries and superstitions, for they pay them much heed, just as their ancestors did.

△ E S S A Y S

Although the two essays in this chapter present very different approaches to the fateful collision of cultures that marked the Iberian conquest of the Americas, both offer new directions in the cultural and social history of the era.

Inga Clendinnen's essay draws attention to the contrasting cultural assumptions embedded in Spanish and Mexican military tactics during Hernan Cortés's campaign against the Mexica capital city of Tenochtitlan. Clendinnen contrasts the Mexicas' view of warfare as a highly ritualized "sacred duel" with the Spaniards' more utilitarian view of warfare as a means to kill the enemy and control his territory. In Clendinnen's view, Cortés's refusal to fight according to the Mexica warriors' code of honor was crucial to his victory, achieved in the end by the most dishonorable method of all, a prolonged siege of Tenochtitlan.

Whereas Clendinnen's essay is primarily concerned with the masculine world of battle, Susan Socolow traces the various ways that the Iberian discovery and conquest of the Americas affected indigenous women beyond the battlefield and outside the royal court. Many Indian women were victimized by European men, but some forged alliances of sex and marriage that benefited them, and many indigenous women took advantage of Spanish law and custom to protect their economic and familial interests. This selection from Socolow's essay focuses on the effect of indigenous women's migration to towns and cities, and their shift from their preconquest religious traditions to Roman Catholicism.

The Culture of Conquest

INGA CLENDINNEN

The conquest of Mexico matters to us because it poses a painful question: How was it that a motley bunch of Spanish adventurers, never numbering much more than four hundred or so, was able to defeat an Amerindian military power on its home ground in the space of two years? What was it about Spaniards, or about Indians, that made so awesomely implausible a victory possible? The question has not lost its potency through time, and as the consequences of the victory continue to unfold has gained in poignancy. . . .

Analysts and participants alike agree that the Conquest falls into two phases. The first began with the Spanish landfall in April of 1519, and Cortés's assumption of independent command in defiance of the governor of Cuba, patron of Cortés and of the expedition; the Spaniards' march inland, in the company of coastal Indians recently conquered by the Mexicans, marked first by bloody battles and then by alliance with the independent province of Tlaxcala; their uncontested entry into the Mexican imperial city of Tenochtitlan-Tlatelolco, a magnificent lake-borne city of 200,000 or more inhabitants linked to the land by three great causeways; the Spaniards' seizing of the Mexican ruler Moctezoma, and their uneasy rule through him for six months; the arrival on the coast of another and much larger Spanish force from Cuba under the command of Panfilo Narváez charged with the arrest of Cortés, its defeat and incorporation into Cortés's own force; a native "uprising" in Tenochtitlan, triggered in Cortés's absence by the Spaniards' massacre of unarmed warriors dancing in a temple festival; the expulsion of the Spanish forces, with great losses, at the end of June 1520 on the so-called "Noche Triste," and Moctezoma's death, probably at Spanish hands, immediately before that expulsion. End of the first phase. The second phase is much briefer in the telling, although about the same span in the living: a little over a year. The Spaniards retreated to friendly Tlaxcala to recover health and morale. They then renewed the attack, reducing the lesser lakeside cities, recruiting allies, not all of them voluntary, and placing Tenochtitlan under siege in

Source: Inga Clendinnen, "'Fierce and Unnatural Cruelty': Cortés and the Conquest of Mexico," *Representations*, 1991 (33), pp. 65–67, 76–84. Reproduced with permission via Copyright Clearance Center.

May of 1521. The city fell to the combined forces of Cortés and an assortment of Indian "allies" in mid August 1521. End of the second phase. . . .

Analysts, save for military historians, have overwhelmingly concentrated on the first phase of the Conquest, assuming the consummation of Spanish victory to be merely a matter of applying a technological superiority: horsemen against pedestrian warriors, steel swords against wooden clubs, muskets and crossbows against bows and arrows and lances, cannon against ferocious courage. I would argue that it is only for the second phase that we have sufficiently solid evidence to allow a close analysis of how Spaniards and Indians made sense of each other, and so to track down issues that must remain will-o'-the-wisps for the first phase. I would also argue that the final conquest was a very close-run thing: a view in which the combatants on both sides, as it happens, would agree. After the Spanish ejection from Tenochtitlan the Mexicans remained heavily favored in things material, most particularly manpower, which more than redressed any imbalance in equipment. Spanish technology had its problems: the miseries of slithering or cold-cramped or foundering horses, wet powder, the brutal weight of the cannon, and always the desperate question of supply. Smallpox, introduced into Mexico by one of Narváez's men, had swept through the native population, but its ravages had presumably affected Spanish "allies" equally with the Mexicans. The sides were approximately matched in knowledge: if Cortés was to profit from his familiarity with the fortifications and functioning of the lake city, the Mexicans at last knew the Spaniards as enemies, and were under the direction of a ruler liberated from the ambiguities that appear to have bedeviled them earlier.

We tend to have a *Lord of the Flies* view of battle: that in deadly combat the veils of "culture" are ripped away, and natural man confronts himself. But if combat is not quite as cultural as cricket, its brutalities are nonetheless rule-bound. Like cricket, it requires a sustained act of cooperation, with each side constructing the conditions in which both will operate, and so, where the struggle is between strangers, obliging a mutual "transmission of culture" of the shotgun variety. And because of its high intensities it promises to expose how one's own and other ways of acting and meaning are understood and responded to in crisis conditions, and what lessons about the other and about oneself can be learned in that intimate, involuntary, and most consequential communication. . . .

Here the usual caveats of overidealization apply. If all social rules are fictions, made "real" through being contested, denied, evaded, and recast as well as obeyed, "rules of war," war being what it is, are honored most earnestly in the breach. But in the warrior societies of Central Mexico, where the battlefield held a central place in the imagination, with its protocols rehearsed and trained for in the ordinary routines of life, the gap between principle and practice was narrow. War, at least war as fought among the dominant peoples of Mexico, and at least ideally, was a sacred contest, the outcome unknown but preordained, revealing which city, which local deity, would rightfully dominate another. Something like equal terms were therefore required: to prevail by mere numbers or by some piece of treachery would vitiate the significance of the contest. So important was this notion of fair testing that food and weapons were sent to the selected target city as part of the challenge, there being no virtue in defeating a weakened enemy.

The warriors typically met outside the city of the defenders. Should the attacking side prevail, the defenders abandoned the field and fled, and the victors swept unresisted into the city to fire the temple where the local deity had its place. That action marked victory in occurrence and record; the formal sign for conquest in the painted histories was a burning temple. Free pillage continued until the increasingly frantic pleas of the spokesmen for the defeated were heard, and terms of tribute set. Then the victors withdrew to their home city with their booty and their captives, including not only the warriors taken in the formal battle but "civilians" seized during the period of plunder. Their most significant captive was the image of the tutelary deity of the defeated city, to be held in the "god captive house" in Tenochtitlan. Defeat was bitter because it was a statement and judgment of inferiority of the defeated warriors, who had broken and run; a judgment the victorious warriors were only too ready to reinforce by savage mockery, and which was institutionalized by the imposition of tribute.

The duration of the decision remained problematic. Defeated towns paid their tribute as a regular decision against further hostilities, but remained independent, and usually notably disaffected, despite the conquering city's conviction of the legitimacy of their supremacy. Many towns in the valley, whether allied or defeated or intimidated by the Mexicans, paid their token tribute, fought alongside the Mexicans in Mexican campaigns, and shared in the spoils, but they remained mindful of their humiliation and unreconciled to their subordination. Beyond the valley the benefits of empire were commonly smaller, the costs greater, and disaffection chronic. The monolithic "Aztec empire" is a European hallucination: in this atomistic polity, the units were held together by the tension of mutual repulsion. (Therefore the ease with which Cortés could recruit "allies," too often taken as a tribute to his silver tongue, and therefore the deep confusion attending his constant use of that meaning-drenched word *vassal* to describe the relationship of subject towns first to Tenochtitlan, and later to the Spanish crown.)

If war was a sacred duel between peoples, and so between the "tribal" gods of those peoples, battle was ideally a sacred duel between matched warriors: a contest in which the taking of a fitting captive for presentation to one's own deity was a precise measure of one's own valor, and one's own fate. One prepared for this individual combat by song, paint, and adornment with the sacred war regalia. (To go "always prepared for battle" in the Spanish style was unintelligible: a man carrying arms was only potentially a warrior.) The great warrior, scarred, painted, plumed, wearing the record of his victories in his regalia, erupting from concealment or looming suddenly through the rising dust, then screaming his war cry, could make lesser men flee by the pure terror of his presence: warriors were practiced in projecting ferocity. His rightful, destined opponent was he who could master panic to stand and fight. There were maneuverings to "surprise" the enemy, and a fascination with ambush, but only as a device to confront more dramatically; to strike from hiding was unthinkable. At the outset of battle Indian arrows and darts flew thickly, but to weaken and draw blood, not to pierce fatally. The obsidian-studded war club signaled warrior combat aims: the subduing of prestigious individual captives in single combat for presentation before the home deity.

In the desperation of the last stages of the battle for Tenochtitlan, the Mexican inhibition against battleground killing was somewhat reduced: Indian "allies" died, and Spaniards who could not be quickly subdued were killed, most often, as the Mexicans were careful to specify, and for reasons that will become clear, by having the backs of their heads beaten in. But the priority on the capture of significant antagonists remained. In other regards the Mexicans responded with flexibility to the challenges of siege warfare. They "read" Spanish tactics reasonably accurately: a Spanish assault on the freshwater aqueduct at Chapultepec was foreseen, and furiously, if fruitlessly, resisted. The brigantines, irresistible for their first appearance of the lake, were later lured into a carefully conceived ambush in which two were trapped. The horses' vulnerability to uneven ground, to attack from below, their panic under hails of missiles, were all exploited effectively. The Mexicans borrowed Spanish weapons: Spanish swords lashed to poles or Spanish lances to disable the horses; even Spanish crossbows, after captive crossbowmen had been forced to show them how the machines worked. It was their invention and tenacity that forced Cortés to the desperate remedy of leveling structures along the causeways and into the city to provide the Spaniards with the secure ground they needed to be effective. And they were alert to the possibilities of psychological warfare, capitalizing on the Spaniards' peculiar dread of death by sacrifice and of the cannibalizing of the corpse. On much they could be innovative. But on the most basic measure of man's worth, the taking alive of prestigious captives, they could not compromise.

That passion for captives meant that the moment when the opponent's nerve broke was helplessly compelling, an enemy in flight an irresistible lure. This pursuit reflex was sometimes exploited by native opponents as a slightly shabby trick. It provided Cortés with a standard tactic for a quick and sure crop of kills. Incurious as to the reason, he nonetheless noted and exploited Mexican unteachability: "Sometimes, as we were thus withdrawing and they pursued us so eagerly, the horsemen would pretend to be fleeing, and then suddenly would turn on them; we always took a dozen or so of the boldest. By these means and by the ambushes which we set for them, they were always much hurt; and certainly it was a remarkable sight for even when they well knew the harm they would receive from us as we withdrew, they still pursued us until we had left the city." That commitment bore heavily on outcomes. Had Indians been as uninhibited as Spaniards in their killing, the small Spanish groups, with no secured source of replenishment, would soon have been whittled away. In battle after battle the Spaniards report the deaths of many Indians, with their own men suffering not fatalities but wounds, and fast-healing wounds at that: those flint and obsidian blades sliced clean. It preserved the life of Cortés: time and again the Spanish leader struggled in Indian hands, the prize in a disorderly tug of war, with men dying on each side in the furious struggle for possession, and each time the Spaniards prevailing. Were Cortés in our hands, we would knife him. Mexican warriors could not kill the enemy leader so casually: were he to die, it would be in the temple of Huitzilopochtli, and before his shrine. . . .

For Cortés the individual challenge had been a histrionic preliminary flourish: he then proceeded to the serious work of using firepower to kill warriors, and to control more territory, which was what he took war to be about. Throughout, Spaniards measured success in terms of body counts, territory controlled, and evidence of decay in the morale of the "enemy," which included all warriors, actively engaged in battle or not, and all "civilians" too. Cortés casually informed the king of his dawn raids into sleeping villages and the slaughter of the inhabitants, men, women, and children, as they stumbled into the streets: these were necessary and conventional steps in the progressive control of terrain, and the progressive demoralization of opposition.

To an Indian warrior, Cortés's riposte to the Indian champions' challenge was shameful, with only the horses, putting themselves within reach of the opponents' weapons, emerging with any credit. Cortés's descents on villages are reported in tones of breathless incredulity.

There is in the *Florentine Codex* an exquisitely painful, detailed description of the Spaniards' attack on the unarmed warrior dancers at the temple festival, the slaughter that triggered the Mexican "uprising" of May 1520. The first victim was a drummer: his hands were severed, then his neck. The account continues: "Of some they slashed open their backs: then their entrails gushed out. Of some they cut their heads to pieces. . . . Some they struck on the shoulder; they split openings. They broke openings in their bodies." And so it goes on. How ought we interpret this? It was not, I think, recorded as a horror story, or only as a horror story. The account is sufficiently careful as to precise detail and sequence to suggest its construction close after the event, in an attempt to identify the pattern, and so to discover the sense, in the Spaniards' cuttings and slashings. (This was the first view the Mexicans had of Spanish swords at work.) The Mexicans had very precise rules about violent assaults on the body, as the range of their sacrificial rituals makes clear, but the notion of a "preemptive massacre" of warriors was not in their vocabulary.

Such baffling actions, much more than any deliberately riddling policy, worked to keep Indians off balance. To return to an early celebrated moment of mystification by Cortés, the display of the cannon to impress the Mexican envoys on the coast with the killing power of Spanish weapons: the men who carried the tale back reported the thunderous sound, the smoke, the fire, the foul smell—and that the shot had "dissolved" a mountain, and "pulverised" a tree. It is highly doubtful that the native watchers took the intended point of the display, that this was a weapon of war for use against human flesh. It was not a conceivable weapon for warriors. So it must have appeared (as it is in fact reported) as a gratuitous assault upon nature: a scrambled lesson indeed. Mexican warriors learned, with experience, not to leap and shout and display when faced with cannon fire and crossbows, but to weave and duck, as the shield canoes learned to zigzag to avoid the cannon shot from the brigantines, so that with time the carnage was less. But they also learned contempt for men who were prepared to kill indiscriminately, combatants and noncombatants alike, and at a secure distance, without putting their own lives in play. . . .

Spanish "difference" found its clearest expression in their final strategy for the reduction of the imperial city. Cortés had hoped to intimidate the Mexicans sufficiently by his steady reduction of the towns around the lake, by his histrionic acts of violence, and by the exemplary cruelty with which resistance was punished, to bring them to treat. Example-at-a-distance in that mosaic of rival cities could have no relevance for the Mexicans—if all others quailed, they would not—so the Spaniards resorted, as Díaz put it, to "a new kind of warfare." Siege was the quintessential European strategy: an economical design to exert maximum pressure on whole populations without active engagement, delivering control over people and place at least cost. If Cortés's own precarious position led him to increase that pressure by military sorties, his crucial weapon was want.

For the Mexicans, siege was the antithesis of war. They knew of encircling cities to persuade unwilling warriors to come out, and of destroying them too, when insult required it. They had sought to burn the Spaniards out of their quarters in Tenochtitlan, to force them to fight after their massacre of the warrior dancers. But the deliberate and systematic weakening of opposition before engagement, and the deliberate implication of noncombatants in the contest, had no part in their experience.

As the siege continued the signs of Mexican contempt multiplied. Mexican warriors continued to seek face-to-face combat with these most unsatisfactory opponents, who skulked and refused battle, who clung together in tight bands behind their cannon, who fled without shame. When elite warriors, swept in by canoe, at last had the chance to engage the Spaniards closely, the Spaniards "turned their backs, they fled," with the Mexicans in pursuit. They abandoned a cannon in one of their pell-mell flights, positioned with unconscious irony on the gladiatorial stone on which the greatest enemy warriors had given their final display of fighting prowess; the Mexicans worried and dragged it along to the canal and dropped it into the water. Indian warriors were careful, when they had to kill rather than capture Spaniards in battle, to deny them an honorable warrior's death, dispatching them by beating in the back of their heads, the death reserved for criminals in Tenochtitlan. And the Spaniards captured after the debacle on the Tacuba causeway were stripped of all their battle equipment, their armor, their clothing: only then, when they were naked, and reduced to "slaves," did the Mexicans kill them.

How Conquest Shaped Women's Lives

SUSAN MIGDEN SOCOLOW

The early years of European discovery and conquest of America was a period of violence, dramatic social change, and profound transformation in the lives of indigenous peoples. The Indian world was conquered, dismantled, and restructured according to the conqueror's vision. The conquest probably had a more varied effect on Indian women than any other single group. But not all Indian women were equally affected by the conquest. The aftermath of conquest severed the lives of some women and reduced others to slavery; still others managed to integrate themselves into European society, in many cases more successfully than the Indian men. Thus, the conquest could be a traumatic experience or a new opportunity. In addition, the effects of conquest varied over time, with those who witnessed the destruction of their world and the imposition of European cultural, religious, and social values being far more affected than succeeding generations, who were born into a world already changed.

European women were for the most part absent from the initial ranks of conquistadors who extended Spanish dominion over the islands of the Caribbean, Aztec Mexico, and Inca Peru, but this did not cause Spanish men to undertake lives of voluntary celibacy. Instead they turned to the available Indian women for immediate sexual pleasure. Many native women were accosted, abused, beaten, and raped. As early as two months into his first voyage to America (1492), Columbus, who had repeatedly remarked upon the beauty and fine figures of the native women, mentioned that Indian women were now being systematically hidden from the Spaniards.

Source: Susan Migden Socolow, *The Women of Colonial Latin America* (New York: Cambridge University Press, 2000), pp. 32–37, 40–42, 46–49, 50. Reprinted with the permission of Cambridge University Press.

Rodrigo Rangel, a member of the De Soto expedition to Florida and the Mississippi Valley (1539–1543), reported that the Spaniards took Indian women "who were not old nor the most ugly" and that "they wanted the women in order to make use of them [as servants] and for their lewdness and lust and that they baptized them more for their carnal intercourse than to instruct them in the faith."

Other women, from tribes allied to the Spanish or those conquered by them, were persuaded to become lovers and concubines of Spanish soldiers. Indeed, chiefs offered their sisters and daughters to Spanish conquistadors, continuing the pre-Columbian pattern of using women to appease the powerful and ally with them. Indian women probably willingly accepted these relationships, for this behavior formed part of their culture. The native rulers of Tlaxcala (Mexico) gave their women to the Spaniards in the hope that the children of these unions, perceived by the Indians to be of a high social rank, would remain within the Indian community. Quetzalmamalitizin, lord of Teotihuacán, married his daughter to a Spaniard to strengthen his family's power. If no women were offered, the Iberian conquerors simply helped themselves to any women they wanted. During the conquest of Spanish America, Indian women were routinely taken captives and distributed as booty among the victorious conquistadors. Jiménez de Quesada in Colombia, for example, gave three hundred Indian women to his minions. . . .

Some European men brutally violated and abandoned Indian women, but others began long-lasting relationships with the conquered women. We should remember that it was not unusual for men in sixteenth-century Spanish society to have stable unions with women of lesser social rank either before or outside of marriage. In addition, Indian women who had grown up in societies that accepted polygamy may have found concubinage with Spaniards to be not all that different from the sexual relations that they had previously known.

Although we have no notion of how the Indian women viewed their new situation, these Spanish-Indian unions at times resulted in enduring romantic attachments or even lifelong companionship. The most famous of these romantic liaisons was that of Hernán Cortés, conqueror of Mexico, and Malintzin, an Indian woman he met in 1519, shortly after arriving in Veracruz. Probably of noble Mayan birth, Malintzin (called "doña Marina" by the Spaniards, and also known disrespectfully as "La Malinche" in present-day Mexico) had been captured and enslaved by Tabascan Indians and then given to the Spaniards, along with nineteen other female captives, as a welcoming gift. She showed her gratitude to her new masters by becoming their principal interpreter and go-between as they made their way to the Aztec capital of Tenochitlán. She also became Cortés's concubine (his wife had remained in Cuba), his trusted adviser, and the mother of his illegitimate son, Martín, born in 1522. In 1524, seeking to improve her situation, Cortés arranged a legitimate marriage for her to Juan Jaramillo de Salvatierra, a Spanish soldier in his army and holder of the *encomienda* (royal grant of Indian labor) of Xilotepec. . . .

Perhaps the most famous Indian woman of her time was Isabel Moctezuma (originally named Techichopotzin), whose dramatic life provides an extraordinary example of the complex role of elite Indian women in the years of the conquest and early settlement of America. Born in 1509 or 1510, she was one of perhaps 150 children sired by Montezuma II, the Aztec emperor. At age eleven, the Aztec princess was married to her uncle, Cuitláhuac. Widowed within two months of marriage, she was quickly remarried to her cousin, Cuauhtémoc, the last Aztec emperor. Cuauhtémoc's defeat and torture by the conquering Spaniards, and subsequent death, left his bride again a widow at age sixteen. Quickly baptized and christened Isabel, the young woman became a symbol of the Hispanization and Christianization of Mexico. She was also granted a major encomienda, that of Tacuba. Combining the necessary attributes of Indian princess and wealthy *encomendera*, Isabel was married to her third husband, a Spaniard. Only nineteen at the time of his death, Isabel joined the Cortés household and briefly became the conquistador's lover. Indeed she was pregnant with Cortés's child when she married for the fourth time. After bearing Cortés's daughter and a son to her legitimate husband, doña Isabel was again widowed by age twenty-one, but within a year she married her fifth husband, a Spanish conquistador. This marriage produced five more children and lasted until Isabel's death in 1550. Isabel was buried in the Church of San Agustín, her favorite religious institution. All of her children, with the exception of two daughters who became nuns, married well and became part of the Mexican colonial nobility.

These examples also show that Spanish men of both middling and modest social and economic background could and did marry Indian women, especially women who belonged to the preconquest indigenous nobility. Although some Indian women refused to be used in these Spanish power games, these women were desirable marriage candidates for lesser conquistadors and others seeking to improve their social position in America, for they knowingly brought a degree of prestige, important social ties, Indian lands or other dowry property, and pre-Hispanic legitimacy to their European husbands. Nearly one-fourth of first-generation Spanish settlers in sixteenth-century Puebla de los Angeles married Indian brides. Indian wives were the most privileged of all conquered people, and it has been suggested that, until the arrival of large numbers of Spanish women, these Indian wives were considered to be honorary Spanish women and were treated as such. Indian women who lacked noble Indian blood, while still desirable as concubines, were less in demand as formal marriage partners.

The female offspring of these first Spanish-Indian unions, especially those mestizas who inherited from their conquistador fathers, were also attractive marital partners. In general their wealth and perceived social status overcame any possible problems associated with legitimacy and race. Francisca Pizarro, the illegitimate mestiza daughter of Francisco Pizarro and Inés Yupanqui, inherited an enormous fortune from her father and had several eager Spanish suitors. Educated in Peru, she was eventually sent to Spain where she married her paternal uncle, Hernando Pizarro, a man approximately thirty years her senior. Widowed seventeen years later, Francisca soon remarried a young Spanish nobleman, son of a Spanish grandee and brother of her own daughter-in-law. Ana García de Loyola, legitimate mestiza daughter of Martin García de Loyola and Beatriz Clara Coya, and granddaughter of the Inca prince Sairi Tupac, also returned to Spain as a young adult. She was named Marquesa de Oropesa and later married the son of the Marques de Alcañises. Other mestizas were married off by their Spanish fathers to create political alliances. The most famous case is that of Governor Irala of Paraguay who forced his defeated political enemies to marry his mestiza daughters. . . .

In the years following the Spanish conquest, large numbers of Indian women were drawn to towns and cities. Probably there was a combination of "push" and "pull" factors that influenced this female migration. In addition to a severe demographic decline, which in turn affected the productive capacities of the indigenous world, the conquest no doubt disturbed gender relations within the Indian community, thus encouraging women to seek their livelihood elsewhere. Other Indian women were coerced by their Spanish encomenderos to move to the city, where they became either domestic servants or concubines. Indian women had traditionally been active in the marketplace, and new opportunities in the provisioning of Spanish towns also drew women to these urban centers. Lastly, late-sixteenth-century changes in the laws of the Viceroyalty of Peru allowed Indian women who had borne children to Spaniards to accompany these men anywhere in the empire, thus encouraging these women to leave their communities.

The end result was that Indian women migrants learned the European's language and his ways and served as cultural interpreters between the conquerors and the conquered. Working as servants, cooks, nursemaids, and laundresses, these women played a crucial role within the households of Spaniards. In many homes they found themselves doing familiar tasks, often surrounded by other Indian women domestics. But some of these "domestic" tasks could be very physically demanding. While in theory Spanish laws such as the Laws of Burgos (1512–1513) protected pregnant women, nursing mothers, and single girls, this humane legislation was never enforced.

In cities, towns, haciendas, farms and ranches, Indian women working within Spanish households were often the first sexual partners, and sometimes longtime companions, of Spanish men, as well as the mothers of their illegitimate children. We can only wonder about the psychological effects on both Indian women and Spanish men. Furthermore, these women were frequently at risk of being sexually molested by Spanish, black, mestizo, mulatto, and nonkin Indian men. The Indian servant Juana, for example, was raped by her master because he wanted "to determine if she was a virgin." When she attempted to resist, she was hung from the roofbeam and beaten.

While Spanish men clearly held the upper hand in these sexual liaisons, some Indian and mestiza women profited from their proximity to power. Inés González, a Peruvian Indian servant of the cleric Rodrigo González Marmolejo, enjoyed such a close relationship with her master that she adopted his name and accompanied him to Santiago when he was named first bishop of the fledgling city. Shortly thereafter he presented her with a *chacara* (farm) on the outskirts of the city. Less than eight years later, Inés owned this farm, two houses in the city, horses, goats, sheep, and swine.

For some Indian women migration to the cities of colonial Latin America created economic opportunities. The emergence of a market economy created new positions for Indian women as small independent sellers, market women, peddlers, producers of foodstuffs or goods, and even long-distance traders. Among these women were those who were able to amass enough capital to invest in real property. Many prospered by participating actively in the real-estate market, using Spanish inheritance laws to will their land on to female kin, although there was no clear, universal pattern. Other women became small-scale entrepreneurs, owning taverns that catered to the urban Indian population, functioning as pawnbrokers, investing their cash, and owning slaves. . . .

Perhaps the most dramatic changes produced by the European conquest occurred in the sphere of religion. Indian women and men were forced to abandon their "heathen" ways and adopt Roman Catholicism. Women had had a relatively minor role in the religious ritual of preconquest societies, but this role was probably further reduced after the conquest. Nonetheless, the Catholic Church provided Indian women with new forms of religious expression and a degree of spiritual continuity. Preconquest female religious cults had linked women of differing social strata together; now *cofradías* (religious sisterhoods) gave these women a Catholic arena in which to organize their social and religious life. Like pre-Columbian forms of female worship, female cofradías were often devoted to a female saint. These native sodalities also provided a ceremonial life, as well as practical help in the form of burials, financial aid, and dowries for impoverished offspring.

The church, under the guise of freedom of choice in marriage, also tried to end the control of the Indian nobility over the marriage choices of commoners. At the same time the church worked to implement its kinship prohibitions on marriage, rules that were probably unintelligible to the Indian population. At first the church tended to accept Indian customs except when they were deemed to be repugnant to natural law and Christian morality. Slowly European ideas of marriage, legitimacy, and inheritance were introduced into Indian society, but they were probably not fully functioning until well into the seventeenth century. . . .

The Spanish church and state also waged a campaign to end polygamy, outlawing the practice of one man taking several wives, but in some districts, such as Alto Peru, polygamy continued well into the seventeenth century. How this change affected the lives of Indian women also is far from clear. While one possible result was the end of the sociability of the household, another result might have been the end of rivalries between wives.

In rural Peru colonial authorities also attempted to end sexual and marital practices they considered immoral. Although they themselves were hardly chaste, both church and state increasingly condemned the widespread Andean practice of trial marriage, cohabitation that could last for years. In the 1570s Viceroy Toledo denounced the practice as "noxious and pernicious." Later authorities would use sermons, the confessional, and even prison to dissuade Indian couples from living together. To judge from ongoing complaints, Spaniards were never able to convince Indian men and women of the virtues of premarital virginity, and trial marriage was never successfully rooted out.

Perhaps no Indian women were as tightly controlled as those who found themselves living on missions directly supervised by religious orders. Their entire lives, including their sex life, marriage, and morality, came under direct religious control. Mission priests viewed adultery, polygamy, and concubinage as immoral and worked to root out these vices while promoting Catholic marriage and morality. Fearing sexual promiscuity, the friars campaigned to stamp out informal unions and promote early marriage. Women were to marry at age fifteen; the result was that these Indian women devoted a greater portion of their lives to bearing and rearing children than did any other group of women in colonial society. Once married couples were forced to live in nuclear households. The friars' goals also served the Spanish state, which counted the married couple as the basic tribute-paying unit.

In frontier regions Spanish missionary priests, unable to understand why Indian women had no shame in being "unclothed from the waist up and the knees down," decried female nudity and encouraged women to adopt "proper" dress. Indeed the repeated use of the word "shame" when referring to nudity and the universal euphemism "shameful parts" reflect Spanish discomfort and fascination with people whose dress code differed greatly from theirs. Missionary teaching introduced European ideas of the weakness of women at the same time as it enforced traditional Indian concepts of female subordination. In the confessional priests also railed against what they saw as female tendencies toward infanticide, abortion, and neglect of their wifely duties.

Mission priests went even further in protecting women from sexual temptation. In many missions there was a *casa de recogidas*, where women whose husbands were absent, or had fled, or whose general whereabouts were unknown, lived. In addition, widows, especially young widows without parents or other living relatives to protect them, were also housed in the casa. The casa de recogidas also served as a prison for female criminals—that is, for women who had in some way disobeyed the priests. Although they were not formally imprisoned, those deemed to have misbehaved were kept handcuffed and could leave the house only when accompanied by the *superiora*. On the other hand, recalcitrant women received better treatment than men; they were whipped only on their backs, only in private (within the confines of the casa), and only by other women.

Although responsible for female conduct, mission priests were enjoined to avoid all contact with Indian women. In the Jesuit missions of Paraguay priests were instructed to speak directly to women only with a witness present. The priest was never to be alone with or to touch any woman, and when handing the rosary to a woman, he used an Indian male as go-between. This did not stop priests from closely supervising the work of women. For example, priests managed to check the quality and quantity of the cotton thread spun by women, punishing those believed guilty of trickery.

The degree to which mission priests actually kept their distance from their female charges is hard to determine, although probably the Jesuits came closest to the ideal. On the other hand, firsthand observers such as Huamán Poma de Ayala depicted Catholic priests in general as sexual hypocrites. The text of his drawing *The Father Confesses* warned that "the fathers confess the Indian women in houses of the church and the baptismal font and the sacristy[;] in the dark and suspicious hidden places [they force] the single women to commit fornication and sin with them."

△ FURTHER READING

Acosta, José de. *Natural and Moral History of the Indies.* Edited by Jane E. Mangan. Introduction and commentary by Walter D. Mignolo. Translated by France M. López-Morillas. Durham, NC: Duke University Press, 2002.

Andrien, Kenneth J. *Andean Worlds: Indigenous History, Culture, and Consciousness Under Spanish Rule, 1532–1825.* Albuquerque: University of New Mexico Press, 2001.

Boxer, C. R. *The Portuguese Seaborne Empire, 1415–1825.* New York: A. A. Knopf, 1969.

Casas, Bartolomé de las. *A Short Account of the Destruction of the Indies.* Translated and edited by Nigel Griffin. Introduction by Anthony Pagden. New York: Penguin, 1992.

Clayton, Lawrence A., Vernon James Knight, Jr., and Edward C. Moore, eds. *The De Soto Chronicles: The Expedition of Hernando de Soto to North America in 1539–1543.* Tuscaloosa: University of Alabama Press, 1993.

Clendinnen, Inga. *Ambivalent Conquests: Maya and Spaniard in Yucatan, 1517–1570.* New York: Cambridge University Press, 2003.

Cortés, Hernán. *Letters from Mexico.* Translated, edited, and with a new introduction by Anthony Pagden. New Haven, CT: Yale Nota Bene, 2001.

Elliott, John Huxtable. *Empires of the Atlantic World: Britain and Spain in America, 1492–1830.* New Haven, CT: Yale University Press, 2006.

Hemming, John. *Red Gold: The Conquest of the Brazilian Indians.* Cambridge, MA: Harvard University Press, 1978,

León-Portilla, Miguel, ed. *The Broken Spears: The Aztec Account of the Conquest of Mexico.* Foreword by J. Jorge Klor de Alva. Boston: Beacon Press, 1992.

Lockhart, James, and Stuart B. Schwartz. *Early Latin America: A History of Colonial Spanish America and Brazil.* New York: Cambridge University Press, 1983.

McAlister, Lyle N. *Spain and Portugal in the New World, 1492–1700.* Minneapolis: University of Minnesota Press, 1984.

Núñez Cabeza de Vaca, Alvar. *Castaways: The Narrative of Alvar Núñez Cabeza de Vaca.* Edited by Enrique Pupo-Walker. Translated by Frances M. López-Morillas. Berkeley: University of California Press, 1993.

Pagden, Anthony. *Lords of All the World: Ideologies of Empire in Spain, Britain and France c. 1500–c. 1800.* New Haven, CT: Yale University Press, 1995.

Prescott, William H. *History of the Conquest of Mexico.* New York: Modern Library, 1998.

Restall, Matthew. *Seven Myths of the Spanish Conquest.* New York: Oxford University Press, 2003.

Sahagún, Bernardino de. *General History of the Things of New Spain: Florentine Codex.* Salt Lake City, Utah: University of Utah, 1950.

Seed, Patricia. *Ceremonies of Possession in Europe's Conquest of the New World, 1492–1640.* New York: Cambridge University Press, 1995.

Thomas, Hugh. *Rivers of Gold: The Rise of the Spanish Empire, from Columbus to Magellan.* New York: Random House, 2003.

Todorov, Tzvetan. *The Conquest of America: The Question of the Other.* Translated from the French by Richard Howard. New York: HarperPerennial, 1992.

Townsend, Camilla. *Malintzin's Choices: An Indian Woman in the Conquest of Mexico* Albuquerque: University of New Mexico Press, 2006.

CHAPTER
4

European Challenges to Iberian Hegemony

In what ways did religious and political conflicts in Europe alter the Atlantic world? How was Europe itself transformed by these new dynamics? The Atlantic world was transformed between 1560 and 1660, and this chapter explores the complex factors that account for these changes. European kingdoms previously characterized by their shared Catholicism were riven with bloody and violent divisions launched by the Protestant Reformation, which Martin Luther started in the Holy Roman Empire (a collection of states based primarily in central Europe, ruled over by an elected emperor) in 1517. As new religious hatreds between Protestants and Catholics fused with longstanding diplomatic, dynastic, and economic rivalries, Europeans took their quarrels off the continent, turning the Atlantic into a vast battlefield for souls and loot. Rivals were eager to challenge the growing power of the Habsburgs, a dynasty with historic roots in Austria but whose domain had expanded through marriage and other strategies to include such areas as the Low Countries and the Iberian peninsula. As a result, English, French, and Dutch competitors seized Iberian holdings where they could (in Brazil, Jamaica, and Elmina, for example) and established rival settlements elsewhere. Although they often emulated prior models of Spanish and Portuguese colonialism, they also criticized Spanish and Portuguese methods and devised their own strategies for territorial and commercial expansion. Evolving European ideas about indigenous people of the Americas shaped their justifications for conquest and provided a new language of cultural criticism for Europeans to deploy among themselves. Often, Americans and Africans controlled the fate of those Europeans who had pushed into the Atlantic in their efforts to dislodge Habsburg power. Their activities thus contributed to the emergence of a new geopolitical scene. The documents and essays in this chapter explore some of these international conflicts and their repercussions throughout the Atlantic world.

DOCUMENTS

Religious divisions in Europe led to terrible civil wars and brutal violence. Document 1 describes the ordeal of Anne Askew, an English Protestant who did not share King Henry VIII's interpretation of scripture. She was tried in 1545–46 and burned at the stake as a heretic. Document 4 illustrates the intersection between European religious rivalries and economic and geopolitical ambitions. The English adventurer Sir Walter Ralegh (1552–1618) asserted that it would be honorable, profitable, necessary, and easy for England to "subdue" Guiana, thus rescuing the inhabitants from Spanish tyranny and Catholicism, as well as enriching and protecting England. Document 6, the seal of the Massachusetts Bay Colony, illustrates the roots of the English self-image as the Indians' liberators.

Europeans' ideas about Indians revealed a great deal about themselves. After several months at sea, the Frenchman Jean de Léry and his Calvinist companions found themselves on the Brazilian coast, where they traded with a hostile Indian nation allied with the Portuguese. Document 2 describes Léry's astonishment at the way the Margaia Indians wore the shirts they purchased from the French, "revealing what should be hidden." Drawing from French eyewitness reports of the Indians in Brazil, the French philosopher Michel de Montaigne (1533–1592) depicts the "noble savage" and questions the concept of "barbarism" in Document 3. Montaigne compares the Indians' cannibalism with the Europeans' own horrific practices.

The English, French, and Dutch all relied heavily on American and African allies to unseat their rivals, as Documents 7 and 8 illustrate. Document 7, an excerpt from Paul Le Jeune's account of Jesuit activity in New France in 1633, recounts the speech of an Indian captain reassuring Samuel de Champlain (1567–1635) that he did not intend to betray his French allies by trading with the English. In Document 8, a Dutch account of their displacement of the Portuguese in Angola in 1647 recognizes the support of Njinga Mbandi of Ndongo (c. 1583–1663) and her warriors. Njinga's enemies had allied with the Portuguese and defeated her in 1626–1629, so when the Dutch West India Company seized Luanda in 1641, Njinga took advantage of the Dutch presence to restore her rule. For their part, the Dutch were ultimately defeated by the Portuguese.

Of all the exploits by Spain's rivals, none matched Piet Heyn's amazing capture of the Spanish silver fleet in 1628. It brought wealth to the Dutch Republic (funding subsequent Dutch activity in Brazil) and fame to the mariner. Document 5 relates the contemporary reception of Heyn on his return home and the enduring legacy of his plunder. A letter from Cardinal De la Cueva (a Catholic prelate based in Brussels) to Philip IV, on December 2, 1628, conveys the impact of Heyn's accomplishment on the Dutch rebels. The second item, a song about Piet Heyn's great triumph composed by J. P. Heije and J. J. Viotta in the heyday of nineteenth-century nationalism, is still sung by Dutch soccer fans.

1. Anne Askew Meets Her Fate, 1546

The Two Examinations of the worthy Servant of God, Mistress Anne Askew, Daughter of Sir William Askew, knight, of Lincolnshire.

Martyred in Smithfield for the Constant and Faithful Testimony of the Truth.

Here next followeth the same year the true examinations of Anne Askew, which here thou shalt have, gentle reader, according as she wrote them with her own hand, at the instant desire of certain faithful men and women: by the which, if thou mark diligently the communications both of her and of her examiners, thou mayest easily perceive the tree by the fruit, and the man by his work.

Source: George Townsend, *The Acts and Monuments of John Foxe* (New York: Arno Press, 1965), volume 5, pp. 537–538, 546–548, 550.

The Sum of the Condemnation of Me Anne Askew at the Guildhall.

They said to me there, that I was a heretic, and condemned by the law, if I would stand in my opinion. I answered, that I was no heretic, neither yet deserved I any death by the law of God. But, as concerning the faith which I uttered and wrote to the council, I would not, I said, deny it, because I knew it true. Then would they needs know, if I would deny the sacrament to be Christ's body and blood. I said, "Yea: for the same Son of God that was born of the Virgin Mary, is now glorious in heaven, and will come again from thence at the latter day like as he went up. And as for that ye call your God, it is a piece of bread. For a more proof thereof (mark it when you list,) let it but lie in the box three months, and it will be mouldy, and so turn to nothing that is good. Whereupon I am persuaded that it cannot be God."

After that, they willed me to have a priest; and then I smiled. Then they asked me, if it were not good; I said, I would confess my faults unto God, for I was sure that he would hear me with favour. And so we were condemned without a quest.

The Cruel Handling and Racking of Anne Askew After Her Condemnation.

The Effect of My Examination and Handling Since My Departure from Newgate.

On Tuesday I was sent from Newgate to the sign of the Crown, where Master Rich, and the bishop of London, with all their power and flattering words went about to persuade me from God: but I did not esteem their glosing pretences. . . .

Then Master Rich sent me to the Tower, where I remained till three o'clock.

Then came Rich and one of the council, charging me upon my obedience, to show unto them, if I knew any man or woman of my sect. My answer was, that I knew none. . . .

Then they did put me on the rack, because I confessed no ladies or gentlewomen to be of my opinion, and thereon they kept me a long time; and because I lay still, and did not cry, my lord chancellor and Master Rich took pains to rack me with their own hands, till I was nigh dead.

Then the lieutenant caused me to be loosed from the rack. Incontinently I swooned, and then they recovered me again. After that I sat two long hours reasoning with my lord chancellor upon the bare floor; where he, with many flattering words, persuaded me to leave my opinion. But my Lord God (I thank his everlasting goodness) gave me grace to persevere, and will do, I hope, to the very end.

Then was I brought to a house, and laid in a bed, with as weary and painful bones as ever had patient Job; I thank my Lord God there-for. Then my lord chancellor sent me word, if I would leave my opinion, I should want nothing: if I would not, I should forthwith to Newgate, and so be burned. I sent him again word, that I would rather die, than break my faith.

Thus the Lord open the eyes of their blind hearts, that the truth may take place. Farewell, dear friend, and pray, pray, pray!

Touching the order of her racking in the Tower thus it was; first she was let down into a dungeon, where sir Anthony Knevet, the lieutenant, commanded his jailor to pinch her with the rack. Which being done as much as he thought sufficient, he went about to take her down, supposing that he had done enough. But Wriothesley, the chancellor, not contented that she was loosed so soon, confessing nothing, commanded the lieutenant to strain her on the rack again: which because he denied to do, tendering the weakness of the woman, he was threatened therefore grievously of the said Wriothesley, saying, that he would signify his disobedience unto the king. And so consequently upon the same, he and Master Rich, throwing off their gowns, would needs play the tormentors themselves; first asking her, if she were with child. To whom she answering again, said, "Ye shall not need to spare for that, but do your wills upon me." And so, quietly and patiently praying unto the Lord, she abode their tyranny, till her bones and joints wore almost plucked asunder, in such sort as she was carried away in a chair. When the racking was past, Wriothesley and his fellow took their horse towards the court. . . .

Hitherto we have entreated of this good woman: now it remaineth that we touch somewhat as concerning her end and martyrdom. After that she (being born of such stock and kindred that she might have lived in great wealth and prosperity, if she would rather have followed the world than Christ) now had been so tormented, that she could neither live long in so great distress, neither yet by her adversaries be suffered to die in secret, the day of her execution being appointed, she was brought into Smithfield in a chair, because she could not go on her feet, by means of her great torments. When she was brought unto the stake, she was tied by the middle with a chain, that held up her body. When all things were thus prepared to the fire, Dr. Shaxton, who was then appointed to preach, began his sermon. Anne Askew, hearing and answering again unto him, where he said well, confirmed the same; where he said amiss, "There," said she, "he misseth, and speaketh without the book."

The sermon being finished, the martyrs, standing there tied at three several stakes ready to their martyrdom, began their prayers. The multitude and concourse of the people was exceeding; the place where they stood being railed about to keep out the press. Upon the bench under St. Bartholomew's church sat Wriothesley, chancellor of England; the old duke of Norfolk, the old earl of Bedford, the lord mayor, with divers others. Before the fire should be set unto them, one of the bench, hearing that they had gunpowder about them, and being alarmed lest the faggots, by strength of the gunpowder, would come flying about their ears, began to be afraid: but the earl of Bedford, declaring unto him how the gunpowder was not laid under the faggots, but only about their bodies, to rid them out of their pain; which having vent, there was no danger to them of the faggots, so diminished that fear.

Then Wriothesley, lord chancellor, sent to Anne Askew letters, offering to her the king's pardon if she would recant; who, refusing once to look upon them, made this answer again, that she came not thither to deny her Lord and Master. Then were the letters likewise offered unto the others, who, in like manner, following the constancy of the woman, denied not only to receive them, but also to look upon them. Whereupon the lord mayor, commanding fire to be put unto them, cried with a loud voice, "Fiat justitia."

And thus the good Anne Askew, with these blessed martyrs, being troubled so many manner of ways, and having passed through so many torments, having now ended the long course of her agonies, being compassed in with flames of fire, as a blessed sacrifice unto God, she slept in the Lord, A.D. 1546, leaving behind her a singular example of christian constancy for all men to follow.

2. A French Expedition Trades with Hostile Indians on the Brazilian Coast, 1557

After that we had a favorable west wind, which lasted so long that on the twenty-sixth of February 1557 (as determined with the astrolabe and planisphere) at about eight o'clock in the morning, we sighted West India, the land of Brazil, the fourth part of the world, unknown to the Ancients: otherwise called "America" (from the name of him who first discovered it in about 1497). You can well imagine that when we saw we were so near the place that we had set out for, with some hope of soon putting foot to ground, we were filled with joy and gave whole-hearted thanks to God. Indeed, since we had been tossing and afloat on the sea almost four months without putting in to port, it had often occurred to us that we were in exile out there, and it seemed as though we would never escape it. After we had ascertained that what we had sighted was, indeed, dry land (for you can often be deceived on the sea by the clouds, which then vanish), having a fair wind and heading straight for the land, the same day (our Admiral having gone on ahead) we cast anchor a half a league from a mountainous place that the savages call *Huuassou*.

After we had taken the boat down out of the ship, and, according to the custom in that land when one arrives, had fired the cannon several times to warn the inhabitants, we suddenly saw a great number of savage men and women on the seashore. However (as some of our seamen who had been there before recognized), they were of the nation called *Margaia*, allies of the Portuguese, and therefore such enemies of the French that if they had had us at their mercy, we would have paid no other ransom except being slain and cut to pieces, and serving as a meal for them.

We also began to see for the first time, even in the month of February (just when over here, and in almost all of Europe, everything is closed up and hidden in the womb of the earth because of the cold and frost), the forests, woods, and plants of that country as green and flourishing as those of our France are in May and June. And it is that way all year long, and in all seasons in that land of Brazil.

Notwithstanding this enmity of our Margaia with respect to the French, which both they and we dissimulated as best we could, our master's mate, who could stammer out a few words in their language, got into the ship's boat with a few other sailors and went over to the shore, where the savages continued to assemble in big troops. However, since our people put no trust in them except for some express purpose, they stayed beyond an arrow's reach from land so as to avoid the danger of being seized and *boucané*—that is, roasted. From a distance, our sailors displayed for them knives, mirrors, combs, and other trifles, and called out to them asking for food supplies in exchange; some of the savages, who had drawn as near as they could, upon hearing this did not wait to be asked again, but hurried off to get food for them. So when he returned, our master's mate brought back flour made from a root (which the savages eat instead of bread), hams, and the meat of a certain kind of boar, with an abundance of other food and fruits that are found in that country. Not only that, but, to present themselves to us, and to bid us welcome, six men and

Source: Jean de Léry, *History of a Voyage to the Land of Brazil, Otherwise Called America*, translation and introduction by Janet Whatley (Berkeley: University of California Press, 1990), pp. 25–28. Reprinted with permission of the University of California Press.

one woman embarked straightaway to come see us on the ship. And because these were the first savages that I had seen up close, you can well imagine that I looked at them and studied them attentively. I will postpone describing them at length until a more appropriate place, but still even now I want to say something in passing.

First, both the men and the woman were as utterly naked as when they came out of their mother's womb; however, to bedeck themselves, they were painted and blackened over the entire body. The men had their heads shaved close in front, like a monk's tonsure, and wore their hair long in back; but, in the style of men's wigs over here, their locks were clipped around the neck. Furthermore, they all had the lower lip pierced, and each one wore in the hole a green stone, well polished, carefully placed, and mounted in the lip as in a setting; the stone was of about the size of a testoon, and they would take it out and put it back whenever they pleased. They wore such things thinking to be the more handsomely adorned; but to tell the truth, when this stone is removed and this great split in the lower lip appears like a second mouth, they are greatly disfigured. As for the woman, besides not having a split lip, she wore her hair long like the women over here; her ears were so cruelly pierced that you could have put a finger through the holes; she wore great pendants of white bone in them, which swung almost to her shoulders. I will wait until later to refute the error of those who would have had us believe that the savages were covered with hair.

However, before these visitors left us, the men, and especially two or three elders who seemed to be the most important men in their parishes (as we say over here), claimed that their region grew the finest brazilwood that could be found in the whole country, and they promised to help us cut and carry it; furthermore, they would provide us with food—in short, they did everything they could to persuade us to load our ship right there. But because, as I have said, they were our enemies, all this was merely to lure us and trick us into coming ashore so that afterwards, having the advantage over us, they could cut us to pieces and eat us. So aside from the fact that we intended in any case to go elsewhere, we had no mind to stop there.

After our Margaia had taken a good look at our artillery and at whatever else they wanted to see in our ship, since we wanted neither to detain them nor to offend them (bearing in mind the consequences of our deeds for other Frenchmen who would come there unwarned in the future and who might suffer as a result of our acts) and since they were asking to return to their people who were waiting for them on the shore, it was a question of paying them what they wished for the food they had brought us. And because they have no use of currency, the payment we made them was in shirts, knives, fishhooks, mirrors, and other merchandise and small wares fit to peddle among this people. But here was the best of it. Upon their arrival these good people, all naked, had not been sparing in showing us everything they had; and now at their departure, not being in the habit of wearing undergarments or, indeed, any other kind of clothes, when they put on the shirts that we had given them and came to seat themselves in the ship's boat, they tucked them clear up to the navel so as not to spoil them, and, revealing what should be hidden, insisted that we see their behinds and their buttocks as they took their farewell of us. Were these not courteous officers, and was this not a fine ambassadorial civility? For notwithstanding the proverb that is so common to us over here, that the flesh is nearer than the shirt, they on the contrary, as if to show us that they were not of that mind, and perhaps as a display of their magnificent hospitality, favored their shirts over their skin by showing us their behinds.

After we had refreshed ourselves a little there (for although the food that they had brought us seemed strange, nonetheless out of necessity we ate heartily of it), the next day, a Sunday, we weighed anchor and set sail. Skirting the land, and working our way toward our destination, we had not sailed more than nine or ten leagues before we found ourselves at the place of a Portuguese fort, called by them *Espirito santo* (and by the savages *Moab*). Recognizing both our equipage and that of the caravel that we had in tow (which they judged correctly that we had taken from their countrymen), they fired three cannon shots at us, and we fired three or four at them in reply. But because we were too far for the reach of their shot, they did us no harm, and I think we did none to them, either.

3. Montaigne Reflects on the Meaning of Barbarism, 1580

I had with me for a long time a man who had lived for ten or twelve years in that other world which has been discovered in our century, in the place where Ville-gaignon landed, and which he called Antarctic France. This discovery of a boundless country seems worthy of consideration. I don't know if I can guarantee that some other such discovery will not be made in the future, so many personages greater than ourselves having been mistaken about this one. I am afraid we have eyes bigger than our stomachs, and more curiosity than capacity. We embrace everything, but we clasp only wind. . . .

This man I had was a simple, crude fellow—a character fit to bear true witness; for clever people observe more things and more curiously, but they interpret them; and to lend weight and conviction to their interpretation, they cannot help altering history a little. They never show you things as they are, but bend and disguise them according to the way they have seen them; and to give credence to their judgment and attract you to it, they are prone to add something to their matter, to stretch it out and amplify it. We need a man either very honest, or so simple that he has not the stuff to build up false inventions and give them plausibility; and wedded to no theory. Such was my man; and besides this, he at various times brought sailors and merchants, whom he had known on that trip, to see me. So I content myself with his information, without inquiring what the cosmographers say about it. . . .

Now, to return to my subject, I think there is nothing barbarous and savage in that nation, from what I have been told, except that each man calls barbarism whatever is not his own practice; for indeed it seems we have no other test of truth and reason than the example and pattern of the opinions and customs of the country we live in. *There* is always the perfect religion, the perfect government, the perfect and

---

accomplished manners in all things. Those people are wild, just as we call wild the fruits that Nature has produced by herself and in her normal course; whereas really it is those that we have changed artificially and led astray from the common order, that we should rather call wild. The former retain alive and vigorous their genuine, their most useful and natural, virtues and properties, which we have debased in the latter in adapting them to gratify our corrupted taste. . . .

These nations, then, seem to me barbarous in this sense, that they have been fashioned very little by the human mind, and are still very close to their original naturalness. The laws of nature still rule them, very little corrupted by ours; and they are in such a state of purity that I am sometimes vexed that they were unknown earlier, in the days when there were men able to judge them better than we. . . . This is a nation, I should say to Plato, in which there is no sort of traffic, no knowledge of letters, no science of numbers, no name for a magistrate or for political superiority, no custom of servitude, no riches or poverty, no contracts, no successions, no partitions, no occupations but leisure ones, no care for any but common kinship, no clothes, no agriculture, no metal, no use of wine or wheat. The very words that signify lying, treachery, dissimulation, avarice, envy, belittling, pardon—unheard of. How far from this perfection would he find the republic that he imagined: *Men fresh sprung from the gods* [Seneca].

These manners nature first ordained.
VIRGIL

For the rest, they live in a country with a very pleasant and temperate climate, so that according to my witnesses it is rare to see a sick man there; and they have assured me that they never saw one palsied, bleary-eyed, toothless, or bent with age. . . . They have a great abundance of fish and flesh which bear no resemblance to ours, and they eat them with no other artifice than cooking. The first man who rode a horse there, though he had had dealings with them on several other trips, so horrified them in this posture that they shot him dead with arrows before they could recognize him. . . .

The whole day is spent in dancing. The younger men go to hunt animals with bows. Some of the women busy themselves meanwhile with warming their drink, which is their chief duty. Some one of the old men, in the morning before they begin to eat, preaches to the whole barnful in common, walking from one end to the other, and repeating one single sentence several times until he has completed the circuit (for the buildings are fully a hundred paces long). He recommends to them only two things: valor against the enemy and love for their wives. And they never fail to point out this obligation, as their refrain, that it is their wives who keep their drink warm and seasoned. . . .

They have their wars with the nations beyond the mountains, further inland, to which they go quite naked, with no other arms than bows or wooden swords ending in a sharp point, in the manner of the tongues of our boar spears. It is astonishing what firmness they show in their combats, which never end but in slaughter and bloodshed; for as to routs and terror, they know nothing of either.

Each man brings back as his trophy the head of the enemy he has killed, and sets it up at the entrance to his dwelling. After they have treated their prisoners well for a long time with all the hospitality they can think of, each man who has a prisoner calls a great assembly of his acquaintances. He ties a rope to one of the prisoner's arms, by the end of which he holds him, a few steps away, for fear of being hurt, and gives his dearest friend the other arm to hold in the same way; and these two, in the presence of the whole assembly, kill him with their swords. This done, they roast him and eat him in common and send some pieces to their absent friends. This is not, as people think, for nourishment, as of old the Scythians used to do; it is to betoken an extreme revenge. And the proof of this came when they saw the Portuguese, who had joined forces with their adversaries, inflict a different kind of death on them when they took them prisoner, which was to bury them up to the waist, shoot the rest of their body full of arrows, and afterward hang them. They thought that these people from the other world, being men who had sown the knowledge of many vices among their neighbors and were much greater masters than themselves in every sort of wickedness, did not adopt this sort of vengeance without some reason, and that it must be more painful than their own; so they began to give up their old method and to follow this one.

I am not sorry that we notice the barbarous horror of such acts, but I am heartily sorry that, judging their faults rightly, we should be so blind to our own. I think there is more barbarity in eating a man alive than in eating him dead; and in tearing by tortures and the rack a body still full of feeling, in roasting a man bit by bit, in having him bitten and mangled by dogs and swine (as we have not only read but seen within fresh memory, not among ancient enemies, but among neighbors and fellow citizens, and what is worse, on the pretext of piety and religion), than in roasting and eating him after he is dead. . . .

Three of these men, ignorant of the price they will pay some day, in loss of repose and happiness, for gaining knowledge of the corruptions of this side of the ocean; ignorant also of that fact that of this intercourse will come their ruin (which I suppose is already well advanced: poor wretches, to let themselves be tricked by the desire for new things, and to have left the serenity of their own sky to come and see ours!)—three of these men were at Rouen, at the time the late King Charles IX was there. The king talked to them for a long time; they were shown our ways, our splendor, the aspect of a fine city. After that, someone asked their opinion, and wanted to know what they had found most amazing. They mentioned three things, of which I have forgotten the third, and I am very sorry for it; but I still remember two of them. They said that in the first place they thought it very strange that so many grown men, bearded, strong, and armed, who were around the king (it is likely that they were talking about the Swiss of his guard) should submit to obey a child, and that one of them was not chosen to command instead. Second (they have a way in their language of speaking of men as halves of one another), they had noticed that there were among us men full and gorged with all sorts of good things, and that their other halves were beggars at the doors, emaciated with hunger and poverty; and they thought it strange that these needy halves could endure such an injustice, and did not take the others by the throat, or set fire to their houses.

I had a very long talk with one of them; but I had an interpreter who followed my meaning so badly, and who was so hindered by his stupidity in taking in my ideas, that I could get hardly any satisfaction from the man. When I asked him what profit he gained from his superior position among his people (for he was a captain, and our sailors called him king), he told me that it was to march foremost in war. How many men followed him? He pointed to a piece of ground, to signify as many as such a space could hold; it might have been four or five thousand men. Did all his authority expire with the war? He said that this much remained, that when he visited the villages dependent on him, they made paths for him through the underbrush by which he might pass quite comfortably.

All this is not too bad—but what's the use? They don't wear breeches.

4. Walter Ralegh Justifies the Voyage to Guiana, 1596

Touching the voyage for Guiana it is to be considered first, whether it bee to be undertaken: secondly, the manner of subduing it: and lastly, the meanes howe to subdue it, and annex it to the Crowne Imperiall of the Realme of England.

That it is to be undertaken will appeare, if it be proved to bee (1) honorable, (2) profitable, (3) necessary, (4) and with no greate chardge, or difficultye accomplished.

It is honorable, both for that by this meanes infinite nombers of soules may be brought from theyr idolatry, bloody sacrifices, ignoraunce, and incivility to the worshipping of the true God aright to civill conversation, and also theyr bodyes freed from the intollerable tirrany of the Spaniards whereunto they are already or likely in shorte space to bee subjected, unlesse her excellent Majestie or some other christian prince doe speedily assiste, and afterward protect them in their just defensive wars against the violence of usurpers which if it please her highnes to undertake, besids that presently it will stopp the mouthes of the Romish Catholickes, who vaunt of theyr great adventures for the propogacion of the gospell, it will add greate increase of honor, to the memory of her Majesties name upon earth to all posterity and in the end bee rewarded with an excellent starlike splendency in the heavens, which is reserved for them that turne many unto righteousnes, as the Prophet speaketh.

2. Likewise it is profitable, for heereby the Queens dominions may bee exceedingly enlarged, and this Realme inestimably enriched, with pretious stones, gold, silver, pearle, and other commodityes which those countryes yeald, and (God giving good successe to the voiage) an entrance made thereby to many other Empyres, (which hapily may prove as rich as this) and it may bee to Peru it selfe and other Kingdomes of which the Spaniards bee now possessed, in those partes and else where.

3. Lastly, the necessity of attempting Guiana in regard of our owne security (albeit noe profite should redound thereby to the Indians, or to ourselves directly from those countryes) ought greatly to weigh with us. For if the Spaniards by the treasure of those Kingdomes which hee hath already, be able to trouble the better parte of Christendome, what would hee doe if hee were once established in Guiana, which is thought to bee more rich then all other lands which hee enjoyeth either in the East or West Indies. Whereas if her Majestie weare seased of it, hee mighte bee soe kepte

Source: Walter Ralegh, *The Discovery of the Large, Rich, and Beautiful Empire of Guiana* (London, Haklyut Society, 1898), 135–139.

occupied in those provinces that hee would not hastely threaten us, with any more of his invincible navies.

But although this voyage were never so honorable, profitable, or necessary for our estate to be undertaken, yet if we had not some possibility for the effecting of our purpose, it were more meete to strengthen our selves at home, then to weaken our forces in seeking to annoy our enemy abroad. But such opportunity and so many encouragements doe now offer themselves unto her highnes that (I suppose) there is no prince in the world but hee would greatly strayne hymselfe, rather then to omitt the advantage of such a booty. Among others, these inducements are to bee weighed.

1. The Bordurers, who are sayd to bee naturalls, and to whom onely the Empire of Guiana doth of right apperteine, are already prepared to joyne with us, having submitted themselves to the Queen's protection both against the Spaniards and Emperor of Guiana who usurpeth upon them.

2. The Spaniards for theyr oppressions and usurpations, are detested and feared both by the Guianians and bordurers, by the former, beecause the Spaniards forced them to fly from theyr owne country of Peru, and by the latter, by experience of the Spanish dealing towardes themselves and theyr adjoyning neighbors. So as it is reported none doe assiste them save the Arwacans, a vagabond, poore, and small people. But it is like that all the countryes of the continent who are not yet inthralled to the Spaniards and have heard of their outrage and especially the Amazones in regarde of their sexe, will be ready to ayd her Majestie against the Spaniards.

3. The voyage is shorte being but 6 weekes sayling from England and the like backe againe, which may so bee contrived as going, abiding, and returning we may bestow an whole yeare without any winter at all by the way, no lee shore, no sandes, or enimies coast.

4. No chardge but onely at the first setting forth which need not be great, especially if the course layd downe in this treatise or some such like, be taken, considering the country yeeldeth store of corne, beasts, fowle, fish, and fruit for victualls, and steele and copper for the making of armor and ordinance, and among the Amapagotos and Caraccas horses may be had and in short time manned for our service in the wars.

5. It is thought the passage to it may bee easely fortifyed by sea and the country by nature is defensed by land with mountaines and multitude of nations, that it is impossible in manner by land to bee evicted, beeing once attayned by us.

6. Though we are not greatly to rely upon prophesies, yet if it weare found in Peru (as Don Anthonio de Beereo told Sir Walter Ralegh) among other prophesies that from Inglatiera the Inga should be restored to Peru, it may fall out to bee true (as many of theyr prophesies did both in Mexico and Peru which indeed foreshewed the altaration of those Empires) at least the prophesy will greatly daunt the Spaniards and make them afrayd of the worst event in these imployments.

7. If it be remembred how the Spaniards have without just title or any wrong at all donne to them by the harmelesse Indians, forceably envaded and wrongfully deteyned their countryes aboute 100 yeares, committing barbarous and exquisite massacres to the distruction of whole nations of people (arising by estimacion of some of accompt among them and acquaynted with theyr proceedings in some few yeares to the number of 20 millions of reasonable creatures made to the Image of God and lesse harmefull then the Spaniards themselves) whereby more fruitfull

land was layd wast and depopulated then is in all Europe and some parte of Asia, in revenge wherof their owne religious men do make accompte that the just God in judgment will one day horribly chasten and peradventure wholy subvert and root out the Spanish nation from the world. Againe if it bee noted that the Spaniards have above 20 severall times in vayne sought the conquest of Guiana, and that it doth by the providence of the Almighty now (as it were) prostrate herselfe before her Majesties feet the most potent enemy that the Spaniards hath, not onely intreating but by unvaluable offers and unanswerable reasons alluring, even urging and forcing her highnes to accept it under her alleigeaunce, who would not bee perswaded that now at length the great judge of the world, hath heard the sighes, grones, lamentacions, teares, and bloud of so many millions of innocent men, women, and children aflicted, robbed, reviled, branded with hot irons, roasted, dismembred, mangled, stabbed, whipped, racked, scalded with hott oyle, suet, and hogsgrease, put to the strapado, ripped alive, beheaded in sport, drowned, dashd against the rocks, famished, devoured by mastifes, burned and by infinite crueltyes consumed, and purposeth to scourge and plague that cursed nation, and to take the yoake of servitude from that distressed people, as free by nature as any Christian. In comtemplacion of all which things, who would not bee incouraged to proceed in this voyage, having in a maner none other enemyes but these Spaniards, abhorred of God, and man, being provoked by so many allurements, occacions, reasons, and opportunityes, in a most just cause, the safety of our dread soveraigne, of our selves, and of a great part of the Christian world thereuppon depending.

5. Piet Heyn Captures the Spanish Fleet, 1628, 1847

Cardinal De la Cueva to His Majesty, Brussels, 2 December 1628.

Majesty,

The news received from Holland, namely that the rebels have captured the fleet and silver of New Spain, has had ruinous effects here, because no one thinks it possible that the money supply is sufficient for our army and fleet, and because they believe that the enemy, in possession of so much treasure, will display even greater courage, thereby and through the general rebellion, which—they surely suppose—shall follow the termination of wages, for now, at the moment, one sees open unrest amongst the soldiers everywhere, and we have news that especially in Zandvliet and in Damme some soldiers have adopted a very bold attitude, for they do not doubt that great disasters shall occur. And indeed there is now more than ever reason to fear, because of what I have just related, and because now there is no relief, for we lost the credit that we enjoyed and the money at hand, and everything that can be borrowed is already borrowed. And therefore I considered it necessary

Source: Samuel Pierre L'Honoré Naber and Irene A. Wright, eds., *Piet Heyn en de Zilvervloot, Bescheiden uit Nederlandsche en Spaansche archieven*. (Utrecht: Kemink and Zoon, 1928), pp. 281–283. English translation for this volume by Danny Noorlander; De Zilvervloot (http://ingeb.org/songs/hebjevan.html). Text: Dr. J. P. Heije [1847]; Melody: J. J. Viotta. English translation for this volume by Henriette de Bruyn Kops.

to take this opportunity to explain it to Your Majesty, for I know that many loyalists here, fearing disaster and expecting it, begin to worry for their safety and so it is easy to understand what the unfaithful will do, who are numerous, and who we know are always seeking a chance to carry out what they have long desired. And because it is true that most of these provinces consider Your Majesty a foreigner and the rebels their countrymen, whom they envy for their freedom, which they so prize, not inclined to obey anyone, least of all those who are not their countrymen, from which flow the difficulties and clear peril that would exist should anyone here attempt to obtain money by the extraordinary means that men elsewhere in similar circumstances have tried, it now appears necessary that Your Majesty command that all necessities be directly provided, to avoid what surely will follow the news, namely a general rebellion of the soldiers and the revolt of the obedient provinces that will be the immediate result thereof and at the same time an attack with much damage, as it is easy to foresee. And everything shall cease if this army just receives its pay, so that it, as necessary, can begin a campaign. And if by these circumstances, which the obedient and disobedient subjects deem hopeless, they display great courage, that would then have an effect of uncommon meaning for the safety of these provinces and even for Your Majesty, not only for prestige, but for the glory with which Your Majesty's greatness before all eyes would be veiled. And now is the best time to show it.

God protect Your Majesty.

The Silverfleet (De Zilvervloot)

1. Did you hear about the silver fleet?
The silver fleet of Spain?
Which carried many Spanish "matten" [coins]
Plus small apples of Orange
Piet Hein, Piet Hein
Piet Hein his name is short
His deeds are grand, his deeds are grand
He won the Silverfleet!

2. Did Piet Hein then not speak an earnest word:
"Well my lads of Orange,
Come on, let's board this and that Spanish ship
And seize those Spanish coins!"
Piet Hein, Piet Hein
Piet Hein his name is short
His deeds are grand, his deeds are grand
He won the Silverfleet!

3. Did the lads not climb the rigging like cats?
And did they not fight like lions?
They put the Spanish to serious shame
All the way to Spain their cries rang out

Piet Hein, Piet Hein
Piet Hein his name is short
His deeds are grand, his deeds are grand
He won the Silverfleet!

4. If ever another such a silver fleet appeared
Say, would you go after it just like that?
Or would you keep yourselves safe and out of harm's way,
quietly in your hammocks?
Well, Dutch blood,
That blood still has the courage!
We may not be tall, we may not be tall, [but]
We would win the Silverfleet

6. English Colonization Liberates Indians, 1629

Source: Increase Mather, *A Brief History of the War with the Indians in New England* (London, 1676), p. 15. Courtesy Library of Congress.

7. An Indian Describes the French Alliance, 1633

On the 24th of May, eighteen canoes of Savages having descended to Kebec, sieur de Champlain, suspecting that they might go on to the English, who had three vessels at Tadoussac and a bark far up the river, went into the Cabins of these Savages, and made to them a very suitable address through sieur Olivier the interpreter, who is an excellent man and well fitted for this country. He said to them through the lips of this interpreter that the French had always loved and defended them, that he had assisted them in person in their wars; that he had greatly cherished the Father of the Captain to whom he was talking, who was killed at his side in a battle where he himself was wounded by an arrow; that he was a man of his word, and that, notwithstanding the discomforts of the sea voyage, he had returned to see them again, as if they were his brothers; as they had expressed a wish that a French settlement should be made in their country, to defend them against the incursions of their enemies, he contemplated granting this desire, and it would already have been granted but for the obstacles created by the English; he was, moreover, then engaged in repairing the ruins that these wicked guests had left behind them; that he would not fail to satisfy them all as soon as he attended to the more urgent affairs; that the Fathers (speaking of us), would remain among them and would instruct them as well as their children. Yet, notwithstanding the great obligations that they [the Savages] were under to the French, they had descended the river with the intention of going to see the thieves who came to pillage the French. He said they should consider well what they were doing; that these robbers were only birds of passage, while the French would remain in the country as it belonged to them. This is a part of the discourse that sieur de Champlain delivered to them, as far as I have been able to learn, from the report made to me by those present.

During this speech, the Captain and his men listened very attentively. He, among others, appeared to be in deep thought, drawing from his stomach from time to time this aspiration, while they were speaking to him, *hám! hám! hám!* as if approving the speech of the interpreter, which, when finished, this Captain arose to answer, but with a keenness and delicacy of rhetoric that might have come out of the schools of Aristotle or Cicero. He won, in the beginning of his discourse, the good will of all of the French by his profound humility, which appeared with exceeding grace in his gestures and in his language.

"I am," said he, "only a poor little animal, crawling about on the ground; you Frenchmen are the great of the earth, who make all tremble. I do not know how I dare to talk before such great Captains. If I had some one behind me who would suggest what I ought to say, I would speak more boldly. I am bewildered; I have never had any instruction; my father left me very young; if I say anything, I go seeking it here and there, at hazard, and it is that which makes me tremble.

"Thou tellest us that the French have always loved us; we know it well, and we would lie if we said the contrary. Thou sayest that thou hast always been true, and we have always believed thee. Thou hast assisted us in our wars, we love thee all the more for it; what dost thou wish that we should answer? All that thou sayest is true.

Source: Paul Le Jeune's account, in Reuben Gold Thwaites, *Jesuit Relations* (Cleveland: The Burrows Brothers, 1898), vol. 5, pp. 202–209.

"Thou sayest that the French have come to live at Kebec to defend us, and that thou wilt come into our country to protect us. I remember well to have heard our fathers say that, when you were below at Tadoussac, the Montagnaits went to see you and invited you, unknown to us, to ascend [the river] above here, where our fathers, having seen you, loved you, and prayed you to make your home there.

"As to the settlement thou sayest we have asked for at the three rivers, I am only a child; I have no recollection, I do not know that I have asked for it! You, you have your Massinahigan; (that is to say, you have a knowledge of writing), which makes you remember everything. But, however that may be, thou wilt always be welcome." Note the discretion of this man, to make it plain that not only the Savages, but the French, desire this settlement. He continued his discourse, saying, "When thou shalt come up there with us thou wilt find a land better than this; thou wilt make, to begin with, a house like this to live in" (he indicated a little space with his hand); "that is to say, thou wilt make a fortress. Then thou wilt make another house like that," designating a large space, "and then we shall no longer be dogs who sleep outside, we shall go into that house." He meant to say an enclosed village. "Then we shall no longer be suspected of going to see those who do not love you. Thou wilt sow wheat; we shall do as thou dost, and we shall no longer go to seek our living in the woods; we shall no longer be wanderers and vagabonds.

"It was sieur de Caën, who believed that I had sent Beavers to the foreigners; I sent to those quarters a few Moose skins, not in trade, but to cut off the arms of our enemies. Thou knowest that the Hiroquois have long arms; if I had not cut them, we should have been taken by them long ago. I send presents to tribes who are their neighbors, to the end that they should not unite with them; it is not to offend the French, but to preserve ourselves.

"Thou sayest that we wish to go to the English; I will tell my men that they should not go there. I promise thee that neither I myself, nor they who have any sense, will do that; but if there is some young man who jumps over there without being seen, I shall not know what to do; thou knowest well that youth cannot be restrained. I shall forbid every one from going there. Any one who does so has no sense. Thou canst do everything, place thy boats in the way and capture the Beavers of those who attempt to go.

"Thou sayest that the Fathers will live among us, and will teach us. This good fortune will be for our children; we, who are already old, shall die ignorant. This blessing will not come as soon as we should like to have it.

"Thou sayest that we must be careful what we do; grasp us by the arm, and we shudder; grasp us afterward by the heart, and the whole body trembles. We do not want to go to the English; their Captain wanted to make an alliance with me and take me for his brother, and I did not desire it; I withdrew, saying that he was too great a Captain. I bethought myself well of a word that thou hadst said to us, that thou wouldst return; therefore I always awaited thee. Thou hast been truthful, thou wilt still be so in coming to see us in our country. I have but one fear; it is that in the association of the French with our people, some one may be killed, then we would be lost: thou knowest all are not prudent, but that the wiser ones will always do their duty."

This is about the answer of this Savage, who astonished our French people. They told me how he raised his voice according to the subjects he treated, then lowered it with so much humility, and with such an attitude of submission, that he won the hearts of all who looked at him, though they did not understand him.

The conclusion was that sieur de Champlain said to them: "When that great house shall be built, then our young men will marry your daughters, and we shall be one people." They began to laugh, answering: "Thou always sayest something cheering to rejoice us. If that should happen, we would be very happy." Those who think that the Savages have dull and heavy intellects will recognize by this speech that they are not so stupid as they may have been painted.

8. Dutch and Africans Triumph in Angola, 1647

The Portuguese, noticing Our weakness and the sober circumstances into which We had fallen, raised a mighty Army of their own Nations, Mulattoes, and Jagas [a people from somewhere around eastern Kongo], this past August, over twenty-five thousand men strong (under the Command and Governance of a certain Portuguese-man named Casper Ambrosius Borges), and encamped nearly on our territory, for no other purpose than to frighten our Sovas [chiefs], draw them away from us and debauch them, and make themselves Master of the whole Land, and trap us and oppress us in this City: but their object and purpose (which they surely would have accomplished according to their intentions, in truth, had they not been immediately stopped by Director Ouman) was simply unsuccessful, and with great damage and loss checked: For as soon as the rumors were heard, it was immediately resolved that our forces be brought to the Field, our Lands defended against the said Armies to the utmost Limits, our Sovas protected, and the same once more inspired with a measure of reverence; a number of whom having come here, on the third of October the forenamed Director personally took the Field, and made his Camp, with two hundred men, first for a few days at Namboaca Lombe, and thereafter marched five miles to Combi and established himself right in the face of the enemy, where our Sovas with their Army had gathered, expecting Captain Gim (who had been commanded to come) with most of the Garrison of Benguale [Benguela], and Queen Nzinga with her People, and awaiting our Soldiers, to arm and strengthen our Army somewhat against theirs.

In these circumstances the enemy, on 25 October, formed a party against Us, dividing into three Troops, and quickly began to advance on Us, and assault us; but they were so pressed by our Blacks, that they were turned back with the loss of over three hundred men, and after this Battle abandoned their Camp three days, moving it higher.

In the meantime we were still gathering our People together, waiting for Queen Nzinga, which took until 29 October, as when the Forenamed Queen lent the assistance a few days before of about four thousand men, but not more than two thousand

Source: *Extract van seeckeren Brief gheschreven uyt Loando St. Paulo, in Angola, van weghen de groote Victorie die de Onse verkregen hebben tegen de Portugesen onder 't beleydt van onsen Directeur Ouman: mitsgaders de assistentie vande Koninginne Zinga aende onse gedaen.* 's-Gravenhage: Ludolph Breeckevelt, 1648.

(*Extract of a certain letter written from Luanda St. Paulo, in Angola, concerning Our great Victory against the Portuguese under the leadership of our own Director Ouman: together with the assistance given us by Queen Nzinga.* The Hague: Ludolph Breeckevelt, 1648. Translated for this volume by Danny Noorlander.)

Archers and able-bodied men, with our Army, about three hundred Whites strong, and ten thousand Blacks from Combi, who were determined to seek the Enemy, and to strike him, and to that end we broke camp and began our march, until on 25 October, about four hours before nightfall, we discovered their army, and the Director himself with a Manly Courage attacked, striking so hard that they fell into disorder after a few charges, took to flight, and were pursued by Us in such a way that more than three thousand were cut down and slain, in addition to the injured, and the multitude of prisoners that were taken prize by our Black Warriors, and disposed of for us.

Even Casper Ambrosius Borges perished, with fifteen of the principal Sovas and all the Portuguese and Mulattoes who had accompanied him, except his Son, who made a narrow escape.

In addition, the Director took five Sovas captive, two of whom got loose and escaped.

In the pursuit five Horses were left behind and fell into our hands.

The burning and scorching of the Portuguese Sovas' Villages was so widespread that over two hundred were left in ashes, their plantations ruined, even Massango, where our Army had encamped, and on our return march Muchinne suffered such a share of the devastation that the entire Lemba was destroyed, right up to the City, all the houses burned, smashed to the ground, and before Muchinne everything razed; truly a wound that they will not easily overcome.

We cannot thank the Lord God enough for this Victory, not only that He gave us the victory over our Enemies; but that he also shined his watchful eye over this City, and took the same into his protection.

Actum Loando St. Paulo, the 16th of December, Anno 1647.

△ E S S A Y S

Wim Klooster and Benjamin Schmidt, experts on the history of the Netherlands and of Dutch activities overseas, take a broad geographical approach to understanding the age of imperial rivalries within the Atlantic world. Klooster probes the link between events in Europe, particularly the economic depression that gripped much of the world after 1610, and the reconfiguration of European holdings in the western Atlantic. He uses this transatlantic perspective to explain the decline of Spain and the ascendancy of its main rivals, France, England, and the Netherlands. His emphasis is less on religious division than on economic, political, and military conflict.

Focusing on the Dutch revolt against the Spanish between 1568 and 1648, Schmidt offers a case study of how events thousands of miles away across the ocean might affect a single nation. The Habsburg crown controlled the Low Countries (the provinces comprising modern Belgium and the Netherlands). Opposition to Spanish rule, organized especially but not exclusively by Protestant subjects, commenced in 1568 and became a focal point for larger European conflicts. Schmidt shows how the Dutch rebels used the writings of the Dominican friar Bartolomé de las Casas, whose work appears in Chapter 3, to articulate their own perception of themselves as victims of Spanish tyranny. The essays by Klooster and Schmidt offer different evaluations of the weight of religious and economic factors in historical change, and they raise the question of how the indigenous people of the Americas figured into the geographical transformation of the Atlantic world as Iberian power began to crack.

Northern Europeans Invade the Americas

WIM KLOOSTER

In the seventeenth century the New World underwent a number of radical political and economic changes. While by 1600 the Spanish king could still believe in his uncontested possession of the Indies, by 1700 large parts had been divided between three foreign contenders: England, France, and the Netherlands. Their arrival set off a number of sweeping economic innovations, especially in the Caribbean. In this paper I will argue that the European colonization was set on a new footing around 1620, after which the Atlantic seaboard of the entire New World entered upon a long period of instability. The new American settlements were not completely consolidated until the 1680s. . . .

Why was it that the non-Iberian powers now succeeded in creating permanent settlements when all previous efforts had been defeated? Could there be a connection between the westward migration and the so-called "general" economic crisis that afflicted Europe after circa 1610? Most economic historians agree that 1610 forms a watershed in European history. If the era between 1450 and 1610 was generally one of economic stability, the half century after 1610 was characterized by a very serious economic depression throughout Europe, borne out by high prices, real wages falling behind the cost of living, and a demographic disaster, that is, rising mortality combined with declining rates of fertility. On top of this, Europe was ravaged by warfare. But did this multiple crisis create a large pool of potential New World immigrants? In the case of England, America indeed provided an outlet for farmers and farm hands hit by under-employment and falling wages in agriculture and for gentry and sons of merchants looking for land. Still, it is clear that reasons of an economic nature were not decisive in all cases. In fact, religious factors may have been as significant. The New World lured both religious separatists and people who were afraid that the Church of England, in the long run, could not avoid being infected by Roman Catholicism.

Economic motives were even less obvious in the Dutch case. Until at least the middle of the seventeenth century, the United Provinces remained outside the crisis. Opportunities for employment were generally excellent. The domestic market could absorb the population explosion occurring in the provinces of Holland and Friesland between 1500 and 1650, when their combined number of inhabitants grew from 350,000 to one million. This increase was unparalleled in Europe. Prosperity, however, was not distributed evenly, and many a family in the rural parts of the east of the country scratched out a living. Still, few Dutchmen were eager to become economic refugees. What numbers did migrate? By the time the Caribbean colony of Curaçao had developed into a major commercial entrepôt in the mid-1660s, that is, after twenty-five years of Dutch presence, its population was 600 men, one-fourth of whom were serving the Company. The other Caribbean islands, which had been in Dutch hands since the 1630s, did not have any immigration of consequence. The Dutch colony *par excellence* in the western hemisphere was, of course, Brazil. But even Brazil did not attract the vast numbers of settlers that had been expected. In

Source: Wim Klooster, "Winds of Change: Colonization, Commerce, and Consolidation in the Seventeenth-Century Atlantic World," *Halve Maen*, 1997, 70(3): 53–56, 58. Reprinted courtesy of The Holland Society of New York.

1639, at the very height of Dutch power, before a local rebellion forced them onto the defensive, 10,000 Company men were living in New-Holland, as the Dutch styled their colony. Before long, this number would drop. Not counting Company personnel, a census of the mid-1640s revealed that 3,399 men, women, and children were living in Dutch Brazil. Compared to these figures, immigration to New Netherland was by no means insignificant, particularly not in the last nine years of the colony's existence, when 2,900 people arrived.

Yet, compared to English migration to New England and the Chesapeake, Dutch migration was hardly impressive, to put it mildly. In addition to the difference in religious climate, an important factor underlying the divergent migration volumes may be the discrepancy in real wages which existed between the two countries. Public purchasing power in the Netherlands increased continuously from the late 1620s through the 1680s, while at least one additional indicator in this connection is in favor of the Dutch republic: wages of artisans in the west of the Netherlands were almost twice as high as those earned in southern England.

At least in terms of migration, therefore, the "general" European crisis does not offer a convincing explanation for the sudden success of the new contenders for American territories. Or did it work in another way? For the crisis did seriously affect a country whose leaders felt it had exclusive rights over large parts of the New World. Spain was passing through an unprecedented economic slump, which manifested itself in the decline of the shipbuilding and textile industries. Its foreign trade was reduced to that of a classic underdeveloped country, with hardware and textiles as major import items and exports made up solely of primary products, such as wool, wine, and olive oil.

Not only were foreign markets lost; the Spanish industry was also unable to meet the needs of both the domestic and colonial markets. Certain sectors of the colonial economies began to develop independently, in Peru and Mexico as well as on the edges of empire. Increased self-sufficiency, exemplified by the rise of domestic American textile manufacturing, and economic diversification went hand in hand. Both developments were speeded up by the decline of the transatlantic trade, which curtailed the supply of European goods. But while Spanish Americans soon found solutions for the changing conditions by setting up textile industries and engaging in contraband trade, the Spanish state relied too much on the transatlantic trade. King Philip IV had simply burdened his state with too many obligations at home and abroad, and he expected the proceeds from the American imports to pay for his wars. But precisely from the time he took office in 1621, their volume and value began to drop.

This change of fortune made it impossible for Spain to fight and be victorious on all fronts. Of course, had the monarchy been financially healthy, the Spanish ministers would undoubtedly have given preference to their European pet projects anyway, but the present situation forced them to neglect Caribbean defenses. France and England could take advantage of the lack of Spanish defensive power and embark on their colonizing missions. It is telling that in both the Caribbean and North America, local Indian groups proved more formidable enemies than the Spanish.

Whatever the push and pull factors may have been behind the establishment of the northern maritime states, their intrusion into mainland North America and the Caribbean was irreversible. In South America their gains were much more modest. They carved out small colonies in Guiana. For several decades, though, it looked like a more substantial chunk of land would be theirs: Brazil. It was the Dutch who, with ardent zeal, espoused the settlement of this Portuguese colony that had become part of the Habsburg world empire with the union of the Spanish and Portuguese crowns in 1580. Dutch-held territory in the northeast gradually expanded after the capture of Recife in 1630, and, as the conflict between the Dutch and the Portuguese continued after Portugal's secession from Spain, the costly war effort almost induced the Portuguese king to give up. However, a rebellion of Portuguese planters broke out, never lost momentum, and forced the Dutch to abandon Brazil in 1654. By that time, the main prizes in the Caribbean had been carried off by England and France, who left some crumbs for the Dutch: islands such as Curaçao, which would never blossom into major plantation colonies. It is tempting to imagine what would have happened if the West India Company and the States General would not have invested so much time and energy in Brazil but rather in the Caribbean.

The Dutch adventure in Brazil, nevertheless, did have important consequences for the West Indies. Because Brazil was the world's leading sugar producer, the Dutch came to control sugar cultivation in all of its aspects and, in the middle decades of the century, transferred their capital, know-how, and technology to Barbados, Martinique, Guadeloupe, and St. Christopher. What did this transfer amount to? Let us take Barbados as an example. When the Dutch came to this English colony, the settlers had just failed to substitute cotton for tobacco. The Dutch now taught them how to produce sugar, loaned them capital to buy land and equipment and set up the sugar mills, supplied them with the slaves who worked the plantations and ground the cane, and shipped their end product to Europe. Looking back on the early decades of English settlement in 1651, the governor and council of Barbados insisted that "all the antient inhabitants know very well, how greatly they have been obliged to those of the Low Countries for their subsistence, and how difficult it would have been . . . without their assistance, ever to have inhabited these places, or to have brought them into order."

In so doing, the Dutch paved the way for a shift in the economic gravity in the New World from the Iberian colonies to those of France and England in the Caribbean. At the same time, they speeded up the rhythm of the Atlantic slave trade, in which they had begun to take part during their colonization of Brazil. After the start of the Portuguese rebellion, the Dutch were left with large supplies of African labor but without a market. The expansion of Caribbean sugar production then created a demand for slave labor which they could satisfy.

The new slave-based economies fitted well into the schemes of mercantilists. Mercantilism pursued commerce, especially foreign commerce, as a means of national enrichment. Growth in the wealth of a society promised to augment the power of a polity, and both wealth and power were considered to be dependent upon a favorable balance in international trade. This balance depended on the profitability of the nation's colonies. The commodities shipped in from the West Indies were primary staples which were processed in the mother country. According to the model, all that the colonies could not produce themselves was imported from the homeland. This ideal functioned better in the Caribbean islands than in the settlement colonies of North America, which were largely lacking in prized cash crops. . . .

This brings us to the scale of the Atlantic empires. Even though the vast majority of Indians died in the wake of the Spanish conquest, the survivors still outnumbered the Europeans by far. Including them all in the new empire required tremendous organizational efforts on the part of Spanish officials. The vastness of the newly gained territories made it all the more difficult. The French faced the same problem in North America toward the end of the century when they occupied three-fourths of the continent, claiming possession over an area stretching "from Louisiana to Hudson's Bay, from Newfoundland to the as yet unexplored territories in the West, beyond the Great Lakes and Detroit."

The Dutch Atlantic empire was never that extensive, and it was already past its prime by the time the Duke of York seized New Amsterdam. Brazil had been abandoned, and in the Caribbean the Dutch were falling victim to their own success. Several measures were taken to remove them from the existing commercial networks. The English Navigation Acts and Colbert's mercantilism seemed to spell the end of the Dutch role of intermediaries, a role that had set them apart from the other European players in the Atlantic world. What were these Navigation Acts? The first act—whose content would not be fundamentally altered by the second one of 1660—was passed by the English Parliament in 1651 and was aimed at Dutch shipping. It decreed that the transport of goods from Asia and Africa and from America to England, Ireland, or other English possessions was only allowed in ships owned by Englishmen. The masters and most of the sailors also had to be subjects of the Commonwealth. The act, likewise, dictated that foreign commodities had to be shipped directly from the port of origin to English settlements.

French officials also took action against the Dutch. In the French part of St. Christopher, over sixty well-stocked Dutch warehouses were set on fire in 1663. The following year saw the founding of the *Compagnie des Indes Occidentales*, a company which would wield power and administer justice in the French Antilles for a period of forty years. A royal ban on mercantile dealings with the Dutch, initially issued under the pretext of an epidemic of plague in Amsterdam, led to regular revolts, first in Martinique and some years later in Saint-Domingue. The planters' wishes were not heeded, and Dutch traders were forced to withdraw.

Although they were on the retreat everywhere, the Dutch did not immediately resign themselves to the role of bystanders. It took them seven years to sign a peace treaty with Portugal, and even then they continued to dream of a large American empire. Shortly after the defeat in Brazil, Dutch authorities tried to involve an inhabitant of Venezuela in their designs. During his three-month stay in Amsterdam, this man had interviews with quite a number of high officials. He could not believe his ears. He learned about the existence of advanced plans to establish an enormous Dutch colony in the region between Brazil and Venezuela. Both the coastal area and the interior would be gradually populated, so that by the time the next war with Spain broke out—it was judged that the peace treaty would not last long—the Dutch would be in a position to conquer northern South America. Likewise, preparations were made to seize the southern cone of the continent. At the outbreak of war, a Dutch fleet would be fitted out that was to leave for Rió de la Plata, sail up the river, and finally occupy Spanish territory. One Dutchman, who was fluent in Spanish, had already been sent to the area to make inquiries. Dressed up as a Spaniard he had walked inland more than 500 miles and later returned to the Netherlands with a map on which all rivers and country lanes he had discovered were indicated.

It is difficult to establish if such plans were seriously discussed in government circles, but, in any case, they never bore fruit. Admittedly, the Dutch conquest of Suriname in 1677 may be seen as a first step toward the fulfillment of the plans that were just outlined. But this accomplishment and the short-lived return to New Amsterdam were the last convulsions of Dutch Atlantic ambitions. Thereafter, very little was left of the Dutch empire in the Americas. What remained were six small Caribbean islands and a string of colonies in northern South America.

After Oliver Cromwell's Western Design had ended in a fiasco, England also buried her aspirations to major territorial gains at the cost of Spain and Portugal. Gradually, a new status quo emerged in the New World as the period of successful outside infiltration into the Iberian world was completed. The establishment of the French, Dutch, and English colonies was not a foregone conclusion. Wars with Native Americans, internecine Western European struggles, attacks by pirates and buccaneers, and other hardships had to be overcome. By no means had all these hardships subsided by the late seventeenth century, but the new economies were in place and so was metropolitan control. What the Navigation Acts had effected for England, Colbert brought about for France. By ending the regime of *propriétaires*, who had been operating independently of government control, and by appointing governors tied to Paris, the colonies were subordinated to the crown. At least for the time being, the winds of change that had been blowing through the New World had stopped.

The Dutch Rebels and America

BENJAMIN SCHMIDT

In early November 1565, there arrived in Brussels the long-awaited response of King Philip II to reports of social, political, and religious unrest in the Low Countries. . . . By the following spring, a league of some two hundred noblemen had rallied together and, in response to the stated position of the Spanish Crown, gathered in Brussels to present to Margaret of Parma, governess-general of the Netherlands and half-sister to Philip, a "Request" for the moderation of the placards and abolition of the Inquisition. These events, which took place against a backdrop of expanding religious disorder and contracting economic growth, traditionally mark the beginning of the Revolt of the Netherlands. On the face of it, they had little to do with events in the New World, where the sway of Habsburg rule also happened to prevail. Yet within a matter of months, another group of Dutch nobles, this time assembled in Rotterdam, offered the case of Spanish abuses in America—"tyranny" as they termed it—to justify their own opposition to Spanish rule in the Netherlands. Resistance was necessary, the nobles maintained, for "the Spanish seek nothing but to abuse our Fatherland as they have done in the New Indies." The Revolt had thus begun, and with it commenced a revolution in Dutch representations of America.

The nobles' complaint of Habsburg misrule in America signaled an audacious shift in the political and geographic imagination of the Dutch. It indicated, too, a dramatic reorientation of Netherlandish notions of the New World. For, later developments notwithstanding, evidence in support of the nobles' position was, by the mid-1560s,

Source: Benjamin Schmidt, *Innocence Abroad: The Dutch Imagination and the New World, 1570–1670* (New York: Cambridge University Press, 2001), pp. 68–69, 73–78, 95–97, 99, 111–113, 121–122. Reprinted with the permission of Cambridge University Press.

hardly overwhelming. On the eve of the Revolt, a number of different visions of the New World coexisted in the books and pamphlets, broadsides and prints, published lately in the Low Countries. The image of "Spanish tyranny in the New World," however, was not necessarily, or even most likely, the preeminent of these. . . . Rather than diminishing the Spanish achievement in America, these works tended to celebrate the heroism, perseverance, and piety of Spanish discoverers and their royal patrons. . . .

Over the course of the 1560s and 1570s, the Dutch vision of the New World evolved from what might loosely be called a Hispanophilic attitude to one decidedly Hispanophobic. The new geographic sensibilities emerged less from any abrupt change that may have occurred in the distant climes of America than from shifting political winds in the Netherlands. As enthusiasm for the Habsburg regime in the Low Countries subsided, criticism for perceived Habsburg abuses in the Indies gathered force. . . .

The nobles' case against Spain in America indicated both a reinvigorated interest in the New World and a reformulation of its significance. It heralded the rebels' creation of a new geography—a usable geography—to accompany their new political aspirations. It also commenced a process of articulating a self-consciously "Dutch" identity partly through reference to "American" history. . . . Dutch pamphleteers and printers, and especially those in the service of the rebel party, now joined these topoi to create an image of intolerable Spanish tyranny visited upon the innocent natives of America. "In the newly discovered lands . . . they have murdered practically all of the natives," wrote a pamphleteer in 1574 of Spain's American adventure. "Whoever wishes to see an example of their tyranny, and to know fully how they would reign," it was suggested, could observe the fate of the New World. The "innocent blood" of the Indians vividly alerted the Dutch; for the experience of America suggested what could yet transpire in the Netherlands. "Let us imagine the example of the Indians," wrote a leading figure of the rebel party in a work brazenly published by the archtypographer to the king, "and let us imagine that our descendants will be abused as are they."

The creation of the rebels' "America" proceeded gradually in the years following the initial Dutch resistance to Habsburg rule. It followed approximately the shape of the campaign against the Spanish government and the progress of political events in Brussels, where the regent, Margaret of Parma, resided. It followed more closely, however, the contours of the war of words waged against "Spanish tyranny" and the progress of printers in Antwerp, where the rebel image-makers reigned. From the start—the "Request" of the nobles published in 1566—the rebels recognized and exploited the power of print in their battle for public opinion. The "flood of publications" noted by contemporaries prompted action first from Margaret and later from her replacement, the duke of Alba, who sought to stem the flow with a sharply worded edict in 1568 against the "mutinous, wretched forgers, enemies and disturbers of the public welfare." Yet these and later Spanish governors scored little success. "The more the court issued edicts against them," wrote a supporter of Orange, "the more the number of such booklets and writings increased." Indeed, the Dutch rebels were extraordinarily prolific writers. . . .

Opposition to Habsburg rule in the Netherlands converged originally around the issue of the Inquisition. Though a mechanism to pursue heresy had existed in the Low Countries from the earliest moments of the Reformation, public reaction remained generally muted throughout the first half of the sixteenth century and reached crisis proportions only by the mid-1560s. The reinvigorated attention paid by Philip II to the "plague" of Protestantism following the Peace of Cateau-Cambrésis (1559), and the concurrent circulation within Calvinist circles of a number of particularly inflammatory attacks on the Holy Office, help to explain the intensified campaign conducted by Dutch Reformers around this time against the Inquisition. . . .

"America" originally entered the repertoire of the rebels as a parallel case of inquisitorial imperiousness. In the New World, it was proposed, the Spanish Inquisition had similarly violated indigenous rights and abused "native privileges." With striking geographic imagination, Dutch pamphleteers posited a didactic connection between Spanish actions taken in America and Habsburg rule in the Netherlands, warning that within the first example lay a lesson for the second. Already in 1566, le Clercq intimated that the Dutch should keep a wary eye on the far-flung advances of their Habsburg enemies. The Spanish Inquisition had spread around the world, and no one lay beyond its reach. A group of nobles who signed a remonstrance against the "inconveniences arising from the Inquisition and the [religious] placards" made the case much more explicitly. The Spanish, they warned, "seek nothing but to use [*bruyken*] our Fatherland as they have done in the New Indies which they have recently won." . . . They claimed to fear, as did other rebel pamphleteers, that Spain would rule without consulting the natural leaders of the Netherlands, that Spain endeavored (to cite the *actual* words of Alba) "to create a New World" in the Netherlands. . . .

One source surfaces repeatedly in Dutch texts, conspicuous particularly in the 1580s and 1590s, in materials as varied as the songs of the *Geuzen* and the testaments of Orange. . . . The prince and the poets alluded to the same cleric: Fray Bartolomé de Las Casas, onetime bishop of Chiapas and longtime "Apostle of the Indians." That cleric's history to which both gestured was the *Brevíssima relación de la destruyción de las Indias*, dedicated to (then) Prince Philip in 1552 and destined to enjoy near canonical status among the sacred texts of the Revolt. Printed repeatedly throughout the late-sixteenth and seventeenth centuries, it ranks among the most successful descriptions of America to appear in early modern Europe. Replete with lurid tales of Spanish tyranny, it also became one of the most commonly cited texts of the Dutch patriotic party. . . .

The *Brevíssima relación* represented but one of the many treatments by Las Casas of the Indian question, and it appears, at first glance, unusual that an otherwise obscure tract written for a royal Spanish audience should end up some thirty years later in the hands of Dutch rebels. Conceived as early as the 1520s, the *Brevíssima relación* was drafted (for Charles V) originally in 1542, printed (for Philip II) ultimately in 1552, and abandoned for all intents and purposes promptly thereafter to languish in the Spanish royal archives. Though Las Casas and his ideas exercised undeniable influence over certain members of the royal circle, and though Philip continued to regard the Dominican with respect and even favor, the "Indianist policy" ultimately ceded to the expediency of financial crisis, and Lascasian rhetoric gave way to the stronger pressures of the colonialist lobby. Little in the mid-sixteenth century would have indicated that Las Casas's account would endure over the next four centuries. Yet that changed dramatically and abruptly in 1578, when the Dutch discovered "the bishop's histories" and their uses. The *Brevíssima relación* fit the rebels' agenda perfectly. It catalogued vividly the "great miseries and wretched destruction" visited upon America and thereby exposed the extent of Spain's perfidy. It addressed directly the emperor Charles V and the future king Philip II and thereby implicated (indirectly) the Spanish crown, which, by 1578, had not altered a course of government that had plainly gone awry. Best of all, it flowed passionately from the pen of a reputable Spanish cleric, an eyewitness to the events described, and thereby lent greater legitimacy to the rebels' case against Spain.

It also worked spectacularly. The rebels consequently not only rehabilitated Las Casas' tract; they also reprinted it tirelessly, translated it quickly, and disseminated it widely across Northern Europe. Following the cautiously produced Dutch translation in 1578, which appeared without the name of the printer or translator or the place of publication, an astonishing twenty-five more Dutch-language editions rolled off the presses of the Low Countries by the time the war with Spain had ended (1648). Over the course of the late-sixteenth and seventeenth centuries, the Dutch published altogether some thirty-three editions of Las Casas, more than did all other European countries combined. Furthermore, those editions produced outside the Netherlands originated largely from texts either translated or printed by the rebels. . . . The rebel publicists incorporated Las Casas into an already growing repertoire of anti-Spanish propaganda, in which the New World occupied a position of honor. From the earlier histories of America—especially that of Benzoni, published in 1565, 1573, and 1578, and that of Martyr, published in 1555, 1574, and 1577—from the references to Spanish tyrannies circulating among the various stations of the international Protestant community, and from the scattered comments of the Spanish governors themselves, the Dutch formulated an image of Spanish tyranny in America that was meant to serve "as an example" for readers in the Habsburg-controlled Low Countries. Las Casas added grist to a propaganda mill already well in motion. Recognizing the obvious use that the *Brevíssima relación* might have in their program, the rebels adopted and popularized what turned out to be one of the most compelling pieces of colonial literature to emerge from the *Conquista*, a work that might otherwise have faded into obscurity. The colonial critique by the bishop of Chiapas filled a need for all those who sought to discredit Spain and its leaders, yet that need predated the Dutch discovery of Las Casas. By 1578, those opponents of Philip II who published the *Brevíssima relación* were merely stoking fires already strongly burning. . . .

The rebels' road to America ran both ways. If the political events in the Netherlands colored Dutch perceptions of the New World, it is also the case that descriptions of the New World, and especially those derived from Las Casas and other popular historians of the *Conquista*, worked their way back into Dutch representations of the Revolt. . . . If the natives of America could appear in Dutch writings as would-be "rebels," stripped of their rights and plundered of their property, the Spaniards stationed in the Netherlands could feature as would-be colonizers, addicted to *conquistadora* violence and committed to the wholesale enslavement of the Netherlands. The Dutch created America in their own image, yet in the process, and by dint of their exposure to certain Americana, they came to reinvent that image based on "America." Increasingly, the language of conquest and the polemic of revolt converged to form a single vocabulary of tyranny used to discredit Spanish behavior at home and abroad. In trope, topos, and metaphor, the rebels allied the Indian with the Orangist and Alba with Cortés.

What might be called the Americanization of the Revolt appears from the earliest years of written opposition to Spain, when descriptions of developments in the Netherlands began to take on many of the features associated with descriptions of the *Conquista*. Foremost among these borrowings was the idiom of conquest itself, used by the rebels to characterize Spain's malevolent intentions toward the Low Countries. A conflict that had all the makings of a limited, domestic contest—a debate over the distribution of patronage, collection of taxes, and policing of religion—took on the shape of a full blown war of conquest. From the rebels' perspective, Spain intended not simpy to regain its leverage in Brussels, but fully to reconquer and colonize the "subject" population of the Netherlands. The notorious "Legend of the Inquisition" circulated the notion that the Holy Office had devised a plan to starve the Netherlands, exterminate its leading nobles, and subject its defenseless population to a yoke of intolerable tyranny. The *Articles and Resolutions of the Spanish Inquisition to Invade and Impede the Netherlands*, a scandalous forgery concocted by the rebels, imputed to Spain the goal of annihilating, literally, the entire native Dutch population. "We shall consider no one in all of the Netherlands, apart from our agents, worthy of living," read the ninth article. "In the end, all will be uprooted, to make room for a new state [*rijk*] and a new nation [*volk*]." Adrianus Saravia, among Orange's stable of propagandists in the late 1560s, insinuated that the recent arrival of Alba bespoke a similar plan of colonization. The iron duke allegedly planned to destroy the entire Netherlands and resettle it with his own men. For his effort, Alba the Conqueror, like any great conquistador, would see the lands renamed in his honor, "The Duke of Alva's Converted, Conquered New Christian Lands." Some dozen years later, Orange employed a nearly identical idiom to portray the king of Spain, whom he dubbed "Devourer of the People." Left unchallenged, Philip II would brutalize the entire native population, "noble men and the Lords of the countrey, as well as the common people." The king had forgotten the difference between lands inherited and those achieved by conquest, Orange asserted. Philip II governed the Low Countries according to the rules of the latter and with disastrous effects. The same metaphor of conquest featured in the pamphlets of Marnix. In an early publication he decried Granvelle's design to turn the land "*en pays de conquest*"; in another he proposed that Philip II would convert the Netherlands into "a second colonie of Castile." The *first* colony, Marnix added knowingly, was that of the Indies.

Once conquered, soon enslaved, went the rebels' logic; and, in much the same polemical spirit, the conquering Castilians were attacked for their plots (purportedly) to "yoke" the Netherlands. Drawing once again on motifs of Lascasian rhetoric, the Dutch projected onto their Habsburg governors a master plan to reduce the Low Countries to a state of "eternal servitude." One particularly imaginative rendition of this theme saw the Catholic King placing all of the land's Calvinists in iron fetters and banishing them to, of all locations, the New World. Other versions imagined domestic bondage, and this sort of invective arose most naturally around the person of Alba, who appeared in allegorical prints as a Pharaonic master lording over the shackled figures of the Seventeen Provinces. A strongly worded pamphlet of 1582 claimed that Alba "intended to treat the [Dutch] not as subjects of a fatherly sovereign, but as a conquered nation and as slaves." . . .

Certainly, [a variety of sources] influenced the myth-makers of the Dutch Revolt. Yet the role of America within the Dutch imagination still deserves to be singled out, if only because the rebels did so themselves. Time and again, they compared their own situation *specifically* with that of the Amerindians. Insistently and incessantly they juxtaposed the image of Spanish tyrannies perpetrated in the New World with those committed in the Netherlands. And with good reason: America had been victimized primarily by Spain, and not simply by a Catholic or Imperial enemy; the Americans did not yet possess any incurably damning religious or political beliefs that might have made them inappropriate models of suffering; and, not least important, reports of American atrocities did, in fact, stand out from much of the literature of conquest available at the time. Nothing matched the *Brevíssima relación* for blood and gore.

Above all, the New World, still novel and forever distant, lent itself to refashioning. The Dutch discovered America in every sense of the word. Shortly after the protests against the Habsburg government in Brussels commenced, patriotic pamphleteers recognized the role America could play in their campaign against Spain, and they quickly seized upon the image of *conquistadora* violence to blacken the Spanish reputation. Once revealed, America and the American predicament quickly took on the shape of the rebels' own situation. Innocent natives, proposed the Dutch, faced an invasive, foreign monarch who had ignored traditional privileges and pillaged private property under the pretense of religion. Yet while the Dutch fashioned their own style of America, the actual Americana that reached the Low Countries, and especially the *Brevíssima relación* of Las Casas, worked its way back into the very texture of patriotic histories. Lascasian language and metaphor colored the history of the Revolt and led to wonderfully exaggerated notions of the Spanish enemy. The invading army of Flanders, it was said, had sought to conquer and enslave the entire Netherlands, commit barbaric feats of butchery, and murder epic numbers of women and children. If the rebels had invented the New World, within time America would help to reinvent the world of the Dutch. By the end of the sixteenth century, "America" not only symbolized the extent of Spanish tyranny abroad, but also provided the model for Spanish behavior in the Netherlands. It had become a shaping force in Dutch political propaganda, coloring countless readers' visions of Spain and its empire.

FURTHER READING

Andrews, Kenneth R. *Trade, Plunder, and Settlement: Maritime Enterprise and the Genesis of the British Empire, 1480–1630.* Cambridge, UK: Cambridge University Press, 1984.

Axtell, James. *The Invasion Within: The Contest of Cultures in Colonial North America.* New York: Oxford University Press, 1985.

Boxer, C. R. *The Dutch in Brazil, 1624–1654.* Oxford: Clarendon Press, 1957.

Davies, K. G. *The North Atlantic World in the Seventeenth Century.* St. Paul: University of Minnesota Press, 1974.

Dunn, Richard S. *The Age of Religious Wars.* New York: W. W. Norton, 1970.

Goslinga, Comelis Ch. *The Dutch in the Caribbean and on the Wild Coast, 1580–1680.* Gainesville: University Press of Florida, 1971.

Israel, Jonathan Irvine. *Dutch Primacy in World Trade, 1585–1740.* New York: Oxford University Press, 1989.

———. *The Dutch Republic and the Hispanic World, 1606–1661.* New York: Oxford University Press, 1982.

Klooster, Wim. *Illicit Riches: Dutch Trade in the Caribbean, 1648–1795.* Leiden: KITLV Press, 1998.

Lane, Kris E. *Pillaging the Empire: Piracy in the Americas 1500–1750.* Armonk, NY: M. E. Sharpe, 1998.

McGrath, John T. *The French in Florida: In the Eye of the Hurricane.* Gainesville: University Press of Florida, 2000.

Paquette, Robert L., and Stanley L. Engerman, eds. *The Lesser Antilles in the Age of European Expansion.* Gainesville: University Press of Florida, 1996.

Phillips, Carla Rahn. *Six Galleons for the King of Spain: Imperial Defense in the Early Seventeenth Century.* Baltimore: The Johns Hopkins University Press, 1986.

Postma, Johannes, and Victor Enthoven, eds. *Riches from Atlantic Commerce: Dutch Transatlantic Trade and Shipping, 1585–1817.* Leiden, Netherlands: Brill, 2003.

Schmidt, Benjamin. *Innocence Abroad: The Dutch Imagination and the New World, 1570–1670.* New York: Cambridge University Press, 2001.

Steele, Ian K. *Warpaths: Invasions of North America.* New York: Oxford University Press, 1994.

Thornton, John K. *The Kingdom of Kongo: Civil War and Transition, 1641–1718.* Madison: The University of Wisconsin Press, 1983.

———. *Warfare in Atlantic Africa, 1500–1800.* London: University College London, 1999.

Weber, David J. *The Spanish Frontier in North America.* New Haven, CT: Yale University Press, 1992.

CHAPTER
5

The Columbian Exchange

Historians of past generations explained European conquests in the Americas and elsewhere around the globe as a consequence of superior European technology. Now, however, we know that technology was only one part of the baggage that Europeans brought with them across the Atlantic. A historian named Alfred W. Crosby opened an entirely new way to understand European expansion and the extraordinary ability of Europeans to impose themselves on distant people and societies in a book entitled The Columbian Exchange, *published in 1972. Focusing on people as biological entities living among all other organisms, Crosby scrutinized the pathogens that accompanied European mariners, traders, and conquerors; helped readers see a transformed landscape in the wake of plant and animal invasions; and sketched the global impact of American foods on diets beyond the Atlantic.*

Long separated by the ancient and on-going shifting of tectonic plates, the flora and fauna of the Eurasian and American landmasses rejoined in the wake of 1492, and they did so in turbulent ways. American populations, previously isolated from endemic Eurasian diseases, were "virgin soil" populations that suffered mortality rates as high as 90 percent in the most devastating outbreaks. These epidemics, bolstered by animal invasions, shaped, facilitated, and sustained European occupation and conquests. But disease environments similarly curtailed European presence in the tropics, where inhabitants had acquired their own relative immunities to endemic diseases. Ecosystems defined the way in which the Atlantic world emerged.

As the essays and documents in this chapter reveal, people, whether European, African, or American, pursued diverse strategies in their responses to unfamiliar and often invasive and deadly diseases, plants, and animals. They sought to make sense of new food and animals by invoking familiar scientific, agricultural, medicinal, and religious frameworks. They responded to unwelcome invaders—animals and pathogens alike—through traditional mechanisms of disease prevention and through the innovative legal and cultural resources available to them in colonial societies. As plants, animals, people, and pathogens crossed and circulated the Atlantic in all directions, they helped to create a distinctive zone of interaction, one defined not by people alone but by other living organisms as well. Understanding the asymmetrical interactions determined by disease environments can help us see the ability of different people within the Atlantic to remain in control in their home territories, as was generally the case for Africans, or to endure the occupation and dominion of outsiders, as was generally the case for Americans.

△ D O C U M E N T S

These documents explore how people and communities within the Atlantic world responded to adverse disease environments, unfamiliar animals, and new foods. Documents 3, 4, 6, and 8 address the new diseases and parasites people encountered within a transformed world. Documents 3 and 4 offer European perspectives on indigenous responses to epidemics in North America. In Document 3, two prominent English inhabitants of New England, the Massachusetts governor John Winthrop and the Plymouth governor William Bradford, describe the course of a harrowing smallpox epidemic in the winter of 1633 and 1634 and how both the indigenous people of southern New England and new European inhabitants responded to the deadly outbreak. The two selections that comprise Document 4 were written by the Jesuit missionary Paul Le Jeune in New France. They reveal contrasting attitudes among the Huron Indians toward epidemic disease and Catholic missionaries. Le Jeune's 1637 report shows that many Indians regarded the Jesuits as bearers of disease, while his 1640 report describes the activities of Catholic nuns tending to sick Indians at the hospital in Quebec. Documents 6 and 8 focus on European experiences with new diseases. William Dampier, an English sailor who became a noted pirate and explorer, contracted a Guinea worm (now known as *dracunculiasis*) while cutting logwood in the Yucatan peninsula in 1676, and a local black healer applied a mysterious remedy to extract the worm. He describes his ordeal in Document 6. Joseph Dupuis, an English trader in West Africa, discusses his struggle with the endemic fevers of the Gold Coast in Document 8. Dupuis' ability to engage in trade largely resulted from his ability to survive the "seasoning" period that plagued European newcomers to tropical Africa.

Documents 1, 2, and 5 focus on the animal invasions that accompanied European migrations to the Americas, and they illustrate the different ways in which Europeans and Americans regarded large domesticated animals. In Document 1, the Spanish priest José de Acosta describes the migration and proliferation of European domestic animals including sheep and cattle in the Spanish territories in the Caribbean and American mainland. Acosta was one of many Catholic missionaries whose interest in converting the people of the Americas led him to desire a deep appreciation of indigenous culture and history. His *Natural History*, from which these excerpts are drawn, remains one of the best sources historians have for this first century of contact. Nathaniel Butler, the governor of Bermuda, offers a chilling glimpse at one consequence of new pests without predators in Document 2, which describes a rat infestation on the English colony of Bermuda. In Document 5, three petitions lodged in English colonial courts in the colonies of Plymouth and Maryland depict the burden these animal invaders posed to Indians.

Finally, Documents 1 and 7 illustrate a third aspect of the Columbian exchange, the migration of plants. In Document 1, Acosta draws on his own religious and medical traditions as he describes at length for European readers the new foods he discovered in America and the Caribbean. In Document 7, the English governor of Sierra Leone marvels in September 1792 at the contents of the gardens planted by the colony's new inhabitants. These men and women were largely part of an exodus of former slaves who had sided with the British during the American War for Independence; they were resettled by the British in Nova Scotia, and then transported to Sierra Leone. Their gardens reflect the geographic diversity of their backgrounds.

1. A Priest Accounts for the Plants and Animals of New Spain, 1590

Chapter 16 * Of Bread in the Indies, and Maize

In speaking of plants we will first discuss those that are most characteristic of the Indies and then those that are common both to those lands and Europe. And because plants were grown chiefly to sustain man's life, and the chief food that sustains him is bread, we need to show what sort of bread there is in the Indies and what they use in place of bread. The word for bread is also used in their languages; in Peru it is called *tanta*, and in other places it is known by other names. But the quality and substance of the bread that the Indians possessed and used is very different from ours, for it has not been discovered that they had any sort of wheat or barley or millet or any of the other grains used for bread in Europe. Instead of this they used other grains and roots; the chief place among them all is rightly held by maize, which in Castile is called "Indies wheat" and in Italy "Turkish grain."

Just as wheat has been the ordinary grain in the ancient parts of the globe, which are Europe, Asia, and Africa, so in the regions of the New World it has been, and is, maize, which has been found in almost all the realms of the West Indies, in Peru, New Spain, the New Kingdom of Granada, Guatemala, Chile, and everywhere on the continent. I do not know whether in olden times they used maize in the Windward Islands, which are Cuba, Hispaniola, Jamaica, and San Juan; today they make more use of yucca and cassava, of which I will speak shortly.

I believe that maize is not inferior to wheat in its strength and power of sustenance, but it is heavier and gives more heat and engenders blood; hence those who first eat it, if they overindulge, often suffer from bloating and the itch. It grows on stalks, each of which bears one or two ears that contain the grains, and although the grains are large there are many of them, for we counted seven hundred grains on some of the ears. It is planted by hand and not scattered freely; it requires a hot and humid land. It grows very abundantly in many parts of the Indies; it is not rare to harvest three hundred bushels from one planting.

There are different kinds of maize just as there are different kinds of wheat: one kind is heavy and nourishing, another small and dry and called *moroche*; maize leaves and its green stalks make excellent fodder for horses and mules and even in dry form serve as straw. The grains themselves are better food for horses and mules than barley, and it is common in those parts to water the animals before they give them corn to eat; for if they drink on top of the corn they will swell up and have cramps, as is also the case with wheat.

The Indians' bread is maize, which they usually eat boiled in the grain and hot, and they call this *mote*; the Chinese and Japanese also eat rice boiled, along with its hot water. . . . And, to show that there is no lack of ingenuity in New World cookery, they have also contrived to make a kind of pastry with this dough by mixing the finest of their flour with sugar, and these biscuits are called *melindres*.

Source: José de Acosta, *Natural and Moral History of the Indies*, ed. by Jane E. Mangan (Durham: Duke University Press, 2002), pp. 197–200, 230–232.

Maize serves the Indians not only as bread but also as wine, for they make drinks out of it with which they become quite drunk and more rapidly than with wine made of grapes. The maize wine that is called *azua* in Peru, and more commonly in the Indies *chicha*, is made in various ways. The strongest is made like beer, first soaking the grains of corn until they start to sprout and then boiling it in a certain way; it becomes so strong that a few drinks leave a man unable to stand. In Peru they call this drink *sora*, and it is forbidden by law owing to the serious consequences that it entails, for it causes violent drunkenness. But the law is of little use, for the Indians drink it regardless and are capable of dancing and drinking for days and nights together. . . .

When the maize is tender on the ear and milky, both Indians and Spaniards eat it as a dainty either boiled or roasted, and they also put it in the pot and in stews, and it is a good food. The grains of maize are very rich and serve as lard in place of oil, so that maize is used in the Indies for animals and men, for bread and wine, and for oil. And that is what the viceroy Don Francisco de Toledo used to say, that Peru had two things of substance and wealth, which were maize and the flocks of that land. And truly he was right, for both of these serve any number of uses. As for how maize came to the Indies, and why this most useful grain is called "Turkish" in Italy, I can ask this question sooner than answer it. . . . Verily, the Creator scattered his largesse everywhere; to this hemisphere he gave wheat, which is the chief nourishment of man, and to the hemisphere of the Indies he gave maize, which holds second place after wheat for the sustenance of men and animals. . . .

Chapter 33 * Of Sheep and Cattle

I find that there are three kinds of animals in the Indies: some that have been taken there by Spaniards; others that, although they have not been brought from Spain, are of the same species as in Europe, and others that are native to the Indies and are not found in Spain. Among the first group are sheep, cattle, goats, pigs, horses, asses, dogs, cats, and other such animals, for all these kinds are found in the Indies. Sheep have multiplied greatly, and if their wool could be utilized by shipping it to Europe it would be one of the Indies' greatest riches, for sheep have a great abundance of pasturage there and in many places the grass never dries up; the freedom of pastures and grazing lands is so great that there is no individual ownership of them in Peru. Each man grazes his flock where he pleases, and for this reason meat is usually cheap and abundant there, as are other products from sheep such as cheese, milk, and so on. For a time all the wool went to waste, until textile workshops were built to make cloth and blankets, which has been of great help to the poor folk in that land, for Castilian clothing is very expensive. There are various textile workshops in Peru and many more in New Spain, although, either because the wool is coarser or because it is not woven as well, clothing from Spain is much better than that made in the Indies. There used to be men who owned seventy thousand and a hundred thousand head of sheep, and even today there are flocks nearly as large; in Europe this would represent great wealth, and there it is only moderate.

In many parts of the Indies, I believe almost everywhere, sheep cannot be raised successfully because the grass is so tall and the vegetation so rank that only cattle can graze there, and so there are innumerable herds of cattle. And there are two kinds of these, the first being domestic cattle in herds, as in the Charcas district and other provinces of Peru, and as in all of New Spain. The herds are made use of, as in Spain, for meat and butter and calves, the oxen are used for plowing, and so on. There is another kind of cattle that has gone wild, and because of the rough country and great thickets as well as their large numbers these are not branded and have no owners; the first man to hunt and kill them, like game, becomes their owner. The cattle of Hispaniola and other neighboring islands have multiplied so greatly in this way that thousands of ownerless animals roam the woods and fields. These cattle are used for their hides; both whites and blacks go out in the country and chase the bulls and cows, and the animal that they hamstring, when it falls, belongs to them. They flay it and take the hide home, leaving the meat to go to waste on the spot, for no one uses it or even wants it owing to the glut of cattle. This happens so frequently on that island that I was told infection existed in some places from the quantities of rotting meat. The hides that are imported into Spain represent one of the chief products of the islands and New Spain. In the fleet that came from Santo Domingo in fifteen hundred and eighty-seven, there were 35,444 cattle hides. From New Spain came 64,350, which were valued at 96,532 pesos. When one of these fleets unloads, it is astonishing to see the river in Seville, and the sandy bank where all those hides and all that merchandise are displayed. . . .

In Hispaniola dogs have multiplied both in number and size to the point that they are the plague of that island, for they eat the cattle and roam the countryside in packs. A bounty is offered to those who kill them, as is done with wolves in Spain. There were no true dogs in the Indies, only an animal similar to a little dog that the Indians called *alco*; and the Indians are so fond of them that they will go hungry in order to feed them, and when they are walking along the roads they will carry them on their backs or in their bosoms. And if they are ill the dog must stay by them, though they use them for nothing, only good friendship and company.

2. Rats Invade Bermuda, 1617–1618

Sone after . . . came a hott alarme from Sandys tribe, of a fierce assault made by the ratts upon their newe sett corne, who scratched it out of the ground in the night as fast as they put it in in the day; thes race of ratts being (as you have heard) first brought in by the runne away frigate from the West Indies, in Mr. Moores time, began presently so sylently and sodainely to encrease (ther being noe place of the world more apt to nourish them, partly by reason of the sweet temper of the aire, but especially through the generall shelter and covert that it affords them) that they then became felt before they wer feared, and yet not so duely feared as befitted; so that litle or noethinge being done against them at that time, and lesse in the lazie dayes of the six Governours, they wer by this time gotten to so ranck a head that swimeinge in huge troupes from iland to iland (for fishes have bin taken three leauges of at sea with whole ratts in ther bellyes), they eate up the whole country before them, whersoever

Source: J. Henry Lefroy, ed. *The Historye of the Bermudaes or Summer Islands*. London: Hakluyt Society, 1882, pp. 90–92.

they went, utterly devoureinge all the corne they mett with all in an instant; so that, in despight of all the catts sent from out of England, and the layeinges of poyson, the Governours often fireinge of the whole ilands, to the huge wast and spoyle of much excellent cæder timber, or whatsoever els could be devised against them, they every day more and more so multiplied and grewe upon the poore amazed people, as that it very litle wanted that the whole place had once againe bin utterly and quite left voide of her reasonable inhabitants: and with out all question, this ill had not fayled to have befallen, had not God (who noe doubt hath an especiall worck in the peopling of thes partes with Christians), by his owne hand, in great mercy, swept them all away in an instant, when it was least expected; for not long after that the Governour, . . . had determined once againe to fall upon another generall burneinge of the whole ilands, to the extreame discontent of all men, and especially of Mr. Lewes the minister, who openly preached against it, so that the Governour could never endure him afterwards; behold, by a soudaine fall of great store of raine, and some cold northerly windes bloweinge with all, in a moment, and when noe man durst so much as hope for so happy a turne, thes mightie armies of ravenous ratts are clean taken awaye, vanish, and are scarce one to be found in a share; but in steed of them, shortly after, come in marchinge towards the houses whole troupes of great and fatt wild catts, who haveinge formerly found foode ynough upon these vermin abroad, and so become wild and sauvage, are now againe in this their necessitie, and by want of wonted reliefe, forced to returne to their first tamenesse; sheweinge themselves herein like thoes unthanckfull badd naturall men who never respect longer nor farther than to serve their owne turnes. And thus was this desperate wound recovered, beinge a blessinge which, comeinge indeed imediately from heaven, not only procured and established the well-fare and very subsistance of this colony, but with all (as fallinge out in his time), carryed with it an accidentall addition of much reputation to the Governour; for, in such events, fewe men trouble themselves to looke out so far as the causes, but rest well ynough contented with the sence of the effects.

3. Two Governors Describe the New England Smallpox Epidemic, 1633–1634

Governor John Winthrop's Account

Nov. 1633   A great mortalitye amonge the Indians: Chickatabut [&] the Sagamor of Naponsett died, & many of his people The disease was the small poxe: some of them were cured by suche meanes as they had from us: many of their children escaped & were kept by the English . . .

John Sagamore died of the smallpoxe: & allmost all his people (above 30: buried by mr maverick of winesementt in one daye) the townes in the Baye tooke awaye many of the Children: but most of them died soone after.

Source: Richard S. Dunn, James Savage, and Laetitia Yeandle, eds., *The Journal of John Winthrop 1630–1649* (Cambridge: Belknap Press of Harvard University Press, 1996), pp. 101, 105, 108–109, and *Winthrop Papers* (Massachusetts Historical Society, 1943), vol. 3, pp. 171–172; William Bradford, *Of Plymouth Plantation, 1620–1647*, ed. Samuel Eliot Morison (New York: Knopf, 1970), pp. 270–271.

James Sagamore of Sagus died allso, & most of his folk. Jo: Sagamore desired to be brought amonge the Englishe (so he was) & promised (if he recovered) to live with the Englishe, & serve their God. he lefte one sonne, which he disposed to mr willson the paster of Boston, to be brought up by him. he gave to the Governor a good quantity of wampompege, & to divers others of the Englishe he gave giftes, & tooke order for the payment of his owne debtes & his mens: he died in a perswasion that he should goe to the Englishe mens God. diverse of them in their sickenesse, confessed that the Englishe mens God was a good God, & that, if they recovered they would serve him.

It wrought muche with them, that when their owne people forsooke them, yet the Englishe came dayly & ministered to them, & yet fewe tooke any Infection by it. Amonge others, mr maverick of winesemett is worthy of a perpetuall remembrance himselfe his wife & servantes went dayly to them, ministerd to their necessityes, & buried their dead, & took home many of their Children, so did other of the neighbors. . . .

Janry. 20:   Hall & the 2: other who went to Conectecott november 3: came now home, havinge lost themselves & endured muche miserye. they enformed us, that the small poxe was gone as farr as any Indian plantation was knowne to the west & muche people dead of it. by reason wherof they could have no trade. At Narigansett (by the Indians report) there died 700. but beyond Pascat. none. to the E: . . .

Jan^ry 30:   Jo: Seales who ranne from his master to the Indians came home againe he was at a place 12: miles off where were 7: Indians whereof 4: died of the poxe while he was there. . . .

John Winthrop to Sir Simonds D'Ewes, July 21, 1634

MUCHE HONORED SIR, . . . But for the natives in these parts, Gods hand hath so pursued them, as for 300 miles space, the greatest parte of them are swept awaye by the small poxe, which still continues among them: So as God hathe hereby cleered our title to this place, and those who remaine in these parts, being in all not 50, have putt themselves under our protection, and freely confined themselves and their interest within certain Limitts.

Governor William Bradford's Account

I am now to relate some strange and remarkable passages. There was a company of people lived in the country up above in the River of Connecticut a great way from their trading house there, and were enemies to those Indians which lived about them, and of whom they stood in some fear, being a stout people. About a thousand of them had enclosed themselves in a fort which they had strongly palisadoed about. Three or four Dutchmen went up in the beginning of winter to live with them, to get their trade and prevent them for bringing it to the English or to fall into amity with them; but at spring to bring all down to their place. But their enterprise failed. For it pleased God to visit these Indians with a great sickness and such a mortality that of a thousand, above nine and a half hundred of them died, and many of them did rot above ground for want of burial. And the Dutchmen almost starved before they could get away, for ice and snow; but about February they got with much difficulty to their trading house; whom they kindly relieved, being almost spent with hunger and cold. Being thus refreshed by them divers days, they got to their own place and the Dutch were very thankful for this kindness.

This spring also, those Indians that lived about their trading house there, fell sick of the small pox and died most miserably; for a sorer disease cannot befall them, they fear it more than the plague. For usually they that have this disease have them in abundance, and for want of bedding and linen and other helps they fall into a lamentable condition as they lie on their hard mats, the pox breaking and mattering and running one into another, their skin cleaving by reason thereof to the mats they lie on. When they turn them, a whole side will flay off at once as it were, and they will be all of a gore blood, most fearful to behold. And then being very sore, what with cold and other distempers, they die like rotten sheep. The condition of this people was so lamentable and they fell down so generally of this disease as they were in the end not able to help one another, no not to make a fire nor to fetch a little water to drink, nor any to bury the dead. But would strive as long as they could, and when they could procure no other means to make fire, they would burn the wooden trays and dishes they ate their meat in, and their very bows and arrows. And some would crawl out on all fours to get a little water, and sometimes die by the way and not be able to get in again. But of those of the English house, though at first they were afraid of the infection, yet seeing their woeful and sad condition and hearing their pitiful cries and lamentations, they had compassion of them, and daily fetched them wood and water and made them fires, got them victuals whilst they lived; and buried them when they died. For very few of them escaped, notwithstanding they did what they could for them to the hazard of themselves. The chief sachem himself now died and almost all his friends and kindred. But by the marvelous goodness and providence of God, not one of the English was so much as sick or in the least measure tainted with this disease, though they daily did these offices for them for many weeks together. And this mercy which they showed them was kindly taken and thankfully acknowledged of all the Indians that knew or heard of the same. And their masters here did much commend and reward them for the same.

4. Indians Respond to Epidemics in New France, 1637, 1640

Of the Persecutions that We Suffered in the Year 1637.

I said a word, last year, about our new Residence in the village which is almost the heart of the country. Our cabin was not yet half finished when it attracted these peoples from all directions to come and see us; the crowd there was so great that it was a more than sufficient occupation to keep watch upon their hands, in addition to the great number of sick persons who continually needed our visits.

Source: Reuben Gold Thwaites, *Jesuit Relations* (Cleveland: The Burrows Brothers, 1898), vol. 15, pp. 17–31, vol. 19, pp. 9–19, 23–25.

Our Fathers had erected a sort of Altar, where they had placed some little pictures, in order thus to secure opportunity to explain to them what was the principal motive that brought us here and had attracted us to their village. The whole Cabin resounded with expressions of admiration at the sight of these extraordinary objects; above all, they could not weary of gazing at two pictures—one of Our Lord, and the other of Our Lady. We had some difficulty in making them believe that these were only flat paintings, especially as these pictures were of life size, for the small figures make but little impression upon their minds. We had to leave them exposed all day, in order to satisfy all the people.

This first view cost us very dear; for, without speaking of the annoyance that inquisitive persons have since caused us,—that is to say, all the people who arrive from other villages,—if we derived thence some advantage for speaking to them of our Holy mysteries and disposing them to the knowledge of the true God, some of them took occasion to spread new reports and to authorize the previous calumnies, namely, that we were causing the death of these peoples by our Images.

In a few days the country was completely imbued with this opinion, that we were, without any doubt, the authors of this so universal contagion. It is very probable that those who invented these slanders did not believe them at all; yet they spoke in so positive terms that the majority no longer doubted them. The women and children looked upon us as persons who brought them misfortune. God be forever blessed, who willed that for the space of three or four months, while these persecutions were at their height, we should be deprived of nearly all human consolation. The people of our village seemed to spare us more than the others, yet these evil reports were so persistent and were such a common subject of conversation in their assemblies that suspicion began to take hold upon them, and the most prominent ones, who had loved us and had been accustomed to speak in our favor, became entirely mute, and when they were constrained to speak, they had recourse to excuses, and justified themselves as well as they could for having built us a cabin.

On the 26th of June, the niece of Pierre, our first Christian, died, notwithstanding the vows and prayers we had offered for her recovery. This was the first blow to this family, which was followed some time afterward by the death of his wife; and after his return from the trade the malady carried off one of his daughters, and his brother-in-law. Several slanderous tongues, which were already of themselves fruitful enough in impostures and calumnies, thought they had a new opportunity to throw the cat at our legs,—alleging as their motive that affliction had not fallen upon this cabin until after the solemn Baptism of Pierre. In fact, they had passed the winter very comfortably, the majority of the other cabins having been very badly treated by the disease.

This idea so deeply entered the minds of some of them that one entire village, according to the report made to us, decided no longer to use French kettles, imagining that everything which came in any way from us was capable of communicating the disease to them.

There came another piece of news from the Tobacco Nation (for these reports continued to increase, even in the surrounding Nations). It was asserted that a Savage, stricken with this pestilential disease, had vomited up in some blood a leaden pellet, whence they concluded that a Frenchman had bewitched him. We were obliged every day to answer the bearers of similar news; and there were very few of them capable of understanding the arguments we brought forward to show them how disinclined we were to these evil thoughts. Their usual answer was that "this was being constantly said everywhere; and that, besides, all the inhabitants of the Island where these peoples live had their brains upset,—that the death of so many of their relatives had unsettled their minds; and so one need not be surprised if, like madmen, they should inconsiderately lay the blame on whatever was at hand." For our own part, we consider ourselves too highly honored to wear the livery of Our Lord; one thing alone afflicted us—to see Hell triumphing for a time, and carrying away so many Souls, whose danger we realized without being able to stretch out our hands and place them in the way of salvation. However, we never ceased making our usual trips until at the very worst, when we saw that our holy Mysteries were not received with the respect that they merited, and we judged that these visits might be prejudicial to the progress of the Holy Gospel.

The mortality prevailed everywhere, but especially in the village of Angoutenc, which was only three-quarters of a league from us. We made two visits there, but without effect; we returned thither on the 3rd of July. We found a considerable number of sick people, but they wrapped themselves in their robes and covered their faces, for fear of speaking to us; others, upon seeing us, hastened to close the doors of their cabins; we already had our feet upon the threshold of two others, when we were driven away, the reason given being that there were sick persons there. Ah! this was precisely what we sought, nor did we lose courage thereat; and the more the devil played his tricks, the more we felt ourselves inspired not to abandon this poor village. All things considered, we judged that this hostile aspect arose only from the fact that they were not yet well informed as to our purpose in these visits,—for they are not accustomed to visit one another in this way during their illnesses, unless they are near relatives; so it was a great novelty to them to see persons who sought out only the sick, and, moreover, the most wretched and most forsaken. Hence, we returned there on the 8th of the same [month], not so much in behalf of the sick as to see some old men and those who had the management of affairs, that we might try to make them understand our purpose. We very fortunately encountered a Captain of great intelligence. He was made to understand how precious our visits ought to be to them. He listened to us willingly, giving us his word that he would communicate with the Old Men,—saying that, as for himself, he already assured us that he would always look upon us kindly. We went immediately to see those who were most ill, but we were no better received than on the former visit. A certain war Captain no sooner saw us at the door of his cabin than he threatened to split our heads if we went any further. . . .

Afterwards, in our visits, we encountered a very sick old man. "My Nephews" (he said to us at first), "be welcome." He soon reversed the compliment when he learned what brought us there, for he said, the angry blood mounting to his face, "It is you people who are making me die; since you set foot in this house, six days ago, I have eaten nothing; and I have seen you in a dream as persons who are bringing us misfortune; it is you who are making me die." Observe that among these peoples nothing more need be said for a man to have his head split. In fact, notwithstanding the fine promises that I have just mentioned, we noticed afterwards so much coldness on all sides, and so great distrust of us, that we judged it wise to desist entirely from our visits; more than this, upon the advice that Our Father Superior sent us, we remained for some time at anchor, during the tempest. He wrote to us also that, at the close of the feast which had interrupted our council, they had again assembled, and had resolved to kill some Frenchman, whoever he might be. . . .

Of the Hospital. [1640]

The hospital Nuns arrived at Kebec on the first day of the month of August of last year. Scarcely had they disembarked before they found themselves overwhelmed with patients. The hall of the Hospital being too small, it was necessary to erect some cabins, fashioned like those of the Savages, in their garden. Not having enough furniture for so many people, they had to cut in two or three pieces part of the blankets and sheets they had brought for these poor sick people. In a word, instead of taking a little rest, and refreshing themselves after the great discomforts they had suffered upon the sea, they found themselves so burdened and occupied that we had fear of losing them and their hospital at its very birth. The sick came from all directions in such numbers, their stench was so insupportable, the heat so great, the fresh food so scarce and so poor, in a country so new and strange, that I do not know how these good sisters, who almost had not even leisure in which to take a little sleep, endured all these hardships. . . . All the French born in the country were attacked by this contagion, as well as the Savages. Those who came from your France were exempt from it, except two or three, already naturalized to the air of this region.

In brief, from the month of August until the month of May, more than one hundred patients entered the hospital, and more than two hundred poor Savages found relief there, either in temporary treatment or in sleeping there one or two nights, or more. There have been seen as many as ten, twelve, twenty, or thirty of them at a time. Twenty poor sick people have received holy Baptism there; and about twenty-four, quitting this house of mercy, have entered the regions of glory. . . .

What I am about to tell is taken from the letters that the Mother Superior has written me.

"All our sick are very careful to pray to God. They urge us often to pray for them. It is a great consolation to us to see them attentive to prayers evening and morning. They waken one another as soon as the time for prayers draws near. There are some who remain alone a long time in the chapel, before the Blessed Sacrament. . . .

"The patience of our sick astonishes me. I have seen many whose bodies were entirely covered with smallpox, and in a burning fever, complaining no more than if they were not sick, strictly obeying the physician, and showing gratitude for the slightest service that was rendered them.

"Among others, Lazare Petikouchkaouat has left us one of the rarest examples of patience that it is possible to see. You have often seen him in his infirmity. He was seven whole months in our hospital, afflicted with very painful sores in several parts of his body, with a fever that continually preyed upon him and so parched him that he could not quench his thirst. He was seized by a ravenous hunger, which he could not satisfy; he ate continually, and the more he ate the more he wasted away. He reached such a state that his bones actually pierced through his skin. Putrefaction took place, both in his bones and in his skin; a large walnut could have been put in some of his bones, uncovered and all hollowed out by putrefaction; his sores were large and deep; he suffered strangely, but with a patience still more strange. He had himself raised once every day; and, after one cry that he uttered through the violence of the pain caused by touching him, he spoke encouragingly to those who held him, and then thanked them with great gentleness. He particularly loved the young man who offered himself to our hospital to assist the poor patients; but then it must be confessed that this good young man succored him with a charity that cannot be sufficiently praised. He called this patient his consolation. You know how offensive to smell he was—I have never known anything so tainted; yet after his death no bad odor arose from his body, which astonished us. He confessed and received communion frequently, doing so even after you gave him extreme unction. In short, he died with these words upon his lips: 'Jesus chauerimir,' 'Jesus have pity upon me; Jesus, have pity upon me.'" Thus far the Mother.

The secrets of God are unfathomable. This large and powerful Savage had been very proud and dissolute. When he first entered the hospital he was still full of self,— he tried to kill himself, to be freed from the torments that he was suffering; but Father Pijard related, every day of Lent, some story of the Passion in the hall of the poor; this wretched man was touched and piously fell into the line of duty. The Nuns have exercised a most signal charity towards this living skeleton; he is one of those whom God has willed to save through the mercy that is exercised in their hospital.

"I have seen in some of them," continues the Mother, "a great steadfastness at death, and a joy founded upon their hope of going to heaven. Among others, Esperance Itauichpich greatly consoled us. When she first entered our hospital, she had an eager desire to recover her health. She seemed very averse to dying; and yet, as soon as she was told that her sickness was mortal, that it was all over with her, she was not at all shocked; she begged that the Father be sent for, and, having confessed two or three times, in a little while she appeared as resolute and firm as a rock. She saw before her eyes four little children that she was leaving, very poor and very young, and her husband exceedingly disconsolate; and all this did not make her waver. The faith operates strongly in these new Christians. You would say that they are sure that, in leaving this life, they go straight to Paradise." . . .

The Savages who leave the hospital, and who come to see us again at St. Joseph, or at the three Rivers, say a thousand pleasant things about these goods Nuns. They call them "the good," "the liberal," "the charitable." The Mother Superior having fallen sick, these poor Savages were very sorry, the sick blaming themselves for it. "It is we who have made her sick," they said; "she loves us too much; why does she do so much for us?" When this good Mother, having recovered, entered the hall of the poor, they knew not how to welcome her enough. They have good reason to love these good Mothers; for I do not know that parents have so sweet, so strong, and so constant an affection for their children as these good women have for their patients. I have often seen them so overwhelmed that they were utterly exhausted; yet I have never heard them complain, either of the too great number of their patients, or of the infection, or of the trouble they gave them. They have hearts so loving and so tender towards these poor people that, if occasionally some little present were given them, one could be very certain that they would not taste it, however greatly they might need it, everything being dedicated and consecrated to their sick. This charity had to be moderated, and an order was given them to eat at least a part of the little gifts that were made to them, especially when they were not strong. I am not surprised if the Savages, who recognize very clearly this great charity, love, cherish, and honor them.

5. Indians Complain About Animal Trespass, 1656–1664

Plymouth Colony, July 3, 1656

Wheras there hath been complaint made from time to time, by the naighboring Indians on the towne of Rehoboth, of great and unsufferable wronges don in theire corn by the horses and other cattle of the inhabitants of Rehoboth aforsaid, and that we are informed that the fences between the English and Indians there are in a good measure finished; but wheras notwithstanding, by the reason that many horses and other cattle have been wonted to goe into the Indians corn, wherby noe reasonable fence will keep them out, as alsoe the horses and other cattle being apte to swime through the water to the said corne, where noe fence can bee sett up, the Court have ordered, that if the horses or other cattle shall breake in one way or other and treaspase the said Indians, then they have heerby liberty to drive any such horses or other cattle soe treaspasing to Rehoboth towns pound, and shall demaund of the owners of such horses or other cattle six pence a peece, sucking foales excepted; and for such treaspas as shalbee don, the said Indians treaspased shall take two English men of Rehoboth to judge theire dammage, and the owners of the said horses or other cattle shalbee lyable to make good the same.

Plymouth Colony, June 11, 1664

An Order sent downe to Sandwich, as followeth.

To Mr Freeman, Richard Bourne, Mr Dexter, James Skiffe, and Wilłam Bassett, greeł, &c.

Wheras Nanquatnumacke hath complained of wrong done to him in his corne by horses of Sandwich, these are to request you to take some serious and effectuall course that the poor man may have his corne preserved from the horses, either by keeping of them away or some other course, this sommer, or otherwise wee shalbee in some straight what to doe in the case.

This is the Courts desire and order.

Ꝑ me,　　　　NATHANIELL MORTON, Clark.

Plymouth, June 11th, 1664.

Maryland, November 17, 1663

By the Leiuetenn^t Generall　Whereas Sundry Complaints have been made unto mee by the Queene of Portaback in behalfe of her Selfe and Indians und^r her, Intimating how that they have not only left their Towne standing by the water, but have removed themselves farther of even to their utmost bownds of their land—Leaving

---

Source: Shurtleff, Nathaniel B., ed., *Records of the Colony of New Plymouth in New England* (Boston, 1885); v. III, p. 106; v. IV, p. 68; *Proceedings of the Council of Maryland*, v. 3 (Baltimore, 1885, 1965), p. 489.

place to the English to Seate on theire ancient plantations by the River side the English not being (as they informe mee) contented with what Land is allready freely granted Doe still take up land and Seate themselves very nigh unto the said Indians whose stocks of Cattle and hoggs doe and will yearely destroy theire Corne feilds by which meanes they must of necessity come to famine they not knowing the way and meanes to fence in theire Corne feilds as the English doe will soon come to destruction

I doe therefore hereby will and require all p^rsons whatsoever inhabitants of this province to take notice hereof and desist from taking up any land or seating any land (though formerly taken up) and surveyed by them) within three miles att the least of any the said Indian habitations or plantations, Given und^r my hand this 17th day of November 1663

6. William Dampier Wrestles with His Worm, 1676

To be short, I kept to my Work by my self, till I was hindred by a hard, red and angry Swelling like a Boyl, in my right Leg; so painful that I was scarce able to stand on it: but I was directed to roast and apply the Roots of White Lillies (of which here is great plenty, growing by the Creek sides) to draw it to a head. This I did three or four Days, without any benefit. At last I perceived two White Specks in the middle of the Boil; and squeezing it, two small white Worms spurted out: I took them both up in my Hand, and perceived each of them to be invested with three Rows of black, short, stiff Hair, running clear round them; one Row near each end; the other in the middle; each Row distinct from other; and all very regular and uniform. The Worms were about the bigness of a Hens Quill, and about three fourths of an Inch long.

I never saw Worms of this sort breed in any Man's Flesh. Indeed *Guinea Worms* are very frequent in some Places of the *West-Indies*, especially at *Curasao*; They breed as well in Whites as Negroes: And because that Island was formerly a Magazin of Negroes, while the Dutch drove that Trade with the Spaniards, and the Negroes were most subject to them; 'twas therefore believed that other People took them by Infection from them. I rather judge that they are generated by drinking bad Water; and 'tis as likely that the Water of the other Island of *Aruba* and *Bonariry* may produce the same Effects; for many of those that went with me from thence to *Virginia* (mentioned in my former Volume) were troubled with them after our arrival there: particularly I my self had one broke out in my Ancle, after I had been there five or six Months.

These Worms are no bigger than a large brown Thread, but (as I have heard) five or six Yards long; and if it breaks in drawing out, that part which remains in the Flesh will putrifie, and be very painful, and indanger the Patients Life; or at least the use of that Limb: and I have known some that have been scarified and cut strangely, to take out the Worm. I was in great torment before it came out: my Leg and Ancle swell'd and look'd very red and angry; and I kept a Plaister, to it, to bring it to a Head. At last drawing off my Plaister, out came about three Inches of the Worm; and my pain abated presently. Till then I was ignorant of my Malady; and the Gentlewoman, at

---

Source: William Dampier, *Voyages and Descriptions* (London: Printed for James Knapton, 1700), vol. 2, 89–91.

whose House I was, took it for a Nerve; but I knew enough what it was, and presently roll'd it up on a small Stick. After that I opened it every Morning and Evening; and strained it out gently, about two Inches at a time, not without some pain, till at length I had got out about two Foot.

Riding with one Mr. *Richardson*, who was going to a Negro to have his Horse cured of a gall'd Back, I asked the Negro if he could undertake my Leg: and which he did readily; and in the mean time I observed his Method in curing the Horse; which was this. First he strok'd the sore Place, then applying to it a little rough Powder, which looked like Tobacco Leaves dryed and crumbled small, and mumbling some Words to himself, he blew upon the part three times; and waving his Hands as often over it said, it would be well speedily. His Fee for the Cure was a White Cock.

Then coming to me, and looking on the Worm in my Ancle, he promised to cure it in three Days, demanding also a White Cock for his pains, and using exactly the same Method with me, as he did with the Horse. He bad me not open it in three Days; but I did not stay so long; for the next Morning the Cloath being rubb'd off, I unbound it, and found the Worm broken off, and the Hole quite healed up. I was afraid the remaining part would have given some trouble, but have not felt any pain there from that day to this.

7. Governor Clarkson Describes the Gardens of Sierra Leone, 1792

September 21st. . . .   The gardens of the settlers begin to look very pleasing, the Nova Scotians brought out with them a quantity of *good seeds*, and have been able to furnish the officers with many vegetables, especially cabbages, besides satisfying their own wants—the English vegetables which *thrive* here best, appear as yet to be the cabbage, the whole pumpkin tribe, purslain, sage, certain kinds of beans, magarone, thyme, cresses, besides all tropical fruits, and some American vegetables. In many of the houses of the settlers are seen great quantities of beef and pork that they have saved out of their allowance, and hung up along the ridges of their houses to smoke, as provisions for the time when they first go upon their lots of land. In the skirts of the town particularly are also in the gardens sweet potatoes, cassava and ground-nuts in abundance, rice, maize, yams, with many other excellent tropical plants in tolerable plenty; in many places rich pastures for cattle. Mr. Afzelius superintends a garden at present dedicated to culinary purposes for the Company's officers, but which will hereafter serve for botanical experiments. I called to-day upon Mr. Wakerell and the other invalids and promised to take them a little trip to sea for a few days in hopes of restoring them to health. Mr. Grey is to attend upon Mr. Wakerell and take all the accounts with him in the hope of decyphering them. . . .

I have been so disappointed in consequence of the illness of the officers and the debility usually attending every one after the fever leaves them, that I dare not reckon upon much progress being likely to be made in our present attempt. If we can get to sea we shall be free at any rate from continual interruptions, which will

Source: "Diary of Lieutenant J. Clarkson, R.N. (Governor, 1792)," *Sierra Leone Studies* 8 (March 1927), 51–53.

greatly aid us, but Mr. Wakerell has been too long ill for me to expect much good for his *exertions* in unravelling intricate accounts.

8. Joseph Dupuis Complains About the Fevers of the Gold Coast, 1824

From January, the month I landed on the Gold Coast, to the following June, my health was unimpaired by the effect of climate, while many sunk under the mortal influence of tropical diseases; yet I courted rather than shunned exposure to the air by night as well as day.* It was the opinion of my friends that the seven or eight years of "seasoning" I had undergone in Mauritania rendered me less susceptible of danger; but in this sentiment I never could agree with them; and I was the more prejudiced in favour of my own way of reasoning when the periodical rains set in, for I was instantly assailed by a fever, which for severity and duration, was of the most dangerous character. When from this attack I emerged to a state of convalescence, which I did only under symptons of extreme debility after the lapse of nearly two months, I retired from the castle to a little cottage in the "bush," where for six ensuing weeks I gradually improved in health. But the season of fogs, mists, and exhalations succeeding the first fall, as it does upon this parallel of latitude, I again relapsed under the malignant influence of the period. The fever at this time attached itself locally† to the liver, spleen, &c., and although the danger was more remote than heretofore, yet as I laboured long under it, and grew gradually worse, I had no hopes of gaining strength sufficient for my contemplated journey to the interior, unless by a change of air. Thus prepossessed, during the height of the ulterior rains which usually set in in the month of September, I embarked on a cruise in his Majesty's ship Pheasant, commanded by Captain Kelly, an officer every way conspicuous for his gentleman-like conduct.

The rains chased us from the coast to the bight of Benin, whither we were bound, and for five ensuing weeks the strides of death among the crew were considerable. My health continued to be seriously bad, and the cruise becoming irksome, I availed myself of an opportunity that offered to transship myself to the Snapper gun-brig, (commanded by a late lamented friend) then on her passage back to Cape Coast. A tornado which we experienced, and the set of the current together, carried us to our destination in two or three days, and when I set foot again on shore at the close of November, I was little improved in health. The rains, however, had ceased, and in less then a week my disorder wholly subsided. I recovered, seemingly, to the most perfect state of health.

---

*I am satisfied, from the result of my own experience in Africa, that many fall victims to the climate from the adoption of a course of training improperly termed prudential; viz. a *sudden* change of diet, from *ship's fare* to a scanty sustenance of vegetable matter, (rejecting even a moderate proportion of wine) and seclusion in their apartments from the sun and atmosphere. Habits of this kind have, at least, a natural tendency to stagnate the flow of healthy juices, and render the body unfit for exertion. Many there are, however, who fall victims to intemperate habits.

†This is a very common symptom of the progress of disease upon the constitution of Europeans between the tropics.

Source: Joseph Dupuis, *Journal of a Residence in Ashantee*, ed. W. E. F. Ward (London: Frank Cass, 1966, second edition), pp. v–vi.

◁ E S S A Y S

These three essays by Alfred W. Crosby, Marcy Norton, and Donald R. Wright convey the complexity and scope of the processes contained within the Columbian exchange. Crosby's essay sketches the contribution of Eurasian plants, animals, and pathogens to facilitating European dominion around the globe. Within the Atlantic world, Europeans found their attempts to inhabit tropical Africa hindered by disease environments well into the nineteenth century, while they were able to settle safely in most parts of the Americas. Crosby's essay might make European domination in the Americas seem almost inevitable, but Norton and Wright remind us that the Columbian exchange went in many directions and was always mediated by factors specific to individual locales and historic moments. Norton and Wright focus on two American plants—cacao and peanuts—and the products generated from them—chocolate, oils, and soap. Marcy Norton argues that the Spanish had to learn to like chocolate, and that they did so within the specific context of Spanish occupation and settlement in the Indies. The asymmetries of conquest, the peculiar demography of early Spanish migration to central America, the reliance of Spanish men on indigenous women, the challenges of Atlantic transport: all helped the Spanish to acquire a taste for the kind of chocolate they would consume in Europe. The peanut, regarded for centuries in The Gambia as good only for animal fodder and the desperately hungry, experienced a revolution in the 1830s and 40s as British manufacturers sought African markets for British goods. These markets required forms of payment, and enterprising men discovered that peanut oils were useful in the cleaning products made popular by a culture that increasingly prized hygiene. Both Norton and Wright illustrate the configuration of variables—familiarity, interest, demand, taste, science, commerce, human initiative, and choice—that dictated how the Columbian exchange occurred.

Europe's Biological Conquest

ALFRED W. CROSBY

Europeans in North America, especially those with an interest in gardening and botany, are often stricken with fits of homesickness at the sight of certain plants which, like themselves, have somehow strayed thousands of miles eastward across the Atlantic. Vladimir Nabokov, the Russian exile, had such an experience on the mountain slopes of Oregon:

> Do you recognize that clover?
> Dandelions, *l'or du pauvre*?
> (Europe, nonetheless, is over.)

A century earlier the success of European weeds in America inspired Charles Darwin to goad the American botanist, Asa Gray: "Does it not hurt your Yankee pride that we thrash you so confoundly? I am sure Mrs. Gray will stick up for your own weeds. Ask her whether they are not more honest, downright good sort of weeds."

The common dandelion, *l'or du pauvre*, despite its ubiquity and its bright yellow flower, is not at all the most visible of the Old World immigrants in North America. Vladimir Nabokov was a prime example of the most visible kind: the *Homo sapiens*

Source: Alfred W. Crosby, "Ecological Imperialism: The Overseas Migration of Western Europeans as a Biological Phenomenon," *Texas Quarterly*, 1978 21(1): 10–22. Reprinted with permission of Dr. Alfred W. Crosby, author of *The Columbian Exchange, Ecological Imperialism,* and *Children of the Sun.*

of European origin. Europeans and their descendants, who comprise the majority of human beings in North America and in a number of other lands outside of Europe, are the most spectacularly successful overseas migrants of all time. How strange it is to find Englishmen, Germans, Frenchmen, Italians, and Spaniards comfortably ensconced in places with names like Wollongong (Australia), Rotorua (New Zealand), and Saskatoon (Canada), where obviously other peoples should dominate, as they must have at one time.

None of the major genetic groupings of humankind is as oddly distributed about the world as European, especially Western European, whites. Almost all the peoples we call Mongoloids live in the single contiguous land mass of Asia. Black Africans are divided between three continents—their homeland and North and South America—but most of them are concentrated in their original latitudes, the tropics, facing each other across one ocean. European whites were all recently concentrated in Europe, but in the last few centuries have burst out, as energetically as if from a burning building, and have created vast settlements of their kind in the South Temperate Zone and North Temperate Zone (excepting Asia, a continent already thoroughly and irreversibly tenanted). In Canada and the United States together they amount to nearly ninety percent of the population; in Argentina and Uruguay together to over ninety-five percent; in Australia to ninety-eight percent; and in New Zealand to ninety percent. The only nations in the Temperate Zones outside of Asia which do not have enormous majorities of European whites are Chile, with a population of two-thirds mixed Spanish and Indian stock, and South Africa, were blacks outnumber whites six to one. How odd that these two, so many thousands of miles from Europe, should be exceptions in *not* being predominantly pure European.

Europeans have conquered Canada, the United States, Argentina, Uruguay, Australia, and New Zealand not just militarily and economically and technologically—as they did India, Nigeria, Mexico, Peru, and other tropical lands, whose native peoples have long since expelled or interbred with and even absorbed the invaders. In the Temperate Zone lands listed above Europeans conquered and triumphed demographically. These, for the sake of convenience, we will call the Lands of the Demographic Takeover.

There is a long tradition of emphasizing the contrasts between Europeans and Americans—a tradition honored by such names as Henry James and Frederick Jackson Turner—but the vital question is really why Americans are so European. And why the Argentinians, the Uruguayans, the Australians, and the New Zealanders are so European in the obvious genetic sense?

The reasons for the relative failure of the European demographic takeover in the tropics are clear. In tropical Africa, until recently, Europeans died in droves of the fevers; in tropical America they died almost as fast of the same diseases, plus a few native American additions. Furthermore, in neither region did European agricultural techniques, crops, and animals prosper. Europeans did try to found colonies for settlement, rather than merely exploitation, but they failed or achieved only partial success in the hot lands. The Scots left their bones as monument to their short-lived colony at Darien at the turn of the eighteenth century. The English Puritans who skipped Massachusetts Bay Colony to go to Providence Island in the Caribbean Sea did not even achieve a permanent settlement, much less a Commonwealth of God.

The Portuguese who went to northeastern Brazil created viable settlements, but only by perching themselves on top of first a population of native Indian laborers and then, when these faded away, a population of laborers imported from Africa. They did achieve a demographic takeover, but only by interbreeding with their servants. The Portuguese in Angola, who helped supply those servants, never had a breath of a chance to achieve a demographic takeover. There was much to repel and little to attract the mass of Europeans to the tropics, and so they stayed home or went to the lands where life was healthier, labor more rewarding, and where white immigrants, by their very number, encouraged more immigration.

In the cooler lands, the colonies of the Demographic Takeover, Europeans achieved very rapid population growth by means of immigration, by increased life span, and by maintaining very high birth rates. Rarely has population expanded more rapidly than it did in the eighteenth and nineteenth centuries in these lands. It is these lands, especially the United States, that enabled Europeans and their overseas offspring to expand from something like eighteen percent of the human species in 1650 to well over thirty percent in 1900. Today 670 million Europeans live in Europe, and 250 million or so other Europeans—genetically as European as any left behind in the Old World—live in the Lands of the Demographic Takeover, an ocean or so from home. What the Europeans have done with unprecedented success in the past few centuries can accurately be described by a term from apiculture: they have swarmed.

They swarmed to lands which were populated at the time of European arrival by peoples as physically capable of rapid increase as the Europeans, and yet who are now small minorities in their homelands and sometimes no more than relict populations. These population explosions among colonial Europeans of the past few centuries coincided with population crashes among the aborigines. If overseas Europeans have historically been less fatalistic and grim than their relatives in Europe, it is because they have viewed the histories of their nations very selectively. Charles Darwin, as a biologist rather than a historian, . . . when he returned from his world voyage on the *Beagle* in the 1830s, wrote, "Wherever the European has trod, death seems to pursue the aboriginal."

Any respectable theory which attempts to explain the Europeans' demographic triumphs has to provide explanations for at least two phenomena. The first is the decimation and demoralization of the aboriginal populations of Canada, the United States, Argentina, and others. The obliterating defeat of these populations was not simply due to European technological superiority. The Europeans who settled in temperate South Africa seemingly had the same advantages as those who settled in Virginia and New South Wales, and yet how different was their fate. The Bantu-speaking peoples, who now overwhelmingly outnumber the whites in South Africa, were superior to their American, Australian, and New Zealand counterparts in that they possessed iron weapons, but how much more inferior to a musket or a rifle is a stone-pointed spear than an iron-pointed spear? The Bantu have prospered demographically not because of their numbers at the time of first contact with whites, which were probably not greater per square mile than those of the Indians east of the Mississippi River. Rather, the Bantu have prospered because they survived military conquest, avoided the conquerors, or became their indispensable servants—and in the long run because they reproduced faster than the whites. In contrast, why did so few of the natives of the Lands of the Demographic Takeover survive?

Second, we must explain the stunning, even awesome success of European agriculture, that is, the European way of manipulating the environment in the Lands of the Demographic Takeover. The difficult progress of the European frontier in the Siberian *taiga* or the Brazilian *sertão* or the South African *veldt* contrasts sharply with its easy, almost fluid advance in North America. Of course, the pioneers of North America would never have characterized their progress as easy: their lives were filled with danger, deprivation, and unremitting labor; but as a group they always succeeded in taming whatever portion of North America they wanted within a few decades and usually a good deal less time. . . .

In attempting to explain these two phenomena, let us examine four categories of organisms deeply involved in European expansion: (1) human beings; (2) animals closely associated with human beings—both the desirable animals like horses and cattle and undesirable varmints like rats and mice; (3) pathogens or microorganisms that cause disease in humans; and (4) weeds. Is there a pattern in the histories of these groups which suggests an overall explanation for the phenomenon of the Demographic Takeover or which at least suggests fresh paths of inquiry?

Europe has exported something in excess of sixty million people in the past few hundred years. Great Britain alone exported over twenty million. The great mass of these white emigrants went to the United States, Argentina, Canada, Australia, Uruguay, and New Zealand. (Other areas to absorb comparable quantities of Europeans were Brazil and Russia east of the Urals. These would qualify as Lands of the Demographic Takeover except that very large fractions of their populations are non-European.)

In stark contrast, very few aborigines of the Americas, Australia, or New Zealand ever went to Europe. Those who did often died not long after arrival. The fact that the flow of human migration was almost entirely from Europe to her colonies and not vice versa is not startling—or very enlightening. Europeans controlled overseas migration, and Europe needed to export, not import, labor. But this pattern of one-way migration is significant in that it reappears in other connections.

The vast expanses of forests, savannahs, and steppes in the Lands of the Demographic Takeover were inundated by animals from the Old World, chiefly from Europe. Horses, cattle, sheep, goats, and pigs have for hundreds of years been among the most numerous of the quadrupeds of these lands, which were completely lacking in these species at the time of first contact with the Europeans. By 1600 enormous feral herds of horses and cattle surged over the pampas of the Río de la Plata (today's Argentina and Uruguay) and over the plains of northern Mexico. By the beginning of the seventeenth century packs of Old World dogs gone wild were among the predators of these herds.

In the forested country of British North America population explosions among imported animals were also spectacular, but only by European standards, not by those of Spanish America. In 1700 in Virginia feral hogs, said one witness, "swarm like vermaine upon the Earth," and young gentlemen were entertaining themselves by hunting wild horses of the inland counties. In Carolina the herds of cattle were "incredible, being from one to two thousand head in one Man's Possession." In the eighteenth and early nineteenth centuries the advancing European frontier from New England to the Gulf of Mexico was preceded into Indian territory by an *avant-garde* of semi-wild herds of hogs and cattle tended, now and again, by semi-wild herdsmen, white and black. . . .

In the Lands of the Demographic Takeover the European pioneers were accompanied and often preceded by their domesticated animals, walking sources of food, leather, fiber, power, and wealth, and these animals often adapted more rapidly to the new surroundings and reproduced much more rapidly than their masters. To a certain extent, the success of Europeans as colonists was automatic as soon as they put their tough, fast, fertile, and intelligent animals ashore. The latter were sources of capital that sought out their own sustenance, improvised their own protection against the weather, fought their own battles against predators and, if their masters were smart enough to allow calves, colts, and lambs to accumulate, could and often did show the world the amazing possibilities of compound interest.

The honey bee is the one insect of worldwide importance which human beings have domesticated, if we may use the word in a broad sense. Many species of bees and other insects produce honey, but the one which does so in greatest quantity and which is easiest to control is a native of the Mediterranean area and the Middle East, the honey bee (*Apis mellifera*). The European has probably taken this sweet and short-tempered servant to every colony he ever established, from Arctic to Antarctic Circle, and the honey bee has always been one of the first immigrants to set off on its own. . . .

Thomas Jefferson tells us that the Indians of North America called the honey bees "English flies," and St. John de Crèvecoeur, his contemporary, wrote that "the Indians look upon them with an evil eye, and consider their progress into the interior of the continent as an omen of the white man's approach: thus, as they discover the bees, the news of the event, passing from mouth to mouth, spreads sadness and consternation on all sides."

Domesticated creatures that traveled from the Lands of the Demographic Takeover to Europe are few. Australian aborigines and New Zealand Maoris had a few tame dogs, unimpressive by Old World standards and unwanted by the whites. Europe happily accepted the American Indians' turkeys and guinea pigs, but had no need for their dogs, llamas, and alpacas. Again the explanation is simple: Europeans, who controlled the passage of large animals across the oceans, had no need to reverse the process.

It is interesting and perhaps significant, though, that the exchange was just as one sided for varmints, the small mammals whose migrations Europeans often tried to stop. None of the American or Australian or New Zealand equivalents of rats have become established in Europe, but Old World varmints, especially rats, have colonized right alongside the Europeans in the Temperate Zones. Rats of assorted sizes, some of them almost surely European immigrants, were tormenting Spanish Americans by at least the end of the sixteenth century. European rats established a beachhead in Jamestown, Virginia, as early as 1609, when they almost starved out the colonists by eating their food stores. In Buenos Aires the increase in rats kept pace with that of cattle, according to an early nineteenth century witness. . . .

Europe, in return for her varmints, has received muskrats and gray squirrels and little else from America, and nothing at all of significance from Australia or New Zealand, and we might well wonder if muskrats and squirrels really qualify as varmints. As with other classes of organisms, the exchange has been a one-way street.

None of Europe's emigrants were as immediately and colossally successful as its pathogens, the microorganisms that make human beings ill, cripple them, and kill them. Whenever and wherever Europeans crossed the oceans and settled, the pathogens they carried created prodigious epidemics of smallpox, measles, tuberculosis, influenza, and a number of other diseases. It was this factor, more than any other, that Darwin had in mind as he wrote of the Europeans' deadly tread.

The pathogens transmitted by the Europeans, unlike the Europeans themselves or most of their domesticated animals, did at least as well in the tropics as in the temperate Lands of the Demographic Takeover. Epidemics devastated Mexico, Peru, Brazil, Hawaii, and Tahiti soon after the Europeans made the first contact with aboriginal populations. Some of these populations were able to escape demographic defeat because their initial numbers were so large that a small fraction was still sufficient to maintain occupation of, if not title to, the land, and also because the mass of Europeans were never attracted to the tropical lands, not even if they were partially vacated. In the Lands of the Demographic Takeover the aboriginal populations were too sparse to rebound from the onslaught of disease or were inundated by European immigrants before they could recover.

The First Strike Force of the white immigrants to the Lands of the Demographic Takeover were epidemics. A few examples from scores of possible examples follow. Smallpox first arrived in the Río de la Plata region in 1558 or 1560 and killed, according to one chronicle possibly more interested in effect than accuracy, "more than a hundred thousand Indians" of the heavy riverine population there. An epidemic of plague or typhus decimated the Indians of the New England coast immediately before the founding of Plymouth. . . . After a series of such lethal and rapidly moving epidemics, then came the slow, unspectacular but thorough cripplers and killers like venereal disease and tuberculosis. In conjunction with the large numbers of white settlers these diseases were enough to smother aboriginal chances of recovery. First the blitzkrieg, then the mopping up.

The greatest of the killers in these lands was probably smallpox. The exception is New Zealand, the last of these lands to attract permanent European settlers. They came to New Zealand after the spread of vaccination in Europe, and so were poor carriers. As of the 1850s smallpox still had not come ashore, and by that time two-thirds of the Maori had been vaccinated. The tardy arrival of smallpox in these islands may have much to do with the fact that the Maori today comprise a larger percentage (nine percent) of their country's population than that of any other aboriginal people in any European colony or former European colony in either Temperate Zone, save only South Africa.

American Indians bore the full brunt of smallpox, and its mark is on their history and folklore. The Kiowa of the southern plains of the United States have a legend in which a Kiowa man meets Smallpox on the plain, riding a horse. The man asks, "Where do you come from and what do you do and why are you here?" Smallpox answers, "I am one with the white men—they are my people as the Kiowas are yours. Sometimes I travel ahead of them and sometimes behind. But I am always their companion and you will find me in their camps and their houses." "What can you do," the Kiowa asks. "I bring death," Smallpox replies. "My breath causes children to wither like young plants in spring snow. I bring destruction. No matter how beautiful a woman is, once she has looked at me she becomes as ugly as death. And to men I bring not death alone, but the destruction of their children and the blighting of their wives. The strongest of warriors go down before me. No people who have looked on me will ever be the same."

In return for the barrage of diseases that Europeans directed overseas, they received little in return. Australia and New Zealand provided no new strains of pathogens to Europe—or none that attracted attention. And of America's native diseases none had any real influence on the Old World—with the likely exception of venereal syphilis, which almost certainly existed in the New World before 1492 and probably did not occur in its present form in the Old World.

Weeds are rarely history makers, for they are not as spectacular in their effects as pathogens. But they, too, influence our lives and migrate over the world despite human wishes. As such, like varmints and germs, they are better indicators of certain realities than human beings or domesticated animals.

The term *weed* in modern botanical usage refers to any type of plant which—because of especially large numbers of seeds produced per plant, or especially effective means of distributing those seeds, or especially tough roots and rhizomes from which new plants can grow, or especially tough seeds that survive the alimentary canals of animals to be planted with their droppings—spread rapidly and outcompete others on disturbed, bare soil. Weeds are plants that tempt the botanist to use such anthropomorphic words as aggressive and opportunistic.

Many of the most successful weeds in the well-watered regions of the Lands of the Demographic Takeover are of European or Eurasian origin. French and Dutch and English farmers brought with them to North America their worst enemies, weeds, "to exhaust the land, hinder and damnify the Crop." By the last third of the seventeenth century at least twenty different types were widespread enough in New England to attract the attention of the English visitor, John Josselyn, who identified couch grass, dandelion, nettles, mallowes, knot grass, shepherd's purse, sow thistle, and clot burr and others. One of the most aggressive was plantain, which the Indians called "English-Man's Foot."

European weeds rolled west with the pioneers, in some cases spreading almost explosively. As of 1823 corn chamomile and maywood had spread up to but not across the Muskingum River in Ohio. Eight years later they were over the river. The most prodigiously imperialistic of the weeds in the eastern half of the United States and Canada were probably Kentucky bluegrass and white clover. They spread so fast after the entrance of Europeans into a given area that there is some suspicion that they may have been present in pre-Columbian America, although the earliest European accounts do not mention them. Probably brought to the Appalachian area by the French, these two kinds of weeds preceded the English settlers there and kept up with the movement westward until reaching the plains across the Mississippi.

Old World plants set up business on their own on the Pacific coast of North America just as soon as the Spaniards and Russians did. The climate of coastal southern California is much the same as that of the Mediterranean, and the Spaniards who came to California in the eighteenth century brought their own Mediterranean weeds with them via Mexico: wild oats, fennel, wild radishes. These plants, plus those brought in later by the Forty-niners, muscled their way to dominance in the coastal grasslands. These immigrant weeds followed Old World horses, cattle, and sheep into California's interior prairies and took over there as well.

They did not push so swiftly into the coastal Northwest because the Spanish, their reluctant patrons, were slow to do so, and because those shores are cool and damp. Most of the present-day weeds in that region had to come with the Russians or Anglo-Americans from similar areas on other coasts. The Northwest has a semi-arid interior, however, into which some European plants like redstem filaree spread quite early, presumably from the prairies of California.

The region of Argentina and Uruguay was almost as radically altered in its flora as in its fauna by the coming of the Europeans. The ancient Indian practice, taken up immediately by the whites, of burning off the old grass of the pampa every year, as well as the trampling and cropping to the ground of indigenous grasses and forbs by the thousands of imported quadrupeds who also changed the nature of the soil with their droppings, opened the whole countryside to European plants. In the 1780s Félix de Azara observed that the pampa, already radically altered, was changing as he watched. European weeds sprang up around every cabin, grew up along roads, and pressed into the open steppe. Today only a quarter of the plants growing wild in the pampa are native, and in the well-watered eastern portions, the "natural" ground cover consists almost entirely of Old World grasses and clovers.

The invaders were not, of course, always desirable. When Darwin visited Uruguay in 1832, he found large expanses, perhaps as much as hundreds of square miles, monopolized by the immigrant wild artichoke and transformed into a prickly wilderness fit neither for man nor his animals. . . .

Thus, many—often a majority—of the most aggressive plants in the temperate humid regions of North America, South America, Australia, and New Zealand are of European origin. It may be true that in every broad expanse of the world today where there are dense populations, with whites in the majority, there are also dense populations of European weeds. Thirty-five of eighty-nine weeds listed in 1953 as common in the state of New York are European. Approximately sixty percent of Canada's worst weeds are introductions from Europe. Most of New Zealand's weeds are from the same source, as are many, perhaps most, of the weeds of Australia's well-watered coasts. Most of the European plants that Josselyn listed as naturalized in New England in the seventeenth century are growing wild today in Argentina and Uruguay, and are among the most widespread and troublesome of all weeds in those countries.

In return for this largesse of pestiferous plants, the Lands of the Demographic Takeover have provided Europe with only a few equivalents. The Canadian water weed jammed Britain's nineteenth century waterways, and North America's horseweed and burnweed have spread in Europe's empty lots, and South America's flowered galinsoga has thrived in her gardens. But the migratory flow of a whole group of organisms between Europe and the Lands of the Demographic Takeover has been almost entirely in one direction. Englishman's foot still marches in seven league jackboots across every European colony of settlement, but very few American or Australian or New Zealand invaders stride the waste lands and unkempt backyards of Europe.

European and Old World human beings, domesticated animals, varmints, pathogens, and weeds all accomplished demographic takeovers of their own in the temperate, well-watered regions of North and South America, Australia, and New Zealand. They crossed oceans and Europeanized vast territories, often in informal cooperation with each other—the farmer and his animals destroying native plant cover, making way for imported grasses and forbs, many of which proved more nourishing to domesticated animals than the native equivalents; Old World pathogens, sometimes carried by Old World varmints, wiping out vast numbers of aborigines, opening the way for the advance of the European frontier, exposing more and more native peoples to more and more pathogens. . . .

There have been few such stories of the success in Europe of organisms from the Lands of the Demographic Takeover, despite the obvious fact that for every ship that went from Europe to those lands, another traveled in the opposite direction.

The demographic triumph of Europeans in the temperate colonies is one part of a biological and ecological takeover which could not have been accomplished by human beings alone, gunpowder notwithstanding. We must at least try to analyze the impact and success of all the immigrant organisms together—the European portmanteau of often mutually supportive plants, animals, and microlife which in its entirety can be accurately described as aggressive and opportunistic, an ecosystem simplified by ocean crossings and honed by thousands of years of competition in the unique environment created by the Old World Neolithic Revolution.

The human invaders and their descendants have consulted their egos, rather than ecologists, for explanations of their triumphs. But the human victims, the aborigines of the Lands of the Demographic Takeover, knew better, knew they were only one of many species being displaced and replaced; knew they were victims of something more irresistible and awesome than the spread of capitalism or Christianity. One Maori, at the nadir of the history of his race, knew these things when he said, "As the clover killed off the fern, and the European dog the Maori dog—as the Maori rat was destroyed by the Pakeha [European] rat—so our people, also, will be gradually supplanted and exterminated by the Europeans." The future was not quite so grim as he prophesied, but we must admire his grasp of the complexity and magnitude of the threat looming over his people and over the ecosystem of which they were part.

Acquiring the Taste for Chocolate

MARCY NORTON

Chocolate—along with tomatoes, potatoes, maize, and tobacco—originated in the Americas. How did chocolate make its way to Europeans and Europe? One might think that Europeans knew a good thing when they saw it, and immediately began exporting chocolate to savor in the "Old World." Or maybe Europeans found chocolate overly bitter and strange-tasting and so thought to sweeten it with sugar and Old World spices and make it "European." Both of these answers are wrong.

Europeans neither found chocolate instantly tantalizing nor did they begin to experiment with Indian chocolate recipes to suit their palates right away. To understand how Europeans developed a taste for chocolate and integrated it into their culture requires understanding something about Mesoamerica, Spanish colonialism, and their interactions. Liking chocolate required learning to like chocolate. And in

Source: Marcy Norton, "Conquests of Chocolate," *Magazine of History* 18, no. 3 (April 2004): 14–17. Copyright © 2004 Organization of American Historians. All rights reserved. Excerpts used with permission.

learning to like the Indian *taste* of chocolate, Europeans also absorbed several important Indian ideas about chocolate.

Chocolate in Native America

Before Europeans arrived in the Americas, chocolate and cacao were restricted to Mesoamerica—the region most famously associated with Aztec and Maya peoples. Mesoamericans greatly esteemed cacao beans and the chocolate beverages they yielded. Fermented and ground cacao "beans," actually the seeds found within the large fleshy fruit pods of the cacao trees, were the basis for many beverages. Though there were countless ways to prepare chocolate, the classic concoction was "finely ground, soft, foamy, reddish bitter," based on cacao and water, mixed with achiote to give it a reddish tint, chili peppers for a spicy edge, and wild bee honey for sweetening effect. Chocolate was also enhanced with the aromatic tropical flowers, designated by their Nahuatl names: *tlilxochitl* (vanilla); *xochinacaztli*; and *mecaxóchitl*. The texture and visual effects of chocolate were just as important, as suggested by the Mesoamerican insistence on the "foamy" head, and the special drinks and serving spoons with which they consumed it.

Chocolate featured in the tribute that the Mexica, as the Aztecs called themselves, required of conquered people. Cacao beans as well as special cups fashioned from hollowed gourds were among tribute items listed in *The Essential Codex Mendoza*. The Mexica also participated in trading networks that crossed Mesoamerica. This long-distance trade was another way for them to procure cacao from trees that did not readily grow in the arid highlands of the Valley of Mexico. Cacao was necessary for chocolate, but it also served as currency throughout Mesoamerica, which is evidence of its status as a precious good throughout the region.

Chocolate in the Mexica world was associated with status within a deeply stratified society. One of the privileges of status was special, perhaps exclusive, access to chocolate. "If he who drank [chocolate] were a common person," the Spanish missionary Bernadino de Sahagún observed of preconquest customs, "it was taken as a bad omen." Chocolate was also used to reward soldiers for heroic service, for which warriors were also entitled to smoke fragrant pipes and carry special flowers, wear cotton cloaks, and adorn themselves with precious stones and feathers. Chocolate was also ritually consumed at betrothal and wedding ceremonies, and presented to visiting dignitaries. It was associated with a lifeforce, originating from or strengthened by its blood red coloring achieved by adding achiote. Chocolate, then, played an important role in Mesoamerican society as a drink that denoted status and that was embedded in a range of social, diplomatic, and religious rituals.

The first recorded European encounter with chocolate took place on Christopher Columbus's fourth voyage in 1502, when he and his crew were near the coast of Mayan Honduras. They captured a trading vessel and found "almond"-shaped objects, cherished by the Mayans, among its cargo. Yet it took more than twenty years for Spaniards to learn more about the uses and taste of these objects. It was during Hernando Cortés's invasion of Mexico that Spaniards acquired their first taste, or at least view, of chocolate. This initial encounter did not predict a great future for the commodity. In the spring of 1519, Cortés and his retinue landed on the coast of Veracruz. Two envoys of Moctezuma presented Cortés and his officers with jewels, precious stones, and feather works as well as abundant dishes of food. The Spaniards delighted in the durable goods, "staring at them with great happiness and contentment," but they expressed hesitation about the foodstuffs. The Spanish missionary, Diego Durán, who heard this story from Indian informants, reported that "when the time came to drink the chocolate that had been brought to them, that most highly prized drink of the Indians, they were filled with fear. When the Indians saw that they dared not to drink they tasted from all the gourds and the Spaniards refreshed themselves with chocolate, because in truth, it is a refreshing beverage."

For all their initial dislike of the drink, the Spanish saw the importance of chocolate in Aztec rites of diplomacy. This education was reinforced during the siege of Tenochtitlan, the Mexica capital and modern-day Mexico City. The men who accompanied Cortés and participated elsewhere in the Spanish conquest of the Americas were men preoccupied with status and eager for opportunities for advancement and fortune. It did not take long for these honor- and status-obsessed men to learn that in Aztec society chocolate connoted, if not conferred, high social rank.

Chocolate and Colonialism

By 1524, the Spanish had consolidated their rule in central Mexico and were busy organizing a colonial regime. Cacao cultivation and consumption survived the conquest, but not without major changes, especially in consumption. Cacao production itself expanded under Spanish rule. Having quickly learned that cacao was a valuable good and an item of tribute, Spaniards encouraged its continued cultivation. In fact, they intensified it, by increasing cacao tribute requirements. But who consumed chocolate? Evidence suggests that consumption spread among native society. With the social upheaval that came in the wake of the Spanish conquest, traditional social hierarchies partly collapsed. In 1553, traditional Indian nobles complained that some Indian commoners were violating social norms by ostentatiously consuming chocolate:

> They give one another a great deal of food, and the chocolate they drink is very thick, with plenty of cacao in it. When they find the chocolate just a little watery, then it is not to their liking and they do not want to drink it. Some pour it on the ground, whereby whoever has given his very good cacao to someone is affronted, but they imagine themselves very grand because of it.

Under Spanish colonialism, new Indian groups had access to chocolate, but the meaning of chocolate consumption remained the same: a reflection of power and prestige.

An increasing number of Spanish migrants also took to the beverage. Chocolate, however, was not instantly appetizing. Those Europeans who had only scant exposure to the drink found it, by and large, disgusting. An Italian traveler, Giralomo Benzoni, who was welcomed with chocolate by Guatemalan Indians, first declared that the drink was fit only for pigs, though he eventually came to like it. The Jesuit writer José de Acosta likewise thought that "those who had not grown up" with chocolate "could not have a taste for it." Particularly revolting to him was the frothy top-layer of chocolate, "foam on top and bubbles like feces."

Spaniards had to learn to like chocolate and they did so through their continued dependence on Indians even as they assumed dominant positions. A distinctive feature of colonial Mexico was the creation of a *mestizo*, or mixed society. The first conquistadores who established homes in New Spain, as they named the colony, often took Indian wives or mistresses who were responsible for the domestic sphere, including cooking, and who introduced Spaniards to chocolate. As Spanish emigration increased and Spanish women began to come in larger numbers in the 1540s, elite Spaniards no longer married Indian women, though commoners continued to do so, but Indian women still were an indispensable part of the household as domestic servants. Early Spanish missionaries also forged close relations to Indian parishioners and reported on their gifts of chocolate.

Chocolate Arrives in Europe

By the second half of the sixteenth century, chocolate was fully part of creole or European colonial life. Chocolate's arrival in Europe was more hesitant. Erratic importations of chocolate occurred throughout the sixteenth century, offered as an exotic novelty by visiting retinues of Indians or brought home by a returning friar. The chocolate "take-off" appears in Seville in the first decades of the seventeenth century. The first publication devoted to chocolate, aimed at Spanish consumers, appeared in Seville in 1624, Santiago de Valverde Turices's *Un Discurso de Chocolate*. By the 1620s, thousands of pounds of cacao and chocolate were imported annually. By 1633, enough of a chocolate manufacturing industry existed in Madrid for city authorities to institute licensing requirements for those who wanted to make and sell chocolate. And by the spring of 1727, Madrid had more than seven hundred thousand pounds of cacao and chocolate in stores and warehouses for a population of about one hundred thirty thousand.

Why did chocolate take so long to get a foothold in Europe? As there was nothing automatically appealing to Europeans about chocolate, a critical mass of chocolate aficionados—those with extensive New World experience for example—needed to develop in Spain before a market for chocolate could exist. This threshold was not crossed until the end of the sixteenth century. Not surprisingly, some of the precocious chocolate consumers came from communities with connections on both sides of the Atlantic. For instance, members of ecclesiastical orders helped disseminate the chocolate habit, as they had people constantly coming and going from far-off places.

There is a common—and erroneous—belief that Europeans needed to "transform" chocolate in order to make it appetizing. While it is true that Spaniards put sugar, which was unknown to indigenous Americans, into chocolate, this additive was not as innovative as it is often taken to be. Mesoamericans already sweetened chocolate with honey, and the step from honey to sugar—increasingly more available than honey because of expanding sugar plantations in the Americas—is a small one. Sugar can be seen as an "import substitute" for honey to approximate the taste of the original. Moreover, Europeans maintained the spice complex used by Mesoamericans. Like Mesoamericans, the first chocolate-drinkers in Europe mixed their chocolate with vanilla, *xochinacaztli*—flowers nicknamed *orejuelas* or "little ears" by the Spanish for their ear-shapes, *mecaxóchitl*, and achiote. Like Mesoamericans, Europeans valued "foam" on chocolate—perhaps the antecedent to the contemporary custom of putting marshmallows in hot chocolate. Spaniards even adopted Mesoamerican chocolate drinking vessels—the special cup named *jícara*, after the Nahua *xicalli*.

There were changes, of course. Spaniards began to use *jícaras* made of porce-
lain, rather than hollowed gourds. They tinkered with the recipes by using Old World
spices—cinnamon, black pepper, anise, and sesame—but even so, the spices they
chose suggest that they were trying to replicate the harder-to-find native flowers.
Black pepper could be used instead of chilies and *mecaxóchitl*; cinnamon and cloves
were found to be adequate substitutions for the *orejuelas*. Sugar replaced honey. Yet
they intended to simulate original tastes, rather than create new palate sensations.

By the end of the eighteenth century, all that remained of the spice complex
was cinnamon and sugar. But there is no indication the Spaniards deliberately tried
to change the original chocolate. Rather, the inconvenience of imports and extension of consumers probably led to its simplification. Moreover, by then enough time
had passed and the preparation of chocolate had become sufficiently simplified that
the origins of the concoction were no longer remembered correctly. The myth that
chocolate had conformed to European taste was consistent with the Spanish ideology of conquest that took for granted that colonialism involved the Europeanization
of Indians. The reality, however, was that Europeans unwittingly developed a taste
for Indian chocolate, which involved not only bodily changes but also the absorp-
tion of cultural material.

Just as Spaniards—in Spain as well as America—learned to replicate the taste,
fragrance, look, and texture of Mesoamerican chocolate, they also learned to attribute
Mesoamerican social meanings to it. For one, they had internalized the association
between chocolate and noble distinction. By the seventeenth century, royal ceremonies in Spain itself involved chocolate. New allocations of household space
similarly underscored chocolate's arrival as part of the requisite trappings for noble
life. The most important aristocrats apportioned living quarters—chocolate rooms—
exclusively for chocolate. These spaces seem to have been conveniently ensconced
between the large hall and a drawing room where guests were received, emphasizing the often social nature of chocolate consumption. Spaniards learned from Aztecs
that chocolate could assist in the maintenance of social distinctions in a heavily
stratified society.

It did not take long before the chocolate habit spread beyond Spain to other
parts of Europe. The European elite were a cosmopolitan bunch, and novel ideas,
goods, and habits could spread quickly. Missionary orders, such as the Jesuits, and
European aristocratic circles were important disseminators who provided a human
network for the transfer of new habits such as chocolate drinking. Once people in
England, Holland, France, Germany, and Italy had developed an appetite for the
stimulating drink of chocolate, they were ready to embrace the caffeinated beverages of tea and coffee that would eventually surpass path-breaking chocolate as the
choice beverage.

The chocolate we consume today does not preserve many of these features
appreciated in seventeenth-century Europe. Hot cocoa is viewed most often as a
children's drink, rather than an adult's delicacy. Our society is a democracy and
so chocolate's "aristocratic" lineage has been forgotten. But there are still vestiges
of chocolate's premodern and pre-Columbian past. The association between chocolate and romantic love continues to hold sway in our collective imagination, as evidenced by the box-of-chocolates' status as the quintessential Valentine's Day gift and
its mythical status as an aphrodisiac. It is quite likely that Spaniards in the sixteenth

and seventeenth century derived these ideas from pre-Columbian uses: chocolate played a role in marriage negotiations among the Maya and in symbolic representations of marriage among the Mixtec. We enjoy a layer of whipped cream or marshmallows that resembles the "foam" of the original drink and we even continue to appreciate the hint of red in chocolate brown. In our own casual consumption of chocolate today, we unconsciously invoke ancient rituals of consumption that predate the European conquest of America and signal the peculiar transformations and continuities alike of commodities in the Atlantic World.

The Peanut Revolution

DONALD R. WRIGHT

Just a year before Niumi's soldiers ran the British garrison out of Fort Bullen, in 1831, British traders had sent a few baskets of locally grown peanuts to the British Institute for Tropical Agriculture in the West Indies. For some time, they had been looking for primary products in world demand that they could obtain along the banks of the Gambia in exchange for the consumer goods being manufactured in western Europe in ever-greater quantity and quality. This time they found one.

Although the Portuguese brought peanuts to West Africa from Brazil as early as the sixteenth century, farmers in Niumi never paid them special attention—nor did anyone else along the Gambia River for quite a long time. Over two centuries and more, peanuts had become just one more of a host of crops grown for local consumption, mainly as a hedge against failure of the grains. When people were *really* hungry, they would eat peanuts. Ruling elites had their slaves feed the tops of the plants to their horses and some believed this made the mounts stronger and likely to live longer than horses who did not have peanut tops in their fodder.

But peanuts in the Gambia would have their day. Through the first third of the nineteenth century, demand grew steadily in Europe for vegetable fats and oils that could be used in candles, cooking oils, lubricants, and, particularly, soap—it was a time when people around the Western world were becoming aware of the relationship of personal hygiene to good health. A popular tropical oil in use for soap production since the latter part of the eighteenth century was palm oil, obtained along the forested coasts of lower Guinea. England's Lever Brothers combined palm oil with olive oil and turned out the famous "Palmolive" brand that sold briskly. In addition, French cooks had begun using peanut oil as a cheaper substitute for olive oil and soon there were experiments with its use in soap manufacture. Four years after the initial British investigation of Gambian peanuts, 213 baskets of the product left the Gambia and ended up at Forster and Smith, the London firm that was to become Britain's leading peanut importer. Forster and Smith had experience in the West African trade; they were importers of palm oil, rice, beeswax, and mahogany. In 1835 the firm built a mill in London to crush peanuts and render their oil, and the demand for peanuts was under way.

Source: Donald R. Wright, *The World and a Very Small Place in Africa: A History of Globalization in Niumi, The Gambia* (Armonk, NY: M. E. Sharpe, 2004, 2d ed.), pp. 139–143. Copyright © 2004 by M. E. Sharpe, Inc. Reprinted with permission.

Other factors relating to the world market aided the rise of Gambian peanut production for export in Niumi. In Europe of the 1830s, factory workers and common laborers made paltry wages, so there were not masses of people with disposable money for the purchase of industry's large and growing output. This was especially true for Britain's leading industry: textiles. Industrialists saw African consumers as candidates to fill the consumption gap. To entice a broader range of Africans to consume European goods, British and French traders offered liberal credit to almost anyone, including many who previously had been outside the commercial network in the Gambia River. Large numbers of people with fewer means and less influence in Niumi found it possible to obtain imported goods for trading. Once peanuts proved to be a major item in demand, common peasants had a clear way to pay their debts and obtain still more inexpensive European manufactures that they increasingly desired. After the 1830s, a much broader segment of Niumi's population became involved in the market, eventually acquiring more products on credit and paying off their debts with peanuts.

For a time, Gambian peanut exports grew with unprecedented speed. A market for Gambian peanuts blossomed in the United States after 1835, and soon three-quarters of the Gambian peanut crop was crossing the Atlantic and ending up for sale in New York and New England, at fruit markets and newsstands, at circuses and shows. A restrictive American tariff in 1842 all but stopped such imports momentarily, and then they fluctuated wildly. But France stepped in as the major buyer of Gambian peanuts, and with the exception of lean years caused by revolution and war, it would remain such for a long time. The initial reason for French interest was that, unlike British consumers, the French did not take to the yellow, palm-oil-based soaps. Until the soap industry could find a method to remove the yellow, such soaps had a small market in France. But after experimentation, Marseilles soap makers found they could make a blue-marble soap with peanut oil as a major ingredient, and not long afterward the rush for the small legume was on. Marseilles imported a ton of peanuts in 1841, 205 tons in 1845, 5,500 in 1854.

As European demand grew, farmers along the Gambia responded. By the 1850s Gambians, who never had exported a nut before 1830, were exporting, on average, over 10,000 tons of peanuts a year with a value in some years of over £130,000; by the end of the century, it was 30,000 tons at £200,000. Providing additional incentive were the falling prices of European manufactured goods, the result of great increases in the efficiency of production and transportation. Between 1817 and 1850 the price of British textiles sold in the Gambia River dropped by 75 percent, for instance, prompting Niumi's growers of cotton and weavers to buy imported cloth, with profits from peanut sales, rather than to produce their own. With world prices for peanuts holding firm in spite of the increased African production, entering the market for a number of years was simply smart economics.

Like other regions of coast-wise Senegambia, Niumi quickly became a region of large-scale peanut exporting. Its male farmers made the transition to export production over a short time and remained the state's major peanut producers thereafter. They did so, argues economist Jan Hogendorn, largely because of particular circumstances of the time and place. Hogendorn believes that such farmers had surplus land and wanted a variety of reasonably priced European products at the very time the world market beckoned. They were able to clear additional land, interplant peanuts with food crops, and produce nuts for export while for a long time continuing to grow sufficient food for their regular consumption. The continuing existence of slavery all about the region played a role, too. By the 1840s captives from regional wars, who once might have been marched toward the coast for sale and shipment across the Atlantic, could be taken to centers of export production like Niumi and sold there. Slave laborers were important elements in Niumi's peanut production; the numbers and proportion of slaves in Niumi grew through the middle and late nineteenth century.

But another phenomenon added considerably to Niumi's peanut exports and became an important part of seasonal life and the workings of the state's peanut-based economy since the 1840s: what locals call "strange farming." This involved persons from elsewhere (the strangers), often some distance away, migrating to Niumi before the beginning of the rainy season, taking up temporary residence in a village, making a peanut crop, selling it, and returning home with cash or goods. The roots of strange farming may extend back even earlier, to the eighteenth century, when the Atlantic slave trade was at its height. Dealers who marched slave caravans down to Juffure in the dry winter months for sale there to Europeans might encounter low demand, and thus low prices, on arrival. One option they had to selling cheaply was to rent land and put the slaves to work growing a crop, which they would sell once harvested and then hope that prices for slaves were better. It is possible that at the same time small handfuls of farmers from the region of the upper Senegal and Gambia rivers moved down toward the Gambia's mouth for a season of farming nearer points of exchange with European merchants. These early strange farmers sold their crop for trade goods and then marched inland with them and became traveling merchants themselves over the dry season.

Once Niumi's farmers began growing peanuts for cash, the banks of the lower river lured persons from as far away as modern Guinea and Mali, intent on bettering their social and economic position at home in ways that required possessing some wealth. A number of young men went strange farming for one or several seasons to acquire the bride price for marriage. Aware of traditional requirements to share wealth with needy kinsmen, they recognized the benefits of improving one's personal economic position some distance away from family demands. Niumi had the advantage of having farming land near the river (meaning transportation costs could be low), coupled with a relatively light population. The prospective strange farmer would come to one of Niumi's villages between late April and early June and inform the village head that he wanted to make a crop with the coming rains. The village head either would assume the role of the individual's landlord or would designate another villager to serve in that position. In either case, the village head collected a custom payment from the stranger, a portion of which went to Niumi's *mansa*. The landlord would provide a dwelling for the stranger, see to it that he had sufficient food for the farming season, designate a plot of land for the stranger to farm, and make sure the stranger had tools and seed. The stranger would be required to work for three or four days of every week in his landlord's fields, and he would give the landlord one-tenth or a little more of the peanuts he produced. The stranger would be gone soon after the sale of his crop, but one strange farmer might return to the same village several years running if the experience was profitable. In this way, the land of Niumi produced more peanuts than its regular, small population could grow.

The merchant populations at Bathurst and Albreda and British officials up and down Africa's west coast encouraged the migration of distant farmers or anything else that would increase peanut production and trade in Niumi. Supplying peanuts for the European market for oils was a worthy engagement for Gambian merchants, but every bit as important were issues related to colonial revenue. British outposts along Africa's coast—like Bathurst—were proving expensive. The troops, gunboats, colonial steamers, constables, and administrators cost money, and it was money that British taxpayers did not want to pay. The key to having funds for such settlements was a bustling commerce. British port authorities at Bathurst levied duties on goods imported; as the quantity of imports rose to exchange for peanuts, so did Bathurst revenues. Then, in 1863, as indigenous warfare threatened trade and production up and down the river, bringing Bathurst merchants to press for expensive military operations to bring order, the British administrator in Bathurst imposed an export tax on peanuts. It was not a large tax, but one that brought in greater revenue as peanut production climbed toward the century's end. Its historical importance was great, however, for taxes on peanut exports of one sort or another would become an important part of Gambian revenues from that time on, through the period of formal British control of its Gambia colony and through the early decades of independence.

There were more reasons for common folk to grow peanuts. Always a supplementary crop for the peasant, the peanut normally was of minor significance and thus was outside the realm of taxation by the ruling elites of African states. Niumi's rulers might get a tenth of a peasant's millet crop, but if they took anything of the peanuts that common farmers grew, it was only the tops of the plants (for fodder), which farmers did not want anyway. Now, with demand for peanuts at the waterside expanding, peasants could grow peanuts and trade them to European buyers and thus, seemingly for the first time, gain access to a significant source of wealth all their own. With such wealth they soon were able to acquire commodities that previously only the ruling elites could afford—metalware and cloth, decorative items and luxury goods, and especially weapons, in this case firearms and gunpowder. These last items turned out to be of particular importance, for such weapons would enable the peasantry at first to resist their frequently oppressive *soninke* rulers, and then, as peanut exports and firearm imports continued to mount, to rise and attempt to overthrow them for good. This seems to be what happened in Niumi over the half century following 1830, when the region experienced one of its most disruptive periods ever: a time of far-reaching political, social, and economic change that Gambians know as the era of the Soninke-Marabout Wars.

△ *F U R T H E R   R E A D I N G*

Acosta, José de. *Natural and Moral History of the Indies.* Edited by Jane E. Mangan. Durham, NC: Duke University Press, 2002.

Anderson, Virginia DeJohn. *Creatures of Empire: How Domestic Animals Transformed Early America.* New York: Oxford University Press, 2004.

Carney, Judith Ann. *Black Rice: The African Origins of Rice Cultivation in the Americas.* Cambridge, MA: Harvard University Press, 2001.

The Columbian Exchange 155

Coe, Sophie D., and Michael D. Coe. *The True History of Chocolate.* London: Thames and Hudson, 1996.

Cook, Noble David. *Born to Die: Disease and New World Conquest, 1492–1650.* New York: Cambridge University Press, 1998.

Cronon, William. *Changes in the Land: Indians, Colonists, and the Ecology of New England.* New York: Hill and Wang, 1983.

Crosby, Alfred W. *The Columbian Exchange: Biological and Cultural Consequences of 1492.* Westport, CT: Greenwood Press, 1972.

———. *Ecological Imperialism: The Biological Expansion of Europe, 900–1900.* New York: Cambridge University Press, 1986.

Curtin, Philip D. *Death by Migration: Europe's Encounter with the Tropical World in the Nineteenth Century.* New York: Cambridge University Press, 1989.

Dean, Warren. *With Broadax and Firebrand: The Destruction of the Brazilian Atlantic Forest.* Berkeley: University of California Press, 1995.

Fenn, Elizabeth A. *Pox Americana: The Great Smallpox Epidemic of 1775–82.* New York: Hill and Wang, 2001.

Kiple, Kenneth F. *The Caribbean Slave: A Biological History.* New York: Cambridge University Press, 1984.

Mancall, Peter C. *Deadly Medicine: Indians and Alcohol in Early America.* Ithaca, NY: Cornell University Press, 1995.

McCann, James. *Maize and Grace: Africa's Encounter with a New World Crop, 1500–2000.* Cambridge, MA: Harvard University Press, 2005.

McNeill, William H. *Plagues and Peoples.* Garden City, NJ: Anchor Press, 1986.

Melville, Elinor. *A Plague of Sheep: Environmental Consequences of the Conquest of Mexico.* Cambridge: Cambridge University Press, 1994.

Mintz, Sidney. *Sweetness and Power: The Place of Sugar in Modern History.* New York: Viking, 1985.

Richards, John F. *The Unending Frontier: An Environmental History of the Early Modern World.* Berkeley: University of California Press, 2003.

Sahagún, Bernardino de. *The Florentine Codex: General History of the Things of New Spain.* 12 books in 13 volumes. Translated by Arthur J. O. Anderson and Charles Dibble. Santa Fe, NM: School of American Research and the University of Utah Press, 1950.

Super, John C. *Food, Conquest, and Colonization in Sixteenth-Century Spanish America.* Albuquerque: University of New Mexico Press, 1988.

C H A P T E R

6

Migrations

Several million people—free, unfree, and enslaved—crossed the Atlantic Ocean in the early modern era, one of the greatest population movements in human history up to that time. War, poverty, ambition, and religious zeal were among the forces that compelled emigrants to leave their homes, while demand for their labor drew millions of them to the mines, plantations, factories, and urban centers of the Atlantic world. A vast and varied business developed around the recruitment of workers, whether conducted in the trading posts of Africa or in the taverns of European ports. It is crucial to understand that free migrants were the minority. Most were unfree in one way or another: convicts, indentured servants, slaves. In fact, the vast majority of people who crossed the Atlantic before 1800 were captive Africans, whose "middle passage" to the Americas was exceptionally degrading and deadly. Migration was thus an ordeal. It generally involved coercion and violence, disorientation and disruption, adaptation, and a determination to survive or perish. Migrants to the Americas often tried to re-create the patterns of life they had known in Europe and Africa, but unfamiliar environments, social ruptures, new patterns of labor, and the mixture of diverse cultures ensured that migrants could seldom replicate the places they left behind. The documents and essays in this chapter highlight the diverse experiences of transatlantic migrants. They illuminate the hopes and fears of the many millions who crossed the ocean, whether they wanted to go or not.

◬ D O C U M E N T S

These documents reveal the diverse experiences of transatlantic migrants from different perspectives. The problems facing unfree English laborers emerge in Documents 2 and 7. Document 2 bears witness to the problem of laborers being enticed overseas under false pretenses and against their will. In Document 7, an English indentured servant named Elizabeth Sprigs writes home to her father in London begging relief from her miserable servitude in the colony of Maryland.

The travail of enslaved Africans was even worse, as Documents 5 and 8 indicate. Thomas Phillip's journal of the voyage of the *Hannibal* presents an English slave trader's candid account of bad conditions and high mortality on board a slave ship. In Document 5 he acknowledges the deep fear and despair of captive Africans, who even went so far as to commit suicide rather than suffer the fate that awaited them in Barbados. Ottobah Cugoano, one of the early leaders of the British antislavery movement, included a brief autobiography in one of his published pamphlets, excerpted in Document 8. He narrates his capture in an inland part of the Fante country, his transportation to the coast, and the horror of slavery in the Caribbean island of Grenada.

Documents 1, 3, 4, and 6 catch a glimpse of the complex motivations guiding European migrants. These illustrate continued attachment to family and patrons in Europe, as well as varied and inconsistent responses to the opportunities, perils, and people of America and Africa. In 1570 Andrés Chacón wrote the letter in Document 1 in Trujillo, Peru, after some forty years in the Indies, and after thirty years as an encomendero. Compare his letter with that in Document 3, written from Quebec City by Marie Guyart Martin, or Marie of the Incarnation (1599–1672), the superior of the Ursuline convent in Quebec, to her son in France on September 9, 1652. She describes her activities in New France, where she had lived for thirteen years.

Documents 4 and 6 present three different perspectives from German-speaking migrants in the Atlantic. In Document 4, two Germans debate the merits of the English colony of Pennsylvania established by the Quaker William Penn. The colony's leaders deliberately recruited Protestants from the European continent. Francis Daniel Pastorius (1651–1720), one of the first Germans to migrate to Pennsylvania, became an ardent promoter of the colony. His favorable view is amply refuted by Christopher Saur (1693–1758), who describes conditions in Germantown in 1738. In Document 6, Peter Kolb (1675–1726), a German astronomer and mathematician, explains why he traveled to the Dutch colony at the Cape of Good Hope and why he returned home again. First published in 1713, his voluminous account details the flora, fauna, and people he encountered at the Cape. It remains one of the most important sources historians have for this period.

1. "Let Them Come and Leave that Misery": Andrés Chacón Writes Home to Spain, 1570

Sir:

For a long time no one there has written me. In this fleet that just came from Spain, I thought there might be some letters, but it seems that none came, because I inquired, and there is no trace of anything. I don't know the reason. It must be that you there don't want to write except when I send money. Truly you should write more often, or at least remember me from time to time if I am neglectful; it seems to me that would be best. Also, I suppose you haven't had letters from me for a long time, because another year I wrote and sent a gold ingot to Licentiate Montalbo who lives in Panamá, and unfortunately for you and the rest who were to have it, the fleet had already departed for Spain; only one ship was left there, and the Licentiate didn't want to send it in a single ship, for which I was very sorry, because in fact he didn't send it, and it was left behind. Later when I sent to Panamá to buy some blacks for some mines I have, there wasn't enough money, and he spent the gold ingot toward the purchase of the blacks. Now at present I don't know if I will send anything, because I am outside my house thirty leagues from Trujillo among my

Source: James Lockhart and Enrique Otte, eds., *Letters and People of the Spanish Indies* (Cambridge, 1976), pp. 65–70.

villages, and the messenger who is going to Spain will not touch in Trujillo, I believe, and for that reason I don't know if anything can be sent. If he should not go at present and there are ships when I go to Trujillo, I will try to send something, even if it shouldn't be much, because at present I don't have much, but with the aid of God if these mines that I'm working do well, I will make up for it, if God gives me life and health. I hope to God that these mines I'm working will yield us enough silver for here and for there both, because I have some silver mines that I think will be good, and if they are, I will make up for what was lost; if you had the money there that I've spent on them, it would take care of you very well. I have a dozen and a half blacks at the mine, and tools and things. So far I have spent more than 7,000 pesos on blacks and the rest, and with the aid of God, the mines will yield silver; until now everything has been spending.

What I would need now is what there is too much of there, which is a boy from among those nephews of mine, to ride about on horseback inspecting my properties and these mines; they need someone to take care of them, because the blacks overlook nothing they can steal, and as to the Spaniards that I have there, each one looks after himself. As I say, I have great need of someone to go about, because I am old and tired and can no longer run everywhere, and as these mines are far from Trujillo in the mountains, it is hard on me to go, and the cold up there doesn't agree with me. To avoid going I would like to have one of those boys here, though none have ever managed to come, and he would flourish and lighten my work, if he is the right person. In case one who wanted to come should be free, I have written to a friend or two of mine in Seville who will help him along his way. When they come, they should bring my letters along. I believe Juan Antonio Corso, a very rich man, will outfit them for the trip, because he wrote me here. He carries on business here, and he will get the boy passage without his paying anything. I will pay here what it should cost, as I am now writing to Corso. Let them come and leave that misery in which they are immersed. Somehow two thousand paupers manage to get here; they look for a way to come across and finally they find it. But in forty years that I have been away from home, not one person from our town has come here except Alonso de Lara, son of Rodrigo de Lara the Red, who became a priest, and he has a living now; if he had wanted to go seek his fortune before he was a priest, he would have things even better. I have written other times that if some of the boys should take to learning, they should be trained up as lawyers or priests. If everything is to be digging and plowing, they and their fathers will be at it their whole lives. And however many of them come or make something of themselves, I will do my part to support them, and I say that when the mines begin to show profit, I will send money for it every year as long as I live.

I've been awaiting news about my papers of nobility, and haven't seen a thing. It must all be a joke, or I don't know what to say, when at the end of ten years there still has been no judgment. I consider it a joke.

As to things here, I am well, and Ana López too, though we are old and tired, and in the end this is very poor country, and all the properties aren't worth two pennies any more. If it weren't for a mulebreeding business I have, I don't know what would come of us, because this has sustained me in my great expenses; to the priest who instructs my Indians and to Spanish employees and Indians, I pay 1,000 pesos for salaries alone, not counting the cost of their food. Consider what I need to keep up with costs, since I have to spend another 2,000 to maintain my household. And now there's the added cost of the mines, but with the aid of God they will yield enough for everything. As I said, I have a mulebreeding business and five or six stud donkeys; there's one they've offered me 1,000 pesos for, but I wouldn't sell him for 1,500, he's so good and so big. Most of the mules he sires are worth 100 pesos to me, and some more. The small livestock I have, sheep and goats, are worth nothing. A ewe can sell for 3 tomines or so, and a mutton brings me a peso at most. Meat is dirt cheap in this country. Every day at the mines the blacks and Christians eat up a goat or mutton. And here at Casma and in Trujillo we eat another every day, so that I have the expense of two head of stock daily and even then, truly, the blacks are not happy with it, so what am I to do with the rest, that is, the other expenses? I've said this so that you there understand that for all a man may have here, he needs it all, and hopes to God it is enough.

I know that those who have been here say that I am rich. Certainly I have more than I deserve from God. But as I said, everything goes for expenses, and at the end of the year the income only covers operations, and even sometimes isn't enough. And as the Indians give me nothing, that is, I take little from them and have expenses for priests and other things for them and they have been destroyed in past wars, since they are on the main highway and have been mistreated and destroyed, few of them remain. Once there were more than 2,000 Indians, and now there are about 200. I considered them as if they were my children; they have helped me earn a living and, as I say, I relieve them of tributes and everything else that I can. I have given them 220 pesos in income, [1?] 60 at my pleasure and 60 perpetually, and if God gives me life, I will leave them free of tributes when I die, so that whoever enjoys the tributes will not mistreat the Indians to get his revenue. Probably you there will say that it would be better to give this to my relatives than to the Indians. But I owe it to these children who have served me for thirty-odd years; it is a debt of life, and if I did not repay it I would go to hell. I am obliged to do what I can for my relatives, but if I don't, I won't go to hell for it.

I am here in this place much of the year because it is so luxuriant. To be able to stay, I have sheep, goats and pigs here, and I did have cows, but recently I sold them because they damaged the Indians' crops. I have a constant supply of milk, cream, and curds. This valley, or rather the Indians and my property, are close to the sea, where the Indians catch a thousand kinds of fish, and have many nets they fish with. And as they like me well, when they have good luck they bring fish to me. I have maize from tributes, and a mill where wheat is ground. And certainly we have very good fare, with the capons they give me as tribute, and the very fat kids and muttons; all is from the harvest and tribute, and praise to God, the excess here could feed all of those boys. I have four pounds of fish and two chickens in tribute daily. In the previous assessment they were obliged to give me 600 bushels of wheat and 500 of maize, but in this assessment that was just made the amounts were reduced by half, because I requested it of the inspector, since if I die, I want them relieved; I have more than enough with the wheat and the maize they give me now.

I have here next to the mill four or five hundred fig trees that yield a harvest of fifty hundredweight, and there are orange trees and some vines that yield grapes to eat. The Indians here suffer because the river of the valley is so variable, full of water in the winter and empty in the spring, and some years they have scarcity, but since they are fishermen, they get everything they need from the neighboring people in exchange for fish.

I have a farm in Trujillo where I grow wheat to maintain my household, and I have a mill in the middle of it to grind the wheat that is harvested and other wheat that is grown by surrounding neighbors. I have there a dozen Indian couples and two blacks, one of whom watches a flock of goats and sheep to supply the house. But since there are many livestock around the town, the animals are thin, and the milk is less abundant than here. And besides I have in Trujillo two black women who make bread and cook for everyone, and a mulatto woman who serves Ana López, embroidering and sewing and serving at table along with the Indian women and girls. There are five or six other Indian women who are laundresses and help the black women make bread, so that there are twenty or twenty-five people eating there, including the Indian women and boys and blacks serving at the house. I have said this so you will see whether or not I have much to maintain and support. You will ask why I never wrote this before. I say that since Trujillo causes it all, Trujillo is what I have written about.

Many salutations to milady sister Mari López and the gentlemen your sons. May our Lord give you the desired contentment and repose. From this valley of Casma, 1st of January, 1570.

Your servant,

Andrés Chacón

2. Colonial Investors Lure Servants Overseas, 1618, 1664

From Domestic Correspondence, James I

1618, Oct. 19, Nethersham.

Sir Edward Hext, Justice of the Peace of Somerset to the Privy Council, Complaint having been made to him that one Owen Evans, had commanded the constable of the hundred of Whitleighe and others to press him divers maidens to be sent to the Bermudas and Virginia, he issued a warrant for his apprehension. Evans on being examined said he was a messenger of the Chamber and showed his badge of office. The constable affirmed that said Owen required him in His M. name to press him five maidens with all speed for the service aforesaid, and on demanding to see his commission reviled and threatened that he should answer it in another place—Another affirmed that Evans delivered 5 to one and 12 to another to press six maidens, and to a third he delivered his badge and required him to press some maidens, else would he procure him to be hanged—Sends an acquittance inclosed—Evans confessed all, and that he had no commission at all and so fell upon his knees and humbly confessed his fault. Has committed him to gaol. His undue proceedings breed such terror to the poor maidens as forty of them fled out of one parish into such obscure and remote places as their parents and masters can yet have no news what is become of them.

Source: "Kidnapping Maidens, to Be Sold in Virginia, 1618," in *Virginia Magazine of History and Biography* 6 (1899): 229; W. Noel Sainsbury, ed., *Calendar of State Papers, Colonial* (London, 1880), July 12, 1664, v. 5 pp. 220–221.

From the Calendar of State Papers

July 12.   Petition of merchants, planters, and masters of ships trading to the Plantations to the King. That there is a wicked custom to seduce or spirit away young people to go as servants to the plantations, which petitioners abominate the very thoughts of. This gives the opportunity to many evil-minded persons to enlist themselves voluntarily to go the voyage, and having received money, clothes, diet, &c., to pretend they were betrayed or carried away without their consents. Pray that persons may be appointed under the Great Seal who may enter the names, age, quality, place of birth, and last residence of those desiring to go to said Plantations, which will be a means to prevent the betraying and spiriting away of people. *With reference* to the Attorney and Solicitor-General to consider what may be done by law, also to call some of the petitioners before them and report thereon. Whitehall, 1664, July 12. *Annexed,*

> I.   Report of Sir Heneage Finch that he finds the mischiefs complained of very frequent, there being scarce any voyage to the Plantations but some are carried away against their wills, or pretend to be so after they have contracted with the merchants and so run away. That a registry of passengers to the Plantations who go by contract with the merchant would be a proper remedy. That the King might by law erect such an office with a small fee annexed, but it will never be effectually executed without an Act of Parliament imposing a fee sufficient to recompense the pains. 1664, July 18.

1664 ?   Memorial of the Lord Mayor and Court of Aldermen to the Privy Council. That usually for the supply of soldiers to divers parts and sending of men to the several Plantations beyond the seas without lawful press, certain persons called "spirritts" do inveigle and by lewd subtilties entice away youth against the consent either of their parents, friends, or masters, whereby oftimes great tumults and uproars are raised within the city of the breach of the peace and the hazard of men's lives, which being of dangerous consequence the memorialists request their Lordships will take into consideration and devote some course for the suppressing of them, either by proclamation or otherwise.

Lady Yarborough to Williamson. A poor boy of whom she had care has been stolen away by spirits, as they call them, who convey such boys to ships for New England or Barbadoes. Begs a warrant for the bearer whose apprentice he was to search ships for him.

Proposals to the King and Council to constitute an office for transporting to the Plantations all vagrants, rogues, and idle persons that can give no account of themselves, felons who have the benefit of clergy, such as are convicted of petty larceny, vagabonds, gipsies, and loose persons, making resort to unlicensed brothels, such persons to be transported from the nearest seaport, and to serve four years according to the laws and customs of those islands, if over 20 years of age, and seven years if under 20. For want of such an office no account can be given of many persons of quality transported in the late times of rebellion, wherefore in future all such persons to be registered under penalty of 20*l.*, no person under 12 years of age to be transported unless their friends and relations shall first personally appear at the office and give good reasons for the same, half the fines paid by merchants, mariners, or planters for persons transported to be given to the King, and the other half to the officers for transport.

3. Marie of the Incarnation Finds Clarity in Canada, 1652

To Her Son [September 9, 1652]

My very dear son, . . .

I find everything you say concerning our remaining in this country or our withdrawal to France as reasonable as prudence could suggest. I share your feelings but the outcome rarely conforms to our thoughts, as those indicate who are familiar with God's conduct in these regions where it seems that his providence plays games with human prudence.

I, too, am certain that his Divine Majesty wants our reestablishment and that the vocation I have to labor here comes from him, just as certain as I am that I will die one day. Yet notwithstanding this certitude and the energy we have expended, we do not know what this country will become. There is, nonetheless, a stronger appearance that it will endure than otherwise and I myself feel as strong in my vocation as ever; yet ready, just the same, for a withdrawal to France whenever it will please God to give me a sign to that effect through those who hold his place on earth. . . .

This morning I spoke to two people experienced in the affairs of this country concerning two young women whom we would like to bring from France as lay sisters. They found no difficulty with this; for myself, I find a great deal. First, because of the perils at sea; second, because of the difficulties in France; and, finally, because of the composition of our group. This is why we still have not come to any decision. The hostility of the Iroquois is not what holds us back. There are some who consider this country to be lost, but I do not see that we have so much to fear on that score as, I am told from France, people of our sex and condition have to fear from French soldiers. I tremble at what I have been told. The Iroquois are barbarians, but they certainly do not deal with persons of our sex as I am told the French have done. Those who have lived among them have told me that they never resort to violence and that they leave free those who do not want to consent to them.

I would not trust them though, for they are barbarians and heathens. We would rather be killed than taken prisoner, for it is in this kind of rebellion that they kill; but thanks to Our Lord we have not reached that point. If we knew of the approach of the enemy, we would not wait for them and you would see us again this year. If I saw only seven or eight French families returning to France, I would consider it foolhardy to remain, and, even were I to have a revelation that there was nothing to fear, I would consider my vision suspect in order to hold to something more certain for my sisters and me. The Hospital Sisters are determined to do the same.

To speak to you frankly, the difficulty of getting the necessities of life and of clothing will be the reason for leaving—if we leave—rather than the Iroquois. But to tell the truth, the latter will always be the fundamental cause, for their incursions and the terror they spread everywhere bring trade in many of its aspects to a halt. It is for this reason that we clear as much land as possible for cultivation. The bread

---

Source: Irene Mahoney, ed., *Marie of the Incarnation: Selected Writings* (New York: Paulist Press, 1989), pp. 246–251.

here has a better taste than that of France, but it is not so white nor so nourishing for the working people. Vegetables are also better here and more abundant. There we are, my dear son, concerning the Iroquois.

I agree wholeheartedly with your feelings concerning the necessity of providing for the observance of our rules in the future. For now, I say to my shame, I do not see in me a single virtue capable of edifying my sisters. I cannot answer for the future but as far as I can see of those who have come from France, I would be as certain of the majority of them as I am of myself. And even should they wish to return—which they are very far from doing—those whom we have professed from this country, having been raised in our rules and never having tasted any other spirit, would be capable of maintaining it.

This is why we are in no hurry to ask for more sisters to come. Further, the wound that the hand of God has inflicted on us is still too fresh and we still feel its inconvenience too keenly. We are also afraid that they might send us subjects who are not suitable for us and who would have difficulty in adjusting to the food, the climate, and the people. What we fear even more is that they would not be docile and that they would not have a strong vocation. For since they have a spirit different from ours, if they do not have a spirit of submission and docility they would have difficulty in adjusting, as we would perhaps in putting up with them.

This vexatious spirit has already caused two hospital sisters to return and having this example before my eyes arouses my fear. For what good is making a display of traveling a thousand or twelve hundred leagues to people of our sex and condition amid the dangers of the sea and of enemies if one is then to retrace those same steps? I would have difficulty in resolving this question unless there were an absolute necessity; for example, if a young woman were so determined to return to France that she could only be restrained with violence and perhaps with detriment to her salvation.

I had a strong desire to have my niece of the Incarnation come here who, I have often been told, is both wise and virtuous and has a stable vocation. I would even like to prepare her for her duties and for everything concerning this country. But the fear I have that she might not be happy as well as that of exposing her to the risk of returning to France has held me back. Furthermore, I am getting old and when I die I would leave her in a solitude which might be too difficult for her. Finally, the hindrance that the Iroquois bring to Christianity does not permit us to have the savage girls as before. This would be a very sharp pain for her to see herself deprived of the very end for which she had come. For to tell you the truth, this is extremely painful and depressing. How would a young woman have the heart to learn these very difficult languages, seeing herself deprived of the very subjects with which she hoped to use them? If hostilities were to last for just a little time, the spirit would make an effort to overcome this repugnance. But death may come before peace does.

This is what prevented me from letting my niece come here in spite of my wish to please her and in spite of the consolation I could have hoped for from her. Since I am so far away from you and any opportunity of seeing you, she would have been for me another you, for you are the two people for whom my spirit most often wanders off to France. But it is rather in the heart of our lovable Jesus that I visit you both, offering my wishes for your sanctification and the complete immolation of yourselves. I offer the sacrifice of this satisfaction to my divine Jesus, leaving everything in his hands both for time and eternity. He knows what he wants to do with us; let us be glad to let him do it. If we are faithful to him, our reunion in heaven will be that much more perfect since we will have broken our ties in this world in order to obey the maxims of his Gospel.

But to come back to our subject. We are not in a hurry, then, to ask for choir sisters from France, for we feel it is necessary to wait a little and take measures so that neither we nor they will have any reason for discontent. Nevertheless, in spite of all the reasons I have listed, we simply have to ask for two lay sisters, perhaps even this year. . . .

All the darkness I encounter makes me see into my vocation more clearly than ever and reveals to me lights which were only obscure and incomprehensible when God gave them to me before I came to Canada. I will speak to you of this in the writings I have promised you, so that you can understand and admire the guidance of the divine goodness on me and how he has wanted me to obey him beyond human reason, losing myself in his ways in a manner I cannot express. . . .

I assure you that despite all our losses, [God] has never yet let me want for the necessities of life, nor even of clothing, and that he has provided for everything most paternally. . . . He is my all and my life wherever I may be.

4. Two Germans Debate the Merits of Pennsylvania, 1684, 1738

Positive Information from America, Concerning the Country of Pennsylvania, from a German Who Has Migrated Thither; Dated Philadelphia, March 7, 1684.

To fulfill my duty as well as my promise made at my departure I will somewhat more circumstantially state what I have found and noted of these lands; and since I am not unaware that by imperfect relations many of you have been misinformed, I give my assurance beforehand that I with impartial pen and without deceptive additions will set forth faithfully both the inconveniences of the journey and the defects of this province, as well as that plentifulness of the same which has been praised by others almost to excess; for I desire nothing more in my little place than to walk in the footsteps of Him who is the way, and to follow His holy teachings, because He is the truth, in order that I may ceaselessly enjoy with Him eternal life. . . .

III. Of the nature of the land I can write with certainty only after one or more years of experience. The Swedes and Low Dutch who have occupied it for twenty years and more are in this as in most other things of divided opinions. . . . Certain it is that the soil does not lack fruitfulness and will reward the labor of our hands as well as in Europe if one will duly work and manure it, both which things are for the most part lacking. For the above mentioned old inhabitants are poor agriculturists. Some of them have neither barns nor stables, and leave their grain for years together

Source: Albert Cook Myers, ed., *Narratives of Early Pennsylvania, West New Jersey and Delaware, 1630–1707* (New York: Charles Scribner's Sons, 1912), pp. 392, 397, 399–401, 410–411; "Two Germantown Letters of 1738," *Pennsylvania Magazine of History and Biography* 56 (1932): 10–11.

unthreshed and lying in the open air, and allow their cattle, horses, cows, swine, etc., to run in the woods summer and winter, so that they derive little profit from them. . . . Inasmuch as in the past year very many people came hither both out of England and Ireland and also from Barbadoes and other American islands, and this province does not yet produce sufficient provisions for such a multitude, therefore all victuals are somewhat dear, and almost all the money goes out of the land to pay for them. Yet we hope in time to have a greater abundance of both things, because William Penn will coin money and agriculture will be better managed. Working people and husbandmen are in the greatest demand here, and I certainly wish that I had a dozen strong Tyrolese to cut down the thick oak trees. . . .

V. As to the inhabitants, I cannot better classify them than into the native and the engrafted. For if I were to call the former savages and the latter Christians, I should do great injustice to many of both varieties. Of the latter sort, I have already mentioned above, that the incoming ships are not altogether to be compared with Noah's Ark. The Lutheran preacher, who ought as a *statua Mercurialis* to show the Swedes the way to heaven, is, to say it in one word, a drunkard. Also there are coiners of false money and other vicious persons here whom nevertheless, it may be hoped, the wind of God's vengeance will in his own time drive away like chaff. On the other hand there is no lack of pious, God-fearing people, and I can with truth affirm that I have nowhere in Europe seen the notice posted up, as here in our Philadelphia, that such an one has found this or that, and that the loser may call for it at his house; often however the converse, Lost this or that; he who returns it again shall receive a reward, etc.

Of these new engrafted strangers I will for the present say no more . . . but will briefly give my account of those who are erroneously called savages. The first who came before my eyes were those two who at Upland came in a canoe to our ship. I presented them with a dram of brandy. They attempted to pay me for it with a sixpence, and when I refused the money they gave me their hands, and said, Thank you, brother. They are strong of limb, swarthy of body, and paint their faces, red, blue, etc., in various ways. In the summer they go quite naked, except that they cover their private parts with a piece of cloth, and now in winter hang duffels upon themselves. They have coal-black hair, while the Swedish children born here have hair snow-white. I was once dining with William Penn where one of their kings sat at table with us. William Penn, who can speak their language fairly fluently, said to him that I was a German, etc. He came accordingly on the third of October, and on the twelfth of December another king and queen came to my house. Also many common persons over-run me very often, to whom however I almost always show my love with a piece of bread and a drink of beer, whereby an answering affection is awakened in them and they commonly call me "Teutsch-mann," also "Carissimo" (that is, brother). N. B. Their language is manly and in my opinion is little inferior to the Italian in gravity, etc. As to their manners and nature, one must so to speak sub-distinguish them into those who have associated for some time with the so-called Christians and those who are just beginning to come forth out of their burrows. For the former are crafty and deceitful, which they owe to the above-mentioned nominal Christians. . . . Those of the second class, on the contrary, are of a reasonable spirit, injure nobody, and we have nothing whatever to fear from them. . . .

Now you might perhaps ask whether I with a pure and undisturbed conscience could advise one and another of you to come over to this place. I answer with good deliberation that I would be heartily glad of your dear presence; yet unless you (1) find in yourselves freedom of conscience to go, (2) can submit to the difficulties and dangers of the long journey, and (3) can resolve to go without most of the comforts to which you have been accustomed in Germany, such as stone houses, luxurious food and drink, for a year or two, then follow my advice and stay where you are for some time yet. But if the things I have mentioned do not come too hard for you, depart the sooner the better from the European Sodom, and remember Lot's wife, who indeed went forth with her feet but left her heart and inclinations there. . . .

Herewith I send a specimen of the Indian money used here, of which six of the white and three of the black make an English farthing; and these Indians will not sell anything more for silver money but will be paid with their own money, since for the most part they wish to quit this land and to withdraw some hundred miles farther into the woods. For they have a superstition, that as many Indians must die each year, as the number of Europeans that newly arrive. . . .

I remain ever your true and devoted servant,

N. N.

Christopher Saur Writes from Germantown, 1738

Germantown [Pennsylvania]

18 October, 1738.

The great numbers of people who have been prevailed upon this year to come to this country are raising a considerable lamentation in the land. Moreover, since so many hundreds have sickened and died on board ship, the members of families remaining behind must pay or go into service; so that there is an unusual shortage of money and a degree of privation among the people that can scarcely be described. And then the captains get hold of the little silver and gold that is to be found here and there in the country as payment for shipping immigrants over everywhere. And still, despite the great drought of the past summer, which has dried up nearly all plants and vegetables, grain and wheat enough has been produced, but it is not being exported at present. So the farmer has nothing with which he can make headway himself or help others; hence borrowing, also among manual laborers, is becoming more and more frequent. What the outcome of this will be, remains to be seen. A great many are regretting bitterly and with tears that they ever came here, especially those who could have got along in some fashion over there. They have left everything, they have been unable to get started here, and are without sufficient help. Many who have never done a day's work, or intended to, must beg. How miserable will it not be this autumn, especially for people with such habits! Oh, if the people on the other side would only consider what they do, and not let their minds be inflamed by cunning and false rumors or by deceiving letters (or by enticing letters—*Lock-Briefe*—of which, if one in twenty gets results, it makes good business)! As above mentioned, a severe drought has persisted throughout the whole summer, so that very many, indeed most, of the wells have dried up. And thus it has been in Carolina, Maryland, Virginia, and in New York, as well. The rumor has been in circulation daily that the war between England and Spain will break out in Carolina or Georgia, but thank God, it has not taken place up to this time. But the embers are glowing strongly. The Elsoffers have not yet arrived. Everybody is wondering where their ship is, and besides that vessel, three or four other ships with people are expected. According to report, these have already been on the sea for three months. The people who have arrived in Georgia are having a hard time of it there. They have little good water. The Savannah river region is reported to be a waste of sand. The people cannot get farther into the country because of the many bogs, morasses, cane [brakes] and dense woods. It takes an unbelievable amount of work to make roads. So too, it is going to take a long time before the soil can be prepared to raise good grain and wheat. More than half of the Salzburgers who have got there have died; likewise the Swiss. The people here have it from reliable witnesses that between here and Virginia is a stretch of country on the Susquehanna which may be reached through Maryland, in which Annapolis, the capital, is situated,—a large strip of uncommonly fertile land. Into that region, people from here and from neighboring lands which are already filled up, have been moving annually for the past five years, and have found things to their liking. The poor people who have been persuaded this year to leave Hesse for Georgia will find themselves sadly disappointed, for they do not even have oat bread there. The chief diet there is Welsh or Indian corn, with rice and melons. Butter, milk, fresh meat, wheat and grain are exceedingly scarce there, when not in season (*nach der Zeit*); all such provisions must be brought there from this country (*i.e.*, Pennsylvania). I have permitted myself this digression for the sake of others who may have a great desire to emigrate. So I close with greetings, etc.

J. Chr. Sauer.

5. Slaves Endure the Middle Passage, 1693

The negroes are so wilful and loth to leave their own country, that they have often leap'd out of the canoos, boat and ship, into the sea, and kept under water till they were drowned, to avoid being taken up and saved by our boats, which pursued them; they having a more dreadful apprehension of Barbadoes than we can have of hell, tho' in reality they live much better there than in their own country; but home is home, &c. We have likewise seen divers of them eaten by the sharks, of which a prodigious number kept about the ships in this place, and I have been told will follow her hence to Barbadoes, for the dead negroes that are thrown over-board in the passage. I am certain in our voyage there we did not want the sight of some every day, but that they were the same I can't affirm. We had about 12 negroes did wilfully drown themselves, and others starv'd themselves to death; for 'tis their belief that when they die they return home to their own country and friends again. . . .

When our slaves are aboard we shackle the men two and two, while we lie in port, and in sight of their own country, for 'tis then they attempt to make their escape, and

---

Source: George Francis Dow, ed., *Slave Ships and Slaving* (Marine Research Society, 1927), pp. 62–63, 65–69.

mutiny; to prevent which we always keep centinels upon the hatchways, and have a chest of small arms, ready loaden and prim'd, constantly lying at hand upon the quarter-deck, together with some granada shells; and two of our quarter-deck guns, pointing on the deck thence, and two more out of the steerage, the door of which is always kept shut, and well barr'd. They are fed twice a day, at 10 in the morning, and 4 in the evening, which is the time they are aptest to mutiny, being all upon deck; therefore all that time, what of our men are not employ'd in distributing their victuals to them, and settling them, stand to their arms; and some with lighted matches at the great guns that yaun upon them, loaden with partridge, till they have done and gone down to their kennels between decks. Their chief diet is call'd dabbadabb, being Indian corn ground as small as oat-meal in iron mills, which we carry for that purpose; and afterwards mix'd with water and boil'd well in a large copper furnace, till 'tis as thick as a pudding. About a peckful of which in vessels, call'd crews, is allow'd to 10 men, with a little salt, malagetta, and palm oil, to relish.

They are divided into messes of ten each, for the easier and better order in serving them. Three days a week they have horse-beans boil'd for their dinner and supper, great quantities of which the African Company do send aboard us for that purpose. These beans the negroes extremely love and desire, beating their breast, eating them, and crying "Pram! Pram!" which is, "Very good!" They are indeed the best diet for them, having a binding quality, and consequently good to prevent the flux, which is the inveterate distemper that most affects them, and ruins our voyages by their mortality. The men are all fed upon the main deck and forecastle, that we may have them all under command of our arms from the quarter-deck, in case of any disturbance; the women eat upon the quarter-deck with us, and the boys and girls upon the poop. After they are once divided into messes, and appointed their places, they will readily run there in good order of themselves afterward. When they have eaten their victuals clean up (which we force them to for to thrive the better), they are order'd down between decks, and every one as he passes has a pint of water to drink after his meat, which is serv'd them by the cooper out of a large tub, fill'd beforehand ready for them. When they have occasion to ease nature, they are permitted by the centinels to come up, and go to a conveniency which is provided for that purpose, on each side of the ship, each of which will contain a dozen of them at once, and have broad ladders to ascend them with the greater ease.

When we come to sea we let them all out of irons, they never then attempting to rebel, considering that should they kill or master us, they could not tell how to manage the ship, or must trust us, who would carry them where we pleased; therefore the only danger is while we are in sight of their own country, which they are loath to part with; but once out of sight out of mind. I never heard that they mutiny'd in any ships of consequence, that had a good number of men, and the least care; but in small tools where they had but few men, and those negligent or drunk, then they surpriz'd and butcher'd them, cut the cables, and let the vessel drive ashore, and every one shift for himself. However, we have some 30 to 40 Gold Coast negroes, which we buy, and are procur'd us there by our factors, to make guardians and overseers of the Whidaw negroes, and sleep among them to keep them from quarrelling, and in order, as well as to give us notice, if they can discover any caballing or plotting among them, which trust they will discharge with great diligence; they also take care to make the negroes scrape the decks where they lodge every morning very clean, to eschew any distempers that may engender from filth and nastiness. When we constitute a guardian, we give him a cat of nine tails as a badge of his office, which he is not a little proud of, and will exercise with great authority. We often at sea, in the evenings, would let the slaves come up into the sun to air themselves, and make them jump and dance for an hour or two to our bag-pipes, harp, and fiddle, by which exercise to preserve them in health; but notwithstanding all our endeavour, 'twas my hard fortune to have great sickness and mortality among them.

Having bought my complement of 700 slaves, viz. 480 men and 220 women, and finish'd all my business at Whidaw, I took my leave of the old king and his cappasheirs, and parted, with many affectionate expressions on both sides, being forced to promise him that I would return again the next year, with several things he desired me to bring from England; and having sign'd bills of lading to Mr. Peirson, for the negroes aboard, I set sail the 27th of July in the morning, accompany'd with the *East India Merchant*, who had bought 650 slaves, for the island of St. Thomas, from which we took our departure, on August 25th, and set sail for Barbadoes.

We spent in our passage from St. Thomas to Barbadoes two months eleven days, in which time there happened such sickness and mortality among my poor men and negroes, that of the first we buried 14, and of the last 320, which was a great detriment to our voyage, the Royal African Company losing ten pounds by every slave that died, and the owners of the ship ten pounds ten shillings, being the freight agreed on to be paid them by the charter-party for every negro delivered alive ashore to the African Company's agents at Barbadoes; whereby the loss in all amounted to near 6500 pounds sterling. The distemper which my men as well as the blacks mostly died of, was the white flux, which was so violent and inveterate, that no medicine would in the least check it; so that when any of our men were seized with it, we esteemed him a dead man, as he generally proved. I cannot imagine what should cause it in them so suddenly, they being free from it till about a week after we left the island of St. Thomas. And next to the malignity of the climate, I can attribute it to nothing else but the unpurg'd black sugar, and raw unwholesome rum they bought there, of which they drank in punch to great excess, and which it was not in my power to hinder, having chastised several of them, and flung over-board what rum and sugar I could find; and was forced to clap one Lord, our trumpeter, in irons, for his being the promoter of their unseasonable carousing bouts, and going in one of his drunken fits with his knife to kill the boatswain in his bed, and committing other enormities; but tho' he remained upon the poop day and night in irons for two months, without any other shelter than the canopy of heaven, he was never troubled with any sickness, but made good the proverb, "That naught's never in danger," or "that he who is born to be hang'd," &c. I have given some account of him elsewhere, therefore shall say no more here.

The negroes are so incident to the small-pox, that few ships that carry them escape without it, and sometimes it makes vast havock and destruction among them; but tho' we had 100 at a time sick of it, and that it went thro' the ship, yet we lost not above a dozen by it. All the assistance we gave the diseased was only as much water as they desir'd to drink, and some palm-oil to anoint their sores, and they would generally recover without any other helps but what kind nature gave them.

One thing is very surprizing in this distemper among the blacks, that tho' it immediately infects those of their own colour, yet it will never seize a white man; for I had several white men and boys aboard that had never had that distemper, and were constantly among the blacks that were sick of it, yet none of them in the least catch'd it, tho' it be the very same malady in its effects, as well as symptoms, among the blacks, as among us in England, beginning with the pain in the head, back, shivering, vomiting, fever, &c. But what the smallpox spar'd, the flux swept off, to our great regret, after all our pains and care to give them their messes in due order and season, keeping their lodgings as clean and sweet as possible, and enduring so much misery and stench so long among a parcel of creatures nastier than swine; and after all our expectations to be defeated by their mortality. No gold-finders can endure so much noisome slavery as they do who carry negroes; for those have some respite and satisfaction, but we endure twice the misery; and yet by their mortality our voyages are ruin'd, and we pine and fret ourselves to death, to think that we should undergo so much misery, and take so much pains to so little purpose.

6. Peter Kolb Explains Why He Migrated to the Cape of Good Hope and Then Returned Home, 1704, 1713

Having felt, in my early Years, an ardent Desire to travel, and long sought in vain for a favourable Opportunity to gratifie so prevailing a Passion, I leave the Reader to imagine the Transport I felt when my generous Patron The Baron *van Krosick*, Privy Councellor to the late King of *Prussia*, whom I had the Honour to serve in Quality of Secretary, communicated to me his Resolution to send a proper Person, at his own Cost, to reside for some Time at the *Cape of Good Hope*; and that he had pitch'd upon me as such; to make and digest the proper Observations on the Heavenly Bodies, as they appear'd from thence, for the Advancement of *Astronomical* Learning.

This Overture of His Excellency, which was accompanied with the most generous Sentiments of my Capacity and Application, was the Crowning of my Wishes, and possess'd me with a treble Pleasure: First, as it gratified my Passion for Travelling; in the next Place, as it gave me an Opportunity of shewing my Attachment to His Excellency by my Activity in a Service he had so much at Heart; and lastly, as it might enable me to oblige the learned and curious Part of the World with an useful and entertaining History of a Country and People, of whom we have had hitherto such various and uncertain Accounts.

I accepted then of this Employment with the highest Expressions of Gratitude. And my Noble Patron having settled on me a yearly Salary, and promised me every kind of Support and Assistance, which might be in his Power, I withdrew to prepare, according to his Directions, immediately for the Voyage; and was employ'd in getting up such Books, mathematical Instruments and other Things as might be useful to me at the *Cape*, while His Excellency prepar'd Letters in my Favour to several Persons of Distinction in *Holland*, . . . To those his old Friends the Baron explain'd and recommended his Intention, requesting them to introduce me to the Directors of the *India* Company at *Amsterdam*, and to employ their Credit with the said Directors for my Obtaining their Warrant for a Passage to the *Cape of Good Hope* on one of their Ships, together with their Letters Recommendatory to the Company's Settlements and

Source: Peter Kolb, *The Present State of the Cape of Good Hope* (London, 1723), ed. W. Peter Carstens (New York and London: Johnson Reprint Corporation, 1968), v. 1, pp. 1–7; v. 2, pp. 363–365.

Factories at or near the *Cape*, in order to my obtaining there such Countenance and Assistance as might be necessary to the Accomplishment of the Design. . . .

On the 22d of *December* 1704 I embark'd, with several other Passengers, in the Company's Ship the *Union* in the *Texel*, where, with eight more of the Company's Ships bound for *India*, we lay for a Wind till *January* the 8th following, when the whole Fleet sail'd out.

It being in the Time of the late War with *France*, to avoid the Enemy as much as possible, we steer'd our Course *North* about, round *Scotland*; but before we had made so far, the whole Fleet was twice or thrice separated by stormy Weather out of Sight of one another; a Thing, which being ordinary enough, I should not have mention'd but for the Sake of observing the Jealousy and Apprehension with which Friends that have been separated at Sea in Time of War, come in View of one another again. For having lost Sight of our Company, every Sail we descry'd afterwards was taken for a Privateer, as, on the other Hand, was the *Union*; and every Ship, on the Sight of her Friends, prepar'd for an Attack as on the Appearance of an Enemy, till we were all happily join'd again.

Being but a Novice in *Low-Dutch* when I left *Amsterdam*, and finding no other Language on board in which I had any Share, I was extremely at a Loss for Conversation and Intelligence in certain Matters till such Time as I had acquir'd a tolerable Knowledge of it by Application at Sea. But before I was Master of this Talent, I suffer'd enough; for using at first all possible Dispatch in the Acquisition of it, and being withal pretty inquisitive, I offended so often against Grammar and Idiom, and was so little understood, that I was grinn'd at from all the Quarters of the Ship, and particularly by the Savages before the Mast, who look'd upon me as a very strange Fellow. This rude Attack of the Ship's Company forc'd me into close Quarters. I retired to my Cabbin, and for some Time rarely stirr'd or look'd out: But wanting the Reliefs of Conversation there, I fell into a deep Melancholy; by means of which and the extremely piercing Cold I suffer'd in the Northern Climates I fell dangerously ill. My Blood was in a Manner frozen in its Channels. For many Days my Life was despair'd of. But after such Medicines and Assistance as I was able to procure at Sea, my Sickness dwindled into an intermitting Fever; from which, by the Blessing of God and the Skill and Care of the Ship's Surgeon, I was recover'd by the End of *February*.

By this Time we were got into a pretty warm Climate, which gave me wonderful Relief; and it was with the highest Satisfaction I perceiv'd, that as I advanc'd towards the *Line*, and within the Sun's Activity, my Health and Vigour were augmented. The Phlegm and Melancholy that oppress'd me vanish'd as I approach'd the Sun, insomuch that under the *Torrid* Zone I found my self perfectly freed from every Incumbrance of either kind, and in Possession of as much Health and Chearfulness as a Man can wish. I shall not trouble the Reader by accounting for this, since, if he is any Thing of a Philosopher, he will easily do it himself. But this was not all my Happiness between the Tropicks; for I had by this Time pick'd up so much *Low-Dutch*, that I could enter a little into Conversation; and as if Change of Climate had introduc'd a Change into the Manners and Sentiments of the Ship's Company, every one (then somewhat appriz'd, I suppose, of the Patronage and Purpose of my Voyage) shew'd me Abundance of Respect, and were so assiduous to please and oblige me, that they not only gave me immediate Satisfaction in every Enquiry I made to which they could answer, but upon any Accident, or the Appearance of any Thing, which they thought deserv'd my Remark, there was a continual Emulation among 'em who should be the first to give me Notice of it. This was fitting my Humour and Design to a great Exactness; and by the help of a little Assiduity to oblige them on my own Side, I had the good Fortune to be so gratified to the End of the Voyage. . . .

April the 9th 1713, I embark'd on board the Company's Ship, call'd the *Stadthouse* of *Enckhuysen* for *Holland*. By the Favour of the Government at the *Cape*, my Accommodations and Privileges on board this Ship were some of the best. I victual'd with the Captain, and was very much caress'd by him and by all the inferiour Officers, as likewise by all the Gentlemen Passengers on Board. These Things, together with my Advances towards my native Country, which I long'd to see again, were a mighty Comfort to me: For I had undergone a great many Fatigues and Disappointments at the *Cape*, and not a little ill Usage. My Friends in *Europe* were much wanting to their Promises to me of Support and Encouragement while I remain'd at the *Cape*; and I was not a little shatter'd and reduc'd thro' their Neglect of me. . . . Near the *Line* we were held for several Days by a stark Calm. Near the *Line* too we had thick Fogs, in which Guns were frequently discharg'd from all the Ships, in order to keep the Ships together; for we knew not then of the Peace in *Europe*. Soon after, we met with several Ships which gave us the agreable News. Nothing remarkable happen'd during the Rest of the Voyage. About the Middle of *August* we arriv'd in the *Flie*; From whence I pass'd in a Yacht, with several Passengers of Distinction, to *Amsterdam*, where we arriv'd on the 22d. Having pass'd some Time at this City, I set out for, and, blessed be God, arriv'd safely in my native Country.

7. Elizabeth Sprigs Begs for Help, 1756

**To Mr. John Sprigs White Smith in White Cross Street
near Cripple Gate London**

MARYLAND Sept'r 22'd 1756.

Honred Father

My being for ever banished from your sight, will I hope pardon the Boldness I now take of troubling you with these, my long silence has been purely owing to my undutifullness to you, and well knowing I had offended in the highest Degree, put a tie to my tongue and pen, for fear I should be extinct from your good Graces and add a further Trouble to you, but too well knowing your care and tenderness for me so long as I retaind my Duty to you, induced me once again to endeavour if possible, to kindle up that flame again. O Dear Father, belive what I am going to relate the words of truth and sincerity, and Ballance my former bad Conduct [to] my sufferings here, and then I am sure you'll pitty your Destress [ed] Daughter, What we unfortunat English People suffer here is beyond the probability of you in England to Conceive, let it suffice that I one of the unhappy Number, am toiling almost Day and Night, and very often in the Horses druggery, with only this comfort that you Bitch

Source: Isabel M. Calder, ed., *Colonial Captivities, Marches and Journeys* (Kennikat Press, Inc: Port Washington, NY, 1935, 1967), pp. 151–152.

you do not halfe enough, and then tied up and whipp'd to that Degree that you'd not serve an Annimal, scarce any thing but Indian Corn and Salt to eat and that even begrudged nay many Neagroes are better used, almost naked no shoes nor stockings to wear, and the comfort after slaving dureing Masters pleasure, what rest we can get is to rap ourselves up in a Blanket and ly upon the Ground, this is the deplorable Condition your poor Betty endures, and now I beg if you have any Bowels of Compassion left show it by sending me some Relief, Cothing is the principal thing wanting, which if you should condiscend to, may easely send them to me by any of the ships bound to Baltimore Town Patapsco River Maryland, and give me leave to conclude in Duty to you and Uncles and Aunts, and Respect to all Friends

Honred Father

Your undutifull and Disobedient Child
ELIZABETH SPRIGS

Please to direct for me
at Mr. Rich'd Crosses to
be left at Mr. Luxes Merc't
in Baltimore Town Patapsco River
Maryland

8. An Afro-British Abolitionist Recalls His Childhood Captivity, 1787

I was born in the city of Agimaque, on the coast of Fantyn; my father was a companion to the chief in that part of the country of Fantee, and when the old king died I was left in his house with his family; soon after I was sent for by his nephew, Ambro Accasa, who succeeded the old king in the chiefdom of that part of Fantee known by the name of Agimaque and Assinee. I lived with his children, enjoying peace and tranquillity, about twenty moons, which, according to their way of reckoning time, is two years. I was sent for to visit an uncle, who lived at a considerable distance from Agimaque. The first day after we set out we arrived at Assinee, and the third day at my uncle's habitation, where I lived about three months, and was then thinking of returning to my father and young companion at Agimaque; but by this time I had got well acquainted with some of the children of my uncle's hundreds of relations, and we were some days too ventursome in going into the woods to gather fruit and catch birds, and such amusements as pleased us. One day I refused to go with the rest, being rather apprehensive that something might happen to us; till one of my play-fellows said to me, because you belong to the great men, you are afraid to venture your carcase, or else of the *bounsam*, which is the devil. This enraged me so much, that I set a resolution to join the rest, and we went into the woods as usual; but we had not been above two hours before our troubles began, when several great ruffians came upon us suddenly, and said we had committed a fault against their lord, and we must go and answer for it ourselves before him.

Source: Ottobah Cugoano, *Thoughts and Sentiments on the Evil and Wicked Traffic of the Slavery and Commerce of the Human Species* (London, 1787), pp. 6–10, 12.

Some of us attempted in vain to run away, but pistols and cutlasses were soon introduced, threatening, that if we offered to stir we should all lie dead on the spot. One of them pretended to be more friendly than the rest, and said, that he would speak to their lord to get us clear, and desired that we should follow him; we were then immediately divided into different parties, and drove after him. We were soon led out of the way which we knew, and towards the evening, as we came in sight of a town, they told us that this great man of theirs lived there, but pretended it was too late to go and see him that night. Next morning there came three other men, whose language differed from ours, and spoke to some of those who watched us all the night, but he that pretended to be our friend with the great man, and some others, were gone away. We asked our keepers what these men had been saying to them, and they answered, that they had been asking them, and us together, to go and feast with them that day, and that we must put off seeing the great man till after; little thinking that our doom was so nigh, or that these villains meant to feast on us as their prey. We went with them again about half a day's journey, and came to a great multitude of people, having different music playing; and all the day after we got there, we were very merry with the music, dancing and singing. Towards the evening, we were again persuaded that we could not get back to where the great man lived till next day; and when bedtime came, we were separated into different houses with different people. When the next morning came, I asked for the men that brought me there, and for the rest of my companions; and I was told that they were gone to the sea side to bring home some rum, guns and powder, and that some of my companions were gone with them, and that some were gone to the fields to do something or other. This gave me strong suspicion that there was some treachery in the case, and I began to think that my hopes of returning home again were all over. I soon became very uneasy, not knowing what to do, and refused to eat or drink for whole days together, till the man of the house told me that he would do all in his power to get me back to my uncle; then I eat a little fruit with him, and had some thoughts that I should be sought after, as I would be then missing at home about five or six days. I enquired every day if the men had come back, and for the rest of my companions, but could get no answer of any satisfaction. I was kept about six days at this man's house, and in the evening there was another man came and talked with him a good while, and I heard the one say to the other he must go, and the other said the sooner the better; that man came out and told me that he knew my relations at Agimaque, and that we must set out to-morrow morning, and he would convey me there. Accordingly we set out next day, and travelled till dark, when we came to a place where we had some supper and slept. He carried a large bag with some gold dust, which he said he had to buy some goods at the sea side to take with him to Agimaque. Next day we travelled on, and in the evening came to a town, where I saw several white people, which made me afraid that they would eat me, according to our notion as children in the inland parts of the country. This made me rest very uneasy all the night, and next morning I had some victuals brought, desiring me to eat and make haste, as my guide and kid-napper told me that he had to go to the castle with some company that were going there, as he had told me before, to get some goods. After I was ordered out, the horrors I soon saw and felt, cannot be well described; I saw many of my miserable countrymen chained two and two, some hand-cuffed, and some with their hands tied behind. We were conducted along by a guard, and when we arrived at the castle, I asked my guide what I was brought there for, he told me to learn the ways of the *browfow*, that is the white faced people. I saw him take a gun, a piece of cloth, and some lead for me, and then he told me that he must now leave me there, and went off. This made me cry bitterly, but I was soon conducted to a prison, for three days, where I heard the groans and cries of many, and saw some of my fellow-captives. But when a vessel arrived to conduct us away to the ship, it was a most horrible scene; there was nothing to be heard but rattling of chains, smacking of whips, and the groans and cries of our fellow men. Some would not stir for the ground; when they were lashed and beat in the most horrible manner. I have forgot the name of this infernal fort; but we were taken in the ship that came from us; to another that was ready to sail from Cape Coast. When we were put into the ship, we saw several black merchants coming on board, but we were all drove into our holes, and not suffered to speak to any of them. In this situation we continued several days in sight of our native land; but I could find no good person to give any information of my situation to Accasa at Agimaque. And when we found ourselves at last taken away, death was more preferable than life, and a plan was concerted amongst us, that we might burn and blow up the ship, and to perish all together in the flames; but we were betrayed by one of our own country-women, who slept with some of the head men of the ship, for it was common for the dirty filthy sailors to take the African women and lie upon their bodies; but the men were chained and pent up in holes. It was the women and boys which were to burn the ship, with the approbation and groans of the rest; though that was prevented, the discovery was likewise a cruel bloody scene. . . .

But I must own, to the shame of my own countrymen, that I was first kid-napped and betrayed by some of my own complexion, who were the first cause of my exile and slavery; but if there were no buyers there would be no sellers. So far as I can remember, some of the Africans in my country keep slaves, which they take in war, or for debt; but those which they keep are well fed, and good care taken of them, and treated well; and, as to their cloathing, they differ according to the custom of the country. But I may safely say, that all the poverty and misery that any of the inhabitants of Africa meet with among themselves, is far inferior to those inhospitable regions of misery which they meet with in the West-Indies, where their hard-hearted overseers have neither regard to the laws of God, nor the life of their fellow-men.

◁ E S S A Y S

Historians of migration need to consider where people came from, where they went, and what they carried with them—their material goods, for those lucky enough to possess them, but also the whole array of practices and beliefs we lump together as culture, including language, religion, diet, clothing, and family relations. Although historians have generally understood the slave trade as driven by demand for labor in the plantation societies of the Americas, John Thornton helps us understand the local context in central Africa. Protracted civil wars in the kingdom of Kongo produced tens of thousands of captives. A leading historian of the "African Atlantic," Thornton examines the ideas enslaved Africans held about those who enslaved them. Drawing on sources that reveal slaves' fears of being eaten, Thornton analyzes central African ideas about witchcraft. Witches were people who were selfish and greedy; hence, rulers and merchants who engaged in the slave trade became identified as witches.

Enslaved people carried their association of slavery, cannibalism, and witchcraft from Central Africa to the Americas.

In her essay, Alison Games looks at some of the challenges migrants faced in their efforts to replicate familiar institutional structures or cultural forms in new places of settlement around the Atlantic. She insists that we consider an array of variables in order to make sense of the new kinds of societies that emerged around the Atlantic: the challenges and constraints of new environments, the demographic features of migrating populations, the freedom or coercion that characterized different migrations. She emphasizes the innovation and adaptation that were essential to survival as migrants struggled to create new homes for themselves in adverse circumstances.

Adaptation and Survival

ALISON GAMES

The Portuguese merchants who settled at trading posts along the coastline of west and central Africa in the fifteenth century were the first European migrants in the Atlantic world. Some of these men chose to live among the local population. They were called *lançados*, from the Portuguese verb *lançar*, to throw oneself, because they insinuated themselves into kinship and patronage networks and became permanent inhabitants. Their descendants, who spoke Portuguese in addition to African languages and who embraced both European and African cultural practices, were important commercial intermediaries between Europeans and Africans for centuries. Other European traders in Africa rejected this model of assimilation and instead sought to remain embedded in the fashions and pastimes of home. In the eighteenth century, a group of British merchants at Bance Island, located in the Sierra Leone River approximately twenty miles from modern-day Freetown, missed the leisure pursuits of their native Britain, and so they built a two-hole golf course, where they strolled the links attended by African caddies in tartan loincloths. The contrasting approaches the *lançados* and the British traders employed to adjust to their new residences far from Europe illustrate a core challenge in understanding migration across and around the Atlantic: to what extent could migrants reproduce Europe or Africa overseas, and to what extent did improvisation and adaptation characterize their response to new settings and new neighbors?

A variety of factors, including cultural attributes, power dynamics, disease environments, and the age and sex ratio of different migrating populations, largely dictated the extent to which newcomers could sustain or replicate their familiar home cultures in the often alien and perilous places they inhabited. The challenge of cultural retention was particularly acute for coerced laborers, European and especially African, who had little control over their place or condition of settlement and were often compelled to adapt to new circumstances in order to survive. Residence in the western Atlantic required cultural accommodation to the unfamiliar customs of strangers. But cultural encounters within the Atlantic also exaggerated people's attachment to their now-distant homes, as they cultivated heightened senses of who or what they were when they unexpectedly met those unlike themselves. These affiliations expressed themselves in newfound ideas about race, nationalism, and ethnicity.

Alison Games, "Atlantic Migrations: Patterns and Flows." Specifically commissioned for this volume.

The millions of migrants who struggled to assert or adapt their old cultural practices were primarily laborers. Before 1800, approximately two million Europeans crossed the Atlantic; during the period in which the slave trade was legal, from the first vessel that departed Africa in the fifteenth century until the last arrival of captives in Cuba in 1866, some twelve million Africans made the same journey. Although all of these Africans were part of a labor migration, so, too, were most of the Europeans. And although the Europeans may have had more choice in their overseas journeys, many of them might well have agreed with the English indentured servant William Moraley, who complained in the eighteenth century that he was a "tennis ball of fortune," vulnerable to forces beyond his control. For the vast majority of transatlantic migrants, the journey to the Americas meant a violent life of hunger, poverty, and brutal toil ending in an early death.

The laboring status of these Atlantic migrants, in addition to the circumstances of their procurement, affected the transmission of culture across the ocean. Merchants in Africa acquired captives from hundreds of miles away from the major trading ports, and as a result, vessels carried people from different language and ethnic groups. Awaiting embarkation from the trading forts that dotted the African coast, captives devised new languages in order to communicate with strangers. This blend of people and cultures sometimes continued in the Americas. In Jamaica in the eighteenth century, slaves from a single slaving voyage and sometimes from a common place of origin in Africa were dispersed to plantations all around the island. These ethnically diverse captives transported a wide range of cultural attributes, and the dynamics of the slave trade made it difficult for any single group of people to transport their culture intact or even to find anyone with whom they might communicate. Ayuba Suleiman, an African from Senegal who was enslaved in Maryland in the 1730s, was left stranded in jail after he ran away from his master, unable to explain himself, until the English could find "an old Negroe man" who spoke Suleiman's language, Wolof.

A second factor inhibiting the transmission of old world cultures was the sex and age structures of laboring populations. Investors, merchants, imperial officials, planters, and property owners who hoped to exploit the economic opportunities of the Americas often preferred agricultural laborers who were young and male. These preferences both hindered and defined the replication of familiar ways of life overseas, because migrants carried only fragments of their cultural traditions with them, each individual transporting only what knowledge was appropriate for his or her age and gender. Glimpses of these gendered cultural habits appear in colonial records. When Thomas Dale arrived to govern the English settlements in Virginia in 1611, he found the young men there pursuing a familiar English recreational activity for their gender: they were bowling in the streets. (What they weren't doing, to Dale's dismay, was planting corn, although that, too, was a gendered activity appropriate for English men. Instead, they starved and bowled.) Soldiers from Africa, especially those captured during the protracted civil wars in Kongo and sold into the slave trade, brought with them strategies, ideologies, and communal structures derived from their military backgrounds, and employed them in acts of resistance in the Americas.

Adults transmitted to children of the appropriate gender any number of crucial and often life-sustaining cultural practices, from religious expertise to food preparation to house construction. Gender divisions of labor varied greatly from one culture to another. In many parts of West Africa, for example, women were in charge of rice cultivation, and without their technological expertise rice production in the Americas would have floundered. In contrast, in England men were responsible for agricultural production. In all cases, parents needed to live long enough to transmit knowledge from one generation to another—and from one side of the Atlantic to another. Free parents could instill their religious beliefs in their children; provide them with the training and education consistent with status, gender, and future expectations; and thereby replicate cultural norms and values. Enslaved Africans could not even be assured of proximity to their children, much less the ability to raise them as they wished. Even European indentured laborers lost legal rights over the children they bore during their terms of service, leaving another person to define that child's religious, occupational, and social identity. Although free parents might name their children in ways that symbolized religious and familial connections—as they did by naming children after their parents or deceased relations, by giving them religious names (Lovethelord, Feargod, Jesus, Moses, or Mohammad), or, in Africa, using name days (Kofi, Cudjo, Quashee)—masters could bestow whatever names they wished upon enslaved children: Nero, Sally, Antonio, Maria, Telemaque. The hostile disease environments that new migrants, free and enslaved, confronted in most parts of the Americas hindered the transmission of European and African cultures from one generation to the next. So common were parental deaths in seventeenth-century Virginia that English colonists devised special orphans' courts to adjudicate the disposition of parental estates and to arrange for an orphaned child's education. Ruptured and reformulated households composed of stepsiblings, half-siblings, and stepparents defined the colonial American family.

Bound laborers were at an acute disadvantage in the power dynamics of colonial societies, because so many features of their lives were controlled by those who owned their labor. Their ability to retain familiar cultural traditions—whether naming their children, practicing religious rituals, or replicating family configurations—was often thwarted by legal restrictions (such as laws in those jurisdictions that refused to recognize slave marriages), the hostility of their owners, and deadly work regimes. But despite the difficulty of finding opportunities to express, re-create, and transmit one's own cultural practices, the horrors of the slave trade did not destroy the vestiges of home cultures. On the contrary, slaves conveyed their cultural heritage in their language, architecture, dress, worship, food preferences, music, art, animal husbandry, and a host of other practices. Memories and tales of a distant home might endure decades after forced migration from Africa. In 1677, John Johnson, the free American-born grandson of an African-born slave named Anthony, named his property in Virginia "Angola." But these memories of an African home were constantly reshaped by new African-born arrivals. Because of the high rates of mortality that slaves endured from the deadly toil and disease environments associated with the mining or sugar industries, most slave populations remained migrant populations, regularly replenished by newcomers from Africa. Cultures in Africa were no more static than cultures anywhere else, and so newcomers brought with them new ideas and fashions.

A complex combination of the composition of migrant groups and the nature and values of the host society determined what cultural characteristics survived—and in what form. Captive Africans from Central Africa, for example, brought many of their familiar religious practices with them. Because Central Africans believed that malevolent spiritual forces caused illness, they employed healing rituals to restore the harmony of the world and of the individual. These practices continued in migrant communities in places such as Brazil, where slaves practiced divination and slaveholders themselves consulted enslaved diviners. But other practices could not withstand the dislocation of forced migration from Central Africa and the hostility of life in a colony such as Brazil governed by a Catholic monarch and populated by priests who sought to impose their moral code. A third gender category existed in Central Africa, a population of men who lived as women known as *jinbandaa*. In Angola, the *quimbanda* (as the *jinbandaas* were known there) seem to have been a powerful religious caste. They lived together, respected by others in the community, and were highly regarded for their spiritual roles. They dressed as women and lived with men. But this important religious group did not survive the transatlantic crossing and resettlement in Portuguese territories. The *jinbandaas* did not migrate in sufficient numbers to re-create their ritual world, but more importantly the Portuguese shared the gender norms of many western Europeans of the period and did not recognize this gender category. Instead, men who dressed as women and pursued sexual relations with other men were condemned in church courts as sodomites and punished, as one Portuguese slave was in 1647, with service in the king's galleys, a labor as deadly and debilitating as work on a sugar plantation.

In contrast to the struggles many Africans confronted in replicating familiar cultural practices, some newcomers—especially Europeans—enjoyed immediate advantages in transplanting fundamental features of their home life. English, Spanish, French, Dutch, and Portuguese migrants who settled in those regions their countries had claimed could continue to speak a familiar language and to be governed by familiar laws. If the transmission of local government institutions was incomplete, these governments were nonetheless for the most part functional. Everywhere the church provided a cultural glue that linked European migrants in the western Atlantic—even religious dissenters—to the different ecclesiastical polities of the eastern Atlantic, whether Catholic or Protestant.

Thanks to the constant flow of ships, news, and letters, European migrants were able to remain embedded in transatlantic networks of kin and community. The encomendero Andrés Chacón demonstrated the tenacity of these ties several decades after he had left Spain for Peru when he wrote home in 1570, reporting on his accomplishments and calling for a nephew to assist him in his labors. Marie of the Incarnation, an Ursuline nun in Quebec, was similarly entwined in a transatlantic community made up, in her case, of her biological family, the son she had left behind in France, and a spiritual family, the transatlantic network of religious women who shared her vocation. Often such networks lured migrants back home again. Some brave people boarded ships again to tend to family affairs, to re-establish themselves in Europe, or to join allies in moments of political, religious, and national urgency. During the English Civil War (in the 1640s) and Commonwealth (in the 1650s), when devout puritans from New England believed that they could best achieve God's will in old England, approximately 15 percent of New Englanders returned home. Not everyone had such a sense of divine mission. For the German astronomer Peter Kolb, personal disappointment and pessimism about future opportunities after some nine years in the Dutch settlement at the Cape of Good Hope encouraged him to make the dangerous trek back home to Germany in 1713.

But for all the apparent advantages of continued political, commercial, and familial ties across the ocean, no European power could transplant itself in its entirety in the Americas. Europeans new to the Americas often renamed the spots they claimed and occupied, christening them after familiar places in Europe: the city of New London, in the English colony of Connecticut, was located on the river Thames; the Dutch colony of New Netherlands boasted New Amsterdam as its capital; the Spanish had New Spain, the Swedes had (briefly) New Sweden, and the French had New France. These names reflect the nostalgia and homesickness newcomers often endured (in addition to the political and territorial aspirations of acquisitive European nations), and they expose the gulf between Europe and the Americas; new names could not transform unfamiliar environments into replicas of Europe.

As Andrés Chacón's letter makes clear, for all the ties that linked the two sides of the ocean, his new world was quite unfamiliar to his curious kin in Spain, so he described carefully the peculiar array of people and the economies that sustained him: enslaved Africans, bound indigenous laborers, mining, and support industries. In letters and reports, writers described unfamiliar food and drink, marveled at the strange people they met (whether other Europeans, Africans, or Indians), lamented the pesky mosquitoes who tormented them, and detailed the plants, animals, and natural resources in their new homes. Although migrants remained attached to their countries of origin, new environments, the demographic peculiarities of migrating populations, and the presence of other strangers all combined to force Europeans in the western Atlantic to innovate and adapt. Even houses looked different from structures in the eastern Atlantic. Available resources required Europeans to modify their architectural preferences. Wealthy English colonial merchants and planters in the eighteenth century sought to emulate the building styles of Britain, for example, but in their colonial houses they used wood, a readily available material in places such as Massachusetts' prosperous North Shore, rather than the brick more commonly used in England. Less affluent colonists in the agricultural hinterlands of North America discarded the variety of regional housing styles they brought from England for a single colonial style: in rural New England, for example, settlers constructed their homes out of wood (not the brick, stone, or thatch that were all commonly used in England), and similarly rejected the great variation in floor plans from England for a common one- or one-and-a-half-story house. Eighteenth-century migrants from the European continent for the most part abandoned their own distinctive building styles, characterized for some by cellars, large central chimneys, and steeply pitched roofs, for simple and functional cabins.

Indeed, for Europeans in the Americas, despite state support of their efforts to reproduce the institutions of home, an important theme is the creation, not the replication, of ethnic identities. German-speaking people from a host of discrete communities in the Rhinelands became "Germans," an ethnic identity they would have found alien in Europe in this period. For one cohort of migrants from the Holy Roman Empire, the process of becoming "German" began in Europe. In 1709, over six thousand migrants departed the southwestern region of the Holy Roman Empire for Britain, lured by what turned out to be erroneous promises that Queen Anne would give them free land in the American colonies. This diverse group of migrants became known collectively in Britain as the Palatines, and, thanks largely to the writings of Daniel Defoe, was depicted as Protestant refugees from French invasions and Catholic oppression. Defoe even transformed these farmers into skilled laborers. In fact, these German-speaking migrants were not all from the Palatinate, few fled the French, and virtually none were victims of religious persecution, yet the refugees ended up embracing this identity. Impoverished and stranded in refugee camps in London, they depended on charity to make the final leg of their journey to North America, and it proved far better to pose as victims of persecution in need of charity from sympathetic British Protestants than to reveal themselves for who they really were—peasants seeking free land. Once the migrants reached their homes in New York and Pennsylvania, the importance of regional origin receded further. Instead, language and religion became the hallmarks of a new, common "German" identity.

Similar processes of identity formation were at work for all populations who traveled around the Atlantic. Regional European identities were muted in favor of national affiliations: Bretons became French and East Anglians became English when they were among strangers. At a larger level, the slave trade created "Africans" from thousands of discrete ethnic groups and shaped new ideas about racial differentiation. Ottobah Cugoano revealed such an awareness when he reflected on the immorality of the slave trade in his narrative. He invoked Africans as "my own countrymen," and drew on markers of racial similarity, an identification that could only emerge as Africans encountered those unlike themselves, when he called African traders people "of [his] own complexion."

A map of languages in the western Atlantic illustrates this complex process of cultural transmission, adaptation, and innovation. Ethnic majorities did not necessarily impose their own language in new places of settlement. Seventeenth-century Montserrat contained an Irish (and Irish-speaking) majority, but most people communicated in English. In the Dutch territory of Suriname, slaves spoke an English-based creole, despite the fact that the region was under English control for no more than two decades and slaves, largely African-born, always outnumbered planters, whether they were Dutch or English. But in other places, migrants from one region of Europe or Africa could have a profound linguistic impact. In Pennsylvania the protracted migration of German-speaking people ensured the continued use of German in this English colony over a century after the first German-speaking migrants (including Francis Daniel Pastorius) arrived. In parts of eighteenth-century Saint Domingue, the language of Kongo became the colony's main tongue because of the dominance of Kongolese slaves. Elsewhere, in places with no ethnic or linguistic majority, pidgins (languages that emerge in places where people speak multiple incompatible languages) developed. This happened with Gullah and Geechee in the Sea Islands of North America (off the coasts of South Carolina, Georgia, and Florida). These two languages share African grammatical features and a mixture of vocabulary from numerous languages. Speakers used English words, but Gullah also contains words with origins in the parts of Africa from which most coastal slaves came, Sierra Leone, Senegambia, and West Central Africa (Angola and Kongo). To this day modern Americans have integrated vocabulary from these eighteenth-century pidgins into their own speech: to badmouth (or curse), for example, is a Gullah word that literally translated into English an African linguistic convention that used body parts to describe behavior.

The importance of finding a common language, of replacing the linguistic isolation a newcomer might experience with the community borne of shared speech, suggests the process of adaptation central to the experience of many Atlantic migrants. For most, it proved impossible to replace what they had left behind and what they had lost through forced removal, and so they built a new world out of the remnants of the old and from practices borrowed from new neighbors. They launched a process of cultural innovation, one sparked by necessity, that redefined people and cultures around the Atlantic, creating new categories (whether African or German), new languages, and new forms of personal and cultural expression. In so doing, they revealed the human element at the center of the creation of a new Atlantic world.

The Mental World of the Captive

JOHN THORNTON

Testifying before an ecclesiastical inquest in 1659, Jose Monzolo, from the small marquisate of Nzolo in the extreme east of the Kingdom of Kongo, then enslaved and residing in Cartagena, described some of his reactions to his passage across the Atlantic. He noted the fear that his fellow slaves had in crossing the sea, for "when they left their own country, they believed that the Spanish, whom they called the whites, brought them to kill them and to make the flags for the ships from their remains, for when they were red it was from the blood of the Moors, and desperately fearing this many threw themselves in the sea on the voyage."

These bloody fears were nearly ubiquitous among Africans forced to cross the Atlantic during the years of the slave trade. . . . It was this chilling fear of being killed, eaten by white cannibals, crushed to make oil, or ground to make gunpowder that drove some of the human cargo on the ship that bore Jose Monzolo to Cartagena to jump into the sea. . . .

The beliefs of slaves from the Kikongo- and Kimbundu-speaking regions of West Central Africa, discernable in a variety of documents from the African side, allow us a further penetration into the mental world of those unfortunate people who found themselves on the slave ships bound for labor in the Americas. These sources show how deeply the ideas of cannibalism as an idiom for exploitation was rooted in West Central African ideology dealing with all aspects of life, not just the slave trade.

For those who hailed from West Central Africa, like Jose Monzolo, cannibalism and other atrocities represented a small facet of a larger social critique of all forms of economic and political exploitation—African, European, and American. This exploitation was connected to a complex series of beliefs that are often dubbed "witchcraft." The critique reached not only the slavers and slaveowners of America and not only the larger business of the slave trade, but also rulers in Africa both in their domestic policies and their participation in the slave trade and all forms of exploitation; indeed, many scholars of contemporary Africa realize that this analysis is still very much in use today. Although African beliefs about witchcraft draw some

Source: John Thornton, "Cannibals, Witches, and Slave Traders in the Atlantic World," *William and Mary Quarterly*, 2003 60(2): pp. 273–275, 277–278, 280–285, 290–294. Reprinted with permission of the Omohundro Institute of Early American History and Culture.

attention to the personal actions of witches who do evil by supernatural means, witchcraft centered around notions of selfishness and thus had a political and social as well as a personal dimension. West Central Africans used both analogy and literal description to make all forms of exploitation into manifestations of witchcraft.

Increasingly, Africanists are viewing the slave trade in the larger context of African society. Seen from the American side of the Atlantic and conditioned by the widespread belief that Europeans can be held solely responsible for the sufferings of the slave trade because they captured Africans directly or forced a fairly direct collaboration with African leaders, the slave trade appears to have been an independent force that shaped Africa and Africans. In the African perspective, it is obvious that Europeans often played a limited role, or no role, in the actual enslavement of Africans, and the slave trade was itself more often a manifestation of local politics—the solution to problems raised by war. To many seventeenth- and eighteenth-century Africans the slave trade was only one of the many consequences of war and disorder, which also included death, injury, rapine, the destruction of property, and famine. Even if one accepts that Europeans' trade and their capacity to manipulate African leaders swayed African decisions about war, this influence might not be obvious to the average African who was enslaved. Not surprisingly, therefore, Africans were unlikely to make the European and American traders responsible for the events that led to their enslavement, but instead shifted the blame to many others, including a good many other Africans. This is why beliefs that linked slavery to cannibalism and witchcraft were already circulating among slaves who had just arrived in America, before they had had a chance to feel the full weight of American slavery. That weight undoubtedly explains why cannibalism stories remained in the African American folk culture, but it is less successful in explaining their presence at the point of enslavement.

Fully to understand slavery as cannibalism and the idiom of cannibalism as a manifestation of witchcraft requires piecing together the ethical world of seventeenth- and eighteenth-century West Central Africans from contemporary sources, despite their limitations. First, because cannibalism was one of the activities of witches, we need to consider the larger issue of what was considered witchcraft in West Central Africa. . . .

Eating people, symbolically or literally, was one of the ways that witches worked their evil. During a campaign in 1692, the Kongolese nobleman Pedro Valle das Lagrimas attacked and killed two rivals, Duke Alexio of Mbamba and Afonso, marquis of Mpemba. Although Capuchin missionaries who were present at the time noted the campaign with sadness, they did not record anything exceptional about it. But an ex-Jesuit priest, Pedro Mendes, writing of the events fifteen years later, added a detail that probably came from Kongolese informants rather than from eyewitnesses. According to Mendes, Valle das Lagrimas had disinterred both Afonso's and Alexio's bodies and eaten their hearts and livers. Whether the story is true or not, it reflects the interpretation or reinterpretation that Kongolese had given the event and represented an accusation of witchcraft; thus Valle das Lagrimas was motivated by greed or wickedness, not by a just cause. . . .

In short, the grinding of the slaves, reducing them to oil, and using their blood to paint flags reported by Jose Monzolo or the cannibalism expected by others represent some of the heinous acts of the greedy. Consuming the bodies of the enslaved was but one of many symbols of avarice and selfishness, and in the context of the slave trade could clearly be applied to or expected of the Europeans who manned the slave ships and delivered the Africans to their American masters. Indeed, the link between slavery and cannibalism might be made even if the slaves were not immediately eaten on arrival—though Monzolo noted that they were certainly relieved to find that this was not the case—for the accusation and rumors of the events were as important as any demonstrated proof.

That these slaves thought there was a connection between the slave trade and witchcraft was noted in the seventeenth century by Alonso de Sandoval, a Jesuit priest whom Jose Monzolo served in Cartagena. Through years of experience meeting slaves on ships in the harbor of Cartagena he knew well what to expect. They all believed, he wrote, that the ocean voyage was "a type of witchcraft" in which upon arrival, "they would be made into oil and eaten." It might be seen figuratively . . . but the imagery and ideology were firmly based on a much larger set of ethical notions in Africa.

We can take these ethical notions as a starting point for penetrating the African understanding of the slave trade in its larger context and from the perspective on slavery in Africa itself. Doing so gives us two perspectives on the slave trade and its critique. Enslaved Africans and historians considering the situation of African slaves in America focus on the exploitation of plantation and related economies and clearly see the plantation owners and slave shippers as the primary exploiters of Africans, the originators of the slave condition, and the perpetrators of its harm. As such, the "whites" are the witches, cannibals, exploiters, and greedy ones. But viewed from the African side, slavery and the slave trade are but two of many possible ways that Africans might be exploited. While witches might be found everywhere, they were especially dangerous among those in authority who had abused their power to exploit the people. Despotic African rulers and nefarious local traders were denounced as cannibals and witches. To the degree that Europeans were ruling (as they did in places in West Central Africa after the Portuguese founded the colony of Angola in 1575) and were exporting slaves, they could also be accused of exploitative behavior and similarly suspected of cannibalism or witchcraft.

Merchants of any race or nationality were especially vulnerable to the charge of being witches because the necessarily individualistic behavior of merchants in the face of a folk ethic of sharing and community service could easily be seen as greed, the root of witchcraft. Not surprisingly, for example, the Vili, professional merchants from the Kingdom of Loango on the coast north of Kongo and who frequently crossed Kongo in search of merchandise, including slaves, were often regarded as witches by the common people of Kongo in the seventeenth century. So, too, might European merchants and their agents based in Angola or visiting the Angolan coast. . . . It was the accusation or suspicion of witchcraft that formed the basis for social criticism as well as a therapeutic technique for illness.

Kings, rulers, and others in political authority were especially vulnerable to such criticism if their public actions were perceived as being rooted in greed. . . .

Kongolese kings might be autocratic and authoritarian, but the autocrats who were also selfish or individualistic could be accused of witchcraft. Absolute rulers who did not take the interests of their subjects into consideration might easily fall into the category of witches. An important function of rulers was to control evildoers, a role that required that they master exactly the same sort of ruthless techniques that the witches used. The idea that a king must also do the things that witches do emerges clearly in a historical myth of the founding of Kongo. In this story, recorded about 1665, Lukeni lua Nimi, the founder of the monarchy, killed his pregnant mother by stabbing her in the womb, the sort of gratuitous cruelty associated with witch-craft. Alternately, King Afonso I (ruled 1509–1542), regarded by eighteenth-century Kongolese as the first Christian king of Kongo, was held, according to a tradition that emerged in the late seventeenth century but has no basis in fact, to have buried his mother alive simply for her refusal to part with a "small idol" that she wore around her neck. These stores not only established that kings, as makers of law, were above the law and the consequences of such actions, but also that they could do things that witches normally did. By being adept at the kinds of activities that witches engaged in, kings had the power necessary to counteract witches and other evildoers. Kings who were autocratic or skilled in witchcraft could overcome charges of being witches by being open handed and just in their application of the power for the public good. . . .

[A]lthough Kongolese might argue, as indeed they did, over how much power the king should have, even when they accepted an arrangement that allowed him great power, he was expected to use that power for the public good. Failure to do so was evidence that he was indulging his greedy appetites and could make him subject to charges of witchcraft that went to the heart of his authority to rule legitimately. In this way, the means to discover and punish the evildoer and the witch, inherent in his office, might be used for selfish, personal aims converting him to a witch himself.

If exported slaves saw their fate as a project of cannibalistic witches, those who remained in Africa might not see the slave trade as the primary problem and would thus not necessarily place the European shippers in the center of the picture. The main problem, more often than not, was the abuse of authority, especially in war, by those in power. Defensive wars were considered just; wars waged for personal gain, including the profits of the slave trade, clearly fell outside the ethical requirements of kings and were cause for criticism. This was particularly true in the Kongo civil wars that erupted intermittently from the battle of Mbwila in 1665 through most of the eighteenth century. . . .

These civil wars not only destroyed the country, but they also contributed might-ily to the slave trade. In the mid-seventeenth century, when the country was united and strong under such kings as Garcia II, relatively few Kongolese were exported from Africa, though some from the eastern edges were shipped across its borders. But when the civil wars broke the country's strength, Kongolese slaves became a veritable flood, leaving Africa both from the Portuguese port of Luanda and through the kingdom of Loango, where they passed into the hands of English, French, and Dutch merchants. Shipping records suggest that as many as 70,000 people were ex-ported from Kongo in the first decade of the eighteenth century, and although slave exports did not always reach these numbers in every decade thereafter, they usually exceeded 50,000 per decade for much of the century. The wars of the 1780s, when as many as 62,000 slaves departed, led to a massive reduction in the adult male population and crippled some regions. In this way, Kongolese became an important component of all the American slave societies.

The warfare that contributed to the enslaved population of the Americas also became widely regarded by the Kongolese as a product of greed rather than a politically necessary restitution of order. But the slave trade was only one of its nefarious byproducts; there were many others, perhaps equally important. King Pedro IV, who had temporarily restored the kingdom in 1709, undoubtedly expressed the sentiments of many of his fellows. He protested that "in no way did he want war because it was precisely because of continuous wars that their kingdom had already been destroyed." The Kongolese were tired, he argued, of "having to live like beasts in the fields and woods: relatives, wives and children on all sides had been outraged, killed, stripped naked, sold, and slaughtered." Being sold as a slave was only one of the possible bad outcomes of civil war. Others included being killed, raped, displaced from one's home, and pillaged, losing crops or even stripped of personal clothing. War was the root problem, and slavery only one of the outcomes. Rather than resist the slave trade specifically, the Kongolese attacked all forms of greed— and war as their immediate manifestation.

Nowhere is such resistance more clear than in the case of Dona Beatriz Kimpa Vita, the "False Saint Anthony," whose preaching won a large following at the same time that Pedro IV was making his protestations against war. In 1704, Beatriz, an eighteen-year-old girl of noble origin, became possessed by Saint Anthony. In this state, she preached against war and for the peaceful restoration of the kingdom. Her movement began by burning witches' charms and was directed specifically against them, but it also had a stern message for the rulers that is best understood in the context of hostility to witchcraft. Jesus was angry with Kongo, she related, because of the wars and the cupidity of the ruling nobles. They could only recover their rights by repenting and following her. "Up to this point," she said, "there had been no king in Kongo, but if all the pretenders were to gather in the church, an angel would appear and appoint the one most worthy with a wreath, and that one would become King of Kongo." Some of her followers, who also felt themselves possessed by saints and were known as "Little Anthonies," proclaimed an even sterner message: the pretenders' greed had cost them all the right to rule, and God would not make his choice from among them. In the end, Beatriz yielded to political exigency and appointed Pedro Constantinho da Silva, a political opportunist who commanded some of the colonists that King Pedro had sent to restore the ruined capital, to be king. She was captured, tried for heresy and witchcraft herself, and in 1706, burned at the stake in King Pedro's temporary fortified base at Evululu in eastern Kongo.

Though Beatriz did not mention the slave trade, her preaching was directed against the war that fostered it. She opposed, not the concept of monarchy itself, but the behavior of the kings. On taking up her call to preach she had disposed of her possessions and followed an "apostolic" lifestyle, devoting herself entirely to the welfare of the ordinary people. She saw the war as the product of greed, deserving of divine punishment, and she was to lead the restoration of a virtuous moral order. Like the rulers she criticized, she was not above demanding obedience and threatening those who opposed her with punishment, but she was confident, as were the thousands who joined her in São Salvador after she moved there in 1705, that she was working on the public's behalf. These ideas were best revealed in her prayer, a reworking of the traditional Christian Salve Regina (Hail Holy Queen), in which she stressed that God judged people's intentions even above their actions in determining salvation.

Thus, if rulers or would-be rulers had the interest of the country at heart, they would be accepted by God and by her, but if they were motivated simply by a desire to defeat their opponents and to rule alone, they would be found out and punished.

West Central Africans who found themselves "passing salt water"—as the expression current in Angola for the slave trade went—surely saw themselves as the exploited victims of greed and evil. But their sense of the sources of this greed probably extended beyond the European and Euroamerican traders on whose ships they were traveling. While sharing little optimism about their likely fate, they might still look back on the Africans who had originally enslaved them and see the origin of their plight in a chain of greedy actions. These actions included those of admitted witches like the Imbangala, whose campaigns accounted for thousands of captives, or like such cynical slave traders and raiders as Mbwa Lau, to the apparently legitimate but still grasping rulers whose wars had resulted in their capture and sale. Across the Atlantic, the political and social idiom of this critique of society would continue, not just in persistent beliefs about the intentions of slaveowners, but also about life in America.

The struggle against witchcraft would continue, both on the personal and the social level. In Haiti, where Kongolese made up a significant percentage of the pre-revolutionary population, many ideas about witchcraft came with the slaves, as did witches, for the remedies against witchcraft were directed not only against the owners of estates but against other slaves as well. . . . [W]hen the revolution broke out, ideas about ideal government were also considered among the Kongolese enslaved in Saint-Domingue, and a panoply of African ideologies including both constitutional thinking and the social role of witchcraft emerged in the great ideological contest that followed the massive social movement. In this way, an African social and personal ethical ideology crossed the ocean to the New World.

FURTHER READING

Altman, Ida. *Transatlantic Ties in the Spanish Empire: Brihuega, Spain, & Puebla, Mexico, 1560–1620.* Stanford, CA: Stanford University Press, 2000.

Altman, Ida, and James Horn, eds. *"To Make America": European Emigration in the Early Modern Period.* Berkeley: University of California Press, 1991.

Bailyn, Bernard. *The Peopling of British North America: An Introduction.* New York: Knopf, 1986.

Brooks, George. *Eurafricans in Western Africa: Commerce, Social Status, Gender, and Religious Observance from the Sixteenth to the Eighteenth Century.* Athens: Ohio State University Press, 2003.

Canny, Nicholas, ed. *Europeans on the Move: Studies on European Migration, 1500–1800.* Oxford: Oxford University Press, 1994.

Davis, Natalie Zemon. *Women on the Margins: Three Seventeenth-Century Lives.* Cambridge, MA: Harvard University Press, 1995.

Eltis, David. *The Rise of African Slavery in the Americas.* Cambridge, UK: Cambridge University Press, 2000.

Eltis, David, Stephen D. Behrendt, David Richardson, and Herbert S. Klein. *The Trans-Atlantic Slave Trade: A Database on CD-ROM.* Cambridge, UK: Cambridge University Press, 1999.

Elitis, David, and David Richardson, eds. *Routes to Slavery: Direction, Ethnicity and Mortality in the Transatlantic Slave Trade.* London: Frank Cass, 1997.

Fogleman, Aaron Spencer. *Hopeful Journeys: German Immigration, Settlement, and Political Culture in Colonial America, 1717–1775.* Philadelphia: University of Pennsylvania Press, 1996.

Games, Alison. *Migration and the Origins of the English Atlantic World.* Cambridge, MA: Harvard University Press, 1999.

Heywood, Linda, ed. *Central Africans and Cultural Transformation in the American Diaspora.* Cambridge, UK: Cambridge University Press, 2001.

Lovejoy, Paul E., ed. *Identity in the Shadow of Slavery.* London: Continuum, 2000.

———. *Transformations in Slavery: A History of Slavery in Africa.* Cambridge, UK: Cambridge University Press, 2000.

Miller, Joseph. *Way of Death: Merchant Capitalism and the Angolan Slave Trade, 1730–1830.* Madison: University of Wisconsin Press, 1988.

Morgan, Jennifer L. *Reproduction and Gender in New World Slavery.* Philadelphia: University of Pennsylvania Press, 2004.

Otterness, Philip. *Becoming German: The 1709 Palatine Migration to New York.* Ithaca, NY: Cornell University Press, 1994.

Smith, Abbot Emerson. *Colonists in Bondage: White Servitude and Convict Labor in America, 1607–1776.* Chapel Hill: University of North Carolina Press, 1947.

Sweet, James H. *Recreating Africa: Culture, Kinship, and Religion in the African-Portuguese World, 1441–1770.* Chapel Hill: University of North Carolina Press, 2003.

Thornton, John. *Africa and Africans in the Making of the Atlantic World, 1400–1800.* Cambridge, UK: Cambridge University Press, 1998.

———. *The Kongolese Saint Anthony: Dona Beatriz Kimpa Vita and the Antonian Movement, 1684–1706.* Cambridge, UK: Cambridge University Press, 1998.

CHAPTER
7

Atlantic Economies

Although Europeans never realized their dream of discovering El Dorado, the legendary City of Gold, in Africa or the Americas, they did find many other sources of wealth in the Atlantic world. Early modern Atlantic economies encompassed a wide array of activities from cod fishing off the Newfoundland coast to slave trading in the Kongo. Indeed, the conventional image of a "triangular trade" linking Europe, Africa, and the Americas drastically oversimplifies the many different economies that crisscrossed the Atlantic world. Diverse ecological conditions, technological constraints, social norms, and political structures shaped the Atlantic economies in ways that defy simple generalization, yet some broad patterns emerged. European state power and private entrepreneurs combined to exploit the natural and human resources of the Atlantic world. In Atlantic Africa, where tropical diseases and Africans' political power kept the Europeans at bay, African chieftains and merchants sold gold, ivory, and other human beings to their European counterparts on terms dictated at least in part by the African traders themselves. On the Atlantic islands and in the Americas, European capitalists employed unfree African and indigenous laborers to mine gold and silver, herd sheep and cattle, and cultivate sugar and tobacco. Many European indentured servants and convict laborers worked alongside them under difficult, often fatal conditions. In western Europe, profits from Atlantic trade stimulated the growth of highly stratified port cities, while the commodities imported from overseas colonies whetted consumer appetites for more and cheaper goods, thus starting the vicious cycle of Atlantic commerce all over again. The documents and essays in this chapter reveal the diversity of the Atlantic economies while emphasizing the centrality of slavery. They show how Europeans, Africans, and Amerindians collaborated and clashed with each other in the initial stages of economic globalization.

DOCUMENTS

Throughout the Atlantic world, entrepreneurs turned plants and animals into commodities for sale, as the first two documents illustrate. In Document 1, the English humanist Thomas More (1478–1535) rebukes sheep farmers for enclosing land and displacing farmers in the English countryside, while the Jesuit missionary Paul Le Jeune (1591–1664), writing from New France, describes the Huron Indians' method for hunting beaver, whose fur was coveted by French traders. Despite their willingness to trade with Europeans, Amerindians sometimes criticized the Europeans' insatiable greed for the fruits of nature, as Jean de Léry (1534–1613?) reports in Document 2.

The arduous labor needed to produce commodities for Atlantic markets varied from place to place depending on technical, environmental, and political circumstances. Cod fishing was a major industry of the sixteenth-century Atlantic. In Document 3, Richard Whitbourne (1579–1628) describes the activities of cod fishermen in Newfoundland as they salted and dried fish to be sold in southern Europe. Another Englishman, Thomas Gage (1596–1656), published an account of his experiences as a Dominican priest in Guatemala and Mexico between 1625 and 1637. In Document 4, Gage decries Spanish oppression of the Indians, arguing that Spanish demand for labor disrupted indigenous families and economies.

Slavery was central to the Atlantic economy. Document 6 presents the report of Arthur Wendover, an agent for the Royal African Company, which describes the buying and selling of slaves in a town called Appa on West Africa's Slave Coast. Across the Atlantic in Barbados, as Richard Ligon (1585?–1662) explains in Document 5, sugar planters faced myriad challenges from disease to mutiny in their effort to develop profitable plantations in the seventeenth century. Ligon does not hide the sugar planters' dependence on slave labor. Laws regulating slavery were established throughout the Americas. Document 7 offers excerpts from Louis XIV's *Code Noir* (Black Code) enacted in 1685.

Two great political economists disagreed over the moral significance of the Atlantic economy, as Document 8 reveals. Writing in 1776, Adam Smith (1723–1790) argued that the discovery of the Americas added to the variety of commodities enjoyed by Europeans and also increased European industriousness. Almost a century later, Karl Marx (1818–1883) agreed that the discovery of America contributed to European economic development, but he emphasized the violence that plagued this history. Pointing to the destruction of aboriginal people and the profits made from the slave trade, Marx memorably concluded that "capital comes dripping from head to foot, from every pore, with blood and dirt."

1. Creatures Become Commodities, 1516, 1634

Thomas More on Sheep

'Your sheep,' I replied, 'that used to be so meek and eat so little. Now they are becoming so greedy and wild that they devour men themselves, as I hear. They devastate and pillage fields, houses, and towns. For in whatever parts of the land the sheep yield the softest and most expensive wool, there the nobility and gentry, yes, and even some abbots though otherwise holy men, are not content with the old rents that the land yielded to their predecessors. Living in idleness and luxury, without doing any good to society, no longer satisfies them; they have to do positive evil. For they leave no land free for the plow: they enclose every acre for pasture; they destroy houses and abolish towns, keeping only the churches, and those for sheep-barns. And as if enough of your land were not already wasted on woods and game-preserves, these worthy men turn all human habitations and cultivated fields back to wilderness.

Source: Thomas More, *Utopia*, ed. Robert M. Adams (New York: Norton, 1975), pp. 12–13. Reuben Gold Thwaites, *Jesuit Relations* (Cleveland: The Burrows Brothers, 1898), vol. 6, pp. 297–305.

Thus one greedy, insatiable glutton, a frightful plague to his native country, may enclose many thousand acres of land within a single hedge. The tenants are dismissed and compelled, by trickery or brute force or constant harassment, to sell their belongings. By hook or by crook these miserable people—men, women, husbands, wives, orphans, widows, parents with little children, whole families (poor but numerous, since farming requires many hands)—are forced to move out. They leave the only homes familiar to them, and they can find no place to go. Since they cannot afford to wait for a buyer, they sell for a pittance all their household goods, which would not bring much in any case. When that little money is gone (and it's soon spent in wandering from place to place), what remains for them but to steal, and so be hanged—justly, you'd say!—or to wander and beg? And yet if they go tramping, they are jailed as sturdy beggars. They would be glad to work, but they can find no one who will hire them. There is no need for farm labor, in which they have been trained, when there is no land left to be plowed. One herdsman or shepherd can look after a flock of beasts large enough to stock an area that would require many hands if it were plowed and harvested.

'This enclosing has had the effect of raising the price of grain in many places. In addition, the price of raw wool has risen so much that poor people who used to make cloth are no longer able to buy it, and so great numbers are forced from work to idleness. One reason is that after the enlarging of the pasture-land, rot killed a great number of sheep—as though God were punishing greed by sending upon the animals a murrain, which in justice should have fallen on the owners! But even if the number of sheep should increase greatly, their price will not fall a penny. The reason is that the wool trade, though it can't be called a monopoly because it isn't in the hands of one single person, is concentrated in few hands (an oligopoly, you might say) and these so rich, that the owners are never pressed to sell until they have a mind to, and that is only when they can get their price.'

Indian Attitudes Toward the Beaver

The Castor or Beaver is taken in several ways. The Savages say that it is the animal well-beloved by the French, English and Basques,—in a word, by the Europeans. I heard my host say one day, jokingly, *Missi picoutau amiscou*, "The Beaver does everything perfectly well, it makes kettles, hatchets, swords, knives, bread; and, in short, it makes everything." He was making sport of us Europeans, who have such a fondness for the skin of this animal and who fight to see who will give the most to these Barbarians, to get it; they carry this to such an extent that my host said to me one day, showing me a very beautiful knife, "The English have no sense; they give us twenty knives like this for one Beaver skin."

In the Spring, the Beaver is taken in a trap baited with the wood it eats. The Savages understand perfectly how to handle these traps, which are made to open, when a heavy piece of wood falls upon the animals and kills it. Sometimes when the dogs encounter the Beaver outside its House, they pursue and take it easily; I have never seen this chase, but have been told of it; and the Savages highly value a dog which scents and runs down this animal.

During the Winter they capture them in nets and under the ice, in this way: They make a slit in the ice near the Beaver's House, and put into the hole a net, and some wood which serves as bait. This poor animal, searching for something to eat, gets caught in a net made of good, strong, double cord; and, emerging from the water to the opening made in the ice, they kill it with a big club.

The other way of taking them under the ice is more noble. Not all the Savages use this method, only the most skillful; they break with blows from the hatchet the Cabin or house of the Beaver, which is indeed wonderfully made. In my opinion no musket ball can pierce it. During the Winter it is built upon the shore of some little river or pond, is two stories high, and round. The materials of which it is composed are wood and mud, so well joined and bound together that I have seen our Savages in Midwinter sweat in trying to make an opening into it with their hatchets. The lower story is in or upon the edge of the water, the upper is above the river. When the cold has frozen the rivers and ponds, the Beaver secludes himself in the upper story, where he has provided himself with wood to eat during the Winter. He sometimes, however, descends from this story to the lower one, and thence he glides out under the ice, through the holes which are in this lower story and which open under the ice. He goes out to drink and to search for the wood that he eats, which grows upon the banks of the pond and in the pond itself. This wood at the bottom is fastened in the ice and the Beaver goes below to cut it and carry it to his house. Now the Savages having broken this house, these poor animals, which are sometimes in great numbers under one roof, disappear under the ice, some on one side, some on the other, seeking hollow and thin places between the water and ice, where they can breathe. Their enemies, knowing this, go walking over the pond or frozen river, carrying a long club in their hands, armed on one side with an iron blade made like a Carpenter's chisel, and on the other with a Whale's bone, I believe. They sound the ice with this bone, striking upon it and examining it to see if it is hollow; and if there is any indication of this, then they cut the ice with their iron blade, looking to see if the water is stirred up by the movement or breathing of the Beaver. If thy water moves, they have a curved stick which they thrust into the hole that they have just made; if they feel the Beaver, they kill it with their big club, which they call *ca ouikachit*; and, drawing it out of the water, go and make a feast of it at once, unless they have great hopes of taking others. I asked them why the Beaver waited there until it was killed. "Where will it go?" they said to me; "its house is broken to pieces and the other places where it could breathe between the water and ice are broken; it remains there in the water, seeking air, and meanwhile it is killed." Sometimes it goes out through its House, or some hole; but the dogs which are there, scenting and waiting for it, have soon caught it.

When there is a river near by, or an arm of water connecting with the pond where they are, they slip into that; but the Savages dam up these rivers when they discover them, breaking the ice and planting a number of stakes near each other, so that the Beaver may not escape in that direction. I have seen large lakes which saved the lives of the Beavers; for our people, not being able to break all the places where they could breathe, therefore could not trap their prey. Sometimes there are two families of Beavers in the same House, that is, two males and two females, with their little ones.

The female bears as many as seven, but usually four, five, or six. They have four teeth, two below, and two above, which are wonderfully drawn out; the other two are small, but these are large and sharp. They are used to cut the wood for their food, and the wood with which they build their house; they sharpen these teeth when they are dull, by rubbing and pressing them against each other, making a little noise which I have myself heard.

The Beaver has very soft fur, the hats made of it being an evidence of this. It has very short feet which are well adapted to swimming, for the nails are united by skin, in the same way as those of river-birds or seals; its tail is entirely flat, quite long and oval-shaped. I measured one of a large Beaver; it was a palm and eight fingers or thereabout in length, and almost one palm of the hand in width. It was quite thick, and was covered, not with hair, but with a black skin looking like scales; however, these are not real scales. The Beaver here is regarded as an amphibious animal, and there-fore it is eaten in all seasons. My idea is that the grease when melted is more like oil than grease; the flesh is very good, but it seems to me a little stale in the Spring, and not so in Winter. But if the pelt of the Beaver excels the pelt of the sheep, the flesh of the sheep is superior, in my opinion, to that of the Beaver,—not only because it tastes better, but also because the Sheep is larger than the Beaver.

2. Jean de Léry Describes the Brazilwood Trade, 1578

First, since brazilwood (from which this land has taken the name that we use for it) is among the most famous trees, and now one of the best known to us and (because of the dye made from it) is the most valued, I will describe it here. This tree, which the savages called *araboutan*, ordinarily grows as high and branchy as the oaks in the forests of this country; some are so thick that three men could not embrace a single trunk. While we are speaking of big trees, the author of the *General History of the West Indies* says that two have been seen in those countries, one of which had a trunk more than eight arm lengths around, and the other a trunk of more than sixteen. On top of the first one, he said, which was so high that you couldn't throw a stone to the top of it, a *cacique* had built a little lodge (the Spaniards who saw him nesting up there like a stork burst out laughing); they also described the second tree as a mar-velous thing. The same author also recounts that in the country of Nicaragua there is a tree called *cerba*, which grows so big that fifteen men could not embrace it.

To return to our brazilwood: it has a leaf like that of boxwood, but of a brighter green, and it bears no fruit. As for the manner of loading it on the ships, take note that both because of the hardness of this wood and the consequent difficulty of cutting it, and because, there being no horses, donkeys, or other beasts to carry, cart, or draw burdens in that country, it has to be men who do this work: if the foreigners who voy-age over there were not helped by the savages, they could not load even a medium-sized ship in a year. In return for some frieze garments, linen shirts, hats, knives, and other merchandise that they are given, the savages not only cut, saw, split, quarter, and round off the brazilwood, with the hatchets, wedges, and other iron tools given to them by the French and by others from over here, but also carry it on their bare shoulders, often from a league or two away, over mountains and difficult places, clear down to the seashore by the vessels that lie at anchor, where the mariners receive it.

Source: Jean de Léry, *History of a Voyage to the Land of Brazil, Otherwise Called America*, translation and introduction by Janet Whatley (Berkeley: University of California Press, © 1990), pp. 100–103. Re-printed with permission of the University of California Press.

I say expressly that it is only since the French and Portuguese have been frequenting their country that the savages have been cutting their brazilwood; for before that time, as I have heard from the old men, they had almost no other way of taking down a tree than by setting fire to the base of it. There are people over here who think that the round logs that you see at the merchants' are of the natural thickness of the trees; to show that they are mistaken, besides saying that these trees are often very thick, I have added that the savages round them off and shape them so that they are easier to carry and to handle in the ships.

During the time that we were in that country we made fine fires of this brazilwood; I have observed that since it is not at all damp, like most other wood, but rather is naturally dry, it gives off very little smoke as it burns. One day one of our company decided to bleach our shirts, and, without suspecting anything, put brazilwood ash in with the lye; instead of whitening them, he made them so red that although they were washed and soaped afterward, there was no means of getting rid of that tincture, so that we had to wear them that way.

If the gentlemen over here with their perfectly starched pleats—those who send to Flanders to have their shirts whitened—choose not to believe me, they have my permission to do the experiment for themselves, and, for quicker results, the more to brighten their great ruffs (or rather, those dribble-catchers more than half a foot wide that they are wearing these days), they can dye them green if they please.

Our Tupinamba are astonished to see the French and others from distant countries go to so much trouble to get their *araboutan*, or brazilwood. On one occasion one of their old men questioned me about it: "What does it mean that you *Mairs* and *Peros* (that is, French and Portuguese) come from so far for wood to warm yourselves? Is there none in your own country?" I answered him yes, and in great quantity, but not of the same kinds as theirs; nor any brazilwood, which we did not burn as he thought, but rather carried away to make dye, just as they themselves did to redden their cotton cord, feathers, and other articles. He immediately came back at me: "Very well, but do you need so much of it?" "Yes," I said (trying to make him see the good of it), "for there is a merchant in our country who has more frieze and red cloth, and even" (and here I was choosing things that were familiar to him) "more knives, scissors, mirrors, and other merchandise than you have ever seen over here; one such merchant alone will buy all the wood that several ships bring back from your country." "Ha, ha!" said my savage, "you are telling me of wonders." Then, having thought over what I had said to him, he questioned me further, and said, "But this man of whom you speak, who is so rich, does he never die?" "Certainly he does," I said, "just as others do." At that (since they are great discoursers, and pursue a subject out to the end) he asked me, "And when he is dead, to whom belong all the goods that he leaves behind?" "To his children, if he has any, and if there are none, to his brothers, sisters, or nearest kinsmen." "Truly," said my elder (who, as you will judge, was no dullard), "I see now that you *Mairs* (that is, Frenchmen) are great fools; must you labor so hard to cross the sea, on which (as you told us) you endured so many hardships, just to amass riches for your children or for those who will survive you? Will not the earth that nourishes you suffice to nourish them? We have kinsmen and children, whom, as you see, we love and cherish; but because we are certain that after our death the earth which has nourished us will nourish them, we rest easy and do not trouble ourselves further about it."

And there you have a brief and true summary of the discourse that I have heard from the very mouth of a poor savage American. This nation, which we consider so barbarous, charitably mocks those who cross the sea at the risk of their lives to go seek brazilwood in order to get rich; however blind this people may be in attributing more to nature and to the fertility of the earth than we do to the power and the providence of God, it will rise up in judgment against those despoilers who are as abundant over here, among those bearing the title of Christians, as they are scarce over there, among the native inhabitants. Therefore, to take up what I said elsewhere—that the Tupinamba mortally hate the avaricious—would to God that the latter might be imprisoned among them, so that they might even in this life serve as demons and furies to torment those whose maws are insatiable, who do nothing but suck the blood and marrow of others. To our great shame, and to justify our savages in the little care that they have for the things of this world, I had to make this digression in their favor.

3. Richard Whitbourne Praises the Newfoundland Fishery, 1622

But the chiefe commodities of *New-found-land* yet knowne, and which is growne to be a settled trade, and that which may be much bettered by an orderly Plantation there, (if the Traders thither will take some better course, then formerly they have done, as shall be declared) is the Codfishing upon that Coast, by which our Nation and many other Countries are enricht and greatly comforted.

And if I should here set downe a valuation of that fish, which the *French, Biscaines,* and *Portugals* fetch yeerely from this Coast of *New-found-land,* and the *Banke,* which lieth within 25. leagues to the *East* of that Countrey, where the *French* use to fish Winter and Summer, usually making two voyages every yeere thither: (To which places, and to the Coast of *Canady,* which lieth neere unto it, are yeerely sent from those Countries, more than 400. saile of ships:)

It would seeme incredible, yea some men are of opinion, that the people of *France, Spaine, Portugall* and *Italy,* could not so well live, if the benefit of the fishing upon that Coast, and your Majesties other Dominions, were taken from them.

But I trust it will bee sufficient, that I give an estimate of our owne trading thither, and partly of the wealth and commodities we reape thereby, without any curious search into other mens profits.

In the yeere 1615. when I was at *New-found-land,* with the Commission before-mentioned, which was an occasion of my taking the more particular observations of that Countrey, there were then on that Coast, of your Majesties subjects, above 250. saile of Ships great and small. The burthens and Tunnage of them al one with another, so neere as I could take notice, allowing every ship to bee at least threescore tunne (for as some of them contained lesse, so many of them held more) amounted to more then 15000. tunnes. Now for every threescore tunne burthen, according to the usuall manning of Ships in those voyages, agreeing with the note I then tooke, there are to

Source: Richard Whitbourne, *A Discourse and Discovery of Newfoundland* (London, 1622), pp. 11–14, 17–21.

be set downe twenty men and boyes: by which computation in 250. saile, there were no lesse then five thousand persons. Now every one of these ships, so neere as I could ghesse, had about 120000. fish, and five tun of Traine oyle one with another.

So that the totall of the fish in 250. saile of those ships, when it was brought into *England*, *France*, or *Spaine*, (being sold after the rate of foure pound, for every thousand of fish, six score fishes to the hundred, which is not a penny a fish, & if it yeeld lesse, it was ill sold) amounted in mony to 120000. pound.

Now, as I have said before, allowing to every ship of 60. tunne, at least five tun of Traine oyle, the totall of all that ariseth to 1250. tunne; each tunne, whether it bee sold in *England*, or elsewhere, being under-valued at twelve pound. So as the whole value thereof in money, amounteth to the summe of 15000. pound, which added to the fish, it will appeare that the totall value of the fish, and Traine oyle of those 250. saile of ships that yeere, might yeeld to your Majesties subjects better then the summe of 135000. pound, omitting to reckon the over-prices which were made and gotten by the sale thereof in forraine Countreys, being much more then what is usually made at home, and so the like in other yeeres.

And this certainely, in my understanding, is a point worthy of consideration, that so great wealth should yeerely be raised, by one sole commodity of that Countrey, yea by one onely sort of fish, and not upon any other trade thither, which must needes yeeld, with the imployments thereof, great riches to your Majesties subjects: And this also to bee gathered and brought home by the sole labour and industry of men, without exchange or exportation of our Coine, and native Commodities, or other adventure (then of necessary provisions for the fishing) as Salt, Nets, Leads, Hookes, Lines, and the like; and of victuals, as Bread, Beere, Beefe, and Porke, in competent measure, according to the number and proportion of men imployed in those voyages.

The converting of these commodities (gotten by fishing) into money, cannot chuse but be a great benefit to all your Majesties Kingdomes in many respects.

What the charge in setting foorth of these 250. saile might amount unto (being onely for victuals, which our Countrey yeeldeth) I hold it not fit heere to set downe, lest I should be accused for breaking a gap into other mens grounds.

And withall, it is to be considered, that the Trade thither (as now it is) doth yeerely set on worke, and relieve great numbers of people, as Bakers, Brewers, Coopers, Ship-Carpenters, Smiths, Net-makers, Rope-makers, Line-makers, Hooke-makers, Pully-makers, and many other trades, which with their families have their best meanes of maintenance, from these *New-found-land* Voyages. Adde unto them the families or servants of divers Owners and Masters of such ships as goe thither, and Mariners with their families, hereby imployed and maintained. . . .

That Countrey may be made a place of great use and advantage for this State, in any action that may ingage us by way of attempt or defence, in regard of those parts of the world.

For the first, this Countrey lyeth so neere the course which the Spanish ships, that come from *Mexico*, *Havona*, and other places of the *West-Indies*, hold in their returne from thence, that they often saile within 190. leagues from the South part thereof.

In the yeere 1615. whilest I was in that Countrey, three ships returning from the *West-Indies*, did arrive there, purposely to refresh themselves with water, wood, fish, and fowle, and so have divers others done at other times to my knowledge.

Sundry *Portugall* ships have also come thither purposely to loade fish from the *English*, and have given them a good price for the same, and sailed from thence with it to *Brasile*, where that kinde of fish is in great request, and they have made great profit thereby.

And divers *Dutch* and *French* ships have also oftentimes come thither, purposely to loade fish from the *English*, which they afterwards transport into *Italy*, *Spaine*, and other parts, whereby they imploy both their shipping and Mariners, making good profit thereof.

Wee have already spoken of the great numbers of *French* and *Portugall* shipping, that usually trade every yeere to this Coast, and the places neere adjoyning in fishing voyages: so that what in all likelihood may be the event of a Plantation to be made there, if either *Spaine* or *France* should breake league with your Majesty, or your royall Progeny; I leave to the consideration of your Majesty. . . .

And I am verily of opinion, if their Audit were truely published to the world, that their trade of fishing upon your Majesties Sea-coasts, hath beene the best meanes of their present strength, having thereby increased their shipping and wealth, and inabled their men for Navigation; For it is well knowne, that the *French* and also the *Dutch*, by their fishing so neere on your Majesties Sea-coasts, doe use a petty kinde of picking away of infinite sums of mony yeerely from your Majesties Kingdomes; not onely from North-Yarmouth, and other places thereby, all the time that the Herring fishing lasteth; but also at other places for Mackerell, Soles, Whitings, and other sorts of fish which they take, in sight of your Majesties Kingdome, and bring it heere to land daily, and sell it for ready money. Such daily gathering away of coyne, may well bee remedied, if your Majesties subjects would but forbeare to buy any fresh fish of other Nations, (which me thinkes they should) then Strangers should bee constrained to bring coyne into your Majesties Kingdomes with their fish, to set poore people a-worke to salt and preserve their Herrings, and other fish withall, when they bring it heere a-land; whereby some Customes and other duties will also grow to your Majesty: or otherwise they will leave their daily fishing so neere your Majesties Kingdomes (as now they doe) and then such fish will be the more plentifull for your Highnesse subjects to take, and thereby greatly incourage them to set forth and imploy many a poore man the more in fishing, then now there is; and it will then not onely preserve great sums of money yeerely from carrying away from your Majesties Kingdomes, but also there will bee much more gotten, than now there is, and greater numbers of Mariners thereby yeerely increased, to bee very serviceable for the Navy, when there may be cause. . . .

4. Indians Toil in Guatemala, 1648

The miserable condition of the Indians of that country is such that though the kings of Spain have never yielded to what some would have, that they should be slaves, yet their lives are as full of bitterness as is the life of a slave. I myself have known some that have come home from toiling and moiling with Spaniards, after many blows, some wounds, and little or no wages, and who have sullenly and stubbornly

---

Source: *Thomas Gage's Travels in the New World.* Ed. J. Eric S. Thompson (Norman, OK: University of Oklahoma Press, 1958), pp. 215–219.

lain down upon their beds, resolving to die rather than live any longer a life so slavish. And they have refused to take either meat or drink or anything else comfortable
and nourishing, which their wives have offered unto them, that so by pining and
starving, they might consume themselves. Some I have by good persuasions encouraged to life rather than to a voluntary and willful death; others there have been
that would not be persuaded, but in that willful way have died.

The Spaniards that live about that country (especially the farmers of the Valley
of Mixco, Pinola, Petapa, Amatitlán, and those of the Sacatepéquez) allege that all
their trading and farming is for the good of the commonwealth, and therefore,
whereas there are not Spaniards enough for so ample and large a country to do all
their work, and all are not able to buy slaves and Blackamoors, they stand in need
of the Indians' help to serve them for their pay and hire. Therefore, a partition of
Indian laborers is made every Monday, or Sunday in the afternoon, to the Spaniards,
according to the farms they occupy, or according to their several employments,
calling, and trading with mules, or any other way. For such and such a district there
is named an officer, who is called *juez repartidor*, who according to a list made of
every farm, house, and person, is to give so many Indians by the week. And here is
a door opened to the President of Guatemala, and to the judges, to provide well for
their menial servants, whom they commonly appoint for this office, which is thus
performed by them. They name the town and place of their meeting upon Sunday
or Monday, to the which themselves and the Spaniards of that district do resort.

The Indians of the several towns are ordered to have in readiness so many
laborers as the Court of Guatemala hath appointed to be weekly taken out of such a
town. These are conducted by an Indian officer to the town of general meeting. They
come thither with their tools, their spades, shovels, bills, or axes, with their provision of victuals for a week (which are commonly some dry cakes of maize, puddings
of *frijoles*, or French beans, and a little chile or biting long pepper, or a bit of cold
meat for the first day or two) and with beds on their backs (which is only a coarse
woollen mantle to wrap about them when they lie on the bare ground). Then they
are shut up in the town-house, some with blows, some with spurnings, some with
boxes on the ear, if presently they go not in.

Now all being gathered together, and the house filled with them, the *juez repartidor*, or officer, calls by the order of the list such and such a Spaniard, and also calls
out of the house so many Indians as by the Court are commanded to be given him
(some are allowed three, some four, some ten, some fifteen, some twenty, according to their employments) and delivereth unto the Spaniard his Indians, and so to
all the rest, till they be all served. When they receive their Indians, they take from
them their tools or mantles, to make sure that they do not run away; and for every
Indian delivered unto them, they give unto the *juez repartidor*, or officer, for his
fees, half a real, which is threepence. Yearly this amounts to a great deal of money,
for some officers make a partition or distribution of four hundred, some of two hundred, some of three hundred Indians every week, and carrieth home with him so
many half hundred reals for one or half a day's work.

If complaint be made by any Spaniard that such and such an Indian ran away
and served him not the week past, the Indian is brought and securely tied to a post
by his hands in the market-place, and there is whipped upon his bare back. But if the
poor Indian complain that the Spaniards cozened and cheated him of his shovel, axe,

bill, mantle, or wages, no justice shall be executed against the cheating Spaniard, neither shall the Indian be righted, though it is true the order runs equally in favor of both Indian and Spaniard.

Thus the poor Indians are sold for threepence apiece for a whole week's slavery, and are not permitted to go home at nights unto their wives, though their work lie not above a mile from the town where they live. Nay, some are carried ten or twelve miles from their home, and they may not return till Saturday night late, and must that week do whatsoever their master pleaseth to command them. The wages appointed them will scarce find them meat and drink, for they are not allowed a real a day, which is but sixpence, but for six days' work and diet they are to have five reals, which is half a crown, and with that they are to find themselves. This same order is observed in the city of Guatemala, and towns of Spaniards, where every family that wants the service of an Indian or Indians, though it be but to fetch water and wood on their backs or to go of errands, is allowed the like service from the nearest Indian towns.

It would grieve a Christian's heart to see how some cruel Spaniards in that week's service wrong and abuse those poor wretches. Some visit their wives at home, whilst their poor husbands are digging and delving; others whip them for their slow working; others wound them with their swords, or break their heads for some reasonable and well-grounded answer in their own behalf; others steal from them their tools; others cheat them of half. Some even cheat them of all their wages, alleging their service cost them half a real, and yet their work is not well performed. I knew some who made a common practice of this, when their wheat was sown, and they had little for the Indians to do. They would have as many as were due unto their farm, and on Monday and Tuesday would make them cut and bring on their backs as much wood as they needed all that week. Then at noon, on Wednesday, knowing the great desire of the Indians to go home to their wives, for the which they would give anything, they would say unto them: "What will you give me now, if I let you go home to do your own work?" Whereunto the Indians would joyfully answer, some that they would give a real, others two reals. This the Spaniards would take and send them home, and so they would have much work done, wood to serve their house a week, and as much money as would buy them meat and cacao for chocolate for two weeks. Thus from the poor Indians do those unconscionable Spaniards practice a cheap and lazy way of living. Others will sell them away for that week unto a neighbor who needs laborers, demanding reals apiece for every Indian, which he that buyeth them will be sure to defray out of their wages.

Similarly, are they in a slavish bondage and readiness for all passengers and travellers, who in any town may demand as many Indians as he needs to go to the next town with his mules, or to carry on their backs a heavy burden as he shall need. Then at the journey's end he will pick some quarrel with them, and so send them back with blows and stripes without any pay at all. They will make those wretches carry on their backs a *petaca*, or leathern trunk, and chest of above a hundredweight a whole day, nay, some two or three days together. This they do by tying the chest on each side with ropes, having a broad leather in the middle, which they cross over the forepart of their head, or over their forehead, hanging thus the weight upon their heads and brows. By the end of the journey this makes the blood stick in the foreheads of some, galling and pulling off the skin, and marking them in the fore-top of their heads. So these carriers, who are called *tamemes*, are easily known in a town by their baldness, that leather girt having worn off all their hair. Despite these hard usages, yet those poor people make shift to live amongst the Spaniards, but with anguish of heart they still cry out to God for justice, and for liberty.

5. Sugar Planters Transform Barbados, 1647–1650

Now for the Masters, I have yet said but little, nor am able to say half of what they deserve. They are men of great abilities and parts, otherwise they could not go through, with such great works as they undertake; the managing of one of their Plantations, being a work of such a latitude, as will require a very good head-peece, to put in order, and continue it so.

I can name a Planter there, that feeds daily two hundred mouths, and keeps them in such order, as there are no mutinies amongst them; and yet of several nations. All these are to be employed in their several abilities, so as no one be idle. The first work to be considered, is Weeding, for unless that be done, all else (and the Planter too) will be undone, and if that be neglected but a little time, it will be a hard matter to recover it again, so fast will the weeds grow there. But the ground being kept clean, 'tis fit to bear any thing that Country will afford. After weeding comes Planting, and they account two seasons in the year best, and that is, *May* and *November*; but Canes are to be planted at all times, that they may come in, one field after another; otherwise, the work will stand still. And commonly they have in a field that is planted together, at one time, ten or a dozen acres. This work of planting and weeding, the Master himself is to see done; unless he have a very trusty and able Overseer; and without such a one, he will have too much to do. The next thing he is to consider, is the Ingenio, and what belongs to that; as, the Ingenio it self, which is the *Primum Mobile* of the whole work, the Boyling-house, with the Coppers and Furnaces, the Filling room, the Still-house, and Cureing-house; and in all these, there are great casualties. If any thing in the Rollers, as the Goudges, Sockets, Sweeps, Cogs, or Braytrees, be at fault, the whole work stands still; or in the Boyling-house, if the Frame which holds the Coppers, (and is made of Clinkers, fastned with plaister of *Paris*) if by the violence of the heat from the Furnaces, these Frames crack or break, there is a stop in the work, till that be mended. Or if any of the Coppers have a mischance, and be burnt, a new one must presently be had, or there is a stay in the work. Or if the mouths of the Furnaces, (which are made of a sort of stone, which we have from *England*, and we call it there, high gate stone) if that, by the violence of the fire, be softned, that it moulder away, there must new be provided, and laid in with much art, or it will not be. Or if the bars of Iron, which are in the floor of the Furnace, when they are red hot (as continually they are) the fire-man, throw great shides of wood in the mouths of the Furnaces, hard and carelesly, the weight of those logs, will bend or break those bars, (though strongly made) and there is no repairing them, without the work stand still; for all these depend upon one another, as wheels in a Clock. Or if the Stills be at fault, the *kill-devil* cannot be made. But the main impediment and stop of all, is the loss of our Cattle, and amongst them, there are such diseases, as I have known in one Plantation, thirty that have dyed in two dayes. And I have heard, that a Planter, an eminent man there, that clear'd a dozen acres of ground, and rail'd

Source: Richard Ligon, *A True and Exact History of the Island of Barbadoes* (1673), pp. 55–57, 85–86.

it about for pasture, with intention, as soon as the grass was grown to a great height, to put in his working Oxen; which accordingly he did, and in one night fifty of them dyed; so that such a loss as this, is able to undo a Planter, that is not very well grounded. What it is that breeds these diseases, we cannot find, unless some of the Plants have a poysonous quality; nor have we yet found out cures for these diseases; Chickens guts being the best remedy was then known, and those being chop'd or minc'd, and given them in a horn, with some liquor mixt to moisten it, was thought the best remedy: yet it recovered very few. Our Horses too have killing diseases amongst them, and some of them have been recovered by Glisters, which we give them in pipes, or large Seringes made of wood, for the same purpose. For, the common diseases, both of Cattle and Horses, are obstructions and bindings in their bowels; and so lingring a disease it is, to those that recover, as they are almost worn to nothing before they get well. So that if any of these stops continue long, or the Cattle cannot be recruited in a reasonable time, the work is at a stand; and by that means, the Canes grow over ripe, and will in a very short time have their juice dryed up, and will not be worth the grinding.

Now to recruit these Cattle, Horses, Camels, and Assinigos, who are all liable to these mischances and decayes, Merchants must be consulted, ships provided, and a competent Cargo of goods adventured, to make new voyages to forraign parts, to supply those losses; and when that is done, the casualties at Sea are to be considered, and those happen several wayes, either by shipwrack, piracy, or fire. A Master of a ship, and a man accounted both able, stout, and honest, having transported goods of several kinds, from *England* to a part of *Africa*, the River of *Gambra*, and had there exchanged his Commodities for *Negroes*, which was that he intended to make his voyage of, caused them all to be ship'd, and did not, as the manner is, shakle one to another, and make them sure, but having an opinion of their honesty and faithfulness to him, as they had promised; and he being a credulous man, and himself good natur'd and merciful, suffered them to go loose, and they being double the number of those in the Ship, found their advantages, got weapons in their hands, and fell upon the Saylers, knocking them on the heads, and cutting their throats so fast, as the Master found they were all lost, out of any possibility of saving; and so went down into the Hold, and blew all up with himself; and this was before they got out of the River. These, and several other wayes there will happen, that extreamly retard the work of Sugar-making.

Now let us consider how many things there are to be thought on, that go to the actuating this great work, and how many cares to prevent the mischances, that are incident to the retarding, if not the frustrating of the whole work; and you will find them wise and provident men, that go on and prosper in a work, that depends upon so many contingents.

This I say, to stop those mens mouths, that lye here at home, and expect great profit in their adventures, and never consider, through what difficulty, industry and pains it is acquired. And thus much I thought good to say, of the abilities of the Planters. . . .

At the time we landed on this Island, which was in the beginning of *September*, 1647. we were informed, partly by those Planters we found there, and partly by our own observations, that the great work of Sugar-making, was but newly practiced by the inhabitants there. Some of the most industrious men, having gotten Plants from *Fernambock*, a place in *Brasil*, and made tryal of them at the *Barbadoes*; and finding them to grow, they planted more and more, as they grew and multiplyed on the place, till they had such a considerable number, as they were worth the while to set up a very small Ingenio, and so make tryal what Sugar could be made upon that soyl. But, the secrets of the work being not well understood, the Sugars they made were very inconsiderable, and little worth, for two or three years. But they finding their errours by their daily practice, began a little to mend; and, by new directions from *Brasil*, sometimes by strangers, and now and then by their own people, (who being covetous of the knowledge of a thing, which so much concerned them in their particulars, and for the general good of the whole Island) were content sometimes to make a voyage thither, to improve their knowledge in a thing they so much desired. Being now made much abler to make their queries, of the secrets of that mystery, by how much their often failings, had put them to often stops and nonplusses in the work. And so returning with most Plants, and better Knowledge, they went on upon fresh hopes, but still short, of what they should be more skilful in: for, at our arrival there, we found them ignorant in three main points, that much conduced to the work; *viz.* The manner of Planting, the time of Gathering, and the right placing of their Coppers in their Furnaces; as also, the true way of covering their Rollers, with plates or Bars of Iron: All which being rightly done, advance much in the performance of the main work. At the time of our arrival there, we found many Sugar-works set up, and at work; but yet the Sugars they made, were but bare Muscavadoes, and few of them Merchantable commodities; so moist, and full of molosses, and so ill cur'd, as they were hardly worth the bringing home for *England*. But about the time I left the Island, which was in 1650. they were much better'd; for then they had the skill to know when the Canes were ripe, which was not, till they were fifteen months old; and before, they gathered them at twelve, which was a main disadvantage to the making good Sugar; for, the liquor wanting of the sweetness it ought to have, caused the Sugars to be lean, and unfit to keep. Besides, they were grown greater proficients, both in boyling and curing them, and had learnt the knowledge of making them white, such as you call Lump Sugars here in *England*; but not so excellent as those they make in *Brasil*, nor is there any likelyhood they can ever make such: the land there being better, and lying in a Continent, must needs have constanter and steadier weather, and the Aire much drier and purer, than it can be in so small an Iland, and that of *Barbadoes*. And now, seeing this commodity, Sugar, hath gotten so much the start of all the rest of those, that were held the staple Commodities of the Iland, and so much over-top't them, as they are for the most part slighted and neglected. And, for that few in *England* know the trouble and care of making it, I think it convenient, in the first place, to acquaint you, as far as my memory will serve, with the whole process of the work of Sugar-making, which is now grown the soul of Trade in this Iland. And leaving to trouble you and my self, with relating the errours our Predecessors so long wandred in, I will in brief set down the right and best way they practiced, when I left the Island, which, I think, will admit of no greater or farther improvement.

But, before I will begin with that, I will let you see, how much the land there hath been advanc'd in the profit, since the work of Sugar began, to the time of our landing there, which was not above five or six years: For, before the work began, this Plantation of Major *Hilliards*, of five hundred acres, could have been purchased for four hundred pound sterling; and now the halfe this Plantation, with the halfe of the Stock upon it was sold for seven thousand pound sterling. And it is evident, that all the land there, which has been imployed to that work, hath found the like improvement. And I believe, when the small Plantations in poor mens hands, of ten, twenty, or thirty acres, which are too small to lay to that work, be bought up by great men, and put together, into Plantations of five, six, or seven hundred acres, that two thirds of the Iland will be fit for Plantations of Sugar, which will make it one of the richest Spots of earth under the Sun.

6. An English Trader Scouts for Opportunities on the Slave Coast, 1682

Arthur Wendover   Appa, 17 July 1682

Seeing how causes went and nothing to do, I desired the favour of Captain Wyborne that I might goe to Appa per the next canoe, which he readily granted mee, telling me the canoe would returne in 10 days, which time I thought would not be long, and knowing that Mr Smith would not goe this month, I did adventure at which place I am now, of which I shall give you the following account and the great advantage that may be made on all accounts whatsoever. Appa is about 30 or 40 leagues at the most from Guidah and is very remarkable for ships to find, there being a single cocarnutt tree standing in the middle of a small bay, and a flag staff by that one [= on] which they hang up an old clout, itt makes off to sea very woody for it is a woody place, but I shall advise the Phidalgoe to make a new St Georges flagg. The Phidalgoes towne is about 3 miles from the sea, which is incompassed round with water and small riverlett issuing from the great river, and is mightily full of ba[m]boo trees which afford wine much like unto palme wyne, of which baboos they build all their houses. There is also a very famous river that goes to Boneen, from whence comes all sorts of cloathes and are sold cheap for any sorts of goods. Boneen is 2 dayes journey from this place per land, all goods that comes to this place are conveyed to the Phidalgoes towne by water, they having canoes of 40, 50 and 60 foot in length. There is noe need of anyones taking care of goods when ashoare as to watch them, for the people are so just that they may be trusted with unsold gold, their honesty is to admiration, and the Phidalgoe takes all the care upon himselfe. Here is good conveniency of wooding and watering just by the seaside. These people never goe to sea in their canoes, for the river being soe large and affording very much fish as mullitts and there is one sort of fish that is large as a good handsome hoge, eats much like our sturgeon and is as good in my judgement, for that if any vessell intends for this place they must be provided with a canoe and men, which said canoe may returne fraighted with Boneen cloathes (and other sorts as the place can afford, which may be much to the advantage of the Royall Company my masters. It is also the chiefest markett for slaves (or the fairo as the blacks call it), from whence the people of Guidah and Ophra are furnisht. Assinah voulgarly called Ardua Grandy and other ajacent places from whence comes most slaves are ajacent to this place, soe that slaves cannot be wanting and are not, and to be bought for a more reasonable rate then either at

Source: Robin Law, ed., *The Local Correspondence of the Royal African Company of England, 1681–1699* (Oxford; New York: Published for the British Academy by Oxford University Press, © 1997), pp. 232–235, 236, 237.

Guidah or Ophra; of rates shall give you an account how I have seen them bought. The Phidalgoe is very desirous of a trade and also the people. Once in 15 or 20 days you shall see the river full of canoes and like unto the River of Thames, some with slaves others with clouts, others with sheap, goats, henns, others with corne etc.

The Phidalgoe is a very good man, and lives in great splendour and much honoured by all his people—your trade is wholly with him and noe man elce, he takeing charge of all, soe the trouble is but small.

The Cappusheers are a very good honest people, very laborious alwayes, and for the Phidalgoe or else themselves, their business is cheifely in building, which they doe very famously and very large houses, and as for the common people they seldome or never trouble you, for they come not within the Kings Court, but they are generally honest, which thing is a rarity amongst them: tis not soe at Guidah, them knaves are always stealing and bringing troublesome palavoras to their King, which is not here. Goods bringing from the Appraye very reasonably with abundance of care, and delivered safe into your house. As for the base exacting of custome as the King of Guidah doth demand, I doe not as yett understand that they desire any, and I shall not make enquiry for feare of putting them in mind of such an evill habuit, but I doe believe the Phidalgoe doth expect something, and also the Cabbisheers, which will not be much. I can assure your Worship this that slaves are not wanting at this place, and could the Phidalgoe have any encouragement and his people they would make it their business to turne the trade. Also the people of Assimah or Uper Arda and severall neighbouring Phidalgoes have been with me, and beg heartily that ships may come, for it is soe far for them to go to Guidah, and likewise they run the hazard of being panjard and robed of their goods and slaves (which are all very good reasons in my opinion). . . .

And having now made you sincible of my goeing to Appa and upon what account, which was noe other then to see what manner of place it was and what sort of people, also if that the place were a place for trade or not, which were my cheiefe intentions, and noe other ends in the least but to make the strictest enquiry as possibly I could, that I might be capable of giveing account of a place that may soe much to the advantage of the Royall Company, which is the truth (as God will help me), having given this account I shall leave it to your wise and prudent considerations and shall remaine here untill your further answer and make what inspection possible I can into the trade; and accordingly shall act and doe as you advice. . . .

Accounts of the rates I have seen paid for slaves at this place Appa
Silks, 1 piece yellow, damaged, containing 48 yards ¾ for 5 slaves; 1 piece greene containing 37¼ yards for 4 slaves; 1 piece of pink and 1 piece cherry, damaged, containing 37 yards for 4 slaves; 1 piece of good slite skye containing 39 yards ¾ for 5 slaves; one piece flowred ditto, good, containing 13 yards ½ for 2 slaves.

All sorts of silks sell well here, especially those that are very rich and gaudy. Sundry other sorts of goods vizt a piece of fine scarlett cloth, 7 slaves; 12 iron barrs, 1 ditto; 3 cases of spiritts, 1 ditto; 2 red perpettuanos 1 ditto; 3 fine India carpetts, ditto; 6 narrow pintadoes, ditto; 4 silke allejars ditto; 12 small baftas, ditto; 4 chints, ditto. These goods I have seen bartered for slaves per Cockro and for the rates above mentioned, butt for the rates of others I cannot tell as yett, but doe presume to be all one, nay and rather cheaper, for good goods they covett much, gaudy and rich, although anything is vendible here, rather than want a trade the people are so desireous. I doe believe that Welch plaines would sell well here, by reason they make all their rich cloathes of them, soe that care must be had to the severall sorts of colours, red, green, yellow, blew, purple and orange, and the Phidalgoe gave me a cloath made of Welch plaine which is very handsome.

7. Louis XIV Regulates Slavery in the Colonies, 1685

The Black Code: Edict of the King
Concerning the enforcement of order in the French American
islands from the month of March 1685
Registered at the Sovereign Council of Saint-Domingue, May 6, 1687

Louis, by the grace of God, King of France and Navarre, to all present and to come, greetings. Since we owe equally our attention to all the peoples that Divine Providence has put under our obedience, We have had examined in our presence the memoranda that have been sent to us by our officers in our american islands, by whom having been informed that they need our authority and our justice to maintain the discipline of the Catholic, Apostolic, and Roman church there and to regulate the status and condition of the slaves in our said islands, and desiring to provide for this and to have them know that although they live in regions infinitely removed from our normal residence, we are always present to them, not only by the range of our power, but also by the promptness of our attempts to assist them in their needs. For these reasons, by the advice of our Council, and by our certain knowledge, full power, and royal authority, We have said, ruled, and ordered, we say, rule, and order, wish, and are pleased by that which follows.

I.   We wish and intend that the edict by the late King of glorious memory our very honored lord and father of 23 April 1615 be enforced in our islands, by this we charge all our officers to evict from our Islands all the Jews who have established their residence there, to whom, as to the declared enemies of the Christian name, we order to have left within three months from the day of the publication of these present [edicts], or face confiscation of body and property.

II.   All the slaves who will be in our Islands will be baptized and instructed in the Catholic, Apostolic, and Roman religion. We charge the planters who will buy newly arrived *negres* to inform the Governor and Intendant of the said islands within a week at the latest or face a descretionary fine, these [officials] will give the necessary orders to have them instructed and baptized within an appropriate time. . . .

IV.   No overseers will be given charge of *negres* who do not profess the Catholic, Apostolic, and Roman religion, on pain of confiscation of the said *negres* from the masters who had given this charge to them and of discretionary punishment of the overseers who accepted the said charge. . . .

VI.   We charge all our subjects, whatever their status and condition, to observe Sundays and holidays that are kept by our subjects of the Catholic, Apostolic, and Roman religion. We forbid them to work or to make their slaves work on these days

Source: http://www.vancouver.wsu.edu/fac/peabody/sd.htm. Translation by John Garrigus.

from the hour of midnight until the other midnight, either in agriculture, the manufacture of sugar or all other works, on pain of fine and discretionary punishment of the masters and confiscation of the sugar, and of the said slaves who will be caught by our officers in their work. . . .

IX.   The free men who will have one or several children from their concubinage with their slaves, together with the masters who permitted this, will each be condemned to a fine of two thousand pounds of sugar; and if they are the masters of the slave by whom they have had the said children, we wish that beyond the fine, they be deprived of the slave and the children, and that she and they be confiscated for the profit of the [royal] hospital, without ever being manumitted. Nevertheless we do not intend for the present article to be enforced if the man who was not married to an other person during his concubinage with his slave would marry in the church the said slave who by this means will be manumitted and the children rendered free and legitimate.

X.   The said solemnities prescribed by the Ordonnance of Blois, Articles XL, XLI, XLII, and by the declaration of November 1629 for marriages will be observed both for free persons and for slaves, nevertheless without the consent of the father and the mother of the slave being necessary, but that of the master alone.

XI.   We forbid priests to officiate at the marriages of slaves unless they can show the consent of their masters. We also forbid masters to use any means to constrain their slaves to marry [them?] against their will.

XII.   The children who will be born of marriage between slaves will be slaves and will belong to the master of the women slaves, and not to those of their husband, if the husband and the wife have different masters.

XIII.   We wish that if a slave husband has married a free woman, the children, both male and girls, will follow the condition of their mother and be free like her, in spite of the servitude of their father; and that if the father is free and the mother enslaved, the children will be slaves the same. . . .

XV.   We forbid slaves to carry any weapons, or large sticks, on pain of whipping and of confiscation of the weapon to the profit of those who seize them; with the sole exception of those who are sent hunting by their master and who carry their ticket or known mark.

XVI.   In the same way we forbid slaves belonging to different masters to gather in the day or night whether claiming for wedding or otherwise, whether on their master's property or elsewhere, and still less in the main roads or faraway places, on pain of corporal punishment, which will not be less than the whip and the *fleur de lys* and which in cases of frequent violations and other aggravating circumstances can be punished with death: this we leave to the decision of judges. We charge all our subjects to approach the offenders, to arrest them and take them to prison, even if they are not officers and there is not yet any decree against them.

XVII.   Masters who are convicted of having permitted or tolerated such assemblies composed of slaves other than those belonging to them will be condemned in their own and private name to pay for all the damage that will have been done to their neighbors by these said assemblies and a fine of 10 *ecus* for the first time and double for repeat offenses.

XVIII.   We forbid slaves to sell sugar cane for whatever reason or occasion, even with the permission of their master, on pain of whipping for the slaves and 10 *livres tournois* for their masters who permitted it, and a similar fine against the buyer.

XIX.　We forbid them also to expose for sale, at the market or to carry to private houses for sale any kind of commodity, even fruits, vegetables, firewood, herbs for their food and animals of their manufacture without express permission of their masters by a ticket or by known marks, on pain of confiscation of the things thus sold, without restitution of the price by their masters, and of a fine of six livres tournois to their profit for the buyers. . . .

XXII.　Each week masters will have to furnish to their slaves ten years old and older for their nourishment two and a half jars in the measure of the land, of cassava flour or three cassavas weighing at least two-and-a-half pounds each or equivalent things, with two pounds of salted beef or three pounds of fish or other things in proportion, and to children after they are weaned to the age of 10 years half of the above supplies. . . .

XXXIII.　The slave who will have struck his master or the wife of his master, his mistress or their children to bring blood, or in the face, will be punished with death.

LV.　Masters twenty years old will be able to manumit their slaves by all [legal] deeds or by cause of death, without being required to provide the reason for this manumission, neither will they need the permission of parents, provided that they are minors twenty-five years of age. . . .

LVIII.　We command manumitted slaves to retain a particular respect for their former masters, their widows and their children; such that the insult that they will have done be punished more severely than if it had been done to another person: we declare them however free and absolved of any other burdens, services and rights that their former masters would like to claim, as much on their persons as on their possessions and estates as patrons.

LIX.　We grant to manumitted slaves the same rights, privileges and liberties enjoyed by persons born free; desiring that they merit this acquired liberty and that it produce in them, both for their persons and for their property, the same effects that the good fortune of natural liberty causes in our other subjects.

This we give and command to our loved and loyal supporters the persons holding our sovereign council established in Martinique, GadeLoupe [sic], Saint Christophe, that they read, publish and register. . . . [signed Louis, Colbert, LeTellier]

8. Two Political Economists Evaluate the Discovery of America, 1776, 1867

Adam Smith

The general advantages which Europe, considered as one great country, has derived from the discovery and colonization of America, consist, first, in the increase of its enjoyments; and, secondly, in the augmentation of its industry.

Source: Adam Smith, *An Inquiry into the Nature and Causes of the Wealth of Nations* (Dublin, 1776), vol. 2, pp. 447–451; Karl Marx, *Capital*, translated from the third German edition by Samuel Moore and Edward Aveling; edited by Frederick Engels; revised and amplified according to fourth German edition by Ernest Untermann (New York, The Modern Library, 1906), 823–824, 825–827, 832–834.

The surplus produce of America, imported into Europe, furnishes the inhabitants of this great continent with a variety of commodities which they could not otherwise have possessed, some for conveniency and use, some for pleasure, and some for ornament, and thereby contributes to increase their enjoyments.

The discovery and colonization of America, it will readily be allowed, have contributed to augment the industry, first, of all the countries which trade to it directly; such as Spain, Portugal, France, and England; and, secondly, of all those which, without trading to it directly, send through the medium of other countries, goods to it of their own produce; such as Austrian Flanders, and some provinces of Germany, which, through the medium of the countries before mentioned, send to it a conderable quantity of linen and other goods. All such countries have evidently gained a more extensive market for their surplus produce, and must consequently have been encouraged to increase its quantity.

But, that those great events should likewise have contributed to encourage the industry of countries, such as Hungary and Poland, which may never, perhaps, have sent a single commodity of their own produce to America, is not, perhaps, altogether so evident. That those events have done so, however, cannot be doubted. Some part of the produce of America is consumed in Hungary and Poland, and there is some demand there for the sugar, chocolate, and tobacco, of that new quarter of the world. But those commodities must be purchased with something which is either the produce of the industry of Hungary and Poland, or with something which had been purchased with some part of that produce. Those commodities of America are new values, new equivalents, introduced into Hungary and Poland, to be exchanged there for the surplus produce of those countries. By being carried thither they create a new and more extensive market for that surplus produce. They raise its value, and thereby contribute to encourage its increase. Though no part of it may ever be carried to America, it may be carried to other countries which purchase it with a part of their share of the surplus produce of America; and it may find a market by means of the circulation of that trade which was originally put into motion by the surplus produce of America.

Those great events may even have contributed to increase the enjoyments, and to augment the industry of countries which, not only never sent any commodities to America, but never received any from it. Even such countries may have received a greater abundance of other commodities from countries of which the surplus produce had been augmented by means of the American trade. This greater abundance, as it must necessarily have increased their enjoyments, so it must likewise have augmented their industry. A greater number of new equivalents of some kind or other must have been presented to them to be exchanged for the surplus produce of that industry. A more extensive market must have been created for that surplus produce, so as to raise its value, and thereby encourage its increase. The mass of commodities annually thrown into the great circle of European commerce, and by its various revolutions annually distributed among all the different nations comprehended within it, must have been augmented by the whole surplus produce of America. A greater share of this greater mass, therefore, is likely to have fallen to each of those nations, to have increased their enjoyments, and augmented their industry.

The exclusive trade of the mother countries tends to diminish, or at least, to keep down below what they would otherwise rise to, both the enjoyments and industry of all those nations in general, and of the American colonies in particular. It is a dead weight upon the action of one of the great springs which puts into motion a great part of the business of mankind. By rendering the colony produce dearer in all other countries it lessens its consumption, and thereby cramps the industry of the colonies, and both the enjoyments and the industry of all other countries, which both enjoy less when they pay more for what they enjoy, and produce less when they get less for what they produce. By rendering the produce of all other countries dearer in the colonies, it cramps, in the same manner, the industry of all other countries, and both the enjoyments and the industry of the colonies. It is a clog which, for the supposed benefit of some particular countries, embarrasses the pleasures, and encumbers the industry of all other countries; but of the colonies more than of any other. It not only excludes, as much as possible, all other countries from one particular market; but it confines, as much as possible, the colonies to one particular market: and the difference is very great between being excluded from one particular market, when all others are open, and being confined to one particular market, when all others are shut up. The surplus produce of the colonies, however, is the original source of all that increase of enjoyments and industry which Europe derives from the discovery and colonization of America; and the exclusive trade of the mother countries tends to render this source much less abundant than it otherwise would be.

Karl Marx

The discovery of gold and silver in America, the extirpation, enslavement and entombment in mines of the aboriginal population, the beginning of the conquest and looting of the East Indies, the turning of Africa into a warren for the commercial hunting of black-skins, signalised the rosy dawn of the era of capitalist production. These idyllic proceedings are the chief momenta of primitive accumulation. On their heels treads the commercial war of the European nations, with the globe for a theatre. It begins with the revolt of the Netherlands from Spain, assumes giant dimensions in England's anti-jacobin war, and is still going on in the opium wars against China, &c.

The different momenta of primitive accumulation distribute themselves now, more or less in chronological order, particularly over Spain, Portugal, Holland, France, and England. In England at the end of the 17th century, they arrive at a systematical combination, embracing the colonies, the national debt, the modern mode of taxation, and the protectionist system. These methods depend in part on brute force, *e.g.*, the colonial system. But they all employ the power of the State, the concentrated and organised force of society, to hasten, hothouse fashion, the process of transformation of the feudal mode of production into the capitalist mode, and to shorten the transition. Force is the midwife of every old society pregnant with a new one. It is itself an economic power. . . .

The treatment of the aborigines was, naturally, most frightful in plantation-colonies destined for export trade only, such as the West Indies, and in rich and well-populated countries, such as Mexico and India, that were given over to plunder. But even in the colonies properly so-called, the Christian character of primitive accumulation did not belie itself. Those sober virtuosi of Protestantism, the Puritans of New

England, in 1703, by decrees of their assembly set a premium of £40 on every Indian scalp and every captured red-skin: in 1720 a premium of £100 on every scalp; in 1744, after Massachusetts-Bay had proclaimed a certain tribe as rebels, the following prices: for a male scalp of 12 years and upwards £100 (new currency), for a male prisoner £105, for women and children prisoners £50, for scalps of women and children £50. Some decades later, the colonial system took its revenge on the descendants of the pious pilgrim fathers, who had grown seditious in the meantime. At English instigation and for English pay they were tomahawked by red-skins. The British Parliament, proclaimed blood-hounds and scalping as "means that God and Nature had given into its hand."

The colonial system ripened, like a hot-house, trade and navigation. The "societies Monopolia" of Luther were powerful levers for concentration of capital. The colonies secured a market for the budding manufactures, and, through the monopoly of the market, an increased accumulation. The treasures captured outside Europe by undisguised looting, enslavement, and murder, floated back to the mother-country and were there turned into capital. . . .

With the development of capitalist production during the manufacturing period, the public opinion of Europe had lost the last remnant of shame and conscience. The nations bragged cynically of every infamy that served them as a means to capitalistic accumulation. Read, *e.g.*, the naïve Annals of Commerce of the worthy A. Anderson. Here it is trumpetted forth as a triumph of English statecraft that at the Peace of Utrecht, England extorted from the Spaniards by the Asiento Treaty the privilege of being allowed to ply the negro-trade, until then only carried on between Africa and the English West Indies, between Africa and Spanish America as well. England thereby acquired the right of supplying Spanish America until 1743 with 4800 negroes yearly. This threw, at the same time, an official cloak over British smuggling. Liverpool waxed fat on the slave-trade. This was its method of primitive accumulation. And, even to the present day, Liverpool "respectability" is the Pindar of the slave-trade which—compare the work of Aikin [1795] already quoted—"has coincided with that spirit of bold adventure which has characterised the trade of Liverpool and rapidly carried it to its present state of prosperity; has occasioned vast employment for shipping and sailors, and greatly augmented the demand for the manufactures of the country" (p. 339). Liverpool employed in the slave trade, in 1730, 15 ships; in 1751, 53; in 1760, 74; in 1770, 96; and in 1792, 132.

Whilst the cotton industry introduced child-slavery in England, it gave in the United States a stimulus to the transformation of the earlier, more or less patriarchal slavery, into a system of commercial exploitation. In fact, the veiled slavery of the wage-earners in Europe needed, for its pedestal, slavery pure and simple in the new world.

Tantæ molis erat, to establish the "eternal laws of Nature" of the capitalist mode of production, to complete the process of separation between labourers and conditions of labour, to transform, at one pole, the social means of production and subsistence into capital, at the opposite pole, the mass of the population into wage-labourers, into "free labouring poor," that artificial product of modern society. If money, according to Augier, "comes into the world with a congenital blood-stain on one cheek," capital comes dripping from head to foot, from every pore, with blood and dirt.

From the era when the Spanish and Portuguese began to seek new trade routes to Asia, the Atlantic economy was always connected to a larger global economy. The two essays in this chapter trace this connection through the histories of silver and sugar, two of the Atlantic world's most important commodities. Economic historians Dennis Flynn and Arturo Giráldez show that after Spanish invaders discovered silver at the mountain of Potosí in Peru in 1545, much of the silver mined in the Americas ended up in China, where demand for the metal was exceptionally high. The key to Chinese demand was the "Single-Whip" tax system implemented by the Ming Dynasty in the 1570s, which required taxes to be paid in silver. Spanish American silver either flowed to China through Europe or was transported directly to Asia on galleons that sailed from Acapulco to Manila.

Like silver, sugar also had a global history. J. H. Galloway, a leading historian of sugar, analyzes Dutch participation in the early modern global economy of sugar traders, producers, and consumers. The Dutch involvement in sugar production began in Asia, where Dutch merchants gained a significant share of the carrying trade in sugar. Around the same time as Dutch planters began to grow sugar in Java, the Dutch West India Company tried to grow sugar in northeastern Brazil. Not only did the Dutch bring technological innovations in sugar processing from Asia to Brazil, but they also provided English sugar planters in Barbados with technical expertise that helped the take-off of that colony. The Dutch imported large quantities of American and Asian sugar into Amsterdam, which became a center of European sugar refining. Not surprisingly, Dutch culture developed a sweet tooth in the seventeenth century.

What Did China Have to Do with American Silver?

DENNIS O. FLYNN AND ARTURO GIRÁLDEZ

The birth of world trade has been described by C. R. Boxer in the following terms: "Only after the Portuguese had worked their way down the West African coast, rounded the Cape of Good Hope, crossed the Indian Ocean and established themselves in the Spice Islands of Indonesia and on the shore of the South China Sea; only after the Spaniards had attained the same goal by way of Patagonia, the Pacific Ocean and the Philippines—then and only then was a regular and lasting maritime connection established between the four great continents."

Although Boxer does not pick a specific date for the birth of global trade, his logic leads us to choose 1571—the year the city of Manila was founded. Manila was the crucial entrepôt linking substantial, direct, and continuous trade between America and Asia for the first time in history.

For our purposes, global trade emerged when all important populated continents began to exchange products continuously—both with each other directly and indirectly via other continents—and in values sufficient to generate crucial impacts on all the trading partners. It is true that there was an important intercontinental

Source: Dennis O. Flynn and Arturo Giráldez, "Born with a 'Silver Spoon': The Origin of World Trade in 1571," *Journal of World History* 1995 6(2): 201–203, 203–204, 209–212, 216–217. Reprinted with permission of the University of Hawaii Press.

trade before 1571, but there was no direct trade link between America and Asia, so the world market was not yet fully coherent or complete. To understand the global significance of the direct Pacific trade between America and Asia—international trade history's "missing link"—it is useful first to discuss the underlying economic forces that motivated profitable world trade in the early modern period. The singular product most responsible for the birth of world trade was silver.

More than the market for any other commodity, the silver market explains the emergence of world trade. China was the dominant buyer of silver. On the supply side, Spanish America (Mexico and Peru) erupted with unprecedented production of the white metal. Conservative official estimates indicate that Latin America alone produced about 150,000 tons of silver between 1500 and 1800, perhaps exceeding 80% of the entire world production over that time span. Despite America's dominance in silver production over three centuries, Japan may have been the primary exporter of silver to China in the late sixteenth and early seventeenth centuries, shipping perhaps 200 tons per year at times. Japanese silver exports, however, fell off dramatically in the second half of the seventeenth century. "The amount of Japanese silver poured into foreign trade in the heyday of Japan's overseas trade, 1615 to 1625, through Japanese, Chinese, Dutch, Portuguese and other ships, reached tremendous value, roughly estimated at 130,000–160,000 kilograms—equal to 30% or 40% of the total world silver production outside Japan. This explains why European and Asian merchants were so enthusiastic about developing trade with Japan." The central point is that all the great silver mines in both hemispheres sold ultimately to China.

　　We intentionally emphasize the role of China—and its tributary system—in the silver trade because the scholarly literature in general has neglected this pivotal country, certainly in terms of recognizing China as a prime causal actor. The literature on New World treasure is huge and multifaceted—sometimes focusing on sixteenth-century price inflation (the price revolution), and/or the rise and fall of Spain, and/or the transition from feudalism to capitalism, and many other issues— but it is unified in one central respect: it focuses virtually exclusively on Europe as the fulcrum. Europe is considered the epicenter of early modern commercial activity. The sixteenth-century price revolution, for example, is mostly thought of in terms of European price inflation, when in reality it was a global phenomenon. In a remarkably clear summary of China's participation in the global price revolution, Geiss provides an exception to the normal Eurocentric focus: "In the late sixteenth century, however, when silver from Mexico and Japan entered the Ming empire in great quantity, the value of silver began to decline and inflation set in, for as the metal became more abundant its buying power diminished. This inflationary trend affected the values of all commodities, everything had been valued in silver and silver lost its value. Ramifications of this change touched the lives of almost everyone in the empire." . . .

　　Acceptance of a global perspective instead of the predominant Eurocentric view outlined above yields a startlingly different view. It becomes clear that Europeans did indeed play an important role in the birth of world trade, but their role was as middlemen in the vast silver trade; they were prime movers on neither the supply side (except Spain in America) nor the demand side of the worldwide silver market.

Europeans were intermediaries in the trade between the New World and China. Massive amounts of silver traversed the Atlantic. After it had reached European soil, the Portuguese in the sixteenth century and Dutch in the seventeenth century became dominant distributors of silver by a multitude of routes into Asia. Attman conservatively estimates that 150 tons of silver passed through Europe into Asia on an annual basis. "The country which reigned supreme in arranging solutions for the deficit problems in world trade was Holland, acting mainly on her own behalf in the Baltic area, the Levant and Asia, but also acting for other nations. . . . Even when other countries needed precious metals Holland acted in many cases as a clearing centre and in the final stage as an exporter of precious metals. . . . But the bulk of the precious metals required for the Asian trade came from Europe around the Cape." It is worthwhile to reflect momentarily on Attman's estimate of 150 tons of silver exported each year from Europe to Asia. Attman emphasizes that his estimates include only specie shipments (i.e., bullion is excluded from consideration) and that he has studied only port records (i.e., overland trade is excluded). If Attman had included bullion shipments through ports, as well as specie and bullion shipments over land routes, his estimate of west-to-east silver flows would have been far greater. He warned readers of the conservative and partial nature of his estimates, but scholars rarely acknowledge this when citing his figures.

The Pacific leg of the China trade has not received the attention it deserves. Writing of the period 1571–1620, TePaske says that an enormous quantity of silver passed over the Pacific, especially out of Acapulco and through Manila on its way to China. "Mexican silver also flowed out to the islands in large sums, far exceeding the 500,000-peso limitation. In fact at the opening of the seventeenth century the drain of pesos from Mexico to the Orient through the Philippines was estimated at 5 million pesos [128 tons] annually, with a reported 12 million pesos [307 tons] being smuggled out in 1597." These are shocking figures because this alleged average of 5 million pesos (128 tons per year) over the Pacific, at the turn of the century, is only 15% less than the 150 tons minimum that Attman says Europe shipped to Asia on an annual basis. Moreover, the 12 million pesos (307 tons) in 1597 is more than double Attman's estimate of the entire European leg of the journey of silver to China. These may seem like fantastic figures to some, but Barrett has pointed out a glaring discrepancy between Spanish American production figures and estimated exports to Europe: production seems to have exceeded exports to Europe by 5.5 million pesos (135 tons) per year. Barrett reasons that this 5.5 million pesos must have either remained in America or been exported through the Philippines. It will become clear shortly that exportation of such a vast amount of silver through Manila makes sense in global terms, while its retention in the New World does not. . . .

The richest silver mine in the history of the world was discovered at more than 15,000 feet altitude in the Andes in Potosí (present-day Bolivia), a one-way journey of two and one-half months via pack animal from Lima. Nothing grew at that altitude, so there was no population at the time silver was discovered in 1545. During the ensuing sixty years, Potosí's population swelled to 160,000, about equal to that of London or Paris. This would be the modern-day equivalent of, say, 20 million people moving to a spot on Alaska's North Slope. Evidently something unusual was going on in Potosí.

Potosí's *cerro rico* (rich mountain) may have produced 60% of all the silver mined in the world in the second half of the sixteenth century. Its veins were incredibly rich. In addition to naturally bountiful deposits, a series of new production technologies—the most famous being the mercury-amalgam "patio process"—combined to render Spanish American mines the world's lowest cost sources of silver. This supply-side phenomenon was particularly fortuitous because it coincided chronologically with the extraordinary rise in the value of silver caused by the Chinese demand-side forces culminating in the Single-Whip tax reform. The combination of low supply-side production costs in Spanish America and Chinese-led demand-side elevation in silver's value in Asia generated probably the most spectacular mining boom in human history. This combination of supply-side and demand-side forces implied enormous profits.

No entity reaped greater rewards from the silver industry than the Spanish crown, which wisely allowed favored "private sector" entrepreneurs to operate New World mines, rather than attempting to do so itself. Instead, the crown took a substantial fraction of mining profits through taxes. The most famous tax was the *quinto*, a 20% severance tax on gross value, but there were many indirect taxes as well. According to Hamilton, 27.5% of total registered precious metals entering Seville between 1566 and 1645 belonged to the crown of Castile. Revenues from overseas mines provided the fiscal foundation for the Spanish empire.

Spain was a small country of perhaps 7.5 million inhabitants by the middle of the sixteenth century, about half the population of France. Elliott has described Castile of 1600 as "an economy closer in many ways to that of an East European state like Poland, exporting basic raw materials and importing luxury products, than to the economies of West European states." Carande and many others classify Spain as backward domestically, substantiating the observation that the financial foundation of the Spanish empire was based on resources outside the Iberian peninsula. Mine profits were enormous, and there was no comparable profit center elsewhere, so we conclude that the New World mines supported the Spanish empire.

This view of Spain leads to surprising but inevitable conclusions. We have already established that domestic developments inside China elevated the value of silver in world markets far beyond what it could have been otherwise. The largest beneficiary of silver's high value must have been the Spanish crown, the institution that reaped enormous profits by way of its control and taxation of the low-cost New World centers of production. Thus, the silver-industry profits that financed the Spanish empire were huge because China had become the world's dominant silver customer. This implies that ultimately China was responsible for a power shift within early modern Europe. In the absence of the "silverization" of China, it is hard to imagine how Castile could have financed simultaneous wars for generations against the Ottomans in the Mediterranean; Protestant England and Holland and the French in Europe, the New World, and Asia; and against indigenous peoples in the Philippines.

Even giant China could not prop up Spain indefinitely. As tens of thousands of tons of silver accumulated on the Asian mainland, its value gradually fell there (as it had already been doing in the West and Japan) toward its cost of production. Imports eventually glutted even China's vast silver market. We know that this portrayal of silver's loss of value is accurate because by about 1635 it took about 13 ounces of silver to buy an ounce of gold in China, while a half century earlier it took 6 ounces of silver. The value of silver also fell relative to other things, not just gold, which is to say that price inflation occurred. "In the late sixteenth century . . . when silver from Mexico and Japan entered the Ming empire in great quantity, the value of silver began to decline and inflation set in, for as the metal became more abundant, its buying power diminished. This inflationary trend affected the value of all commodities; everything had been valued in silver and silver lost its value. Ramifications of this change touched the lives of almost everyone in the empire." As silver lost value, more silver money was required to purchase items that had maintained their value. Price inflation is defined as the surrender of more pieces of money for a given set of items, so the descent of silver to its cost of production is what ultimately caused prices to inflate in China to about the same extent as in Europe and elsewhere.

The unavoidable fall in the value of silver is a crucial issue because each year as it descended closer to its cost of production in America, profit per unit of silver also shrank. Declining profits were not due to inefficient operations; rather, they were the inevitable result of the laws of demand and supply. The existence of arbitrage profits motivated the trade, and the trade itself, in turn, led to the elimination of such profits. Faced with declining profits from its silver industry, Castile could no longer afford its vast empire. China contributed mightily to the duration of the Spanish empire, but even China's prodigious demand for silver could not prevent the eventual erosion of mine profits and therefore the decline of Spain. Spanish American silver production may have peaked in the 1590s, but large production coupled with vanishing profits per ounce of silver still implied a vanishing overall profit level by this time.

Historians tend to focus too much attention on the quantity of silver shipments, while the participants themselves cared only about the profits associated with the trade. In the words of an executive in a standard business joke today, "Since we are losing money on each item sold, we simply must make up for it in volume!" Spain experienced multiple bankruptcies in the late sixteenth and early seventeenth centuries, during a time of record silver production, because the value of each unit of silver continued to decline. When profit per unit of a product declines to zero, multiplication of zero per-unit profit times any quantity of output must yield zero total profit. Spanish American mines were not yet yielding zero profits per unit of product, but the trend was clearly in that direction. Silver's declining value affected the crown so profoundly that interest payments on Castile's federal debt alone—"the equivalent of at least ten years' revenue" by 1623—eventually exceeded total crown receipts. Spain vanished as a serious Western power as its silver basis eroded, but the Iberian surge to power had been lengthy and impressive. The fact that Spain's empire owed its financial foundation to distant Ming China is a forceful reminder that much of what passes for local history in the early modern period can only be understood in terms of world history. . . .

We have consciously neglected any attempt to tie the African continent into the global trade of silver. Nonetheless, it seems that the Portuguese swapped huge numbers of (mostly smuggled) African slaves directly for (mostly smuggled) New World silver via the Rio Plata in Brazil:

> During the decade 1616–1625, recorded imports for Buenos Aires (the sum of legal and confiscated goods) were 7,957,579 pesos, while exports for the same period amounted to only 360,904 pesos. The annual trade deficit, which was met with smuggled silver from Upper Peru, amounted to at least three-quarters of a million pesos per year. Between

1619 and 1623, port officials seized a total of 3,656 slaves from illegally landing vessels; their market value in Lima would have approached two million pesos. These numbers do not include those slaves legally imported and those which evaded port officials. The size of these figures clearly indicates a flourishing and considerable illicit trade up the Rio Plata from the 1580s until probably the 1640s. During its most successful years, no less than 1–2 million pesos (roughly 25,000 to 50,000 kg) flowed illegally from the mines of Peru out through the port of Buenos Aires. These totals equalled from 15% to 30% of the silver output of Potosí.

Not all the slaves remained in Brazil, nor were all of them plantation laborers. Palmer has provided demographic information suggesting that between 10,000 and 20,000 Africans were domestic slaves in Mexico City in the early seventeenth century. Since, as we have argued, the Spanish enterprise in America was financed by the world silver market (as were the activities of the Portuguese traders), and since China was the dominant factor in the global silver market, then it appears that the trans-Atlantic slave trade was heavily, though indirectly, influenced by monetary and fiscal developments in Ming China. In other words, end-customer China created profitable trade in the New World, and profitable trade in America created the demand for African slaves. Clearly, a global view of early modern trade may suggest many research topics that might otherwise be overlooked.

What Did the Dutch Have to Do with Sugar in the Caribbean?

J. H. GALLOWAY

In the early sixteenth century, the Spanish and Portuguese took the sugar industry to America, the Spanish at first tentatively to Hispaniola, and the Portuguese very successfully to Brazil. In tropical America, with its year-round rainfall, abundance of land, and seemingly unlimited fuel, the industry took on a far larger scale that required innovations in technology and a great increase in labor, a demand which was satisfied by Africa. The large slave-worked plantation was the basic unit of production. This experience demonstrated to the Spanish and Portuguese, and to the other European powers who observed, that the sugar industry could be lucrative, both a means of paying the expenses of colonization and a motive for acquiring colonies. The Dutch, among others, wished to participate.

The Dutch as Traders

In medieval Europe, Venetians and Genoese at first controlled the sugar trade. Sugar was then a luxury product which only the elite could afford. Nevertheless, the virtues of sugar were well-known: it satisfies the craving for sweetness, it sweetens without altering the taste of the food and drink to which it is added, and it is a preservative. Many customers also believed sugar had medicinal value. The market was there if more sugar could be imported at a lesser price.

Source: J. H. Galloway, "The Role of the Dutch in the Early American Sugar Industry," *Halve Maen*, 2003, 76(2): 25–32. Reprinted courtesy of The Holland Society of New York.

In the late fourteenth century and into the fifteenth, sugar began to arrive in Northern Europe in greater quantities, at first from Granada and soon also from Madeira, recently discovered by the Portuguese. Bruges and London were the main ports through which this sugar was distributed. The Venetians and Genoese were still prominent in the trade, but ships from Flanders had become involved. Documents from 1498 show that by this time Flanders was the major market for Madeiran sugar. São Tomé, still further south off the African coast, became in the 1500s another Portuguese sugar colony, and it too helped supply Flanders. The Spanish in turn produced sugar in the Canaries. By the late 1500s Antwerp had become the main center of sugar refining in Northern Europe. The Dutch entered the sugar trade in their own right after the beginning of the Eighty Years' War, at first with the Portuguese Atlantic colonies and then with Asia. Their vehicle for doing so was the East India Company—the VOC, to use its Dutch initials—founded in 1602 after a few Dutch traders had made exploratory voyages in the last years of the sixteenth century.

The Dutch encountered in Asia, as indeed had the Portuguese a century before them, an active, sophisticated trading network extending from the Persian Gulf to Japan and involving the ships of many peoples and the exchange of a vast array of goods. Sugar was one of the items traded. In Asia, in contrast to the Atlantic Islands and America, an indigenous sugar industry existed that in a number of localities produced a surplus for export. At this time, the trade in sugar was divided into two separate spheres, east and west of the great port of Malacca on the Malay peninsula. To the east, the Chinese provinces of Fujian and Guangdong were the major exporters with Taiwan, the Philippines, Java, Sumatra, Vietnam, and Thailand playing lesser roles. The markets were Japan, mainly supplied from China, and other ports to the east and south of Malacca. To the west, Bengal was the major exporter, supplying markets around the Bay of Bengal, along the west coast of India, in Persia, and onto the Middle East. The Portuguese approach to breaking into the Asian trade had been to seize a network of fortified ports from the Persian Gulf to Malacca for the protection of their own ships and from which they could exact taxes and protection costs from other shipping. The acquisition of Macao in 1554 and of port facilities at Nagasaki in 1571 extended their influence into the Far East and enabled them to secure for a time a dominant position in the trade between China and Japan. Portuguese intervention in the sugar industry was limited to participation in the carrying trade: they did not engage in the production of sugar nor did they import significant amounts of Asian sugar to Europe. Portuguese resources, however, were too meager to support a major role in the inter-regional Asian trade. The heralded connection with Japan, maintained by voyages between Goa and Nagasaki, was symptomatic of this problem: trade was soon reduced to one *não*, or large ship, a year. The lack of resources is also evident in the tenuous contacts with Lisbon: between 1500 and 1634 an average of seven ships a year left Portugal for the East, and only an average of four ships a year made the voyage home. The ships that failed to return were either lost at sea or served for a time along the Asian sea routes. Despite the Portuguese crown's pretentious claims to be Lord of the Conquest, Navigation and Commerce of Ethiopia, Arabia, Persia, and India, the Portuguese during the sixteenth century made relatively little impact on the patterns of Asian maritime traffic which, in effect, they joined in a modest way rather than changed. Change was to come with the arrival of the Dutch. . . .

The Dutch were already experienced traders in sugar before they founded the VOC, but their experience in Asia helped to create a worldwide market in sugar in which a change of price in one part of the system would affect prices and orders for sugar elsewhere. The VOC shipped cargoes of Asian sugar to the Netherlands as ballast, an indication of the weight of sugar and its ability not only to withstand long distance travel but to pay for the costs. The quantities the VOC shipped home depended on prices in Amsterdam of Brazilian and, later, West Indian sugar. When these prices were low, there was little call on Asian sources. When they rose as they did in the late 1620s and into the 1630s, the VOC ordered from Asia. The Directors would specify to their officials in Batavia the quantity, quality, and provenance of the sugar to be ordered. China, Bengal, and Siam were the suppliers. The VOC added to the complexities of the trade by becoming a producer of sugar, around Batavia, from the late 1630s and, briefly, also in Taiwan. The VOC then had an interest in finding markets for its own Java sugar. High prices in Amsterdam would attract sugar from Java; times of low prices would force the VOC to find markets for its Javanese sugar in Asia. It successfully competed with Bengali sugar in western India and in Persia and after the 1660s could undersell Chinese sugar in Japan. One period of high prices in Amsterdam, from 1645–1655, occasioning the import of a large amount of sugar from Java, was the result of the war in Brazil between the Dutch and the Portuguese that ended the Dutch attempt to become a major producer of sugar in America.

The Dutch as Sugar Producers in America

At about the same time the Dutch were beginning to produce sugar in Java, the West India Company (WIC) decided to become producers of sugar in America. Given that land in mainland tropical America was already claimed by Spain and Portugal and various European powers were fighting over ownership of islands in the Caribbean, the Dutch, if they were to have sugar colonies, had to be prepared to seize land and hold onto it. The WIC decided that São Tomé was not worth the trouble of taking and turned its attention to the largest sugar colony of the time, Brazil. The founding of Dutch Brazil was controversial from the very beginning and proved to be an adventure expensive both in treasure and lives.

The Dutch were accustomed from the late sixteenth century to importing sugar from Brazil via Portugal and even directly and found in Brazil a market for their linen and textiles. They estimated they carried between a half and two thirds of all Brazilian trade with Europe in their ships. During the truce of 1609–1621 between the United Provinces and Spain, trade with Brazil greatly increased. The Dutch also depended on salt from Setúbal, in Portugal, for their herring trade. Understandably, some Dutch, particularly in Amsterdam and North Holland, were very concerned that an attack on Brazil by the WIC would jeopardize these profitable trade relations with Portugal for what might be very modest gains. The motives of the WIC were not only to capture a major sugar-growing region that would provide them with big profits but also to secure a base from which to attack other Spanish and Portuguese possessions in America. In 1624 a WIC expedition captured the city of Salvador, the colonial capital of Brazil, but had to abandon it a few months later in 1625 on the arrival of a Spanish and Portuguese fleet. The WIC returned in force in 1630 and this time captured and held Recife on the northeast coast. Over the next few years the Dutch extended their control slowly in the face of guerilla warfare over the sugar-growing coastlands to the north and south. At the height of their power in Brazil from 1637 to 1644, during the years of the rule of Count Johan Maurits, the Dutch held the coast from Sergipe to Maranhâo. Their control, however, never extended more than a few miles inland and was most secure around the city of Recife. After the departure of Johan Maurits the fortunes of Dutch Brazil rapidly declined because of poor administration, lack of support from the WIC and the States-General, and the resumption of guerilla warfare. For the last years of its existence, Dutch Brazil was reduced to the besieged city of Recife. It finally capitulated to the Portuguese in 1654. . . .

There are two important questions to ask in relation to Dutch Brazil and sugar technology. What techniques, if any, did they bring to Brazil from Asia? And, secondly, what techniques did they introduce to the Caribbean as they prepared new sources of the sugar supply as their hold on Brazil weakened? Before answering these questions there is one point to make: the Dutch entered on their occupation of northeast Brazil just as a technological innovation, the three-roller mill, was sweeping through the region, an innovation which had nothing to do with the Dutch. This design of the mill could be adapted to different types of power—animal, water, wind—and be built in various sizes. It was economical in its use of labor and, in general, was far more efficient and better suited to the large scale of the sugar industry in the Americas than the edge-runners and screw presses that the colonizers had brought with them from the Mediterranean and the Atlantic Islands. The first record of the three-roller mill in America dates to 1613 in Peru. There is controversy over its origin. Long-standing claims that it was invented in Sicily in the mid-fifteenth century have probably now finally been set aside, but debate continues. Christian Daniels has put forward the case for a Chinese origin of a two-roller vertically-mounted mill to which a third roller was added in America, and Mazumdar has replied with a very effective case for a European/American origin of vertically-mounted mills. Whatever the origin, the vertical roller mill may well have been "one of the most productive inventions of mankind for agricultural processing."

Records show that three-roller mills had already gained rapid acceptance in Brazil by 1618 and within ten more years had largely replaced the old types of mills and presses. Dutch artists confirm this rapid acceptance. An illustration from 1636, if not from a year or two earlier, shows in the background an edge-runner crushing sugar cane and in the foreground two slaves and several Dutchmen. Frans Post provides abundant evidence of the transition: he only showed three-roller mills. Maybe he ignored any surviving edge-runners, wishing to emphasize the modernizing policies of the Dutch regime. Perhaps the most famous of his drawings of sugar mills is the one that appeared originally on Markgraf's map of Brazil, published in Barlaeus's book. He drew an even more detailed picture of a water-powered three-roller mill that is now in the Musée Royal des Beaux Arts in Brussels. The ox-powered mill in Piso's part of the *Historia Naturalis Brasiliae* is by Post. There are two curious points about these illustrations: there are no windmills and the Dutch overseers are shown, despite the tropical heat, fully dressed as if they were in Amsterdam.

The Dutch were responsible for the second improvement recorded in the illustrations. In the early years in the Americas, the Spanish and Portuguese had continued the practice brought over from Europe of reducing the juice in a single cauldron over an open fire. The Dutch illustrations do not record any examples of this practice. They show something very different. The Chinese system in the seventeenth century for boiling the juice was to build a brick furnace and to set on top of it three large pans in a triangular pattern. The masonry conserved the heat, and the furnace was fuel-efficient with one fire serving the three pans. The juice was transferred from one pan to the next, reaching the strike point in the third. The work could be carried on continuously by refilling the empty first pan with fresh juice from the mill. Chinese sugar-making technology was spreading through South East Asia at this time. The Dutch must have seen these furnaces in operation in Java and Taiwan and to bring this technology to Brazil was a logical step. Piso's illustration shows brick furnaces and what seems to be the Chinese system in operation. This Asian system greatly increased the efficiency of the manufacture of sugar and was a necessary accompaniment of the three-roller mill to deal with the greater scale that the sugar industry had assumed in America.

The transfer of technology from Brazil to the Caribbean was the final contribution of the Dutch to sugar technology in colonial America. Barbados was their point of entry where in the late 1640s they helped the English set up sugar plantations with advice on all aspects of sugar-making from cultivating cane to designing the complex of mill, boiling house, and curing house to ensure the continuous flow of work. They introduced the three-roller mill with one significant modification: they built windmills to make use of the Trade Winds that waft reliably over the island. The Dutch, however, did not bring the Chinese style of furnace to Barbados. Instead, in Barbados there appears the first record in America of yet another design of furnace in which the cauldrons are arranged in a linear battery, starting with the largest and ending with the smallest. The juice was transferred from one cauldron to the next as it condensed to reach the strike-point in the last cauldron. There could be four, five, or even more cauldrons in the battery. Each cauldron was heated by its own fire. This arrangement gave the sugar master even greater control over the work and was another step forward in the efficiency of what was an industrial activity. Within a few years the design was modified so that one fire heated all cauldrons through an internal flue. The place of origin of the linear battery is still debated. Mazumdar and Daniels see Asian antecedents. Given that the English in Barbados learned how to make sugar from the Dutch in Brazil, the supposition is that the Dutch were responsible for the introduction of the linear battery. Yet, the Dutch artists did not record the linear batteries. Is it possible the Dutch brought this furnace to Brazil from Asia after the Johan Maurits era but just in time to pass it on to Barbados? The timing seems very tight. The linear battery did in time come into general use in Brazil. The issue of its origins has been further complicated by the results of the excavation of large sugar mills in Cyprus which functioned from the mid-fourteenth century, if not earlier, to the end of the sixteenth. They have been found to have had furnaces that were organized in a linear battery similar to those of the seventeenth-century Caribbean.

In addition to helping the English on Barbados, the Dutch sought to found replacement sugar colonies for Dutch Brazil along the "Wild Coast" that stretched from the mouth of the Orinoco to the Amazon and which at that time no one European power controlled. The Dutch fought with the French and English over colonies that were little more than trading posts at the estuaries of the many rivers. These posts were conquered, destroyed, and reclaimed in an almost endless round of war. The Dutch were most successful in holding onto Surinam, Berbice, and Essequibo where they accomplished very little in the second half of the seventeenth century— only Berbice had the beginnings of a sugar industry—but which they managed to make something of during the eighteenth. These were to become the only Dutch sugar colonies in the Americas, but they were of minor importance compared to the larger islands of the Caribbean. There the Dutch were only able to secure St. Martin, Saba, St. Eustatius, and Curaçao, which were too small to be of any significance agriculturally but made good ports for smuggling and trade.

Another consequence of the loss of Dutch Brazil was a further stage in the dispersal of the Sephardic Jewish diaspora. Sephardic Jews emigrated from Portugal in the sixteenth century to escape the attention of the Inquisition. Some went to the Ottoman Empire, some to France, Antwerp, and Amsterdam. Others made their way to Brazil as "New Christians" after a pro-forma conversion to Christianity. There they became involved in the sugar industry, particularly in finance. In Dutch Brazil they supported the Dutch, a natural alliance given the presence of the Sephardic community in Amsterdam. In 1654, 600 Jews left Recife for Amsterdam, but for many of them this was a temporary sojourn. A few appear in the Dutch colonies on the Wild Coast where they tried to establish sugar production. Later in the next century, Sephardic Jews were to become prominent in Surinam. The Jewish community in Curaçao was founded in 1659. Sephardic Jews were also present in St. Eustatius and in the English colonies of Nevis, Jamaica, and Barbados. Their knowledge of the sugar industry, their capital, and their trading connections with Amsterdam played an important role in the establishment of the sugar industry in the Caribbean and in the supply of sugar to the United Provinces during the second half of the sixteenth century. The Jews were accepted because of their importance to the economies of these colonies and also because Sephardic Jews were investors in the WIC. However, the first Jewish refugees from Brazil who arrived in New Amsterdam in 1654 met with anti-semitism but were allowed to remain in the colony through the intervention of the directors of the WIC.

A review of this activity leads to the conclusion that the Dutch were not very successful as sugar producers in America. This, of course, stands in great contrast to what they were to achieve later in Java. Before the Brazilian adventure began they were traders in sugar, bringing it home to the refineries and sending some of it on to markets in northern Europe. They continued as traders during their attempts to become producers in America but reverted to trading again as their main role after the Brazilian adventure was over. But during these years they made for themselves an important place in the history of the American sugar industry both as introducers of technology from southeast Asia to Brazil and as introducers of sugar-making technology to Barbados and the Caribbean.

Dutch as Consumers

The Dutch trade in sugar made Amsterdam a major center of sugar refining. The city's refining industry had indeed benefited from the decline of Antwerp as a port during the wars with Spain in the late sixteenth century. At first the Amsterdam refineries were supplied from Madeira and São Tomé and later from Asia, Brazil, and the Caribbean. By the 1640s there were more than fifty refineries in the city. Much of this sugar was sold outside the Netherlands—to Germany and Scandinavia and even to England. But from an early date in the 1600s sugar was comparatively abundant in the Netherlands, more so quite possibly than in any other European country at that time. Indeed, a painting from about 1610, a still life of an opulent dessert table, shows prominently a plate of sugar-encrusted biscuits and tarts. Sugar, however, was not just a luxury of the rich: even those much lower down the scale of wealth could afford it in modest quantities. It was used in the making of all manner of cakes, tarts, and biscuits. Marzipan was a festive treat. Sugar sweetened wine and even beer. On special occasions there was sugared Rhine wine flavored with cinnamon, ginger, and cloves. A good number of recipes survive of the abundant use of sugar in the making of fruit preserves and marmalade. The popularity of coffee and tea came a little later and caused a further increase in the demand for sugar. Neither the censure of Calvinists nor the protectionist arguments of the distinguished medical doctor Johan van Beverwijck, concerned less about the fate of Dutch teeth than the future of Dutch apiarists, could stem the craving for sweetness that only the import of cane sugar could satisfy. But it was not only in the consumption of sugar that the Dutch were doing well: they also enjoyed an abundance of food, so much so that foreign travellers commented on how well the Dutch ate. What explains this situation? There are several strands to the answer. Domination of the Baltic grain trade and the huge fishing fleet which ensured a reliable supply of staple foods were important factors. The riches of the East India trade were another. Dutch agriculture, too, was very productive, thanks in part to the investment of capital and the willingness to be innovative. The policy of training workers in various skills brought its reward during the early 1600s in more productive labor. Wages in the Netherlands were high compared to other parts of Europe so that even the middling Dutch could afford to eat well and buy what elsewhere were still luxuries. . . .

Conclusion

The role of the Dutch in the early American sugar trade provides another example of the extraordinary importance of sugar in the first decades of European imperialism. Compared to the English, French, Spanish, and Portuguese, the Dutch were only minor producers of sugar in the Americas for the basic reason that they failed to secure a satisfactory territorial base. Perhaps Geyl was right. Dutch Brazil was too ambitious an undertaking in that the Dutch could never have controlled the vast interior where guerillas could always find safe refuge before emerging to attack again. The WIC would possibly have found better use for its capital and manpower in joining the scramble for Caribbean islands. However, the Dutch experience shows that a sugar colony was not an essential requisite for a secure supply of sugar, given the success of their refining industry and the relative abundance of sugar in the Netherlands compared to other European countries during the seventeenth century. The carrying trade and finance produced results. In Asia, the story was different. In Java the Dutch found a sugar colony, and there they remained major producers of sugar until the end of the European overseas empires.

FURTHER READING

Berlin, Ira, and Philip D. Morgan. *Cultivation and Culture: Labor and the Shaping of Slave Life in the Americas.* Charlottesville: University Press of Virginia, 1993.

Blackburn, Robin. *The Making of New World Slavery: From the Baroque to the Modern, 1492–1800.* New York: Verso, 1997.

Brewer, John, and Roy Porter, eds. *Consumption and the World of Goods.* New York: Routledge, 1993.

Carney, Judith Ann. *Black Rice: The African Origins of Rice Cultivation in the Americas.* Cambridge, MA: Harvard University Press, 2001.

Christopher, Emma. *Slave Ship Sailors and Their Captive Cargoes, 1730–1807.* New York: Cambridge University Press, 2006.

Coclanis, Peter, ed. *The Atlantic Economy During the Seventeenth and Eighteenth Centuries: Organization, Operation, Practice, and Personnel.* Columbia: University of South Carolina Press, 2005.

Cole, Jeffrey A. *The Potosí Mita, 1573–1700: Compulsory Indian Labor in the Andes.* Stanford, CA: Stanford University Press, 1985.

Curtin, Philip D. *The Rise and Fall of the Plantation Complex: Essays in Atlantic History.* New York: Cambridge University Press, 1998.

Davis, Ralph. *The Rise of the Atlantic Economies.* Ithaca, NY: Cornell University Press, 1973.

Eltis, David. *The Rise of African Slavery in the Americas.* New York: Cambridge University Press, 2000.

Hancock, David J. *Citizens of the World: London Merchants and the Integration of the British Atlantic Community, 1735–1785.* New York: Cambridge University Press, 1995.

Innis, Harold A. *The Cod Fisheries: The History of an International Economy.* New Haven, CT: Yale University Press, 1940.

Klein, Herbert S. *The Atlantic Slave Trade.* New York: Cambridge University Press, 1999.

Kurlansky, Mark. *Cod: A Biography of a Fish that Changed the World.* New York: Walker and Co., 1997.

Linebaugh, Peter, and Marcus Rediker. *The Many-Headed Hydra: Sailors, Slaves, Commoners, and the Hidden History of the Revolutionary Atlantic.* Boston: Beacon Press, 2000.

Matson, Cathy, ed. *The Economy of Early America: Historical Perspectives and New Direction.* University Park: The Pennsylvania State University Press, 2006.

McCusker, John J., and Kenneth Morgan, eds. *The Early Modern Atlantic Economy.* New York: Cambridge University Press, 2000.

Miller, Joseph Calder. *Way of Death: Merchant Capitalism and the Angolan Slave Trade, 1730–1830.* Madison: University of Wisconsin Press, 1988.

Mintz, Sidney Wilfred. *Sweetness and Power: The Place of Sugar in Modern History.* New York: Viking, 1985.

Pope, Peter Edward. *Fish Into Wine: The Newfoundland Plantation in the Seventeenth Century.* Chapel Hill: The University of North Carolina Press for the Omohundro Institute of Early American History and Culture, 2004.

Saunt, Claudio. *A New Order of Things: Property, Power, and the Transformation of the Creek Indians, 1733–1816.* New York: Cambridge University Press, 1999.

Schwartz, Stuart B. *Sugar Plantations in the Formation of Brazilian Society: Bahia, 1550–1835.* New York: Cambridge University Press, 1985.

Stein, Stanley J., and Barbara H. Stein. *Silver, Trade, and War: Spain and America in the Making of Early Modern Europe.* Baltimore: The Johns Hopkins University Press, 2000.

Williams, Eric Eustace. *Capitalism & Slavery.* Chapel Hill: University of North Carolina Press, 1994.

Pirates, Runaways,
and Rebels

The expansion of European political authority, commercial ambition, and religious zealotry fell heavily on poor, enslaved, and heterodox people throughout the Atlantic world. Many fought back in desperate attempts to lift themselves out of poverty, free themselves from exploitation, or preserve their systems of belief. This chapter reveals the violent struggles between authority and the many forms of outlawry that challenged it. Living "a merry life and a short one," pirates preyed on transatlantic and coastal vessels carrying rich cargoes of silver and other booty. The pirates' world was rough, but it could also be surprisingly egalitarian and democratic. On land, servants and slaves frequently ran away from their employers and owners. Communities of runaways, known as "maroons," formed on the outskirts of plantation societies throughout the Americas. Servants and slaves occasionally conspired to overthrow their masters through outright rebellion. Africans and American Indians (as well as many Europeans themselves) defied clergymen who sought to convert them to Christianity or to regulate their worship. These forms of resistance challenged colonial power, offered alternative visions of justice and right, and extended the realm of freedom to the downtrodden.

If pirates, runaways, and rebels used violence and terror to achieve their goals, they faced even greater violence and terror when they failed. Captured pirates faced the gallows. Returned runaways were whipped and mutilated. Frustrated rebels were burned and beheaded. From its stormy seas to its riotous port cities to its forbidding mountains and swamps, the Atlantic world dripped with blood.

D O C U M E N T S

These documents illustrate an array of challenges to constituted authority in the Atlantic world, beginning with piracy at sea. Document 1 reveals pirates marauding on both sides of the ocean in the late seventeenth and eighteenth centuries. The first excerpt shows one group of pirates' sense of equity in the distribution of booty. The second describes Captain Henry Morgan's vicious assaults on Porto Bello (Panama) in 1667 and on Maracaibo (Venezuela) in 1669. An Englishman, Morgan (1635–1688) was technically not a pirate but rather a privateer, which means that his attacks were licensed by the English government and were an extension of inter-European warfare. The third example of piracy comes from depositions in a 1743 court case in Newport, Rhode Island. They tell the cautionary tale of Captain John Cutler, who was purchasing slaves in the Sierra Leone River when he was murdered by Afro-Portuguese pirates.

Documents 2 and 4 describe indigenous resistance to Spanish religious mission-ary activity and economic exploitation in New Spain. Document 2 presents the des-perate report of Father Antonio Carbonel, a priest living at Nambé among the Pueblo Indians in 1696, who complained that the Indians were resisting Spanish authority and harassing his mission. One Indian slapped him in the face; others stole his livestock and supplies from the mission. Three months later, Carbonel was killed in the Pueblo uprising. Document 4 provides Ilarione da Bergamo's (1727?–1778) eyewitness ac-count of a revolt that erupted at the Real del Monte silver mine in 1766. An Italian Capuchin friar, Bergamo observed that the angry mob of Indian men and women wanted to burn the mine and kill its owner and all of his officials, but that "God did not permit such ravaging to occur."

Documents 3, 5, and 6 point to resistance among servants and slaves. Colonial newspapers were routinely peppered with advertisements for runaway servants and slaves. The ads from the *Pennsylvania Gazette* in the eighteenth century offer highly detailed descriptions of a diverse lot of runaways, including people of European, Amer-ican Indian, and African descent. In Document 5, Lady Anne Barnard, the wife of the Secretary of the Cape Colony in southern Africa, describes a slave's murderous ram-page. She commends what she perceived as the temperate and efficient punishment inflicted by the English. The final document, discovered by the eminent historian of Brazil, Stuart Schwartz, offers a glimpse of how Afro-Brazilian slaves would have liked to live. In 1806, a group of slaves who had run away from the Santana plantation in Ilhéus presented a peace treaty to their former owner outlining the conditions under which they would agree to return. Among other demands, they wanted to "play, relax, and sing any time we wish."

1. Pirates Sail Under the Jolly Roger, 1684, 1743

The Code of the Pirate Ship

The ship being well victualled, they call another council, to deliberate towards what place they shall go, to seek their desperate fortunes. In this council, likewise, they agree upon certain Articles, which are put in writing, by way of bond or obligation, which every one is bound to observe, and all of them, or the chief, set their hands to it. Herein they specify, and set down very distinctly, what sums of money each par-ticular person ought to have for that voyage, the fund of all the payments being the common stock of what is gotten by the whole expedition; for otherwise it is the same law, among these people, as with other Pirates, *No prey, no pay*. In the first place, therefore, they mention how much the Captain ought to have for his ship. Next the salary of the carpenter, or shipwright, who careened, mended and rigged the vessel. This commonly amounts to one hundred or an hundred and fifty pieces of eight, being, according to the agreement, more or less. Afterwards for provisions and

Source: John Exquemelin, *The Buccaneers of America* (1684, repr. 1951), pp. 59–60, 144–145, 158–159; Elizabeth Donnan, ed., *Documents Illustrative of the History of the Slave Trade to America* (Washington, D.C.: Carnegie Institution of Washington, 1930–1933), vol. 3, pp. 52–65.

victualling they draw out of the same common stock about two hundred pieces of eight. Also a competent salary for the surgeon and his chest of medicaments, which usually is rated at two hundred or two hundred and fifty pieces of eight. Lastly they stipulate in writing what recompense or reward each one ought to have, that is either wounded or maimed in his body, suffering the loss of any limb, by that voyage. Thus they order for the loss of a right arm six hundred pieces of eight, or six slaves; for the loss of a left arm five hundred pieces of eight, or five slaves; for a right leg five hundred pieces of eight, or five slaves; for the left leg four hundred pieces of eight, or four slaves; for an eye one hundred pieces of eight, or one slave; for a finger of the hand the same reward as for the eye. All which sums of money, as I have said before, are taken out of the capital sum or common stock of what is got by their piracy. For a very exact and equal dividend is made of the remainder among them all. Yet herein they have also regard to qualities and places. Thus the Captain, or chief Commander, is allotted five or six portions to what the ordinary seamen have; the Master's Mate only two; and other Officers proportionate to their employment. After whom they draw equal parts from the highest even to the lowest mariner, the boys not being omitted. For even these draw half a share, by reason that, when they happen to take a better vessel than their own, it is the duty of the boys to set fire to the ship or boat wherein they are, and then retire to the prize which they have taken.

They observe among themselves very good orders. For in the prizes they take, it is severely prohibited to every one to usurp anything in particular to themselves. Hence all they take is equally divided, according to what has been said before. Yea, they make a solemn oath to each other not to abscond, or conceal the least thing they find amongst the prey. If afterwards any one is found unfaithful, who has contravened the said oath, immediately he is separated and turned out of the society. Among themselves they are very civil and charitable to each other. Insomuch that if any wants what another has, with great liberality they give it one to another.

Henry Morgan Attacks Spanish Ports

Henry Morgan's Attack on Porto Bello

The assault of this castle where the Governor was continued very furious on both sides, from break of day until noon. Yea, about this time of the day the case was very dubious which party should conquer or be conquered. At last the Pirates, perceiving they had lost many men and as yet advanced but little towards the gaining either this or the other castles remaining, thought to make use of fireballs, which they threw with their hands, designing, if possible, to burn the doors of the castle. But going about to put this into execution, the Spaniards, from the wall let fall great quantities of stones and earthen pots full of powder and other combustible matter, which forced them to desist from that attempt. Captain Morgan seeing this generous defence made by the Spaniards, began to despair of the whole success of the enterprize. Hereupon many faint and calm meditations came into his mind; neither could he determine which way to turn himself in that straitness of affairs. Being involved in these thoughts, he was suddenly animated to continue the assault, by seeing the English colours put forth at one of the lesser castles, then entered by his men, of whom he presently after spied a troop that came to meet him, proclaiming victory with loud shouts of joy. This instantly put him upon new resolutions of making new efforts to take the rest of the castles that stood out against him; especially seeing the chief citizens were fled to them, and had conveyed thither great part of their riches, with all the plate belonging to the churches, and other things dedicated to divine service.

To this effect, therefore, he ordered ten or twelve ladders to be made, in all possible haste, so broad that three or four men at once might ascend by them. These being finished, he commanded all the religious men and women whom he had taken prisoners to fix them against the walls of the castle. Thus much he had beforehand threatened the Governor to perform, in case he delivered not the castle. But his answer was: *He would never surrender himself alive.* Captain Morgan was much persuaded that the Governor would not employ his utmost forces, seeing religious women and ecclesiastical persons, exposed in the front of the soldiers to the greatest dangers. Thus the ladders, as I have said, were put into the hands of religious persons of both sexes; and these were forced, at the head of the companies, to raise and apply them to the walls. But Captain Morgan was fully deceived in his judgment of this design. For the Governor, who acted like a brave and courageous soldier, refused not, in performance of his duty, to use his utmost endeavours to destroy whoever came near the walls. The religious men and women ceased not to cry to him and beg of him by all the Saints of Heaven he would deliver the castle, and hereby spare both his and their own lives. But nothing could prevail with the obstinacy and fierceness that had possessed the Governor's mind. Thus many of the religious men and nuns were killed before they could fix the ladders. Which at last being done, though with great loss of the said religious people, the Pirates mounted them in great numbers, and with no less valour; having fireballs in their hands, and earthen pots full of powder. All which things, being now at the top of the walls, they kindled and cast in among the Spaniards. . . .

Henry Morgan's Attack on Maracaibo

As soon as they had entered the town the Pirates searched every corner thereof, to see if they could find any people that were hidden who might offend them unawares. Not finding anybody, every party, according as they came out of their several ships, chose what houses they pleased to themselves, the best they could find. The church was deputed for the common *corps de garde*, where they lived after their military manner, committing many insolent actions. The next day after their arrival, they sent a troop of one hundred men to seek for the inhabitants and their goods. These returned the next day following, bringing with them to the number of thirty persons, between men, women and children, and fifty mules laden with several good merchandize. All these miserable prisoners were put to the rack, to make them confess where the rest of the inhabitants were and their goods. Amongst other tortures then used, one was to stretch their limbs with cords, and at the same time beat them with sticks and other instruments. Others had burning matches placed betwixt their fingers, which were thus burnt alive. Others had slender cords or matches twisted about their heads, till their eyes burst out of the skull. Thus all sort of inhuman cruelties were executed upon those innocent people. Those who would not confess, or who had nothing to declare, died under the hands of those tyrannical men. These tortures and racks continued for the space of three whole weeks; in which time they ceased not to send out, daily, parties of men to seek for more people to torment and rob; they never returning home without booty and new riches. . . .

The Case of the Jolly Batchelor

Deposition of Alexander McKenzie

Alexander McKenzie aged about 35 years, testifieth and Saith that at farron Bay on Serrelone River on the Coast of Guinea abt the 8th of March last past, he went on board the Snow, called the *Jolly Batchelor* John Cutler Commr with a design to get a pasage with sd Cutler (the vessel he was before in being lately taken by the Spainyards) the sd Cutler accordingly shipt him, and in two or three Days after the sd Cutler being then in good health, Sent on shore the Yawl to look for the Long boat, (in wch he the Deponent went with two Blacks) wch had been mising a day or two before, in looking for wch he was sent out one Day about 9 a Clock in the morning and returnd the next Day about 7 a Clock with the Long boat with the two negroes before mentioned. when he came on board two Portuguese Negroes laid hold on him the Deponent and presented two Cockt pistoles at his breast, and forced him on board the Snow where were about twenty other negroes who were Confederates in the murder of Cap Cutler, who's body half an hour after he saw dead upon the half deck and some of the negroes tying stones about his hands and then they threw him over. In an hour or two after this all the slaves in the vessel to the number of about Seventy or Eighty were Caried on shore in the Long boat and Yawl, while some others were plundering the sd Vessel, and in the Evening they caried the deponent with some others on shore at atown called Senr Lewis's[?] town and kept them there till the next day, when the deponent one Rich'd Smith and Jno Kendall had leave to go from them and they by the direction of two negroes in three Days and a half arrived at a place called the Bannanoes where they inform'd Cap Burchall and Cap Wickham that Cutler was murdered With two of his men and his vessel taken. In seven or Eight Days after the sd Burchall fixed out three shallop and a smaller boat with abt thirty men black and white with fire arms within three or four days, after they arrived at Sarelone river where they found the vessel Lying like a wreck without any running riging or Sails to the Yard. when they came on Board there was no person there, then Mr. Burchall and Capt Wickham borrowed a Shallops Main Sail and fore Sail and brought the Vessel to White Mans Bay about four Miles distant and then said Burchall and Wickham procured the Forestay Sail Main Sail and Fore Sail and Maintop Sail, with about Thirty five of the Slaves that were carried out of the Vessel, and the Foretopsail Cut to pieces, and proceeded with the Vessel to the Island of Bananos and their bought Rigging etc. and refitted the Vessel. But wanting provision and some other Necessaries were obliged to keep sd Vessel thereabouts Six Weeks and upon Arival of Capt Pitman in a Ship from Bristol were Supplied and then they returned to Serralone River to Water the Vessel, and Capt. Wickham Sailed from [*illegible*] with Twenty Slaves on the Owners account, for Newport in Rhode Island where We arrived the Eleventh Day of this Instant August and further saith not.

Deposition of Charles Wickham

Charles Wickham of Newport, Mariner On Oath in Open Court Declared, That he was at the Bannanoes on the 12th or 13th Day of March last at the House of Mr. George Burchall, and saw an English Ensign hoisted over upon the Main and as soon as he saw it Capt. Burchall dispatched a Canoe over which returned in about two Hours and brought three White Men Over with him, who travelled by Land from Serralone who told us they belonged to the Snow *Jolly Batchelor* and declared that Capt. John Cutler the Master of sd Snow had been about four Days before cut off by about twenty Portugese and Negroes who came aboard sd Snow armd and killed the sd Cutler and two of his Men and carried away the running Rigging and Sails of sd Snow together with the Slaves and Cargo and forced all the Seamen and Mariners on Shoar at Senr Lewis' Town in Sierra Leon River. About the 28th of the same Month of March Capt. George Burchall fitted out from the Bonanas three Shallops and a Yawl maned with about thirty men blacks and Whites well armed in order to go to the sd River and retake sd Snow. About eight and forty Hours after we arrived at Whiteman's Bay in Sierra Leon River were Capt Burchell and the Deponent immediately went on shoar to John Cumberbur's Town and upon advising with him went in our Shallops and Yawl to a Portugese negro named Joseph Lopez and desired him to Assist us that we might recover sd Snow. He promisd he would Whereupon we returned to Whiteman's Bay where we expected him the next Day there. We waited about Eight Days without hearing anything of sd Lopez and then one of his Men came with Orders to Senr Lewis to deliver up the Vessel and Slaves And the same Day sd Lewis sent Word to Us that we might go up to Farrons Bay and take the Vessel. The next Day we went in two of our Shallops and Yawl only the other Shallop being gone to get Provision and took possession of the Snow, Likewise her Main sail and Foresail were delivered at the same Time, Top sails and Forestaysail We purchased of the Natives and a small Quantity of the running Rigging and after we had got her a small matter fitted we carried her down to the Bannanoes and after we had been there some Time Came Capt Pitman from Bristol, who supplied us with Cordage sails and provisions to fit her for the Sea. There was no English Vessel at the River Sierolone at the Time the sd Snow was taken and for some Time afterwards. I received at several Times Thirty four Slaves of Senr. Lewis, two of which Died and twelve were Sold for the Necessary Stores and provisions for the Vessel, to wit Eight to Capt. Burchall and four to Capt. Pitman and the remaining Twenty the Deponent [hath ?] now brought into this port in sd Snow. And the Deponent further Saith That One of the Mariners belonging to sd Snow told the Deponent that the Slaves on Board sd Snow were Numbered the Night before sd Capt. Cutler was Murdered and that there were Seventy five of them then on Board and further the Deponent saith that after they had taken possession of sd Snow they went and lay at Whiteman's Bay about Ten Days in Order to recover the Slaves of sd Vessel but could not get any more than the above Thirty four, and one that was sent down to sd Snow at the Bannanoes who afterwards run away.

2. A Spanish Priest Among the Pueblo Indians Complains of Harassment and Danger, 1696

Our very reverend father custodian and ecclesiastical judge. I am grateful for the paternal love and watchfulness with which Your Paternal Reverence seeks the good of your sheep, as the vigilant shepherd over the small flock which our holy mother church has entrusted to Your Paternal Reverence. I state below what motivated me to

Source: From *The Pueblo Indian Revolt of 1696 and the Franciscan Missions in New Mexico: Letters of the Missionaries and Related Documents*, edited and translated by J. Manuel Espinosa, 1988, University of Oklahoma Press, pp. 219–223. Reprinted with permission of the University of Oklahoma Press.

return to the mission of Our Father San Francisco of Nambé even without the guard that was requested of the lord governor and captain general of this kingdom, who did not grant it because he indicates that he does not have sufficient soldiers for his own protection and that of the horses, despite the fact that His Majesty (may God protect him) spends from the royal treasury for soldiers to protect the ministers of the gospel when wars are taking place, as they are taking place in this kingdom. As His Lordship knows and has witnessed, for three days he was summoning [*requiriendo*] the Tanos Indians of the pueblo of San Cristóbal, who were in the mountains in rebellion, and they said that they wanted only to fight, and most of them are still joined with the bandits, who have no intention of coming down. This I know, for I saw it with my own eyes, having gone to said pueblo in the company of Reverend Father Fray José Arbizu and the lord captain Roque Madrid, and of the over six hundred Indians of that pueblo there were only ten or twelve who, because of fear, did not go, because they were certain that they would be killed for having given advance notice to the Spaniards; therefore, this is evidence of revolt and not presumption or rumors. I also know for certain that an Indian *tlatolero* of this pueblo went with them to the mountains with ten or twelve Indian men and women who do not appear to be from this pueblo, and on various occasions they have come to stir up the Indians of this pueblo to revolt, and although they say that they have not admitted the said *tlatoles*, "if the jug goes too many times to the fountain, it finally is broken." And when all of these people act like bandits, I do not know what protection there is for a poor religious alone at his mission, for even if the Indians of this pueblo might wish to defend me, assuming that they are good, "What can an ant do against a thousand bloodthirsty wolves?"

Notwithstanding all of what has been referred to above, I returned to my mission so that they would not profane the sacred vessels and vestments and the other articles pertaining to the divine religion and in case a child might be born in danger of not being baptized, so that he might be saved, but without applying the holy oils, because being close to apostates I do not know whether I may administer any other holy sacrament, because in administering it we should follow the surest course, following the published apostolic decrees.

I recognize manifest danger for the ministers, because punishment is lacking for those who so much deserve it. Some eight months ago, while I was engaged in my holy duties in the mission of Cochití, an Indian slapped me in the face, and it was the same day that the lord governor paid a visit to the said pueblo, and having notified him of the said boldness and impudence on the part of the said Indian, the lord governor gave it the same notice as one would give to a corpse. When this is overlooked and His Lordship lets apostate rebels go without punishment, what can the poor ministers do, seeing their sacerdotal dignity thus outraged? What can be presumed other than that the vile acts and wickedness of the said Indians are swept aside and they are left to commit other greater shameful acts, for which the ministers are continuously struggling with the Indians, as they know and experience their dissoluteness and wickedness? What the lord governor experiences on a one-hour visit, accompanied by one hundred armed men and only passing through, is not the same as being there over a period of time, alone, contending with the Indians. On a passing visit they act like gentle sheep, and over a longer period they are wild bears. Idolatry is continued, they continue their depraved concubinage, and the time has come to remedy all of this, for we have been among them now for three years, and every day they are worse, because the Indians know who should punish them and who is observing and suffering their wicked acts. And so it is my view that what is taking place is going more against the crown of our royal monarch than in his favor.

I say, as for me, that when they took me from my mother the Province of Santo Evangelio, it was to go to a conquered and pacified land, which it is not nor has it been nor will it be until it may serve God our Lord to free it from danger. And if they had told me then that I was coming to die among infidels, I would have premeditated the undertaking and would have followed the dictates of the Lord. I now confess that I was deceived, because if the goal that our Catholic monarch (may God keep him) hopes for it is not attained, how can we justly receive the very considerable alms which he spends from his royal treasury, with so much generosity, on the ministers of the gospel only for the purpose of teaching these Indians the catechism and instructing them under the impression that much fruit is being harvested, whereas there is none because of the very many thorns and brambles? These can not be pulled out, because the strength to do so is lacking. I also state that since I am a poor friar minor without a house or home or anything else from which I can pay back to my king what he is spending on me from the treasury, in the belief that I am gathering some fruit, and I know that I have accomplished nothing, these are points that weigh very heavily and are a burden on my conscience. I unburden it in this letter for the rigorous tribunal, our father. I speak with all of this clearness so that at no time may it be said that our sacred religion has deceived its king, to whom we should look with piety, for he looks upon us with compassion.

I recognize that the said Indians do not seek peace but rather to perturb the peace, for every day the ministers are on the verge of being lost. The same day that the lord governor and captain general made a visit to this pueblo, the Indians killed the best cow of three that Your Paternal Reverence charitably gave me for this mission, and during the period of three months they have stolen twenty-seven head of sheep, not small ones but large ones and the best ones, and I fear that they may consume all of them, for they go unpunished. This was the payment I received from them for having them place their trust in the lord governor. Also, twice they have broken into the convent and have stolen from me a quantity of food, chocolate, and sugar. Does this show that the Indians are good? When they look for incidents to confound the minister so that they may say that it is because of the minister that they are in rebellion? It appears to me that all of their ill will is toward the ministers, because they are the ones who seek to lead them to live as Christians. Their idolatries continue, and it is very difficult to root them out. They do not like Christians nor those who subject them to the law of God; rather, they wish to flee to freedom. This should not be permitted, because of what I have said, that the reason that His Majesty (may God keep him) is spending from the royal treasury is in conformity with the successful winning of souls. To deal and bargain with the Indians is not the same as to teach them the law of God, for the heretics deal and bargain with Christians, but in dealing with the matter of whether they wish to be Catholics, most of them refuse. I speak from experience.

They mock the ministers and even Christ transubstantiated in the host. If this is tolerated among Catholics, ponder on it as a point to be given thought. Although they have not yet revolted, because their plan has been foreseen, sooner or later they will carry it out, and they will begin with the ministers, who are alone at their missions.

And so, if it is going astray to change one's opinion, I change mine, and I state that it is now of concern to change such opinion, because if these few Indians of this pueblo are communicating with the many perverse and evil ones for fear of these others, they will kill millions of priests, who cost dearly and are not found easily, whereas soldiers are found abundantly. Your Reverence may be sure that your ministers have their reputation guaranteed by my mother religion and not by the boldness of the lord governor, who in wishing to pursue difficult undertakings must support them with the spilling of the blood of ministers of the gospel, who could in another land profit in the winning of souls. It is not my word but that of the gospel, when Christ ordered us, in our lives as ministers of the gospel, that if we should find ourselves in a city where the people refused to accept the divine law, we should flee to another where we would be received and welcomed, and since these people do not wish to accept it, let us go to another place where they accept it. And our father Saint Francis orders us likewise: Ubi no fuerint accepti fugiam in alia terra cum benedictione Dei. We read the same in the writings of many other saints, and therefore we are not the ones who flee when we are thus ordered, when finding no success for conversion to our holy gospel among these natives.

I cannot speak more clearly, because I am not able to do so with my limited ability. Your Very Reverend Paternity knows very well what should be done; I only say that we are spending our time writing letters, nothing is being carried out, help is very distant, the travails and needs are very great, and death is very close at hand; all rests on entrapping time, and it will entrap us in our tombs. For already two of the religious have died within a short time, and perhaps one has died more from grief and the other from being bewitched than from anything else, as is presumed. And there are others who walk about with the same ailment, and if here they kill us and bewitch us to flee from being among these people, before they destroy us and make us unfit for service, let the will of God be done, from whom I request the good direction and wisdom of Your Reverend Paternity.

At this mission of our father San Francisco of Nambé, March thirty-one, the year sixteen hundred ninety-six. Our very reverend father custodian, your most humble and lowly son and subject kisses your feet.

Fray Antonio Carbonel

3. Employers Advertise for the Return of Runaways in Pennsylvania, 1739–1753

October 11, 1739
The Pennsylvania Gazette

RUN away on the 20th of Aug. past, from the Subscriber near the Head of Bush River in Baltimore County, Maryland, an Indian Man, named Pompey, aged about 24 Years, of middle Stature, well set, speaks nothing but English, very much scarrified on the Body with whipping in Barbadoes; he had on his Neck when he went away an Iron

Source: *Pennsylvania Gazette*, Accessible Archives. Pennsylvania Gazette (CD-ROM). Provo, Utah: Folio Corp, 1991. Items 3655, 4714, 5397, 8991, 10856, 15303.

Collar, but its suppos'd he has got it off. Also a lusty Negro Woman named Pegg, aged about 22 Years, this Country born and speaks plain English; They carried away with them a striped Duffle Blanket, an old Ticken Jacket and Breeches with black Buttonholes, a Felt Hat near new, a coarse linnen Bag, a new white Linsey woolsey Petticoat and other coarse Negro Apparel. Whoever secures the said Indian and Negro so that their Master may have them again, shall have Five Pounds Reward and reasonable Charges paid by Richard Ruff.

September 10, 1741

RUN away the 21st of August, from the Subscribers, of Kingsess, Philadelphia County, a White Man and a Negro, it is supposed they are gone together; the White Man's Name is Abraham Joseph, a Yorkshire Man, a Shoemaker by Trade, aged about 24 Years, of middle Stature: Had on, a ratteen Jacket and Breeches of a light colour, a castor Hat pretty much worn, a check Shirt with white patches on the Back, two pair of yarn Stockings, one pair of grey colour and t'other pair blue, a pair of thin Shoes round toed, and a pair of Boots. The Negroe's Name is Tom, of a yellowish colour, pretty much pitted with the Small Pox, thick set: Had on, a light coloured cloth Coat, a linnen Jacket and Breeches, a pair of check Trowsers, good Shoes sharp toed. Two Nights before there were several things Stolen, and it's supposed they have them, a List whereof follows, viz. a suit of Drugget of a snuff colour half trim'd, a light coloured cloth Coat, two linnen Jackets, a pair of leather Breeches, two pair of check Trowsers, two Hats, a drab coloured broad Cloth Coat pretty much worn, a Jacket of the same colour of the first mentioned Suit, a dark brown Wig, two napt Caps, a Gun, and a Pocket Book with two Bonds in it, one of Ten Pounds, the other of Eight Pounds, with a Note written at the end of the Sixteen Shillings, with several other small things. Any Person or Persons that will take up and secure the said Men, so that they may be had again, shall have for the White Man Three Pounds, and for the Negro Five Pounds Reward, and reasonable Charges, paid by James Hunt, Peter Elliot.

   N.B. They took a Cedar Canoe with them, broken at the Stern and split at the Head.

October 28, 1742

RUN away from the Subscriber, living at Elk Ridge in Anne Arundel County, Maryland, the 26th of September, 1742, the following Servants, viz. John Simms, a Convict Servant Man, well set, about 30 Years of Age, and is of a pale Complexion; he is without his Hair, and had on when he went away, a Castor Hat, a ruffled Holland Shirt, a Flower'd Vest, a Pair of round Pumps, and blue ribb'd Stockings. Also, Thomas Handfield, a Convict Servant, he is a young raw Youth, about 18 or 20 Years of Age, fresh coloured and somewhat pitted with the small Pox, wears his own yellow curl'd Hair, had on a Castor Hat with a Gold Button and Loop, his other Cloaths unknown. Likewise, a negro Woman named Jenny, supposed to be dressed in Man's Cloaths; if so, she has on a Felt Hat, an Ozenbriggs Jacket, a Pair of check'd Trowsers, and an old Pair of Mens Pumps. If she is in Woman's Apparel, she has on a Country Cloth Habit, a Hempen Roll Petticoat, she is a slim young Wench, looks smooth, with large Eyes. Whoever apprehends the said Servants and brings them to the Subscriber shall have Ten Pounds Reward for the Three; or Three Pounds each for the Men, besides what the Law allows, and Four Pounds Reward for the Woman. John Howard.

October 1, 1747

RUN away, on the 20th of September last, from Cohansie Bridge, a very big Negroe man, named Sampson, about 50 years of age, has some Indian blood in him, is hip shot, and goes very lame; he had taken his son with him, a boy about 12 or 14 years of age, named Sam; he was born of an Indian woman, and looks much like an Indian, except in his hair; both belonging to Silas Parvin of Philadelphia, and are both well clothed, only the boy is barefoot; they have taken with them a gun and ammunition, and two rugs; can both talk Indian very well, and it is likely they have dressed themselves in Indian dress, and gone towards Carolina. Whoever secures said slaves, so that their master may have them again, shall have Five Pounds reward, and all reasonable charges, paid by Silas Parvin.

August 31, 1749

Westmoreland County, Virginia, August 17, 1749.

Run way from the subscriber, on Monday last, a convict servant, named Thomas Winey; he is a middle siz'd fellow, about five foot, seven inches high, of a swarthy complexion, has had a piece cut out of one side of the end of his nose, which is very remarkable; he says it was done by the kick of a horse; he professes farming, was imported lately in the Litchfield, Capt. Johnson, and came from Maidstone gaol, in the county of Kent, Great Britain; his dress when he went off, was a brown cloath coat, with a small cape, a pair of sailor's trowsers, a brown wig, check shirt, and dark coloured worsted stockings. The above mentioned servant took with him a Molattoe slave, nam'd James, a well set fellow, 21 years old, about five foot seven inches high, is very apt to stutter when closely examin'd, having a stoppage in his speech; he has on his back a large white scar: His dress was a dowlas shirt, and a brown linnen coat and breeches, and has been us'd to drive a chariot for several years. I have been inform'd by their confederates, since they went off, that they intend to Pennsylvania, and from thence to New England, unless they can on their way get a passage in some vessel to Great Britain, where the Molattoe slave pretends to have an uncle, who escap'd from his master in this colony near 20 years ago, and is said to keep a coffee house in London. Whoever apprehends the said runaways, and secures them, so that they may be had again, if taken in Maryland or Pennsylvania, shall have Ten Pounds sterling reward, besides what the law allows, or Five Pounds for either of them; and if taken in any government to the northward of Maryland and Pennsylvania, the reward shall be Twenty Pounds sterling for both, or Ten Pounds sterling for either, which shall be paid on demand, by WILLIAM FITZHUGH.

February 20, 1753

Virginia, Lancaster County, Sept. 22, 1752.

RUN away from the subscriber, at the Glebe of the said county, in the 4th of May, A convict servant woman, named Sarah Knox (alias Howard, alias Wilson) of a middle brown complexion, short nose, talks broad, and said she was born in Yorkshire, has been in the army for several years, with the camp in Flanders, and at the battle of Colloden, where she lost her husband. She may pretend to be a dancing mistress; will make a great many courtesies, and is a very deceitful, bold, insinuating woman, and a great liar.

In reading of the Virginia Gazette, No. 87, I find an extract of a letter from Chester, in Pennsylvania, July 13, 1752, mentioning a quack Doctor, by the name of Charles Hamilton, pretending to be brought up under Dr. Green, a noted Mountebank in England, who turns out to be a woman in mens cloaths, and now assumes the name of Charlotte Hamilton, and calls herself about 28 years of age, tho'seems to be about 40: Thus much of the letter; and if she talks broad, I have reason to believe that she is the very servant who belongs to me. Whoever apprehends my said servant, and has her convey to me, shall have Two Pistoles, besides what the law allows, paid by DAVID CURRIE.

N.B. This Sarah Knox was imported from Whitehaven, in the Duke of Cumberland, with other convicts, among whom was one William Forrester, who, I have heard her say, was sometime with the above Dr. Green.

4. Silver Miners Revolt in New Spain, 1766

I will conclude the subject of mining with a brief account of an uprising that occurred in 1766 in Real del Monte, where I was living. There were some dissensions, the reason for which I do not know, that erupted between the mineworkers and officials acting on behalf of the owner, Don Pedro Romero de Terreros. Before long, on a certain day, a large number of Indians gathered in this mining camp. All of them were mine workers, not just from this location but from other nearby areas as well. The intention of these people (as was later determined) was to kill the owner, i.e., Señor Terreros, and all of his officials and burn down the mines. Had this occurred, it would have been their own ruination and that of the whole country as well. But God did not permit such ravaging to occur.

So, on August 15, [1766,] the day set by that rabble for the total destruction of Real del Monte, many of them gathered in the mine of San Cayetano. There, after some quarrels between them and a miner, or mine official, they stoned him so that he died a few hours later. When the alcalde mayor or *podestà* of Pachuca, a young man recently arrived from Spain who happened to be there, attempted to bring these people to a halt by drawing his sword, they flung themselves on him with such ferocity and cruelty that they left him there dead, completely crushed by stones.

Señor Terreros, having heard about the uprising and the two fatalities that had already occurred, hid in a room where he kept plenty of fodder for the horses, burying himself up to his neck in this. However much the rebel Indians tried to hunt him down and kill him, they could not find him. It was necessary for the parish priest to lead a procession with the Blessed Sacrament, which I also accompanied, so as

Source: Robert Ryal Miller and William J. Orr, eds., *Daily Life in Colonial Mexico: The Journey of Friar Ilarione da Bergamo, 1761–1768*, trans. William J. Orr. Norman: University of Oklahoma Press, 2000, pp. 161–163. Reprinted with permission of the University of Oklahoma Press.

to convey Señor Romero de Terreros from his hiding place and guide him into the church, underneath the baldachin, as a sanctuary for himself and his general foreman. It was a gratifying sight arriving in certain places with the Blessed Sacrament. There were many women and children, [and] listening to their wailing and weeping one would have thought it was the final day [of judgment].

While all this was going on, other women, enraged like their husbands, were going about tossing lighted embers onto the piles of straw of the mines to set them ablaze. There was no damage, thanks to the diligence of a few individuals. The insurgents moved on to a house where they believed a certain mine official was hidden, whom they had vowed to kill. They smashed in the door and windows and went inside, but they did not find the one they were looking for. They moved on to the jails, ecclesiastical as well as secular, forced them open, and removed all the prisoners, their accomplices.

Then they passed on to Pachuca, where they did the same thing, i.e., forcibly liberate all the prisoners. They then headed to the home of the foreman of the mines to burn it down. Those enraged individuals only desisted from their design because some Reformed fathers, who have a monastery in that town, had promptly arrived on the scene, loudly threatening to bring down the wrath of God, while hoisting a crucifix above their heads.

The matter ended with the mines being closed down for some time, and the first to experience the devastation were the instigators of the uprising. As day laborers in the mines with no other means of livelihood, they were compelled to suffer from the damage they themselves had wrought.

Some troops were sent up from Mexico City with orders to put down the revolt. Some [instigators] were hanged in Mexico City; others less culpable were sent to labor in the garrison. And finally I made my little rounds, not finding alms at this time except by happenstance.

I have mentioned a few things about the mines, but there is a lot more that could be written about them. I refer the reader to Gemelli, who treats these matters in greater detail. I will only say that, after these lands were conquered by the Spaniards, such was the quantity of gold, silver, and other precious articles coming from there that all Europe has felt the effects and still feels the benefit.

5. Lady Anne Barnard Praises the Swift Punishment of a Slave, 1797

The day before yesterday a sad accident happened, or rather a wicked act, the son of our butcher being killed by his slave in revenge for having been refused liberty to go out on Sunday, though it was *not* his turn to do so. After he had stabbed him he attempted to murder his mistress, and stabbed one of her slaves. I suppose the unfortunate wretch would have "run muck" (as is the term in this country of frenzy from despair and the certainty of death), and would have killed every one he met, (it is some years since an instance of this kind has happened); but the man had been

Source: W. H. Wilkins, ed., *South Africa a Century Ago: Letters Written from the Cape of Good Hope (1797–1801) by the Lady Anne Barnard* (London: Smith, Elder, & Co., 1901), pp. 78–79.

wounded in his attempts, and must have died, had not his life been cut short by the gallows an hour after the affair happened, to deter others. Thank God, the days of torture are over, and the sad evidences of what *was* practised by the Dutch Government only remain on a high ground hard by the entrance to the Castle; it froze my blood at first, but habit hardens the nerves, I hope without hardening the heart.

6. Manoel da Silva Ferreira's Slaves Propose a Treaty, 1806

Arquivo Público do Estado
da Bahia: Secção histórica

Cartas ao Governo, 207

Illustrious and most Excellent Sir

The Supplicant Gregorio Luís, a *cabra* finds himself a prisoner in the jail of this High Court where he was sent by his master, Captain Manoel da Silva Ferreira, resident on his Engenho called Santana in the district of the Town of Ilhéus; there coming at the same time with him, as I remember, some fifteen or sixteen other slaves. These were sent to the merchant José da Silva Maia, his commercial agent, so that he could sell them in Maranhão while the Supplicant came with the recommendation that he be held in prison while the Court of that district prepared the charges so that he could be given exemplary punishment. Taking a preliminary investigation of the Supplicant, I have determined the following facts. The above mentioned Manoel da Silva Ferreira being master and owner of the aforesaid *engenho* with three hundred slaves, including some of the Mina nation discovered the majority of them in rebellion refusing to recognize their subordination to their master. And, the principal leader of this disorder was the Supplicant who began to incite among them the partisan spirit against their master and against the Sugar Master. The Supplicant was able with a few of his followers to kill the latter and until now none know where they buried him. Taking control of part of the *engenho*'s equipment, they fled to the forest refusing not only to give their service or to obey their master, but even placing him in fear that they would cruelly take his life. For this reason the *engenho* has remained inactive for two years with such notable damage that its decadence is dated from that time forward, and, moreover, these damages added to the danger that the rest of the slaves might follow the terrible example of those in rebellion. Thus the majority of the slaves persisted divided into errant and vagabond bands throughout the territory of the *engenho*, so absolute and fearless that the consternation and fright of their master increased in consideration that he might one day fall victim to some disaster. Matters being in this situation, the rebels sent emissaries to their Master with a proposal of capitulation contained in the enclosed copy to which he showed them that he acceded: some came and others remained. The Supplicant as the most astute was able to extort from him a letter of Manumission which was granted at the time without

Source: From Stuart B. Schwartz, "Resistance and Accommodation in Eighteenth-Century Brazil: The Slaves' View of Slavery [excerpts]," in *Hispanic American Historical Review*, Vol. 57, No. 1, pp. 76–79.

the intention that it have any validity, at the same time he [the Supplicant] sought the District Judge who entering the *engenho* with eighty-five armed men sought out the house of his Master: The latter who could not now confide in the principal leaders of that uprising took advantage of a stratagem of sending the Supplicant Gregorio and fifteen others with a false letter to the Captain major of the militia, João da Silva Santos, who was in the Vila of Belmonte, telling them that they would receive from him some cattle and manioc flour for the *engenho*. Arriving at the said Vila all were taken prisoner with handcuffs despite the great resistance that they made almost to the point of much bloodshed. They were finally conducted to the jail of this High Court as I have said, that is, the Supplicant as the prime mover to be held until his charges were seen and the others with orders to the aforementioned merchant to be sold to Maranhão as they were.

Twice there has been required from this court an order to be sent the investigation or any other charges against the Supplicant and until now they have not arrived.

I must also tell Your Excellency that the Master of the said Engenho has on repeated occasions recommended with the greatest insistence that the Supplicant not be released from prison except by a sentence that exiles him far away because if he is freed he will unfailingly return to the *engenho* to incite new disorders, that may be irreparable.

That which is reported here seems to me enough to give Your Excellency a sufficient idea concerning the Supplicant and the reasons for his imprisonment. God Protect Your Excellency. Bahia 22 of January of 1806.

The Desembargador Ouvidor geral do Crime

Claudio Jose Pereira da Costa

Treaty Proposed to Manoel da Silva Ferreira by His Slaves During the Time that They Remained in Revolt

My Lord, we want peace and we do not want war; if My Lord also wants our peace it must be in this manner, if he wishes to agree to that which we want.

In each week you must give us the days of Friday and Saturday to work for ourselves not subtracting any of these because they are Saint's days.

To enable us to live you must give us casting nets and canoes.

You are not to oblige us to fish in the tidal pools nor to gather shellfish, and when you wish to gather shellfish send your Mina blacks.

For your sustenance have a fishing launch and decked canoes, and when you wish to eat shellfish send your Mina blacks.

Make a large boat so that when it goes to Bahia we can place our cargoes aboard and not pay freightage.

In the planting of manioc we wish the men to have a daily quota of two and one half hands and the women, two hands.

The daily quota of manioc flour must be of five level *alqueires*, placing enough harvesters so that these can serve to hang up the coverings.

The daily quota of sugarcane must be of five hands rather than six and of ten canes in each bundle.

On the boat you must put four poles, and one for the rudder, and the one at the rudder works hard for us.

The wood that is sawed with a hand saw must have three men below and one above.

The measure of firewood must be as was practiced here, for each measure a woodcutter and a woman as the wood carrier.

The present overseers we do not want, choose others with our approval.

At the milling rollers there must be four women to feed in the cane, two pulleys, and a *carcanha*.

At each cauldron there must be one who tends the fire and in each series of kettles the same, and on Saturday there must be without fail work stoppage in the mill.

The sailors who go in the launch beside the baize shirt that they are given must also have a jacket of baize and all the necessary clothing.

We will go to work the canefield of Jabirú this time and then it must remain as pasture for we cannot cut cane in a swamp.

We shall be able to plant our rice wherever we wish, and in any marsh, without asking permission for this, and each person can cut jacaranda or any other wood without having to account for this.

Accepting all the above articles and allowing us to remain always in possession of the hardware, we are ready to serve you as before because we do not wish to continue the bad customs of the other *engenhos*.

We shall be able to play, relax and sing any time we wish without your hinderance nor will permission be needed.

△ E S S A Y S

One hallmark of recent historiography has been the celebration of marginalized people's resistance to oppression. The two essays in this chapter analyze resistance in contrasting settings. Peter Linebaugh and Marcus Rediker, leading historians of Anglo-Atlantic radicalism, observe that European and Euro-American writers often likened the task of maintaining social order to Hercules' combat with the Hydra, a monster with many regenerating heads. Cut one head off and two more grew back. Sympathizing with the monster, Linebaugh and Rediker identify the diverse forms of workers' protest that emerged in Atlantic port cities in British North America and Great Britain, where sailors, slaves, and other urban denizens plotted conspiracies, staged riots, dodged impressment, and cried out for liberty. These dissidents frequently endured harsh punishment for their protests. Here Linebaugh and Rediker take a closer look at London's port "strike" of 1768, which was heavily influenced by the rebellious Irish Whiteboy movement of the previous decade. The London uprising provides a good example of the links between agrarian and urban unrest, and of the resilience of resistance from below.

Far from the riotous ports of the Atlantic world, small bands of runaway Africans and Afro-Americans formed semi-autonomous settlements, or "maroon" communities, on the edges of plantation regions. Maroons often attempted to re-create microcosmic African societies on the edges of American slavery, and they constituted a standing threat to the plantation order wherever they existed. The largest was probably Palmares in northeastern Brazil, which harbored as many as 20,000 people in the late seventeenth century, but maroon communities could also be found in the mountains of Jamaica in the eighteenth century and the swamps of Florida in the early nineteenth century. Paul Lokken's essay examines a maroon outpost in the western coast of Guatemala. Although not commonly included in the story of New World slavery, many thousands of African slaves were imported into Guatemala between 1590 and 1640, where they displayed the same propensity for running away from their owners as did slaves elsewhere. An outgrowth of this resistance, a maroon community coalesced at Tulate on Guatemala's western coast. It drew the attention of Guatemalan officials in the first decade of the seventeenth century, and in 1611 they sent a military expedition to crush the settlement—the fate of many maroons throughout the Americas.

The Atlantic's Working Class

PETER LINEBAUGH AND MARCUS REDIKER

Through the harsh winter of 1740–41, as food riots broke out all over Europe, a motley crew of workers met at John Hughson's waterside tavern in the city of New York to plan a rising for St. Patrick's Day. The conspirators included Irish, English, Hispanic, African, and native American men and women: they spoke Gaelic, English, Spanish, French, Dutch, Latin, Greek, and undoubtedly several African and Indian languages. They were a mixture of mostly slaves and wage laborers, especially soldiers, sailors, and journeymen. During their deliberations, David Johnson, a journeyman hatter of unknown European background, swore that "he would help to burn the town, and kill as many white people as he could." John Corry, an Irish dancing-master, promised the same, as, apparently, did John Hughson himself and many others, a large number of African-Americans among them. And they eventually put at least part of their plan into action, burning down Fort George, the Governor's mansion, and the imperial armory, the symbols of Royal Majesty and civil authority, the havens and instruments of ruling-class power in New York. They did not succeed, as evidenced by the 13 burned at the stake, the 21 hanged, and the 77 transported out of the colony as slaves or servants. The corpses of two of the hanged dangled in an iron gibbet on the waterfront as a lesson to others. As the bodies decayed in the open air, observers noted a gruesome, yet instructive, transformation. The corpse of an Irishman turned black and his hair curly while the corpse of Caesar, the African, bleached white. It was accounted a 'wondrous phemenonon'.

One of the many remarkable things about this upheaval is the way in which it confounds much of contemporary historical understanding. Here we have a polyglot community of workers who by current wisdom should never have been able to conceive, much less execute, a joint rebellion. Here we have "white" Europeans pledging themselves to the destruction of "the white people" of New York, by which they obviously meant *the rich people*. Here we have, not a slave revolt or a "great Negro Plot" (as it has long been called), not a mutiny by soldiers and sailors nor a strike by wage laborers, but rather a many-sided rising by a diverse urban

Source: Peter Linebaugh and Marcus Rediker, "The Many-Headed Hydra: Sailors, Slaves, and the Atlantic Working Class in the Eighteenth Century," *Journal of Historical Sociology*, 1990 3(3): 225–228, 229–232, 236–240. Reprinted with permission of Blackwell Publishing.

proletariat—red, white, and black, of many nations, races, ethnicities, and degrees of freedom.

The events of 1741 were part of a broader history of the Atlantic working class in the eighteenth century, a class that suffered not only the violence of the stake, the gallows, and the shackles of a ship's dark hold, but now the violence of abstraction in the writing of history. For concepts such as "nationality," "race," and "ethnicity" have obscured essential features of the history of the working class in the early modern era. Historians who consciously or unconsciously posit static and immutable differences between workers black and white, Irish and English, slave and free in the early modern era, have frequently failed to study the actual points of contact, overlap, and cooperation between their idealized types. Without such cooperation, of course, the economy of the transatlantic world could never have functioned.

Our study starts from the material organization of many thousands of workers into transatlantic circuits of commodity exchange and capital accumulation and then proceeds to look at the ways in which they translated their cooperation into anticapitalist projects of their own, as did those who gathered and whispered 'round the fire at Hughson's tavern in New York. It is thus a study of *connections* within the working class—connections that have been denied, ignored, or simply never seen by most historians. It is also an effort to remember, literally to *re-member*, to reconnect as a way of overcoming some of the violence, some of the dismembering the Atlantic working class has undergone. Our effort to remember begins with a myth about dismemberment.

The Myth of the Many-Headed Hydra

The slaying of the Hydra was the second of the twelve labors of Hercules. A Greek version of the story is perhaps best known. Confronted with the monstrous, many-headed Hydra, a water snake with nine to a hundred heads, Hercules found that as soon as he cut off one head, two grew in its place. With the help of his nephew Iolaus, he learned to use a firebrand to cauterize the stump of the beast's neck. Thus they killed the Hydra. Hercules dipped his arrows in the blood of the slain beast, whose venom gave to his arrows their fatal power.

Allusions to the story appear often in the annals of European conquest in the seventeenth and eighteenth centuries. For instance, in 1751, a former governor of Surinam returned to Holland, where he wrote poetic memoirs recollecting his defeat at the hands of the Saramaka, the victorious maroons:

> There you must fight blindly an invisible enemy
> Who shoots you down like ducks in the swamps.
> Even if an army of ten thousand men were gathered, with
> The courage and strategy of Caesar and Eugene,
> They'd find their work cut out for them, destroying a
> Hydra's growth
> Which even Alcides would try to avoid.

Mauricius was a European conqueror writing to and for other Europeans assumed to be sympathetic to the project of conquest. He likened their labor to that of Hercules, here called Alcides. Hydra is identified with the former slaves who had freed themselves, and who in subsequent war assured their freedom—a first permanent victory over European masters in the New World, preceding by a generation the victory of the Haitian people.

The Hydra comparison came easily to the pens of slaveholders worried about rebellion. Thus, in the aftermath of Bussa's Rebellion (Barbados, 1816) a planter wrote that Wilberforce and the African Institute "have pierced the inmost recesses of our island, inflicted deep and deadly words in the minds of the black population, and engendered the Hydra, Rebellion, which had well nigh deluged our fields with blood."

The Hydra analogy was restricted, however, neither to the West Indies, nor only to Afro-American slaves. In 1702 when Cotton Mather published his history of Christianity in America (*Magnalia Christi Americana*) he entitled his second chapter on the sectarian opposition to the New England Puritans, "Hydra Decapita." "The church of God had not long been in this wilderness, before the dragon cast forth several floods to devour it," he wrote of the antinomian controversy of the 1630s. The theological struggle of "works" against "grace" subverted "all peaceable order." It prevented an expedition against the Pequot Indians; it raised suspicions against the magistrates; it confused the drawing of town lots; and it made particular appeals to women. To Cotton Mather, therefore, the Hydra challenged legal authority, the demarcations of private property, the subordination of women, and the authority of ministers who refused to permit open discussions of sermons. The antinomians of America had begun to call the King of England "the King of Babylon." The struggle in Massachusetts was thus a theological dress-rehearsal for the English Revolution of the 1640s.

Thus in many different contexts did various ruling classes use the ancient myth of the many-headed Hydra to understand their metropolitan and colonial problems, usually referring to the proletariat whom European powers were either conquering or disciplining to the life of plantation, regiment, estate, workshop, and factory. The capitalists of London, Paris, and the Hague thus cast themselves as Hercules. . . .

1747: Seamen, Slaves, and the Origins of Revolutionary Ideology

Free wage laborers, mostly seamen and others who congregated in urban areas, and unfree unwaged laborers, slaves who lived in city and countryside, were two of the rowdiest heads of the Hydra in Britain's North American colonies. Seamen and slaves each engineered their own cycles of rebellion during the course of the eighteenth century. The revolts that made up these cycles were not only connected in important ways, they were, taken together, much more crucial to the genesis, process, and outcome of the American Revolution than is generally appreciated.

Jesse Lemisch made it clear years ago that seamen were one of the prime movers in the American Revolution. They played a major part in a great many of the patriot victories between 1765 and 1776. Seamen led a series of militant riots against impressment between 1741 and 1776, and indeed their agency was acknowledged by both Tom Paine (in *Common Sense*) and Tom Jefferson (in the Declaration of Independence), both of whom listed impressment as a major grievance and spur to colonial liberation.

But what has been less fully appreciated is how the sailor's involvement in revolutionary politics was part of a broader, international cycle of rebellion that spanned the better part of the eighteenth century. For merchant seamen entered the revolutionary era with a powerful tradition of militancy well in place. They had already learned to use portside riots, mutiny, piracy, work stoppage, and desertion to assert their own ends over and against those mandated from above by merchants, captains, and colonial and royal officials. They would soon learn new tactics.

After the declaration of war against Spain in 1739, struggles against impressment took on a new intensity as seamen fought pitched battles against press gangs all around the Atlantic. Seamen rioted in Boston twice in 1741, once when a mob beat a Suffolk County Sheriff and a Justice of the Peace for their assistance to the press gang of *H.M.S. Portland* and again when 300 seamen armed with "axes, clubs, and cutlasses" attacked the commanding officer of the *Astrea*. They rose twice more in 1745, first roughing up another Suffolk County sheriff and the commander of *H.M.S. Shirley*, then, seven months later, engaging Captain Forest and *H.M.S. Wager* in action that resulted in two seamen being hacked to death by the press gang's cutlasses. Seamen also animated crowds that attacked the Royal Navy and its minions in Antigua, St. Kitts, Barbados, and Jamaica throughout the 1740s.

The most important early development in the seaman's cycle of rebellion took place in Boston in 1747, when Commander Charles Knowles of *H.M.S. Lark* commenced a hot press in Boston. A mob, initially consisting of 300 seamen but ballooning to "several thousand people," quickly seized some officers of the *Lark* as hostages, beat a deputy sheriff and slapped him into the town's stocks, surrounded and attacked the Provincial Council Chamber, and posted squads at all piers to keep naval officers from escaping back to their ship. The mob was led by laborers and seamen, black and white, armed with "clubs, swords, and cutlasses"; the "lower class," observed Thomas Hutchinson, "were beyond measure enraged." The sailors originally assembled for "self-defense," but there was a positive element to their protest as well. As Knowles remarked:

> The Act [of 1746] against pressing in the Sugar Islands, filled the Minds of the Common People ashore as well as Sailors in all the Northern Colonies (but more especially in New England) with not only a hatred for the King's Service but [also] a Spirit of Rebellion *each Claiming a Right* to the same indulgence as the Sugar Colonies and declaring they will maintain themselves in it.

Maintain themselves in it they did: sailors defended their "liberty" and justified their resistance in terms of "right."

This was the essential idea embodied in the seamen's practical activity, in their resistance to unjust authority. Sam Adams, who watched as the maritime working class defended itself, began to translate its "Spirit of Rebellion" into political discourse. According to historians John Lax and William Pencak, Adams used the Knowles Riot to formulate a new "ideology of resistance, in which the natural rights of man were used for the first time to justify mob activity." Adams saw that the mob "embodied the fundamental rights of man against which government itself could be judged." But the self-activity of some common tars, "zealous abetters of liberty," came first. Their militant resistance produced a major breakthrough in libertarian thought that would ultimately lead to revolution.

This was only the beginning, for both the cycle of seamen's rebellion and for the articulation of a revolutionary ideology in the Atlantic world. In the aftermath of the 1740s, Jack Tar proceeded to take part in almost every port-city riot in England and America for the remainder of the century. Whether in Newport, Boston, New York, Philadelphia, Charleston, London, Liverpool, Bristol, or in the Caribbean, tars took to the streets in rowdy and rebellious protest on a variety of issues, seizing in practice what would later be established as "right" by law.

The years leading up to the Knowles Riot were ones in which the winds of rebellion also slashed through many of the slave societies of the New World. The struggles included the First Maroon War of Jamaica (1730–1740), slave rebellions on St. John in the Danish Virgin Islands and in Dutch Guyana (1733), a plot in the Bahama Islands (1734), a slave conspiracy in Antigua (1735–36), a rebellion in Guadeloupe (1736–38), the Stono Rebellion (1739), the St. Patrick's Day rising in New York (1741), and a series of disturbances in Jamaica (early 1740s). The connections among these events are not always easy to discover, but the life of a slave named Will, who took part in the rebellion of St. John, then the conspiracy of Antigua, and finally the plot of New York, suggests something important about the movement and exchange of subversive experience among slaves. Another Antigua conspirator, banished from his own island, turned up as a leader of a plot on the Danish Island of St. Croix in 1759.

The movement toward rebellion among African-Americans accelerated after 1765, as demonstrated in some important recent work by Peter Wood, who has argued that "black freedom struggles on the eve of white independence" intensified as slaves seized the new opportunities offered by splits between imperial and colonial ruling classes. Running away increased at a rate that alarmed slaveholders everywhere, and by the mid-1770s, a rash of slave plots and revolts sent the fears of their masters soaring. Slaves organized risings in Perth Amboy, New Jersey, in 1772; in St. Andrews Parish, South Carolina, and in a joint African-Irish effort in Boston, in 1774; in Ulster County, New York, Dorchester County, Maryland, Norfolk, Virginia, and the Tar River region of North Carolina, in 1775. In the last of these, a slave named Merrick plotted with a white seafarer to get the arms that would make the intended revolt possible.

Such conspiracy and exchange was facilitated by the strategic position that many urban slaves or free blacks occupied in the social division of labor in the port towns, as day laborers, dockworkers, seamen, and river pilots. Northern ports, with their promise of anonymity and an impersonal wage in the maritime sector, served as a magnet to runaway slaves and free blacks throughout the colonial period and well into the nineteenth and even twentieth centuries. Many found work as laborers and seamen. Slaves too were employed in the maritime sector, some with ship masters as owners, others hired out for a given time. By the middle of the eighteenth century, slaves dominated Charleston's maritime and riverine traffic, in which some 20 percent of the city's adult male slaves labored. The freedom of Charleston's "Boat negroes" had long upset Charleston's rulers, at no time more than when they involved themselves in subversive activities. as alleged against Thomas Jeremiah, a river pilot, in 1775. Jeremiah was accused of stockpiling guns as he awaited the imperial war that would "help the poor Negroes." Jeffrey J. Crow has noted that black pilots were "a rebellious lot, particularly resistant to white control."

Peter Wood concludes that between 1765 and 1776 North American slaves generated a "wave of struggle" that became "a major factor in the turmoil leading up to the Revolution": "It touched upon every major slave colony, and it was closely related to—even influential upon—the political unrest gripping many white subjects in these years." Wood's treatment of this cycle of rebellion as "a significant chapter in the story of worker and artisan political unrest" invites us to link it to the revolutionary struggles of other workers. . . .

1768: From Ireland to London, Where the Serpent Learns to Strike

Patrick Carr, another Boston worker who was to be a martyr of the coming revolution, represented that part of the Atlantic working class that hailed from Ireland. Carr, like many others, left Ireland in the 1760s well-experienced in the ways of mobs and their confrontations with British military power. Many of his compatriots went to London, where they helped to make the London port strike of 1768.

Indeed, the strike in London cannot be understood apart from Ireland, where the hangman's noose and the woodsman's axe had centuries before been the principal tools of the English Ascendency. Following the Williamite confiscations of the 1690s, the forests, and the human culture dependent upon them, were largely destroyed; the agrarian policy subsequently introduced into Ireland promoted pasturage for the export of cattle rather than an arable farming that could feed the population. As a result, a large population, having neither forests nor lands to subsist upon, either left the land altogether or submitted to a standard of subsistence so utterly mean that it beggared the powers of description of independent observers and caused even the rulers to *wonder* at how an oppressed population could tolerate such conditions. The Irish language was "banished from the castle of the chieftain to the cottage of the vassal," from whence in hard times it migrated to the boozing kens of London and the "low tippling houses" of American and Caribbean ports. The "Hidden Ireland"— its conspiratorial tradition and willingness to act outside the law—was carried along in the diaspora within people like Patrick Carr.

The "Whiteboy Outrages," the name given to the largest and longest of agrarian rebellions in Ireland (1761–1765, with sporadic outbursts through 1788), were a major part of the subversive experience of the mobile Irish. These protests took place in a period of increased expropriation and accumulation, intensified by the demands of two world wars. With the outbreak of cattle disease, the murrain, in continental Europe, and the passage in 1759 of the Cattle Exportation Act, the value of Irish land increased greatly. The poorest of the cottiers who had a potato patch or a cow kept on the common land, suddenly found that even these were to be denied, as landlords, their agents, and bailiffs evicted them in search of new grazing lands, taking over whole baronies, and erecting walls, hedges, and fences to keep their herds in and the former tenants out. Against this, the Irish cottier and laborer reacted with what Lecky called "an insurrection of despair."

In October, 1761, nocturnal bands of 200–400 people, dressed in flowing white frocks and white cockades, threw down fences enclosing lands in Tipperary. The movement quickly expanded to new areas in Cork, Kilkenny, Limerick, and Waterford, and to actions designed to redress other grievances, such as the manifold tithes (of potatoes, agistment, turf, or furze) imposed by an alien religious establishment. Sounding horns, carrying torches, and riding commandeered horses, the Whiteboys opened gaols, rescued prisoners, attacked garrisons, stole arms, released 'prentices, maimed cattle, ploughed wasteland, prevented export of provisions, burned houses, reduced prices, and everywhere tore down walls, fences, hedges, and ditches. These rebels were originally known as, and often called, "the Levellers."

The overall strength of the Whiteboys remains unknown, though it was reported that 14,000 insurgents lived in Tipperary in 1763. Their largest gatherings, 500–700 strong, took place in 1762 in Cork and Waterford. Using military techniques, the poorest cottiers and laborers (many of them spalpeens, or migratory laborers) formed themselves into an autonomous organization quite separate from the middling and upper classes. Indeed, the proletarian experience of the hundreds of thousands of Irishmen who had soldiered in the French army since 1691 lay behind the White-boy movement.

Of necessity much of their movement was anonymous and mysterious. It was conducted "under the sanction of being fairies," it was said in 1762, and led by mythological figures such as "Queen Sieve" who wrote,

> We, levellers and avengers for the wrongs done to the poor, have unanimously assembled to raze walls and ditches that have been made to inclose the commons. Gentlemen now of late have learned to grind the face of the poor so that it is impossible for them to live. They cannot even keep a pig or a hen at their doors. We warn them not to raise again either walls or ditches in the place of those we destroy, nor even to inquire about the destroyers of them. If they do, their cattle shall be houghed and their sheep laid open in the fields.

Whiteboy captains who would carry out these threats called themselves "Slasher," "Lightfoot," "Fearnot," and "Madcap Setfire."

Theirs was a movement inspired by strong notions of justice. The High Sheriff of Waterford, for instance, could find no person willing to whip a convicted White-boy, though he offered 20 Guineas and though a large body of troops was present for the occasion. When English law was enforced, as in the hanging of Father Sheehy in 1766, the people undermined its effect. The earth over his grave was treated as holy ground; a "Sheehy Jury" became proverbial for partiality. Four years later his executioner was stoned to death and ten years later his prosecutor killed, by people who refused to forget.

The Whiteboy movement attacked tithes and alarmed many Protestants, but it ought not be interpreted as a sectarian phenomenon, since both Catholics and Protestants were present among both the Whiteboys and their victims, and since wealthy Catholics and Protestants cooperated to stop the risings. And although it began in rural settings against enclosures, the movement ought not be interpreted exclusively as "agrarian unrest." Just as the creation of a landless proletariat is a necessary corollary to the expropriation of land, so the forms and experience of that struggle will move with the wandering, roving proletariat thus created. An historian of the transported convicts to Australia wrote, "The Whiteboy Associations were, in a sense, a vast trades union." Whiteboy sabotage, according to Constantia Maxwell, was taken up by Dublin journeymen. The Friendly Society of Philadelphia's ship carpenters, its historian avers, was also associated with the Whiteboys. Therefore, when in the late 1760s, the terms of exchange between England and Ireland included one and a half million pounds in remittances to absentee landlords, three million pounds worth of exports, and thousands of hungry laboring people, we need to add to such material commerce, a cultural exchange that is broader than coleric playwrights and sad balladeers, and which includes the rebellious organizations of "hidden Ireland," because these surfaced in London in 1768 with great effect.

Proletarian labors in London were characterized by high turnover, by absence of guild fellowships, be ethnic heterogeneity, and by working conditions that were seasonal, dangerous, and subject to harsh discipline. The productive power of such social labor arose from the assembly of many people in one place at one time. Harvesting and road-making, canal-digging and soldiering required such labor, as did the loading, sailing, and unloading of ships. The Irish concentrated in the mass labor of coalheaving, a hot, filthy, back-breaking line of work, but crucial to the energizing of England's greatest city. Individually weak and pitiful, as a collective mass such wage laborers had power and posed danger. "A body of men working in concert has hands and eyes both before and behind, and is, to a certain degree, omnipresent," wrote Karl Marx.

In the 1760s it took more money to eat, and the hungry people of London began to act directly against price increases. River workers led the groups who stole fresh vegetables, forced vendors to sell their wares at popular prices, and intimidated merchants into both closing down their shops and burying their plate. On 11 May a group of sailors assembled at the Stock Exchange "and would not suffer any Person except their own Body to enter it." These actions were not peaceful: murder was a frequence occurrence during the spring and summer. Thomas Davis, for instance, said he "did not care who they killed, rather than his family should starve." When a "Gentleman" asked a young man whether it was foolish for people to risk their lives, he was answered: "Master, Provisions are high and Trade is dead, that we are half starving and it is as well to die at once, as die by Inches."

Otherwise, the hungry took indirect actions to increase their wages. The sailors petitioned and marched upon Parliament to increase their wage payments. The shoemakers met often in mass meeting in Moorfields as part of their attempts to get greater wages. The bargemen struck for more money. The sawyers were threatened by the recent introduction of a steam-powered engine installed in Limehouse. They destroyed it. A thousand glass grinders petitioned for higher wages; thousands of London tailors did the same. Leaders were sent to prison, like the three tailors sent to Bridewell "for irritating their Brethren to Insurrection, abusing their Masters, and refusing to work at the stated prices."

In many ways, the riots of the spring and early summer of 1768 appear to be classic instances of the eighteenth-century plebeian "mob" in action: the forms (petitioning, marching, illuminations, smashing of windows), the heterogeneity of the "trades" (tailors, shoemakers, carpenters), and, generally, the subordination of its demands and actions to the middle-class reform movement led by John Wilkes. Yet the activities of that year need to be seen not only as the licensed outrages of the plebeian mob, but as something new, unlicensed, insurrectionary, and proletarian. "The Extremities to which the Cry of Liberty is carried, seem to threaten the Destruction of all Civil Society," as one newspaper put it. Wilkes and his men could not control the protests of 1768, as demonstrated when some sailors chanted, "No Wilkes, No King." Nor did artisans lead these events. The river workers led them, closing river shipping for a time, and almost causing a general strike. In July "A Spectator" observed the pattern of recent months: "Thus Sailors, Taylors, Coopers,

Lightermen, Watermen, &c. follow one another, the adventurous Coalheavers leading the Van."

The leaders of the coalheavers, many knew, were "of the Gang of White Boys in Ireland, driven out from thence for the most Enormous Crimes, as they have bragg'd and given it out themselves," to quote the Solicitor-General of England. The involvement of Whiteboys among the coalheavers was reported by several newspapers and assumed by Samuel Foote, who wrote *The Tailors: A Tragedy for Warm Weather* about the strikes of '68–'69. Horace Walpole, the Earl of Orford, noted that the coalheavers "are all Irish Whiteboys"; his certainty of this fact allowed him to use the terms coalheavers and Whiteboys interchangeably. Thus the Hydra-head slain by the noose and the axe in Ireland re-appeared with doubled force in London, as insurgent Irish wage labor. It may have been little enough solace to John Brennan's wife, who had carried the severed Whiteboy's head through the streets and shops of Kilkenny "collecting money from the populace" after his execution. But the inescapable truth remained, as recognized by the Chief Baron of Ireland's Exchequer: in Ireland, "England has sown her laws like dragon's teeth, and they have sprung up, armed men."

The working men and women of riverside London came out of 1768 armed in a new way. The sailors, who collectively decided to "strike" the sails of their vessels and thereby halt the commerce and international accumulation of capital in the empire's leading city, had in conjunction with Irish coalheavers and others made a major addition to the political language and activity of the working-class movement: the strike.

Resistance on the Margins

PAUL LOKKEN

The modern republic of Guatemala has often been viewed as the product of colonial relations between "Spaniards" and "Indians" exclusively, but the territory it occupies was home in the early seventeenth century to communities of escaped African slaves along both the Pacific and Caribbean coasts. Those maroon communities were the source of frequent headaches for officials of the Spanish Audiencia seated in Santiago de Guatemala, capital of a region stretching from Chiapas to Costa Rica for more than two centuries and now the town of Antigua, Guatemala. The period during which settlements of escaped slaves flourished is characterized here as Guatemala's "maroon moment," a moment which occurred, not coincidentally, in conjunction with the era during which imports of African slaves into mainland Spanish America peaked. That moment ended suddenly when imports were almost entirely cut off after 1640 and—shortly thereafter—free blacks and mulattos in Guatemala began to be mustered formally into local militia units, developments which contributed to a transformation in the status of people of African origins. The historical circumstances that allowed for the emergence of outlaw bands of escaped slaves in colonial Guatemala,

Source: Paul Lokken, "A Maroon Moment: Rebel Slaves in Early Seventeenth-Century Guatemala," *Slavery & Abolition* 25:3 (December 2004): 44–53. Reprinted by permission of the publisher, Taylor & Francis Ltd., http://www.informaworld.com.

in other words, were fleeting. While those circumstances persisted, however, local society exhibited more than a passing resemblance to others in the Americas that were more heavily reliant in the long term on enslaved African labour.

Documentation of the "maroon moment" discussed here is relatively sparse. Happily, though (at least for historians), an extensive description exists of a small settlement of outlaw slaves that was established near Guatemala's Pacific coast during the first decade of the seventeenth century. The description of the settlement, which was located somewhere upriver from the present-day coastal hamlet of El Tulate in the Guatemalan department of Retalhuleu, resulted from the pursuit by the Spaniard who oversaw its destruction in 1611 of a lengthy legal process aimed at obtaining the *encomienda* he believed he had been promised as a reward for his services to the Crown. The paper trail created by the efforts of the aggrieved petitioner, Juan Ruiz de Avilés, to obtain what he believed to be his just deserts indicates that the Tulate community had much in common with other settlements of escaped slaves in the Americas. It also provides some basis for imagining the circumstances of the maroon bands that were reported to have threatened the flow of trade goods on the road linking Santiago to the Caribbean coast, whose documentary traces are much less pronounced. Enough of those traces exist, nevertheless, to reveal that the activities of the Tulate maroons were not isolated, but instead formed part of a larger local pattern of collective resistance to enslavement via *marronage*, often characteristic of immigrant-based slave populations. This article focuses first on that larger local pattern before examining the specific case bequeathed to us by a would-be encomendero's sense of injustice.

African Slavery and Caribbean Coast Maroons in Early Seventeenth-Century Guatemala

Slaves of African origins probably accompanied the forces of Pedro de Alvarado during his invasion of Guatemala in 1523–24, and they were in any case present in the region within a decade. Their numbers grew slowly but steadily during the remainder of the sixteenth century, as demand for imported labour rose in the wake of severe demographic decline among the indigenous population and the Spanish Crown's efforts to restrict exploitation of Indian workers. Imports then picked up sharply between 1595 and 1640, when nearly 270,000 slaves, many from West Central Africa, are estimated to have arrived in Spain's American realms, and an average of 150 *piezas de indias* may have been brought into Spanish Central America annually. While Veracruz and Cartagena handled most of the seaborne commerce in slaves to Spanish America, ships carrying human cargoes showed up from time to time at the Honduran ports of Trujillo and Puerto de Caballos or, after its opening in 1604, at Santo Tomás de Castilla, located in Guatemala's Amatique Bay and thus much closer than its Honduran counterparts to Santiago. Early in 1613, for example, the latter port witnessed the unexpected arrival of a vessel carrying 97 men and boys and 39 women and girls from Angola who, although originally destined for Veracruz, were eventually sold locally. Nine more ships are known to have carried another 1,000 or so Africans directly to the region between 1614 and 1628 alone, with at least three of those ships also having proceeded from Angola. Other slaves, meanwhile, entered the Audiencia overland from New Spain and Panama.

Demand for imported African labour in Central America had arisen mostly in the silver-mining regions of Honduras and Nicaragua during the sixteenth century, but by 1600 it was intensifying in Santiago's wealthier households and on nearby agricultural operations, especially sugar plantations located in the vicinity of Lake Amatitlán, just south of modern Guatemala City. The impact of this growing demand is evident in a 1630 inventory from the sugar plantation that was probably Central America's largest in the early seventeenth century: the "ingenio de Anís," located near the lake and owned by the heirs of its founder, Juan González Donis (de Onís). This plantation, home to a water-powered sugar mill that had been constructed during the 1590s (hence the designation "ingenio"), held 191 slaves at the time the inventory was taken. A contemporary English observer said it resembled "a little Town by it selfe for the many cottages and thatched houses of *Blackmore* slaves which belong unto it." Roughly half of those slaves—and, more tellingly, two-thirds of the 137 individuals said to be at least 18 years of age—were African-born, while 128 men and boys outnumbered 63 women and girls two to one. Along with a skewed sex ratio, the prevailing patterns of the Atlantic slave trade had also imparted a distinctively West Central African cast to the plantation's workforce. No fewer than 48 of its members were identified as "angola' and 16 others as either "congo" or "anchico."

Hundreds of other Africans and their descendants worked either on nearby sugar-producing properties in the Amatitlán region or on the large Dominican-owned ingenio of San Jerónimo, located well to the north in the Verapaz. Available inventories indicate the immigrants who were largely of West Central African origins also dominated the ranks of adult workers on these operations, while sex ratios were, if anything, even more skewed than on the Anís plantation. On one relatively small property lying to the southwest of Lake Amatitlán along the route to the Pacific coast, near the town of Escuintla, three enslaved women worked alongside 25 male counterparts, at least 17 of them African-born. Such circumstances proved fertile ground for the emergence of maroon communities in many societies in the Americas, and Guatemala's was no exception.

Early seventeenth-century documentation is replete with evidence of slaves' propensity for escaping their masters whenever possible. The records of Pantaleón de Herrera's shipbuilding exploits in the Pacific coast district of Guazacapán between 1602 and 1604, for example, include frequent references to expenditures of both time and money on the recovery of slaves who repeatedly fled their exasperated owner. Some slaves were so incorrigible in the matter of flight that masters did not bother to try to hide this defect when selling them, as in the case of Isabel, an Arará woman sold openly as a "crazy runaway" by don Francisco Manso de Contreras to the priest Nicolás Sánchez in 1621. Indeed, the degree to which *cimarronaje* was simply a fact of life for local slave owners is indicated in documentation of inspections made by Audiencia officials of the jail in Santiago. Records of nine inspections conducted between October 1624 and June 1625 reveal that nearly half of the prisoners defined as black or mulatto—who in turn made up, depending on the day, between one-fifth and two-fifths of the entire inmate population—had committed the crime of attempting to escape bondage.

Many of these escaping slaves were probably uninterested in pursuing life in the remote and generally unattractive areas where maroon bands were most likely to flourish. There must, nevertheless, have been a steady supply of recruits. In 1642,

Diego de Avendaño, then president of the Audiencia of Guatemala, complained to the Crown in Madrid that maroons had been operating for 70 years in mountainous terrain near the Golfo Dulce (now known as Lake Izabal), in spite of numerous efforts to eliminate their outlaw settlements. One of his chief concerns, perennial among local officials, was that maroons operating in this area near the Caribbean coast might make common cause with the Dutch, French and English privateers who had begun to plague the region. Avendaño's fear was made especially acute by the fact that the author of several recent enemy incursions along the coast was the notorious mulatto privateer Dieguillo, an ally of the Dutch who had himself escaped slavery in Cuba in 1629. Whether or not Dieguillo harboured any special affinity for other rebel slaves, or desire to make common cause with them, he was viewed by Spanish officials as a particularly dangerous adversary.

Documentary traces of the maroon history alluded to by Avendaño are lamentably scarce, but enough references exist to confirm that the Golfo Dulce region was a redoubt for escaped slaves for, at the very least, more than two decades. In 1617, the *cabildo* (city council) of Santiago complained that maroons were threatening commerce along the crucial trade route between the capital and its closest outlet to the Caribbean, whereupon don Antonio Peraza Ayala Castilla y Rojas, Count of La Gomera and Audiencia president from 1611 to 1627, sent out an expedition that led, he claimed, to the capture of "the guiltiest ones, and the burning of their settlement and cornfields, which they had made in the mountains many leagues from any populated areas." The president's suggestion that his actions had "cleansed" the region of a maroon presence was clearly premature, however. Audiencia officials were forced to undertake at least two more efforts to wipe out the rebels by military means over the course of the next 15 years, in the process embroiling themselves in a lengthy dispute with merchants in the capital over who should bear the costs of securing the road to the gulf.

The fullest portrait, although still brief, of the outlaws who caused such trouble to royal officials along the road to the Caribbean coast appears in the memoirs of Thomas Gage, the Englishman and renegade Dominican friar who lived in Guatemala from 1627 to 1637. In 1629–30, Gage participated in a missionizing expedition into the territory of the Chol Maya, north of the Spanish-controlled Verapaz, travelling thereafter via the Golfo Dulce to the Caribbean coast and, eventually, the port of Trujillo. He learned along the way that as many as 300 escaped slaves lived in the mountains near the gulf, where they survived in part by holding up passing mule trains and helping themselves to "Wine, Iron, clothing and weapons." The audacious outlaws were furthermore said to appeal to slaves working on the mule trains, "being of one colour, and subject to slavery and misery which [the maroons] ha[d] shaken off," to join the rebel band in a life of freedom. Gage, it should be made clear, was writing in the 1640s for an English audience which he hoped to convince of the wisdom of invading Central America, and thus played up the notion that the maroons he described were eager to "joyne with the *English* or *Hollanders*, if ever they land in that Golfe." Propaganda or not, his observation echoed concerns expressed on numerous occasions by at least three Audiencia presidents.

But the maroon issue appears to have dropped suddenly from view in Guatemala before Gage's memoirs were even published in England. Why? One possibility emerges in the 1642 report of the Audiencia president Diego de Avendaño, who said he had decided to forego further military expeditions against the Golfo Dulce maroons and had instead despatched a friar to persuade them to settle permanently in the area and serve as scouts on behalf of the very regime they had sought so tirelessly to escape. Perhaps this shift in tactics bore fruit. It is notable in this regard that a contemporary account of a Dominican expedition into Chol Maya territory in 1674–76 made reference to a Christianized community known as the Village of the Mulattos "because the Indians are darkened (*amulatados*) and distinct from others who are whiter." Even if something along the lines proposed by Avendaño did occur, however, it would not necessarily account for what appears to have been the complete disappearance of maroon settlements in Guatemalan territory soon after. A full explanation for this phenomenon would have to include other factors mentioned earlier: the near-total cessation of slave imports into Central America between the 1630s and the 1690s owing initially to imperial setbacks suffered by Spain during the Thirty Years' War, and the formal induction of free blacks and mulattos into militia units during the 1640s in response to hostile activities carried out along the Caribbean coast by Dieguillo and an assortment of English, French, and Dutch corsairs.

In the long term, these developments, in combination with ongoing processes of *mestizaje*, helped obscure the significance of the African presence in mid-colonial Guatemala. In the early seventeenth century, though, local Spaniards had no doubts about the significance of that presence: they found it deeply threatening, and too large. Three times between 1612 and 1620 the cabildo of Santiago requested a halt in imports of new slaves from Africa. These requests represented a sudden turnabout in attitude, for the cabildo members had long sought to increase the number of slaves sent to the region because of the ongoing decline of the indigenous labour force and royal efforts to protect what remained of it. As late as 1609, they had asked for 2,000 slaves to be shipped to Central America. Suddenly, though, not enough African immigrants were evidently too many. The explanation for this sudden unease may lie in a litany of complaints aired during the first years of the seventeenth century about threats to social order created by feuding gangs of "disrespectful" slaves in the capital, dangerously skilled black and mulatto horsemen—both free and enslaved—who slaughtered cattle at will in defiance of the law on the ranches of the Pacific coastal lowlands, and, perhaps worst of all, maroons.

The Maroons of Tulate

Concern among residents of Santiago de Guatemala about the threat that escaped slaves posed, not only to commerce but to social order in general, may have reached its peak in the autumn of 1611. Upon taking up his new post as President of the Audiencia of Guatemala that year, the Count of La Gomera was forced almost immediately to give his attention to the problem posed by a band of outlaw slaves living near the Pacific coast southwest of the capital, whose activities in the surrounding area, and even in Santiago itself, had alarmed local Spaniards. According to the new President, during his initial round of visits to the churches of the capital he heard urgent pleas from the pulpits "to conquer the black and mulatto runaways [of the Pacific coast] because of the harm they were doing to Indians and other people on the roads and elsewhere." At least two previous efforts to dislodge the rebels from their adopted home had failed, although a total of eight escaped slaves had been recaptured. Resolving to destroy the settlement once and for all, the Count accepted an offer from Juan Ruiz de Avilés, a native of Spain who had gained military experience in and around Cartagena de las Indias before relocating with his family to Guatemala, to raise a militia force on the coast and track down and destroy the outlaw community.

Ruiz de Avilés, himself the owner of a threatened indigo *obraje* near the Pacific coast, raised a force among the local population of nearly 40 men of varying Spanish, African and indigenous origins. Most lived in the nearby communities of Chipilapa, Texcuaco and Xicalapa. These villages were Pipil in origin, although the first two were already home to many Spanish, mestizo and mulatto residents, to judge by the identifications of the men summoned to serve in the expedition, while Xicalapa, the closest of the three to the maroon settlement, was nearly defunct in the early seventeenth century, and soon would be. Its Indian governor, one don Luis, accompanied Ruiz de Avilés and his men and served as translator in cases where indigenous witnesses were required to give testimony.

Having pulled together a group of militiamen, Ruiz de Avilés then moved quickly to locate, interrogate and impress into his service a number of people reported to have maintained illicit contacts with the maroons. Among these individuals were two indigenous men named Juan and Francisco, identified in conflicting testimony as natives of Mazatenango, Quezaltenango or Huehuetenango, who were reputed to have worked as lookouts for the runaways in the territory that lay between their coastal redoubt and the capital. Two other key intermediaries between the rebel community and the outside world were Diego Pizarro and Diego del Castillo, local Spaniards from the regional commercial centre of San Antonio Suchitepéquez. Both Pizarro and Castillo had travelled back and forth between San Antonio and the maroons' fishing grounds at the coast for at least a year, conducting a thriving trade with the outlaws.

With these men serving as guides and spies, Ruiz de Avilés organized an overnight march through difficult coastal terrain and led an ambush of the rebel settlement's men at their fishing grounds on the morning of 9 November 1611. Two maroons were said to have died in the ensuing mêlée, including Diego, "captain" of the band. After leading a brief but evidently intense resistance during which the rebel slaves fought with knives, spears and machetes against their attackers, Diego was apparently shot and killed while trying to escape across the Tulate inlet, probably with the intention of fleeing upriver to warn the band's remaining members. Those unfortunates, left unsuspecting, were surprised and captured the following day by Ruiz de Avilés and a small contingent of his men, who had quickly headed several leagues inland to the rebel encampment under the guidance of one of the prisoners seized at the coast.

Seventeen band members were taken alive during the course of the expedition, including seven maroon men, six maroon and two free women, a male youth of undetermined age and a one-year-old boy. According to the testimony of these captives, a ninth woman and her child had died not long before the assault—perhaps in childbirth—and, counting the two men killed at the coast, no one else remained. The band's reputed founder, significantly, was an Angolan named Francisco who had fled an owner in the town of Sonsonate (now in El Salvador) nearly ten years earlier, and appears to have been sharing leadership duties with Diego when the end came. While none of the other rebels was identified clearly as an African immigrant, at least six belonged to prominent owners of agricultural enterprises situated near the Pacific coast. These included Pedro, slave of a wealthy merchant named Francisco de Mesa who counted among his properties the small sugar plantation near Escuintla remarked upon earlier for its extremely skewed sex ratio, and Juan Gómez, the only man among the outlaws to be identified as a mulatto, whose reputation as the band member most responsible for terrorizing landowners and other coastal inhabitants may have been testimony to experience gained on the *estancia* of his owner, Luis Aceituno de Guzmán. A few years earlier, investigators of illicit cattle slaughter on the Pacific coast had identified the mostly black and mulatto ranch-hands on that operation in Guazacapán as some of the most notorious offenders in the entire region.

Witnesses from the party of militiamen that trekked inland to the home territory of the rebel slaves said the latter had lived in a well-ordered settlement consisting of nine houses and a small storage hut, all stocked with corn, cotton, chiles, squashes, sugar cane and plantains harvested from plots maintained nearby. This location had been abandoned not long before the ambush at the coast, however, in favour of a more remote encampment, after the inhabitants picked up news of impending trouble through their communications network. The nature of that network reveals the extent to which this maroon community was forced, like others throughout the Americas, to maintain links to the very society its members sought to escape. In order to enhance the quality of a subsistence lifestyle cobbled together under harsh conditions, rebel slaves often had to rely at least in part either on trading with outsiders or taking what they wanted or needed by force. The Tulate maroons were said to have sent iguanas and fish inland to Mazatenango—where iguanas were especially scarce—and perhaps even as far as Quezaltenango in the Maya highlands, in exchange for clothing, axes, machetes, arrows and tobacco. But, led by Juan Gómez, they also extorted goods from local fishermen and residents of nearby indigenous villages and Spanish-owned estancias, held up travellers on the roads, and threatened revenge against anyone who dared report them, or so witnesses claimed. Whatever the precise mix of trading and raiding was in the economy of the outlaw settlement, its success can be measured in part by the community's survival for close to a decade. One imagines that the Angolan founder, Francisco, found the destruction of the settlement and the return to "civilization" after years of independent life especially bitter.

If the short-term success of the maroon band at Tulate owed a good deal to contacts with outsiders, so its demise followed upon betrayal by those who knew it best. While none of the people who had maintained relations with the rebels was given much choice about assisting Ruiz de Avilés once he had tracked them down, Diego Pizarro appears to have been the most eager to help the militia commander in the interests of saving his own skin. His sometime partner, Diego Castillo, seems on the other hand to have deliberately discouraged the expeditionaries from attaining their objective and was in fact accused of having warned the maroons of impending trouble. As a consequence, he was kept under especially close surveillance. Both Spaniards, nevertheless, were forced to play key roles in the ambush at the Tulate inlet, luring the maroon fishermen into a trap under the pretext that they had arrived with promised trade goods. It would be difficult to find a better example to illustrate

Price's suggestion that "inability to disengage themselves fully from their enemy was the Achilles' heel of maroon societies throughout the Americas."

The most vital reason for maintaining contact with the outside world may have been expanding, or at the very least sustaining, the numbers of the Tulate settlement. Any such activity, though, was also likely to make the settlement's elimination a priority for the authorities. Felipe Ruiz del Corral, dean of the Cathedral in Santiago, was said to have assured the Count of La Gomera prior to the latter's decision to send out a maroon-hunting expedition that "no owner had a secure slave" as long as the outlaws on the Pacific coast succeeded from time to time in attracting others to their ranks. His warning was given force by the fact that, not long before, the rebels had "stolen" a *mulata* from the house of Jerónimo de Aldaña in the capital itself, an action perhaps motivated by the recent deaths which band members reported to Ruiz de Avilés following their capture.

Such "theft" was evidently aimed not only at gaining new recruits for the maroon band, but also at establishing a balance between the sexes, a concern revealed in the character of the adult population at the time of the rebel settlement's demise: eight women and nine men. It is striking, furthermore, that only two of those 17 adults were not escaped slaves, while just one was not of African origins: an "yndia" from San Salvador named Juana who was said to be the mulatto Juan Gómez's partner. The risks taken by the community's men to "steal" enslaved women from the capital, then, may have suggested a commitment to maintaining the band's "African" character in addition to a desire to retain a balance between the sexes. Those "stolen" women, moreover, may have played an active role in their own "theft" by men whom they already knew. The inherent threat posed to the interests of slaveholders by such moves toward expansion of the community (let alone its very existence) was clear. In spite of the band's relatively small size, the repressive measures launched against it seem in retrospect to have been inevitable.

◢ *F U R T H E R   R E A D I N G*

Brading, David A. *Miners and Merchants in Bourbon Mexico, 1763–1810.* Cambridge, UK: Cambridge University Press, 1971.

Craton, Michael. *Testing the Chains: Resistance to Slavery in the British West Indies.* Ithaca, NY: Cornell University Press, 1982.

Diouf, Sylviane, ed. *Fighting the Slave Trade: West African Strategies.* Athens, OH: Ohio University Press, 2003.

Franklin, John Hope, and Loren Schweninger. *Runaway Slaves: Rebels on the Plantation.* New York: Oxford University Press, 1999.

Genovese, Eugene D. *From Rebellion to Revolution: Afro-American Slave Revolts in the Making of the Modern World.* Baton Rouge: Louisiana State University Press, 1979.

Jones, Grant D. *Maya Resistance to Spanish Rule: Time and History on a Colonial Frontier.* Albuquerque: University of New Mexico Press, 1989.

Knaut, Andrew L. *The Pueblo Revolt of 1680: Conquest and Resistance in Seventeenth-Century New Mexico.* Norman: University of Oklahoma Press, 1995.

Ladd, Doris M. *The Making of a Strike: Mexican Silver Workers' Struggles in Real del Monte, 1766–1775.* Lincoln: University of Nebraska Press, 1988.

Lane, Kris E. *Pillaging the Empire: Piracy in the Americas, 1500–1750.* Armonk, NY: M.E. Sharpe, 1998.

Lepore, Jill. *The Name of War: King Philip's War and the Origins of American Identity.* New York: Knopf, 1998.

Linebaugh, Peter, and Marcus Rediker. *The Many-Headed Hydra: Sailors, Slaves, Commoners, and the Hidden History of the Revolutionary Atlantic.* Boston: Beacon Press, 2000.

Mullin, Michael. *Africa in America: Slave Acculturation and Resistance in the American South and the British Caribbean, 1736–1831.* Urbana: University of Illinois Press, 1992.

Price, Richard, ed. *Maroon Societies: Rebel Slave Communities in the Americas.* Baltimore: The Johns Hopkins University Press, 1979.

Rediker, Marcus. *Villains of All Nations: Atlantic Pirates in the Golden Age.* Boston: Beacon Press, 2004.

Ritchie, Robert C. *Captain Kidd and the War Against the Pirates.* Cambridge, MA: Harvard University Press, 1986.

Rudé, George F. E. *The Crowd in History: A Study of Popular Disturbances in France and England, 1730–1848.* New York: Wiley, 1964.

Taylor, Eric Robert. *If We Must Die: Shipboard Insurrections in the Era of the Atlantic Slave Trade.* Baton Rouge: Louisiana State University Press, 2006.

Taylor, William B. *Drinking, Homicide & Rebellion in Colonial Mexican Villages.* Stanford, CA: Stanford University Press, 1979.

Religion, Culture, and Society

European, African, and American worldviews came into contact with each other around the Atlantic world and were reshaped as a result. This chapter emphasizes the diversity, creativity, innovation, and mixture that marked the cultural encounters among the people of the Atlantic, with special attention to the confrontation of different religious traditions. Christianity accompanied Europeans as they expanded into the Atlantic, often legitimating their conquest and occupation of "heathen" lands. Spanish officials expected their indigenous subjects in the Americas to convert to the new faith; failure to do so became a pretext for war and enslavement. When Central African rulers expressed interest in Catholicism, the Portuguese sent priests to instruct them. Protestant missionaries also spread throughout the Atlantic to wage a spiritual battle against Catholicism and to win souls for their brand of Christianity. Cultural heterogeneity and creative mixing, whether forced or voluntary, characterized the Atlantic world. People learned new languages and customs from each other; they adopted new forms of dress and worship; they tried new foods; they lived with unfamiliar people who came from distant parts of the Atlantic. It was a new world for all. The documents and essays in this chapter illustrate cultural expressions of both resistance and adaptation to new circumstances. To what extent did cultural change reflect the power dynamics of conquest and contact?

DOCUMENTS

These documents explore the different ways people made sense of the unfamiliar belief systems, practices, and people they met within the Atlantic world. Religion presented some of the deepest challenges. In Document 3, two items reveal Christian missionaries' interest in non-Christians' views of the afterlife. In the first, the Jesuit missionary Jean Brebeuf describes the Huron Indians' idea that the souls of the dead gather in a village that is ordinary in every way except that the souls complain all the time. In the second, the Moravian missionary Christian Georg Andreas Oldendorp describes the various West African beliefs of the immortality of the soul, noting that some Africans in the West Indies would commit suicide in the belief that they would be reincarnated back in Africa.

Understanding was a prelude to conversion efforts rather than "tolerance." The two items in Document 1 provide European accounts of the conversion of Africans to Christianity on different sides of the Atlantic. The first is taken from the Portuguese chronicler Duarte Lopez's account of the conversion of the Prince of Sogno in the Kingdom of Kongo in 1491, while the second comes from a Moravian history of the Christian "awakening" of the blacks on the Dutch island of St. Thomas in the Caribbean in 1736. Many of the whites on St. Thomas opposed the Moravians' efforts to convert the slaves, fearing it would lead to rebellion. In Document 6, the poet Phillis Wheatley of Boston exemplifies the conversion of black men and women to Protestant Christianity in the northern colonies of North America. One of her poems thanks God for bringing her out of Africa, and the other eulogizes the Reverend George Whitefield, one of the leaders of the Anglo-Atlantic "Great Awakening" in the eighteenth century.

One of the most famous converts in the English colonies was Pocahontas, the daughter of the chief Powhatan. Kidnapped by the English in 1613, Pocahontas converted to Christianity at the same time that she met John Rolfe, an English settler who reached Virginia in 1610. In Document 2, a letter to Governor Thomas Dale, Rolfe explains and justifies his decision to marry Pocahontas. Although many people endured pressure to convert to Christianity as part of imperial conquest and occupation, others were promised freedom of worship. In 1657, the Zeeland Chamber of the Dutch West India Company granted a charter to a group of Portuguese Jews who had fled Brazil when the Portuguese gained control of the colony in 1654. The DWIC wanted to entice them to settle in Suriname, and so granted the Jews privileges, excerpted in Document 4, including freedom of religion and favorable terms for the importation of slaves.

Documents 5, 7, and 8 illustrate the cultural heterogeneity of the Atlantic world. Africans and Indians sometimes found their way to Europe as free people, and Document 5 shows us three of them, all portrayed in dramatically different costumes and cast as royalty. The first image, from an engraving made by John Simon based on the portrait by John Verelst, is that of Sa Ga Yeath Qua Peth Ton, an Iroquois who visited London in 1710, dubbed the "king of the Maquas." The other two men, described for this 1750 image in the *Gentleman's Magazine* as "Two African Princes," were Job Ben Suleiman and William Unsah Sessarakoo. Suleiman (or Solomon) was a Muslim who was captured and sold into slavery in Maryland but who through a series of improbable adventures and lucky contacts with powerful English patrons ended up in London before he found his way home. Sessarakoo was sold as a slave in Barbados in 1744. After his father pleaded for his redemption, he was brought to London, where he sat for a portrait in 1749.

Documents 7 and 8 depict the diversity of colonial populations. Of Scots and Dutch parentage, John Stedman sailed to Suriname in 1772 for a four-year stint as a soldier. Suriname was a sugar colony whose population consisted primarily of African-born laborers; they outnumbered Europeans by as much as 65:1 in the agricultural districts. Stedman describes the capital city of Paramaribo and its varied inhabitants in Document 7. Hector St. John de Crèvecoeur argues in Document 8 that the American is a "new man" who often has a "strange mixture" of European blood. Who is left out of Crèvecoeur's definition of Americanness?

1. Africans and Afro-Caribbean People Convert to Christianity, 1491, 1736

Duarte Lopez's Account

The K. of *Portingal Don Giovanni* the secód, being desirous to discover the *East Indies*, sent forth divers ships by the coast of *Africa* to search out this Navigation, who having founde the *Islands of Capo Verde*, and the Isle of Saint *Thomas*, and running all along that coast, did light upon the River *Zaire*, whereof we have made mention before, and there they had good trafficke, and tryed the people to bee very courteous and kinde. Afterwards he sent fourth (for the same purpose) certaine other vesselles, to entertaine this trafficke with *Congo*, who finding the trade there to be so free and profitable, and the people so frendly, least certaine *Portingalles* behinde them, to learne the language, and to trafficke with them: among whom one was a Masse-priest. These *Portingalles* conversing familiarly with the Lorde of *Sogno*, who was uncle to the King, and a man well stroken in yeares, dwelling at that time in the Port of *Praza* (which is in the mouth of *Zaire*) were very well entertained and esteemed by the Prince, and reverenced as though they had beene earthly *Gods*, and descended downe from heaven into those Countries. But the *Portingalles* told them that they were men as themselves were, and professors of *Christianitie*. And when they perceyved in how great estimation the people held them, the foresaide *Priest* & others beganne to reason with the Prince touching the Christian religion, and to shew unto them the errors of the Pagan superstition, and by little and little to teach them the faith which wee professe, insomuch as that which the *Portingalles* spake unto them, greatly pleased the Prince, and so he became converted.

With this confidence and good spirit, the prince of *Sogno* went to the Court, to enforme the King of the true doctrine of the Christian *Portingalles*, and to encourage him that he would embrace the Christian Religion which was so manifest, and also so holesome for his soules health. Hereupon the king commanded to call the Priest to Court, to the end he might himself treat with him personally, and understand the truth of that which the Lord of *Sogno* had declared unto him. Whereof when he was fully enformed, he converted and promised that he would become a Christian.

And nowe the *Portingall* shippes departed from *Congo*, and returned into *Portingall*: and by them did the King of *Congo* write to the King of *Portingall, Don Giovanni* the second, with earnest request, that he would send him some Priestes, with all other orders and ceremonies to make him a Christian. The Priest also that remayned behind, had written at large touching this busines, and gave the King ful information of all that had happened, agreeable to his good pleasure. And so the King tooke order for sundry religious persons, to be sent unto him accordingly,

---

Source: Duarte Lopez, *A Report of the Kingdom of Congo* (London: John Wolfe, 1597), 118–121; Johann Jakob Bossart, ed., *C. G. A. Oldendorp's History of the Mission of the Evangelical Brethren on the Caribbean Islands of St. Thomas, St. Croix, and St. John*, with translation by Arnold R. Highfield and Vladimir Barac (Ann Arbor, Mich.: Karoma Publishers, 1987), 198–199. Reprinted with permission of Arnold R. Highfield.

with all ornaments for the Church and other service, as *Crosses* and *Images*: so that hee was throughly furnished with all thinges that were necessary and needefull for such an action. . . .

At the last the shippes of *Portingall* arrived with the expected provisions (which was in the yeare of our salvation 1491) and landed in the port which is in the mouth of the River *Zaire*. The Prince of *Sogno* with all shewe of familiar joy, accompanied with all his gentlemen ran downe to meete them, and entertained the *Portingalles* in most courteous manner, and so conducted them to their lodgings. The next day following according to the direction of the Priest that remayned behinde, the Prince caused a kinde of Church to bee builded, with the bodies and braunches of certayne trees, which he in his owne person, with the helpe of his servantes, most devoutly had felled in the woode. And when it was covered, they erected therein three Altars, in the worshippe and reverence of the most holy *Trinitie*, and there was baptised himselfe and his young sonne, himselfe by the name of our Saviour, *Emanuel*, and his child by the name of *Anthonie*, because that Sainte is the Protector of the Cittie of *Lisbone*.

The Christian Awakening on St. Thomas

Now the time had come for the first Negroes to be received by the brethren into the community of the church of Jesus Christ by means of holy baptism and to be assured of the forgiveness of their sins. Among the Blacks, the Brethren **Spangenberg** and **Martin** found three who were ready to receive the divine blessing, namely **Immanuel**, **Jost**, and **Clas**. The men were once again instructed regarding the meaning of the sacrament of baptism and recommended to the grace of God in a prayer meeting on the preceding night. Their baptism took place on Sunday, September 30, 1736, on Mr. Carsten's plantation at Mosquito Bay, after the governor had been notified and permission had been received from him. This important and blessed event occurred in the presence of a number of brethren and sisters from St. Croix, who were there, as well as several awakened Negroes. After the baptismal candidates had joyfully and openly responded to a number of questions, thus expressing their belief in Jesus Christ, they were duly baptized by Spangenberg, in the name of the Father, the Son, and the Holy Spirit. Immanuel was given the name **Andreas**, Clas was named **Petrus**, and Jost became **Nathanael**. At the conclusion of that ceremony, the baptized men were given the kiss of peace and the blessing of the Church. After their return to Tappus, they were guests of honor at the first lovefeast. Therefore, that day marked the beginning of the first Negro congregation on St. Thomas, of which these three men were the first fruits. . . .

The influence of the gospel then spread rapidly among the Negroes. There were already some two hundred of them who were eager for a closer understanding of God in Christ, providing an attentive audience for the brethren. The meetings were held daily in Tappus during the evening hours and were eagerly anticipated by many Negroes who made a long journey in the dark of night to attend, despite their full day's work. Before everyone assembled together, some time was usually devoted to instruction in reading and writing. The enthusiasm to learn such things was widespread among the Negroes. Everyone wanted to have a textbook. Whoever was lucky enough to obtain one carried it with him everywhere and devoted every free moment to studying it. One young man found that his book had disappeared, and all his efforts to recover it turned out to be in vain. No scholar could have been more upset about the loss of his entire library than that young man was about the disappearance of his little book. All the more admirable, therefore, was his attitude that led him to wish its new possessor no ill but to desire that the new owner find in it the opportunity to know Christ and to experience salvation. Nor were the brethren in any way ever displeased by the efforts which they expended to teach their Negro students how to read, for, in addition to the fact that their newly-acquired reading skills enabled the Negroes to read the Bible, it also induced many of those who had come to the meetings with the sole purpose of learning to read to partake of the desire to get to know Christ and to share in his grace. . . .

In addition to the many blessed means employed in the missionary efforts to extend the work of God among the Negroes, the major contribution came from the Negroes themselves. It was they who spread the good news throughout the island about Jesus Christ and His faithful teachers whom He had sent to them. One light kindled another, and he who had tasted of the divine love of Jesus Christ sought to help those around him enjoy it also. And since at the same time their behavior had undergone a marked change, their words accordingly fell upon eager ears. **Andreas** and **Petrus**, the two men who had recently been baptized, proved to be particularly effective in furthering the Lord's work. They led many souls to Christ, they strengthened the weak, and they showed the right path to those who had gone astray. . . .

While the brethren were engaged in spreading the light of the gospel among the Negroes who had lived in the darkness and in the shadow of death for so long a time, the lovers of darkness did their best to hamper their progress. . . .

This opposition to the missionary work, which manifested itself in a variety of ways, stemmed from a single cause, even though it was covered up with various pretexts. In fact, inconceivable as it may seem, many Whites were actually said to have believed that the Blacks were a creation of the devil and were thus incapable of eternal salvation. At any rate, there can be no doubt that the ignorant rabble had no compunction about making that reproach to the poor Negroes in order to point out to them the great chasm that separated them from the Whites. Once, the Negro Mingo, who had often heard this rebuke himself, inquired of Spangenberg in all earnestness, if the accusation had any substance. Later on, he brought a great deal of abuse on himself when, on many occasions, he asserted on the authority of his teacher that black men were no less creatures of God and beneficiaries of the promise of eternal salvation, bought by the blood of Jesus Christ, than were the Whites. As a consequence, detractors sought to represent the endeavors of the Brethren in converting the Negroes as illegal and harmful, because those efforts were detrimental to their interests, as well as the security of the masters. At one time, it was customary in the West Indies and in the Danish and English islands alike that a baptized slave was given his freedom. And even though that practice was abandoned, it was still to be feared, according to the beliefs of those opposed to the practice, that converted slaves might become too clever, too similar to the Whites, and therefore, more inclined to rebellion.

2. John Rolfe Explains Why He Wants
to Marry Pocahontas, 1614

Honourable Sir, and most worthy Governor:

. . . It is a matter of no small moment, concerning my own particular, which here I impart unto you, and which toucheth mee so neerely, as the tendernesse of my salvation. . . .

But (my case standing as it doth) what better worldly refuge can I here seeke, than to shelter my selfe under the safety of your favourable protection? And did not my ease proceede from an unspotted conscience, I should not dare to offer to your view and approved judgement, these passions of my troubled soule, so full of feare and trembling is hypocrisie and dissimulation. . . . And for my more happie proceeding herein, my daily oblations shall ever be addressed to bring to passe so good effects, that your selfe, and all the world may truely say: This is the worke of God, and it is marvelous in our eies. . . .

Let therefore this my well advised protestation, which here I make betweene God and my own conscience, be a sufficient witnesse, at the dreadfull day of judgement (when the secret of all mens harts shall be opened) to condemne me herein, if my chiefest intent and purpose be not, to strive with all my power of body and minde, in the undertaking of so mightie a matter, no way led (so farre forth as mans weakenesse may permit) with the unbridled desire of carnall affection: but for the good of this plantation, for the honour of our countrie, for the glory of God, for my owne salvation, and for the converting to the true knowledge of God and Jesus Christ, an unbeleeving creature, namely Pokahuntas. To whom my hartie and best thoughts are, and have a long time bin so intangled, and inthralled in so intricate a laborinth, that I was even awearied to unwinde my selfe thereout. But almighty God, who never faileth his, that truely invocate his holy name hath opened the gate, and led me by the hand that I might plainely see and discerne the safe paths wherein to treade.

To you therefore (most noble Sir) the patron and Father of us in this countrey doe I utter the effects of this my setled and long continued affection (which hath made a mightie warre in my meditations) and here I doe truely relate, to what issue this dangerous combate is come unto, wherein I have not onely examined, but throughly tried and pared my thoughts even to the quicke, before I could finde any fit wholesome and apt applications to cure so daungerous an ulcer. I never failed to offer my daily and faithfull praiers to God, for his sacred and holy assistance. I forgot not to set before mine eies the frailty of mankinde, his prones to evill, his indulgencie of wicked thoughts, with many other imperfections wherein man is daily insnared, and oftentimes overthrowne, and them compared to my present estate. Nor was I ignorant of the heavie displeasure which almightie God conceived against the sonnes of Levie and Israel for marrying strange wives, nor of the inconveniences which may thereby arise, with other the like good motions which made me looke about warily and with good circumspection, into the grounds and principall agitations, which thus should provoke me to be in love with one whose education hath bin rude, her

---

Source: "Letter of John Rolfe, 1614" in *Narratives of Early Virginia*, ed. by Lyon Gardiner Tyler (New York: C. Scribner's Sons, 1907), 239–244.

manners barbarous, her generation accursed, and so discrepant in all nurtriture from my selfe, that oftentimes with feare and trembling, I have ended my private controversie with this: surely these are wicked instigations, hatched by him who seeketh and delighteth in mans destruction; and so with fervent praiers to be ever preserved from such diabolical assaults (as I tooke those to be) I have taken some rest.

Thus when I had thought I had obtained my peace and quietnesse, beholde another, but more gracious tentation hath made breaches into my holiest and strongest meditations; with which I have bin put to a new triall, in a straighter manner then the former: for besides the many passions and sufferings which I have daily, hourely, yea and in my sleepe indured, even awaking mee to astonishment, taxing mee with remisnesse, and carelesnesse, refusing and neglecting to performe the duetie of a good Christian, pulling me by the eare, and crying: why dost not thou indevour to make her a Christian? And these have happened to my greater wonder, even when she hath bin furthest seperated from me, which in common reason (were it not an undoubted worke of God) might breede forgetfulnesse of a farre more worthie creature. Besides, I say the holy spirit of God hath often demaunded of me, why I was created? If not for transitory pleasures and worldly vanities, but to labour in the Lords vineyard, there to sow and plant, to nourish and increase the fruites thereof, daily adding with the good husband in the Gospell, somewhat to the tallent, that in the end the fruites may be reaped, to the comfort of the laborer in this life, and his salvation in the world to come? And if this be, as undoubtedly this is, the service Jesus Christ requireth of his best servant: wo unto him that hath these instruments of pietie put into his hands, and wilfully despiseth to worke with them. Likewise, adding hereunto her great apparance of love to me, her desire to be taught and instructed in the knowledge of God, her capablenesse of understanding, her aptnesse and willingnesse to receive anie good impression, and also the spirituall, besides her owne incitements stirring me up hereunto.

What should I doe? shall I be of so untoward a disposition, as to refuse to leade the blind into the right way? Shall I be so unnaturall, as not to give bread to the hungrie? or uncharitable, as not to cover the naked? Shall I despise to actuate these pious dueties of a Christian? Shall the base feare of displeasing the world, overpower and with holde mee from revealing unto man these spirituall workes of the Lord, which in my meditations and praiers, I have daily made knowne unto him? God forbid. I assuredly trust hee hath thus delt with me for my eternall felicitie, and for his glorie: and I hope so to be guided by his heavenly graice, that in the end by my faithful paines, and christianlike labour, I shall attaine to that blessed promise, Pronounced by that holy Prophet Daniell unto the righteous that bring many unto the knowledge of God. Namely, that they shall shine like the starres forever and ever. A sweeter comfort cannot be to a true Christian, nor a greater incouragement for him to labour all the daies of his life, in the performance thereof, nor a greater gaine of consolation, to be desired at the hower of death, and in the day of judgement.

Againe by my reading, and conference with honest and religious persons, have I received no small encouragement, besides *serena mea conscientia*, the cleerenesse of my conscience, clean from the filth of impurity, *quæ est instar muri ahenei*, which is unto me, as a brasen wall. If I should set down at large, the perturbations and godly motions, which have striven within mee, I should but make a tedious and unnecessary volume. But I doubt not these shall be sufficient both to certifie you of my tru intents, in discharging of my dutie to God, and to your selfe, to whose gracious providence I humbly submit my selfe, for his glory, your honour, our Countreys good, the benefit of this Plantation, and for the converting of one unregenerate, to regeneration; which I beseech God to graunt, for his deere Sonne Christ Jesus his sake.

Now if the vulgar sort, who square all mens actions by the base rule of their own filthinesse, shall taxe or taunt me in this my godly labour: let them know, it is not any hungry appetite, to gorge my selfe with incontinency; sure (if I would, and were so sensually inclined) I might satisfie such desire, though not without a seared conscience, yet with Christians more pleasing to the eie, and lesse fearefull in the offence unlawfully committed. Nor am I in so desperate an estate, that I regard not what becommeth of mee; nor am I out of hope but one day to see my Country, nor so void of friends, nor mean in birth, but there to obtain a mach to my great content: nor have I ignorantly passed over my hopes there, or regardlesly seek to loose the love of my friends, by taking this course: I know them all, and have not rashly overslipped any.

But shal it please God thus to dispose of me (which I earnestly desire to fulfill my ends before sette down) I will heartely accept of it as a godly taxe appointed me, and I will never cease, (God assisting me) untill I have accomplished, and brought to perfection so holy a worke, in which I will daily pray God to blesse me, to mine, and her eternall happines. . . .

> At your commaund most willing
> to be disposed off
> JOHN ROLFE.

3. Christians Discover "Heathen" Ideas of the Afterlife, 1636, 1777

Jean Brebeuf's Description of Huron Beliefs

The Ideas of the Hurons Regarding the Nature and Condition of the Soul, Both in This Life and After Death

It is amusing to hear them speak of their souls—or rather, I should say, it is a thing quite worthy of compassion to see reasonable men, with sentiments so low concerning an essence so noble and bearing so distinct marks of Divinity. They give it different names according to its different conditions or different operations. In so far as it merely animates the body and gives it life, they call it *khiondhecwi*; in so far as it is possessed of reason, *oki andaérandi*, "like a demon, counterfeiting a demon;" in so far as it thinks and deliberates on anything, they call it *endionrra*; and *gonennoncwal*, in so far as it bears affection to any object; whence it happens that they often say *ondayee ihaton onennoncwat*, "That is what my heart says to me, that is what my appetite desires." Then if it is separated from the body they call it *esken*, and even the bones of the dead, *atisken*—in my opinion, on the false persuasion entertained by them that the soul remains in some way attached to them for some time

Source: Reuben Gold Thwaites, *Jesuit Relations* (Cleveland: The Burrows Brothers, 1898), vol. 10, pp. 141–147; Johann Jakob Bossart, ed., *C. G. A. Oldendorp's History of the Mission of the Evangelical Brethren on the Caribbean Islands of St. Thomas, St. Croix, and St. John*, with translation by Arnold R. Highfield and Vladimir Barac (Ann Arbor, Mich.: Karoma Publishers, 1987), 198–199. Reprinted with permission of Arnold R. Highfield.

after death, at least that it is not far removed from them; they think of the soul as divisible, and you would have all the difficulty in the world to make them believe that our soul is entire in all parts of the body. They give to it even a head, arms, legs—in short, a body; and to put them in great perplexity it is only necessary to ask them by what exit the soul departs at death, if it be really corporeal, and has a body as large as that which it animates; for to that they have no reply.

As to what is the state of the soul after death, they hold that it separates in such a way from the body that it does not abandon it immediately. When they bear it to the grave, it walks in front, and remains in the cemetery until the feast of the Dead; by night, it walks through the villages and enters the Cabins, where it takes its part in the feasts, and eats what is left at evening in the kettle; whence it happens that many, on this account, do not willingly eat from it on the morrow; there are even some of them who will not go to the feasts made for the souls, believing that they would certainly die if they should even taste of the provisions prepared for them; others, however, are not so scrupulous, and eat their fill.

At the feast of the Dead, which takes place about every twelve years, the souls quit the cemeteries, and in the opinion of some are changed into Turtledoves, which they pursue later in the woods, with bow and arrow, to broil and eat; nevertheless the most common belief is that after this ceremony, of which I shall speak below, they go away in company, covered as they are with robes and collars which have been put into the grave for them, to a great Village, which is toward the setting Sun—except, however, the old people and the little children who have not as strong limbs as the others to make this voyage; these remain in the country, where they have their own particular Villages. Some assert that at times they hear the noise of the doors of their Cabins, and the voices of the children chasing the birds in the fields. They sow corn in its season, and use the fields the living have abandoned; if any Village takes fire, which often happens in this country, they take care to gather from the middle of this fire the roasted corn, and lay it by as a part of their provisions. . . .

According to them the Village of souls is in no respect unlike the Village of the living—they go hunting, fishing, and to the woods; axes, robes, and collars are as much esteemed as among the living. In a word, everything is the same; there is only this difference, that day and night they do nothing but groan and complain. They have Captains, who from time to time put an end to it and try to moderate their sighs and groans. God of truth, what ignorance and stupidity! *Illuminare his qui in tenebris, et in umbra mortis sedent.*

Christian Georg Andreas Oldendorp's Description of West African Beliefs

There is almost no nation in Guinea that does not believe in the immortality of the soul. It is also understood by them that the soul continues living after its separation from the body, that it has certain needs, that it carries on various activities, and that it is capable of experiencing both happiness and misery. On the other hand, there is no denying that there are some nations, including in particular the Fida, the Watje, the Wawu, and possibly others as well, which make no distinctions between the death of a human being and that of an animal. Therefore, they do not reflect on the circumstances in which they will find themselves after death. The Amina use the same term for soul and shadow, and some members of the Watje nation have told me that they consider the soul to be as delicate as a shadow.

Almost all Negroes believe that the souls of the good go to God after their separation from the body, while those of bad persons go to the evil spirit. That is why the
death of the former is commented on with the expression that "God has taken their
souls." The Loango consider the region of the blessed to be the dwelling place of
Sambianpungo (God), while hell is located up in the air, whereas others think of it
as somewhere deep under the earth. It is also believed that the souls allotted to the
evil spirit are destined to become ghosts, reappearing as such with evil intentions,
plaguing, for instance, those to whom they are ill-disposed, in their sleep. They are
also found fluttering in the air and making a great deal of clutter and noise in the
bush. If a person reappears on the third day after his death, then that fact serves as a
proof that his soul has not reached God. The body of such a Negro will not be buried
according to the honorable rites of the Amina nation, even if it had been only ru-
mored by a malicious old neighbor woman that she had seen his ghost. The Negroes
also imagine that even good souls often find it difficult to pass by the evil spirit on
their way to God, for the former tries to bring them under his control. From this
derives the already discussed custom among the members of the Amina nation,
whereby the survivors come to an understanding with **Didi**. According to the Mokko,
it is possible to be insured against the claims of the evil spirit by having one's body
marked with signs which indicate that the person so marked belongs to God. Against
these marks, the evil spirit is supposedly incapable of doing anything. According to
the belief of the Ibo, every soul is accompanied by two spirits, a good one and an
evil one, on the way to its destiny. In the course of that journey, the soul has to pass
a dangerous place, a wall which blocks its way. A pious soul is then helped by the
good spirit past the obstacle, whereas a bad one bashes its head on the barrier. After
that, two roads are opened up. One is a narrow road, along which the better soul is
taken to God by its benevolent guide. The other is a wider road along which the
bad soul is led to a dark place by a malevolent spirit.

The conceptions of these ignorant people about the condition of the blessed
dead resembles their other ideas concerning life after death. Their treatment of the
deceased reveals the fact that they consider their condition to be little different from
that of the living, attributing to the former the very same needs whose fulfillment was
necessary for them when alive. Hence, they not only place food on their graves but
also provide them with other necessities, such as their wives, servants, and slaves to
be taken with them into the other world.

The doctrine of the **migration of souls** from one body to another is widely accepted by the Karabari and by several other black nations. They maintain that the
soul of a deceased person is reincarnated in the infant born most immediately after
his demise. I was also assured by some Negroes of the widespread belief in the
reincarnation of a human soul in fowl, fish, or some other animal body. This belief
in the migration of souls has a very harmful effect on some Negroes. Thus, when
slavery in the West Indies becomes too hard for them, they take their own life in the
hope that their souls will wander back to their homeland and be reincarnated there
in a newborn child. Some even imagine their own bodily resurrection in Guinea.
The only persons thought to be excluded from the opportunity to start a successful
new life in another body are murderers and comparable criminals. **Abarre** (as they
call the evil spirit) will not let them get away with it nor will he let them find their
way to God. As punishment, they must flutter around as ghosts, and, for pleasure,
they frighten people with their terrifying appearance.

4. The Dutch West India Company Recruits Jews to the "Wild Coast" of America, 1657

Privileges Granted to the People of the Hebrew Nation That Are to Goe to the Wilde Cust

1. That thei shall have Libertie of Conscience with exercise of their laws and writes and ceremonies according to the doctrine of their Ancients without anny Prohibition, and that they shall have a place apointed for the Building of their Sinagoga or Sinagogas and Schooles, as allso sutch ground as thei shall make choice for their Burring in a separatte place according to their fashion, all according to the use and Fashion thei doe Possesse in Amsterdam.

2. That on the day of their Sabbath and the Rest of their festivicall dayes thei shall not be obliged to apeare in the court upon anny sutte at lawe or cause, and that what deligence or Acts that shall bee made against them or Past, on the said dayes shall bee given voide, and without force, and thei shall be execused of going to the Garde, except if (which God forbid) should bee urgent necessitie.

3. That all The Hebrews shall bee admitted for Burgezes as The People of the Province of Zeeland that shall live in the said Coste and that they shall with them enjoy, all the Previledges which thei shall enjoy.

4. That thei may make choice among themselves of sutch number of Persons as thei shall think convenient to Governe their Sinagogues, and to Administave the Causes of their nation, butt it is to bee understood that the execution shall be made of the officers of the Justice.

5. And whereas the intension of the said Hebrews is to Preserve themselves Peasibly, it shall be granted to them that if their should be among them anny Person or Persons of badd Proceedings and that should give them anny scandall, giving his or their names to the Governour or to the justice whom it shall apartaine, with knowledgement of the cause, shall imbarque sutch Person or Persons for those Provinces, or for sutch Place as the Deputies of the said nation shall apointe.

6. That at all the generall meetings concerning the generall and comerse the said Lords commissiones shall be pleased to order that 2 of the Hebrews be called to Represent the body of their Nation that with the rest of the Burges, thei may allsoe serve the Publick with their advise.

7. Granting to anny Persons of anny Nation anny Previlledges the Hebrews shall enjoy them allsoe.

8. That what constitutions and Customes that the Hebrew nation shall make among themselves, them that shall goe to live there, of their nation, shall be oblidged to observe them.

9. That noe one may be opressed nor putt to Lawe for debts caused in Brazil or in other Kingdomes and States, except for them that shall bee caused in the said Provinces or on the said Cust.

10. That sutch as shall be willing to goe shall have free Passage, as well in the States ships as in them that shall be fraighted for the purpose, with their Bagage and their

Source: Robert Cohen, "The Egerton Manuscript," *American Jewish Historical Quarterly*, 1973, 62(4): pp. 341–343.

Provisions, as allsoe of their matterialls for their land and building of a house for his famillie and thei all shall carrie sword and moskett.

11. That as soone as anny bee aRived at the said Cust shall appeare beefore the Governour or Commissioner, whome shall apoint each one soe mutch Land as thei cann Command and Purchase.

12. That each one shall Possesse as their owne the lands which shall bee appointed and given to them, and that thei may dispose of them that shall succede them, for ever, as well by will as by contract, or obligation, or other wayes, in the same manner as each one may dispose of their owne goods in those Parts.

13. That every one shall have Libertie to goe hunting and fishing each one in their Lands and Rivers, for ever as allsoe in the Mountains that are not subjected and in woods and open sea.

14. That every one shall bee, for the time of Seaven yeares, free from all taxes, and customes, and duties, or anny other charges that cann bee named, hee that shall make a Plantation of Sugar with 50 negroes shall enjoy 12 years of the same Libertie, hee that shall make a Plantation of Oxen, with 30 negroes, 9 yeares, and if it be less—accordingly, butt after the said time thei shall Pay the tenth parte of the fruttes.

15. Each one shall injoy for the time of five years the same Liberties of the Mines of Gould and Silver and Precious Stones allsoe of the fishing of perles and Corall, butt after the 3rd yeares—thei shall Pay the fift Parte of what thei shall gett, or the vallew of it, at allsoe it shall bee Lawfull to Trade with the Indians.

16. That each one may freely goe with anny ships as well Their owne as fraighted from those Parts with sutch goods as thei shall thinke good, as allso to the Cust of Guiny to Transport negroes to the said Coste, and transport them where thei shall think fit.

17. That each one shall be provided of the wherehouse (which shall bee sett at the said Cust) in the first six months of all Provisions, Clothes and instruments for their lands, at a reizonable Ratte and thei shall make the Paiment of the first fruttes of the Cuntri.

18. Also it is Granted to anny Person to have there in their service all kinds of shipping which thei shall neede.

A Rulle in What Manner and Condition That the Negroes Shall Be Delivered in the Wilde Cust

1. That there shall bee delivered in the said Cust soe many negroes as each shall have occasion for, The which shall be Paide heere shewing the Receipt, in ready money at one hundred and fifty guilders for each man or whoman.

2. Children from eight to twelve years thei shall counte, two for one piece, under the eight yeares three for one the breeding goeth with the mothers.

3. Hee that shall advance the paiment before the Reeceipt comes shall enjoy the discounnte of teen Percent.

4. To all them that shall Paye and buy for Ready mony if thei will thei shall have sutch number of negroes. Trusted to pay within five years and after them shall Pay for each man, whoman or child as above the sume of two hundred and fifty and he that shall advanse the Paiment shall have discount of Tean Per Cent a yeare and them that shall buy for ready money shall bee ingaged for the Paiment of the others.

5. Artists Depict Three Visitors to London, 1710, 1750

Sa Ga Yeath Qua Pieth Ton King of the Maquas

Source: Engravings of Sa Ga Yeath Qua Peth Ton King of the Maquas, in John Simon, *Portraits of the four Indian kings of Canada* (engravings after the John Verelst portraits), London, 1710; and of Ayuba Suleiman and William Mansah Sessarakoo (*Gentleman's Magazine*, v. 20, 1750, facing p. 272).

6. A Christian Convert Celebrates Her Faith, 1768–70

On being brought from Africa to America.

'Twas mercy brought me from my *Pagan* land,
Taught my benighted soul to understand
That there's a God, that there's a *Saviour* too:
Once I redemption neither sought nor knew,
Some view our sable race with scornful eye,
"Their colour is a diabolic die."
Remember, *Christians*, *Negroes*, black as *Cain*,
May be refin'd, and join th' angelic train.

On the Death of the Rev. Mr. GEORGE WHITEFIELD. 1770.

Hail, happy saint, on thine immortal throne,
Possest of glory, life, and bliss unknown;
We hear no more the music of thy tongue,
Thy wonted auditories cease to throng.
Thy sermons in unequall'd accents flow'd,
And ev'ry bosom with devotion glow'd;
Thou didst in strains of eloquence refin'd
Inflame the heart, and captivate the mind.
Unhappy we the setting sun deplore,
So glorious once, but ah! it shines no more.
   Behold the prophet in his tow'ring flight!
He leaves the earth for heav'n's unmeasur'd height,
And worlds unknown receive him from our sight.

Source: "On Being Brought from Africa to America," and "On the Death of the Rev. Mr. George White-field" in Phillis Wheatly, *Poems on Various Subjects, Religious and Moral* (Philadelphia, 1786), 12, 15–16.

There *Whitefield* wings with rapid course his way,
And sails to *Zion* through vast seas of day.
Thy pray'rs, great saint, and thine incessant cries
Have pierc'd the bosom of thy native skies.
Thou moon hast seen, and all the stars of light,
How he has wrestled with his God by night.
He pray'd that grace in ev'ry heart might dwell,
He long'd to see *America* excell;
He charg'd its youth that ev'ry grace divine
Should with full lustre in their conduct shine;
That Saviour, which his soul did first receive,
The greatest gift that ev'n a God can give,
He freely offer'd to the num'rous throng,
That on his lips with list'ning pleasure hung.
    "Take him ye wretched, for your only good,
"Take him ye starving sinners, for your food;
"Ye thirsty, come to this life-giving stream,
"Ye preachers, take him for your joyful theme;
"Take him my dear *Americans*, he said,
"Be your complaints on his kind bosom laid:
"Take him, ye *Africans*, he longs for you,
"*Impartial Saviour* is his title due:
"Wash'd in the fountain of redeeming blood,
"You shall be sons, and kings, and priests to God."
    Great *Countess*,* we *Americans* revere
Thy name, and mingle in thy grief sincere;
New England deeply feels, the *Orphans* mourn,
Their more than father will no more return.
    But, though arrested by the hand of death,
Whitefield no more exerts his lab'ring breath,
Yet let us view him in th' eternal skies,
Let ev'ry heart to this bright vision rise;
While the tomb safe retains its sacred trust,
Till life divine re-animates his dust.

7. John Stedman Describes Paramaribo, 1770s

Being once more arrived at Paramaribo, and having now the leisure, I think it will
be high time to give some account of that beautiful town. . . .

    The Protestant church, where divine worship is done both in Low Dutch and
French, has a small spire, clock, and dial, besides which there is a Lutheran chapel,
and two elegant Jewish synagogues, the one German and the other Portuguese. . . .

---

*The Countess of *Huntingdon*, to whom Mr. *Whitefield* was Chaplain.

Source: From Richard Price and Sally Price (eds.), *Stedman's Surinam: Life in an Eighteenth-Century
Slave Society. An Abridged, Modernized Edition of a Narrative of a Five Years Expedition Against the
Revolted Negroes of Surinam*, by John Gabriel Stedman (The Johns Hopkins University Press, 1992).
Reprinted with permission of Richard Price and Sally Price.

Paramaribo is a very lively place, the streets being crowded with planters, sailors, soldiers, Jews, Indians, and Negroes, while the river swarms with canoes, barges, yawls, ships, boats, &c., constantly going and coming from the different estates, and crossing and passing each other like the wherries on the Thames, and mostly accompanied with bands of music. . . . But nothing so much displays the luxury of the inhabitants of Surinam as the quantity of slaves that constantly attend them, sometimes in one family to the number of twenty and greatly upwards, a European man- or maidservant being almost never to be met with in the Colony. . . .

The fair or European inhabitants in this whole colony, who reside mostly in town, are computed (including the garrison) to be five thousand, and the Negro slaves about seventy-five thousand people.

For a better idea of the town of Paramaribo, I shall now say a word or two more of its inhabitants. Here the guard mounts regularly every morning at eight o'clock by the military in the fortress, besides the burghers or militia who keep watch all night in the middle of the town. At six o'clock A.M. and at the same hour P.M., the morning and evening gun is fired by the commanding ship in the roads, when that instant down come all the flags, and all the bells on board the vessels are set a-ringing, while the drums and fifes keep beating and playing the tattoo through the streets. From this time, viz., from sunset to sunrise, the watch is set, and no Negro whatever of either sex is allowed to appear in the streets or on the river without a proper pass, signed by the master or mistress that he belongs to, without which he is taken up and, without further ceremony, flogged the next morning. And at ten o'clock at night, a band of black drums beat the burgher or militia retreat through Paramaribo.

But it is after this time that the ladies chiefly begin to make their appearance, who delight (as I have mentioned) above all things to have a *tête-à-tête* in the moonshine, where they entertain you with sherbet, sangaree, and wine and water, besides the most innocent and unequivocal discourse, such as the circumstance of their last lying-in, the mental and bodily capacities of their husbands, and the situation of their young female slaves, of whom they propose you the acceptance, at the price of so much money per week, payable to themselves according to their value in their own estimation. For instance, having ordered half a dozen of the girls to stand in a row, the lady tells you "Sir, this is a *caleebasee* (that is, a maid), and this is not. This has only had one husband, but this had three, &c." Thus are they not only unreserved in their conversation, but even profuse in bestowing their encomiums on the figures and sizes of such gentlemen as have the honor to profit by their entertaining and instructive company. I ought not to omit that, to give a proof of their keeping discipline and good order, they sometimes order the girls to strip as naked as they were born, when you may have a better opportunity of seeing the marks of the whip, which indeed some of them are barbarously covered over with from neck to heel. As for the Negro men, they always go entirely stripped, a small slip of cotton that serves as a fig leaf only excepted, in which dress they attend their mistresses at tea tables, breakfast, dinner, and supper, unless it should happen that some of them had found the means of purchasing a pair of Holland-trousers, but in this case, should they chance to forfeit a flogging, they are by their ladies industriously ordered to take them off in their presence, while the other covering being soon whipped to atoms, she has the better chance of beholding the effects of flagellation, besides the preservation of the poor young man's breeches. Thus much for the humanity, and modesty, of the Creole ladies in this colony, and which, however much it may astonish some readers, is nevertheless an incontrovertible fact, but every country has its customs, yet from these customs exceptions are to be made, and I have seen ladies in Surinam whose polite conversation and delicate feelings would have graced the first circles in all Europe. . . .

When speaking about slaves, I must here also mention one class of them, called *Quadroons*, that are in general very much respected, on account of their affinity to Europeans, a Quadroon being between a white and a Mulatto, and which are very frequent in this colony. These young men are frequently put to some good trade such as a joiner, a silversmith, or a jeweler, while the girls are employed as waiting women, and taught the arts of sewing, knitting, and embroidery to perfection. They are generally very handsome and well-behaved, and being (both sexes) not divested of pride, they dress with a great degree of neatness, and even elegance. In short, one sees at Paramaribo not only white and black, but meets

> the Samboe dark, and the Mulatto brown,
> the Mesti fair—the well-limbed Quaderoon. . . .

All these fine women have Europeans for their husbands, to the no small mortification of the Creoles and fair sex, while should it ever be known that a female European had kept a carnal intercourse with a slave of whatever denomination, the first is detested, and the last loses his life without mercy. Such is the despotic law of men in Dutch Guiana, if not in the whole world, over the weaker species. . . .

But I must not leave Paramaribo without mentioning that, during my stay here, nine Negro slaves had one leg cut off each, for having run away from their work at a plantation. This punishment is part of the Surinam administration of justice, viz., at the master's desire, and was executed by Mr. Greber, the surgeon of the hospital, while the poor devils were deliberately smoking a pipe of tobacco, and for which, he told me, he was regularly paid at the rate of about six pounds per limb. Query: How many would not do the office of Jack Catch for less money? However, independent of his great abilities, four of them died after the operation, while a fifth killed himself by plucking the bandages from the stump, and bleeding willfully to death during the night. These amputated Negroes are frequent in this colony, where they are equally useful in rowing the boats or barges of their masters, while others are sometimes met with that want a hand, but this is for having dared to lift it against any of the Europeans, and this verifies what Voltaire says in his *Candide*. . . .

8. Hector St. John de Crèvecoeur Contrasts Americans and Europeans, 1782

What attachment can a poor European emigrant have for a country where he had nothing? The knowledge of the language, the love of a few kindred as poor as himself, were the only cords that tied him: his country is now that which gives him land, bread, protection, and consequence: *Ubi panis ibi patria*, is the motto of all emigrants. What then is the American, this new man? He is either an European, or the descendant of an European; hence that strange mixture of blood, which you will find in no other

Source: J. Hector St. John de Crèvecoeur, *Letters from an American farmer* . . . (Philadelphia: Mathew Carey, 1793), 46–47, 51–55.

country. I could point out to you a man, whose grandfather was an Englishman, whose wife was Dutch, whose son married a French woman, and whose present four sons have now four wives of different nations. *He* is an American, who, leaving behind him all his ancient prejudices and manners, receives new ones from the new mode of life he has embraced, the new government he obeys, and the new rank he holds. He becomes an American by being received in the broad lap of our great *Alma Mater.*

Here individuals of all nations are melted into a new race of men, whose labours and posterity will one day cause great changes in the world. Americans are the western pilgrims, who are carrying along with them that great mass of arts, sciences, vigour, and industry, which began long since in the east; they will finish the great circle. The Americans were once scattered all over Europe; here they are incorporated into one of the finest systems of population which has ever appeared, and which will hereafter become distinct by the power of the different climates they inhabit. The American ought, therefore, to love this country much better than that wherein either he or his forefathers were born. Here the rewards of his industry follow with equal steps the progress of his labour; his labour is founded on the basis of nature, *self-interest*; can it want a stronger allurement? Wives and children, who before in vain demanded of him a morsel of bread, now, fat and frolicsome, gladly help their father to clear those fields whence exuberant crops are to arise to feed and to clothe them all; without any part being claimed, either by a despotic prince, a rich abbot, or a mighty lord. Here religion demands but little of him; a small voluntary salary to the minister, and gratitude to God; can he refuse these? The American is a new man, who acts upon new principles; he must therefore entertain new ideas, and form new opinions. From involuntary idleness, servile dependance, penury, and useless labour, he has passed to toils of a very different nature, rewarded by ample subsistence.—This is an American. . . .

As I have endeavoured to show you how Europeans become Americans; it may not be disagreeable to show you likewise how the various christian sects introduced, wear out, and how religious indifference becomes prevalent. When any considerable number of a particular sect happen to dwell contiguous to each other, they immediately erect a temple, and there worship the divinity agreeably to their own peculiar ideas. Nobody disturbs them. If any new sect springs up in Europe, it may happen that many of its professors will come and settle in America. As they bring their zeal with them, they are at liberty to make proselytes if they can, and to build a meeting and to follow the dictates of their consciences; for neither the government nor any other power interferes. If they are peaceable subjects, and are industrious, what is it to their neighbours how and in what manner they think fit to address their prayers to the Supreme Being? But if the sectaries are not settled close together, if they are mixed with other denominations, their zeal will cool for want of fuel, and will be extinguished in a little time. Then the Americans become as to religion, what they are as to country, allied to all. In them, the name of Englishman, Frenchman, and European is lost: and in like manner, the strict modes of christianity, as practised in Europe, are lost also. This effect will extend itself still farther hereafter; and though this may appear to you as a strange idea, yet it is a very true one. I shall be able perhaps hereafter to explain myself better: in the mean while, let the following example serve as my first justification.

Let us suppose you and I to be travelling; we observe that in this house, to the right, lives a catholic, who prays to God as he has been taught, and believes in transubstantiation; he works and raises wheat, he has a large family of children, all hale and robust; his belief, his prayers offend nobody. About one mile farther on the same road, his next neighbour may be a good honest plodding German Lutheran, who addresses himself to the same God, the God of all, agreeably to the modes he has been educated in, and believes in consubstantiation; by so doing he scandalizes nobody; he also works in his fields, embellishes the earth, clears swamps, &c. What has the world to do with his Lutheran principles? He persecutes nobody, and nobody persecutes him: he visits his neighbours and his neighbours visit him. Next to him lives a seceder, the most enthusiastic of all sectaries; his zeal is hot and fiery; but, separated as he is from others of the same complexion, he has no congregation of his own to resort to, where he might cabal and mingle religious pride with worldly obstinacy. He likewise raises good crops; his house is handsomely painted; his orchard is one of the fairest in the neighbourhood. How does it concern the welfare of the country, or of the province at large, what this man's religious sentiments are? He is a good farmer; he is a sober, peaceable, good citizen. William Penn himself would not wish for more. This is the visible character; the invisible one is only guessed at, and is nobody's business. Next again lives a Low Dutchman, who implicitly believes the rules laid down by the synod of Dort. He conceives no other idea of a clergyman than that of an hired man; if he does his work well, he will pay him the stipulated sum; if not, he will dismiss him, and do without his sermons, and let his church be shut up for years. But notwithstanding this coarse idea, you will find his house and farm to be the neatest in all the country; and you will judge by his waggon and fat horses, that he thinks more of the affairs of this world than of those of the next. He is sober and laborious; therefore he is all he ought to be as to the affairs of this life; as for those of the next, he must trust to the great Creator.

Each of these people instruct their children as well as they can: but these instructions are feeble compared to those which are given to the youth of the poorest class in Europe. Their children will therefore grow up less zealous and more indifferent in matters of religion than their parents. The foolish vanity, or rather the fury, of making proselytes, is unknown here; they have no time: the seasons call for all their attention; and thus in a few years, this mixed neighbourhood will exhibit a strange religious medly, that will be neither pure catholicism nor pure Calvinism. A very perceptible indifference even in the first generation, will become apparent; and it may happen, that the daughter of the catholic will marry the son of the seceder, and settle by themselves at a distance from their parents. What religious education will they give their children? A very imperfect one. If there happens to be in the neighbourhood any place of worship, we will suppose a quaker's meeting; rather than not show their fine clothes, they will go to it; and some of them may perhaps attach themselves to that society. Others will remain in a perfect state of indifference; the children of these zealous parents will not be able to tell what their religious principles are, and their grandchildren still less. The neighbourhood of a place of worship generally leads them to it; and the action of going thither, is the strongest evidence they can give of their attachment to any sect.

The quakers are the only people who retain a fondness for their own mode of worship; for be they ever so far separated from each other, they hold a sort of communion with the society, and seldom depart from its rules, at least in this country.

Thus all sects are mixed as well as all nations; thus religious indifference is imperceptibly disseminated from one end of the continent to the other; which is at present one of the strongest characteristics of the Americans. Where this will reach, no one can tell; perhaps it may leave a vacuum, fit to receive other systems. Persecution, religious pride, the love of contradiction, are the food of what the world commonly calls religion. These motives have ceased here; zeal in Europe is confined; here it evaporates in the great distance it has to travel; there it is a grain of powder inclosed; here it burns away in the open air, and consumes without effect.

△ E S S A Y S

In these essays, Nancy M. Farriss and James H. Sweet explore the power and appeal of Christianity to non-European people in different contexts. Farriss looks at how the Maya of the Yucatan Peninsula adapted and incorporated Christianity into their lives, while Sweet argues that although the people of Central Africa may have incorporated some elements of Christian practice, they never became Christians. As early as the fifteenth century, Kongo rulers expressed interest in Catholicism and invited the Portuguese to send missionaries. Their missions bore fruit. The kingdom converted to Catholicism at the insistence of its ruler, Nzinga Nkuwu, in 1490. Thereafter Catholic priests dwelled in Central Africa only with the permission of African political rulers, and some Africans became priests. Sweet's exploration of Catholicism among the people of Central Africa offers a close analysis of Central African religious practices prior to Catholic missionary efforts. He argues that the core elements of African cosmology endured, unaltered by Catholic belief or practice.

A different dynamic existed in the Yucatan, where the indigenous Mayans' complex faith with a rich array of deities was dependent on a highly educated class of specialized religious practitioners. Their protracted struggle with Spanish power shaped the Maya response to this new faith. In this excerpt from her study of the Maya under Spanish rule, Farriss examines the adoration of Catholic saints in Mayan religious observance. She suggests that the importance of these religious figures sprang from a unique combination of the structure of Mayan religion, the collective nature of worship, and Catholicism as it was introduced to the Maya. Farriss emphasizes how religious practice among the Maya was shaped by a dynamic interaction of customary ritual and theology with Catholicism; Sweet rejects this model and argues instead that two parallel belief systems existed. To what extent did the different configurations of political power shape the reception of Christianity in each region? Or does each historian simply have a different measure of what it means to be Christian?

Catholic Saints Among the Maya

NANCY M. FARRISS

The colonial Maya continued to concentrate their collective attention on the middle range of the cosmos, on the tutelary beings identified with their own communities. Within this public sphere no shift in emphasis toward universality can be discerned. On the contrary, universality withdrew further into the background once it lost its only class of adherents within Maya society.

Source: Nancy M. Farriss, *Maya Society Under Colonial Rule: The Collective Enterprise of Survival* (Princeton: Princeton University Press, 1984), pp. 309–313, 321, 324, 327–328, 330–333. Reprinted with permission of the author.

The evangelistic zeal of the friars, backed by the military power of the conquerors, ensured that the parochial level of religion would eventually be expressed exclusively within the framework of Christianity. The outward transformation was accomplished rapidly. Within a decade or so after the friars' arrival the pagan temples, except the ones already long abandoned to the bush, had been destroyed and their stones incorporated into the fabric of the Christian churches erected on their platforms. The old idols had also been destroyed or hidden away. Their place had been taken by effigies of Christian saints adorned with European finery and served by foreign priests with a whole new array of vestments, ritual objects, and sacred symbols. Even if the indigenous long-distance trade had not been destroyed, the new temples had no place for the jade masks, jaguar-pelt draperies or the iridescent plumage of the quetzal bird. Moreover, the ceremonial round that focused on the new temples, the various feasts and rites that marked the passage of time were not only new; they also moved to the different rhythm of the Christian calendar.

The pagan cults that had persisted as a clandestine rival were no match for the officially sanctioned cult, for the more stealthy and exclusive the ritual, the less it fulfilled its purpose. Hidden worship can sustain a personal relationship with a supreme deity; secret gifts to the corporate gods that no one else knows about or shares in, although possibly satisfying to the individual, cannot express and sustain an entire community's links with the sacred. The Maya's corporate relationship with the supernatural was triadic, consisting of deities, elite mediators, and the rest of the community. With the third element removed by the vigilance of the friars, the mediators would become superfluous. They might as well cease their intercessions—and, incidentally, renounce their claim to legitimacy—unless they could transfer them elsewhere.

The ancient calendar round that the gods sustained may have been forgotten; the gods themselves were not. They were transformed into the particular collections of Catholic saints assigned to each town or village according to the whim or special devotion of the friars who established its church. . . .

Much of the rich lore of Christian hagiography was lost in the transfer to Yucatan. Whatever information may have been transmitted to the Maya about the life histories, the personalities, the special powers, and other idiosyncrasies of their designated patrons, it seems to have had little impact. There is no evidence that Saint Anthony's power to trace lost objects or cure sore throats was ever appealed to, or that Saints Michael, Peter, and Gregory were distinguished in any way other than as patrons of different Maya communities. And their importance, like that of the various local images of the Virgin, was measured purely in terms of the inter-village hierarchy.

The physical images of these saints were as foreign to the Maya as the names and particular miraculous traditions they bore. Few if any were produced in the peninsula, even after Spanish craftsmen had begun to settle there and teach their skills to the Maya. Carved and painted in pure European style, the images were imported from Guatemala and Mexico, to be deposited in the village churches ready made for local veneration. Although through the centuries silver halos, silk robes and canopies, and other locally made adornments were added, and arms were replaced and faces retouched, none of the later embellishments reveals any influence of local styles or visual symbolism. . . .

As alien as the Iberian saints were originally—in name, in physical appearance, and in the whole devotional apparatus surrounding them—the Maya were able to merge them with their traditional gods. We have no reliable guide to which particular gods might have merged with which saints, or even whether there was a one-to-one correlation. Whatever ordered complexity the popular cosmology of the colonial Maya may have had, we must be content with lumping the saints together into more or less undifferentiated assemblages and concentrate on their collective role as community guardians, rather than on any specialized attributes and powers that might have been assigned to them within that category.

Some have seen in the Christianized religion of postconquest Mesoamerica simply a cover for the old gods, who as "idols behind altars" have remained hidden in the saints' shrines or at least in the minds of the Indians. The evidence suggests a more subtle and complex process of gradual fusion, at least among the Yucatec Maya.

Few areas under Spanish rule had the freedom enjoyed by the east coast Maya to work out on their own terms a satisfactory combination of the new cult with their pagan practices. In more closely supervised areas those who were prepared to accept the Christian God, even as supreme being, had no easier a time than those who rejected him. The sticking point was his jealous nature, the idea that all divinity was concentrated in this one remote figure to the exclusion of all the more familiar and more intimate deities that permeated the Maya's world. We can only guess at the disorientation and anxiety the Maya must have suffered as the first shock of conquest became deepened by the friars' assault on their deities, indeed on their whole world order. One assumes that their earliest reactions were what has been termed "culture shock," or loss of "plausibility structure," or what Anthony Wallace has described in the psychological terms of personal loss as "Disaster Syndrome": the destruction of one's familiar world first brings about disorientation and numbness, followed by a denial of the loss, then severe anxiety, and finally anomie or despair, unless the world can be pieced together again, albeit with an altered configuration.

The creative process of reconstruction, adaptation, and fusion that the Maya pursued in order to adjust their "reality" to the new circumstances created by evangelization is almost as obscure as the earliest responses, since only a few clues surface now and then from the records. The early adaptation of certain ritual elements from Christianity is well documented, such as the famous cases of human sacrifice in the Sotuta region in which the Maya priests added crucifixion to their standard repertoire and performed these and other sacrifices inside the Christian churches. Idols were still being discovered through the first half of the seventeenth century, and according to the Spanish, as soon as they were smashed, the Maya would fashion new ones of clay or wood "overnight" and simply place them in a different cave. There they would continue to nourish them with copal incense, the ritual drink *balche*, maize, and offerings of turkey and deer (apparently the menu had ceased to include human hearts). These might seem to indicate that Christianity and paganism were still perceived and practiced as two entirely separate, parallel cults. In fact, the fusion was already well underway, in the caves as well as in the churches.

Rather than simply addressing their community gods through Christian stand-ins, the Maya had given them a dual identity, smuggling idols into churches and also giving saints' names to the idols that they were at the same time worshiping in the caves, where they had no need for pretense. Indeed, the Catholic clergy found these syncretic mutations, whenever they learned of them, even more offensive than unadulterated paganism. The "chameleon" nature of Maya gods has made the task of sorting out the pre-Columbian pantheon a frustrating puzzle. It may also have facilitated the process of fusion in this early stage of dual identity. The addition of one more guise to the multiple permutations each deity already possessed would hardly have fazed the Maya theologians.

What I suggest is a gradual shift in emphasis from the old, risky, and increasingly dysfunctional (because necessarily secret) idolatry, which itself was becoming infused with Christian elements, to the less obviously syncretic worship of saint-deities in the churches. The shift would have received a major push from Fray Diego de Landa's vigorous campaign against paganism in the 1560s, which included the wholesale destruction of Maya codices as well as the more easily reproduced idols. The loss of the major part of these "books of the devil," the gradual extinction of a priestly class who could interpret them, and the general decline in literacy after the conquest (including a total loss of the ability to decipher the pre-Columbian glyphs) all facilitated innovation and adaptation, as oral tradition began to replace written texts in the transmission of sacred lore. . . .

The cult of the saints was the colonial Maya's chief corporate enterprise, the one to which they devoted most of their collective energies and material resources. The major part of all the surplus goods and labor they contributed under various headings was destined in one way or another for support of the saints, their churches, and their ministers. . . .

The saints were endowed with very human attributes. They were not unfailingly benevolent. Like the pre-Columbian gods, they were capricious, morally neutral beings whose well-being and good will required careful attention to their physical comfort as well as deference to their high status. Their linen had to be washed and their worn garments replaced; it was thought that the Virgin would be displeased if her dress were allowed to become shabby.

The fiestas were designed as much to entertain as to honor the saints. After high mass they were taken out in procession accompanied by their "servants" (the officers of the *cofradía* and *república*) and the band of musicians they had hired. Homage was paid by community members and invited guests, who might include saints from subordinate villages, and then the images were installed under a temporary arbor or pavilion to witness the festivities. Bishops repeatedly objected to these "profane amusements": the bullfights, mock battles, dances, theatrical performances, banquets, and fireworks displays on which the *cofradías* expended so large a part of their income. The bishops would undoubtedly have found them even more lamentable had they suspected that the Maya invested these amusements with more than profane value. . . .

Most of the colonial Maya lived a threadbare existence with little above the bare necessities of life in good years and no cushion against lean ones. Their expenditure of cash, goods, and labor in honor of the saints must seem extravagant, not to say wildly improvident. The money spent on a silver crown for the Virgin could have paid half the annual assessment for a town's tribute; the cost of such ephemera as candles and fireworks for the year's fiestas could represent everybody's wages for *servicio personal.* The Maya certainly were not constantly on the verge of starvation, but for subsistence farmers existence can never be secure. If existence depended in large part on propitiating the divine powers that controlled the universe and the fate of the community in particular, then such expenditure was a sound investment. The fiestas and adornments for the saints were the main installments in the purchase of survival.

Anyone tempted to mutter caveat emptor should consider that, within the terms of their belief system, the Maya got their money's worth. The universe did continue to hold together in a more or less orderly fashion, and so did the community; and world order and social order were mutually sustaining. In a secular age the slogan "The family that prays together stays together" offers an ominous prognosis for the future of the family. For the colonial Maya, who had not yet lost a sense of the sacred, prayer in its widest sense could still be a powerful social bond.

For reasons that may remain stubbornly obscure, the Maya saw survival as a collective enterprise. The saints on whom survival depended were community guardians, not universal deities whom an individual might approach on his own. The direct, personal relationship with a supreme god or his mediators that Christianity stresses in common with other "world" religions seems to have remained as alien as the concept of universality itself. Any communal expression of religion is likely to be better documented than private devotions. But there is evidence that the Maya placed little reliance on such private relationships to help them either in this world or the next. . . .

The cult of the saints was the shared experience that most clearly defined group boundaries in Maya society and the roles and statuses of members within the group. Most especially it defined the boundaries of the community, translating the geographical fact of shared territory into the social fact of community. The church itself was the physical token of community status, its presence or absence marking the difference between autonomy and dependence for any population cluster, regardless of size. The church housed the community's collection of divine guardians, who might be similar in name and appearance to those belonging to adjacent groups, but were not shared by them. . . .

What gave life to the community as a social organism was the shared effort of sustaining their relationship with the saints. The saints did not bestow their benefits gratuitously. One shared in them only because one had contributed to the collective effort of obtaining them. The cult of the saints was thus more than a mere emblem of group identity. Active participation in the common endeavor gave subjective reality to the territorial boundaries separating one Maya group from another. It also distinguished the Maya from any non-Indians who might share the same territory. . . .

The reciprocal nature of the relationship with the saints helps to account for the territorial limitations of the saints' advocacy. They were tied to the locale not because they were associated with a particular terrain or feature of the landscape like the lesser spirits, but because their supporters were organized by territory rather than lineage, occupation, or some other principle. They were portable only when the entire community moved, as in the congregation program when any resettled town that had already been evangelized brought its saints with it to the new church.

The family or individual who migrated independently simply switched saints along with the change in community affiliation. Fiestas did not ordinarily attract former community members, nor were the friars successful in extending the cults of what they considered particularly efficacious images beyond the images' own territories, even though they tried to encourage regional sales of scapularies and pilgrimages to the Virgin of Motul and other saints besides the Virgin of Izamal. The jurisdiction of the saints was as limited as the horizons of their Maya devotees, and for the same reason. . . .

Saints and fiestas provided the one formal intercommunity link that remained in Yucatan from the preconquest systems of alliances and overlordships. Visits to neighboring fiestas were common, especially within the same parish. They did not, however, blur community boundaries. The guests came as ambassadors from one polity to another, sometimes accompanying their own patron saints. They would reciprocate with invitations to their own fiestas but without sharing in the maintenance of each others' saints. . . .

No one willingly missed his village fiestas, no matter how far from home. Men might be gone for months on a distant wax-collecting expedition, but if anyone failed to show up for a major fiesta it was assumed that he was injured or gravely ill, if not already dead, or had permanently decamped to the unpacified zones. . . .

The Maya were and are drawn from their *ranchos* and from temporary migrations for the show itself: the ear-splitting rounds of fireworks and the bullfights, real or mock (when they cannot afford to purchase a bull); the music that provides an unrelenting accompaniment to all the festivities (musicians are and were well paid by local standards, but they work hard for their fees); the feasting and drinking; the processions and solemn liturgies with colored streamers, masses of flowers and candles, and the saints in their best finery. Fiestas are a time of plenty and pageantry in otherwise drab, pinched lives, and even if designed to entertain the saints the celebrations cannot fail to please the human participants. But the Maya did not and do not come solely to be entertained. These ephemeral delights betokened the general benefits that the saints were expected to provide and in which all could share because all had shared in their purchase. Even the most marginal *macehual* had all through the year been making his own small contribution either through fiesta preparations, repairs to the church and other *cofradía* projects, or through the chores and taxes that maintained the whole apparatus of community governance, which in turn organized the cult of the saints.

Parallel Belief Systems in Kongo

JAMES H. SWEET

As the number of Muslim slaves arriving in the ports of the Portuguese colonial world began diminishing in the second half of the sixteenth century, there arrived new waves of Africans whose religious beliefs were unlike those of most slaves the Portuguese had previously encountered. The overwhelming majority of these slaves were from the Central African areas of present-day Angola, Congo, Gabon, and

Source: James H. Sweet, *Recreating Africa: Culture, Kinship, and Religion in the African-Portuguese World, 1441–1770*. Copyright © 2003 by the University of North Carolina Press. Used by permission of the publisher.

Cabinda. These Africans brought with them to the Americas certain core beliefs and practices that were undeniable products of their indigenous pasts. When we discuss core beliefs and practices, we must attempt to distinguish those cultural beliefs that were central to one's sense of personhood from those that were secondary and thus more malleable. In the case of Central Africa, these core beliefs and practices included a religious cosmology based on the division between the world of the living and the world of the spirits, with a particular emphasis on the importance of ancestral spirits. . . . By comparing the ritual practices and beliefs of Central Africans in Africa with the beliefs and practices of their brethren in the Americas, we can demonstrate that certain core beliefs were not destroyed by the influences of Western Christianity. . . .

One of the distinguishing features of Central African cosmologies was the belief that secular structures were intimately bound to religious ideas. Political, social, economic, and cultural ideologies were all animated by a tightly woven cosmology that explained the origins of the universe, the constitution of the person, and the connections between the worlds of the living and the dead. This broad cosmology dictated codes of behavior and ritual practices; explained the sources of illness, infertility, or other malevolence; and delineated the relationships between human beings and the various deities.

In more specific terms, the universe was conceived as divided between the world of the living and the world of the dead. These two worlds were separated by a large body of water through which the dead had to pass in order to reach the other world. Though the souls of the dead moved on to the other realm to join the souls of deceased ancestors, they never completely abandoned the world of the living. There was a fluidity between the two worlds that allowed ancestral spirits to remain engaged in the everyday lives of their surviving kinsmen. Indeed, ancestral spirits were believed to be among the most powerful influences in shaping the fortunes of their surviving kin. Ancestors witnessed village disputes, sometimes intervening to uphold moral codes and community standards. They watched over hunters in the forests, protected women during childbirth, and insured bountiful harvests. In return, the ancestors expected to be loved and remembered. They required food at communal feasts, expected to be consulted in important family decisions, and demanded proper burials and frequent offerings at their graves. In this way, the living and the dead formed a single community, with social and moral obligations flowing in both directions.

The Central African conception of humanity was closely related to the model of the divided world. Human beings were considered "double beings," consisting of a visible outer shell and an inner, invisible entity that was the actual or essential person. The "soul" was an eternal force that could act independently of the outer being. When the outer person slept, the soul flew off to pursue its own labors and adventures, thereby explaining what Westerners understood to be dreams.

On earth, the most powerful people were thought to possess whole and complete souls. To maintain the well-being of the soul, humans relied on the dead to protect them from evil. These appeals occurred at grave sites or in other ritual settings where the living made offerings to the dead in exchange for power and protection of the life force. When illness, misfortune, or other signs of weakness occurred, it was interpreted to mean that the spiritual protection of the soul was no longer effective. Because good health was viewed as a sign of social and spiritual power, sickness was interpreted as a symbol of a much broader and more general social failure. Sometimes, ancestral spirits invoked illness as punishment for those who failed in their obligations to their kin. At other times, the weakening of the soul was attributed to witches and even spirits who separated the soul from its body by stealing it, often while the person was sleeping. The longer the soul was away from its shell, the risk of illness and death increased, as the witches continued to "eat" away at the soul.

To counteract the depletion of the life force by disgruntled ancestors and witches, individuals might rely on ritual healers or diviners to intervene on their behalf. The diviners, in addition to being able to predict past and future occurrences, were able to determine which spirits were plaguing the body of an individual. After determining the cause of the "illness," the healer prescribed a variety of remedies, including treatment of the witchcraft through natural medicines (roots, herbs, etc.), appeasement of ancestral spirits with feasts in their honor, or ritual judgments of the suspected living witches. . . .

By using the proper medicines and engaging in carefully choreographed rituals, individuals could protect themselves from a wide array of malevolent forces. . . .

The transfer of Central African ideas and their associated rituals across the Portuguese world is clearly shown in the Inquisition records and in the writings of various travelers, clerics, and merchants who resided in those areas, but reading these accounts presents difficulties. One must recognize and filter out Western biases that flaw these otherwise useful documentary sources. Descriptions of African practices, both in Africa and in the African-Portuguese diaspora, were not only condemned and marginalized as "sin" and "idolatry," they also were misinterpreted as the work of the Devil, thereby distorting and omitting important elements crucial to understanding ritual processes. . . .

Though African and European cosmologies were largely incompatible, some scholars are now suggesting that the key to religious exchange had little to do with replacing one belief system in favor of another. Rather, religious exchange between Africans and Europeans depended upon a series of shared revelations, revelations that resonated within both the African and European spiritual traditions. . . .

Where Catholic priests were willing to make spiritual concessions and admit the validity of certain African revelations, some Kongolese were drawn into the Christian fold. . . . But the Catholic priests validated only a very small number of Kongolese revelations, declaring all other revelations to be the work of the Devil. While the Catholic Church considered revelations to be extraordinarily rare and miraculous expressions of God's will on earth, the Kongolese depended upon continuous revelation for their daily survival. . . .

The cosmology of Central Africa was *built* upon the necessity of continuous revelation, while Christianity increasingly was becoming a religion based on communion with the one "true" God. In the Christian context, sources of revelations were finite, limited to God, Jesus, the Virgin Mary, and various saints. The revelations that were proffered by this limited cast were so rare and extraordinary that when they did occur, they were judged to be miraculous. When the Catholic saints revealed themselves, the validity of the revelation had to be confirmed by the Catholic clergy, an irritating obstacle that had no precedent in African thought. Central African revelation, on the other hand, was ordinary, continuous, and included a variety of local deities and ancestral spirits whose function was to intervene from the other world on behalf of those in the temporal world. This constant dialogue between laypeople and the spirit world was the linchpin of African cosmology and became the primary target of Catholic extirpation campaigns. . . .

Everyday forms of curing, healing, and divination were often considered the work of the Devil. Even so-called African "Christians" continued to practice these rituals, prompting commentary from Catholic clergymen. In a 1612 letter to the King of Portugal, the Bishop of Congo, Manuel Baptista, wrote that the people of Kongo were "incapable" of serving God "because the vices are so old and the barbarism is so great that they cannot be cured." Some years later, Father Cavazzi wrote that there were "bad Christians" from Kongo who were "apparently avowed to our religion, but, hidden, they protect the *feiticeiros,* the foundation and support of all the idolatry." As Cavazzi makes clear, those Kongolese who embraced the Catholic faith clearly did so on their own terms, persisting in their beliefs in indigenous African forms.

Catholic priests had little tolerance for African rituals and practices. Across Central Africa, priests burned "idol houses" and "fetish objects" in grand public displays meant to demonstrate the impotence of African spirits and religious leaders (*nganga*). In 1716, Father Lorenzo da Lucca, who had been in Kongo for over ten years as a missionary, complained bitterly about the proliferation of "diabolical witchcraft" in the region around Luanda. He argued that if the African healers were not punished, the city would be "boiling over in a few years swollen from the assembly [of witches]." . . . Father da Lucca predicted that there would be dire consequences if African practices were not curtailed. He wrote that there was not only the "fear of losing the law of God, but moreover of His Majesty losing the Reign, because if these witches (*feiticeiros*) multiply themselves they can corrupt all of these people." The attempts to crush traditional practices and reduce the number of African revelations to acceptable levels illustrate the narrowness of the European Catholic conversion project in Central Africa. Despite a growing indigenous Catholic priesthood, and even millenarian challengers like Dona Beatriz Kimpa Vita, interpretation of Christian doctrine ultimately rested in the hands of European priests and missionaries. While Europeans embraced some African revelations as valid in the Catholic tradition, the vast majority were rejected as being the Devil's work. Thus, the core of African religious belief—continuous, everyday forms of revelation used to explain, predict, and control the temporal world—was viewed by European priests as a "diabolical" oppositional threat.

Despite the rejection of traditional African practices and beliefs by most Catholic priests, some Kongolese still embraced a Catholic identity, especially vis-à-vis their "heathen" neighbors to the north and east. As noted earlier, this was a distinct brand of African Christianity, with strong influences from traditional Kongolese cosmology. Some of the Kongolese elite became well-versed in the commandments, prayers, and sacraments of the church. Others were Christians "only in name." At the very least, many Kongolese were familiar with the "broad outlines of the Faith" and readily added these elements of Catholicism to their arsenal of spiritual beliefs.

But to argue that the Kongolese were Christians, and leave it at that, is to strip them of their spiritual core. Catholicism simply could not meet the here-and-now needs of most Kongolese, even into the eighteenth century, after more than two centuries of practice as the official state religion.

Catholicism and traditional Kongolese beliefs remained discrete cosmologies because their ends were vastly different. Christian revelations, when they occurred, demonstrated and validated the power of a largely unknowable, mysterious, other-worldly God. And this most often required blind faith—communion with an ideal-ized apparition dwelling in the heavens. Kongolese revelation, on the other hand, was a dialogue between the living and the world of the spirits, including the spirits of ancestors, whose powers and foibles were familiar and well known, in real life as well as in death. Faith in a particular deity was verified by the bounty, or lack thereof, that was offered by the deity. If the deity was not producing, then those in the temporal world were failing to accede to his or her wishes. The followers of the deity could either acquiesce to the demands required by the spirit, or they could seek sustenance in another spirit. In this way, African cosmology was based upon an intimate, dynamic relationship between the living and those in the other world. . . .

I am not arguing that there were no Kongolese Christians. There were. But they were not *just* Christians. A more plausible theoretical explanation for Kongolese beliefs is that Christianity and indigenous Kongolese religion operated in *parallel* fashion, with the broad Central African cosmology still being the dominant reli-gious paradigm for most Kongolese, especially in the process of conversion to Christianity. Without doubt, there was some overlap in these traditions, especially at the symbolic level. The Kongolese were quick to recognize the Christian God as *nzambi mpungu*, the creator of all things. They also drew parallels between the Catholic saints and their ancestral deities. The Catholic priests and their superiors in Rome accepted these spiritual convergences as expressions of Catholic orthodoxy. But despite what the priests believed, the Kongolese were likely using Christian symbols to represent their own deities, and they continued to worship them as they always had. . . .

In the initial stages of conversion, just as the Europeans believed that the Kongo-lese were embracing God and the Catholic saints, the Kongolese probably believed that the Europeans were embracing their deities. Wyatt MacGaffey has quite accu-rately called this stage of Kongolese-Portuguese interaction "dialogues of the deaf." The worldviews of Africans and Europeans were so radically different that religious meanings probably were misinterpreted on both sides. Over the course of several generations, the blending of various aspects of the two traditions eventually led to the development of a distinctly Africanized form of Christianity that began to be seen as a religious movement independent of traditional Kongolese cosmol-ogy. Nonetheless, the *core* elements of Kongolese cosmology, even for those who were self-identified "Christians," remained explanation, prediction, and control. Christian faith was, at best, a parallel system of belief that served to complement Kongolese worldviews.

Conversion to this Africanized form of Christianity did not render the Kongolese solely Christian; Christian and Kongolese spheres continued to operate separately, with most adherents being "bi-religious." . . . Kongolese Christians and practitioners of traditional beliefs were often one and the same, sliding seamlessly from one belief system to another, a process that was informed by a common core cosmology that emphasized earth-bound pragmatism over faith.

The phenomenon of parallel religious practices and shifting arenas is perhaps best illustrated in a case from a late seventeenth-century mission in Kongo. Capuchin priest Andrea da Pavia was losing patience with his parishioners, who persisted in visiting indigenous diviners and healers. The priest confronted his flock, demanding to know if they "wished to observe the Laws of God or their superstitious ceremonies." In a telling response, the majority responded that "they firmly believed in God and everything that was taught to them [by missionaries] but that they also believed in their ceremonies and . . . observances." Clearly, this was an indication that the Kongolese were practicing Christianity as well as their indigenous religious beliefs. The two were discrete systems of belief, but they were not necessarily incompatible.

We should emphasize that Europeans also practiced parallel beliefs, especially when Christian cosmology ceased to be an effective remedy to temporal concerns. When Portuguese Christians exhausted all possibilities of prayer and faith in their attempts to control their environments, they were quick to turn to African diviners and curers. Nevertheless, the core of their belief system remained communion with God. Ultimately, the differences in Christian and African cosmologies boiled down to a conflict over the hierarchy of worship, particularly when addressing temporal concerns beyond human control. Africans worshipped multiple deities (including Christian ones in some cases) in an effort to control their daily environments, while Christians depended upon the mercy of the one true God and a finite group of saints to aid them in their daily travails.

FURTHER READING

Axtell, James. *The Invasion Within: The Contest of Cultures in Colonial North America.* New York: Oxford University Press, 1985.

Brooks, George. *Eurafricans in Western Africa: Commerce, Social Status, Gender, and Religious Observance from the Sixteenth to the Eighteenth Century.* Athens: Ohio State University Press, 2003.

Clendinnen, Inga. *Ambivalent Conquests: Maya and Spaniard in Yucatán, 1517–1550.* Cambridge, UK: Cambridge University Press, 1987.

Curtin, Philip D. *Africa Remembered: Narratives by West Africans from the Era of the Slave Trade.* Madison: University of Wisconsin Press, 1967.

Farriss, Nancy M. *Maya Society Under Colonial Rule: The Collective Enterprise of Survival.* Princeton, NJ: Princeton University Press, 1984.

Greer, Allan. *Mohawk Saint: Catherine Tekakwitha and the Jesuits.* New York: Oxford University Press, 2005.

———— and Jodi Bilinkoff, eds. *Colonial Saints: Discovering the Holy in the Americas, 1500–1800.* New York: Routledge, 2003.

Hinderaker, Eric. "The 'Four Indian Kings' and the Imaginative Construction of the First British Empire." *William and Mary Quarterly,* 3rd Series, 53 (1996): 487–526.

Lewis, Laura A. *Hall of Mirrors: Power, Witchcraft, and Caste in Colonial Mexico.* Durham, NC: Duke University Press, 2003.

Price, Richard. *Alabi's World.* Baltimore: The Johns Hopkins University Press, 1990.

Richter, Daniel K. *Facing East from Indian Country: A Native History of Early America.* Cambridge, MA: Harvard University Press, 2001.

Schwartz, Stuart B., ed. *Implicit Understandings: Observing, Reporting, and Reflecting on the Encounters Between Europeans and Other Peoples in the Early Modern Era.* Cambridge, UK: Cambridge University Press, 1994.

Sensbach, Jon. *Rebecca's Revival: Creating Black Christianity in the Atlantic World.* Cambridge, MA: Harvard University Press, 2005.

Stedman, John Gabriel. *Narrative of a Five Years Expedition: Transcribed for the First Time from the Original 1790 Manuscript Against the Revolted Negroes of Surinam.* Edited by Richard Price and Sally Price. Baltimore: The Johns Hopkins University Press, 1988.

Sweet, James H. *Recreating Africa: Culture, Kinship, and Religion in the African-Portuguese World, 1441–1770.* Chapel Hill: University of North Carolina Press, 2003.

Thornton, John K. *The Kongolese Saint Anthony: Dona Beatriz Kimpa Vita and the Antonian Movement, 1684–1706.* Cambridge, UK: Cambridge University Press, 1998.

Townsend, Camilla. *Pocahontas and the Powhatan Dilemma: An American Portrait.* New York: Hill and Wang, 2004.

C H A P T E R
10

Imperial Contests

While European powers vied for supremacy around the Atlantic world in the seventeenth and eighteenth centuries, they also struggled to govern their empires. Disputes originating in Europe were carried into the Atlantic arena by the currents of empire, just as disputes originating in the Americas and Africa could provoke serious repercussions within Europe. Contested borderlands and lucrative or strategically important places around the Atlantic, such as West African trade factories and sugar islands in the Caribbean, offered especially tempting targets of attack. Hence war was a nearly incessant feature of the era, especially in the eighteenth century, plaguing many regions of the Atlantic world with chaos and violence. Yet war also forced Europeans to compete for American and African support, and occasionally gave slaves a rare opportunity to seek their own freedom. The pressures of war proved crucial for imperial "state formation"—the development of political structures capable of surviving the pressures of a dangerous world—but holding an empire together required more than military prowess. Imperial administrators pursued a wide array of peaceful strategies to ensure the loyalty of subjects and the collection of taxes. They were always hindered by their distance from their overseas territories, measured not only in miles but also in understanding. Empire, J. R. McNeill has written, is "the product of metropolitan logic and decisions imperfectly inflicted on people and places poorly understood by the metropolitans." By the middle of the eighteenth century, France, Spain, Portugal, and Britain embarked on sustained efforts to reform their empires. Imperial rulers sought to regulate commerce, organize territory, and control their subjects, but those subjects—whether slave or free, black or white, Indian or mestizo, creole or European—had their own perspective on the advantages or disadvantages such reforms might impose. They protested undesirable imperial reforms and initatives through organized petitions, appeals, protest movements, crowd action, and overt violence, and in their objections articulated different models of imperial governance. Reform, like war, exposed fissures within empires.

△ **D O C U M E N T S**

These documents explore the challenges and opportunities imperial subjects and empires confronted within the volatile Atlantic world of the seventeenth and eighteenth centuries. Document 1 introduces the problems of life in a war zone. In 1666, war broke out between England and France, and in 1667, a French force invaded Antigua. In a letter to his brother John, the governor of Connecticut, Samuel Winthrop describes the

288

attack, the destruction of his estate by the French and their Indian allies, and his family's evacuation to Nevis. Almost a hundred years later, Joseph Sewall, pastor of the South Church in Boston, preached a sermon thanking God for the English capture of Havana in 1762, excerpted in Document 5. Sewall hails it as a providential victory for the Protestant world over the combined Catholic powers of France and Spain.

Strategic locations and alliances shaped European commitments in Africa as well as in the Caribbean. In Document 2, the director-general of the West India Company protests the possible abandonment of Dutch forts on the Gold Coast. He argues that abandonment would alienate African allies and trading partners, leave Dutch interests vulnerable to attack, and allow the English, who were waiting for just such an opportunity, to take over the coastal trade. Document 7 provides another claim for the importance of Africa to European interests. Lady Anne Barnard, whose husband was the first Secretary of the Cape Colony, lived four years in South Africa, and while she was there, she corresponded with Henry Dundas, who was the man primarily responsible for the British annexation of the Cape. In this excerpt from a letter of November 29, 1797, Lady Anne insists on the strategic value of England's possession of the Cape Colony.

Imperial conflict pushed people around, as Document 3 illustrates. One excerpt shows that enslaved blacks in the English colony of South Carolina fled to Spanish Florida in the 1730s, where they hoped to take advantage of a Spanish royal edict granting them liberty. In a second excerpt, Jemima Howe, a resident of New England, recounts her captivity in 1755 during the French and Indian War. Her small children in tow, Howe trekked north and lived as a captive among both the Indians and the French. A final excerpt explores the ordeal of the Acadians, French inhabitants of the region that became Nova Scotia who were expelled when the British took control of the province. Some of the Acadians settled west of New Orleans, where they have become known as "Cajuns."

Another major theme explored in these documents is imperial reform and colonial resistance. Document 4 samples "Bourbon" reforms intended to reinforce metropolitan cultural authority in mid-eighteenth-century Spanish America. In the first excerpt, the king of Spain imposes a requirement of "purity of blood" in 1768 for matriculation in the high schools and universities in Lima, Peru; in the second, the king demands that Spanish be spoken in Mexico in preference to the multitude of indigenous languages. Imperial subjects protested taxes and other efforts at administrative reform in a variety of ways, as Document 6 reveals. In 1765, British colonists objected to the Stamp Act, which imposed duties on all paper (newspapers, college diplomas, legal documents). Their protests were collective, violent, and theatrical, as these three examples from Nevis, Jamaica, and Portsmouth indicate. In the aftermath of an indigenous revolt in Peru, the Spanish magistrate in Cuzco, José Antonio de Areche, ordered the public execution of Túpac Amaru and his family in 1781. He also issued new regulations intended to prevent the indigenous population from affirming their Incan history and culture.

1. Samuel Winthrop Deplores the French Attack on Antigua, 1667

Samuel Winthrop to John Winthrop, Jr.

[April, 1667]

DEARE BROTHER,—The differences in Europa between o^r countrymen & ye Dutch gave ye French oppertunity of molesting us here in ye Cariba Islands; & being a people verry watchfull tooke hold of y^t advantage (wee haveing no shipping in

Source: Samuel Winthrop to John Winthrop, Jr. [April 1667], *Collections of the Massachusetts Historical Society*, 5th Series, v. 8 (Boston: The Massachusetts Historical Society, 1882), pp. 355–357.

theis parts) to invade ye Island Antigua, wch they beganne upon ye 25th daie of October last, at Five Island harbor. After some small dispute wth o^r fortes, they landed their soldiers, & possessed themselves of that place, burning first Go^{rs}, & after y^t all ye houses in y^t division. Next morning they advanced to Johns Harbor by land, where ye Go^r wth a party encountred them, but were presently put to flight, & ye Go^r wth some others taken prisoners in Capt. Mugs house, wch they plundered & burnt & so retreated. One shallop belonging to ye London marchants plantac̃on, bound for Nevis, called at my landing place, in wch I sent my wife & children to Nevis, where they have remayned ever since. Y^e 27th daie the French advanced againe to Lt Coll Bastiaen Bayers, upon Johns Harbor, being about 600 men. O^r islanders, not 200, rec^d them. Y^e contention was verry smart for about ½ an hour, & o^r men wthstood them verry resolvedly, but, being overpowered wth men, were put to flight, many slayne on both sides, but most on o^{rs}, tooke many prisoners, plundered ye house, fired all y^t was combustable, & retreated againe. This was their 3^d daies worke. O^r soldiers repayered to my house, haveing now no other place left for defence, expecting ye enemy ye next morning. About noone came a trumpet wth a summons importing y^t if wthin 2 dayes ye island should not be surrendered to ye obedience of ye French king they would destroy it by fire & sword, & give no quarter. . . . When ye officers & cheife of ye island had deliberated upon ye matter, they finding themselves not able to resist ye French & ye cruell Indian who lay burning & massacaring upon ye windward while ye French were to leward, tooke into considerac̃on ye after part of ye sum̃ons, wch promised hansom condic̃ons if wee would treat wth them. So that way seeming now y^t wch necessity compelled, they commissionated six persons to treat & articulate wth them. Two dayes were spent in ye treaty. Y^e articles (though many) were in short but this, y^t ye inhabitants y^t would take an oath of fealty should injoye all their estates; those y^t would not should have liberty for to sell in six monthes & depart; or to leave their estates to an agent, y^t would take ye s^d oath, to manage it for their use; 200 thousand pounds of sug^r to be payed in six monthes, for wch ye islanders to be freed from guarding, building fortes, or takeing up armes against their country men. Whilst theis things were in action, a party of Barbadian souldiers, inflamed wth wine, impeded ye islanders complyance, whereupon ye French departed upon ye 4th Novemb^r, & left word y^t, when they came againe, if ye islanders would stand to their articles they should have them; in the mean time they should take up their armes to defend themselves against ye Indians. The 23^d daie of Novemb^r ye French fleet came againe; upon whoes appearance one Daniel Fitch, whom ye Lt Generall, Henery Willoughby, had sent up from Nevis to be go^r, called ye people in armes & drew them up against ye French; but seing them to be stronger then he thought for, & seeing ye Indians fireing on ye other side, he ran away from ye companyes, gott into a little boat, & made his escape. When ye soldiers perceived y^t, they faced about & fled also. The French forces, com̃anded by Mon^{sr} de Clodore, Governo^r of Martinque, remayned still upon ye baye, &, not knowing o^r men were fled, came to some termes wth Lt Coll. Bayer & my selfe, to this effect, y^t if ye islanders would submitt they should have good quarter & faire treatm^t; whereupon wee went after them, &, finding some scattered people lurkeing in ye waye, not knowing where to hide themselves, acquainted them wth what was proposed, & they to ye rest, so y^t ye next morning most of them layed their armes in ye path, for ye French to receive them. Clodore, understanding o^r people were fled, marched throug ye country to my house, where he sett up his flag on ye top of my house & incamped round about it. He possest himselfe of 24 of my slaves, (ye rest escaped,) & of most of ye slaves in ye island, destroyed most of my stock, his soldiers plundering ye country round about. My coppers & sug^r worke he medled not w^th, nor fired any houses more in ye island except of those y^t runne off ye island. Haveing encamped there seven dayes, he imbarqued his soldiers, & upon ye 1 of Decemb^r sett sayle for Guardalupa. One memorable thing I omitted, wch was: when he had convened most of ye inhabitants to my house, he told them y^t o^r lives & estates were at his mercy: neverthelesse such as would take an oath of fealty to his master should injoye their estates; ye others he would carry away prisoners of warre of Fraunce. Whereupon all present, except 4 or 5 of those called Quakers, tooke ye oath. The Barbadian soldiers he carryed away prisoners wth him. Thus ye French left Antigua. In this sadd condiçon wee remained; & y^t wch added to o^r afflictions were ye murthers & rapes wch ye Indians comĩtted upon ye inhabitants after ye French departed, haveing, as they said, liberty so to doe for five daies. . . .

2. A Dutch West India Company Official Defends the Company's Fort System in West Africa, 1717

8th April 1717.

D-G. (Engelgraaff Robbertsz) remonstrated that the Directors had considered abandoning a number of forts on the Gold Coast; he argued that the power of the Company here does not in the first place derive from its European servants but rather from a good harmony with the Natives . . . that those of them who have settled under our forts or have continuously been trading with us would not refuse us to help us, as long as we do not refuse to help them: if we were to abandon or demolish forts, they would take their own measures. The power of the Company is not more redoubtable on sea than it is on land, as was demonstrated recently, when in broad daylight two big interlopers dared to sail quietly along the coast and within the sight of this Castle, having "greeted" the Company's Cruiser "Jacoba Galey" off the Upper Coast in such a manner that the latter was not ready, or at least not very eager, for another encounter. If we were to abandon some forts, it would become difficult to travel between (the remaining ones) with canoes, and to maintain proper contact with the outlying tradeposts might become impossible, because the Negroes would not only become complete masters of the passages on land, but also of those on the sea, which up to now has at least been prevented by the interspersed forts. We are therefore of the opinion that none of the forts should be abandoned, and stress that certainly none of them should be demolished. . . . It should also be noted, that at only a few forts more than 3 soldiers are stationed: at Moure: one Merchant, one corporal and four soldiers; at Cormantyn: one Merchant, one Sergeant and nine soldiers; at Commany: one Oppercommies, one ondercommies, one corporal, one constable and two soldiers; at Zacconde: one ondercommies, one corporal and four soldiers; at Boutry: one Commies, one ondercommies and because of the war between the remnant of

Source: A. Van Dantzig, *The Dutch and the Guinea Coast 1674–1742* (GAAS: Accra, 1978), pp. 189–193.

Adjase who have remained faithful to us, and their enemies, ten soldiers (who otherwise would be stationed at Elmina). In this Castle there are at the moment not more than sixteen military men. It should also be noted, that from 1st January 1705 to 31st December 1716 a sum of ƒ775,596 has been traded at the above mentioned five forts. The decline of the trade may be explained chiefly from the growth of the navigation of foreign Nations, as for instance can be seen from the trade figures extracted by a certain English captain from their books, which were shown to Chief Merchant Butler: from January 1702 to August 1708 they took to Barbados: 11256 slaves and to Jamaica 18885, making a total number of not less than 30141, and in this figure are not even included the transactions made for other ships sailing to such islands as Nevis, Montserrat, St. Christopher, for the South Sea Company, the New Netherlands and others, which would increase the above number considerably, and of which Annemaboe (alone) could provide about one third. The R.A.C. has sent hither General Johnson with a large number of new servants and soldiers on board of 6 ships (of which 3 are still being expected from Sierra Lione . . . clearly with the intention of restoring that at present decayed Company) . . . Hereupon the Book-keeper General produced a neat account of the gold, slaves and ivory purchased over the period 1705–1716: (at the aforementioned forts which the Directors propose to abandon).

	MOURE		CORMANTYN		BOUTRY		ZACONDE		COMMANY	
	GOLD	SLAVES	GOLD	SLAVES	GOLD	SLAVES	GOLD	SLAVES	GOLD	SLAVES
1705	Mk. 26	12	Mk. 36	36	Mk. 16	9	Mk. 6	2	Mk. 23	0
1706	40	92	30	30	27	16	15	10	16	33
1707	20	9	33	43	25	30	14	40	18	34
1708	14	20	17	15	14	11	28	64	9	13
1709	20	13	44	21	29	18	39	93	24	29
1710	32	5	29	1	60	31	96	57	34	21
1711	24	0	76	0	46	7	147	5	71	4
1712	20	0	48	0	20	0	32	0	22	0
1713	13	0	31	3	20	4	28	10	21	0
1714	10	1	31	0	17	2	50	11	32	6
1715	34	2	42	0	5	0	56	60	28	10
1716	50	1	64	0	11	28	47	52	22	1

. . . Our fortresses are situated in such a way, that they seem to be mixed with those of others, nay, at some places, such as Commany, Zacconde and Accra so close to those of others, that a buccaneer-shot fired from one (fort) can reach the other. The Natives have also founded special croms under each fort, depending on the profit they expect from either us or the English, and each has its Caboceer who maintains contacts with other Natives in the interior . . . and who brings those to whom he feels most inclined to the forts to sell their gold, slaves and tusks . . . If we were to abandon such forts, it would be regarded as a sign of impotence of the Company, and those under our protection would join the remaining Nation, which they would regard as much more powerful . . . the rumour would also spread to the interior, and our esteem would much decline; and what opposition could three soldiers and a flag offer when such an abandoned place were to be attacked by a band of armed Negroes? The English would also regard this as an opportunity to make themselves masters of the entire Coast and its trade, because we have often enough seen that all our contracts and agreements (with the Africans) hold only as long as they see advantage in them; and even if they did not violate those contracts on their own, the English could easily arrange it at such places as Zacconde and Commany, through the powerful Negro John Cabes, who, as everybody knows, is with the Brandenburg rogue John Conny virtually master of the entire Upper Coast . . . it should be added, that if we abandoned Commany the whole business of collecting and sawing wood on the river of Chama would collapse as a result of the intrigues and the power of the Negroes of that region. Apart from Chama and Boutry there are no other places for the supply of firewood for the ships. Moreover, if Boutry were abandoned, what bad name the Company would make for itself, leaving as a prey to their cruel foes the small number of Adjase who are still defending themselves courageously under Caboceer Zieba and the Braffo against many enemies!

It would be virtually impossible to execute the Noble Company's orders concerning Moure and Cormantyn: in between those places is Annemaboe, that important trading town from which English ships take every year a nearly unbelievable number of slaves. The Negroes of Cormantyn and Moure are simply too careful and also too powerful to let the Dutch depart like that: those two fortresses are, after St. George, the strongest along the whole Coast, and the Negroes, in particular the Saboese around Moure, consider them also a safe refuge against the weapons of the English subjects, whilst the Fantyn natives at Cormantyn would not allow us to go because of their annual claim of ships' gifts which have been paid since 1665 in recognition for the help they gave (in that year) to Admiral De Ruyter to liberate that fortress from its unjust usurpation by the English. Concerning the behaviour of the Natives, long experience has taught us that the Negroes are by nature slavish, and that they want nothing but to submit themselves to a mighty yoke and to serve only those who have the power to put loads on their backs and spurs into their sides. Up to now it seems that they consider the esteem and power of the Noble Company greater than that of the R.A.C., because they always find that the Coast is being well provided with good merchandise every time we have the good fortune of the arrival of the Company's ships and cruisers, . . . whilst the arrival of English ships is much more irregular; their Company sends no or hardly any ships, and for a long time it has not sent any new servants or military men; the English now find themselves compelled to trade with all sorts of ships in order to make it possible for their own men to subsist. Although we have not yet given any sign of abandoning any—let alone so many of our forts—the English are nevertheless watching us . . . Three soldiers without a proper commander would not instill much fear in the Natives, and from our own experience we know only too well how these people have mastered the art of handling firearms; they would by no means be afraid of the empty barrels of the mounted cannons, and these bloodthirsty, cruel and unbridled creatures, once they know that they are stronger, would not hesitate to denude such fortresses of their tradegoods and other effects. It should also be noted, that due to their long experience in trade, the Negroes are very well aware that they can buy the goods much more cheaply on board of the ships than in the forts, and knowing very well where lies their own interest and that of some of the Europeans, they go with their canoes far out into the sea, disregarding the dangers, in order to trade on board of passing or anchored ships whenever they see the least profit in it. They would see nothing with greater pleasure than that the Coast were deprived of all its fortresses. It is no use to contradict that at least 50 times as many English ships as ships of our Company cruise along this Coast, but in fact the Dutch Company is the only one which distracts them a little from the booty; and although they dare not anchor within the reach of the guns of our fortresses, the Natives subject to our fortresses do not hesitate to sail to those (English) ships whilst our servants are looking on. But at least they do know that if they are caught they have to give up all they bought in this manner to the Noble Company. But everybody knows, and it has also been shown on many occasions, like in the case of the sugar, indigo and cotton plantations, that the jurisdiction of the Company does not reach beyond the area covered by its cannons . . .

3. Imperial Wars Challenge Colonial Subjects, 1738–1757

Dispatches of Spanish Officials in Florida

Señor

All the Negroes fugitives from the English plantations, obedient and loyal Slaves of Your Majesty, state that Your Majesty gave us the Royal Charity of ordering that they give us our liberty for our having come to their region: to be Christians and follow the True Religion in which We are Saved; and Disobeying so high and sacred an Order, they have kept us as Slaves for many years, experiencing many miseries and hungers. In Slavery: and obeying the Royal mandates of Your Majesty: the current Governor Don Manuel de Montiano put us in Liberty, of which we give Your Majesty many thanks and gratitudes: because of this Royal Charity the Governor has offered us and assured us that we can form a place called Gracia Real where we can Serve God and Your Majesty Cultivating the land so that there will be fruits in this region. And we promise Your Majesty that we will Always be the Most cruel enemies of the English: And that we will Risk our Lives in Service to Your Majesty until the last drop of Blood is shed to defend the Great Crown of Spain and our Holy faith And thus Your Majesty may Order us wherever may be to Serve as We are All Your loyal Slaves All our Lives And we Forever Pray to our Lord to Keep Your Majesty and all the Royal Family the many years that we the poor need, San Agustin Florida, June 10, 1738

Señor

With the motive of having appeared before me the black Slaves that in distinct times had come as fugitives from San Jorge and other English Populations asking me to place them in liberty in virtue of Royal Orders that Your Majesty had sent for this

Sources: I. A. Wright, "Dispatches of Spanish Officials Bearing on the Free Negro Settlement of Gracia Real de Santa Teresa de Mose, Florida," *Journal of Negro History*, 1924, 9(2): 175–177. Translated for this volume by Okezi Otovo; Narrative of Jemima Howe, in Francis Chase, ed., *Gathered Sketches from the Early History of New Hampshire and Vermont* (Claremont, NH: Tracy, Kenney & Co., 1856; reprinted Somersworth, NH: New Hampshire Publishing Company, 1970), pp. 75–81, 84–88; Thomas B. Atkins, ed., *Selections from the Public Documents of the Province of Nova Scotia* (Halifax, NS: Charles Arnand, 1869), pp. 267–269, 301.

purpose, I inquired of and examined various Royal Documents in which Your Majesty piously favored all who came to profess the Catholic Religion; and having created acts to precede with the due Justification, I put them in liberty, published in an Edict that those who from here forward come from those populations for that end, be put in liberty, which is expressed in a Royal Order of October 29 of 1733. From here, Your Majesty informed on May 31, 1733, and stipulated that they go to live in a territory called Mose, a half a league or so to the north of this town, and form a Pueblo there.

The motive for which I was required to publish Your Majesty's Royal decision in an Edict was the immediacy with which we had been preparing to go to expel the intrusive English in Your Majesty's dominions and to make their Slaves favorable and pleasant such that they would join our Arms; and that assured of their liberty they would determine to come to receive the Royal Pardon and embrace the Catholic Religion, and that the Pueblo in which we are establishing them would grow.

Notified of this Royal grace, the blacks seek by all possible methods to escape, and 23 persons, men, women, and children did that from Puerto Real and that came to this city on November 21 of last year. And I protected them and helped them in the Royal name of Your Majesty sending them to live in Mose, it seemed convenient to the service of God and Your Majesty to have them separated so that they could occupy themselves in farming and augment the Pueblo. As so that they would become accustomed to the mysteries of our Holy faith living alone, to that purpose the Bishop and I have communicated and agreed to give them Don Joseph de Leon so that he may instruct them in the doctrine, good habits. And his being a person who studied the Ecclesiastical course, of recognized quality, of good characteristics and not having a stipend, as he is not ordained, and voluntarily assists the ministers of the Church. And while Your Majesty resolves whether or not to give them a Parish Priest or not, indicating 250 pesos for his stipend which seems enough to me, and is the same that Your Majesty has assigned for alms to each of the Religious Doctrinaires. Or give what would be the Royal will of Your Majesty, I have ordered he receive the same alms.

Likewise, I bring to the Royal attention of Your Majesty that it has been indispensable and it seemed to me convenient for the first foundation of this population, that is composed of 31 men most married, to help them with some provisions from those in the Royal warehouses until they can bear enough fruits to maintain themselves, and reintegrate them; whose provision I hope will be to the approval of Your Majesty as the Zeal of growing these Provinces has reached me and the greatest glory of the Christian generosity of Your Majesty lovingly deciding that which is most to your Royal will.

God keep the Catholic Royal Person of Your Majesty for the most happy years that Christianity needs. San Agustin, Florida, February 16, 1739.

The Narrative of Jemima Howe

Taken Prisoner by the Indians at Bridgman's Fort, in the Present Town of Vernon, Vt. Communicated to Dr. Belknap by the Rev. Bunker Gay.

1755.

As Messrs. Caleb Howe, Hilkiah Grout, and Benjamin Gaffield, who had been hoeing corn in the meadow, west of the river, were returning home a little before sunset, to a place called Bridgman's Fort, they were fired upon by twelve Indians, who had ambushed their path. Howe was on horseback, with two young lads, his children, behind him. A ball, which broke his thigh, brought him to the ground. His horse ran a few rods, and fell likewise, and both the lads were taken. The Indians, in their savage manner, coming up to Howe, pierced his body with a spear, tore off his scalp, stuck a hatchet in his head, and left him in this forlorn condition. . . . Flushed with the success they had met with here, the savages went directly to Bridgman's Fort. There was no man in it, and only three women and some children, viz., Mrs. Jemima Howe, Mrs. Submit Grout, and Mrs. Eunice Gaffield. Their husbands I need not mention again, and their feelings at this juncture I will not attempt to describe. . . . [I]n rushed a number of hideous Indians, to whom they and their tender offspring became an easy prey, and from whom they had nothing to expect but either an immediate death or a long and doleful captivity. The latter of these, by the favor of Providence, turned out to be the lot of these unhappy women, and their still more unhappy, because more helpless, children. Mrs. Gaffield had but one, Mrs. Grout had three, and Mrs. Howe seven. The eldest of Mrs. Howe's was eleven years old, and the youngest but six months. The two eldest were daughters which she had by her first husband, Mr. William Phipps, who was also slain by the Indians. It was from the mouth of this woman that I lately received the foregoing account. She also gave me, I doubt not, a true, though, to be sure, a very brief and imperfect history of her captivity, which I here insert for your perusal. . . .

The Indians (she says) having plundered and put fire to the fort, we marched, as near as I could judge, a mile and a half into the woods, where we encamped that night. . . . Early the next morning we set off for Canada, and continued our march eight days successively, until we had reached the place where the Indians had left their canoes, about fifteen miles from Crown Point. This was a long and tedious march; but the captives, by divine assistance, were enabled to endure it with less trouble and difficulty than they had reason to expect. From such savage masters, in such indigent circumstances, we could not rationally hope for kinder treatment than we received. Some of us, it is true, had a harder lot than others; and, among the children, I thought my son Squire had the hardest of any. He was then only four years old; and when we stopped to rest our weary limbs, and he sat down on his master's pack, the savage monster would often knock him off, and sometimes, too, with the handle of his hatchet. Several ugly marks, indented in his head by the cruel Indians at that tender age, are still plainly to be seen.

At length we arrived at Crown Point, and took up our quarters there for the space of near a week. In the mean time some of the Indians went to Montreal, and took several of the weary captives along with them, with a view of selling them to the French. They did not succeed, however, in finding a market for any of them. They gave my youngest daughter, Submit Phipps, to the governor, De Vaudreuil, had a drunken frolic, and returned again to Crown Point, with the rest of their prisoners. . . .

Our next movement was to St. Francis, the metropolis, if I may so call it, to which the Indians who led us captive belonged. Soon after our arrival at their wretched capital, a council, consisting of the chief sachem and some principal warriors of the St. Francis tribe, was convened; and after the ceremonies usual on such occasions were over, I was conducted and delivered to an old squaw, whom the Indians told me I must call my mother—my infant still continuing to be the property of its original Indian owners. I was nevertheless permitted to keep it with me a while longer, for the sake of saving them the trouble of looking after it, and of maintaining it with my milk. When the weather began to grow cold, shuddering at the prospect of approaching winter, I acquainted my new mother that I did not think it would be possible for me to endure it if I must spend it with her, and fare as the Indians did. Listening to my repeated and earnest solicitations that I might be disposed of among some of the French inhabitants of Canada, she at length set off with me and my infant, attended by some male Indians, upon a journey to Montreal, in hopes of finding a market for me there. But the attempt proved unsuccessful, and the journey tedious indeed. . . . While we were at Montreal, we went into the house of a certain French gentleman, whose lady, being sent for, and coming into the room where I was, to examine me, seeing I had an infant, exclaimed suddenly in this manner: *"Damn it, I will not buy a woman that has a child to look after."* . . . Somewhere, in the course of this visit to Montreal, my Indian mother was so unfortunate as to catch the small pox, of which distemper she died, soon after our return, which was by water, to St. Francis.

And now come on the season when the Indians began to prepare for a winter's hunt. I was ordered to return my poor child to those of them who still claimed it as their property. This was a severe trial. The babe clung to my bosom with all its might; but I was obliged to pluck it thence, and deliver it, shrieking and screaming, enough to penetrate a heart of stone, into the hands of those unfeeling wretches, whose tender mercies may be termed cruel. It was soon carried off by a hunting party of those Indians to a place called Messiskow, at the lower end of Lake Champlain, whither, in about a month after, it was my fortune to follow them. I had preserved my milk, in hopes of seeing my beloved child again; and here I found it, it is true, but in a condition that afforded me no great satisfaction, it being greatly emaciated and almost starved. I took it in my arms, put its face to mine, and it instantly bit me with such violence that it seemed as if I must have parted with a piece of my cheek. I was permitted to lodge with it that and the two following nights; but every morning that intervened, the Indians, I suppose on purpose to torment me, sent me away to another wigwam, which stood at a little distance, though not so far from the one in which my distressed infant was confined but that I could plainly hear its incessant cries and heart-rending lamentations. In this deplorable condition I was obliged to take my leave of it. . . .

When the winter broke up, we removed to St. John's; and through the ensuing summer our principal residence was at no great distance from the fort at that place. In the mean time, however, my sister's husband, having been out with a scouting party to some of the English settlements, had a drunken frolic at the fort when he returned. . . . he laid hold of me, and hurried me to the fort, and, for a trifling consideration, sold me to a French gentleman whose name was Saccappee. . . . I had been with the Indians a year lacking fourteen days; and if not for my sister, yet for me 'twas a lucky circumstance indeed which thus at last, in an unexpected moment, snatched me out of their cruel hands, and placed me beyond the reach of their insolent power. . . .

My service in the family to which I was now advanced was perfect freedom in comparison of what it had been among the barbarous Indians. My new master and mistress were both as kind and generous towards me as I could any ways expect. . . . I had received intelligence from my daughter Mary, the purport of which was, that there was a prospect of her being shortly married to a young Indian of the tribe of

St. Francis, with which tribe she had continued from the beginning of her captivity. These were heavy tidings, and added greatly to the poignancy of my other afflictions. However, not long after I had heard this melancholy news, an opportunity presented of acquainting that humane and generous gentleman, the commander-in-chief, and my illustrious benefactor, with this affair also, who, in compassion for my sufferings, and to mitigate my sorrows, issued his orders in good time, and had my daughter taken away from the Indians, and conveyed to the same nunnery where her sister was then lodged, with his express injunction that they should both of them together be well looked after and carefully educated, as his adopted children. In this school of superstition and bigotry they continued while the war in those days between France and Great Britain lasted; at the conclusion of which war the governor went home to France, took my oldest daughter along with him, and married her to a French gentleman, whose name is Cron Louis. He was at Boston with the fleet under Count d'Estaing (1778) as one of his clerks. My other daughter still continuing in the nunnery, a considerable time had elapsed after my return from captivity, when I made a journey to Canada, resolving to use my best endeavors not to return without her. I arrived just in time to prevent her being sent to France. She was to have gone in the next vessel that sailed for that place; and I found it extremely difficult to prevail with her to quit the nunnery and go home with me; yea, she absolutely refused; and all the persuasions and arguments I could use with her were to no effect until after I had been to the governor and obtained a letter from him to the superintendent of the nuns, in which he threatened, if my daughter should not be immediately delivered into my hands, or could not be prevailed with to submit to my maternal authority, that he would send a band of soldiers to assist me in bringing her away. Upon hearing this, she made no further resistance; but so extremely bigoted was she to the customs and religion of the place, that, after all, she left it with the greatest reluctance and the most bitter lamentations, which she continued as we passed the streets, and wholly refused to be comforted.

The Ordeal of the Acadians

Governor Lawrence to Col. Monckton.

HALIFAX, 31 July, 1755.

* * * The Deputies of the French inhabitants of the districts of Annapolis, Mines and Piziquid, have been called before the Council, and have refused to take the oath of allegiance to His Majesty, and have also declared this to be the sentiments of the whole people, whereupon the Council advised and it is accordingly determined that they shall be removed out of the Country as soon as possible. . . .

In the mean time, it will be necessary to keep this measure as secret as possible, as well to prevent their attempting to escape, as to carry off their cattle &c.; and the better to effect this you will endeavour to fall upon some stratagem to get the men, both young and old (especially the heads of families) into your power and detain them till the transports shall arrive, so as that they may be ready to be shipped off; for when this is done it is not much to be feared that the women and children will attempt to go away and carry off the cattle. But least they should, it will not only be very proper to secure all their Shallops, Boats, Canoes and every other vessel you can lay your hands upon; But also to send out parties to all suspected roads and places from time to time, that they may be thereby intercepted. As their whole stock of Cattle and Corn is forfeited to the Crown by their rebellion, and must be secured & apply'd towards a reimbursement of the expense the government will be at in transporting them out of the Country, care must be had that nobody make any bargain for purchasing them under any colour or pretence whatever; if they do the sale will be void, for the inhabitants have now (since the order in Council) no property in them, nor will they be allowed to carry away the least thing but their ready money and household furniture.

The officers commanding the Fort at Piziquid and the Garrison of Annapolis Royal have nearly the same orders in relation to the interior Inhabitants. But I am informed those will fall upon ways and means in spite of all our Vigilance to send off their Cattle to the Island of St. John & Louisbourg (which is now in a starving condition) by the way of Tatmagouche. I would therefore, have you without loss of time, send thither a pretty strong detachment to beat up that quarter and to prevent them. You cannot want a guide for conducting the party, as there is not a Frenchman at Chignecto but must perfectly know the road. . . .

I would have you give orders to the Detachment you send to Tatmagouche, to demolish all the Houses &c. they find there, together with all the Shallops, Boats, Canoes or Vessels of any kind which may be lying ready for carrying off the inhabitants & their Cattle, & by this means the pernicious intercourse and intelligence between St. Johns Island & Louisbourg and the inhabitants of the interior part of the Country, will in a great measure be prevented.

Extract from Letter Board of Trade to Governor Lawrence, dated March 10, 1757.

We are extremely sorry to find, that notwithstanding the great expence which the public has been at in removing the French inhabitants, there should yet be enough of them remaining to molest and disturb the Settlements, and interrupt and obstruct our partys passing from one place to another; It is certainly very much to be wished, that they could be entirely driven out of the Peninsula, because untill that is done, it will be in their power, by the knowledge they have of the country, however small their numbers, to distress and harrass the out-settlements, and even his Majesty's Troops so as greatly to obstruct the establishment of the Colony; As to the Conduct of the Southern Colonys in permitting those who were removed to coast along from one Province to another in order that they might get back to Nova Scotia, nothing can have been more absurd and blameable, and had not the Governors of New York and Massachusetts Bay prudently stopped them, there is no attempt however desperate and cruel which might not have been expected from Persons exasperated as they must have been by the treatment they had met with.

We entirely agree in Opinion with you that in the present situation of things, and vexed and harrassed as the Province is by the Hostilities of the French and Indians, it will be in vain to attempt to induce hardy and industrious People to leave Possessions, which perhaps they may enjoy in peace in other Colonies, to come and settle in a Country where they must be exposed to every distress and calamity which the most inveterate enemy living in the Country, and knowing every Pass and Corner of it, can subject them to; and therefore we do not desire, nor mean to press the measure upon you further than the circumstances of the province & of the times will admit of it.

4. Spain Reasserts Control over Colonial Affairs, 1768, 1770

Imposing a "Purity of Blood" Requirement on Lawyers in Lima, 1768

Royal Order on the Proposal for the Statute of Legitimacy and Purity of Blood for Entrance into High Schools and Graduation from the Universities to Receive the Degree of Law

Madrid, 14 of July 1768

The King, Viceroy, President and Judges of the High Court of the City of Lima. In the letter dated November 8 of the previous year, you, my Viceroy, informed me of the pernicious consequences that occur due to the multitude of lawyers of obscure birth and bad customs that exist in abundance in this Kingdom that prejudice the Republic and good governance. They have suffocated and depressed the most honest lawyers which are very few in comparison of the others. You expressed that this disorder comes from the facility with which the high schools admit these subjects without the least objection. Thus given scholarships, they are given the degrees of licentiate and lawyer in the Universities without contradiction and holding those degrees they are admitted to the number of lawyers in the High Court because they consider the contrary wrong in such circumstances: That desiring to remedy this damage at its root so harmful to the public and shameful to those who are not stained with the ugly blemish of a vile birth of zambos, mulattos, and other worse castes with whom the most mediocre men are embarrassed to mix and associate. You considered it very important that I prohibit as a general point and with the most severe penalty that any subject is received into the high schools without first determining his legitimacy and purity of blood, principally in this capital where the three schools that exist are Royal schools and one of which is a superior school. And this same test is repeated in the Universities for admittance to the degrees and in the courtrooms of the High Courts. Therefore although there are constitutions, ordinances, and laws in all these bodies that carefully point this out, mitigation and abuses have became nonetheless so common, that one could call it custom. It is necessary to return things to their original state. All my Royal authority is sent with force of law to observe these laudable and premeditated statutes. And seen in my Council of the Indies, with that which my fiscal has told me, I have resolved to observe this punctually. As will you, my Viceroy, and this High Court each in your respective parts, observe the constitutions, ordinances or statutes that have been formed with legitimate authority for the governing of the three schools in this capital, the Universities of this Kingdom and for exercising the profession of law and that if there are not any in each or any one of these bodies, do not make alterations neither with the subjects that have already been admitted. Therefore it is my Royal purpose that is understood from here forward, and likewise neither you, my current Viceroy nor your successors, this High

Sources: Richard Konetzke. *Colección de Documentos para la Historia de la Formación Social de Hispanoamérica, 1493–1810.* Volumen III, Primer Tomo (1691–1779). (Madrid: Consejo Superior de Investigaciones Científicos, 1962), pp. 340–341, 364–368. Translated for this volume by Okezi Otovo.

Court, nor any other person will intrude with any pretext to disturb the observance of the legitimately approved statutes. And given to not have found the statutes of the three schools of this capital that you cited in your letter in the offices of my aforementioned Council, I have resolved that you, my Viceroy, will collect and send a model or copy of those of each one.

Promoting Spanish over the Indigenous Languages in America, 1770

Royal Order that in the Kingdoms of the Indies the Use of Different Languages Be Eradicated for the Sole Use of Spanish

Aranjuez, May 10, 1770.

The King. For what the most Reverend Archbishop of Mexico represented to me in a letter of June 25 of the last year, that ever since the Catholic faith has been propagated in the vast kingdoms of America, all my effort and that of the Kings, my glorious predecessors, and my Council of the Indies has been to publish laws and send Royal ordinances to the Viceroys and diocesan prelates to instruct the Indians in the dogmas of our religion in Spanish. And that they are taught to read and write in this language and that they should extend it and make it the sole and universal language in those same dominions, being the language of the monarchs and conquistadors. And to facilitate the administration and spiritual doctrine of the natives and that they may be understood by their superiors, and love the conquering nation, eliminate idolatry, civilize themselves for trade and commerce. And that with much diversity of languages, men would not confuse themselves like in the Tower of Babel. To this end, all the hierarchies have been ordered many times to establish schools in Spanish in all the pueblos, and that the bishops and parish priests watch over their observance. That these holy, just and repeated Royal resolutions and decrees have not been effective and it seems that every day they lose more spirit. Given that more than two and a half centuries have passed and several and various languages are still maintained in the most discovered and civilized [regions] such as Mexico and Puebla where the Indians are closed, refusing to learn Spanish and to send their children to school, and even in the areas closest to the capital of Mexico, within two leagues in one parish there are Mexica and Otomi pueblos, this can be verified in other places as well, not because the natives do not understand Spanish but because they do not want to speak it. And they never speak Spanish to the priest or their vicars and the same happens with the municipal administrators and justices, using the service of the interpreter. That the root of this problem is the meticulous provision of priests secured of native languages. And as their parish priests and ministers whom they always see and deal with speak their language and preach and explain the doctrine in it, little or nothing has advanced nor will advance if the remedy is not applied because the parish priests and ministers display every day more facility in the languages in frequent communication with the natives, and there is no one promoting Spanish in the pueblos. . . . That it is true that the shepherd should understand the voice of his sheep, and for this rule some have come to believe that the strongest obligation is that the parish priests know the language of each pueblo of America; but this reason is not convincing, because the bishops are the first ministers that have to visit all the pueblos and cure all the sicknesses of their sheep, they do not understand nor could understand all the different languages. And neither my predecessors nor I ever thought to place those who do know with preference because no use could come of it and it causes many problems. If it were that only Mexica was spoken in one diocese, it would be natural and more urgent to provide parish priests with this language. But, in addition to that, there are in the same archbishopric other very distinct ones such as Otomi, Huastec, Mazahuu, Tepehua and Totonaco, and in each diocese many other different ones. In Puebla, in addition to those mentioned, there are Chocho, Mixtec, Tlapaneco, Olmec, two types of Totonaco and in Oaxaca, Tarasco and Zapotec. The result is a disorder of which only with experience can one understand, seeing pueblos very near to each other and each one maintains its own language as if they were leagues apart. . . . That the priest who is Castilian and knows no other language, endeavors with diligence to extend his language, charges and specifies that his parishioners speak in it, promotes schools in Spanish. On the contrary, he who knows another language, always speaks in it, looks upon Spanish with little appreciation, and teaches the doctrine in that language and many times makes errors because it is very difficult if not nearly impossible to explain the dogmas of our holy Catholic faith well in another language, as the Holy Fathers and theologians have dealt with this many times, especially to consolidate and purify the expressions in the mysteries of the Incarnation and Eucharist. By not attempting to eradicate the other languages, it occurs that a priest with lower merit, of low birth and perhaps poor customs, achieves a parish because he knows a language when it should be the reward of a more decorated priest. That young people, distinguished in birth and ability, are educated in the schools of Mexico, Puebla and other capitals and it is a difficult thing that after tiring themselves in the study of high subjects, they see priests of language promoted to parishes who at most have studied one moral lesson. And that it is difficult work and effort for Spaniards to learn another language when they have not been raised among natives. Therefore, it was not his report, nor could it be, to leave the pueblos without ministers of language for now, but rather that the greatest care is taken so that parish priests do not lose for only knowing Spanish. . . . And finally with that which was expressed, in few years all my Royal ministers can understand the natives without the need for interpreters that easily corrupt. The bishops will be equally understood in all the pueblos of their diocese. The Indians will not be left so vulnerable to being cheated in their deals, commerce, and lawsuits. The parish priests will be more uniform. The schoolboys of so many respectful communities of those dominions will see the reward of their efforts. And with emulation the progress will increase and all the territory will be governed more easily. . . . Therefore, for the present I order my Viceroys of Peru, New Spain and the New Kingdom of Granada, the Presidents, Courts, Governors and other ministers, judges and justices of those same districts and of the Philippine Islands and other adjacent places; I request and charge the most Reverend Archbishops, Reverend Bishops, and Town Councils, their stewards in vacant seats in their churches, and general vicars, the local prelates of the Religions and whatever other ecclesiastical judges of those my dominions, that each one in his respective part, guard, comply and execute and make others guard, comply, and punctually and effectively execute my Royal resolution. Providing that from now they observe and put the methods that were expressed and proposed by the aforementioned most Reverend Archbishop of Mexico in practice, so that finally the extinction of the different languages used in those same dominions will be accomplished, and only Spanish will be spoken, as ordered by repeated laws, Royal documents and orders issued on that topic, and be warned that in those places where this is inconvenient, you must inform me with justification, with the goal that in your intelligence you comply to that which is my Royal wish, as this is my will.

5. Joseph Sewall Praises God for English Success, 1762

When *Austria* and *France* were united with *Russia* and *Sweden* against the King of PRUSSIA, and the Armies under him; there was a strong Combination against the *Protestant* Interest: But behold the Lord who cuts off the Spirit of Princes, and takes away their Breath as He pleaseth, sets up another *Head* over that vast Empire, who favours our Cause. A seasonable Interposition of divine Providence! And we are informed, that *Sweden* also is brought to Terms of Reconciliation. However, the Alliance appeared formidable, when the Wealth and Forces of *Spain* were added to the Powers of *Austria* and *France*, those great Supporters of *Antichrist*. Accordingly, the Day after War was proclaimed with *Spain*, our honoured Rulers, being in General Court assembled, met with us in the House of God, *April* 15, last, to seek Direction and Help from God in this important Conjuncture. And now in less than half a Year, the *Great and General Court* again assemble with God's People in the House of Prayer, to unite with us, and lead in Songs of Praise to the God of Victory for signal Successes lately granted against *France* and *Spain*.

We have an authentick Account, that the accomplished General Prince FERDINAND, tho' much inferior in Numbers, yet by a superior Reach of military Conduct and Skill, surprised and encompass'd the *French* Army, and put them to flight; and such of them as boldly opposed their Pursuit, tho' the Flower of the *French* Infantry, were blasted, and in a great Measure cut to Pieces, or made Prisoners: Our Joy is the greater in that the valiant Lord GRANBY, who commanded the English Troops had a great Share in the Victory. We praise the Lord, the God of Salvation, Exod. 15. 3, *The Lord is a Man of War: The Lord is his Name.* Our Joy is much increased by the great and good News of the Conquest of the HAVANNAH, a rich City in *Spanish America*, very strongly fortified, and resolutely defended by numerous Forces. A City of *great Importance*, it being *the Key* which opens a Communication between *Old and New Spain*, where, it is said, the Enemy lay up vast Treasures from *Mexico* and *Peru*, till *they* have a convenient Opportunity for transportation. Accordingly, we have an Account of great Sums of Money already found, from which our Forces, under the General Lord ALBERMARLE, and Admiral POCOCKE, we hope will reap a rich Reward of their great Toils and Valour. By this Conquest, our Enemies are also greatly weakened as to their *Naval Force*, Nine Ships of the Line being taken, others sunk to defend the Harbour, others on the Stocks, or lately launched; together with great naval and other military Stores.

Source: Joseph Sewall, *A sermon preached at the Thursday-lecture in Boston, September 16, 1762: Before the Great and General Court of the Province of the Massachusetts-Bay, in New-England. On the joyful news of the reduction of the Havannah.* (Boston, New-England: Printed by John Draper, printer to His Excellency the governor, and the Honourable His Majesty's Council; and by Edes and Gill, printers to the Honourable House of Representatives, 1762), pp. 27–32.

Let us then sacrifice Praise to the GOD of Armies, who has led our victorious Troops into this strong City, of which our Enemies were ready to boast, as if it was invincible. The Royal Psalmist inquired, *Who will bring me into the strong City; who will lead me into Edom? Wilt not Thou, O God?** Yes, surely. *This is the Lord's Doing, it is marvellous in our Eyes. Who is like unto Thee, O Lord, fearful in Praises, doing Wonders. Thy right Hand, O Lord, is become Glorious in Power; Thy right Hand, O Lord, hath dashed in Pieces the Enemy.*

May we be directed to make a wise Improvement of such remarkable Appearances of God for us! May the Lord preserve us from Pride, and all carnal Confidence in an Arm of Flesh! Let us humble ourselves under the mighty Hand of God, and with deep Abasement acknowledge our own Sinfulness and great Unworthiness, saying, *Not unto us, O Lord, not unto us; but unto thy Name give Glory.*† While we render due *civil Praise* to the brave Commanders and Soldiers, whom God has made Instruments in this glorious Work, let our *religious Praises* ascend to GOD by JESUS CHRIST, our great High-Priest. O may we yield to him, the God of Salvation, not only the Fruit of our Lips; but the Love of our Hearts, and the Obedience of our Lives. O may his Goodness lead us to Repentance, and we not be suffered to abuse the Riches of it, and so to treasure up Wrath. May we by his Spirit be formed as a peculiar People to shew forth his Praise. Thus we may hope further to see the Good of His Chosen, to rejoice with the Gladness of his Nation, and to glory with his Inheritance.

6. Colonial Subjects Resist Reform, 1765, 1781

British Colonists Protest the Stamp Act in Nevis, 1765

Extract of a Letter from Philadelphia, Nov. 26

In my last I informed you Capt. Gregory was below from St. Kitts. I believe you will rejoice to see the spirit of liberty arising in the West-Indies, which you have an account of in the following letter from St. Kitts. Besides which I can with certainty inform you, that at Nevis, liberty reigns, where they also burnt the horrible stamps, but they having but few of them, and thinking it would not make a fire large enough, they seized a man of war's boat, hauled her up, put the stamps in her, and set the whole on fire. . . .

British Colonists Respond to the Stamp Act in Jamaica, 1765

Extract of a letter from Jamaica, Octob. 23. 1765.

Dr. Howell, collector of the stamp-duty, is arrived.—Great are the murmurings against the stamp-law, but we dare not proceed to such violences as the people of Boston and Virginia.

*Psalm 108. 10, 11.

†Psalm 115. 1.

Sources: *The Boston Gazette and Country Journal*, November 11, 1765; *The Boston Evening Post*, December 2, 1765, December 9, 1765; Jose Antonio de Areche, "All Must Die [excerpts only]," in *The Peru Reader: History, Culture, Politics* [ed. by Starn et al.], pp. 157–161. Copyright © 1995, Duke University Press. All rights reserved. Used by permission of the publisher.

The Benignity which appears in the whole Behaviour of our new Governor, endears him to the People of this Colony: His ordering the hostile preparations at the Fort, to be entirely stopt, and, above all, his declaring he had nothing to do with the Stamps, has rid the People of those Fears which Proceedings anterior to his Arrival, had justly suggested to them. The Sons of Liberty, last Friday gave him the most expressive Marks of their Joy, by their meeting, in great Numbers, in the Fields, where they erected Pyramids and Inscriptions to his Honour, and one of the grandest Bonfires ever exhibited in this City. They had previously sent him a congratulatory Address on his Arrival, which being dictated by the most sincere Gratitude, was not the less pathetic for being destitute of the Pageantry, which often attends those of more regular Bodies. His Excellency received it with the greatest Politeness, and made a complaisant Answer.

These Sons of Liberty, ever vigilant for their Country's Good, being again alarmed at a second Importation of Stamps in the Minerva, Capt. Tillet, were indefatigable in their Endeavours to have them lodged with the First, in the City-Hall. A respectful Application was made to the Mayor and Corporation, who worthily exerting themselves, they were accordingly landed on Saturday Morning last, and deposited there. The Magistrates cannot be too much praised for their noble Endeavours to preserve Peace, and quiet the Minds of the People, while they can do it without making any Sacrifice of our Liberties to Despotism.

Tuesday last arrived here the Ship Hope, Capt. Christian Jacobson, from London, —*without Stamps*. He is the first Commander who, to our Knowledge, has had the Honour of refusing to bring those instruments of Oppression into the Country.

The English Papers (which we have received by Capt. Jacobson) contain no very material Intelligence—We find many virulent Aspersions against the colonies in them, as cruel as unjust.—However, we are not without some worthy Advocates in England, who being armed with Truth and Justice, we hope will confound the wicked designs of our Adversaries.

British Colonists Protest the Stamp Act in Portsmouth, 1765

Portsmouth.

Nov. 4. Friday last being the first of November, the Day on which the fatal and never-to-be-forgotten Stamp-Act *was intended* to take Place, the Morning began with tolling all the Bells in this Town, and at Newcastle, Greenland, Kittery, &c. the Colours on board the Shipping in the Harbour were hoisted half mast, and Notice given to the Friends of *Liberty*, to attend her Funeral, which was to be at 3 o'Clock P. M. a Coffin having been previously prepared and neatly ornamented, on the Lid of which was wrote LIBERTY, aged 145. STAMP'D, computing from the Æra of our Forefathers landing at Plymouth from England,—and having with the greatest Difficulty procured a *Stamp-Act*, re-printed at Boston, (no Original having ever been seen in this Province) the same was carried to the Grave by a Person who preceeded the Corps.—The Procession began from the Statehouse, attended by a great Concourse of People of all ranks, with 2 unbrac'd Drums, and after marching through the principal Streets, it passed the Parade, on which Minute Guns were fired, and continued till the Corps arrived at the Place of Interment, which was about half a Mile out of Town, when after much Sorrow express'd for our *expired Liberty*, a Funeral *Oration* was pronounced greatly in favor of the Deceas'd, which was hardly ended before the Corps was taken up, it having been perceived that some Remains of Life were left, at which the Inscription was immediately altered, and then appeared to be *Liberty Revived*—and the *Stamp Act* was thrown into the Grave and buried,—at which the Bells immediately altered their melancholy to a more joyful Sound, and the greatest Pleasure and Satisfaction were diffused into every Countenance. The whole was conducted with the utmost Decency, and in the Evening, a Number of Gentlemen assembled at the King's Arms Tavern, where several Healths adapted to the Occasion, were drank, such as *LIBERTY, PROPERTY,* &c. &c.

The stamp'd Papers sent for the Use of this Province, are lodged in the Fort at Newcastle, where they are to remain as a dead inactive Lump of Matter, till they are sent back to their native Country.

The execution of Túpac Amaru in Cuzco, 1781

I must and do condemn José G. Túpac Amaru to be taken out to the main public square of this city, dragged out to the place of execution, where he shall witness the execution of the sentences imposed on his wife, Micaela Bastidas; his two sons, Hipólito and Fernando Túpac Amaru; his uncle, Francisco Túpac Amaru; and his brother-in-law, Antonio Bastidas, as well as some of the principal captains and aides in his iniquitous and perverse intent or project, all of whom must die the same day.

And once these sentences have been carried out, the executioner will cut out his tongue, and he will then be tied or bound by strong cords on each one of his arms and feet in such a way that each rope can be easily tied or fastened to others hanging from the saddle straps of four horses so that, in this position, each one of these horses, facing opposite corners of the square, will pull toward his own direction; and let the horses be urged or jolted into motion at the same time so that his body be divided into as many parts and then, once it is done, the parts should be carried to the hill or high ground known as "Picchu," which is where he came to intimidate, lay siege to, and demand the surrender of this city; and let there be lit a fire which shall be prepared in advance and then let ashes be thrown into the air and a stone tablet placed there detailing his main crimes and the manner of his death as the only record and statement of his loathsome action.

His head will be sent to the town of Tinta where, after having been three days on the gallows, it shall be placed on a stake at the most public entrance to the town; one of his arms will go to the town of Tungasuca, where he was chief, where it will be treated in like manner, and the other in the capital of the province of Carabaya; one of the legs shall likewise be sent for the same kind of demonstration to the town of Libitaca in the province of Chumbivilcas, while the remaining one shall go to Santa Rosa in the province of Lampa along with an affidavit and order to the respective chief magistrates, or territorial judges, that this sentence be proclaimed publicly with the greatest solemnity as soon as it arrives in their hands, and on the same day every year thereafter; and they will give notice in writing of this to their superiors in government who are familiar with the said territories. . . .

To this same end, it is prohibited that the Indians wear heathen clothes, especially those who belong to the nobility, since it only serves to symbolize those worn by their Inca ancestors, reminding them of memories which serve no other end than to increase their hatred toward the dominant nation; not to mention that their appearance is ridiculous and very little in accordance with the purity of our relics, since they place in different parts images of the sun, which was their primary deity; and this prohibition is to be extended to all the provinces of this southern America, in order to completely eliminate such clothing, especially those items which represent the bestialities of their heathen kings through emblems such as the *unco*, which is a kind of vest; *yacollas*, which are very rich blankets or shawls of black velvet or taffeta; the *mascapaycha*, which is a circle in the shape of a crown from which they hang a certain emblem of ancient nobility signified by a tuft or tassel of red-colored alpaca wool, as well as many other things of this kind and symbolism. All of this shall be proclaimed in writing in each province, that they dispose of or surrender to the magistrates whatever clothing of this kind exists in the province, as well as all the paintings or likenesses of their Incas which are extremely abundant in the houses of the Indians who consider themselves to be nobles and who use them to prove their claim or boast of their lineage.

These latter shall be erased without fail since they do not merit the dignity of being painted in such places, and with the same end in mind there shall also be erased, so that no sign remains, any portraits that might be found on walls or other solid objects; in churches, monasteries, hospitals, holy places or private homes . . . and in their place it would be best to replace such adornments with images of the king and our other Catholic sovereigns should that be necessary.

Also, the ministers and chief magistrates should ensure that in no town of their respective provinces be performed plays or other public functions of the kind that the Indians are accustomed to put on to commemorate their former Incas. . . . In like manner shall be prohibited and confiscated the trumpets or bugles that the Indians use for their ceremonies and which they call *pututos*, being seashells with a strange and mournful sound that celebrate the mourning and pitiful memorial they make for their antiquity; and there shall also be prohibited the custom of using or wearing black clothing as a sign of mourning, a custom that drags on in some provinces in memory of their deceased monarchs and also of the day or time of the conquest which they consider disastrous and we consider fortunate since it brought them into the company of the Catholic Church and the very loving and gentle domination of our kings.

With the same goal it is absolutely forbidden that the Indians sign themselves as "Incas," since it is a title that anyone can assume but which makes a lasting impression on those of their class; and it is ordered, as is required of all those who have genealogical trees or documents that prove in some way their descent, that they produce them or send them certified and without cost by mail to the respective secretaries of both viceroyalties. . . .

And so that these Indians renounce the hatred that they have conceived against the Spaniards, and that they adhere to the dress which the laws indicate, adopting our Spanish customs and speaking Castilian, we shall introduce more vigorously than we have done up to now the use of schools, imposing the most rigorous and fair penalties on those who do not attend once enough time has passed for them to have learned the language . . . and there will be established a term of four years for the people to speak fluently or at least be able to explain themselves in Castilian, the bishops and chief magistrates being required to report on all this to their respective superior governing body, and it being left up to the sovereign discretion of His Majesty to reward and honor those towns whose inhabitants have rendered, under the present circumstances, their due loyalty and faithfulness.

Finally, the manufacture of cannons of all kinds shall be prohibited under the penalty that any noble found manufacturing such items will be sentenced to ten years of prison in one of the presidios in Africa and any commoner will receive two hundred lashes as well as the same penalty for the same time period; reserving for a future time a similar resolution with regards to the manufacture of powder. . . . Thus have I visualized, ordered, and signed: this is my final judgment. José Antonio de Areche.

7. Lady Anne Barnard Praises the Strategic Value of the Cape, 1797

I must therefore conclude by saying that I hope it will be found possible to keep the Cape; that barren and ill-cultivated as it now is, it strikes both Mr. Barnard and me to have great powers in itself to become one of the finest countries in the world. How far it will be the wisdom of England to encourage it to become so is for England's Sovereign and his Ministers to determine. Whether it will be more for England's advantage, and that of our possessions in India, to keep it subordinate, so that it may never interfere, while it aids and assists the to-and-fro constantly going on between England and India, is for you to determine, and you only. The choice climate and fertile soil here might certainly make it a second India, but whether in that point of view Ceylon might not be a better *pis aller*, supposing anything to go wrong with us in the East, is a point I have heard questioned. If the world was at peace, and was I a monarch, I should like to portion a younger son with the Cape, supposing him little, for a ten years' minority would produce a vast difference in this country, if it was as much encouraged as it has been repressed. Yet it is possible (if we keep it) that you may be obliged from policy to adhere to the same selfish considerations which governed the Dutch. The most enlightened of the inhabitants complain of the late *régime*. Their hands were tied up from being possessed of the riches they might so easily have enjoyed from their industry. They tell me there is nothing this place is not equal to, particularly if we can suppose the intercourse between the inner parts of the country and Cape Town rendered more easy. It is certainly a healthy climate.

⊿ *E S S A Y S*

In these essays, J. R. McNeill and Pamela Voekel explore the constraints within which Atlantic empires operated. McNeill shows that a new ecology in the American tropics reshaped imperial warfare. The European tactic of the siege, he argues, failed in environments where yellow fever proved deadly to invading armies. American-born "creoles" and Africans held an advantage under these conditions, which dictated how European empires could fight each other and, ultimately, how American colonists could fight Europeans. Reform accompanied warfare as a strategy of imperial consolidation and control. In the second half of the eighteenth century, imperial officials in

---

Source: W.H. Wilkins, ed., *South Africa a Century Ago: Letters Written from the Cape of Good Hope (1797–1801) by the Lady Anne Barnard* (London: Smith, Elder, & Co., 1901), pp. 143–144.

France, Britain, Spain, and Portugal sought to rationalize systems of taxation, develop and control frontier regions, and diversify colonial economies. They also tried to limit the power of American-born colonial leaders and in some instances attacked what they identified as unfair privileges. The so-called "Bourbon" reforms (after the Bourbon monarchs of Spain and France) even included new policies regulating marriage. Voekel probes a little-studied aspect of those reforms, policing the poor in Mexico City. She sets these reforms in the context of the racial hierarchies of colonial society and the unique setting of Mexico City. Voekel emphasizes the efforts by Mexico City's popular classes to resist the reformers' impositions, while McNeill emphasizes the environmental features that determined the outcome of warfare in the tropics. Together these essays raise important questions about the extent and limits of imperial governance and power, and they offer different sorts of answers.

Constraints on Reform

PAMELA VOEKEL

In the late eighteenth century, the Spanish Crown defined Mexico City's demotic culture as a nemesis to the state's economic aspirations for the colony. The Bourbon bureaucracy engineered unprecedented campaigns to extirpate the vices of the people and to inculcate in them the new virtues of hard work, sobriety, and proper public propriety. The Alcaldes de Barrio, a neighborhood police force established by Viceroy Martin de Mayorga in 1782 to monitor the daily lives of the poor, provided the chief weapon in the campaign against moral turpitude—a campaign reformers regarded as crucial to the success of their efforts to extract more wealth from the city. Although its seventeenth-century Hapsburg predecessor had deferred to powerful corporate interests, especially the Church, the more interventionist Bourbon state attacked the privileges of the nobility, the Church, and the guilds, and attempted to create an unmediated, educative relationship between the state and the new social identity that emerged from that effort: the individual. Traditional historiography has focused on the administrative and economic aspects of the Bourbon reforms. I contend that these reforms involved more than the promulgation of new tax laws, the trimming of corporate privileges, and the rationalization and expansion of the bureaucracy. Reformers—through new institutions like the Alcaldes de Barrio—engaged in radical social engineering to produce a more rational and productive citizen.

The Bourbon State justified its unprecedented interventions into daily life by claiming to act in the interest of "the public," a concept foreign to previous regimes. While in the seventeenth century people sinned against the king by sinning against God, in the late eighteenth century they began to be seen as sinning against the public. Bourbon discourse was threaded through with references to the public good and "sins against the public order." The concept of the public sphere ideally implies neutrality, a place of free cultural exchanges, multiple kaleidoscopic meanings, and a welter of opinions and practices. But in late eighteenth-century Mexico City, the reconstitution of social order under the sign of "the public" involved pitched battles between

Source: Pamela Voekel, "Peeing on the Palace: Bodily Resistance to Bourbon Reforms in Mexico City." *Journal of Historical Sociology* v. 5, no. 2 (June 1992), pp. 183–185, 193–197, 199–202. Reprinted with permission of Blackwell Publishing.

elite and popular culture for both symbolic and literal occupation of city space. The creation of the public was not a neutral process.

In the state's efforts to forge this new generic unity termed "the public" out of the social atomization that its attacks on traditional corporate groups fostered, its hammer fell hardest on those whose conception of public behavior differed from that of reformers, namely the popular classes. But morality and urban renovation campaigns not only sought to transform the poor, they simultaneously provided elites with a means of self and class identity during a time when distinctions based on caste or race had lost their saliency. In particular, the idiom of morality enabled wealthy Mexico City residents to distinguish themselves from the poorer members of the city's burgeoning white population. . . . Thus, morality campaigns were animated by elites' desire to avow their superiority through cultural attitudes about hygiene, alcohol, and public propriety. Their stance would both police the poor and define the social boundaries between them and themselves.

But reform efforts were more than just rhetoric: the new division between high and low culture cut across not only the social formation, but also the topography of the city, and even the body of the individual, as the lower classes became bracketed with the now shameful functions of the lower body. Therefore, although it is important not to over-inflate the competency of reformers or to suggest an elite conspiracy, it is equally short-sighted to ignore the very real power to define social reality wielded by the state. Reformers' unprecedented social intervention can be understood only in light of both the state's economic intentions for the colony and their own perceived need publicly to proclaim their higher social status.

Creating the Public Gaze

Reformist zeal in New Spain reached its apogee under the leadership of King Charles III (1759–1788) and Viceroy Revillagigedo (1789–1794), who sought to extend the many recent reforms in Spain to its overseas empire. Their country's position in the world economy provided the impetus: in the latter half of the eighteenth century, Spain found it increasingly difficult to compete in the world market with the more dynamic economies of France, Holland, and England. In an effort to exploit Spain's colonies as efficiently as its rivals were thought to exploit theirs, Charles III's advisers instituted reforms in industry, taxation, and defense. As part of this campaign, corporate bodies that competed with the state for popular loyalties, such as the church and trade guilds, were stripped of privileges and status while those promoting fidelity to the state, such as the military, were bolstered. The state sought to erase old social loyalties and replace them with its new ordering concept of uniform public behavior regardless of social position.

The project proved daunting in a Mexico City that contained a large number of impoverished residents who understood order and rationality differently. Its 1790 population of 112,926 was twice that of Puebla, the second largest urban area of the colony. While 46 percent of the populace were classified as Spanish and Creole (28 percent were Indian, 19 percent Mestizo, and 7 percent Mulatto), only 4 percent ranked as *gente culta*, that is, employed more than four servants. The remaining *pueblo bajo* consisted of middle class clerks, the lower clergy, merchants, and the *leperos*—approximately 85 percent of the population who were the workers, unemployed, and ragged poor earning low wages in shops and factories. Between the years 1784 and 1787 alone, 40,000 immigrants arrived in the metropolis, largely as a consequence of an agricultural crisis in the neighboring territories.

This wave of urban growth, with its attendant social dislocations, exacerbated the perceived need to monitor and control the poor. Immigrants and the already established poor became the particular objects of the authorities' initiatives to create the new, generic, "public man." In particular, elite discourse was larded with references to the filth of the city and its lower class inhabitants. The untidiness and toilet habits of the poor were constant themes of reformers. Describing the central city in 1790, Francisco Sedaño lamented that "with complete liberty and during all hours of the day, the people throw trash buckets, excrement, and dead dogs and horses into the streets and gutters. In addition, people are seen defecating in the street with complete disregard for the *public gaze*." (italics mine). . . .

The streets of Mexico City became a stage for reformers to display their power to create a clean, ordered, and rational world, a place for them to make a spectacle of themselves. It was a daunting task. The higgledly-piggledly markets and streets had been shockingly promiscuous; food vendors, vagrants, and servants jostled for position with the gente culta, so that, to employ Bakhtin's phrase, decorum and the grotesque "peered into each other's faces." This perceived hodge-podge violated the new social divisions between high and low culture: the inundation of trash and dogs in the Plaza Mayor, wrote one elite observer, "was alarming for those passing by, especially if they were not of the blanket-clad and the naked classes that inhabited that enclosure."

A labyrinthine jumble of shacks and food stands occupied this central plaza, sheltering the men and women who "committed excesses of various types, as it was impossible to exercise vigilance over . . . that disordered and confused space." Criminals were said to elude apprehension by expertly weaving through the tortuous passageways; one married woman concealed herself there for days from the city police and her frantic husband until she decided to summon him to her hideout. If the plaza rendered the poor invisible to the law, alarmed observers noted with even greater disgust the exposed orifices of the "men and women, their clothing pulled up, who urinated and defecated in the plaza without shame or embarrassment." Scandalous, pell-mell, and filthy from the point of view of elites, the plaza had until then been controlled by the popular classes. . . .

In the early 1790s, reformers removed the pulque stalls, the garbage and ordure, and the numerous dogs, cows, and pigs from the central plaza and palace courtyard and relocated the large market to the Volador plaza. Smart cobble stones lined this new square and seventy-four stately crystal street-lamps glowed at night, when the market closed to the public. To police the area, Revillagigedo created the post of Juez de Plaza (plaza judge), who carefully patrolled the new market, ensuring that "nothing happened in the plaza without his notice." Bedizened in uniforms with "old Spanish style" plumed hats, two plaza guards enforced detailed regulations governing the symmetric locations of the stalls, their grouping by type of merchandise sold, and even the fresh paint and numbers that decorated their walls. While the Volador plaza now housed the city's largest market, the Plaza Mayor hosted a monument to elite occupation: in the plaza's center, the Marqués de Branciforte, Revillagigedo's successor, erected a wooden statue of Charles IV surrounded by an elliptical stone balustrade which deterred the undesirable coagulation of crowds; in 1803, Viceroy Iturrigaray replaced the statue with a sturdier bronze version of the original. The protean, motley representations of popular culture that once occupied the center of the Plaza Mayor became redefined as dirty and crude and as the antithesis of the emerging public space.

As reformers expelled the plebe from the public sphere, they also prevented them from entering the spaces designed for the more refined pleasures of the elite. During Revillagigedo's tenure the verdant walkways of the centrally located Alameda were cleaned and entrance denied to the dirty, the unshod, or the scantily-attired. Villarroel had been scandalized by the transgression of elite and popular boundaries that had previously occurred in the small park. Rather than provide tranquility and genteel enjoyment, the park, a distraught Villarroel reported, "served more to anger and bother one because of the lack of political order there; as a rule it fills with the lowest of the plebe, dirty and almost naked, no man of position dares to sit by them, for fear of dirtying oneself with the inundation of fleas." Villarroel hoped the park would be a space for the new public, an orderly cultural island amidst a sea of raucous streets and taverns. As in Paris, where Daniel Roche states that the police regulated popular morals in an attempt to "immobilize the popular classes in time and space," in Mexico City new cultural divisions were literally mapped onto urban geography.

The growing bifurcation of elite and popular culture was also represented at the theater, as reformers strove to replace the lascivious dancing on stage and the raucous laughter, ribaldry, and drunkenness of spectators with sober, specular intensity. Although proceeds went to a public hospital, and comedies and light-hearted works drew enormous, lucrative crowds, elites found these productions "prejudicial to the state." . . . Viceregal edicts established special guards for performances, banned excessive mingling of the sexes, and required all productions to obtain a license from the city. The new license laws, Viceroy Gálvez declared in June 1786, ensured that the public would be "both entertained and taught good habits and customs." The theater reflected the antagonism between elite and popular culture, and, as in the plazas and streets, constraints were imposed upon the behavior of the boisterous lower classes.

Not surprisingly, the new theater regulations constantly rehearsed the dominant themes of reform efforts. The 1786 edict, the first state-sponsored effort to regulate New Spain's theatrical performances, declared that actors be properly attired so as to set an example for viewers; that the theater be cleaned daily; that no satires of public figures be presented; and that the audience refrain from heckling and cajoling the actors, whistling, stomping, shouting, wearing large hats, or mingling with the opposite sex. Women were allowed to leave their section of the theater only twice during the show. Editorialists groused about rowdy performances, believing the theater lost its didactic effect if the plebeian public participated in the spectacle; that is, if they actively contested the meaning of the production. Theater regulations were to create a docile audience who would accept elite rules of public conduct without playing a role in the decolage's creation, who would forfeit their own sense of public propriety and adopt another. The correct stance towards the new public spectacles was to be one of polite distance, not direct participation, a cultural stance corresponding to, or perhaps reflecting, elite distance from the actual physical labor of production.

Reformers expressed unease about the inverisimilitude of theatrical works, fearing it encouraged the transgression of social boundaries. A 1794 edict urged accurate portrayals of social life, rather than Baroque disregard for realism: if real servants removed their hats in the presence of masters, their thespian counterparts were to do the same. More importantly, the rules stipulated that maids should never appear on stage better dressed than their mistresses. The stage, as Father Ramón Fernández del Rincón, the official censor appointed by Revillagigedo, suggested, was to be "an entertaining school of private and public virtues." But, as they did in other parts of the city, the poor continued to act out their own notions of public propriety in the theater, prompting one refined patron to lament that, although significant progress had been made, "in this capital it is necessary to accommodate oneself to the depraved tastes of the plebe." . . .

Reflecting the state's new desire to establish an unmediated relationship with its citizens, the Alcaldes de Barrio fixed clearly numbered, handsome ceramic tiles at a uniform height on all house doors and streets. In the state's attempt to reconstitute social order under the sign of the "public," every individual would now have his proper place with its own number. During the judicial review of Revillagigedo's tenure, his detractors in the City Council, angered at not being consulted about the numbering project, reported that the expensive markers now adorned even "the worst houses in the worst neighborhoods, including Indian hovels." So, numbered and visible, the poor found it increasingly difficulty to elude the public gaze and the state's documentation projects.

The culturally-rich banquet of the street, like that of the plazas, also became increasingly dyspeptic to reformers. Open-air comedies and puppet shows, which provoked raucous laughter from boisterous crowds, and even rope walking, now required a license from the city and permission from the appropriate Alcalde de Barrio; more importantly, no spectacles could be held after dark. The official licenses specified that no pulque be served at events; that no musical instruments be used to convene the public; that actors dress only in the clothing of their own sex; and that the gathering disperse before night-fall. Popular culture, licensed and regulated, began to disappear from the emerging public streets of the city. To ensure that only "rational beings" were visible on the increasingly fashionable avenues of the capital, reformers initiated energetic campaigns to rid the city of cows, dogs, and pigs, with whom the poor were linked by the elite, as references to the "pigsties" in the plaza demonstrate. Unlike the poor, however, animals could not be remade in the image of elites but had to be removed: in one year alone the city exterminated 20,000 dogs and banished all cows to the outskirts of the city. . . .

Peeing on the Palace: Bodily Resistance

If the public streets, plazas, and processions became the battleground between high and low culture, no changes in the city's topography so succinctly symbolized the reformers' desire to make dirt and excrement invisible to the public as the new sewer system, garbage and sewage carts, and public toilets. Official edicts and reports referred obsessively to the toilet habits of the poor as was true also for elite observers who limned the vices of the city and its unenlightened pueblo bajo. Furthermore, as they did in their descriptions of the poor's eating habits, lack of cleanliness, and disregard for public propriety, reformers repeatedly expressed disgust, sheer physical revulsion, upon witnessing the uncultured defecate and urinate in public. . . .

The poor's behavior in public, especially that concerning the body, became systematically redefined as a private matter, and exiled to special spatial enclaves away from public view. A government proclamation issued in 1791 allowed home and tenement owners with access to the new sewer lines three months to build latrines, after which time the Junta de Policia ordered them constructed at the owners' expense. Private efforts in personal homes, however, proved difficult to monitor and the same edict lamented that "despite these measures and the public's interest in their resolution they have not yet been verified."

Public taverns quickly became the focus of efforts to conceal natural bodily functions. A 1793 edict echoed earlier efforts in calling for the construction of separate toilets in the taverns for men and women. Roughly a year later, district magistrates in two districts reported that owners were complying with the order. Ignacio Castera, the dedicated urban planner, understood the relationship between physical and moral order and also fancied himself an architect of human behavior, stating that the "liberty in which in the bars of the city people of all types engage their natural functions is a great scandal, a threat to the public's health, and a bad custom that is against natural and civil order." Castera's notion that public incontinence was a bad habit reflected the hope that the ideal individual would mirror the segmentation of society in a bifurcation of the self: emotional reactions to parades and plays as well as physical processes had to be carefully, and individually, contained and controlled. Thus, toilets in the pulquerías both reflected and contributed to campaigns to train the new urban, public man in proper comportment and to draw cultural class boundaries. Although the success of the new spaces is difficult to gauge, the judges who evaluated Revillagigedo's administration reported that before his renovations of public space "it was as if the entire plaza could have been called a common latrine." . . .

Mexico City's poor, however, continued to embody alternative cultural rules from those of the gente culta and their sense of disgust had to be assiduously cultivated. Rewriting the body's codes, creating in the poor a new threshold of shame and disgust, was another critical, although not clearly articulated or systematically elaborated, component of reform rhetoric. New edicts not only required pulquería owners to construct separate toilets for men and women, but public urination and defecation became punishable with a stint in the stocks, strategically placed in public view outside the new guard-houses of the city. The public gaze would thus be used to impose a new sense of embarrassment and disgust upon the poor, to inscribe the ordering principles of the regime into their very bodies. Towards the end of his rule, Revillagigedo hopefully declared the stocks obsolete, as their employment had succeeded in eliminating "that piggy practice [incontinence] in the city." Presumably, the Viceroy felt that what began as an external constraint, fear of punishment, had become internalized. Toilet habits and sanitation joined sobriety, providence, and cleanliness as part of the package to achieve better control of one's character. Thus, revulsion for the low was diagrammed onto the social body, the landscape of the city, and the anatomy of the individual.

But the popular classes were not passive spectators of the social engineering performed for their supposed benefit. They took their protest right to the doors, and walls—of the viceregal palace, the most visible symbol of Bourbon authority. Perhaps unconsciously recognizing that the Bourbon reforms sought to control their bodies, the pueblo bajo responded with their bodies. Despite the ordinances concerning public lewdness, during Revillagigedo's tenure three armed guards had to be posted around the palace—not to control armed mobs clamoring for revolution, but to prevent the return of the socially repressed: the army of pueblo bajo who daily urinated and defecated against its walls. In late eighteenth-century Mexico City, the compliance of the poor with the judicious enemas of rationality was not total, nor were they completely blinded by the enlightenment.

Yet a new relationship between elite and popular culture did emerge at the end of the eighteenth century, as reformers attempted to foist a would-be-dominant culture on to people with their own distinct notions of time, space, and the body. The state brooked no opposition in its quest for an unmediated, educative relationship with individuals, engaging in radical social engineering to create the newly imagined public. Drinking, outrageous clamor, and incontinence were subject to surveillance and control, as reformers strove both to forge a citizenry conducive to their economic agenda for Mexico City and to publicly avow their own gente culta status. This new antagonism between elite and popular culture manifested itself both in the changing topography of the city and in the new threshold of shame and embarrassment of the body. Through new institutions like the Alcaldes de Barrio, elites maintained a firm, albeit contested, monopoly on the cultural tickets for access to the new public spaces. Reform rhetoric also policed the boundaries between the gente culta and the pueblo bajo during a time of rapidly shifting social identities. The idiom of morality spelled out the cultural aspects of elite class membership as the pueblo bajo, unwilling or economically prevented from acquiring elite cultural accouterments, became the social foil of the gente culta.

Constraints on War

J. R. McNEILL

In this brave new century of emerging viruses and expeditionary warfare it may prove interesting to cast a backward glance to an earlier age when a rampaging virus thwarted imperial ambitions and assisted in revolutions. The setting was the Atlantic American tropics and the virus was yellow fever, known to sailors and soldiers as Yellow Jack, a disease far more lethal than Severe Acute Respiratory Syndrome (SARS). Its historical prominence in the Americas required an ecological and demographic makeover that came with sugar and slavery.

When sugar boomed in tropical Atlantic America, starting in the 1640s, it began a new chapter in the story of ecological transformation of the Americas. It created extremely propitious environmental conditions for the propagation of yellow fever,

Source: J. R. McNeill, "Yellow Jack and Geopolitics: Environment, Epidemics, and the Struggles for Empire in the American Tropics, 1650–1825," *OAH Magazine of History* 18, no. 3 (April 2004), pp. 9–13. Copyright

and thereby a new set of governing conditions for international relations in the American tropics. Those little Amazons, the female mosquitoes *Aedes aegypti*, carriers of yellow fever, structured the geopolitical order of the American tropics from 1660 to 1780. After 1780, they undermined it.

Spain acquired an empire in the Americas after 1492, built on revenue from silver mines. Acute silver envy inspired England, France, Holland, and lesser powers to contest these Spanish dominions. By 1655, they acquired several Caribbean islands, usually through conquest, and created settlements of only a few hundred people. This was the age of buccaneers, when even modest efforts with minimal support from European states could change the political map of the Caribbean. That age ended when sugar, slaves, and sieges came to the Atlantic American tropics.

Sugar first took root in the Americas in northeastern Brazil, but by the 1640s had started to colonize parts of the Caribbean, beginning in Barbados. A social revolution followed, as the plantation complex—Philip Curtin's phrase to describe the world centered around sugar and slaves—spread throughout suitable lowlands. This revolution involved creating slave societies that introduced politically unreliable majorities into many islands and coastlands, changing the nature of war and politics. The comparative scarcity of whites and their fear of arming blacks led to a pattern of warfare by European expeditionary forces. To protect their colonies, all European empires upgraded their fortifications. Spanish silver and everyone's sugar made it possible to afford this in the seventeenth century and made many colonies and ports too valuable not to fortify. Thus, the Vauban revolution in fortification, named for the French military engineer, Sebastien le Prestre de Vauban (1633–1707), came to the Americas and, with it, the necessity of siege warfare.

Siege warfare in the Atlantic American tropics proceeded under conditions very different from those prevailing in Europe or European outposts elsewhere around the world. A Vauban-style fortress in Europe was intended to hold out for six weeks, by which time, the theory went, relief columns might march to the rescue. In the far-flung Portuguese, Dutch, and British strongholds in the Indian Ocean, relief could never arrive in time and so besiegers often succeeded. But in the tropical Atlantic, siege warfare after 1655 favored the defenders.

In 1655, the English took Spanish Jamaica, part of Oliver Cromwell's "Western Design" intended to weaken Spain. This conquest involved a force of some seven thousand men, far more than any previous action in the Caribbean. The days of buccaneers were passing, although another seventy years would elapse before they were finally extinguished. The era of expeditionary forces, of systematic and large-scale warfare, was just beginning. Cromwell's legions needed only a day to take the main Spanish settlement on Jamaica and a week to control the entire island, although guerilla resistance continued to flicker. But six months after this easy conquest, half the troops were dead and half the survivors sick. Subsequently, very few successful invasions took place in tropical America, despite repeated wars and upwards of fifty attempts. The main reason for this lies in another unsuspected consequence of the arrival of sugar: yellow fever.

Yellow fever is a viral infection probably native to tropical West Africa. Its symptoms can be mild or serious, and, in classic cases, consist of fever, headache, jaundice, and internal hemorrhage. It is primarily a disease of tree-dwelling monkeys. In vulnerable human populations, case mortality may be as high as 85 percent. Young adults are the most at risk. Children normally experience it only mildly, and their prospects for survival are excellent. In survivors, it produces lifelong immunity—a very effective vaccination has been available since 1936. The virus has long been endemic in tropical African forests and is now endemic in tropical American ones as well, circulating among monkeys and species of mosquito that are not very attracted to human blood. Yellow fever becomes an epidemic among humans when it circulates among urban populations via the vector, or carrier, *A. aegypti*, which does find human blood appealing.

Yellow fever's geographic range and distribution are determined mainly by characteristics of the vector. The female *A. aegypti* lives close to humans and breeds in water containers, preferably clay-bottomed ones. It rarely travels more than three hundred meters from its birthplace, except on ships or airplanes. It needs warm temperatures to prosper. It also needs water every few days. Yellow fever, then, is a disease of the humid tropics, although it used to make seasonal forays to temperate ports around the Atlantic basin—as far north as Quebec—in summer months.

Epidemic yellow fever has other, more stringent requirements. The virus must establish a cycle of transmission from mosquito to human host to mosquito. This requires a lot of mosquitoes. Without them, the virus will not move from person to person rapidly enough: people have the disease only seven to ten days, after which they are either immune or dead. Their blood is infectious for only three to six days. The transmission cycle also needs a favorable ratio of nonimmune to immune people available for mosquitoes to bite. To perpetuate the cycle, an infected *A. aegypti* must behave like Count Dracula; it must find virgin blood and find it fast. The mosquito only lives a few weeks. Immune people are virus-killers: the cycle of transmission is broken when mosquitoes inject the virus only into immunized blood streams. So a yellow fever epidemic requires suitable mosquitoes in sufficient quantity and susceptible hosts in both sufficient quantity and proportion. From the virus's point of view, its opportunities are sadly limited by the fragility of this cycle. Indeed, despite the warmth and rainfall, conditions in the Atlantic American tropics before 1640 left a lot to be desired: not enough clay-bottomed water vessels; not enough, if any, *A. aegypti*; not enough human bloodstreams; and, among those bloodstreams, not enough who spent their childhoods in places where cold temperatures precluded exposure and, therefore, immunity to the virus.

Sugar and geopolitics set the table very nicely for the yellow fever virus after 1640. Sugar wrought an ecological revolution upon dozens of islands and stretches of adjacent continental lowlands. Armies of slaves hacked down and burned off millions of hectares of forest to plant cane. Their efforts led to multiple ecological changes. Soil erosion accelerated. Wildlife vanished. More importantly from the human point of view, as plantations replaced forests, conditions came to favor the vector of yellow fever. Although fewer birds meant fewer predators for all mosquitoes, breeding conditions matter more than predation for the mosquito population dynamics. So the most crucial development was what replaced the destroyed forests—the spread of the plantations themselves. Plantations made excellent *A. aegypti* incubators.

Sugar production in the seventeenth and eighteenth centuries involved initial refining on the spot, using clay pots. A small plantation needed hundreds of clay pots. A big one used tens of thousands. They were empty except for three or four months after the harvest. Presumably they often broke, as they were brittle and handled by people who had no interest in their preservation. Clay pots and fragments of clay pots caught the rain and made ideal homesteads for *A. aegypti*. Eventually many ports and forts were ringed by plantations producing tons of sugar and clouds of *A. aegypti*. The mosquito—an African by origin—may have successfully colonized the Atlantic American tropics before 1640, but in any case appropriate breeding grounds were far easier to find after 1640.

So was good food, in the form of human blood. Sugar meant slaves and population growth. The Caribbean population had crashed after 1492 and by 1640, was perhaps two hundred thousand. By 1800, it had surpassed two million. Beyond blood, *A. aegypti* can also eat sucrose. It likes sweet fluids, the sweeter the better. It can live off honey or sugar indefinitely, although that diet is insufficient for ovulation. So while individual mosquitoes can live off sugar alone, *A. aegypti* populations require blood as well. After 1640, there was more and more sugar, more and more human blood, and more and more clay-bottomed water vessels in the Atlantic American tropics. For that matter, there were more and more slave ships arriving from West Africa, bringing yet more mosquitoes as stowaways. Things were looking up for *A. aegypti*.

Conditions for the yellow fever virus improved too, with one catch that geopolitics soon addressed. More mosquitoes, more human bloodstreams, and more ships from Africa favored the establishment of yellow fever. The first clear epidemic of yellow fever in the Americas came in 1647, striking Barbados—then the main sugar island—first, and over the ensuing months and years, Guadeloupe, St. Kitts, Cuba, the Yucatan, and the east coasts of Central America generally. It killed perhaps 20 to 30 percent of the local populations. But after this outbreak, yellow fever disappeared for almost forty years. Presumably, it worked its way through the susceptible hosts, leaving behind a higher proportion of immune people. It could not flourish again without a sufficient proportion of nonimmune people. This, for the yellow fever virus, was problematic.

The virus's problem was compounded by the resistance of West Africans. Yellow fever confers immunity upon all survivors. Almost all slaves arriving in the Caribbean had grown up in endemic yellow fever zones in Africa and were virus stoppers. So while the population growth of the sugar zones helped the mosquitoes find food, it did not provoke epidemics because so many of the people bitten by mosquitoes were West Africans. Raging epidemics required an influx of inexperienced immune systems. This is what expeditionary warfare provided.

Participants in the interimperial wars of the seventeenth and eighteenth centuries normally regarded yellow fever epidemics as acts of God. But differential immunity made yellow fever systematically partisan. A large contingent of Africans, or, less reliably, of Caribbean-born whites, could serve as a shield for individuals highly vulnerable themselves to yellow fever by interrupting the transmission cycle— this is known as "herd immunity" to epidemiologists. Yellow fever favored populations without blacks as opposed to those with them; it preferred invaders and immigrants to local populations; and it favored populations without children. Yellow fever was most dangerous to unadulterated populations of young adult Europeans— precisely the composition of expeditionary forces.

Beginning in the 1680s, in the context of the struggles between England and France, expeditions to the West Indies became more frequent. Most West Indies expeditions were British. Almost all were failures. After the successes, victors usually evacuated quickly, suffering from epidemics, and conquered ports were restored to their previous masters at the next peace treaty. A single example from the many wars of the long eighteenth century illustrates the mortality that accompanied expedition forces. In a famous expedition in 1739–1742, during the War of Jenkins's Ear, Admiral Edward Vernon took Portobelo and Chagres, ill-defended ports, each of which surrendered within two days of sighting Vernon's fleet. He arrived in November, well before the rains, and he had the largest force ever seen in these seas—nearly twenty-five thousand counting sailors and soldiers. In April 1741, he tried to take Cartagena but lost 41 percent of all men under his command, 70 percent of all disembarked soldiers, and 77 percent of those hailing from Britain. Three thousand six hundred colonial troops fared slightly better, including one colonist, Lawrence Washington of Virginia, who named his plantation Mount Vernon after the admiral. About six hundred fifty died in combat. Fleeing Cartagena, Vernon attempted to take Santiago de Cuba as a consolidation prize and lost 50 percent of his surviving troops to yellow fever. In all, Vernon lost about three-fourths of the men under his command in 1740–1742, fewer than one thousand of these died in combat.

The power of yellow fever was such that defenders, if comprised of local troops with hardened immune systems, generally had only to hold out for three to six weeks to be assured of victory. Their chances improved if the siege took place during the rainier parts of the year, May–November in the Caribbean, when mosquito strength peaked. Expeditionary fleets tried their best to avoid the hurricane season, July–October, in the American tropics. Strategists in Europe well knew—at least from the 1690s—that prospects for success receded if one failed to get the troops to the scene between December and May. But organizing and providing for a force according to schedule was no easy business in an age of private contracting and uncertain stocks of food and ships. Finding men willing to take the king's shilling proved especially challenging if prospective recruits thought their destination might be the Caribbean. Hence, many expeditions arrived later than planned and suffered the consequences.

The geopolitical significance of yellow fever changed toward the end of the eighteenth century, facilitating the fall of empires and the rise of new republics. The restiveness of slave populations acquired more political forms and more often led to organized violence. Once people of West African birth began to make war on their own behalf in the American tropics, their relative immunity to yellow fever and to *falciparum malaria*, if shrewdly exploited, magnified their power. That power soon shook the foundation of imperial order in the American tropics. In Saint Domingue, after 1791, slaves and ex-slaves engineered a revolution against French planters that the British soon attempted to undo. In the course of their invasion, British forces lost about fifty thousand men, the majority from yellow fever. After the British gave up, the French tried to reclaim Haiti in 1802 and suffered great losses in turn. The army's leader, Toussaint Louverture, was no fool: he knew that if he did not give battle, yellow fever would destroy the French, as it had done the British. His lieutenant and successor, Jean-Jacques Dessalines, knew it too: he told his followers to take courage, that "The French will not be able to remain long in San Domingo. They will do well at first, but soon they will fall ill and die like flies." And this is exactly what happened. Louverture and Dessalines would have been poor commanders indeed not to shape their strategy to exploit the overwhelming power of their insect and viral allies. Haiti's independence was declared in 1804.

The vulnerability of expeditionary forces to tropical infection probably also helped create the United States. Britain fought the American Revolutionary War with an expeditionary force that the rebels could not match. They did not have to. Here, malaria rather than yellow fever took sides. The installation of an irrigated rice economy, based on West African technique and cultigens, in the Carolina coastlands in the eighteenth century helped improve conditions for malarial mosquitoes. Malaria and yellow fever became common scourges in the hot and rainy months of July through September. In 1780, British forces occupied the port cities of the Carolinas, hoping to ignite the spirit of Loyalists against the Revolution. They prudently campaigned in the spring, aware of the enhanced disease toll of the hotter months, taking Savannah and Charleston by April. They found the summer of 1780 lethal. Lord Cornwallis's chief surgeon, John Hayes, procured antimalarial medicine in November for the dangerous months ahead. Fears of fevers sent Cornwallis into the Carolina Piedmont, where his troops lost more battles than they won. Against his wishes, he was ordered to Williamsburg and Yorktown, which he correctly regarded as a "sickly" and "unhealthy swamp." In his account of Yorktown, the battle that effectively ended the war, Cornwallis credited the Americans with skillful siegecraft but noted "Our numbers had been diminished by the Enemy's fire, but particularly by sickness. . ." . Revolutionary soldiers, especially those who had grown up in the southern colonies, although affected by disease in the Carolina campaigns, enjoyed relatively stronger immunities than did British soldiers. Repeated mild infection by malaria from childhood had equipped them to resist the disease. Armies did not have to contain large numbers of blacks to exploit differential disease immunity, although it helped. They did not have to understand what they were exploiting, although that helped too. They did not have to have yellow fever on their side. White armies with seasoned immune systems could profit in the same way, if less reliably and less thoroughly.

A grass from New Guinea (sugarcane), a mosquito, and a virus from Africa wrought an ecological transformation after the mid-seventeenth century that stabilized the geopolitics of the Caribbean basin. They helped keep the Spanish Empire intact after 1655 and prevented first France and then Britain from acquiring a choke hold on Spanish silver and a near monopoly position on American sugar. After the 1770s, differential disease immunity assisted insurgent populations of the American tropics as they sought to end European empires in the New World. In the environmental and epidemiological changes these empires wrought, they sowed the slow-germinating seeds of their own destruction. After 1898, a new empire arose in the Caribbean, made possible, or at least inexpensive, by further environmental and epidemiological change—the mosquito control and yellow fever prevention undertaken by the United States Army.

FURTHER READING

Anderson, Fred. *Crucible of War: The Seven Years' War and the Fate of Empire in British North America, 1754–1766.* New York: Knopf, 2000.
Banks, Kenneth J. *Chasing Empire Across the Sea: Communications and the State in the French Atlantic, 1713–1763.* Montreal: McGill-Queen's University Press, 2002.
Brading, D. A. *Church and State in Bourbon Mexico: The Diocese of Michoacán, 1749–1810.* New York: Cambridge University Press, 1994.

Bridenbaugh, Carl, and Roberta Bridenbaugh. *No Peace Beyond the Line: The English in the Caribbean, 1624–1690.* New York: Oxford University Press, 1972.

Canny, Nicholas, and Anthony Pagden, eds. *Colonial Identity in the Atlantic World, 1500–1800.* Princeton, NJ: Princeton University Press, 1987.

Demos, John. *The Unredeemed Captive: A Family Story from Early America.* New York: Alfred Knopf, 1994.

Dunn, Richard S. *Sugar and Slaves: The Rise of the Planter Class in the English West Indies, 1624–1713.* Chapel Hill: The University of North Carolina Press for the Omohundro Institute of Early American History and Culture, 1972.

Elliott, J. H. *Empires of the Atlantic World: Britain and Spain in America, 1492–1830.* New Haven, CT: Yale University Press, 2006.

Faragher, John Mack. *A Great and Noble Scheme: The Tragic Story of the Expulsion of the French Acadians from Their American Homeland.* New York: W. W. Norton & Co., 2005.

Farriss, Nancy M. *Crown and Clergy in Colonial Mexico 1759–1821: The Crisis of Ecclesiastical Privilege.* London: Athlone Press, 1968.

Fisher, John R., Allan J. Kuethe, and Anthony McFarlane. *Reform and Insurrection in Bourbon New Granada and Peru.* Baton Rouge: Louisiana State University Press, 1990.

Hinderaker, Eric. *Elusive Empires: Constructing Colonialism in the Ohio Valley, 1673–1800.* New York: Cambridge University Press, 1997.

Law, Robin. *The Ọyọ Empire, c. 1600–c. 1836: A West African Imperialism in the Era of the Atlantic Slave Trade.* Brookfield, VT: Ashgate, 1991.

Liss, Peggy K. *Atlantic Empires: The Network of Trade and Revolution, 1713–1826.* Baltimore: The Johns Hopkins University Press, 1983.

Maxwell, Kenneth. *Conflicts & Conspiracies: Brazil and Portugal 1750–1808.* New York: Routledge, 2004.

———. *Pombal, Paradox of the Enlightenment.* New York: Cambridge University Press, 1995.

McNeill, J. R. *Atlantic Empires of France and Spain: Louisbourg and Havana, 1700–1763.* Chapel Hill: University of North Carolina Press, 1985.

Plank, Geoffrey Gilbert. *An Unsettled Conquest: The British Campaign Against the Peoples of Acadia.* Philadelphia: University of Pennsylvania Press, 2001.

Seed, Patricia. *To Love, Honor, and Obey: Conflicts over Marriage Choice, 1574–1821.* Stanford, Calif.: Stanford University Press, 1988.

Steele, Ian. *Warpaths: Invasions of North America.* New York: Oxford University Press, 1994.

White, Richard. *The Middle Ground: Indians, Empires, and Republics in the Great Lakes Region, 1650–1815.* New York: Cambridge University Press, 1991.

CHAPTER

11

Empires and Independence

The late eighteenth and early nineteenth centuries saw remarkable changes in transatlantic politics. Revolutionary movements in the Americas and Europe shook the twin pillars of the traditional order: monarchy and empire. Subversive ideas of popular self-government, civic virtue, individual rights, and free trade circulated throughout the Atlantic world, gaining favor among European radicals and the "creole" populations of the British, French, and Spanish American colonies. As imperial governments sought greater control over their overseas possessions, colonial people began to develop a new sense of their own power and distinct interests. The first colonies to break free from metropolitan rule were the thirteen colonies of British North America that became the United States. The British North American Revolution (1776–1783) erupted into a transatlantic struggle with repercussions as far away as West Africa. Just as the American Revolution involved Europe, so too did the French Revolution and the wars that followed (1789–1815) involve the Americas. French republican ideas of liberty, equality, and fraternity ignited a civil war in the Caribbean, culminating in the independence of Haiti (1804) and the over-throw of slavery in what had been the richest sugar plantation colony of the Atlantic world. Finally, Napoleon's invasion of Spain in 1808 sparked the revolt of Spain's mainland American colonies. Spanish American wars for independence raged until the 1820s, and a slate of new Latin American nation-states emerged from Mexico to Argentina. Brazil gained its independence from Portugal in 1822 but remained a monarchy until the late nineteenth century, proving that independence and repub-licanism did not always march together. Despite all these shocks, European colonial-ism survived the "age of revolution" in the Atlantic world. Britain retained Canada, its Caribbean colonies, and the Cape Colony in southern Africa, while France held on to Martinique and Guadeloupe, and Spain kept Cuba and Puerto Rico. Across the ocean, Sierra Leone's establishment by British abolitionists signaled a new era of European intervention in Africa—one that would fundamentally alter the con-nections among Europe, Africa, and the Americas.

DOCUMENTS

Nobody expressed the republican ideas of the British North American Revolution better than Thomas Paine (1737–1809). Document 1 presents some of the most influential argu-ments of his 1776 pamphlet *Common Sense*. A recent immigrant himself, Paine imagined

America as "an asylum for mankind" in a tyrannical world. Document 2 compares the United States Declaration of Independence in 1776 with the Haitian Declaration of Independence in 1804. What are the similarities and differences between the two declarations? Both revolutions were also civil wars that disgorged refugees into the Atlantic world. Document 3 introduces two sets of revolutionary refugees: the white colonists, slaves, and Indians who remained loyal to the crown during the British North American Revolution, and inhabitants of the French colony of Saint Domingue who fled to Cuba and then made a second migration in 1809 to New Orleans.

Ideas traveled along with people, and advocates of revolution often expressed new ideas in old ways. Catechisms were familiar tools for the religious education of children and new converts. During the 1790s, French radicals adopted secular catechisms, which popularized revolutionary ideology. Document 4 offers an example of a catechism from the failed revolution of the United Irishmen in 1798.

In the Caribbean, the high mortality of European soldiers in the revolutionary era stimulated the British to deploy soldiers of African descent. Document 5 presents one British officer's explanation of the advantages of using black soldiers in tropical combat.

Documents 6–8 shift the focus to the Iberian Atlantic empires. Document 6 offers an epic poem from New Spain defending the Church and the Crown. In contrast, Document 7 presents the vision of one of Spanish America's leading revolutionaries, Simón Bolívar (1783–1830). Like Paine, Bolívar foresaw an independent and republican America. In contrast to the rest of the Americas, Brazil's path to independence was relatively peaceful and politically conservative, as Document 8 reveals. In the first selection, the Prince Regent of Brazil elevates the colony to co-equal status with Portugal, and in the second, Brazil makes a clean break from its mother country, achieving independence without war or revolution.

1. Thomas Paine Justifies American Independence, 1776

Volumes have been written on the subject of the struggle between England and America. Men of all ranks have embarked in the controversy, from different motives, and with various designs; but all have been ineffectual, and the period of debate is closed. Arms, as the last resource, decide the contest; the appeal was the choice of the king, and the continent hath accepted the challenge. . . .

The sun never shined on a cause of greater worth. 'Tis not the affair of a city, a county, a province, or a kingdom, but of a continent—of at least one eighth part of the habitable globe. 'Tis not the concern of a day, a year, or an age; posterity are virtually involved in the contest, and will be more or less affected, even to the end of time, by the proceedings now. Now is the seed time of continental union, faith and honor. The least fracture now will be like a name engraved with the point of a pin on the tender rind of a young oak; the wound will enlarge with the tree, and posterity read it in full grown characters. . . .

I have heard it asserted by some, that as America hath flourished under her former connexion with Great-Britain, that the same connexion is necessary towards her future happiness, and will always have the same effect. Nothing can be more fallacious than this kind of argument. We may as well assert that because a child

---

Source: Thomas Paine, *Common Sense* (Philadelphia, 1776), 14–18, 20, 27.

has thrived upon milk, that it is never to have meat, or that the first twenty years of our lives is to become a precedent for the next twenty. But even this is admitting more than is true, for I answer roundly, that America would have flourished as much, and probably much more, had no European power had anything to do with her. The commerce, by which she hath enriched herself are the necessaries of life, and will always have a market while eating is the custom of Europe. . . .

But Britain is the parent country, say some. Then the more shame upon her conduct. Even brutes do not devour their young, nor savages make war upon their families; wherefore the assertion, if true, turns to her reproach; but it happens not to be true, or only partly so, and the phrase *parent* or *mother country* hath been jesuit-ically adopted by the king and his parasites, with a low papistical design of gaining an unfair bias on the credulous weakness of our minds. Europe, and not England, is the parent country of America. This new world hath been the asylum for the perse-cuted lovers of civil and religious liberty from *every part* of Europe. Hither have they fled, not from the tender embraces of the mother, but from the cruelty of the monster; and it is so far true of England, that the same tyranny which drove the first emigrants from home, pursues their descendants still. . . .

I challenge the warmest advocate for reconciliation, to shew, a single advantage that this continent can reap, by being connected with Great Britain. I repeat the chal-lenge, not a single advantage is derived. Our corn will fetch its price in any market in Europe, and our imported goods must be paid for buy them where we will.

But the injuries and disadvantages we sustain by that connection, are without number; and our duty to mankind at large, as well as to ourselves, instruct us to re-nounce the alliance: Because, any submission to, or dependance on Great-Britain, tends directly to involve this continent in European wars and quarrels; and sets us at variance with nations, who would otherwise seek our friendship, and against whom, we have neither anger nor complaint. As Europe is our market for trade, we ought to form no partial connection with any part of it. It is the true interest of America to steer clear of European contentions, which she never can do, while by her dependance on Britain, she is made the make-weight in the scale of British politics.

Europe is too thickly planted with kingdoms to be long at peace, and whenever a war breaks out between England and any foreign power, the trade of America goes to ruin, *because of her connection with Britain.* The next war may not turn out like the last, and should it not, the advocates for reconciliation now will be wishing for separation then, because, neutrality in that case, would be a safer convoy than a man of war. Every thing that is right or natural pleads for separation. The blood of the slain, the weeping voice of nature cries, 'TIS TIME TO PART. Even the distance at which the Almighty hath placed England and America, is a strong and natural proof, that the authority of the one, over the other, was never the design of Heaven. The time likewise at which the continent was discovered, adds weight to the argument, and the manner in which it was peopled encreases the force of it. The reformation was preceded by the discovery of America, as if the Almighty graciously meant to open a sanctuary to the persecuted in future years, when home should afford neither friendship nor safety. . . .

Small islands not capable of protecting themselves, are the proper objects for kingdoms to take under their care; but there is something very absurd, in supposing a continent to be perpetually governed by an island. In no instance hath nature made the satellite larger than its primary planet, and as England and America, with respect to each other, reverses the common order of nature, it is evident they belong to different systems: England to Europe, America to itself. . . .

Ye that tell us of harmony and reconciliation, can ye restore to us the time that is past? Can ye give to prostitution its former innocence? Neither can ye reconcile Britain and America. The last cord now is broken, the people of England are presenting addresses against us. There are injuries which nature cannot forgive; she would cease to be nature if she did. As well can the lover forgive the ravisher of his mistress, as the continent forgive the murders of Britain. The Almighty hath implanted in us these unextinguishable feelings for good and wise purposes. They are the guardians of his image in our hearts. They distinguish us from the herd of common animals. The social compact would dissolve, and justice be extirpated the earth, or have only a casual existence were we callous to the touches of affection. The robber, and the murderer, would often escape unpunished, did not the injuries which our tempers sustain, provoke us into justice.

O ye that love mankind! Ye that dare oppose, not only the tyranny, but the tyrant, stand forth! Every spot of the old world is overrun with oppression. Freedom hath been hunted round the globe. Asia, and Africa, have long expelled her.—Europe regards her like a stranger, and England hath given her warning to depart. O! receive the fugitive, and prepare in time an asylum for mankind.

2. The United States and Haiti Declare Independence, 1776, 1804

The Declaration of Independence of the United States of America

IN CONGRESS, JULY 4, 1776.

THE UNANIMOUS DECLARATION OF THE THIRTEEN UNITED STATES OF AMERICA.

When, in the course of human events, it becomes necessary for one people to dissolve the political bands which have connected them with another, and to assume, among the powers of the earth, the separate and equal station to which the laws of nature and of nature's God entitle them, a decent respect to the opinions of mankind requires that they should declare the causes which impel them to the separation.

We hold these truths to be self-evident: that all men are created equal; that they are endowed, by their Creator, with certain unalienable rights; that among these are life, liberty, and the pursuit of happiness. That to secure these rights, governments are instituted among men, deriving their just powers from the consent of the governed; that whenever any form of government becomes destructive of these ends, it is the right of the people to alter or to abolish it, and to institute a new government, laying its foundation on such principles, and organizing its powers in such form, as to them shall seem most likely to effect their safety and happiness. Prudence, indeed,

Sources: *The Public Statutes at Large of the United States of America.* (Boston: Charles C. Little and James Brown, 1845), vol. 1, pp. 1–3; "Act of Independence," *The Louverture Project.* [http://thelouvertureproject.org/index.php?title=Act_of_Independence. Accessed January 9, 2007.]

will dictate, that governments long established, should not be changed for light and transient causes; and accordingly all experience hath shown, that mankind are more disposed to suffer, while evils are sufferable, than to right themselves by abolishing the forms to which they are accustomed. But when a long train of abuses and usurpations, pursuing invariably the same object, evinces a design to reduce them under absolute despotism, it is their right, it is their duty, to throw off such government, and to provide new guards for their future security. Such has been the patient sufferance of these colonies; and such is now the necessity which constrains them to alter their former systems of government. The history of the present King of Great Britain is a history of repeated injuries and usurpations, all having in direct object the establishment of an absolute tyranny over these states. . . .

In every stage of these oppressions we have petitioned for redress in the most humble terms. Our repeated petitions have been answered only by repeated injury. A prince, whose character is thus marked by every act which may define a tyrant, is unfit to be the ruler of a free people.

Nor have we been wanting in attentions to our British brethren. We have warned them, from time to time, of attempts by their legislature to extend an unwarrantable jurisdiction over us. We have reminded them of the circumstances of our emigration and settlement here. We have appealed to their native justice and magnanimity, and we have conjured them by the ties of our common kindred to disavow these usurpations, which would inevitably interrupt our connexions and correspondence. They too have been deaf to the voice of justice and of consanguinity. We must, therefore, acquiesce in the necessity which denounces our separation, and hold them, as we hold the rest of mankind, enemies in war, in peace friends.

We, therefore, the representatives of the UNITED STATES OF AMERICA, in General Congress assembled, appealing to the Supreme Judge of the world for the rectitude of our intentions, do, in the name, and by the authority of the good people of these colonies, solemnly publish and declare, That these United Colonies are, and of right ought to be, FREE and INDEPENDENT STATES; that they are absolved from all allegiance to the British crown, and that all political connexion between them and the State of Great Britain, is and ought to be, totally dissolved; and that, as FREE and INDEPENDENT STATES, they have full power to levy war, conclude peace, contract alliances, establish commerce, and to do all other acts and things which INDEPENDENT STATES may of right do. And for the support of this Declaration, with a firm reliance on the protection of DIVINE PROVIDENCE, we mutually pledge to each other our lives, our fortunes, and our sacred honour.

JOHN HANCOCK.

New Hampshire.—Josiah Bartlett, William Whipple, Matthew Thornton.

Massachusetts Bay.—Samuel Adams, John Adams, Robert Treat Paine, Elbridge Gerry.

Rhode Island, &c.—Stephen Hopkins, William Ellery.

Connecticut.—Roger Sherman, Samuel Huntington, William Williams, Oliver Wolcott.

New York.—William Floyd, Philip Livingston, Francis Lewis, Lewis Morris.

New Jersey.—Richard Stockton, John Witherspoon, Francis Hopkinson, John Hart, Abraham Clark.

Pennsylvania.—Robert Morris, Benjamin Rush, Benjamin Franklin, John Morton, George Clymer, James Smith, George Taylor, James Wilson, George Ross.

Delaware.—Cæsar Rodney, George Read, Thomas M'Kean.

Maryland.—Samuel Chase, William Paca, Thomas Stone, Charles Carroll of Carrollton.

Virginia.—George Wythe, Richard Henry Lee, Thomas Jefferson, Benjamin Harrison, Thomas Nelson, Jun., Francis Lightfoot Lee, Carter Braxton.

North Carolina.—William Hooper, Joseph Hewes, John Penn.

South Carolina.—Edward Rutledge, Thomas Hayward, Jun., Thomas Lynch, Jun., Arthur Middleton.

Georgia.—Button Gwinnett, Lyman Hall, George Walton.

Declaration of Independence of Haiti

Liberty or Death

Gonaïves, January 1, 1804
Year I of Independence

Today, January 1, 1804, the General in Chief of the Indigenous Army, accompanied by generals and army chiefs convoked in order to take measures tending to the happiness of the country:

After having made known to the assembled generals his true intention of forever ensuring to the natives of Haiti a stable government—the object of his greatest solicitude, which he did in a speech that made known to foreign powers the resolution to render the country independent, and to enjoy the liberty consecrated by the blood of the people of this island; and, after having gathered their opinions, asked each of the assembled generals to pronounce a vow to forever renounce France; to die rather than to live under its domination; and to fight for independence with their last breath.

The generals, imbued with these sacred principles, after having with one voice given their adherence to the well manifested project of independence, have all sworn before eternity and before the entire universe to forever renounce France and to die rather than live under its domination.

Signed:

Dessalines
General-in-Chief

Christophe, Pétion, Clerveaux, Vernet, Gabart
Major Generals

P. Romain, G. Gérin, L. Capois, Jean-Louis François, Férou, Cangé, G. Bazelais, Magloire Ambroise, J. J.Herne, Toussaint Brave, Yayou
Brigadier generals

Bonet, F. Paplier, Morelly, Chevalier, Marion
Adjutants-general

Magny, Roux
Brigade chiefs

Chaperon, B. Goret, Macajoux, Dupuy, Carbonne, Diaquoi aîné, Raphaël, Malet, Derenoncourt
Army officers

Boisrond Tonnerre
Secretary

3. Refugees Flee from Revolutions, 1779–1809

Letter of John Stuart

Montreal, October 13th, 1781

Sir,

No doubt but the venerable Society is surprised that they have not heard from me during the four years past; yet I flatter myself the following Narrative of my Situation will sufficiently apologise for my Silence.

At the Commencement of the unhappy Contest betwixt Great Britain & her Colonies, I acquainted the Society of the firm Reliance I had on ye Fidelity and Loyalty of my Congregation; which has justified my Opinion:—For the faithful Mohawks, rather than swerve from their Allegiance, chose rather to abandon their Dwellings & Property; and accordingly went in a Body to Genl. Burgoyne, & afterwards were obliged to take Shelter in Canada. While they remained at Fort Hunter I continued to officiate as usual, performing the public Service intire, even after the Declaration of Independence, notwithstanding by so doing I incurred the Penalty of High-Treason, by the new Laws.

As soon as my Protectors *i.e.* the Mohawks were fled, I was made a Prisoner, within the Space of four Days, or be put into close Confinement; and this only upon Suspicion that I was a loyal Subject of the King of Great Britain. Upon this, I was admitted to Parole, and confined to the Limits of the Town of Schenectady, in which Situation I remained for upwards of three years. My House has been frequently broken open by Mobs;—my Property plundered, and indeed every Kind of Indignity offered to my Person by the lowest of the Populace;—At length my Farm and the Produce of it was formally taken from me in May last, as forfeited to the State, and as the last Resource I proposed to open a Latin School for the Support of my Family; But this Privilege was denied, on Pretence that as a Prisoner of War, I was not intitled to exercise any lucrative Occupation in the State. I then applied for Permission to remove to Canada, which after much Difficulty & Expence I obtained upon the following Conditions:—to give Bail in the Sum of £400 to send a rebel Colonel in my

Sources: Letter to John Stuart to the S. P. G., October 13, 1781, in James J. Talman, ed., *Loyalist Narratives from Upper Canada* (Toronto: The Champlain Society, 1946), pp. 341–344; Memoir of Boston King (originally published in serial form in *The Methodist Magazine* 21 (1798); http://collections.ic .gc.ca/blackloyalists/documents/diaries/king-memoirs.htm; *The Methodist Magazine* 21 (1798), p. 261; James Mather to William Claiborne, July 18, 1809; William Claiborne to James Mather, August 4, 1809; James Mather to William Claiborne, August 7, 1809 in Dunbar Rowland, ed., *Official Letter Books of W. C. C. Claiborne, 1801–1816* (Jackson, MS: State Department of Archives and History, 1917), 4: 387–389.

Room [place], or else return to Albany, and surrender myself Prisoner whenever required. In Consequence of which, I set out on my Journey from Schenectady on the 19th of September last with my Wife & three small Children; and after suffering much Fatigue & Difficulty we arrived safe at St. John's in Canada on the 9th instant. The Mohawks are extremely happy at my Arrival, & flatter themselves that I will reside among them; But, having left the most Part of my private Property, by the depretiation of the Paper Currency & other Accidents peculiar to the Times,— And having a Family to maintain in this very expensive Place, I shall be under the Necessity of accepting of a Chaplaincy, which Sr. John Johnson (with his wonted Kindness) is pleased to offer me in his Second Battalion.

I cannot omit to mention that my Church was plundered by the Rebels, & the Pulpit Cloth taken away from the Pulpit—it was afterwards imployed as a Tavern, the Barrel of Rum placed in the Reading Desk,—the succeeding Season it was used as a Stable—And now serves as a Fort to protect a Set of as great Villains as ever disgraced Humanity. . . .

As soon as I can settle my Family in a convenient Situation I expect to visit the Mohawks (distant 7 Miles from hence) and shall continue to officiate occasionally for them, bestowing as much Attention on them as possible. I shall endeavour to write again to the Society this Fall, and shall from Time to Time give an Account of my Proceedings. In the mean Time I am,

> With great Respect,
> Sir,
>
> your very huml. Servant
>
> JOHN STUART

The Memoir of Boston King

My master being apprehensive that Charles-Town was in danger on account of the war, removed into the country, about 38 miles off. Here we built a large house for Mr. Waters, during which time the English took Charles-Town. Having obtained leave one day to see my parents, who had lived about 12 miles off, and it being late before I could go, I was obliged to borrow one of Mr. Waters's horses; but a servant of my master's, took the horse from me to go a little journey, and stayed two or three days longer than he ought. This involved me in the greatest perplexity, and I expected the severest punishment, because the gentleman to who the horse belonged was a very bad man, and knew not how shew mercy. To escape his cruelty, I determined to go Charles-Town, and throw myself into the hands of the English. They received me readily, and I began to feel the happiness, liberty, of which I knew nothing before, altho' I was grieved at first, to be obliged to leave my friends, and reside among strangers. In this situation I was seized with the smallpox, and suffered great hardships; for all the Blacks affected with that disease, were ordered to be carried a mile from the camp, lest the soldiers should be infected, and disabled from marching. This was a grievous circumstance to me and many others. We lay sometimes a whole day without any thing to eat or drink; but Providence sent a man, who belonged to the York volunteers whom I was acquainted with, to my relief. He brought me such things as I stood in need of; and by the blessing of the Lord I began to recover.

By this time, the English left the place; but as I was unable to march with the army, I expected to be taken by the enemy. However when they came, and understood that we were ill of the smallpox, they precipitately left us for fear of the infection. Two days after, the wagons were sent to convey us to the English Army, and we were put into a little cottage, (being 25 in number) about a quarter of a mile from the Hospital. . . .

[In 1783] the horrors and devastation of war happily terminated and peace was restored between America and Great Britain, which diffused universal joy among all parties; except us, who had escaped from slavery and taken refuge in the English army; for a report prevailed at New-York, that all the slaves, in number 2000, were to be delivered up to their masters altho' some of them had been three or four years among the English. This dreadful rumour filled us all with inexpressible anguish and terror, especially when we saw our old masters coming from Virginia, North Carolina, and other parts, and seizing upon their slaves in the streets of New York, or even dragging them out of their beds. Many of the slaves had very cruel masters, so that the thoughts of returning home with them embittered life to us. For some days we lost our appetite for food, and sleep departed from our eyes. The English had compassion upon us in the day of distress, and issued out a Proclamation, importing, That all slaves should be free, who had taken refuge in the British lines, and claimed the sanction and privileges of the Proclamations respecting the security and protection of Negroes. In consequence of this, each of us received a certificate from the commanding officer at New-York, which dispelled all our fears, and filled us with joy and gratitude. Soon after, ships were fitted out, and furnished with every necessary for conveying us to Nova Scotia. We arrived at Birch Town in the month of August, where we all safely landed. Every family had a lot of land, and we exerted all our strength in order to build comfortable huts before the cold weather set in.

Report on Caribbean Refugees in Louisiana

From James Mather

New Orleans,
July 18th 1809.

Sir,

In answer to your much esteemed favour of yesterday, I beg leave to enclose herein for the information of your Excellency, a general statement of the People brought here from the Island of Cuba by thirty four vessels, two of whom were from Baracoa and the Havannah and thirty two from St. Yago.—To that statement I must refer your Excellency, as containing whole number of whites, free people of Colour, & Slaves, and viewing at the same time each class, under the several heads of men, women and children under 15 years of age.—

It is hardly possible to form as yet a Judgement on the general character of the different classes.—It may however be inferred from their conduct since they have lived among us, as also from various other circumstances.—

1stly   In what regards the Blacks, they are trained up to the habits of strict discipline, and consist wholly of affricans bought up from Guineamen in the Island of Cuba, or of faithful slaves who have fled with their masters from St. Domingo as early as the year 1803.

2dly A few characters among the free People of Colour have been represented to me as dangerous for the peace of this Territory; I must however own to your Excellency that in every other Territory but this, the most part of them would not, I think, be viewed under the same light if due attention should be paid to the effects of the difference of language, and if it should be considered that these very men possess property, and have useful trades to live upon.—

In the application of the Territorial law relative to free people of Color, I have been particular in causing such of them as had been informed against, to give bond for their leaving the Territory within the time allowed in such cases.—In the mean time there has not been one single complaint that I know of, against any of them concerning their conduct since their coming to this place.

3rdly The whites persons, consisting *chiefly of Planters*, and *merchants of St. Domingo* who took refuge on the shores of Cuba about six years ago, appear to be an *active, industrious People*. They evince till now, upon every occasion, their respect for our Laws, and their confidence in our Government.—They have suffered a great deal from the want of Provisions both at sea, and in the River.—Several of them have died, and many are now yet a prey to diseases originating, as it appears, from the use of unwholesome food, and from the foul air they have breathed, while heaped up together with their slaves, in the holds of small vessels during their passage from Cuba.—Since a period of nearly three months there have been no less than four hundred poor widows, sick, orphans, or old men, supported by the charity of our Citizens, who have hastened in procuring subscriptions for their relief, and have been as forward in standing securities, in the amount required, for the forthcoming of their negroes, so that the whole number of slaves in the enclosed statement has been delivered agreeably to your directions.—

Your Excellency well knows that it is the fate of every large community never to be totally exempt of some bad members.—We must therefore conclude that time, & perhaps the rather mild features of our Criminal Jurisprudence may give us room to discover at some future Day, among the whites from St. Yago, individuals unworthy of the protection afforded them by the American Government.—But I will observe to your Excellency on the one hand, that I know of no provision established by our Laws, to prevent free white persons who have means for their living, to come and settle in the United States; and farther that I could not anticipate the possibility of future offences, to form a rule in the present case.—

I have the honor to be, very respectfully,
Sir,
your very obedt. hble Servt—

Signed, James Mather Mayor.

Postscript. You will perhaps see with astonishment the number slaves contained in the general statement, to exceed considerably the proportion which it was at first thought they would bear in the emigration from Cuba.—But I request your Excellency to consider that this is the consequence of the great mass of the french population in that Island, having finally given the preference to this part of the Union over the other States, so that the surplus of slaves coming here, will lessen proportionally the number which was expected to take a passage to the Ports of the Atlantic.—

J.M.

To his Excellency W– C. C. Claiborne)
Govr of the Territory of Orleans   )

4. Irish Revolutionaries Adopt a Radical Catechism, 1797

Question: *What is that in your hand?*
Answer: *It is a branch.*
Question: *Of What?*
Answer: *Of the Tree of Liberty.*
Question: *Where did it first grow?*
Answer: *In America.*
Question: *Where does it bloom?*
Answer: *In France.*
Question: *Where did the seeds fall?*
Answer: *In Ireland.*
Question: *Where are you going to plant it?*
Answer: *In the Crown of Great Britain*

5. A British Officer Recommends the Use of Black Soldiers in the British West Indies, 1801

Whatever prejudices may have existed, or may still be entertained, among the Planter or other Residents in the West India Colonies, against the establishment of Black regiments, the utility of them, has in every instance been fully proved, whether by their services in the field or by their capability of performing every other description of Military duties.

Chance having thrown me into the situation of forming and disciplining a Regiment of the above description, it may justly have been expected from me, that while engaged in that particular duty, my attention would be directed to the various circumstances which appear'd to promise any degree of improvement to the establishment, which like every other of whatever nature, cannot fail to derive benefit from experience.

The Corps of Blacks which were first formed, during the present War, and employed in the service of His Majesty, were raised in the French conquer'd Islands, and consequently composed of the People of colour who had attached themselves

Source: Kevin Whelan, *Fellowship of Freedom: The United Irishmen and 1798* (Cork, 1998), p. 1.

Source: Roger N. Buckley, ed., "Brigadier-General Thomas Hislop's Remarks on the Establishment of the West India Regiments: 1801," *Journal of the Society for Army Historical Research*, 1980, 58(236): 211–215.

to the Royalist party, and of such Negro slaves as belonged to the Royalists, who themselves took up Arms in the cause. The Corps of Soter, Druault & Malcolm were of this description. Those, together with the old Carolina Black Corps, which at the end of the late War was withdrawn with the Army from America, on every occasion were distinguished for their intrepidity and alacrity.

As the extraordinary and unprecedented circumstances of the times, produced the unavoidable necessity of embodying & training those people to Arms, so it alike became requisite to afford every possible support to the measures (however dangerous at any former period, such a step would have been consider'd) as the only possible means which afforded any hope of averting the destruction which through Treason and Rebellion were about completing the annihilation of the whole of the British West-Indies. Independent, however, of the several Corps above mentioned, great and essential services were performed by such as were for the moment raised in the different Islands by the Proprietors for their immediate protection. St. Vincent, Grenada and Tobago had recourse to this measure, and were much indebted for their safety to the fidelity, activity and boldness of their Black-Rangers.

Their utility was then universally acknowledged, and it is not improbable but that many persons, whose principal reliance was then on the exertions of the Black Troops, have since, (the danger being passed) been among the most strenuous in representing them as dangerous to ourselves, and contemptible in the eyes of an Enemy.

But this misrepresentation must have long since discover'd itself. It is therefore unnecessary to dwell thereon. Being myself persuaded of its want of Truth, I shall proceed to point out the advantages which a permanent establishment of West India Regiments must produce, and what appears to me necessary for its further improvement. An essential benefit will therefore, in the first place, be generally acknowledged by the saving of the many lives of our Countrymen, who must otherwise compose the whole of the Army in the West-Indies.

How dreadfully fatal the Climate has (in the course of the war) proved to our European Regiments, is unfortunately a fact too well established to make it requisite to bring forward any particular instances thereof; or at the present day do we find that the Mortality diminishes.

The state of the several Corps, last arrives, is a sufficient proof of this melancholy truth. The two Battalions of the 60th Regiment arrived about the time alluded to, and suffer'd dreadfully at Fort Royal, Martinique.

The first circumstance which presents itself as meriting attention with the view of improving the establishment of West-India Regiments is the mode of recruiting them in future.

By far the most eligible plan, as I conceive, will be to purchase new African. The lower order of free coloured people, from which it might be expected to recruit, are very generally of a disorderly and dissolute description, on whom little dependence could be placed, and in late times are strongly suspected of possessing a rooted antipathy to the Whites, with whom they fain would consider themselves entitled to equal priviledges, but from which they are, by the Laws prohibited.

It is therefore in few instances that Recruits should be taken from this Class and certainly only from such whose general behaviour and conduct is known & approved of. Very few however will be found inclined to exchange their actual condition to subject themselves to Military discipline.

Among other circumstances favorable to the measure of forming the Regiments from new imported Africans, one deserving notice is, that they are received, wholly unacquainted with and uncontaminated by the Vices which prevail among the Slaves in the Towns and Plantations, having no acquaintance or connection of any sort, but such as they form in the Regiment. I have invariably found them to make the most orderly, clean and attentive Soldiers. Out of Two hundred and upwards, which have been received into the Regiment in the course of Five years and a half, there are not above three or four instances of any of them being punished, and not one for any serious offence, whereas many of those who are furnished by the Planters, when the Regiment [the 11th] was formed, have very frequently deserved (as some have met) Capital punishment.

The new African recruit becomes gradually initiated into the habits of a Military life, and ere long discovers the superiority of his situation above the Slave, whose debased state he has never been subject to. He likewise feels himself proportionably elevated, from the rank which his officers hold in Society, and the respect which he sees is paid to them.

In recruiting the Regiments, attention should be given to the national character, peculiar to the People; some there are of a more tractable disposition than others, and who, in their own Country are habituated to the dangers and hardships of a Soldier's life, while others again are distinguished for stupidity, obstinacy, indolence & other bad qualities.

The Coromantees are reckoned amongst the most intrepid & hardy, being trained from their Infancy to War.

The Fantees and Angolas are also esteemed a spirited and an active race of People. On the other hand the Ebos and a few others are of a contrary turn. . . .

Among other ideas which have occurr'd to me, with a view of improving the establishment, I shall here mention one, which however at the first glimpse, may possible appear outrè, will on full consideration, I doubt not, clearly convince, that the greatest advantage may be deriv'd from its adoption. It is that of purchasing and attaching a certain number of Women, to each Company, who should have liberty to choose a Husband, from amongst the most regular and well behav'd Men belonging to it, with the approbation of the Commanding officer of the Regiment.

When such connexions are formed, every possible protection should be afforded them, and the severest punishment, should await those, who should venture to trespass on their domestic happiness. And as this arrangement is intended eventually to afford very material benefit to the Publick service, it would be necessary to notice as a serious offence, any instances of infidelity.

The utility of those Women towards the Economy of the Regiment, would be very great, and as before observed, in progress of time, must naturally prove of considerable advantage and profit to the Publick. The Children would of course, be the property of Government, and whether Male or Female, should remain constantly with the Regiment, and be considered as belonging to it. Boys would be trained to arms, and become in time excellent Soldiers.

The Girls, when at a proper age, would be allowed to marry in the Regiment, and during their younger years might be taught such employment as would make them useful to it. It would also be but just to allow the same ration of provisions to them, as to the Wives and Children of Soldiers in European Regiments. . . .

6. Our Lady of Pueblito Supports the Crown, 1801

Triumphant Querétaro in the Countryside of Pueblito. Sacred Historical Poem in Four Cantos. On the Miraculous Image of Our Lady of Pueblito,

Come, distant pueblos, come to see the works of the Lord, and the marvels that He has done for us upon the earth: He has banished war until the ends of the earth . . .

36.
Remove, o Holy Mother, the rumors
Of the error whose source is of the eternal ills:
Inhabitants of this your Kingdom do not weaken,
Your devoted faithful,
In your faith, and your constancy, and victors
Facing the most fatal strikes
That wicked impiety may put forth
Against the Religion, that is so sacred.

37.
Dispel, o beautiful Virgin, the clouds
Of the bloody infernal revolution,
That has so many Pueblos in ruins,
And attempts almost all the Universe
Its rage subverts everywhere:
Atrocious rage, that error moves and foments,
That offends God, and his holy Laws,
Disheartens the Vassals and the Kings.

38.
Never arrive to this fortunate land
The fierce boldness of human pride,
Making fatal war on the holy
Glory of God, and honor of the Sovereign.
Faith maintains your force and power,
Great beloved Mother. At the strike of your hand
The wicked disbelievers of the day
Fall vile victim of their persistence.

39.
Those with their false doctrine
And vain detestable reason,
Whose infernal principle does not concur
With the divine adored Laws,
While with a knowledge that perturbs
They need respectable, wise men,
With this all declare them
Ignorant and foolish in a thousand ways.

Source: Don Francisco María Colombini y Camayori, *Querétaro Triunfante en los Caminos del Pueblito* (Mexico: Zuñiga y Ontiveros, 1801), verses 36–53. Translated for this volume by Okezi Otovo.

40.
But that Holy God that inhabits
The Heavens, with His wisdom
That is righteous, incomprehensible, and infinite,
He will ridicule their Philosophy;
And while His mercy is not irritated
Mocks their stubborn persistence
Until finally tired He will give death
To those godless with His holy and strong arm.

42.
What men are these celebrated sages?
That to deny almost reach God himself,
When the most neglected ignorant ones
Recognize all in the abyss
Of His power, and remain admirers?
Until Paganism sounded in the voice,
That ignoring a God, true God,
Is the greatest plague of the entire World.

45.
Grand God, infernal furies have armed
Against your sacrosanct Temple.
Heavens, tremble from pure fright
Cry, gates of Heaven, so many wrongs.
Piety, Lord: save your holy Pueblo,
Mortals have corrupted.
But no, all of Hell cannot
Prevail against the great Eternal Being.

46.
The Church of the Lord Column endures,
That maintains the Omnipotence,
And established in the most pure truth,
That to suffer may not decline,
Will also be triumphant and very sure
Against the fierce blows and insolence
Of this infernal mob that combats it
In open country, but does not overthrow it.

47.
MARY, great beloved Mother of Pueblito,
With the same power which you defeated
The false Idols of Cerrito,
Defeat the blind furor, that does not desist
From the prideful accursed sinner,
That of God and your fierce piety resists,
And with such impiety, such dishonor
Elevates altars to silver and gold.

49.

To complete the marvels and feats
Defend your invincible eternal right
Of the Royal Monarchy of the two Spains,
That happily and justly govern us.
In their works, enterprises and campaigns
Accompany the glory and internal peace,
Fruit of the piety and Christian faith,
Honors of their sovereign house.

50.

But it is you, Pure MARY,
Defender of your vast Empires,
If to protect your sovereignty
Your Immaculate Conception adore,
Defend, shelter a King that has faith in you,
That swore to you as his special Lady:
A King that grants all, and that delights in all
Related to your holy glory.

51.

Declare, o fortunate Querétaro,
The royal sovereign privileges
Worthy of the heart of a pious King,
And of your very Christian sentiments.
For a Monarch so great and religious
Tribute your affection, o people of Querétaro,
Pray to MARY your Patroness
For the happiness of her Crown.

52.

Mary Holy Virgin, I repeat,
Guard the life of the Catholic King.
Your holy blessing, dear Mother
Arrives To his Court, from your Pueblito.
Your power, that extends to infinity,
Defend Spain: Spain combated
Sings to your eternal honor, sings victory,
And this will be the seal of your holy History.

53.

Of this thousand fortunes and many others,
By your favor, originated fulfilled.
All this Empire to your sacred designs
Tributes to you rendered prayers
Pueblos, Towns, Cities, all
Sing your graces, distinguished graces;
Such that all this America, o MARY,
You have declared our Mother and guide.

7. A South American Revolutionary Looks to the Future, 1815

With what a feeling of gratitude I read that passage in your letter in which you say to me: "I hope that the success which then followed Spanish arms may now turn in favor of their adversaries, the badly oppressed people of South America." I take this hope as a prediction, if it is justice that determines man's contests. Success will crown our efforts, because the destiny of America has been irrevocably decided; the tie that bound her to Spain has been severed. Only a concept maintained that tie and kept the parts of that immense monarchy together. That which formerly bound them now divides them. The hatred that the Peninsula has inspired in us is greater than the ocean between us. It would be easier to have the two continents meet than to reconcile the spirits of the two countries. The habit of obedience; a community of interest, of understanding, of religion; mutual goodwill; a tender regard for the birthplace and good name of our forefathers; in short, all that gave rise to our hopes, came to us from Spain. As a result there was born a principle of affinity that seemed eternal, notwithstanding the misbehavior of our rulers which weakened that sympathy, or, rather, that bond enforced by the domination of their rule. At present the contrary attitude persists: we are threatened with the fear of death, dishonor, and every harm; there is nothing we have not suffered at the hands of that unnatural step-mother—Spain. The veil has been torn asunder. We have already seen the light, and it is not our desire to be thrust back into darkness. The chains have been broken; we have been freed, and now our enemies seek to enslave us anew. For this reason America fights desperately, and seldom has desperation failed to achieve victory.

Because successes have been partial and spasmodic, we must not lose faith. In some regions the Independents triumph, while in others the tyrants have the advantage. What is the end result? Is not the entire New World in motion, armed for defense? We have but to look around us on this hemisphere to witness a simultaneous struggle at every point. . . .

It is even more difficult to foresee the future fate of the New World, to set down its political principles, or to prophesy what manner of government it will adopt. Every conjecture relative to America's future is, I feel, pure speculation. When mankind was in its infancy, steeped in uncertainty, ignorance, and error, was it possible to foresee what system it would adopt for its preservation? Who could venture to say that a certain nation would be a republic or a monarchy; this nation great, that nation small? To my way of thinking, such is our own situation. We are a young people. We inhabit a world apart, separated by broad seas. We are young in the ways of almost all the arts and sciences, although, in a certain manner, we are old in the ways of civilized society. I look upon the present state of America as similar to that of Rome after its fall. Each part of Rome adopted a political system conforming to its interest and situation or was led by the individual ambitions of certain chiefs, dynasties, or associations. But this important difference exists: those dispersed parts later reestablished their ancient nations, subject to the changes imposed by circumstances

Source: Simón Bolívar, "Reply of a South American to a Gentleman of this Island [Jamaica]," in Harold A. Bierck, Jr., ed., *Selected Writings of Bolívar* (New York: The Colonial Press Inc., 1951), vol. 1, pp. 104–105, 109–110, 115–116, 118–119.

or events. But we scarcely retain a vestige of what once was; we are, moreover, neither Indian nor European, but a species midway between the legitimate proprietors of this country and the Spanish usurpers. In short, though Americans by birth we derive our rights from Europe, and we have to assert these rights against the rights of the natives, and at the same time we must defend ourselves against the invaders. This places us in a most extraordinary and involved situation. Notwithstanding that it is a type of divination to predict the result of the political course which America is pursuing, I shall venture some conjectures which, of course, are colored by my enthusiasm and dictated by rational desires rather than by reasoned calculations. . . .

It is harder, Montesquieu has written, to release a nation from servitude than to enslave a free nation. This truth is proven by the annals of all times, which reveal that most free nations have been put under the yoke, but very few enslaved nations have recovered their liberty. Despite the convictions of history, South Americas have made efforts to obtain liberal, even perfect, institutions, doubtless out of that instinct to aspire to the greatest possible happiness, which, common to all men, is bound to follow in civil societies founded on the principles of justice, liberty, and equality. But are we capable of maintaining in proper balance the difficult charge of a republic? Is it conceivable that a newly emancipated people can soar to the heights of liberty, and, unlike Icarus, neither have its wings melt nor fall into an abyss? Such a marvel is inconceivable and without precedent. There is no reasonable probability to bolster our hopes.

More than anyone, I desire to see America fashioned into the greatest nation in the world, greatest not so much by virtue of her area and wealth as by her freedom and glory. Although I seek perfection for the government of my country, I cannot persuade myself that the New World can, at the moment, be organized as a great republic. Since it is impossible, I dare not desire it; yet much less do I desire to have all America a monarchy because this plan is not only impracticable but also impossible. Wrongs now existing could not be righted, and our emancipation would be fruitless. The American states need the care of paternal governments to heal the sores and wounds of despotism and war. The parent country, for example, might be Mexico, the only country fitted for the position by her intrinsic strength, and without such power there can be no parent country. Let us assume it were to be the Isthmus of Panama, the most central point of this vast continent. Would not all parts continue in their lethargy and even in their present disorder? For a single government to infuse life into the New World; to put into use all the resources for public prosperity; to improve, educate, and perfect the New World, that government would have to possess the authority of a god, much less the knowledge and virtues of mankind.

The party spirit that today keeps our states in constant agitation would assume still greater proportions were a central power established, for that power—the only force capable of checking this agitation—would be elsewhere. Furthermore, the chief figures of the capitals would not tolerate the preponderance of leaders at the metropolis, for they would regard these leaders as so many tyrants. Their resentments would attain such heights that they would compare the latter to the hated Spaniards. Any such monarchy would be a misshapen colossus that would collapse of its own weight at the slightest disturbance. . . .

It is a grandiose idea to think of consolidating the New World into a single nation, united by pacts into a single bond. It is reasoned that, as these parts have a common origin, language, customs, and religion, they ought to have a single government to permit the newly formed states to unite in a confederation. But this is not possible. Actually, America is separated by climatic differences, geographic diversity, conflicting interests, and dissimilar characteristics. How beautiful it would be if the Isthmus of Panamá could be for us what the Isthmus of Corinth was for the Greeks! Would to God that some day we may have the good fortune to convene there an august assembly of representatives of republics, kingdoms, and empires to deliberate upon the high interests of peace and war with the nations of the other three-quarters of the globe. This type of organization may come to pass in some happier period of our regeneration. But any other plan, such as that of Abbé St. Pierre, who in laudable delirium conceived the idea of assembling a European congress to decide the fate and interests of those nations, would be meaningless.

Among the popular and representative systems, I do not favor the federal system. It is over-perfect, and it demands political virtues and talents far superior to our own. For the same reason, I reject a monarchy that is part aristocracy and part democracy, although with such a government England has achieved much fortune and splendor. Since it is not possible for us to select the most perfect and complete form of government, let us avoid falling into demagogic anarchy or monocratic tyranny. These opposite extremes would only wreck us on similar reefs of misfortune and dishonor; hence, we must seek a mean between them. I say: Do not adopt the best system of government, but the one that is most likely to succeed. . . .

8. Brazil Becomes an Independent Monarchy, 1815, 1822

Prince Regent João VI's 1815 Decree

D. João, by the Grace of God, Prince Regent of Portugal and the Algarves, in Africa and Guinea, and of the Conquest, Navigation, and Commerce of Ethiopia, Arabia, Persia, and India, &c. make known to those to whom this present Letter of Law shall come, that there being constantly in my royal mind the most lively desire to cause to prosper those States which the Divine Providence has confided to my sovereign rule; and giving, at the same time, its due importance to the magnitude and locality of my domains in America, to the copiousness and variety of the precious elements of wealth which it contains; and knowing besides how advantageous to my faithful subjects in general will be a perfect union and identity between my kingdom of Portugal, the Algarves, and my dominions of Brazil, by raising them to that grade and political class, which, by the aforesaid proposition, they ought to aspire to, and in which my said dominions have been already considered by the plenipotentiaries of the powers which form the Congress at Vienna, also in the Treaty of Alliance concluded on the 8th of April in the current year, as in the final treaty of the same Congress; I am therefore minded, and it is my pleasure, to ordain as follows:

1st. That from the publication of this Letter of Law, the State of Brazil shall be elevated to the dignity, preeminence, and denomination of the Kingdom of Brazil.

Source: E. Bradford Burns, *A Documentary History of Brazil* (New York: Alfred A. Knopf, 1966), 189–191, 198–200.

2dly. That my kingdom of Portugal, the Algarves, and Brazil, shall form from henceforth one only and united kingdom, under the title of The United Kingdom of Portugal, Brazil, and the Algarves. 3dly. That for the titles inherent in the crown of Portugal, and of which it has hitherto made use in all its public acts, the new title shall be substituted of Prince Regent of the United Kingdoms of Portugal, Brazil, and the Algarves, &c.

Given in the Palace of Rio de Janeiro, the 16th of December, 1815.

THE PRINCE
MARQUES DO AGUIAR.

Father Belchior Pinheiro de Oliveira's Account of the Declaration of Brazilian Independence in 1822

The Prince ordered me to read aloud the letters brought by Paulo Bregaro and Antônio Cordeiro. They consisted of the following: an instruction from the Côrtes, a letter from D. João, another from the Princess, another from José Bonifácio and still another from Chamberlain, the secret agent of the Prince. The Côrtes demanded the immediate return of the Prince and the imprisonment and trial of José Bonifácio; the Princess recommended prudence and asked the Prince to listen to the advice of his minister; José Bonifácio told the Prince that he must choose one of two roads to follow: leave immediately for Portugal and make himself the prisoner of the Côrtes, as was the situation of D. João VI, or remain and proclaim the independence of Brazil becoming either its Emperor or King; Chamberlain gave information that the party of D. Miguel, in Portugal, was victorious and that they spoke openly of the disinheritance of D. Pedro in favor of D. Miguel; D. João advised his son to obey the Portuguese law. D. Pedro, trembling with rage, grabbed the letters from my hands and crumpling them up threw them on the ground and stomped on them. He left them lying there, but I picked them up and kept them. Then, after buttoning up and arranging his uniform (he had just been to the edge of the stream of Ypiranga agonized by a painful attack of dysentery), he turned toward me and asked: "What now, Father Belchior?"

I quickly responded, "If your Highness does not declare himself King of Brazil, you will be made a prisoner of the Côrtes and perhaps disinherited by them. The only course is independence and separation."

Accompanied by me, Cordeiro, Bregaro, Carlota, and others, D. Pedro silently walked toward our horses at the side of the road. Suddenly he halted in the middle of the road and said to me, "Father Belchior, they asked for it and they will get it. The Côrtes is persecuting me and calling me an adolescent and a Brazilian. Well, now let them see their adolescent in action. From today on our relations with them are finished. I want nothing more from the Portuguese government, and I proclaim Brazil forevermore separated from Portugal."

With enthusiasm we immediately answered, "Long live liberty! Long live an independent Brazil! Long live D. Pedro!"

The Prince turned to his adjutant and said, "Tell my guard that I have just declared the complete independence of Brazil. We are free from Portugal."

Lieutenant Canto e Melo rode toward a market where most of the soldiers of the guard remained. He returned to the Prince with them shouting enthusiastically in favor of an independent and separate Brazil, D. Pedro, and the Catholic Religion.

D. Pedro before the guard said, "The Portuguese Côrtes wants to enslave and to persecute us. Henceforth our relations are broken. Not one tie unites us!" And tearing from his hat the blue and white emblem decreed by the Côrtes as the symbol of the Portuguese nation, he threw it on the ground, saying, " Throw away that symbol, soldiers! Long live independence, liberty, and the separation of Brazil!"

We responded with a shout in favor of an independent and separate Brazil and another for D. Pedro.

The Prince unsheathed his sword, and the civilians removed their hats. D. Pedro said, "By my blood, by my honor, and with God's help, I swear to liberate Brazil."

"We all swear to it," shouted the rest.

D. Pedro sheathed his sword, an act repeated by the guard, went to the head of the crowd, turned, and rose up in the stirrups to cry, "Brazilians, our motto from this day forward will be 'Independence or Death.'"

Seated firmly in his saddle, he spurred his handsome horse and galloped, followed by his retinue, toward São Paulo, where he was lodged by Brigadier Jordão, Captain Antônio Silva Prado, and others, who worked miracles in order to cheer up the prince.

After dismounting, D. Pedro ordered his adjutant to go at once to the goldsmith Lessa and have made a small disk in gold bearing the words "Independence or Death" to be fastened on the arm with ribbons of green and gold.

Wearing the emblem he appeared at the theatre where my dear friends Alfêres Aquins and Father Ildefonso acclaimed him the King of Brazil.

Throughout the theatre were yellow and green ribbons. They hung from the walls, from the boxes, from the arms of the men and from the hair and dresses of the women.

◁ *E S S A Y S*

Why did some Americans revolt and others remain "loyal" to the empires in which they were embedded? The two essays in this chapter look at both sides of the coin. In a chapter from his seminal book *Imagined Communities*, Benedict Anderson argues that the ideology of nationalism originated in the British North American and Spanish American independence movements of the late eighteenth and early nineteenth centuries. What were the circumstances that made this "creole" nationalism possible? Anderson argues that the administrative structure of the colonies provided self-contained units of allegiance for American-born elites to identify with. Creoles' exclusion from positions of power in Europe reinforced their identification with their homelands. Moreover, the rise of a vigorous print culture, and especially the appearance of provincial newspapers, helped the creole public to imagine themselves as a separate and distinct people, with their own economic and political interests and identities. Yet Anderson's essay does not explain why many Americans chose not to join in revolutionary movements for national independence. During the American War for Independence, for instance, approximately half of all British colonies in the Caribbean and western Atlantic opted to stay in the British empire, and a sizable number of people in the rebellious colonies of North America remained loyal to Britain. In this excerpt from his book on the American Revolution and the British Caribbean, *An Empire Divided*, Andrew Jackson O'Shaughnessy explains why the British colonies in the Caribbean, after some initial support for the mainland rebels, ultimately decided to remain loyal to the empire. His essay raises important issues about the limits to ideology. Many revolutionary constraints (like their fear of slave revolts) blocked white islanders' impulse toward independence. Overall they realized that membership in the British empire had its privileges.

Where Did American Nationalism Come From?

BENEDICT ANDERSON

Here then is the riddle: why was it precisely *creole* communities that developed so early conceptions of their nation-ness—*well before most of Europe*? Why did such colonial provinces, usually containing large, oppressed, non–Spanish-speaking populations, produce creoles who consciously redefined these populations as fellow-nationals? And Spain, to whom they were, in so many ways, attached, as an enemy alien? Why did the Spanish-American Empire, which had existed calmly for almost three centuries, quite suddenly fragment into eighteen separate states?

The two factors most commonly adduced in explanation are the tightening of Madrid's control and the spread of the liberalizing ideas of the Enlightenment in the latter half of the eighteenth century. It is undoubtedly true that the policies pursued by the capable "enlightened despot" Carlos III (r. 1759–1788) increasingly frustrated, angered, and alarmed the upper creole classes. In what has sometimes sardonically been called the second conquest of the Americas, Madrid imposed new taxes, made their collection more efficient, enforced metropolitan commercial monopolies, restricted intra-hemispheric trade to its own advantage, centralized administrative hierarchies, and promoted a heavy immigration of *peninsulares*. Mexico, for example, in the early eighteenth century provided the Crown with an annual revenue of about 3,000,000 pesos. By the century's end, however, the sum had almost quintupled to 14,000,000, of which only 4,000,000 were used to defray the costs of local administration. Parallel to this, the level of peninsular migration by the decade 1780–1790 was five times as high as it had been between 1710–1730.

There is also no doubt that improving trans-Atlantic communications, and the fact that the various Americas shared languages and cultures with their respective metropoles, meant a relatively rapid and easy transmission of the new economic and political doctrines being produced in Western Europe. The success of the Thirteen Colonies' revolt at the end of the 1770s, and the onset of the French Revolution at the end of the 1780s, did not fail to exert a powerful influence. Nothing confirms this "cultural revolution" more than the pervasive *republicanism* of the newly independent communities. Nowhere was any serious attempt made to recreate the dynastic principle in the Americas, except in Brazil; even there, it would probably not have been possible without the immigration in 1808 of the Portuguese dynast himself, in flight from Napoléon. (He stayed there for 13 years, and, on returning home, had his son crowned locally as Pedro I of Brazil.)

Yet the aggressiveness of Madrid and the spirit of liberalism, while central to any understanding of the impulse of resistance in the Spanish Americas, do not in themselves explain why entities like Chile, Venezuela, and Mexico turned out to be

Source: Benedict Anderson, *Imagined Communities: Reflections on the Origin and Spread of Nationalism* (London: Verso Books, 1991, rev. ed.), 50–53, 56–59, 61–64. Reprinted with permission of Verso Books.

emotionally plausible and politically viable, nor why San Martín should decree that certain aborigines be identified by the neological "Peruvians." Nor, ultimately, do they account for the real sacrifices made. For while it is certain that the upper creole classes, *conceived as historical social formations*, did nicely out of independence over the long haul, many actual members of those classes *living* between 1808 and 1828 were financially ruined. (To take only one example: during Madrid's counter-offensive of 1814–16 "more than two-thirds of Venezuela's landowning families suffered heavy confiscations.") And just as many willingly gave up their lives for the cause. This willingness to sacrifice on the part of comfortable classes is food for thought.

What then? The beginnings of an answer lie in the striking fact that "each of the new South American republics had been an administrative unit from the sixteenth to the eighteenth century." In this respect they foreshadowed the new states of Africa and parts of Asia in the mid twentieth century, and form a sharp contrast to the new European states of the late nineteenth and early twentieth centuries. The original shaping of the American administrative units was to some extent arbitrary and fortuitous, marking the spatial limits of particular military conquests. But, over time, they developed a firmer reality under the influence of geographic, political and economic factors. The very vastness of the Spanish American empire, the enormous variety of its soils and climates, and, above all, the immense difficulty of communications in a pre-industrial age, tended to give these units a self-contained character. (In the colonial era the sea journey from Buenos Aires to Acapulco took four months, and the return trip even longer; the overland trek from Buenos Aires to Santiago normally lasted two months, and that to Cartagena nine.) In addition, Madrid's commercial policies had the effect of turning administrative units into separate economic zones. "All competition with the mother country was forbidden the Americans, and even the individual parts of the continent could not trade with each other. American goods en route from one side of America to the other had to travel circuitously through Spanish ports, and Spanish navigation had a monopoly on trade with the colonies." These experiences help to explain why "one of the basic principles of the American revolution" was that of "*uti possidetis* by which each nation was to preserve the territorial status quo of 1810, the year when the movement for independence had been inaugurated." Their influence also doubtless contributed to the break-up of Bolívar's short-lived Gran Colombía and of the United Provinces of the Rio de la Plata into their older constituents (which today are known as Venezuela–Colombia–Ecuador and Argentina–Uruguay–Paraguay–Bolivia). Nonetheless, *in themselves*, market-zones, "natural"-geographic or politico-administrative, do not create attachments. Who will willingly die for Comecon or the EEC? . . .

The pattern is plain in the Americas. For example, of the 170 viceroys in Spanish America prior to 1813, only 4 were creoles. These figures are all the more startling if we note that in 1800 less than 5% of the 3,200,000 creole "whites" in the Western Empire (imposed on about 13,700,000 indigenes) were Spain-born Spaniards. On the eve of the revolution in Mexico, there was only one creole bishop, although creoles in the viceroyalty outnumbered *peninsulares* by 70 to 1. And, needless to say, it was nearly unheard-of for a creole to rise to a position of official importance in Spain. Moreover, the pilgrimages of creole functionaries were not merely vertically barred. If peninsular officials could travel the road from Zaragoza to Cartagena, Madrid, Lima, and again Madrid, the "Mexican" or "Chilean" creole typically served only in the territories of colonial Mexico or Chile: his lateral movement was as cramped as his vertical ascent. In this way, the apex of his looping climb, the highest administrative centre to which he could be assigned, was the capital of the imperial administrative unit in which he found himself. Yet on this cramped pilgrimage he found travelling-companions, who came to sense that their fellowship was based not only on that pilgrimage's particular stretch, but on the shared fatality of trans-Atlantic birth. Even if he was born within one week of his father's migration, the accident of birth in the Americas consigned him to subordination—even though in terms of language, religion, ancestry, or manners he was largely indistinguishable from the Spain-born Spaniard. There was nothing to be done about it: he was *irremediably* a creole. Yet how irrational his exclusion must have seemed! Nonetheless, hidden inside the irrationality was this logic: born in the Americas, he could not be a true Spaniard; *ergo*, born in Spain, the *peninsular* could not be a true American.

What made the exclusion appear rational in the metropole? Doubtless the confluence of a time-honoured Machiavellism with the growth of conceptions of biological and ecological contamination that accompanied the planetary spread of Europeans and European power from the sixteenth century onwards. From the sovereign's angle of vision, the American creoles, with their ever-growing numbers and increasing local rootedness with each succeeding generation, presented a historically unique political problem. For the first time the metropoles had to deal with—for that era—vast numbers of "fellow-Europeans" (over three million in the Spanish Americas by 1800) far outside Europe. If the indigenes were conquerable by arms and disease, and controllable by the mysteries of Christianity and a completely alien culture (as well as, for those days, an advanced political organization), the same was not true of the creoles, who had virtually the same relationship to arms, disease, Christianity and European culture as the metropolitans. In other words, in principle, they had readily at hand the political, cultural and military means for successfully asserting themselves. They constituted simultaneously a colonial community and an upper class. They were to be economically subjected and exploited, but they were also essential to the stability of the empire. One can see, in this light, a certain parallelism between the position of the creole magnates and of feudal barons, crucial to the sovereign's power, but also a menace to it. Thus the *peninsulares* dispatched as viceroys and bishops served the same functions as did the *homines novi* of the proto-absolutist bureaucracies. Even if the viceroy was a grandee in his Andalusian home, here, 5,000 miles away, juxtaposed to the creoles, he was effectively a *homo novus* fully dependent on his metropolitan master. The tense balance between peninsular official and creole magnate was in this way an expression of the old policy of *divide et impera* in a new setting. . . .

Our attention thus far has been focussed on the worlds of functionaries in the Americas—strategically important, but still small worlds. Moreover, they were worlds which, with their conflicts between *peninsulares* and creoles, predated the appearance of American national consciousnesses at the end of the eighteenth century. Cramped viceregal pilgrimages had no decisive consequences until their territorial stretch could be imagined as nations, in other words until the arrival of print-capitalism.

Print itself spread early to New Spain, but for two centuries it remained under the tight control of crown and church. Till the end of the seventeenth century, presses existed only in Mexico City and Lima, and their output was almost exclusively ecclesiastical. In Protestant North America printing scarcely existed at all in that century. In the course of the eighteenth, however, a virtual revolution took place. Between 1691 and 1820, no less than 2,120 "newspapers" were published, of which 461 lasted more than ten years.

The figure of Benjamin Franklin is indelibly associated with creole nationalism in the northern Americas. But the importance of his trade may be less apparent. Once again, Febvre and Martin are enlightening. They remind us that "printing did not really develop in [North] America during the eighteenth century until printers discovered a new source of income—the newspaper." Printers starting new presses always included a newspaper in their productions, to which they were usually the main, even the sole, contributor. Thus the printer-journalist was initially an essentially North American phenomenon. Since the main problem facing the printer-journalist was reaching readers, there developed an alliance with the post-master so intimate that often each became the other. Hence, the printer's office emerged as the key to North American communications and community intellectual life. In Spanish America, albeit more slowly and intermittently, similar processes produced, in the second half of the eighteenth century, the first local presses.

What were the characteristics of the first American newspapers, North or South? They began essentially as appendages of the market. Early gazettes contained— aside from news about the metropole—commercial news (when ships would arrive and depart, what prices were current for what commodities in what ports), as well as colonial political appointments, marriages of the wealthy, and so forth. In other words, what brought together, on the same page, *this* marriage with *that* ship, *this* price with *that* bishop, was the very structure of the colonial administration and market-system itself. In this way, the newspaper of Caracas quite naturally, and even apolitically, created an imagined community among a specific assemblage of fellow-readers, to whom *these* ships, brides, bishops and prices belonged. In time, of course, it was only to be expected that political elements would enter in.

One fertile trait of such newspapers was always their provinciality. A colonial creole might read a Madrid newspaper if he got the chance (but it would say nothing about his world), but many a peninsular official, living down the same street, would, if he could help it, *not* read the Caracas production. An asymmetry infinitely replicable in other colonial situations. Another such trait was plurality. The Spanish-American journals that developed towards the end of the eighteenth century were written in full awareness of provincials in worlds parallel to their own. The newspaper-readers of Mexico City, Buenos Aires, and Bogota, even if they did not read each other's newspapers, were nonetheless quite conscious of their existence. Hence a well-known doubleness in early Spanish-American nationalism, its alternating grand stretch and particularistic localism. The fact that early Mexican nationalists wrote of themselves as *nosotros los Americanos* and of their country as *nuestra América*, has been interpreted as revealing the vanity of the local creoles who, because Mexico was far the most valuable of Spain's American possessions, saw themselves as the centre of the New World. But, in fact, people all over Spanish America thought of themselves as "Americans," since this term denoted precisely the shared fatality of extra-Spanish birth.

At the same time, we have seen that the very conception of the newspaper implies the refraction of even "world events" into a specific imagined world of vernacular readers; and also how important to that imagined community is an idea of steady, solid simultaneity through time. Such a simultaneity the immense stretch of the Spanish American Empire, and the isolation of its component parts, made difficult to imagine. Mexican creoles might learn months later of developments in Buenos Aires, but it would be through Mexican newspapers, not those of the Rio de la Plata; and the events would appear as "similar to" rather than "part of" events in Mexico.

In this sense, the "failure" of the Spanish-American experience to generate a permanent Spanish-America-wide nationalism reflects both the general level of development of capitalism and technology in the late eighteenth century and the "local" backwardness of Spanish capitalism and technology in relation to the administrative stretch of the empire. (The world-historical era in which each nationalism is born probably has a significant impact on its scope. Is Indian nationalism not inseparable from colonial administrative-market unification, after the Mutiny, by the most formidable and advanced of the imperial powers?)

The Protestant, English-speaking creoles to the north were much more favourably situated for realizing the idea of "America" and indeed eventually succeeded in appropriating the everyday title of "Americans." The original Thirteen Colonies comprised an area smaller than Venezuela, and one third the size of Argentina. Bunched geographically together, their market-centres in Boston, New York, and Philadelphia were readily accessible to one another, and their populations were relatively tightly linked by print as well as commerce. The "United States" could gradually multiply in numbers over the next 183 years, as old and new populations moved westwards out of the old east coast core. Yet even in the case of the USA there are elements of comparative "failure" or shrinkage—non-absorption of English-speaking Canada, Texas's decade of independent sovereignty (1835–46). Had a sizeable English-speaking community existed in California in the eighteenth century, is it not likely that an independent state would have arisen there to play Argentina to the Thirteen Colonies' Peru? Even in the USA, the affective bonds of nationalism were elastic enough, combined with the rapid expansion of the western frontier and the contradictions generated between the economies of North and South, to precipitate a war of secession *almost a century after the Declaration of Independence*; and this war today sharply reminds us of those that tore Venezuela and Ecuador off from Gran Colombía, and Uruguay and Paraguay from the United Provinces of the Rio de la Plata.

Why Did the British West Indies Remain Loyal?

ANDREW JACKSON O'SHAUGHNESSY

The posturing of the island colonists on behalf of the North Americans in 1774–75 virtually ceased by August 1776. This was also true in London, where pro-American sentiment "was evidently on the wane." In June 1776, an address of the assembly of Grenada admitted that the island initially accepted that the North Americans were fighting a war to claim redress of grievances but that the subsequent conduct

Source: Andrew Jackson O'Shaughnessy, *An Empire Divided: The American Revolution and the British Caribbean* (Philadelphia: University of Pennsylvania Press, 2000), pp. 147–149, 151–155, 157–159. Reprinted by permission of the University of Pennsylvania Press.

of the patriots revealed "that redress of Grievances had been the pretext [and] . . . Independance the Object of their pursuit." After leaving the West Indies in June, an anonymous planter wrote a pro-government pamphlet to refute the petitions of the previous year and to demonstrate that the islands were able to survive without provisions from North America.

The unpopularity of the American cause was reflected in the hostile treatment of captured Americans in the British West Indies. Silas Deane warned Robert Morris that American patriots "were not safe in Antigua and Barbados if they were known to be friendly to the continental Interest." He claimed that the island colonists "exult in the prospect or rather [the] hopes of a total reduction of the colonies by the Administration" because they expected to confine "American Commerce in the West Indies absolutely to the English Islands." An American merchant in Dominica fled when his belongings were seized and "it was likewise said that all the monies lying in the hands of the merchants in the English islands belonging to America, will be taken hold of by proclamation."

Antigua, the island formerly most closely connected with North America, was especially zealous in arresting anyone suspected of "attachment to the American cause," such as Charles Hobby Hubbard of Boston. Hubbard was "apprehended and confined to Gaol upwards of six Months, a great part of the Time in a Dungeon" after his ship was forced to land by a storm and letters to "the leaders of the American faction" were discovered in his mattress. . . .

Antiguans arrested and executed a man who, "falsely imagining that he might declare his mind here as freely as he did in England, being a favourer of the Americans," had publicly condemned the government. He was taken into custody where a body search revealed papers from British merchants to members of Congress. His punishment was particularly severe because he had tried "to inflame the minds of the people against the government, which might be a means of overturning all order and regularity in this island, and throwing us all into the greatest consternation." An indignant Captain Robert Campbell complained of gratuitous unpleasantness when his ship *America* was condemned by the vice-admiralty court at Antigua. He was imprisoned for over eight weeks "with fellons, at a short allowance of raw provisions, which were . . . dressed by the common Negro Hangman" and he suffered "continual insults and the utmost contempt, being shunned by the men with whom he had been acquainted, who would scarcely deign to speak to him."

There was an outburst of loyal rhetoric and petitions in the British West Indies in 1776. Six hundred and three "friends of government," a high proportion of the adult white population, dined at a tavern in Antigua where they drank twenty-one toasts to the royal family, the government, colonial officials, and military commanders in North America, "success to his Majesty's Arms in America," and finally "Confusion to the Congress." This was a far cry from only two years earlier when local planters had refused to do business with one of the East India ship captains who had transported the infamous tea cargo to Boston.

"Many Gentleman of Large Estates & property in the different West India Collonies . . . expressed their surprise" that the government did not ask them to supply slaves for military service in North America. The inhabitants of Nevis presented British troops with fifty hogsheads of rum "to inspire [them] with courage to beat the Yankee Rebels." Two former members of the assembly of Jamaica offered their advice to the government on how to crush the rebellion in North America. Some of the large planters in Jamaica were willing to provide a thousand slaves for military service on the mainland, "such is their detestation at the present Rebellion in America." A loyal planter wrote that the safety of Jamaica was in jeopardy from both the slaves and the foreign islands until the "sons of sedition [in America] are checked."

The island assemblies began to send addresses to Britain affirming their loyalty to the king. These addresses were generally pro forma but they began to include clauses specifically denouncing the rebellion in North America. In December 1775, Jamaica led all the islands in sending a declaration of loyalty to the king in which it also requested more troops. George III replied by publicly expressing his pleasure at the dutiful behavior of the Jamaican assembly. In December 1776, the assembly passed another loyal address, proclaiming that "it must be and is our desire as well as our interest, to support maintain and defend your Majesty in your just rights, with the greatest loyalty and affection, and thereby render ourselves truly deserving of your Royal favor and protection." They again asked for more military assistance. Their tone was now very different from that of their radical petition of December 1774. . . .

Another indication of British West Indian loyalty was the welcome extended to loyalist refugees from North America. The most exotic group of loyalists were the actors of the American Company of Comedians, who relocated to Jamaica after the Continental Congress banned theatrical performances (October 1774). This was the celebrated troupe founded by Lewis Hallam. As early as February 1775, actor David Douglas led the company to Jamaica, where they opened with a performance of *Romeo and Juliet* in Kingston in July. In October, several families arrived in Jamaica from North America "on account of troubles in their own country." In March 1776, following the flight of Governor Sir James Wright, many loyalists quitted Georgia for the West Indies and the Bahamas. American loyalists in the West Indies influenced local opinion, such as Douglas, who, in partnership with Alexander Aikman, became the king's printer for Jamaica. They published the *Jamaican Mercury and Kingston Weekly Advertiser* beginning in 1779, which they renamed the *Royal Gazette* in 1780.

Why did the posturing of the island colonies on behalf of North America in 1774–75 cease in 1776? The conservative backlash against North America was in part caused by the great Jamaican slave rebellion of 1776. The rebellion was led by skilled creole slaves who, the governor wrote, "never were before engaged in Rebellions and in whose fidelity we had always most firmly relied." They included black drivers, coopers, distillers, millwrights, penkeepers, cartmen, carpenters, and cooks. Jamaica had "never been in such imminent Danger since the English conquest."

The slave leaders confided their plans to no more than two "chiefs" on each estate in the parish of Hanover, in northwest Jamaica, where most of the planters were recent settlers with new plantations and where there were "more sugar works than some [parishes] of three times the extent." Furthermore, the Hanover black-white ratio was an extraordinary twenty-five to one. From Hanover, the leaders aimed to incite an island-wide insurrection beginning in late July. The revolt broke out prematurely. It did not cause immediate panic and the governor thought the danger almost over when he received notice of a general rebellion. The governor declared martial law during which the noise of trumpets and drums beating to arms filled the air, "rousing the most insensible human beings" and causing terror. He placed an embargo on all shipping including the sugar convoy, a drastic measure because it hurt the credit of the island among the merchant community in Britain. The leeward maroons at Trelawny Town were suspected of involvement in the rebellion. Governor Keith found them "restive" during the rebellion and warned of the "very high idea the slaves entertain of them."

The revolt widened when some of the conspirators spread the word elsewhere on the island. In the parish of Vere, on the south side of Jamaica, two slaves were tried and convicted for attempting to obtain guns with the intent to rebel. At Montego Bay, someone tried to poison the market water with arson. At the request of the governor, Admiral Gayton sent two ships to the port of Lucea in Hanover to quell the rebellion. Panic ensued for almost seven weeks. The governor called off martial law even though he was not confident that the danger had passed. Of 135 slaves subsequently tried for the rebellion, 17 were executed, 45 transported, and 11 suffered "severe corporal punishment." Some of those executed were burnt alive and others gibbeted.

The 1776 Jamaican rebellion was a direct consequence of the American Revolution. The loss of food imports from the mainland colonies, together with a severe drought, provoked the slaves to rebel because, according to Pontack of the Blue Hose Estate in the parish of Hanover, "they were angry too much with the white people, because they had taken from them their bread." A report in an English newspaper claimed that American emissaries encouraged the slaves, giving them ammunition and guns. Silas Deane, an American diplomat, had indeed advocated American support for an uprising of the Caribs in St. Vincent and a slave revolt in Jamaica.

Several planters blamed the ideology of the mainland patriots for the revolt. The Rev. John Lindsay, rector of the parish of St. Catherine and Spanish Town, wrote to Dr. William Robertson (the principal of Edinburgh University who became a distinguished historian of the Revolutionary War), attributing the participation of creole slaves to "disaffected" whites who openly expressed their sympathy for the mainland patriots at their dinner tables. Lindsay pondered the impact on slaves who heard some whites praise "the Blood split by Rebells extoll'd as precious drops" and heard "Men toasted into Immortal Honours for Encountering Death in every form, rather than submit to Slavery." A merchant asked, "Can you be surprised that the Negroes in Jamaica should endeavour to Recover their Freedom, when they dayly hear at the Tables of their Masters, how much the Americans are applauded for the stand they are making for theirs." His correspondent agreed and replied, "We are too often unguarded in our conversation when our Servants are present."

Slaves hardly needed to import ideas of liberty; the favorable circumstances created by the outbreak of war was the primary cause of the Jamaican rebellion in 1776. The slaves planned the rising to coincide with both the removal of British troops from Jamaica to North America and the withdrawal of naval ships escorting the merchant convoy to Britain against the new menace of American privateers: "The taking away the few soldiers we had left, at a time when there was a great scarcity of provisions . . . was the chief cause of the late conspiracy among the Negroes in Hanover."

The Jamaican revolt dramatically illustrated the dependence of the white island colonists on the presence of the British army to police the slave population. The revolt began when the Fiftieth Regiment, representing almost half the military force on the island, was about to embark for North America as reinforcements for General Sir William Howe. Nine of the total ten companies were already onboard the troop transports where they were awaiting the other company before sailing from the Hanover port of Lucea for service in America. The military strength of the island was consequently reduced to about 360 soldiers and some parishes were left totally denuded of any protection by regulars.

The slave conspirators recognized that there were fewer troops on the island "than at any other time in their memory" while their own numbers had increased. They knew that "the English were engaged in a desperate war, which would require all their force elsewhere [so that] . . . they could not have a better opportunity of seizing the country to themselves." They knew that the British troops were scheduled to depart before the end of July and that naval ships were due to escort the troops and the homeward-bound convoy. Governor Keith—apparently fearful that his report to the secretary of state would appear too far-fetched—apologized that "this train of Reasoning may seem above negro comprehension." Later examinations of the conspirators uniformly supported the evidence that the rebellion was planned around the anticipated departure of the soldiers. An inquiry by the assembly of Jamaica concluded unanimously that the withdrawal of the troops, upon which the slaves had "placed their strongest hopes," was the primary cause of the conspiracy.

The garrison mentality of the white island colonists intensified in the aftermath of the Jamaican slave rebellion and contributed to the backlash against the American Revolution. A letter from Barbados, written at the time of the Jamaican rebellion, described the slaves there as "in a state of rebellion." In September 1776, the president of the council of St. Kitts sought the help of the British navy when he suspected that the fires on two or three plantations were part of an intended slave insurrection. Others suspected slave involvement in the great fire in Basseterre, the capital of St. Kitts, which caused over £200,000 sterling worth of damage and was widely believed to be arson. Montserrat increased its guards to check the "outrages" committed by slaves and to apprehend any slave found without a ticket after 8:30 at night. Whites in Antigua stayed up all night to prevent a slave uprising. Some estate owners sent their wives and daughters back to England for safety. In December, four slaves in Montserrat were executed for attempting to murder their master. Maroons in Grenada were committing "outrages and Depredations [of the] . . . most alarming Nature." There was "seldom a week passes but we hear of some estates being plundered by them."

The posturing of the white island colonists on behalf of the North Americans in 1774–75 also ceased in 1776 because of the effects of the American War in the Caribbean. It became treason to openly avow sympathy for the North Americans after the king proclaimed them in rebellion on August 23, 1775. It was not safe to express political sentiments in correspondence. The North Americans were no longer fighting a war for the redress of grievances but a war of independence that was less comprehensible to the island colonists, whose self-interest dictated their loyalty to the British Empire.

American privateers intercepted the trade of the islands, which "naturally incline[d] those who were their friends to become their enemies" in the British West Indies. In November 1775, Massachusetts led the other provinces by issuing commissions to privateers and by setting up prize courts. In March 1776, the Continental

Congress also began to issue commissions. It initially tried to exempt the property of the British Caribbean from seizure but found the distinction unworkable. In July, it passed a resolution for the confiscation of the property of the British "and particularly the inhabitants of the British West Indies" taken at sea. . . .

Some American privateers were bold enough to launch raids on the outer ports of the British islands where they cut merchant vessels and fishing boats from their moorings "in sight of the inhabitants" and where they mounted landing parties. They briefly invaded Nassau (New Providence) in the Bahamas in 1776 and twice tried to capture Tobago in 1777. St. Anne's Bay in Jamaica experienced almost daily alarms of an imminent enemy landing and several ships were snatched from their moorings. A raid against Speights Town in Barbados netted fishing boats and slaves valued at £2,000. John Pinney of Nevis was stunned to witness, from his own breakfast table, a St. Kitts–bound brig taken by a privateer off his plantation wharf. He protested that the islands were "subject to be pilfered and robbed by Pirates in the night, who may, with ease, carry off our slaves to the utter ruin of the Planters." . . .

British West Indian merchants pursued their own solution to the problem of privateers in a hostile backlash against the American revolutionaries. They soon began to arm their own vessels to annoy "his Majesties Rebellious Subjects." Antigua took the initiative. By January 1777, the Antiguan sloop *Reprisal* had taken three American vessels and it was said that "seven others will be ready to sail from the Island . . . before the end of the present week." The owners of the *Reprisal* declared that they were "zealously disposed to assist in reducing his Majesty's rebellious colonies in America to lawful obedience." The owners included prominent merchants and planters in the assembly. Antigua and Tortola led the other British islands in arming ships against American privateers. . . .

American privateers were not deterred by these countermeasures, and they continued to disrupt the plantation economy and compound the effects of the loss of North American trade for the British West Indies. It became dangerous to sail across the Atlantic and even between islands. American privateers took an estimated 25,000 hogsheads of sugar aboard ships sailing from the British Caribbean in 1776. Two captured ships from Barbados alone were reckoned to be worth £20,000. By February 1777, the American privateers had taken some 250 British West India merchant ships, contributing to the collapse of four major West India merchant companies in London.

The British West Indies stood to gain nothing from the American Revolutionary War. They dreaded the approach of a conflict in which the colonies were wrenched apart in what contemporaries commonly termed a civil war. They wanted most of all to maintain the integrity of the empire and blamed extremists on both sides for the war. They wanted "a happy reconciliation." . . .

The British West Indies eagerly desired a settlement between the contestants. There were many trimmers who wanted to offend neither Britain nor the United States. Some advocated appeasing the United States, "at least [to] convince our neighbours, that we are not *inimical* to their interests [and] not [to] furnish *reasons* for an hostile disposition on her part nor provoke her just resentment." In 1778, they were tempted by an offer of neutrality from Congress, which the Society of West India Merchants considered but found impractical.

West Indians supported the 1778 British peace initiative led by the earl of Carlisle. The commission was empowered to negotiate directly with Congress and to offer the suspension of all colonial acts passed since 1763. However, Britain was unwilling to grant the independence of the United States and was negotiating from a position of weakness with the imminent declaration of war by France. West Indian hopes of reconciliation were dashed and they became frustrated spectators in a war that promised them nothing but trouble.

FURTHER READING

Anderson, Fred. *Crucible of War: The Seven Years' War and the Fate of Empire in British North America, 1754–1766.* New York: Alfred A. Knopf, 2000.

Bailyn, Bernard. *The Ideological Origins of the American Revolution.* Cambridge, MA: Belknap Press of Harvard University Press, 1967.

Dubois, Laurent. *Avengers of the New World: The Story of the Haitian Revolution.* Cambridge, MA: Belknap Press of Harvard University Press, 2004.

Foner, Eric. *Tom Paine and Revolutionary America.* New York: Oxford University Press, 1977, 2004.

Geggus, David P., ed. *The Impact of the Haitian Revolution in the Atlantic World.* Columbia: University of South Carolina, 2001.

Gould, Eliga H., and Peter S. Onuf. *Empire and Nation: The American Revolution in the Atlantic World.* Baltimore: The Johns Hopkins University Press, 2005.

Hobsbawm, E. J. *The Age of Revolution, 1789–1848.* Cleveland, OH: World, 1962.

James, C. L. R. *The Black Jacobins: Toussaint L'Ouverture and the San Domingo Revolution.* New York: Vintage Books, 1989.

Langley, Lester D. *The Americas in the Age of Revolution, 1750–1850.* New Haven, CT: Yale University Press, 1996.

Liss, Peggy K. *Atlantic Empires: The Network of Trade and Revolution, 1713–1826.* Baltimore: The Johns Hopkins University Press, 1983.

Lynch, John. *Simón Bolívar: A Life.* New Haven, CT: Yale University Press, 2006.

———. *The Spanish American Revolutions, 1808–1826.* New York: Norton, 1973.

Middlekauff, Robert. *The Glorious Cause: The American Revolution, 1763–1789.* New York: Oxford University Press, 1982.

Nash, Gary B. *The Unknown American Revolution: The Unruly Birth of Democracy and the Struggle to Create America.* New York: Viking, 2005.

O'Shaughnessy, Andrew Jackson. *An Empire Divided: The American Revolution and the British Caribbean.* Philadelphia: University of Pennsylvania Press, 2000.

Palmer, R. R. *The Age of the Democratic Revolution.* Two volumes. Princeton, NJ: Princeton University Press, 1959–64.

Pybus, Cassandra. *Epic Journeys of Freedom: Runaway Slaves of the American Revolution and Their Global Quest for Liberty.* Boston: Beacon Press, 2006.

Rodríguez O., Jaime E. *The Independence of Spanish America.* New York: Cambridge University Press, 1998.

Schultz, Kirsten. *Tropical Versailles: Empire, Monarchy, and the Portuguese Royal Court in Rio de Janeiro, 1808–1821.* New York: Routledge, 2001.

Whelan, Kevin. *The Tree of Liberty: Radicalism, Catholicism, and the Construction of Irish Identity, 1760–1830.* Notre Dame, IN: University of Notre Dame Press in association with Field Day, 1996.

CHAPTER
12

Social Revolution

*Just how revolutionary were the American revolutions? Some colonial elites were
able to maintain power while others saw their power erode and crumble. As transatlantic empires fractured in the late eighteenth and early nineteenth centuries, revolutionary movements challenged traditional social hierarchies of class, race, and
gender. Not only did the crisis and tumult of the wars for independence mobilize all
ranks of people in unprecedented ways, but the emerging republican nation-states
had to decide who would be included as citizens and on what terms. Should poor
people enjoy the right to vote? Should slaves be liberated? Should married women
own property? Should Indians have representation? The revolutionary era saw
tremendous pressure "from below" on these questions and others like them. Drawing from transatlantic rhetoric of universal liberty and equality, historically dis-
enfranchised people seized the opportunity to claim their natural and civil rights.
Poor people, Indians, free and enslaved people of African descent, and radical
women battled against the privileges of wealth, whiteness, and manhood. They
wrote, sang, pleaded, petitioned, marched, mobbed, rioted, and fought to improve
their place in society. Their voices widened the promise and meaning of freedom.
Even when they did not get their way, their activities expanded the boundaries of
politics and shaped the post-revolutionary order.*

DOCUMENTS

The republican revolutions challenged not just empire and monarchy, but also traditional
social distinctions. One keen observer of these repercussions was Francisco de Miranda
(1750–1816), a military officer from New Spain, who visited the new United States in
1783–1784. Document 1 presents his view of the North Americans' simple, egalitarian
manners. Miranda later took part in Venezuela's independence effort in 1810, promoting
the colony's 1811 Declaration of Independence from Spain. The republican challenge to
traditional mores extended to the concept of time itself. French revolutionaries devised
an entirely new republican calendar to replace the familiar Christian one. Displayed in
Document 4, the calendar began on September 22, 1792, the day the First Republic was
declared, and remained in use for twelve years. Document 6 vividly depicts a moment
of revolutionary conflict in New Spain in October 1810, when Father Miguel Hidalgo's
motley rebel army besieged the town of Guanajuato. A letter from a parish priest bears
witness to a scene of terror and violence.

354

The enunciation of revolutionary ideals of universal freedom and equality gave people of African descent new opportunities and strategies to claim their own rights. During the tumultuous first months of the French Revolution in the summer of 1789, the free black residents of Paris, like their white neighbors, sought inclusion in the egalitarian promise of the Declaration of the Rights of Man. They insisted upon full rights of citizenship for all free people of color in France and its colonies. Their address to the National Assembly in October 1789 is contained in Document 2. Almost sixty years later, former slaves from the United States who had settled in the colony of Liberia in West Africa demanded their independence from the American Colonization Society. A Virginian named Hilary Teague authored the Liberian Declaration of Independence, presented in Document 7.

Like black people, white women in North America sought a meaningful place in the new republic. In Document 3, Priscilla Mason, a graduate of the new Philadelphia Young Ladies Academy in 1793, proposed an innovative role for women in the republican government of the United States, while the song "The Rights of Woman" from *The Philadelphia Minerva* in 1795 draws directly on the transatlantic world of letters, invoking the pioneering English feminist Mary Wollstonecraft in its adamant call for the freedom of women.

How, then, did the new nation-states of the Atlantic world decide who would be included in the idea of "the people" and what rights they would enjoy? Document 5 presents citizenship clauses from the Constitutions of New Jersey, Haiti, Venezuela, Brazil, and Liberia.

1. Francisco de Miranda Comments on Republican Manners, 1783–1784

New York

I will not forget to record an anecdote which took place here, worthy of immortality. A farmer, owner of the land near Crown Point on which the French had their encampment, made his application to them for the rent. The officers paid no attention to the pretension and did not even give a satisfactory answer; seeing this, the republican rustic withdrew from the scene and went in search of the sheriff. And see you here these two poor peasants coming without a single weapon in their hands, but rather with the palladium and authority of the law, determined with heroic firmness to arrest the French General M. de Rochambeau in front of his entire army for the damages and rent. The General was effectively detained by the sheriff and instantly paid the amount owed to the poor rustic (some ten or fifteen pesos was the entire sum), with which the proceeding ended. How is it possible that under similar protections the most arid and barren countries would not flourish? And that the most pusillanimous and abject men would not within a short time be honest, just, industrious, wise, and brave? . . .

In Transit in New England

At six o'clock in the morning we left Hartford in beautiful and moderate weather. A young girl thirteen or fourteen years old, my servant, and I were the only passengers.

Source: John S. Etzell, ed., *The New Democracy in America: Travels of Francisco de Miranda in the United States, 1783–84* (Norman: University of Oklahoma Press, 1963), pp. 89–90, 112, 158, 166–167.

We arrived shortly after seven o'clock at Windsor, a small town of about sixty inhabitants, where we had breakfast. An hour later, we continued twelve miles farther to Suffield, a similar town; here we halted to feed the horses. Finally, after crossing the Connecticut River on a barge, we arrived at Springfield, in Massachusetts. I will not forget to mention that the spirit of republicanism is such in this region that the coachman sat down with the rest of us at the table, and it was with no little difficulty that I arranged for my servant to be fed separately. . . .

Boston

We also visited the city hall, called the State House, at the head of State Street. It is a brick building without any grace whatsoever, ample enough for the purpose it was built for, but not to contain the two branches of the Legislature, which meet there now. In the Senate Room are some bad pictures of the leading personages who founded this colony (clerics for the most part) and an engraving representing the Swiss scene in which the Governor obliged William Tell to shoot at the apple on the head of his young son. (From this resulted the revolution through which those happy people recovered their liberty—the idea cannot be less than pleasing to these! And should be so to all humanity.) There are no more ornaments nor cleanliness than one commonly sees in a good European barracks! The Assembly Room is larger, in the same style as the preceding, and full of benches for the representatives to sit on. In the middle, hanging from a chain, is the figure of a codfish in natural size, made of wood, and in bad taste. This idea is an imitation of the wool sacks in the English Parliament. . . .

On various occasions I attended the General Assembly of the state legislative body, where I saw clearly the defects and inconveniences to which this democracy has subjected itself by placing the legislative power in the hands of ignorance. One member recited couplets in the middle of a debate he did not understand. Another, at the end of this debate and after the matter had been discussed for two hours, asked what the motion was so he could vote. And thus it is for the most part, with the result that the most absurd and unjust points have been debated, proposed, and approved in these democratic assemblies throughout the continent. All the influence being given by the constitution to property, the leading members do not have to be the wisest, and the Senators and Assemblymen are generally people destitute of principles and education. One, B–k, was a tailor four years ago; another, M–n, an innkeeper; another, B–n, a porter; another was a smith, etc.

2. Free Citizens of Color Claim Their Rights, 1789

Address to the National Assembly, to Our Lords, the Representatives of the Nation

Our lords, the free citizens and landowners of color of the French islands and colonies are honored to inform you that there still exists in one of the lands of this empire a species of men scorned and degraded, a class of citizens doomed to rejection,

Source: Laurent Dubois and John D. Garrigus, eds., *Slave Revolution in the Caribbean, 1789–1804* (Boston: Bedford/ St. Martin's, 2006), pp. 68–70.

to all the humiliations of slavery: in a word, Frenchmen who groan under the yoke of oppression.

Such is the fate of the unfortunate American colonists known in the islands under the name of mulattos, quadroons, etc.

Born citizens and free, they live as foreigners in their own fatherland. Excluded from all positions, from honors and professions, they are even forbidden to practice some of the mechanical trades. Set apart in the most degrading fashion, they find themselves enslaved even in their liberty.

The Estates General has been summoned.

All France has hastened to support the king's benevolent plans; citizens of all classes have been called to the great work of public regeneration; all have contributed to writing complaints and nominating deputies to defending their rights and set forth their interests.

The call of liberty has echoed in the other hemisphere.

It should certainly have erased even the memory of these outrageous distinctions between citizens of the same land; instead, it has brought forth even more appalling ones.

For an ambitious aristocracy, liberty means only the right to rule other men, without sharing power.

The white colonists have acted according to this principle, which even today consistently guides their behavior.

They have taken upon themselves the right to elect colonial representatives.

Excluded from these meetings, the citizens of color have been deprived of the ability to look after their own interests, to discuss things that affect them too, and to carry their wishes, complaints, and demands to the National Assembly.

In this strange system, the citizens of color find themselves represented by the white colonists' deputies, although they have still never been included in their partial assemblies and they have not entrusted any power to these deputies. Their opposing interests, which sadly are only too obvious, make such representation absurd and contradictory.

You, our lords, must weigh these considerations; you must return to these oppressed citizens the rights that have been unjustly stripped from them; you must gloriously complete your work, by ensuring the liberty of French citizens in both hemispheres.

The Declaration of the Rights of Man and Citizen has awakened the colonists of color to their past condition; they have shown themselves worthy of the dignity that you have assigned to them; they have learned their rights and they have used them. . . .

The citizens of color are clearly as qualified as the whites to demand this representation.

Like them they are all citizens, free and French; the edict of March 1685 accords them all such rights and guarantees them all such privileges. It states "that the freedmen (and all the more so their descendants) have earned their liberty; let this liberty produce in them, as much in their persons as for their property, the same effects as the fortune of liberty that is natural to all Frenchmen." Like them they are property owners and farmers; like them they contribute to the relief of the state by paying the levies and bearing all expenses that they and the whites share. Like them they have already shed their blood and are prepared to spill it again for the defense of the fatherland. Like them, finally, though with less encouragement and means, they have proven their patriotism again and again. . . .

They beseech you, our lords, not to forget them, and to act strictly on principle. They ask for no favors.

They claim the rights of man and of citizen, those inalienable rights based on nature and the social contract, those rights that you have so solemnly recognized and so faithfully established when you established as the foundation of the constitution "that all men are born and remain free and equal in rights.

"That the law is the expression of the general will; that all citizens have the right to participate personally, or through their representatives, in its formation;

"That each citizen has the right to certify the necessity of public contribution, and to freely consent to it, either personally or through his representatives."

Is it your intent to reject these fundamental principles, setting the interests of the whites against those of the colonies? Do we want to muffle nature's voice with the calculations of sordid profit?

Can we not recognize the language of ambition and greed, whose speakers do not value the prosperity of the state unless they profit personally?

But this is not the place to conduct such serious discussions about basics of the rights of the citizens of color.

After you have agreed to their preliminary claims: when they have descended into the arena to fight their adversaries, they will easily show that the legitimate interests of the whites themselves, like those of the colonies, lie in guaranteeing the status and the liberty of the citizens of color. For a state's good fortune consists in the peace and harmony of its constituent members, and there can be no true peace or strong union between a strong group that oppresses and a weak one that yields; between a commanding master and an obedient slave.

3. Women in the United States Assert Themselves, 1793, 1795

The SALUTATORY ORATION, Delivered by Miss MASON.

A female, young and inexperienced, addressing a promiscuous assembly, is a novelty which requires an apology, as some may suppose. I therefore, with submission, beg leave to offer a few thoughts in vindication of female eloquence.

I mean not at this early day, to become an advocate for the species of female eloquence, of which husbands so much, and so justly, stand in awe,—a species of which the famous Grecian orator, Xantippe, was an illustrious example. Although the free exercise of this natural talent, is a part of the rights of woman, and must be allowed by the courtesy of Europe and America too; yet it is rather to be *tolerated* than *established*; and should rest like the sword in the scabbard, to be used only when occasion

Source: Miss Priscilla Mason's Salutatory Oration, in *The Rise and Progress of the Young Ladies' Academy of Philadelphia* (Philadelphia, 1794), pp. 90–95; "Rights of Woman," *The Philadelphia Minerva*, October 17, 1795.

requires.—Leaving my sex in full possession of this prerogative, I claim for them the further right of being heard on more public occasions—of addressing the reason as well as the fears of the other sex.

Our right to instruct and persuade cannot be disputed, if it shall appear, that we possess the talents of the orator—and have opportunities for the exercise of those talents. Is a power of speech, and volubility of expression, one of the talents of the orator? Our sex possess it in an eminent degree.

Do personal attractions give charms to eloquence, and force to the orator's arguments? There is some truth mixed with the flattery we receive on this head. Do tender passions enable the orator to speak in a moving and forcible manner? This talent of the orator is confessedly ours. In all these respects the female orator stands on equal,—nay, on *superior* ground. . . .

Our high and mighty Lords (thanks to their arbitrary constitutions) have denied us the means of knowledge, and then reproached us for the want of it. Being the stronger party, they early seized the sceptre and the sword; with these they gave laws to society; they denied women the advantage of a liberal education; forbid them to exercise their talents on those great occasions, which would serve to improve them. They doom'd the sex to servile or frivolous employments, on purpose to degrade their minds, that they themselves might hold unrivall'd, the power and pre-eminence they had usurped. Happily, a more liberal way of thinking begins to prevail. The sources of knowledge are gradually opening to our sex. Some have already availed themselves of the privilege so far, as to wipe off our reproach in some measure.

A M'Caulley, a Carter, a Moore, a Rowe, and other illustrous female characters, have shown of what the sex are capable, under the cultivating hand of science. But supposing now that we possess'd all the talents of the orator, in the highest perfection; where shall we find a theatre for the display of them? The Church, the Bar, and the Senate are shut against us. Who shut them? *Man*; despotic man, first made us incapable of the duty, and then forbid us the exercise. Let us by suitable education, qualify ourselves for those high departments—they will open before us. They *will*, did I say? They have done it already. Besides several Churches of less importance, a most numerous and respectable Society, has display'd its impartiality.—I had almost said gallentry in this respect. With *others*, women forsooth, are complimented with the wall, the right hand, the head of the table,—with a kind of mock pre-eminence in small matters: but on great occasions the sycophant changes his tune, and says, "Sit down at my feet and learn." Not so the members of the enlightened and liberal Church. They regard not the anatomical formation of the body. They look to the soul, and allow all to teach who are capable of it, be they male or female. . . .

But Paul forbids it! Contemptible little body! The girls laughed at the deformed creature. To be revenged, he declares war against the whole sex: advises men not to marry them; and has the insolence to order them to keep silence in the Church—: afraid, I suppose, that they would say something against celibacy, or ridicule the old bachelor.

With respect to the bar, citizens of either sex, have an undoubted right to plead their own cause there. Instances could be given of females being admitted to plead the cause of a friend, a husband, a son; and they have done it with energy and effect. I am assured that there is nothing in our laws or constitution, to prohibit the licensure of female Attornies; and sure our judges have too much gallantry, to urge *prescription* in bar of their claim. In regard to the senate, prescription is clearly in our favour. We have one or two cases exactly in point.

Heliogabalus, the Roman Emperor; of blessed memory, made his grand-mother a Senator of Rome. He also established a senate of women; appointed his mother President; and committed to them the important business of regulating dress and fashions. And truly me-thinks the dress of our own country, at this day, would admit of some regulation, for it is subject to no rules at all—It would be worthy the wisdom of Congress, to consider whether a similar institution, established at the seat of our Federal Government, would not be a public benefit. We cannot be independent, while we receive our fashions from other countries; nor act properly, while we imitate the manners of governments not congenial to our own. Such a Senate, composed of women most noted for wisdom, learning and taste, delegated from every part of the Union, would give dignity, and independence to our manners; uniformity, and even authority to our fashions.

It would fire the female breast with the most generous ambition, prompting to illustrious actions. It would furnish the most noble Theatre for the display, the exercise and improvement of every faculty. It would call forth all that is human—all that is *divine* in the soul of woman; and having proved them equally capable with the other sex, would lead to their equal participation of honor and office.

Rights of Woman.
[By a Lady.]
Tune—"God save America."

God save each Female's right,
Show to her ravish'd sight
          Woman is free;

Let Freedom's voice prevail,
And draw aside the veil,
Supreme Effulgence hail,
          Sweet Liberty.

Man boasts the noble cause,
Nor yields supine to laws
          Tyrants ordain:

Let woman have a share
Nor yield to slavish fear,
Her equal rights declare,
          And well maintain,

Come forth with sense array'd
Nor ever be dismay'd
          To meet the foe,

Who with assuming hands
Inflict the iron bands,
To obey his rash commands,
        And vainly bow.

O let the sacred fire
Of Freedom's voice inspire
        A Female too:

Man makes the cause his own,
And Fame his acts renown,
Woman thy fears disown,
        Assert thy due.

Think of the cruel chain,
Endure no more the pain
        Of slavery:

Why should a tyrant bind
A cultivated mind,
By Reason well refin'd
        Ordained Free.

Why should a woman lie
In base obscurity,
        Her talents hid;

Has providence assign'd
Her soul to be confin'd,
Is not her gentle mind
        By virtue led?

With this engaging charm,
Where is so much the harm
        For her to stand,

To join the grand applause
Of truth and equal laws,
Or lend the noble cause,
        Her feeble hand.

Let snarling cynics frown,
Their maxims I disown,
        Their ways detest:

By man, your tyrant lord,
Females no more be aw'd.
Let Freedom's sacred word,
        Inspire your breath.

Woman aloud rejoice.
Exalt thy feeble voice
                In cheerful strain;

See Wolstoncraft, a friend.
Your injur'd rights defend.
Wisdom her step attend,
                The cause maintain.

4. France Devises a New Republican Calendar, 1793

The NEW FRENCH CALENDAR for the present Year, commencing Sept. 22.

MONTHS.	ENGLISH.	AUTUMN.	TERM.			
Vindemaire	Vintage Month	from	Sept.	22	to	Oct. 21
Brumaire	Fog Month	——	Oct.	22	to	Nov. 20
Frumaire	Sleet Month	——	Nov.	21	to	Dec. 20
		WINTER.				
Nivos	Snow Month	——	Dec.	21	to	Jan. 19
Pluvios	Rain Month	——	Jan.	20	to	Feb. 18
Ventos	Wind Month	——	Feb.	19	to	March 20
		SPRING.				
Germinal	Sprouts Month	——	March	21	to	April 19
Floreal	Flowers Month	——	April	20	to	May 19
Priareal	Pasture Month	——	May	20	to	June 18
		SUMMER.				
Messidor	Harvest Month	——	June	19	to	July 18
Fervidor	Hot Month	——	July	19	to	Aug. 17
Fructidor	Fruit Month	——	Aug.	18	to	Sept. 16

Sans Culotides, as Feasts dedicated to

Les Vertus	The Virtues	Sept. 17.
Le Genie	Genius	Sept. 18.
Le Travail	Labour	Sept. 19.
L'Opinion	Opinion	Sept. 20.
Les Recompenses	Rewards	Sept. 21

The intercalary day of every fourth year is to be called *La Sans Culotide*; on which there is to be a national renovation of their oath, "To live free or die." The month is divided into three decades, the days of which are called, from the Latin numerals,

1. *Primidi.*   2. *Duodi.*   3. *Tridi.*   4. *Quartidi.*
5. *Quintidi.*   6. *Sextidi.*   7. *Septidi.*   8. *Octodi.*
9. *Nonodi.*   10. *Decadi*, which is to be the day of rest.

Source: *An Impartial History of the Late Revolution in France* (Boston, 1794), p. 496.

5. New Nations Define Citizenship, 1776–1847

New Jersey Constitution of 1776

IV. That all inhabitants of this Colony, of full age, who are worth fifty pounds proclamation money, clear estate in the same, and have resided within the county in which they claim a vote for twelve months immediately preceding the election, shall be entitled to vote for Representatives in Council and Assembly; and also for all other public officers, that shall be elected by the people of the county at large. . . .

XVIII. That no person shall ever, within this Colony, be deprived of the inestimable privilege of worshipping Almighty God in a manner agreeable to the dictates of his own conscience; nor, under any pretence whatever, be compelled to attend any place of worship, contrary to his own faith and judgment; nor shall any person, within this Colony, ever be obliged to pay tithes, taxes, or any other rates, for the purpose of building or repairing any other church or churches, place or places of worship, or for the maintenance of any minister or ministry, contrary to what he believes to be right, or has deliberately or voluntarily engaged himself to perform.

XIX. That there shall be no establishment of any one religious sect in this Province, in preference to another; and that no Protestant inhabitant of this Colony shall be denied the enjoyment of any civil right, merely on account of his religious principles; but that all persons, professing a belief in the faith of any Protestant sect, who shall demean themselves peaceably under the government, as hereby established, shall be capable of being elected into any office of profit or trust, or being a member of either branch of the Legislature, and shall fully and freely enjoy every privilege and immunity, enjoyed by others their fellow subjects.

Haitian Constitution of 1805

Art. 1. The people inhabiting the island formerly called St. Domingo, hereby agree to form themselves into a free state sovereign and independent of any other power in the universe, under the name of empire of Hayti.

2. Slavery is forever abolished.

3. The Citizens of Hayti are brothers at home; equality in the eyes of the law is incontestably acknowledged, and there cannot exist any titles, advantages, or privileges, other than those necessarily resulting from the consideration and reward of services rendered to liberty and independence.

4. The law is the same to all, whether it punishes, or whether it protects.

5. The law has no retroactive effect.

Source: "The Constitution of New Jersey (1776), in *The Constitutions of the Sixteen States which Compose the Confederated Republic of America, According to their Latest Amendments* . . . (Boston: Manning & Loring, 1797), 150, 152–153; "Haitian Constitution" in *New York Evening Post*, July 15, 1805; "Federal Constitution for the States of Venezuela . . ." in *Interesting Official Documents Relating to the United Provinces of Venezuela* . . . (London, 1812), 157, 261, 277, 279, 281, 291; "Brazilian Constitution of 1824," Political Database of the Americas. Online at http://pdba.georgetown.edu/Constitutions/Brazil/brazil1824 .html. Accessed August 3, 2006, translated for this volume by Bryan McCann; "Liberian Constitution of 1847," Liberian Collections Project. Online at http://onliberia.org/con_1847.htm. Accessed August 3, 2006.

6. Property is sacred, its violation shall be severely prosecuted.
7. The quality of citizen of Hayti is lost by emigration and naturalization in foreign countries and condemnation to corporal or disgrace punishments. The first case carries with it the punishment of death and confiscation of property.
8. The quality of Citizen is suspended in consequence of bankruptcies and failures.
9. No person is worthy of being a Haitian who is not a good father, a good son, a good husband, and especially a good soldier.
10. Fathers and mothers are not permitted to disinherit their children.
11. Every Citizen must possess a mechanic art.
12. No whiteman of whatever nation he may be, shall put his foot on this territory with the title of master or proprietor, neither shall he in future acquire any property therein.
13. The preceding article cannot in the smallest degree affect white women who have been naturalized Haytians by Government, nor does it extend to children already born, or that may be born of the said women. The Germans and Polanders naturalized by government are also comprized (sic) in the dispositions of the present article.
14. All acception (sic) of colour among the children of one and the same family, of whom the chief magistrate is the father, being necessarily to cease, the Haytians shall hence forward be known only by the generic appellation of Blacks.

1811 Constitution of Venezuela

1. The Catholic, Apostolic, and Roman religion, is also that of the State, and the only and exclusive one of the inhabitants of Venezuela. Its protection, conservation, purity, and inviolability, shall be one of the first duties of the national Representation, who shall not, at any time, allow within the limits of the Confederation, any public, or private, worship or doctrine, contrary to that of Jesus Christ. . . .

169. All foreigners, of whatever nation they may be of, shall be received into the State. Their persons and properties shall enjoy the same security as those of the other citizens, provided they respect the Catholic religion, the only one tolerated; that they acknowledge the independence of this country, its sovereignty, and the authorities constituted by the general will of the inhabitants. . . .

200. As that class of citizens, hitherto denominated *Indians*, has not till now, reaped the advantage of certain laws which the Spanish Monarchy dictated in their favour, in consequence of the functionaries of the government having forgotten their execution, and as the basis of the system of government, which Venezuela has adopted in this Constitution, is no other than that of justice and equality, the provincial governments are hereby most particularly enjoined, that in like manner as they are to apply their cares and endeavours, in order to obtain the instruction of all the inhabitants of the State, to provide for them schools, academies, and colleges, where all may learn the principles of religion, of sound morality, of policy, of science, and of the useful and necessary arts, such as are conducive to the maintainance and prosperity of the people; that they in like manner endeavour by every possible means to draw to the same houses of tuition, the said citizen-natives, to cause them to comprehend the intimate union by which they are bound to the rest of the citizens, to teach them that they merit the same considerations from Government, to inculcate to them the rights

which they enjoy, by the simple act of their being men equal to all others of the same kind; to the end, that by this means, they may be raised from the abject and ignorant state in which they have been kept by the ancient order of things, and that they may no longer remain isolated and fearful of dealing with other men; it being hereby prohibited for them henceforward to be employed against their own will, in the service of the curates of their parishes, or of any other person; they being also allowed to divide and lay out the grounds granted to them, and of which they hold possession; that the same may be proportionably parcelled out amongst the fathers of families of each town, for their own uses and purposes, and in conformity to the regulations which may be established by the provincial Governments.

201. Consequently, hereby are revoked, and rendered null and void, all the laws which under the former Government granted to the natives, certain tribunals, protectors, and the privilege of their always being considered as minors, which privileges, though apparently directed to protect, have nevertheless been extremely injurious to them, as experience has proved.

202. The vile traffic of slaves, prohibited by decree of the Supreme Junta of Caracas, on the 14th of July 1810, is hereby solemnly and constitutionally abolished in the whole territory of the Union, without it being lawful in any manner to import slaves of any kind, for the purposes of mercantile speculation.

203. In the same manner are revoked and annulled, in every sense, the ancient laws which imposed a civil degradation on that part of the free population of Venezuela, hitherto known under the denomination of *persons of colour*; these shall all remain in the possession of their natural and civil rank and be restored to the imprescriptible rights belonging to them, in like manner as the rest of the citizens. . . .

223. In all public acts the Columbian Era shall be used, and in order to avoid all mistakes in calculations, in comparing this period with the common Christian Era, generally used by civilized countries, the former shall date from the first day of January of the year of our Lord, one thousand eight hundred and eleven, which shall be the first of our Independence. . . .

1824 Constitution of Brazil

On Brazilian Citizens

Article 6: The following are Brazilian citizens:

1. Those born in Brazil, including *ingênuos* (children born to freed slaves) and *libertos* (freed slaves), even if the father is a foreigner, as long as the father is not posted in Brazil in the service of a foreign nation.
2. The children of Brazilian fathers, and the illegitimate children of Brazilian mothers, born in foreign lands, who establish residency within the Empire.
3. The children of Brazilian fathers who were posted in foreign lands in the service of the Empire, even if they do not establish residency in Brazil.
4. All those born in Portugal and its possessions, who, resident in Brazil at the time of the proclamation of Independence in the Provinces, where they lived, adhered to Independence either expressly, or implicitly through continued residency.
5. Naturalised foreigners, whatever their Religion. The Law will determine the precise qualities necessary to obtain a Letter of naturalisation.

Article 7: The following lose Rights of Brazilian Citizenship:

1. Anyone naturalized in a foreign land.
2. Anyone who, without the permission of the Emperor, accepts Employment, Pension or Decoration from any Foreign Government.
3. Anyone banished by Judicial Sentence.

Article 8: The Exercise of Political Rights is suspended in the following instances:

1. For moral or physical incapacity.
2. For judicial sentence to prison or exile, for the duration of the sentence.

Liberian Constitution of 1847

Sec. 13th. The great object of forming these Colonies, being to provide a home for the dispersed and oppressed children of Africa, and to regenerate and enlighten this benighted continent, none but Negroes or persons of Negro descent shall be eligible to citizenship in this Republic.

6. A Radical Priest Marches in New Spain, 1810

Guanajuato, October 2, 1810

On Friday the 28th of September at 10:00 o'clock there came to the Castle 2 envoys of Hidalgo, who said they were ambassadors, of the same rank as a Colonel or possibly a Lieut. Colonel; they signaled the Castle and an official having come out, he received some sheets of paper which were directed to the Intendant in which he was told that he commanded a considerable number of troops, that the object which was proposed in this war was the independence of the nation, that he assured the Europeans that he did not wish to injure or harm them but would show them kindness just as though he were embracing them firmly; that he gave himself to them in good faith, he would consider their persons and were anything to be taken from them because of the needs of the army, those things would be replaced later; that independence would be attained and the citizens would remain the same; that already it had been heard said that the many Europeans which he had with him were being treated well and that the homes of the rebels were the only ones which had been pillaged; but besides, he would take charge of the peace, and in good faith he would weigh the right of good Government for them. Beyond this he wrote a friendly letter to the Intendant offering him assurance that although they may struggle, the Intendant would receive consideration in refuge. In his office he continued to sign as he always did MIGL. HIDALGO CAPTAIN GENERAL OF AMERICA. The Intendant answered him that he recognized no other than Captain Gral [General], only Senor Virrey [Viceroy] de Mexico, and like a good soldier he was for the present ready to struggle; he answered the letter in friendly fashion, telling him that under these circumstances he was taking care of the safety of his family. Before dispatching the

Source: From "Hidalgo and the Cry of *El Grito*: Fact and Fiction," by Justin G. Turner, *Southern California Quarterly*, December 1962, pp. 338–340. Reprinted with permission of Southern California Quarterly, published by The Historical Society of Southern California.

message and the papers, he sent everything to the municipal council which at that time had congregated at the home of Alferes Real with the curates; we told him although we were without arms and without protection we would use all of our strength to defend him. The Intendant ordered the flag of war to be raised and readied his men and arms. At 1:00 in the afternoon of this same day, Friday [September 28], there began to enter an infinite number of Hidalgo's men; much cavalry, infantry, and Indians so that as many as 20,000 men arrived and there were another 10,000 which he had left posted. Immediately upon their approaching the Castle a skirmish started, but longer and more terrible than anything I have seen in my life. The Priest posted his artillery in good spots and in an hour and a half they almost broke into the Castle because the enemy was assembled in groups and threw themselves forward like furious lions, with no concern about how many of their numbers might die; they forced open the doors, entered, and then the Intendant ordered the white flag raised and said that he surrendered; but the moment his word was taken and they entered, the Intendant started a fire in order to burn the mines and many of Hidalgo's men perished; but infuriated because of this they killed the Intendant with a bullet wound in the head and a great many of the Europeans and Creoles, and the Assessor in accord with many others made a sign of peace, but they had no confidence and killed, as I say, many of them and the rest were wounded; and then some were bound and carried to the prison, one by one, subjected to a thousand insults and affronts, they sacked the Castle and were so inflamed that they set fire to all of the powder that there was there so that it seemed that the greater part of the city was exploding. The Castle was taken at 5:00 in the afternoon and they surrendered to the plundering of the homes of the Europeans, in which they removed everything but the doors. There were a few which possibly escaped and a few of the Creoles through error perished. Immediately the people set about to capture every European, and actually all were imprisoned and many offered their services for fear that the city which was so deeply against them would be torn to bits. Many of the Europeans from Silao, Leon and Irapuato, who had come here to take refuge, fell into the same predicament again. It is estimated that more than 2,000 men died, of them approximately 200 Europeans, and some 200 Europeans were taken prisoner. The pillage amounted to 1,500,000 pesos and now you must realize what our struggle was and the perturbation of our spirit. I went into the prison where most of the Europeans were and I was grieved to see such a sight. I aided them in any way I could, some with help and some by talking to Hidalgo for some of the elderly people, some of the worthy, and for their families.

Saturday [September 29] in the evening deep ditches were dug in 3 places to bury the dead because all of them were stripped including the Intendant, and those most mutilated were the Indians. All was horror and grimness.

I neglected to say that we do not know anything of the inner country or of the troops, rather they affirm that Senor Callejas is prepared and that Hidalgo bears the flag of our Senora de Guadalupe and underneath a placard which says "long live the Catholic religion," "Long live Fernando 7th," "Long live our country." Far from plundering the shrines, they have been treated with much reverence, mass is heard every day which is said at a portable altar in the presence of the entire army and they conclude that it was victory which they brought to the Virgin of the parish, and they ring all of the bells. . . .

Only last night we had another scare so that no one slept, because to arms was sounded and we were told that a good sized army was moving down the road; a world of men were posted in Valencia and other places and we came to the most probable conclusion that there were 8,000 Indians who had come to join them. I see it as a very bad situation because I see what is happening right here, and I can imagine what it is like in other places because as soon as Hidalgo arrives all of the soldiers they have defending themselves change their allegiance, just as we counted on 12,000 men, and finally only came up with the Europeans. It is the opinion here for sure that those who killed the Intendant were the same soldiers who were supposed to come to your defense. It seems to me that if one goes to Valladolid he will be harmed because it is said that Senor Obispo is ready for the Inquisition and under orders from the audience chamber, and he wishes to avoid that. May your honor not enter into war until you closely examine your strength or else you may be victims to insolence such as Senor Riano was. I cannot write more. May God be with you.

7. African-American Exiles Declare Independence in Liberia, 1847

In Convention.
Declaration of Independence.

We the representatives of the people of the Commonwealth of Liberia, in Convention assembled, invested with authority for forming a new government, relying upon the aid and protection of the Great Arbiter of human events, do hereby, in the name, and on the behalf of the people of this Commonwealth, publish and declare the said Commonwealth a FREE, SOVEREIGN, AND INDEPENDENT STATE, by the name and title of the REPUBLIC OF LIBERIA.

While announcing to the nations of the world the new position which the people of this Republic have felt themselves called upon to assume, courtesy to their opinion seems to demand a brief accompanying statement of the causes which induced them, first to expatriate themselves from the land of their nativity and to form settlements on this barbarous coast, and now to organize their government by the assumption of a sovereign and independent character. Therefore we respectfully ask their attention to the following facts.

We recognise in all men, certain natural and inalienable rights: among these are life, liberty, and the right to acquire, possess, enjoy and defend property. By the practice and consent of men in all ages, some system or form of government is proven to be necessary to exercise, enjoy and secure those rights; and every people have a right to institute a government, and to choose and adopt that system or form of it, which in their opinion will most effectually accomplish these objects, and secure their happiness, which does not interfere with the just rights of others. The right therefore to institute government, and to all the powers necessary to conduct it, is, an inalienable right, and cannot be resisted without the grossest injustice.

We the people of the Republic of Liberia were originally the inhabitants of the United States of North America.

Source: Charles Henry Huberich, *The Political and Legislative History of Liberia* (New York: Central Book Corp., 1947), vol. 1, pp. 828–832.

In some parts of that country, we were debarred by law from all the rights and privileges of men—in other parts, public sentiment, more powerful than law, frowned us down. . . .

All hope of a favorable change in our country was thus wholly extinguished in our bosoms, and we looked with anxiety abroad for some asylum from the deep degradation.

The Western coast of Africa was the place selected by American benevolence and philanthropy, for our future home. Removed beyond those influences which depressed us in our native land, it was hoped we would be enabled to enjoy those rights and privileges, and exercise and improve those faculties, which the God of nature has given us in common with the rest of mankind.

Under the auspices of the American Colonization Society, we established ourselves here, on land acquired by purchase from the Lords of the soil. . . .

Under the auspices and guidance of this institution, which has nobly and in perfect faith redeemed its pledges to the people, we have grown and prospered.

From time to time, our number has been increased by migration from America, and by accessions from native tribes; and from time to time, as circumstances required it, we have extended our borders by acquisition of land by honorable purchase from the natives of the country.

As our territory has extended, and our population increased, our commerce has also increased. The flags of most of the civilized nations of the earth float in our harbors, and their merchants are opening an honorable and profitable trade. Until recently, these visits have been of a uniformly harmonious character, but as they have become more frequent, and to more numerous points of our extending coast, questions have arisen, which it is supposed can be adjusted only by agreement between sovereign powers.

For years past, the American Colonization Society has virtually withdrawn from all direct and active part in the administration of the government, except in the appointment of the Governor, who is also a colonist, for the apparent purpose of testing the ability of the people to conduct the affairs of government, and no complaint of crude legislation, nor of mismanagement, nor of mal-administration has yet been heard.

In view of these facts, this institution, the American Colonization Society, with that good faith which has uniformly marked all its dealings with us, by a set of resolutions in January, in the Year of Our Lord One Thousand Eight Hundred and Forty-Six, dissolve all political connexion with the people of this Republic, return the power with which it was delegated, and left the people to the government of themselves.

The people of the Republic of Liberia then, are of right, and in fact, a free, sovereign and independent State; possessed of all the rights, powers, and functions of government.

In assuming the momentous responsibilities of the position they have taken, the people of this Republic, feel justified by the necessities of the case, and with this conviction they throw themselves with confidence upon the candid consideration of the civilized world. . . .

Liberia is already the happy home of thousands, who were once the doomed victims of oppression, and if left unmolested to go on with her natural and spontaneous growth; if her movements be left free from the paralysing intrigues of jealous, ambitious, and unscrupulous avarice, she will throw open a wider and yet a wider door for thousands, who are now looking with an anxious eye for some land of rest.

Our courts of justice are open equally to the stranger and the citizen for the redress of grievances, for the remedy of injuries, and for the punishment of crime.

Our numerous and well attended schools attest our efforts, and our desire for the improvement of our children.

Our churches for the worship of our Creator, every where to be seen, bear testimony to our piety, and to our acknowledgement of His Providence.

The native African bowing down with us before the altar of the living God, declare that from us, feeble as we are, the light of Christianity has gone forth, while upon that curse of curses, the slave trade, a deadly blight has fallen as far as our influence extends.

Therefore in the name of humanity, and virtue and religion—in the name of the Great God, our common Creator, and our common Judge, we appeal to the nations of Christendom, and earnestly and respectfully ask of them, that they will regard us with the sympathy and friendly consideration, to which the peculiarities of our condition entitle us, and to extend to us, that comity which marks the friendly intercourse of civilized and independent communities.

DONE IN CONVENTION, at Monrovia, in the County of Montserrado, by the unanimous consent of the people of the Commonwealth of Liberia, this twenty-sixth day of July, in the year of our Lord, One thousand, eight hundred and forty-seven.

IN WITNESS WHEREOF we have hereto set our names.

Montserrado County

S. Benedict, President	J. N. Lewis,
H. Teage,	Beverly R. Wilson,
Elijah Johnson,	J. B. Gripon

Grand Bassa County

John Day	A. W. Gardiner
Amos Herring	Ephraim Titler

Sinoe County

R. E. Murray

Jacob W. Prout, Secretary
to the Convention.

▲ E S S A Y S

What did the "age of revolution" mean to the poor and the enslaved? The essays in this chapter address this question in two quite different contexts. Alfred F. Young's biography of a modest shoemaker in Boston shows that there was more to the history of the American Revolution than the so-called Founding Fathers. For many ordinary people of the middling and lower classes in British North America, the revolt against Great Britain gave political meaning to their lives. George Robert Twelves Hewes participated in some of the major events leading up to the Revolution in Boston, including the Massacre of 1770 and the Tea Party of 1773. By participating in these affairs, Hewes shook off colonial habits of deference and became an active and equal citizen in the community, on par with such Boston luminaries as the wealthy merchant John Hancock. Almost fifty years later, Hewes was transformed from a citizen to a celebrity when he gained recognition as one of the last living members of the Revolutionary generation.

Although there are similarities between the revolutions in British North America and elsewhere, we should not assume that all revolutionaries were fighting for the same ideals. In the case of Haiti, some historians have questioned the idea that slaves were fighting for French republican principles. Observing that Kongolese men figured prominently in the slave revolts in St. Domingue, John Thornton traces their political ideas back to the Kingdom of Kongo in West Central Africa. He argues that Kongolese political theory embraced two different concepts of kingship, one authoritarian and the other more egalitarian, and that these opposing concepts informed the struggle for political power in Kongo. Enslaved Kongolese men and women transported to St. Domingue carried these rival concepts of royal authority with them. Rather than fighting to overthrow monarchy, many Africans involved in the civil war in St. Domingue sought to establish new elective kingships in their local communities. Both of these essays raise the issue of sources and evidence. How do historians figure out what ordinary people thought?

How a Shoemaker Became a Citizen

ALFRED F. YOUNG

George Robert Twelves Hewes was born in Boston in 1742 and died in Richfield Springs, New York, in 1840. He participated in several of the principal political events of the American Revolution in Boston, among them the Massacre and the Tea Party, and during the war he served as a privateersman and militiaman. A shoemaker all his life, and intermittently or concurrently a fisherman, sailor, and farmer, he remained a poor man. He never made it, not before the war in Boston, not at sea, not after the war in Wrentham and Attleborough, Massachusetts, not in Otsego County, New York. He was a nobody who briefly became a somebody in the Revolution and, for a moment near the end of his life, a hero.

Hewes might have been unknown to posterity save for his longevity and a shift in the historical mood that rekindled the "spirit of '76." To Americans of the 1830s the Boston Tea Party had become a leading symbol of the Revolution, and Hewes lived long enough to be thought of as one of the last surviving participants, perhaps the very last. In 1833, when James Hawkes "discovered" him in the "obscurity" of upstate New York, Hewes was ninety-one but thought he was ninety-eight, a claim Hawkes accepted when he published the first memoir of Hewes that year. Thus in 1835 when Hewes was invited to Boston, people thought that this survivor of one of the greatest moments of the Revolution was approaching his one hundredth birthday and on "the verge of eternity," as a Fourth of July orator put it. He became a celebrity, the guest of honor on Independence Day, the subject of a second biography by [Benjamin Bussey] Thatcher and of an oil portrait by Joseph Cole, which hangs today in Boston's Old State House.

To Thatcher, Hewes was one of the "humble classes" that made the success of the Revolution possible. How typical he was we can only suggest at this point in our limited knowledge of the "humble classes." Probably he was as representative a member of the "lower trades" of the cities and as much a rank-and-file participant

Source: From Alfred F. Young, "George Robert Twelves Hewes (1742–1840): A Boston Shoemaker and the Memory of the American Revolution," *William and Mary Quarterly* 3rd Series, 38, 1981 (4): 561–564, 585–600. Reprinted with permission of the Omohundro Institute of Early American History and Culture.

in the political events and the war as historians have found. The two biographies, which come close to being oral histories (and give us clues to track down Hewes in other ways), provide an unusually rich cumulative record, over a very long period of time, of his thoughts, attitudes, and values. Consequently, we can answer, with varying degrees of satisfaction, a number of questions about one man of the "humble classes." About the "lower trades": why did a boy enter a craft with such bleak prospects as shoemaking? what was the life of an apprentice? what did it mean to be a shoemaker and a poor man in Boston? About the Revolution: what moved such a rank-and-file person to action? what action did he take? may we speak of his "ideology?" does the evidence of his loss of deference permit us to speak of change in his consciousness? About the war: how did a poor man, an older man, a man with a family exercise his patriotism? what choices did he make? About the results of the Revolution: how did the war affect him? to what extent did he achieve his life goals? why did he go west? what did it mean to be an aged veteran of the Revolution? What, in sum, after more than half a century had passed, was the meaning of the Revolution to someone still in the "humble classes"? . . .

Between 1768 and 1775, the shoemaker became a citizen—an active participant in the events that led to the Revolution, an angry, assertive man who won recognition as a patriot. What explains the transformation? We have enough evidence to take stock of Hewes's role in three major events of the decade: the Massacre (1770), the Tea Party (1773), and the tarring and feathering of John Malcolm (1774).

Thatcher began the story of Hewes in the Revolution at the Stamp Act but based his account on other sources and even then claimed no more than that Hewes was a bystander at the famous effigy-hanging at the Liberty Tree, August 14, 1765, that launched Boston's protest. "The town's-people left their work—and Hewes, his hammer among the rest—to swell the multitude." The only episode for which Thatcher seems to have drawn on Hewes's personal recollection was the celebration of the repeal of the act in May 1766, at which Hewes remembered drinking from the pipe of madeira that John Hancock set out on the Common. "Such a day has not been seen in Boston before or since," wrote Thatcher. . . .

The presence of British troops in Boston beginning in the summer of 1768—four thousand soldiers in a town of fewer than sixteen thousand inhabitants—touched Hewes personally. Anecdotes about soldiers flowed from him. He had seen them march off the transports at the Long Wharf; he had seen them every day occupying civilian buildings on Griffin's Wharf near his shop. He knew how irritating it was to be challenged by British sentries after curfew (his solution was to offer a swig of rum from the bottle he carried).

More important, he was personally cheated by a soldier. Sergeant Mark Burk ordered shoes allegedly for Captain Thomas Preston, picked them up, but never paid for them. Hewes complained to Preston, who made good and suggested he bring a complaint. A military hearing ensued, at which Hewes testified. The soldier, to Hewes's horror, was sentenced to three hundred fifty lashes. He "remarked to the court that if he had thought the fellow was to be punished so severely for such an offense, bad as he was, he would have said nothing about it." And he saw others victimized by soldiers. He witnessed an incident in which a soldier sneaked up behind a woman, felled her with his fist, and "stripped her of her bonnet, cardinal muff and tippet." He followed the man to his barracks, identified him (Hewes remembered him as Private Kilroy, who would appear later at the Massacre), and got him to give up the stolen goods, but decided this time not to press charges. Hewes was also keenly aware of grievances felt by the laboring men and youths who formed the bulk of the crowd—and the principal victims—at the Massacre. From Hawkes and Thatcher three causes can be pieced together.

First in time, and vividly recalled by Hewes, was the murder of eleven-year-old Christopher Seider on February 23, ten days before the Massacre. Seider was one of a large crowd of schoolboys and apprentices picketing the shop of Theophilus Lilly, a merchant violating the anti-import resolutions. Ebenezer Richardson, a paid customs informer, shot into the throng and killed Seider. Richardson would have been tarred and feathered, or worse, had not whig leaders intervened to hustle him off to jail. At Seider's funeral, only a week before the Massacre, five hundred boys marched two by two behind the coffin, followed by two thousand or more adults, "the largest [funeral] perhaps ever known in America," Thomas Hutchinson thought.

Second, Hewes emphasized the bitter fight two days before the Massacre between soldiers and workers at Gray's ropewalk down the block from Hewes's shop. Off-duty soldiers were allowed to moonlight, taking work from civilians. On Friday, March 3, when one of them asked for work at Gray's, a battle ensued between a few score soldiers and ropewalk workers joined by others in the maritime trades. The soldiers were beaten and sought revenge. Consequently, in Thatcher's words, "quite a number of soldiers, in a word, were determined to have a row on the night of the 5th."

Third, the precipitating events on the night of the Massacre, by Hewes's account, were an attempt by a barber's apprentice to collect an overdue bill from a British officer, the sentry's abuse of the boy, and the subsequent harassment of the sentry by a small band of boys that led to the calling of the guard commanded by Captain Preston. Thatcher found this hard to swallow—"a dun from a greasy barber's boy is rather an extraordinary explanation of the origin, or one of the occasions, of the massacre of the 5th of March"—but at the trial the lawyers did not. They battled over defining "boys" and over the age, size, and degree of aggressiveness of the numerous apprentices on the scene.

Hewes viewed the civilians as essentially defensive. On the evening of the Massacre he appeared early on the scene at King Street, attracted by the clamor over the apprentice. "I was soon on the ground among them," he said, as if it were only natural that he should turn out in defense of fellow townsmen against what was assumed to be the danger of aggressive action by soldiers. He was not part of a conspiracy; neither was he there out of curiosity. He was unarmed, carrying neither club nor stave as some others did. He saw snow, ice, and "missiles" thrown at the soldiers. When the main guard rushed out in support of the sentry, Private Kilroy dealt Hewes a blow on his shoulder with his gun. Preston ordered the townspeople to disperse. Hewes believed they had a legal basis to refuse: "they were in the king's highway, and had as good a right to be there" as Preston.

The five men killed were all workingmen. Hewes claimed to know four: Samuel Gray, a ropewalk worker; Samuel Maverick, age seventeen, an apprentice to an ivory turner; Patrick Carr, an apprentice to a leather breeches worker; and James Caldwell, second mate on a ship—all but Christopher Attucks. Caldwell, "who was shot in the back was standing by the side of Hewes, and the latter caught him in his arms as he fell," helped carry him to Dr. Thomas Young in Prison Lane, then ran to Caldwell's ship captain on Cold Lane.

More than horror was burned into Hewes's memory. He remembered the political confrontation that followed the slaughter, when thousands of angry townspeople faced hundreds of British troops massed with ready rifles. "The people," Hewes recounted, "then immediately chose a committee to report to the governor the result of Captain Preston's conduct, and to demand of him satisfaction." Actually the "people" did not choose a committee "immediately." In the dark hours after the Massacre a self-appointed group of patriot leaders met with officials and forced Hutchinson to commit Preston and the soldiers to jail. Hewes was remembering the town meeting the next day, so huge that it had to adjourn from Fanueil Hall, the traditional meeting place that held only twelve hundred, to Old South Church, which had room for five to six thousand. This meeting approved a committee to wait on the officials and then adjourned, but met again the same day, received and voted down an offer to remove one regiment, then accepted another to remove two. This was one of the meetings at which property bars were let down.

What Hewes did not recount, but what he had promptly put down in a deposition the next day, was how militant he was after the Massacre. At 1:00 A.M., like many other enraged Bostonians, he went home to arm himself. On his way back to the Town House with a cane he had a defiant exchange with Sergeant Chambers of the 29th Regiment and eight or nine soldiers, "all with very large clubs or cutlasses." A soldier, Dobson, "ask'd him how he far'd; he told him very badly to see his townsmen shot in such a manner, and asked him if he did not think it was a dreadful thing." Dobson swore "it was a fine thing" and "you shall see more of it." Chambers "seized and forced" the cane from Hewes, "saying I had no right to carry it. I told him I had as good a right to carry a cane as they had to carry clubs."

The Massacre had stirred Hewes to political action. He was one of ninety-nine Bostonians who gave depositions for the prosecution that were published by the town in a pamphlet. Undoubtedly, he marched in the great funeral procession for the victims that brought the city to a standstill. He attended the tempestuous trial of Ebenezer Richardson, Seider's slayer, which was linked politically with the Massacre. ("He remembers to this moment, even the precise words of the Judge's sentence," wrote Thatcher.) He seems to have attended the trial of the soldiers or Preston or both. . . .

Four years later, at the Tea Party on the night of December 16, 1773, the citizen "volunteered" and became the kind of leader for whom most historians have never found a place. The Tea Party, unlike the Massacre, was organized by the radical whig leaders of Boston. They mapped the strategy, organized the public meetings, appointed the companies to guard the tea ships at Griffin's Wharf (among them Daniel Hewes, George's brother), and planned the official boarding parties. As in 1770, they converted the town meetings into meetings of "the whole body of the people," one of which Hutchinson found "consisted principally of the Lower ranks of the People & even Journeymen Tradesmen were brought in to increase the number & the Rabble were not excluded yet there were divers Gentlemen of Good Fortunes among them." . . .

Those in the officially designated parties, about thirty men better known, appeared in well-prepared Indian disguises. As nobodies, the volunteers—anywhere from fifty to one hundred men—could get away with hastily improvised disguises. Hewes said he got himself up as an Indian and daubed his "face and hands with coal dust in the shop of blacksmith." In the streets "I fell in with many who were dressed, equipped and painted as I was, and who fell in with me and marched in order to the place of our destination."

At Griffin's Wharf the volunteers were orderly, self-disciplined, and ready to accept leadership. . . . But for Hewes there was something new: he was singled out of the rank and file and made an officer in the field. . . .

This was Hewes's story, via Hawkes. Thatcher, who knew a good deal more about the Tea Party from other sources, accepted it in its essentials as an accurate account. He also reported a new anecdote which he treated with skepticism, namely, that Hewes worked alongside John Hancock throwing tea overboard. And he added that Hewes, "whose whistling talent was a matter of public notoriety, acted as a boatswain," that is, as the officer whose duty it was to summon men with a whistle. That Hewes was a leader is confirmed by the reminiscence of Thompson Maxwell, a teamster from a neighboring town who was making a delivery to Hancock the day of the event. Hancock asked him to go to Griffin's Wharf. "I went accordingly, joined the band under one Captain Hewes; we mounted the ships and made tea in a trice; this done I took my team and went home as any honest man should." "Captain" Hewes—it was not impossible. . . .

A month later, at the third event for which we have full evidence, Hewes won public recognition for an act of courage that almost cost his life and precipitated the most publicized tarring and feathering of the Revolution. The incident that set it off would have been trivial at any other time. On Tuesday, January 25, 1774, at about two in the afternoon, the shoemaker was making his way back to his shop after his dinner. According to the very full account in the *Massachusetts Gazette,*

> Mr. George-Robert-Twelves Hewes was coming along Fore-Street, near Captain Ridgway's, and found the redoubted John Malcolm, standing over a small boy, who was pushing a little sled before him, cursing, damning, threatening and shaking a very large cane with a very heavy ferril on it over his head. The boy at that time was perfectly quiet, notwithstanding which Malcolm continued his threats of striking him. which Mr. Hewes conceiving if he struck him with that weapon he must have killed him out-right, came up to him, and said to him, Mr. Malcolm I hope you are not going to strike this boy with that stick.

Malcolm had already acquired an odious reputation with patriots of the lower sort. A Bostonian, he had been a sea captain, an army officer, and recently an employee of the customs service. He was so strong a supporter of royal authority that he had traveled to North Carolina to fight the Regulators and boasted of having a horse shot out from under him. He had a fiery temper. As a customs informer he was known to have turned in a vessel to punish sailors for petty smuggling, a custom of the sea. In November 1773, near Portsmouth, New Hampshire, a crowd of thirty sailors had "genteely tarr'd and feather'd" him, as the *Boston Gazette* put it: they did the job over his clothes. Back in Boston he made "frequent complaints" to Hutchinson of "being hooted at in the streets" for this by "tradesmen"; and the lieutenant governor cautioned him, "being a passionate man," not to reply in kind.

The exchange between Malcolm and Hewes resonated with class as well as political differences:

> Malcolm returned, you are an impertinent rascal, it is none of your business. Mr. Hewes then asked him, what had the child done to him. Malcolm damned him and

asked him if he was going to take his part? Mr. Hewes answered no further than this, that he thought it was a shame for him to strike the child with such a club as that, if he intended to strike him. Malcolm on that damned Mr. Hewes, called him a vagabond, and said he would let him know he should not speak to a gentleman in the street. Mr. Hewes returned to that, he was neither a rascal nor vagabond, and though a poor man was in as good credit in town as he was. Malcolm called him a liar, and said he was not, nor ever would be. Mr. Hewes retorted, be that as it will, I never was tarred nor feathered any how. On this Malcolm struck him, and wounded him deeply on the forehead, so that Mr. Hewes for some time lost his senses. Capt. Godfrey, then present, interposed, and after some altercation, Malcolm went home.

Hewes was rushed to Joseph Warren, the patriot doctor, his distant relative. Malcolm's cane had almost penetrated his skull. Thatcher found "the indentation as plainly perceptible as it was sixty years ago." So did Hawkes. Warren dressed the wound, and Hewes was able to make his way to a magistrate to swear out a warrant for Malcolm's arrest "which he carried to a constable named Justice Hale." Malcolm, meanwhile, had retreated to his house, where he responded in white heat to taunts about the half-way tarring and feathering in Portsmouth with "damn you let me see the man that dare do it better."

In the evening a crowd took Malcolm from his house and dragged him on a sled into King Street "amidst the huzzas of thousands." At this point "several gentlemen endeavoured to divert the populace from their intention." The ensuing dialogue laid bare the clash of conceptions of justice between the sailors and laboring people heading the action and Sons of Liberty leaders. The "gentlemen" argued that Malcolm was "open to the laws of the land which would undoubtedly award a reasonable satisfaction to the parties he had abused," that is, the child and Hewes. The answer was political. Malcolm "had been an old impudent and mischievous [*sic*] offender—he had joined in the murders at North Carolina—he had seized vessels on account of sailors having a bottle or two of gin on board—he had in other words behaved in the most capricious, insulting and daringly abusive manner." He could not be trusted to justice. "When they were told the law would have its course with him, they asked what course had the law taken with Preston or his soldiers, with Capt. Wilson or Richardson? And for their parts they had seen so much partiality to the soldiers and customhouse officers by the present Judges, that while things remained as they were, they would, on all such occasions, take satisfaction their own way, and let them take it off." The references were to Captain Preston who had been tried and found innocent of the Massacre, the soldiers who had been let off with token punishment, Captain John Wilson, who had been indicted for inciting slaves to murder their masters but never tried, and Ebenezer Richardson, who had been tried and found guilty of killing Seider, sentenced, and then pardoned by the crown.

The crowd won and proceeded to a ritualized tarring and feathering, the purpose of which was to punish Malcolm, force a recantation, and ostracize him. . . .

Hewes had precipitated an electrifying event. It was part of the upsurge of spontaneous action in the wake of the Tea Party that prompted the whig leaders to promote a "Committee for Tarring and Feathering" as an instrument of crowd control. The "Committee" made its appearance in broadsides signed by "Captain Joyce, Jun.," a sobriquet meant to invoke the bold cornet who had captured King Charles in 1647. The event was reported in the English newspapers, popularized in three or four satirical prints, and dramatized still further when Malcolm went to England, where he campaigned for a pension and ran for Parliament (without success) against John Wilkes, the leading champion of America. The event confirmed the British ministry in its punitive effort to bring rebellious Boston to heel. . . .

The denouement of the affair was an incident several weeks later. "Malcolm recovered from his wounds and went about as usual. 'How do you do, Mr. Malcolm?' said Hewes, very civilly, the next time he met him. 'Your humble servant, Mr. George Robert Twelves Hewes,' quoth he,—touching his hat genteely as he passed by. 'Thank ye,' thought Hewes, 'and I am glad you have learned *better manners at last.*'" Hewes's mood was one of triumph. Malcolm had been taught a lesson. The issue was respect for Hewes, a patriot, a poor man, an honest citizen, a decent man standing up for a child against an unspeakably arrogant "gentleman" who was an enemy of his country. . . .

What moved Hewes to action? It was not the written word; indeed there is no sign he was much of a reader until old age, and then it was the Bible he read. "My whole education," he told Hawkes, "consisted of only a moderate knowledge of reading and writing." He seems to have read one of the most sensational pamphlets of 1773, which he prized enough to hold onto for more than fifty years, but he was certainly not like Harbottle Dorr, the Boston shopkeeper who pored over every issue of every Boston newspaper, annotating Britain's crimes for posterity.

Hewes was moved to act by personal experiences that he shared with large numbers of other plebeian Bostonians. He seems to have been politicized, not by the Stamp Act, but by the coming of the troops after 1768, and then by things that happened to him, that he saw, or that happened to people he knew. Once aroused, he took action with others of his own rank and condition—the laboring classes who formed the bulk of the actors at the Massacre, the Tea Party, and the Malcolm affair—and with other members of his family: his uncle Robert, "known for a staunch Liberty Boy," and his brother Daniel, a guard at the tea ship. Shubael, alone among his brothers, became a tory. These shared experiences were interpreted and focused more likely by the spoken than the written word and as much by his peers at taverns and crowd actions as by leaders in huge public meetings. . . .

But what ideas did Hewes articulate? He spoke of what he did but very little of what he thought. In the brief statement he offered Hawkes about why he went off to war in 1776, he expressed a commitment to general principles as they had been brought home to him by his experiences. "I was continually reflecting upon the unwarrantable sufferings inflicted on the citizens of Boston by the usurpation and tyranny of Great Britain, and my mind was excited with an unextinguishable desire to aid in chastising them." When Hawkes expressed a doubt "as to the correctness of his conduct in absenting himself from his family," Hewes "emphatically reiterated" the same phrases, adding to a "desire to aid in chastising them" the phrase "and securing our independence." This was clearly not an afterthought; it probably reflected the way many others moved toward the goal of Independence, not as a matter of original intent, but as a step made necessary when all other resorts failed. Ideology thus did not set George Hewes apart from Samuel Adams or John Hancock. The difference lies in what the Revolution did to him as a person. His experiences transformed him, giving him a sense of citizenship and personal worth. Adams and Hancock began with both; Hewes had to arrive there, and in arriving he cast off the constraints of deference.

What Were the Africans in St. Domingue Fighting For?

JOHN K. THORNTON

Shortly after a body of rebellious slaves had sacked Le Cap François (now known as Cap Haitien) in June 1793 at the behest of the republican commissioners, their leader, known as Macaya, retreated to the hills and swore allegiance to the king of Spain, who had supported the rebellion for some time. When the commissioner Étienne Polverel tried to persuade him to return to the republic, Macaya wrote back: "I am the subject of three kings: of the King of Congo, master of all the blacks; of the King of France who represents my father; of the King of Spain who represents my mother. These three Kings are the descendants of those who, led by a star, came to adore God made Man."

These sentiments, seconded by other revolutionary leaders from time to time, have led many analysts of the Haitian revolution, from the venerable Thomas Madiou onward, to consider that the rebel slaves were inveterate royalists. Some scholars have proposed that royalism was a product of the slaves' African background, where kings were the rule. Nor was this observation confined to modern historians: the same civil commissioners who were rebuffed by Macaya wrote to Pierrot, one of his associates, at about the same time begging him to consider "the lot which you are preparing for the blacks [*nègres*] who surround you. . . . They follow the banner of kings and therefore of slavery. Who sold you on the coast of Guinea? It was the kings." They continued, "Who is it that gives you freedom? It is the French nation . . . that has cut off the head of its king who sells slaves." A bit later they returned to the same theme: "You know our intentions, they are pure, they are favorable to the unfortunate ones whom the kings of Guinea sold to the white kings."

In a larger context, Eugene Genovese has viewed slave revolts in the Americas in a similar way. Earlier revolts, he argues, were largely backward-looking and restorationist, seeking to recreate an African past in the Americas, including its kings. On the other hand, perhaps ignoring this piece of evidence, Genovese sees the Haitian revolution as ultimately the product of the dissemination of "bourgeois-capitalist" ideas diffusing from Europe and eventually reaching even the slaves. C. L. R. James, whose classic treatment of the revolution was fired by both republican and socialist thought, saw the royalism of the slaves as an inherent problem of their African background, from which heroes like Toussaint Louverture gradually and patiently weaned them. In both scholars' view, backwards Africa confronted forward-looking Europe in the origins and ideology of the Haitian revolution.

However one views the Haitian revolution in its totality, there is no question that many of the revolutionary leaders expressed royalist sentiments, that their followers carried royalist banners and called themselves *gens du roi*, and that they even demanded the restoration of the monarchy. These as well as other elements of the slaves' outlook may well reflect their African background. It is worthy of consideration, after

---

Source: John K. Thornton, " 'I Am the Subject of the King of Congo': African Political Ideology and the Haitian Revolution." *Journal of World History* vol. 4 (1993): 181–191, 198–201, 206–210, 213. Reprinted with permission of the University of Hawaii Press.

all, that perhaps as many as two-thirds of the slaves in Saint-Domingue (Haiti) on the eve of the revolution had been born, raised, and socialized in Africa. Attention to the ideological orientation of the mass of the slaves might be important even if many of their leaders were creoles with no immediate African background, since they would still have to appeal to their followers in terms that resonated with their ideology. Taking this into consideration, Carolyn Fick, whose recent history of the revolution focuses on the mass participation of the slaves, proposes that much could be learned about the revolution and the slaves' background by studying the eighteenth-century Kongo, from which a large number ultimately hailed.

It is appropriate, as Fick suggests, to start with the ideology of the kingdom of Kongo, the central African state to whom Macaya was referring in his celebrated reply to Polverel. Kongo is a particularly good starting point both because it is an extremely well-documented kingdom (including texts dealing with political philosophy) and because it provided thousands of slaves to the island colony of Saint-Domingue on the eve of the revolution. These slaves were exported in large measure as a result of civil war in the kingdom of Kongo. People enslaved through war or as a result of the decline of public order created by constant warfare and resulting brigandage were sold to local merchants, who brought them to the coast for resale. French and English shippers who supplied Saint-Domingue bought slaves primarily along what they called the "coast of Angola," which included not only modern Angola, but also Zaire, Congo-Brazzaville, and southern Gabon. The region around the kingdom of Loango, north of the Zaire River, was the main base for operations, and after 1770 most of the coast north of the Portuguese colony of Angola was being visited by French shipping. African merchants, known as *Mobires* (*Vili* in modern terminology), brought slaves to the northern ports of Cabinda, Malemba, or Loango from inland, many transporting them from Kongo where the civil wars made slaves plentiful. Perhaps more than half of the total exports from the area came from the kingdom of Kongo itself. Certainly the wars had an impact in Kongo, since the exports were witnessed and denounced by the Portuguese missionary Rafael de Castello de Vide, who served in Kongo from 1780 to 1788 and who sought to persuade the king of Kongo to ban the sale of slaves outside the country.

Slaves from this region made up the majority of those imported into Saint-Domingue for the last twenty years before the revolution. David Geggus has studied plantation inventories and concluded that in the 1780s "Congos" made up 60 percent of the slaves in North Province, where the revolution began, and about the same percentage in the south. They were common enough among the rebels that *Congo* became a generic term for the rank and file of the slave insurgents. That Macaya was a Kongolese might be inferred from his name, which can be attested as a personal name in Kongo from the late seventeenth century. It is further indicative of the role of Kongolese in the early stages of the revolution that the most popular early leader, Boukman Dutty, though certainly not a Kongolese himself, was still known by a Kikongo nickname, Zamba (probably *nzamba*, or "elephant," from his large and powerful stature), perhaps because so many of his followers were Kongolese.

The role of Kongo is also important because it can be seen as a source of revolutionary Haiti's ideology—not just its royalism, as an archaic throwback to obsolete political forms, but also its positive movement toward a better society. In this way, Kongo might be seen as a fount of revolutionary ideas as much as France was, even though the idiom of Kongolese ideology was royalist and, being alien to most researchers, has been overlooked.

Indeed, it was to political philosophy that Kongo owed its late eighteenth-century participation in the slave trade. The civil wars that punctuated most of the eighteenth century were fought at least in part to resolve constitutional issues and determine who was the king of Kongo and what were his powers. Many of those enslaved and eventually sent to Saint-Domingue had served in Kongo's civil wars or were caught up by them. The issues that shaped the civil wars in Kongo might well have shaped a different civil war in the Caribbean. . . .

In common with many other political systems, Kongo political philosophy alternated between two opposing concepts: an absolutist one that granted the king full powers and the right to manage all the affairs of the country (at least in theory), and a much more limited one that required the king to rule by consent of the governed and to make decisions only after consultation with at least some of those he governed.

Like eighteenth-century Europe, Kongo thus had both an "absolutist" and a "republican" tendency in its political thought. Which one prevailed depended very much on who exercised power, in both Africa and Europe, though at most times there was a dynamic tension between the two. The interplay of these ideas shaped ideological struggle in Africa as in Europe. Major turning points of European political history, such as the French revolution, the Napoleonic empire, the Restoration, and the revolutions of 1830 or 1848, all were exercises in working out the contradictions of these opposed ideas. Ultimately, the triumph of republican forms of government and democracy resulted in the acceptance of one of these traditions, though even after this victory the authoritarian concept remained and resurfaced from time to time.

Kongo also possessed such opposed traditions, though there was no question of dispensing with kings, as European republicanism proposed. Rather, it was a question of the nature of the king's rule. Analysis based on an understanding of European ideology has difficulty comprehending this dynamic because its idiom was substantially different from that of Europe. It is necessary, therefore, to examine Kongolese political philosophy in order to see how it might have contributed to the African side of the ideology of the Haitian revolution. . . .

Kongolese looked back to the foundation stories of the kingdom to explain basic political philosophy, much as eighteenth-century Europeans looked back to republican or imperial Rome for their own ideas. As the Kongolese understood it, the character of the founder formed a charter for the proper governance of the state.

In some versions of the story, the founder was described as a conqueror. Such kings exercised absolute power and could not be controlled by society; they could act with complete impunity. One symbolic statement of this sort of power appeared in tales of kings who killed people arbitrarily. According to one of the starkest versions of this story, recorded by the Capuchin priest Giovanni Cavazzi da Montecuccolo about 1665, the founder stabbed his pregnant aunt through the womb for refusing to pay a crossing toll, thus committing a double homicide. He went unpunished for this heinous crime, and was even admired; followers flocked to his standard, allowing him to conquer Kongo and establish his rule. . . .

Such stories were appropriate to a highly centralized and autocratic kingdom, such as Kongo was from the time it first came into contact with Portugal in 1483 until the civil wars of the mid- to late seventeenth century. But in the civil war period, a new version of Kongo history began to emerge, especially as King Pedro IV (ruled 1694–1718) attempted to reunite the kingdom through a policy of reconciliation. Unlike the conqueror king of the centralized state, the new founder needed to be a more republican sort of ruler, one who recognized the rights of numerous families and local powers and ruled by consensus and consent. Hence, the stories of Kongo's foundation told in Pedro's court presented the founder as a blacksmith king.

A memorial of about 1710 originating in Pedro IV's court described the royal family as descendants of a "wise and skillful blacksmith" who "gathered the Congolese People as their arbitrator of their differences and suits." Modern anthropologists recognize the widespread central African image of the blacksmith as a conciliatory figure who resolves conflict and is gentle, generous, and unselfish. To emphasize the gentleness of blacksmiths, they were associated with women. Furnaces were often decorated as women with breasts to heighten the imagery. It occurs in foundation stories from other places besides Kongo. The traditions of the kingdom of Ndongo, Kongo's southern neighbor, recorded in the mid-seventeenth century, also speak of a kind and generous blacksmith who is elected king by popular acclaim after relieving a famine from his personal stock of goods and settling disputes. The Kongolese north of Zaire developed regional regulatory mechanisms using these principles in the healing cult of Lemba in the eighteenth century. This cult managed the affairs of the area through a decentralized system of adjudication.

The contrasting constitutional principles were cross-cut by larger moral ideas of political philosophy, which held that whatever powers kings might have, they should use them in the public interest. Thus, no matter how absolute his rule, a Kongolese king was expected to rule fairly and to share unselfishly in his wealth and power. . . .

These ideas did not vanish when those unfortunate soldiers who served in the civil wars were captured and transported to Saint-Domingue, nor did they cease to operate when the conspiracy of 1791 resulted in the slave revolution in Saint-Domingue that eventually led to the independence of Haiti. In the environment of the New World, however, they combined with other ideas to constitute an ideological undercurrent of the revolution. The ideas did have to be translated to fit a new environment, since the social structure of Saint-Domingue was different from that of Kongo. There were, however, ideologically identifiable similarities between the two.

The original leaders of the conspiracy were probably not recently enslaved Kongolese from the civil wars, and indeed they may well have been moved as much by ideas of the French revolution as by those of the Kongo civil wars. According to testimony of the time, the original conspiracy was led by some 200 men, all of whom were *commandeurs d'atelier*, or the leaders of slave gangs. Such men were privileged among slaves in Saint-Domingue, forming a distinct class in a highly unequal slave society, which the Swiss visitor Girod de Chantrans compared to the hierarchy of the Ottoman empire, a favorite absolutist analogy of the eighteenth century. According to occupational listings in estate inventories, over three-quarters of the occupations that either required high skill or involved supervision and personal service were held by creoles. These slaves, born in the colony, were more in touch with the local and European ideological environment than with events in Africa. The official report on the revolt suggested that mulattos played a role in inspiring the revolt and that papers relating events in France were read in the meetings of the conspiracy.

These creole and mulatto supervisors and managers exercised authority in the society of prerevolutionary Saint-Domingue largely through the estate organization. Although they viewed the masters and the white overseers (*économes*) as opponents, much of the revolution from their point of view involved replacing leadership in the plantation, but not necessarily replacing the plantation system itself.

The slaves, especially the common field hands, while certainly required to obey the men their masters had appointed over them, did not necessarily confer legitimacy on them. Their goals certainly included the end of the plantation economy and forced labor, and thus they and the creoles could not share the same ultimate vision for postrevolutionary society.

The newly arrived African field hands often looked to organizations formed by their "nation"—a loose grouping of people from the same part of Africa or the same ethnolinguistic group—to provide leadership and perform mutual aid functions. One way of maintaining leadership of nations was through the election of kings and queens. These elections were widespread in the society of Afro-American slaves in all parts of the Americas. In Iberian America the annual elections were public events, while in other areas they were acknowledged if not recognized. The elected officials certainly had democratic potential, for those in New England in the nineteenth century operated a shadow government and were subject to democratic restraints. In Saint-Domingue, where colonial legislation made open ceremony by national leadership illegal in the interests of security, national leadership was vested in the heads of secret societies. Moreau de Saint-Méry's description of the secret societies on the eve of the revolution notes that they were often nationally organized, while their leaders were selected on a religious basis but served both as oracles and as arbitrators of slave society.

These secret societies, with their kings and queens and their religious orientation, and perhaps also with their potential to form what people might have considered a legitimate government, had strong links to the ideology of African societies. They were also capable of organizing plots, since members of the same nation were typically scattered across many plantations and could be mobilized through the national element of the society. The closet Caribbean analogy to the Haitian revolution in terms of size and scale of mobilization, the Jamaica revolt of 1760, was organized through Akan (Coromanti) national organizations, including an elected king and queen.

Two principles therefore competed in the making of the revolution: the estates headed by creole leadership and relying on the hierarchical organization of plantations for authority, and the nation with a looser but more popular organization. But the two types of organization could not operate independently, for the creoles could not stage a revolt alone. They had to obtain the support of the masses of slaves, and any ideology had to take their beliefs into account. The interesting dual meeting, first between creoles and then among field hands, that started the Haitian revolution was but the first manifestation of the alliance and difficulties between the two groups. . . .

In the complicated world of revolutionary Saint-Domingue, then, rival organizational principles as well as rival leaders from different social strata struggled for supremacy. But even among the independent bands of rebels and the inhabitants of the areas they controlled there was ideological ferment that matched the military maneuvering. While Macaya mentioned serving the king of Kongo, he did not say whether the king he served was a conqueror or a blacksmith. Indeed, a leader like Macaya might see the value of both in different contexts: to his followers perhaps he was a conqueror, but to those who would lead a united Haiti, he was an advocate of the blacksmith.

For Macaya and his Kongolese followers, as for other leaders of nationally organized groups, the revolution and its aftermath raised in a new context the same issues that had divided Kongolese in Africa. Was the new society to be an authoritarian state where the plantation economy continued with or without slavery? Or was it to be a more egalitarian society of smallholders where estates were broken up and redistributed? Clearly the Kongolese ideology of blacksmith versus conqueror kings and related ideas could serve in this context as well as republican or imperial ideas of Europe.

Although explicit evidence is lacking, there are hints that at least some of the generals and elite presented themselves as conqueror kings or leaders. These are found in the innumerable atrocity stories that fill whole cartons in the archives and were the stock in trade of travelers, journalists, and analysts of the time. Of course, atrocities can have many explanations that have nothing to do with ideology or revolution. The brutality of the slave regime and the excesses of those suppressing it could easily create a cycle of increasingly bloody acts of revenge that fueled the atrocity stories. Such stories might even be made up to secure the sympathies of a French public that might be moved from its support for the rebels by revelations of their inhumanity. . . .

Military commanders, however, were not the only leaders created by the revolution. From the beginning kings and queens were elected in various areas whenever the insurgents succeeded in gaining political control. These elections harked back to the older kings and queens of national organizations, which in Saint-Domingue had been the secret societies.

L'Acul, Macaya's original base of operations, seems to have been organized in just this way shortly after the outbreak of the revolution, perhaps by the Kongo nation. A detailed diary of a French militiaman from the start of the revolution noted that the rebels chose a king for each quarter that they had captured. He provided an account of the election conducted in L'Acul on 5 September 1791, shortly after its capture. "Yesterday, being Sunday," he wrote, "the negroes celebrated two marriages in the church at L'Acul. On the occasion they assumed titles, and the titled blacks were treated with great respect, and the ceremony was performed in great pomp. A Capuchin [whose name was Cajetan] retained among them, has been obliged to officiate. Their colours were consecrated and a king was elected. They have chosen one for each quarter." No mention is made of the nationality of the insurgents at L'Acul, but the Christian ceremony, especially one conducted by a Capuchin, suggests a Kongolese presence, for the Capuchin order was greatly honored and respected in Christian Kongo. That L'Acul may have been a specifically Kongolese base is suggested by Macaya's decision to escape to the area in 1795 after having been imprisoned by Louverture. There he met with his nation at their dances and assemblies, as Louverture believed, to plan further revolt. . . .

Their presence as elected leaders in the areas occupied in the early days of the revolution may represent a tentative movement in the direction of a local limited monarchy based on African ideological views, though surely tempered by the military necessities of the moment and the power this gave to more ruthless and less democratic men, who seem to have often held or taken the title of king. Insofar as preexisting African nations played a role in the election and in organizing support, the ideas might have been less authoritarian, since such organizations lacked the capacity to enforce discipline that the plantation system gave to the creoles. The Kongolese rites of modern Voodoo may also reflect the decentralized nature of the rule of secret societies. John Janzen argues that elements of the Lemba cult, which managed political affairs in a decentralized manner in Kongolese societies north of the Zaire, were also transferred to Haiti. Indeed, Haitian secret societies, no longer nationally specific, continue to rule rural life, adjudicate disputes, and even punish malefactors. . . .

It is interesting to note, finally, that among the leaders who strongly resisted the restoration of forced labor by Louverture and Dessalines were the Kongolese, such as Sans Souci, Scylla, and the inevitable Macaya. This may well explain the creole leaders' hostility to the national organizations, which they often did not control and which may have expressed ideological ideas contrary to their own.

△ *F U R T H E R　R E A D I N G*

Armitage, David. *The Declaration of Independence: A Global History.* Cambridge, MA: Harvard University Press, 2007.

Branson, Susan. *Those Fiery Frenchified Dames: Women and Political Culture in Early National Philadelphia.* Philadelphia: University of Pennsylvania Press, 2001.

Davis, David Brion. *The Problem of Slavery in the Age of Revolution, 1770–1823.* Ithaca, NY: Cornell University Press, 1975.

Dubois, Laurent. *Avengers of the New World: The Story of the Haitian Revolution.* Cambridge, MA: Belknap Press of Harvard University Press, 2004.

Fick, Carolyn E. *The Making of Haiti: The Saint Domingue Revolution from Below.* Knoxville: University of Tennessee Press, 1990.

Foner, Eric. *Tom Paine and Revolutionary America.* New York: Oxford University Press, 1977, 2004.

Garrigus, John D. *Before Haiti: Race and Citizenship in French Saint Domingue.* New York: Palgrave Macmillan, 2006.

Gaspar, David Barry, and David Patrick Geggus, eds. *A Turbulent Time: The French Revolution and the Greater Caribbean.* Bloomington: Indiana University Press, 1997.

James, C. L. R. *The Black Jacobins; Toussaint L'Ouverture and the San Domingo Revolution.* New York: Vintage Books, 1963.

Kerber, Linda K. *Women of the Republic: Intellect and Ideology in Revolutionary America.* Chapel Hill: Published for the Institute of Early American History and Culture by the University of North Carolina Press, 1980.

Landes, Joan B. *Women and the Public Sphere in the Age of the French Revolution.* Ithaca, NY: Cornell University Press, 1988.

Linebaugh, Peter, and Marcus Rediker. *The Many-Headed Hydra: Sailors, Slaves, Commoners, and the Hidden History of the Revolutionary Atlantic.* Boston: Beacon Press, 2000.

Nash, Gary B. *The Unknown American Revolution: The Unruly Birth of Democracy and the Struggle to Create America.* New York: Viking, 2005.

Racine, Karen. *Francisco de Miranda: A Transatlantic Life in the Age of Revolution.* Wilmington, DE: SR Books, 2003.

Thompson, E. P. *The Making of the English Working Class.* New York: Pantheon Books, 1963.

Wood, Gordon S. *The Radicalism of the American Revolution.* New York: A. A. Knopf, 1991.

Young, Alfred Fabian. *The Shoemaker and the Tea Party: Memory and the American Revolution.* Boston: Beacon Press, 1999.

C H A P T E R
13

Twilight of Slavery

Atlantic slavery died a long, slow, fitful, and sometimes violent death. Antislavery pressure came from numerous sources: Enlightenment ideas of universal freedom and natural rights, religious ideas that regarded slavery as a sin, and the objections of enslaved people themselves. Although there had been scattered denunciations of slavery in the seventeenth and early eighteenth centuries (and Spain had legally prohibited the enslavement of American Indians in the sixteenth century), organized opposition to the enslavement of Africans emerged in the revolutionary era of the late eighteenth and early nineteenth centuries. A watershed in the history of abolitionism came in 1772, when Lord Chief Justice Mansfield ruled in Somerset v. Stewart that British law did not permit the existence of slavery in Great Britain. Still, it took another sixty years for Great Britain to abolish slavery in the British West Indies. War and revolution overthrew slavery in St. Domingue in the 1790s, but slavery survived in other French colonies until 1848. In the United States, slavery faded away in the northern states after the American Revolution but flourished in the South until the Civil War uprooted it. The Thirteenth Amendment to the U.S. Constitution finally ended slavery in the United States in 1865. The end of slavery elsewhere in the Americas came with abolition in Cuba in 1886 and Brazil in 1888, but slavery persisted well into the twentieth century in much of Africa. And despite legal, diplomatic, and naval pressure against the transatlantic slave trade, slavers carried almost three million captive Africans across the Atlantic in the nineteenth century. As slaveowners struggled against the antislavery tide of progress, abolition and emancipation invited new questions about labor and citizenship in the Atlantic world. What would happen to freed people? Would they work for wages, or would they prefer to work for themselves? Would freedom bring equality and an end to racism, or would it lead to new inequalities and hatreds? The documents and essays in this chapter reveal the death throes of slavery in the Atlantic world.

◁ *D O C U M E N T S*

The ideas and struggles of the revolutionary era sparked criticism of slavery, proposals for emancipation, and defensive reactions from slavery's advocates. One key figure who wrestled with the problem of slavery was Thomas Jefferson (1743–1826), author of the United States' Declaration of Independence. In Document 1, taken from his *Notes on the State of Virginia* (1784), Jefferson attacks slavery, but his proposed solution, gradual emancipation and the deportation of freed people outside the United States, also reveals a deep racism.

Despite the rhetoric of the American Revolution, it was Great Britain that took the lead in promoting abolition in the Atlantic world. In 1807, Great Britain legally ended its participation in the Atlantic slave trade and began a lengthy diplomatic and military campaign against it. The British met with resistance from slave traders around the Atlantic world, including in Africa. In Document 2, Joseph Dupuis, a British emissary to western Africa, records a conversation with Osei Bonsu, the King of Asante (a powerful empire on the Gold Coast), who expressed dismay at Britain's sudden repudiation of a longstanding commerce.

In the 1830s, Britain finally abolished slavery in its West Indian colonies, converting slaves into "apprentices" and establishing special magistrates to oversee the transition to freedom. Document 3 comes from the journal of one such magistrate. John Colthurst, who served in St. Vincent, contrasts conditions on a plantation where the former slaves were treated poorly with one where the former slaves were treated well. Drawing lessons from the British West Indian experience, the French liberal Alexis de Tocqueville (1805–1859) endorsed emancipation in France's colonies in 1843. But as Document 5 indicates, Tocqueville's proposal would have prevented newly freed people from owning their own land in order to force them to continue working on sugar plantations.

The nineteenth-century antislavery movement relied heavily on the testimony and witness of slaves and free people of color. Document 4 includes excerpts from the autobiographies of two former slaves, Frederick Douglass (1818–1895) of the United States and Juan Manzano (1797–1854) of Cuba, which show the importance of literacy to enslaved people. Document 6 presents one leg of the transatlantic odyssey of Mahommah Gardo Baquaqua, an African who was transported to Brazil and sold into slavery. He was eventually purchased by a sea captain, who made the mistake of taking Baquaqua to New York in 1847, where he seized his freedom. After a brief sojourn in Haiti, Baquaqua returned to the United States and co-authored his biography with the aid of Samuel Moore, an American abolitionist.

Slavery ended in different ways in different places, as the letters in Document 7 indicate. Spotswood Rice was an African-American soldier fighting for the Union army in 1864. Emboldened by his newfound power, Rice sought to recover his children from their former owner. More than twenty years later, a Brazilian planter saw a smooth transition to freedom following abolition in 1888. Despite some initial disruptions to the coffee plantation economy, Conselheiro Paula Souza indicated that the newly freed workers were more productive and less expensive than he had expected. By the end of the nineteenth century, Africa remained as the last bastion of slavery in the Atlantic world, as Document 8 suggests. Thomas Phipson (1815–1876), a British officer in Natal in southern Africa, condemned the indigenous practices of polygamy and slavery. Writing a letter to the *Natal Witness* in 1876, Phipson called for a more active British effort to eradicate these evils. For Phipson and many other Europeans in Africa, abolitionism justified imperialism.

1. Thomas Jefferson Wrestles with Slavery, 1785

Query XIV. Laws

To emancipate all slaves born after passing the act. The bill reported by the revisors does not itself contain this proposition; but an amendment containing it was prepared, to be offered to the legislature whenever the bill should be taken up, and further directing, that they should continue with their parents to a certain age, then be brought up,

Source: Merrill D. Peterson, ed., *The Portable Thomas Jefferson* (New York: Penguin Books, 1975), pp. 185–187, 193, 214–215.

at the public expence, to tillage, arts or sciences, according to their geniusses, till the females should be eighteen, and the males twenty-one years of age, when they should be colonized to such place as the circumstances of the time should render most proper, sending them out with arms, implements of household and of the handicraft arts, seeds, pairs of the useful domestic animals, &c. to declare them a free and independent people, and extend to them our alliance and protection, till they have acquired strength; and to send vessels at the same time to other parts of the world for an equal number of white inhabitants; to induce whom to migrate hither, proper encouragements were to be proposed. It will probably be asked, Why not retain and incorporate the blacks into the state, and thus save the expence of supplying, by importation of white settlers, the vacancies they will leave? Deep rooted prejudices entertained by the whites; ten thousand recollections, by the blacks, of the injuries they have sustained; new provocations; the real distinctions which nature has made; and many other circumstances, will divide us into parties, and produce convulsions which will probably never end but in the extermination of the one or the other race.—To these objections, which are political, may be added others, which are physical and moral. The first difference which strikes us is that of colour. Whether the black of the negro resides in the reticular membrane between the skin and scarf-skin, or in the scarf-skin itself; whether it proceeds from the colour of the blood, the colour of the bile, or from that of some other secretion, the difference is fixed in nature, and is as real as if its seat and cause were better known to us. And is this difference of no importance? Is it not the foundation of a greater or less share of beauty in the two races? Are not the fine mixtures of red and white, the expressions of every passion by greater or less suffusions of colour in the one, preferable to that external monotony, which reigns in the countenances, that immoveable veil of black which covers all the emotions of the other race? Add to these, flowing hair, a more elegant symmetry of form, their own judgment in favour of the whites, declared by their preference of them, as uniformly as is the preference of the Oranootan for the black women over those of his own species. The circumstance of superior beauty, is thought worthy attention in the propagation of our horses, dogs, and other domestic animals; why not in that of man? . . .

This unfortunate difference of colour, and perhaps of faculty, is a powerful obstacle to the emancipation of these people. Many of their advocates, while they wish to vindicate the liberty of human nature, are anxious also to preserve its dignity and beauty. Some of these, embarrassed by the question "What further is to be done with them?" join themselves in opposition with those who are actuated by sordid avarice only. Among the Romans emancipation required but one effort. The slave, when made free, might mix with, without staining the blood of his master. But with us a second is necessary, unknown to history. When freed, he is to be removed beyond the reach of mixture. . . .

Query XVIII. Manners

It is difficult to determine on the standard by which the manners of a nation may be tried, whether *catholic*, or *particular*. It is more difficult for a native to bring to that standard the manners of his own nation, familiarized to him by habit. There must doubtless be an unhappy influence on the manners of our people produced by the existence of slavery among us. The whole commerce between master and slave is a perpetual exercise of the most boisterous passions, the most unremitting despotism on the one part, and degrading submissions on the other. Our children see this, and learn to imitate it; for man is an imitative animal. This quality is the germ of all education in him. From his cradle to his grave he is learning to do what he sees others do. If a parent could find no motive either in his philanthropy or his self-love, for restraining the intemperance of passion towards his slave, it should always be a sufficient one that his child is present. But generally it is not sufficient. The parent storms, the child looks on, catches the lineaments of wrath, puts on the same airs in the circle of smaller slaves, gives a loose to his worst of passions, and thus nursed, educated, and daily exercised in tyranny, cannot but be stamped by it with odious peculiarities. The man must be a prodigy who can retain his manners and morals undepraved by such circumstances. And with what execration should the statesman be loaded, who permitting one half the citizens thus to trample on the rights of the other, transforms those into despots; and these into enemies, destroys the morals of the one part, and the amor patriæ of the other. For if a slave can have a country in this world, it must be any other in preference to that in which he is born to live and labour for another: in which he must lock up the faculties of his nature, contribute as far as depends on his individual endeavours to the evanishment of the human race, or entail his own miserable condition on the endless generations proceeding from him. With the morals of the people, their industry also is destroyed. For in a warm climate, no man will labour for himself who can make another labour for him. This is so true, that of the proprietors of slaves a very small proportion indeed are ever seen to labour. And can the liberties of a nation be thought secure when we have removed their only firm basis, a conviction in the minds of the people that these liberties are of the gift of God? That they are not to be violated but with his wrath? Indeed I tremble for my country when I reflect that God is just: that his justice cannot sleep for ever: that considering numbers, nature and natural means only, a revolution of the wheel of fortune, an exchange of situation, is among possible events: that it may become probable by supernatural interference! The Almighty has no attribute which can take side with us in such a contest.—But it is impossible to be temperate and to pursue this subject through the various considerations of policy, of morals, of history natural and civil. We must be contented to hope they will force their way into every one's mind. I think a change already perceptible, since the origin of the present revolution. The spirit of the master is abating, that of the slave rising from the dust, his condition mollifying, the way I hope preparing, under the auspices of heaven, for a total emancipation, and that this is disposed, in the order of events, to be with the consent of the masters, rather than by their extirpation.

2. The King of Asante Explains the Importance of the Slave Trade, 1820

"Now," said the king, after a pause, "I have another palaver, and you must help me to talk it. A long time ago the great king liked plenty of trade, more than now; then many ships came, and they bought ivory, gold, and slaves; but now he will not let the ships come as before, and the people buy gold and ivory only. This is what I have in my head, so now tell me truly, like a friend, why does the king do so?" "His majesty's

---

Source: Joseph Dupuis, *Journal of a Residence in Ashantee*, ed. W. E. F. Ward (London: Frank Cass, 1966, second edition), pp. 162–164.

question," I replied, "was connected with a great palaver, which my instructions did not authorise me to discuss. I had nothing to say regarding the slave trade." "I know that too," retorted the king; "because, if my master liked that trade, you would have told me so before. I only want to hear what you think as a friend: this is not like the other palavers." I was confessedly at a loss for an argument that might pass as a satisfactory reason, and the sequel proved that my doubts were not groundless. The king did not deem it plausible, that this obnoxious traffic should have been abolished from motives of humanity alone; neither would he admit that it lessened the number either of domestic or foreign wars.

Taking up one of my observations, he remarked, "the white men who go to council with your master, and pray to the great God for him, do not understand my country, or they would not say the slave trade was bad. But if they think it bad now, why did they think it good before. Is not your law an old law, the same as the Crammo* law? Do you not both serve the same God, only you have different fashions and customs? Crammos are strong people in fetische, and they say the law is good, because the great God made the book; so they buy slaves, and teach them good things, which they knew not before. This makes every body love the Crammos, and they go every where up and down, and the people give them food when they want it. Then these men come all the way from the great water†, and from Manding, and Dagomba, and Killinga; they stop and trade for slaves, and then go home. If the great king would like to restore this trade, it would be good for the white men and for me too, because Ashantee is a country for war, and the people are strong; so if you talk that palaver for me properly, in the white country, if you go there, I will give you plenty of gold, and I will make you richer than all the white men."

I urged the impossibility of the king's request, promising, however, to record his sentiments faithfully. "Well, then," said the king, "you must put down in my master's book all I shall say, and then he will look to it, now he is my friend. And when he sees what is true, he will surely restore that trade. I cannot make war to catch slaves in the bush, like a thief. My ancestors never did so. But if I fight a king, and kill him when he is insolent, then certainly I must have his gold, and his slaves, and the people are mine too. Do not the white kings act like this? Because I hear the old men say, that before I conquered Fantee and killed the Braffoes and the kings, that white men came in great ships, and fought and killed many people; and then they took the gold and slaves to the white country: and sometimes they fought together. That is all the same as these black countries. The great God and the fetische made war for strong men every where, because then they can pay plenty of gold and proper sacrifice. When I fought Gaman, I did not make war for slaves, but because Dinkera (the king) sent me an arrogant message and killed my people, and refused to pay me gold as his father did. Then my fetische made me strong like my ancestors, and I killed Dinkera, and took his gold, and brought more than 20,000 slaves to Coomassy. Some of these people being bad men, I washed my stool in their blood for the fetische. But then some were good people, and these I sold or gave to my captains: many, moreover, died, because this country does not grow too much corn like Sarem, and what can I do? Unless I kill or sell them, they will grow strong and kill my people. Now you

---

*Moslem law.

†Niger.

must tell my master that these slaves can work for him, and if he wants 10,000 he can have them. And if he wants fine handsome girls and women to give his captains, I can send him great numbers."

3. A British Magistrate Oversees Freedom in St. Vincent, 1835–1838

The great success attending the island cultivation since the abolition of slavery and since the commencement of the Apprenticeship defeats the assumption that the abolition of slavery would lay the foundation of the ruin of the West India colonies. What has come to my knowledge, since my arrival in the island as Special Magistrate, confirms me in my preconceived anticipations of the favorable results flowing from the abolition of slavery. All admit the estates are in excellent order generally; for, although the apprentices are at this moment passing through an ordeal, which is neither absolute freedom nor positive slavery, it is most gratifying to observe (all things considered) how willingly and manfully they perform their duty, and, in many instances, under masters and employers of tempers and habits which could only be acquired in slavery. It is lamentable to be obliged, as a Special Magistrate, to legislate between parties so circumstanced. The trials his temper undergoes upon those occasions are vexatious to a degree. To discharge this duty correctly, and at the same time justly, is extremely critical. On the one hand, he has to encounter ignorance, irritation of temper, and all the tyrannical feelings in the master, as a former slave owner; on the other hand, profound ignorance in the apprentice, lately a slave. This unpleasant state of things is, I rejoice to say, by no means general. It is only the case upon estates which are conducted by an inferior description of agents or managers of property; for I have found it invariably the case that whenever estates were superintended by men of common humanity, the very best understanding prevailed between them and their apprentices, and a most respectable feeling of propriety grew up amongst all.

As some proof of the above remarks, I will relate the particulars of two cases of estate management, which occurred within the last ten days, both in my own district: the first shewing the effects of steady and good conduct in the immediate manager, and the second exhibiting the reverse of all this.

First case: A very respectable young man, a Mr. King, had confided to him the management of three large estates some time prior to my taking the Special Chair of the district in 1835. The number of apprentices upon those estates was over 400, and consequently, Mr. King's duties and responsibilities were extremely onerous; and during several months' residence in the district, and before I had the pleasure of knowing Mr. King personally, it was a matter of surprise to me that for nearly eight months I never had a complaint from any of the estates under his direction brought before me. I then visited the properties in question, and soon discovered the true source from whence this particularly pleasing occurrence flowed—the manager. I met Mr. King by appointment, on the day I allude to, on the principal estate; and recollect with pleasure the scene I there witnessed, of busy hands, willing hearts, and cheerful countenances;

Source: John Bowen Colthurst, *The Colthurst Journal: Journal of a Special Magistrate in the Islands of Barbados and St. Vincent, July 1835–September 1838*, edited by Woodville K. Marshall (Millwood, NY: KTO Press, 1977), pp. 103–108.

every hand industriously employed at the same time exhibiting a deference and respect in the presence of Mr. King, clearly shewing that the negro, like all other men,
can fully appreciate considerate treatment, and resolve to repay it in kind.

This gentleman still continues to conduct these properties most successfully,
and still no complaints. The secret seems to lie in three words—temper, steadiness,
and humanity. The negro population, in their habits and feelings as a body, are precisely the same. Divide them into smaller bodies, these feelings are not altered. This
cannot be the case with those individuals who, as individuals, direct and command
them. Here no two conductors of property scarcely resemble one another; and all
this the Special Magistrate has to contend with.

This excellent understanding having existed for so many months (as detailed
above) between Mr. King and his apprentices, I could not fail to be surprised to see
Mr. King enter my office yesterday, and lodge a complaint upon the file, at the same
time pointing to a negro in the custody of the estate constables, having been that
morning taken in the act of stealing sugar canes. The culprit, being put to the bar, I
enquired how it happened that the character the estate had so justly acquired was now
for the first time to be broken in upon. On my saying this, one of the constables (an
old negro) with a fair feeling of decent pride, said, "Massa, massa Major, dat man is
not belong to de property—he is bad man, he only dare upon de estate two, three day
ago—de damn black nigger." Here, then, was the old story of the pot and the kettle;
yet it was most gratifying to observe the constable's anxiety to vindicate the character of the estate he laboured on. The trial proceeded—the prisoner had no defence to
make, and was consequently convicted of entering the cane field, and there cutting
and stealing therefrom as many canes as he well could carry away, and was taken in
the fact. In the course of this trial, it was satisfactorily proved that this fellow was a
man of bad character, having been convicted of theft in another district twice before.
I therefore sentenced him to receive fifteen stripes on the estate in the presence of the
gangs on the following morning. The prosecuting parties then left the office. However,
in a couple of hours afterwards, three of the principal superintendents of the estate (all
negroes) entered the office, and requested me to attend for a few moments to a "petition" they had to make, saying they had been deputed by the whole body of apprentices "not to disgrace them and the property, by flogging the fellow I had convicted in
the morning *on the estate*, but to give him as many stripes as ever I liked in the prison."
It may be easily supposed how readily I acceded to this request, at the same time directing these sable delegates to tell the people how much I approved such conduct, and
that I should be always happy to oblige them upon any occasion. Here, then, is subject
for comfortable reflection—slaves of yesterday, jealous of their good name!! . . .

Second case, as contrasted with the first case, shewing the evil effects of injudi-
cious management: On Monday evening last, a female negro apprentice came to my
house to make complaint against the manager of the Pine Estate, Mr. Corbin. This is
one of the most extensive properties in the island, and upon which there are upwards
of 200 negroes. . . .

On asking the woman what brought her before me, she said, "Massa, I am shamed
to tell you; for 'tis very dirty thing," and seemed to hesitate to disclose the nature of
her complaint against Mr. Corbin. After much pressing, I collected from this woman
that, for nearly three weeks, he had ordered the superintendent of the field not to
allow any individual of the gang under his charge to retire into the bush to perform

their natural occasions, but compel them to do so in presence of one another upon the rows they were respectively at work on, *both men and women*, showing the barbarous system this odious fellow seemed resolved to adopt, and proving, beyond doubt, that persons of his description, educated in slavery, know nothing of the usages of civilized life, and are prepared by such training to commit the most disgusting acts, subversive of all decency and morals. This woman related the story so circumstantially, and with such evident reluctance, that truth was borne on the face of it. She told me that twenty-eight of her fellow labourers, including herself, were subjected to this disgrace and punishment, and had quietly submitted to it for nearly three weeks. I lost no time, on the following morning, in sending Mr. Corbin notice that a complaint of this nature had been made against him, and that I should be on the estate the next day at 10 in the morning to hear it, and trusted he would be enabled to disprove the charge. I attended accordingly, entered into the merits of the complaint, and called upon him for his defence. He made none. Far from it, he acknowledged he issued the order complained of, and that he took care it was carried into effect by the superintendent of the field. This acknowledgement was made in the most unblushing and unhesitating manner, and I really believe this old disciple of slavery did not think he had done anything exceedingly wrong. It is unnecessary for me to say that I expressed my disgust. In addition to which, I reported his conduct both to the owner and the attorney of the estate, *who took no notice whatever of the transaction, and still continued him in his management*. However, after this affair he was evidently subdued, and things proceeded better. The negroes were satisfied that redress was at hand, which was promptly given, and they were content.

It may be asked why this complaint was not made before it was. Terror of the manager was, no doubt, the chief cause; and I am convinced a native sense of delicacy also prevented them from making it known to me sooner. This disgraceful mode of punishment was one of the many adopted in slavery. What, then, has not abolition effected? Everything; for the final event be what it may, the total overthrow of such acts as these has been accomplished. This barbarian was not long permitted to exercise his cruelties, for, in some weeks after the above transaction, he was taken ill of a fever, very nearly lost his life, and from subsequent ill health was obliged to resign the management which fell into better hands, and all things worked smoothly.

4. Two Slaves Learn to Read, 1839, 1845

Juan Francisco Manzano

After some time, we went to Havana and I was left in the service of Don Nicolás, who loved me, not as a slave, but as a son, notwithstanding his young age. That sadness, rooted so deeply in my soul, began to dissipate then; but I was diagnosed with a chest disease and a somewhat spasmodic cough, which Don Francisco Luvián cured. Time, aided by my youth, drove off all my ailments. I was well-treated, better-dressed, and more loved. I had a coat that my new master had ordered made for me, and I

Sources: Juan Francisco Manzano, *The Autobiography of a Slave*, introduction and modernized Spanish version by Ivan A. Schulman; translated by Evelyn Picon Garfield, pp. 103–105, with permission of Wayne State University Press; Frederick Douglass, *Narrative of the Life of Frederick Douglass, an American Slave* (Boston: 1845), pp. 33–34, 38–40.

had many *reales*. It was my duty to mend all his clothes, clean his shoes, tidy up his room, and arrange his clothing for him. Because this gentleman observed proper and irreproachable habits since his early years, he wanted everything within reach to be just so. He only forbade my going out alone, entering the kitchen, and mixing with indecent people. I never received even the slightest reprimand from him. My affection for him knew no bounds.

At daybreak when I saw him arise, I would prepare his desk, chair, and books before anything else, so he could devote himself to his studies. I began identifying with his habits so thoroughly that I, too, began my own study regimen. Throughout all the stages of my life, poetry—sometimes happy, sometimes sorrowful—afforded me verses in harmony with my situation. I used his rhetoric books and learned my lesson by heart. I learned it like a parrot and even believed that I knew something. However, I recognized how few were the fruits of my labor, since I never had the opportunity to use the information. It was then that I decided to dedicate myself to something more useful, learning to write.

That was another problem. I did not know how to start. I did not know how to cut quills and refrained from taking any from my master. I, nevertheless, bought myself a penknife, quills, and very fine paper, which I placed over a discarded sheet written in my master's hand in order to accustom myself to the feel of fashioning letters. I worked along tracing the shapes on the paper below. With this method, in less than a month I could already write lines that imitated my master's handwriting. For that reason there are certain similarities between his penmanship and mine.

Very happy with my successful experiment, I spent from five to ten o'clock practicing my hand at making small letters. Even during the day, when I had time, I also practiced. I would station myself at the foot of some painting whose title was in capital letters. With many strokes I was able to imitate the most beautiful letters. I succeeded then in making them look more like engravings than handwriting.

The marquis discovered me one time, and from what he said even I believed that I already knew how to write. Then my master found out, from those who used to see me in the act of writing from five on, that I was spending all my time engrossed in my papers. More than a few times he caught me at the head of a table that was in a corner. He ordered me to abandon that pastime, which did not correspond to my class, and to look for something to sew. As for sewing, I would take care to always have some at hand. So as not to interfere with my productivity, I was prohibited from writing; but it was in vain. For when everyone went to bed, I would light my candle stump and indulge myself, copying the prettiest verses from Arriaza, whose writing I always imitated. I figured that if my writing looked like his, I was already a poet or knew how to compose verses. Once they got hold of some scraps of papers full of décimas, and Don Coronado was the first to predict that I would be a poet, even though everyone was against it. He found out how I learned to write and why, and confirmed that most had begun the same way.

Frederick Douglass

Very soon after I went to live with Mr. and Mrs. Auld, she very kindly commenced to teach me the A, B, C. After I had learned this, she assisted me in learning to spell words of three or four letters. Just at this point of my progress, Mr. Auld found out what was going on, and at once forbade Mrs. Auld to instruct me further, telling her, among other things, that it was unlawful, as well as unsafe, to teach a slave to read. To use his own words, further, he said, "If you give a nigger an inch, he will take an ell. A nigger should know nothing but to obey his master—to do as he is told to do. Learning would spoil the best nigger in the world. Now," said he, "if you teach that nigger (speaking of myself) how to read, there would be no keeping him. It would forever unfit him to be a slave. He would at once become unmanageable, and of no value to his master. As to himself, it could do him no good, but a great deal of harm. It would make him discontented and unhappy." These words sank deep into my heart, stirred up sentiments within that lay slumbering, and called into existence an entirely new train of thought. It was a new and special revelation, explaining dark and mysterious things, with which my youthful understanding had struggled, but struggled in vain. I now understood what had been to me a most perplexing difficulty—to wit, the white man's power to enslave the black man. It was a grand achievement, and I prized it highly. From that moment, I understood the pathway from slavery to freedom. It was just what I wanted, and I got it at a time when I the least expected it. Whilst I was saddened by the thought of losing the aid of my kind mistress, I was gladdened by the invaluable instruction which, by the merest accident, I had gained from my master. Though conscious of the difficulty of learning without a teacher, I set out with high hope, and a fixed purpose, at whatever cost of trouble, to learn how to read. The very decided manner with which he spoke, and strove to impress his wife with the evil consequences of giving me instruction, served to convince me that he was deeply sensible of the truths he was uttering. It gave me the best assurance that I might rely with the utmost confidence on the results which, he said, would flow from teaching me to read. What he most dreaded, that I most desired. What he most loved, that I most hated. That which to him was a great evil, to be carefully shunned, was to me a great good, to be diligently sought; and the argument which he so warmly urged, against my learning to read, only served to inspire me with a desire and determination to learn. In learning to read, I owe almost as much to the bitter opposition of my master, as to the kindly aid of my mistress. I acknowledge the benefit of both. . . .

The plan which I adopted, and the one by which I was most successful, was that of making friends of all the little white boys whom I met in the street. As many of these as I could, I converted into teachers. With their kindly aid, obtained at different times and in different places, I finally succeeded in learning to read. When I was sent of errands, I always took my book with me, and by going one part of my errand quickly, I found time to get a lesson before my return. I used also to carry bread with me, enough of which was always in the house, and to which I was always welcome; for I was much better off in this regard than many of the poor white children in our neighborhood. This bread I used to bestow upon the hungry little urchins, who, in return, would give me that more valuable bread of knowledge. I am strongly tempted to give the names of two or three of those little boys, as a testimonial of the gratitude and affection I bear them; but prudence forbids;—not that it would injure me, but it might embarrass them; for it is almost an unpardonable offence to teach slaves to read in this Christian country. It is enough to say of the dear little fellows, that they lived on Philpot Street, very near Durgin and Bailey's ship-yard. I used to talk this matter of slavery over with them. I would sometimes say to them, I wished I could be as free as they would be when they got to be men. "You will be free as soon as you are twenty-one, but I am a slave for life! Have not I as good a right to be free as you have?" These words used to trouble them; they would express for me the liveliest sympathy, and console me with the hope that something would occur by which I might be free.

5. Alexis de Tocqueville Advocates Emancipation in the French West Indies, 1843

The committee of which the duc de Broglie was the organ recognized that the uncertainty in which the colonists, the slaves, and the metropole have been living for several years could not safely last much longer and believes that the moment has arrived to set a time for the abolition of slavery. But how should it be abolished? Here the committee is divided. Two plans are proposed. We shall limit ourselves to describing the one the majority adopted.

A law would set the irrevocable termination of slavery ten years from today. These ten years would be used to prepare the Negroes and the colonists to uphold the new social state destined for them. While remaining subjected to forced and usually unpaid labor, the principal sign of slavery, the Negro would, however, acquire certain rights that until now he has never enjoyed, and without which there can be no progress in morals and in civilization: such as rights to marry, to acquire [property], to buy his freedom; schools would be open to him; religious education and instruction would be furnished abundantly.

You can see that between the end of slavery and independence properly speaking, the committee, like the British government, thought it appropriate to place an intermediate period principally dedicated to the education of Negroes; but the committee conceived this intermediate state differently from the English. The latter had begun by declaring slavery abolished, but each slave, transformed into an apprentice, nonetheless remained under his former master and worked for him without wages. This mixed condition, where freedom, after having been granted, seemed to have been retracted, was not well understood by anyone. It gave birth to interminable discussions between the races: the Negroes grew exasperated, and the whites were not the least bit satisfied. Enlightened by this experience, the committee judged that the name of slavery should not be suppressed until the moment that the principal traits that characterize it are truly erased; instead of announcing more than one is giving, as the English have done, the committee found it wiser to grant in reality more than seems to be promised.

At the end of this preparation period, the forced relations between servant and master would end; work would become productive; servitude would cease in fact as in name.

But this does not mean that colonial society must all at once take on exactly the same appearance as greater French society, nor that the emancipated Negro is to enjoy on the spot all the rights that our worker possesses. The English example is there to prevent us from making such an error. The committee understood this perfectly; it judged that the greatest danger for the colonies at the time of the emancipation did

Source: From Alexis de Tocqueville, edited and translated by Jennifer Pitts, *Writings on Empire and Slavery*, pp. 218–221. Copyright © 2000 Jennifer Pitts. Reprinted with permission of The Johns Hopkins University Press.

not stem, as had been thought until then, from the bad inclinations of the blacks, and that, even though during the last years of slavery the slaves had achieved all the progress in morals and civilization of which experience had shown them capable, it would still be imprudent to accord them all at once the same independence that the French working classes enjoy. The committee understood that if, at the moment when forced labor no longer existed, artificial means were not used to attract and retain Negroes in the sugar refineries, and to prevent an excessive rise in wages, sugar production would receive a sudden and grave blow, and that the colonies, exposed to a sudden perturbation in their principal and almost only industry, would suffer greatly.

In the years immediately following the abolition of slavery, the committee therefore proposes to qualify the freedom of the emancipated Negroes in the following three main ways:

The former slaves will be required to reside in the colony.

Although free to choose their profession and the master under whose direction they want to work, they will neither be permitted to remain idle nor to work only for themselves.

Each year, the maximum and minimum wages will be fixed by the governor in council. Prices will be debated between these limits.

The motives behind these three transitional resolutions are easy to grasp.

With the first, the committee seeks to prevent English recruitment, which would quickly and significantly diminish the laboring population of our islands.

The goal of the second is to prevent the Negroes of our colonies from imitating those of the English colonies and abandoning large industries to settle on portions of fertile soil they would acquire at a very low price or usurp.

The principal object of the third, finally, is to prevent the masters, for their part, from abusing the blacks' obligation to hire out their services, and from abusing their ability, given their small number, to join forces and impose excessively low wages on their workers.

It is understood that these arrangements are transitional: they are intended only to facilitate the colonies' passage from one social state to another and to prevent a rapid decline of workers and, as a result, an industrial disturbance just as prejudicial, it cannot be said too often, to the black race as to the white race.

When the Negroes, after having adopted a fixed residence, have conclusively chosen a profession and learned its customs; when practice has imposed certain limits on wages, the last traces of servitude can disappear. The committee estimates that this transitional state could end after five years.

The Chambers will have to examine whether, instead of having recourse to this set of exceptional measures, they might not restrict themselves, on the one hand, to rigorously implementing the existing laws against vagabondage, and, on the other, to prohibiting Negroes from buying or occupying land for a few years. This would seem simpler, clearer, and perhaps just as effective.

It is principally the possession and cultivation of land that, in the English colonies, has caused blacks to leave the sugar refineries. The same causes infallibly would lead to the same effects in ours.

Of the 263,000 hectares in Martinique and Guadeloupe, 180,000 are not cultivated.

Guyana, which is 125 leagues by nearly 200 leagues, has only cultivated 12,000 hectares. Thus there is not a Negro in the colonies who could not procure land, and who would not procure it if he were given liberty to do so. For as long as the trace of slavery is not erased, the blacks naturally will have little desire to work for the benefit of a master. They will prefer to live independently in their little domain, even if by doing so they live less comfortably. If on the contrary the emancipated Negroes were neither allowed to live as vagabonds nor to procure a little domain for themselves, and were reduced to hiring out their services for a living, it is very likely that most of them would remain in the sugar refineries, and that the cost of running these establishments would not increase immeasurably.

When one examines it closely, the temporary prohibition on landownership is not only the most effective but also in reality the least oppressive of all the exceptional measures to which we could have recourse.

It is not by any natural or necessary consequence of freedom that the Negroes of the colonies could pass all at once from the state of slaves to that of landowners: it is as a result of a very extraordinary circumstance, that is, the proximity of fertile lands that belong so to speak to the first occupant. Nothing like it has ever happened in our civilized societies.

Despite all the efforts we have made in France to put real property within reach of the working classes, land has remained so costly that it is only with great effort that the worker can acquire some. He manages to do so only in the long term and after having earned money by his industry. In all European nations, it is almost unheard of for a worker to become a landowner. For him, the land in a sense lies beyond reach.

In temporarily prohibiting Negroes from possessing land, what are we doing? We are placing them artificially in the position in which the European worker finds himself naturally.

Assuredly, that is no tyranny, and the man on whom only this obstacle is imposed as he leaves slavery would not seem to have any right to complain.

6. A Brazilian Slave Escapes to Freedom in New York, 1847

When the cargo was landed, an English merchant having a quantity of coffee for shipment to New York, my master was engaged for the purpose, and it was arranged, after some time that I should accompany him, together with several others to serve on ship board.

We all had learned, that at New York there was no slavery; that it was a free country and that if we once got there we had nothing to dread from our cruel slave masters, and we were all most anxious to get there.

Previous to the time of the ship's sailing, we were informed that we were going to a land of freedom. I said then you will never see me any more after I once get there. I was overjoyed at the idea of going to a free country, and a ray of hope dawned

Source: Samuel Moore, *Biography of Mahommah G. Baquaqua, a Native of Zoogoo* . . . (Detroit, 1854), pp. 48–57. This source is available at *Documenting the American South*, online at http://docsouth.unc.edu/neh/baquaqua/baquaqua.html.

upon me, that the day was not far distant when I should be a free man. Indeed I felt myself already free! How beautifully the sun shone on that eventful morning, the morning of our departure for that land of freedom we had heard so much about. The winds too were favorable, and soon the canvass spread before the exhilerating breeze, and our ship stood for that happy land. The duties of office, on that voyage, appeared light to me indeed, in anticipation of seeing the goodly land, and nothing at all appeared a trouble to me. I obeyed all orders cheerfully and with alacrity.

That was the happiest time in my life, even now my heart thrills with joyous delight when I think of that voyage, and believe that the God of all mercies ordered all for my good; how thankful was I. . . .

The first words of English that my two companions and myself ever learned was F-r-e-e; we were taught it by an Englishman on board, and oh! how many times did I repeat it, over and over again. This same man told me a great deal about New York City, (he could speak Portuguese). He told me how the colored people in New York were all free, and it made me feel very happy, and I longed for the day to come when I should be there. The day at length came, but it was not an easy matter for two boys and a girl, who could only speak one word of English, to make their escape, having, as we supposed, no friends to aid us. But God was our friend, as it proved in the end, and raised up for us many friends in a strange land.

The pilot who came aboard of our vessel treated us very kindly,—he appeared different to any person I had ever seen before, and we took courage from that little circumstance. The next day a great many colored persons came aboard the vessel, who inquired whether we were free. The captain had previously told us not to say that we were slaves, but we heeded not his wish, and he, seeing so many persons coming aboard, began to entertain fears that his property would take in their heads to lift their heels and run away, so he very prudently informed us that New York was no place for us to go about in—that it was a very bad place, and as sure as the people caught us they would kill us. But when we were alone we concluded that we would take the first opportunity and the chance, how we would fare in a free country.

One day when I had helped myself rather freely to wine, I was imprudent enough to say I would not stay aboard any longer; that I would be free. The captain hearing it, called me down below, and he and three others endeavored to confine me, but could not do so; but they ultimately succeeded in confining me in a room in the bow of the vessel. I was there in confinement several days. The man who brought my food would knock at the door, and if I told him to come in he would do so, otherwise he would pass along, and I got no food. I told him on one occasion that I would not remain confined there another day with my life; that out I would get; and there being some pieces of iron in the room, towards night I took hold of one of them—it was a bar, about two feet long—with that I broke open the door, and walked out. The men were all busy at work, and the captain's wife was standing on the deck when I ascended from my prison. I heard them asking one another who had let me out; but no one could tell. I bowed to the captain's wife, and passed on to the side of the ship. There was a plank from the ship to the shore. I walked across it and ran as if for my life, of course not knowing whither I was going. I was observed during my flight by a watchman who was rather lame, and he undertook to stop me, but I shook him off, and passed on until I got to a store, at the door of which I halted a moment to take breath. They inquired of me what was the matter, but I could not tell them, as I knew nothing of English but the word F-r-e-e. Soon after, the lame watchman and another came up to me. One of them drew a bright star from his pocket and shewed it to me, but I could make nothing of it. I was then taken to the watch-house and locked up all night, when the captain called next morning, paid expenses, and took me back again to the ship along with him. The officers told me I should be a free man, if I chose, but I did not know how to act; so after a little persuasion, the captain induced me to go back with him, as I need not be afraid. This was on a Saturday, and on the following Monday afternoon three carriages drove up and stopped near the vessel. Some gentlemen came aboard from them, and walked about the deck, talking to the captain, telling him that all on board were free, and requesting him to hoist the flag. He blushed a good deal, and said he would not do so; he put himself in a great rage and stormed somewhat considerably. We were afterwards taken in their carriages, accompanied by the captain, to a very handsome building with a splendid portico in front, the entrance to which was ascended by a flight of marble steps, and was surrounded by a neat iron railing having gates at different points, the enclosure being ornamented with trees and shrubs of various kinds; it appeared to me a most beautiful place, as I had never seen anything like it before. I afterwards learned that this building was the City Hall of New York. When we arrived in the large room of the building it was crowded to excess by all kinds of people, and great numbers stood about the doors and steps, and all about the court-yard—some in conversation, others merely idling away the time walking to and fro. The Brazilian Consul was there, and when we were called upon I was asked if we wished to remain there or go back to Brazil. I answered for my companion and myself that we did not wish to return; but the female slave who was with us said she would return. I have no doubt she would have preferred staying behind, but seeing the captain there, she was intimidated and afraid to speak her mind, and so also, was the man, but I spoke boldly out that I would rather die than return into slavery!! After a great many questions had been asked us, and answered, we were taken to a prison, as I supposed it was, and there locked up. A few days afterwards we were taken again to the City Hall, and asked many more questions. We were then taken back to our old quarters the prison-house, I supposed preparatory to being shipped off again to Brazil, but of that I am not sure, as I could not understand all the ceremonies of locking us up and unlocking us, taking us to the court-house to ask questions and exhibit us before the audience there assembled—all this was new to me; I, therefore, could not fully understand the meaning of all this, but I feared greatly that we were about to be returned to slavery—I trembled at the thought! Whilst we were again locked up, some friends who had interested themselves very much in our behalf, contrived a means by which the prison-doors were opened whilst the keeper slept, and we found no difficulty in passing him, and gaining once more "the pure air of heaven," and by the assistance of those dear friends, whom I shall never forget, I was enabled to reach the city of Boston, in Massachusetts, and remained there under their protection about four weeks, when it was arranged that I should either be sent to England or Hayti, and I was consulted on the subject to know which I would prefer, and after considering for some time, I thought Hayti would be more like the climate of my own country and would agree better with my

health and feelings. I did not know exactly what sort of a place England was or perhaps might have preferred to have gone there, more particularly as I have since
learned that nearly all the English are friends to the colored man and his race, and
that they have done so much for my people in the way of their welfare and advancement, and continue to this day to agitate anti-slavery and every other good cause.
As it was, I determined to go to Hayti; accordingly, a free passage was procured for
us, and considerable provisions were collected for my use during the voyage.

7. Slavery Crumbles in the United States and Brazil, 1864, 1888

Spotswood Rice Demands the Return of His Children

[Benton Barracks Hospital, St. Louis, Mo.,
September 3, 1864]

I received a leteter from Cariline telling me that you say I tried to steal to plunder
my child away from you   now I want you to understand that mary is my Child and
she is a God given rite of my own and you may hold on to hear as long as you can
but I want you to remembor this one thing that the longor you keep my Child from
me the longor you will have to burn in hell and the qwicer youll get their   for we
are now making up a bout one thoughsand blacke troops to Come up tharough and
wont to come through Glasgow and when we come wo be to Copperhood rabbels
and to the Slaveholding rebels for we dont expect to leave them there root neor
branch   but we thinke how ever that we that have Children in the hand of you
devels we will trie your [vertues?] the day that we enter Glasgow   I want you to
understand kittey diggs that where ever you and I meets we are enmays to each
orthere   I offered once to pay you forty dollars for my own Child but I am glad
now that you did not accept it   Just hold on now as long as you can and the worse it
will be for you   you never in you life befor I came down hear did you give Children
any thing not eny thing whatever not even a dollers worth of expencs   now you call
my children your pro[*per*]ty   not so with me   my Children is my own and I expect
to get them and when I get ready to come after mary I will have bout a powrer and
autherity to bring hear away and to exacute vengencens on them that holds my
Child   you will then know how to talke to me   I will assure that and you will know
how to talk rite too   I want you now to just hold on to hear if you want to   iff
your conchosence tells thats the road go that road and what it will brig you to kittey
diggs   I have no fears about geting mary out of your hands   this whole Government gives chear to me and you cannot help your self

Spotswood Rice

Sources: Spotswood Rice letters in Ira Berlin et al., *Free At Last: A Documentary History of Slavery, Free-dom, and the Civil War* (New Press, 1992), pp. 481–482; "A Planter's Account of the Ending of Slavery in Sao Paulo, March 19, 1888," in Robert E. Conrad, *Children of God's Fire: A Documentary History of Black Slavery in Brazil* (Pennsylvania State University Press, 1994), pp. 476–480.

A Sao Paolo Planter Marks the End of Slavery in Brazil

Remanso, March 19, 1888.

My dear Zama,

I wrote not just one letter to you while you were campaigning for reelection in the 13th district, but two. By now you must have received the second one. I thought of writing a third to you to congratulate you on your victory; but I didn't, because the great amount of work I have recently had has taken all my time.

I'm going to give you some news that should please you, and at the same time some information concerning free labor.

Since the first of January I have not possessed a single slave! I liberated all of them, and bound them to the property by means of a contract identical to the one that I have with the foreign colonists and that I intend to have with those whom I will hire. You can see that my slavocratic tendencies are moderate and tolerable.

I joyfully inform you that my new colonists have not yet given me the least reason for complaint. I am living happy and content among them, and they shower me with attention and respect.

I granted them total and unconditional freedom, and in the short speech which I made to them when I passed out their letters, I spoke to them of the grave responsibilities that freedom imposed upon them, and I spoke some words to them that came from my heart and were completely different from those that I had prepared for the occasion. From the literary point of view it was a total fiasco, because I also wept. I ended up granting them a week to make the arrangements that would suit them best, while at the same time informing them that my place would always remain open to those among them who wished to work and behave themselves.

With the exception of three, who went to search for their sisters in São Paulo, and of two others, including an *ingênuo*, who joined their father, whom I freed ten years ago, all stayed with me, and they are the same whom I find about me, and with whom I am now happy and content, as I said above.

And now to the information that will benefit the planters in the north, who soon will be faced by that social necessity: the total and immediate emancipation of the slave.

Tell the others in your province not to fool themselves with a half-measure of freedom in the hope of not disorganizing work that has already been started. With conditional liberation they will get nothing from the slaves. They want to feel free, and to work under a new system only, and with total responsibility.

Conditional liberation, even with a very short period of continuing obligations, does not have any effect upon those people who have been tormented by such a long captivity. They suspect—and with reason in regard to some—that that kind of freedom is a mere trick to keep them in that slavery from which circumstances have now freed them. They work, but lazily and with a poor attitude. The body functions, but not the spirit.

When they are completely free they cause a bit of trouble, but in the end they establish themselves at one place or another. What does it matter? What difference does it make if my ex-slaves go in search of another patron, if at least they work, and others come to take their place!

We here in São Paulo have a complete experience with the matter and a total understanding of every form of liberation. There is only one reasonable and profitable kind of freedom, and that is total, immediate, and unconditional freedom. The liberated people must themselves take responsibility for the error of leaving the place where they were slaves. It is obvious that there are masters who have lost all their workers, and the only reason for this is that they did not deserve to possess them. But the great majority will be settled someplace within a month.

I have excellent examples in my own family. My brother freed all that he owned. Some of these left and looked for work at some distant place. A week later they came to me, or to my brother himself, and they reached agreements with us, bringing unfavorable impressions of the vagabond life which they had led during that week.

So as not to annoy you further with such matters, let me sum up by saying that during the month of February we endured hours of bitterness and terror in this province, witnessing the most complete disorganization of labor imaginable.

The whole body of workers deserted the plantations, which were almost all abandoned! I do not exaggerate when I say that 80 out of every 100 were deserted, while the blacks went to the cities or followed wicked seducers. Sadly we wondered what was to become of us.

Little by little they grew tired of roaming about, and in turn the seducers grew weary of providing for them without any advantage to themselves, and today, March, all are more or less settled. Understand that when I say "all," I am excluding proprietors with bad reputations. These, in fact, will be eliminated and replaced by the force of circumstances, and the agricultural system will not miss them.

It is possible that there will be some loss of fruit to the present coffee crop. However, the crop is so large that this loss will not be important, and will be mostly compensated for by the benefits of freedom. Something else that you should tell your fellow provincials is that they are laboring under a serious error when they imagine that they will suffer great damage through the loss of slave property.

You will remember that my major argument as a pro-slavery man was that the slave was the only force we could count on for constant and indispensable agricultural labor, and that if we could always rely upon free workers I would willingly give up the slaves.

Anyone who argued in this way could be considered a pessimist, but not obstinate.

Very well, your people should give up this fear. Workers are not lacking to those who know how to find them. First, we have the slaves themselves, who do not melt away or disappear, and who need to live and feed themselves, and, therefore, to work, something they will understand in a brief time.

Then we have an enormous body of workers whom we did not count upon. I do not mean the immigrant, who today is seeking us in abundance; I refer to the Brazilian, a sluggard yesterday, living upon the scraps of slave labor and the benevolence of the rural proprietor, whom he served in the capacity of a hanger-on, a hired gunman, or in some other way. Today this Brazilian devotes himself heroically to labor, either because it has become more respectable with the advent of freedom, or because he has been denied his former options. This is what we are witnessing today.

Concerning myself, I have gathered many of them together, fearful that in the present circumstances I will not be adequately supplied with workers.

Many people who were living from four hills of beans and a quarter of corn are now appearing for work in the coffee fields, and cheerfully at the coffee drying grounds, and those I have hired have established their quarters perfectly well in the old slave buildings. It is true that mine are good ones; but they were built in the shape of a quadrangle—until now a hated arrangement.

It remains the same, except without the lock, and today they even prefer the quadrangle, because they gather their provisions inside it without fear of damage from their animals. My quadrangle is a large courtyard surrounded by clean, white houses, whose doors I now intend to open toward the outside.

Your fellow provincials must also know that free labor is not as expensive as it seemed at first. This point was my greatest surprise in the transformation that we are passing through.

As I told you, with my ex-slaves I have the same contract that I had with my colonists.

I give them nothing and sell them everything, even their supplies of cabbage or milk.

Understand that I am only doing this to teach them the value of labor, and so that they will understand that they have only themselves to depend upon, and never for personal profit, since only one visit from the doctor, whom I am paying, costs me much more than all the cabbages I possess, and all the milk my cows produce.

In any case, this ration of cattle or milk, the cattle that I slaughter, the produce that I buy wholesale and sell them retail, and cheaper than in the cities, are almost enough to pay for the costs of labor.

None of this was understood under the system of slavery!

There goes the second sheet of paper, and I am still on the same topic! But this topic does in fact deserve the full attention of the people of Bahia, who soon will find themselves face to face with the problem which not long ago caused me such fears for the future. They should not hesitate, they should emancipate and establish contracts. In the production of sugar cane the method will be even more advantageous for the owner than in the production of coffee. I have at the far side of a pasture a small cane-producing property which belongs to my sister, very good for this region but probably inferior to those of Bahia. I took charge of the place, and from it my little sister derives proportionally more profit than I do on my coffee plantation of 250,000 trees!

Enough, you will scream! All right, enough. From here I welcome an embrace from the abolitionist, Zama, for the slavocrat, *Paula Souza*.

8. Thomas Phipson Condemns Polygamy and Slavery in Natal, 1876

To the Editor   *Natal Witness* 21 January 1876

Sir,

The letter of your Biggarsberg correspondent, and your sub-leader in to-day's issue have recalled my attention to this painful topic.

To a new-comer or a passing traveller it must seem incredible that such a "peculiar domestic institution" as that above-named should exist here, under the patronage of

Source: Thomas Phipson's letter to the editor in the *Natal Witness*, 21 January 1876, in R.N. Currey, ed., *Letters and Other Writings of a Natal Sheriff Thomas Phipson 1815–1876* (Cape Town: Oxford University Press, 1968), pp. 193–195.

the Secretary for Native Affairs, who is, I suppose, the pet protégé of the Anti-Slavery and Aborigines' Protection Societies. But whether it does exist let the following instances (among others) decide.

Several years ago I went up to Ladysmith to attend the Circuit Court there, in my then capacity of Sheriff. While I was sitting on the stoop of an hotel, Dr T. T. Kelly, then Resident Magistrate there, came and sat by me, and entered into conversation about his official duties and vexations. Among other things he mentioned a case which had then been recently tried before him. A Kafir man had bought a Kafir woman for cows, and had let her out (according to their abominable law or custom) on hire to another man, who was too poor to buy himself a wife. This pair had cohabited together for several years, and had had two daughters, who had grown up to marriageable age, when the woman's original purchaser and owner came and claimed the girls, in order to sell them for his own profit. Their parents applied to Mr. Kelly, who decided in their favour; but the old slave-owner appealed to the Secretary for Native Affairs, who reversed this judgment, and ordered the girls to be torn away from their progenitors and delivered up to be sold, by one who was a stranger to them in blood and acquaintance, as concubines to any that would buy them.

That there might be no mistake about this case, I put the facts into the form of a letter to Dr Kelly; and before sending it to him showed it to the Secretary for Native Affairs, who (after keeping it for about a week) returned it to me without a single word of comment; and the Doctor, having been, as I suppose, previously warned, in reply merely declined entering into any correspondence on the subject.

Now a few things are plain about this matter. If this was Kafir Law fifteen or more years ago, it is so now; and it will be put into the new promised code. No alteration has been made in this respect by the Legislative Council; and if the Secretary for Native Affairs has power to alter Kafir Law by his own mere *ipse dixit*, he can alter it for the worse as well as for the better. And if cases like these are constantly occurring (as no doubt they are) in Klip River County and elsewhere, can it be wondered at that married women are taken into execution as chattels (like cows), and sold again in order to get cows for Cetywayo?

Another thing Dr Kelly told me at the same time was, that many of the Kafirs under his jurisdiction were living on the farms of Boers; and could not leave those farms to reside anywhere else without his permission, which he had instructions not to grant; and that, while living on such farms, they were obliged to yield compulsory service to the owners thereof. Now if this is not praedial serfdom, where in the world is there any such thing? And if this was Kafir Law then (though in a matter between white and black, and not between Kafir and Kafir, mark) it is Kafir Law (or some law) still; for no lawful power has ever altered it.

Dr Kelly is dead; but it would be easy for me to supplement these dreadful disclosures by others more or less similar, communicated to me by living Magistrates; were it not that, by so doing, I might betray their confidence and bring them into trouble.

Yours, &c.,

Thomas Phipson

New England, Jan. 18th 1876

△ E S S A Y S

Looking at the Atlantic world in 1750, an observer would have found it hard to imagine that opposition to slavery would eventually result in its abolition. Slavery was a profitable and widespread institution at the core of the Atlantic economy, so how did it come to an end? Martin Klein, a leading historian of French West Africa, emphasizes the change in European values that made abolition possible and the exercise of European power that stamped slavery out. Klein insists that slavery remained economically viable in the nineteenth century; it expanded in some places at the same time that it was abolished in others, and it persisted into the late nineteenth century in Cuba, Brazil, and much of Africa. As slavery declined, other forms of unfree labor took its place, ranging from indentured servitude to convict labor. Former slaves generally refused to work in the same ways they had as slaves. Many established themselves as peasants while others who did not have access to land forced their former owners to negotiate with them for wages.

Whereas Klein's essay generally treats "slaves" as a single category, Diana Paton and Pamela Scully argue that enslaved men and women had different experiences of emancipation. Two innovative scholars of gender in the British empire, Paton and Scully draw attention to the ways that ideas about the proper relations between men and women shaped the history of emancipation throughout the Atlantic world. They show that concepts of patriarchal authority were embedded in the patterns of military service, organization of households, and liberal visions of citizenship that accompanied emancipation. As a consequence, freedwomen's experience of emancipation differed from that of freedmen. Not only did freedwomen continue to suffer from their subordination as women, but emancipation may even have confirmed and reinforced inequality between the sexes. Ultimately both essays raise the question: What was the meaning of freedom in the era of emancipation?

How Did Atlantic Slavery Come to an End?

MARTIN KLEIN

The creation of a world economy by European capitalism and the reconstruction of economic relations in almost all parts of the world created in their wake tremendous demands for labour, which could only be met by various forms of labour coercion. European expansion brought in its train an increase in the use of unfree labour in Asia and Africa as well as in the Americas. If the Atlantic world experienced the greatest demands it was because large fertile areas were underpopulated and because some densely populated areas were decimated by disease. There were large movements of free labour, but they were inadequate to the demands of an expanding European economy. Both in the Atlantic basin and elsewhere in the world, slavery was the most common form of unfreedom, in large part because slavery gave the slave's owner greater control over the slave's productive labour. In the Atlantic basin, slaves were also attractive because they could be moved long distances and because Africans had a lower mortality rate than Europeans in such

Source: Martin Klein, "Slavery, the International Labor Market and the Emancipation of Slaves in the Nineteenth Century," *Slavery & Abolition* Vol. 15, No. 2 (August 1994): 197, 201–213. Reprinted by permission of the publisher, Taylor & Francis Ltd., http://www.informaworld.com.

movement. Other forms of unfree labour coexisted with slavery, for example, indentured labour and peonage in the Americas, bondage in India, debt servitude in South-East Asia, pawnship in Africa, and these forms were used to control labour when slavery was abolished.

None of these types was unique, all were widespread and few were ever actively questioned anywhere before the eighteenth century. It is not slavery that was unique, but emancipation. Ironically, slavery was systematically questioned only after a capitalist Europe created in the Americas a particularly systematic form of slavery. The major arenas of the battle over emancipation were in the Atlantic basin, but it shaped all parts of the world. This paper tries to set the question of emancipation in an international and comparative context. It will argue that the struggle for emancipation involved not simply the imposition of a policy that was in the interests of the very powers that created a modern form of slavery, but that acceptance also required the acceptance of different ideological systems. . . .

There were times in many parts of the world when slavery declined, often replaced or absorbed by other forms of exploitation. During the late medieval period, slavery disappeared in northern Europe, and in seventeenth-century Russia it was absorbed within a rather harsh form of serfdom. The use of slaves was declining in South-East Asia during the nineteenth century, most strikingly in Thailand. There is no evidence, however, that slavery was seriously attacked in any part of the world before the eighteenth century. The abolition movement had its origins in a change in European consciousness. In the eighteenth century, Enlightenment thinkers in England and on the Continent increasingly called slavery into question. Montesquieu dissected classical justifications of slavery and attacked it as contrary to natural law. Adam Smith and his followers argued that free labour was more productive because it was better motivated. More important for its later consequences, in 1758 the Philadelphia Yearly meeting of the Quakers voted to exclude any members who bought or sold slaves. Within a generation, abolition had a solid base in evangelical Protestant churches on both sides of the Atlantic.

Slavery was held to be illegal in England in 1772 and by the end of the century upper Canada and most of the northern United States had abolished it. In 1794 revolutionary France followed. The abolitionists were hostile to slavery, but they focused first on ending the trade. The United States constitution provided for the end of slave imports in 1808. The Danes abolished the colonial slave trade in 1803, the British in 1807, and the Dutch in 1814. There was a difference between the British and French abolition movements. In Britain, a powerful movement based in the dissenting churches developed methods of shaping public opinion and was a major force in British politics for 50 years. On the Continent, it remained more a movement of ideas, which never mobilized the masses. Napoleon re-established slavery in the French colonies in 1802, and the Catholic Church was hostile to abolition for much of the nineteenth century. Nevertheless, for the heirs of the Enlightenment throughout the nineteenth century, slavery was seen as contrary to natural law and reason. The revolutionary regime in 1848 again abolished slavery throughout the French empire. It did so without any hesitation, without any transition period, and without any qualifications.

The success of the British abolitionists in persuading Parliament to abolish colonial slavery in 1833 did not end their struggle. The law passed was less than the abolitionists wanted. They were opposed to its apprenticeship provisions. The slaves in the West Indies, however, quickly undercut any idea of a transitional status, but that still left slavery elsewhere. Rival nations reaped the benefits of British abolition. The slave trade continued in foreign ships, only slightly riskier due to the efforts of the Royal Navy, and slave-based production remained prosperous in Brazil, the United States and Spanish Cuba. The British and Foreign Anti-Slavery Society was formed in 1839. During its early years, it was concerned primarily with the Americas, particularly with Cuba, Brazil and the United States. Increasingly, however, it confronted other issues. European explorers described the horrors of the slave trade in Africa. The 1833 abolition did not affect India, Burma or Ceylon, which were controlled by the East India Company. And wherever British authority was extended on the African mainland, concern about relations with slave-holding neighbours compromised British policy.

By 1839 Great Britain had treaties with all major maritime powers except the United States providing for the right to search each other's merchant vessels. The Royal Navy eliminated the trade in some areas, but the skill of the slavers and international law, which required that slaving ships be taken to a Prize Court, limited these efforts. The only Court in West Africa was at Freetown. Under Palmerston, however, as the Royal Navy began to cut more deeply into the trade, British pressure extended its field of operations. In 1845, Sayyid Said of Zanzibar agreed to prohibit the export of slaves from his African territories. Similar treaties were signed with various West African rulers. . . .

It was not just British pressure. The British were often resented, but abolition made steady, if sometimes slow progress. Haitian slaves rose in revolt in 1791 and freed themselves in a bitter and violent revolution that ended only with recognition of Haitian independence in 1804. The leaders of the revolutions against Spain were less radical, but all of the newborn American republics abolished the slave trade after independence. Chile abolished slavery in 1823, and Mexico and Central America followed soon afterwards. The others passed gradual emancipation laws, which freed all children born after the law was enacted. These free womb laws involved a long transition period. As a result, in countries with important slave systems slave prices remained high and planters bitterly and successfully resisted emancipation for a generation. In spite of this, the Hispanic republics ended slavery one by one, finishing with Peru in 1854. Denmark abolished slavery in 1848, the Netherlands in 1863, and the United States between 1863 and 1865. When slavery was abolished in Cuba in 1886 and Brazil in 1888, it was partly a result of internal forces, in Brazil's case a mass abolition movement subsidized by the British. In Cuba, David Eltis argues, it was because the price of sugar was no longer adequate to cover the costs of importing slaves.

Also in 1888, a series of Catholic abolition societies were founded in Europe under the leadership of Cardinal Lavigerie and with the blessing of Pope Leo XIII. The French Catholic abolition movement used quiet pressure more than open propaganda, but it was backed by a strong missionary presence. In France, the Catholic abolitionists refused to collaborate with the more secular movement that had long existed, but they were probably able to put more pressure on the government because they could mobilize Catholic public opinion. More important than any single movement was the equation in late nineteenth-century Europe of bondage with backwardness and the belief held throughout Europe that slavery was profoundly immoral.

The major debate on abolition has been whether it was a triumph of moral principle or a victory of economic interest. The debate was provoked by Eric Williams' *Capitalism and Slavery*, which argued that accumulation of capital in the slave trade and in slave-based production was crucial to the industrial revolution, but that by the end of the eighteenth century the West Indian slave plantations had declined in profitability and in their importance to Great Britain. Most contemporary writers accept the link between anti-slavery and industrial capitalism, while rejecting the economic determinism of Eric Williams. Thus Seymour Drescher has proven that there was no such decline at the time of the anti-slavery debate; "The key to the timing of slavery's ultimate demise in the Western economy lies not in its economic functioning but in its social peculiarity." Eltis argues that the period from 1820 to 1860 was the most profitable period for the Atlantic slave trade. None the less, as David Brion Davis has observed, "antislavery cannot be divorced from the vast economic changes that were intensifying social conflicts and heightening class consciousness . . . in Britain it was part of a larger ideology that helped to ensure stability while accommodating society to political and economic change."

For Howard Temperley, the key question is not what the abolitionists thought but why they were so successful at convincing others. It was not, after all, the market that ended slavery, but the state. The two leaders of abolition, Great Britain and the northern United States, were free labour zones which had experienced extraordinary growth, and the dominant political leaders in both were convinced that individual freedom was crucial to that growth. Continental Europe was still freeing itself from traditional restraints on labour. The abolition movement lacked the organizational base provided by evangelical Protestantism, but a similar capitalist, free labour ideology predominated in Europe by the end of the nineteenth century. Slavery was seen as both immoral and irrational. Public opinion shaped the strategies of imperial statesmen and proconsuls. Leopold, the King of the Belgians, made alliances with slave-dealers when he first penetrated the Congo, but when confronted by the problem of how to finance his colony, he found it necessary to wrap himself in an anti-slavery cloak. The French officers, who gave slaves to their soldiers and allies after military victories, often justified their actions in terms of an eventual abolition. Lugard proposed eventual abolition in northern Nigeria and sold himself at home as an anti-slavery crusader, but in the short run he reinforced the control of slave-owners over their slaves. The contrast between metropole and colony was quite sharp. By the end of the nineteenth century, an Enlightenment discourse on slavery was generally accepted within Europe, but not always in the colonies.

This is most vividly illustrated by the Brussels conference of 1889–90, at which the major European powers agreed to measures against the internal African slave trade, the export of slaves from Africa and the trade in arms and liquor. The Brussels Act came a decade before most colonial powers were willing to act against the slave trade within Africa. It provided a cloak of moral legitimacy for the partition of Africa, but there was a gap between the rhetoric and the reality of Europe's moral crusade. The problem was that Europe's proconsuls lacked resources. The quest for

African empire was often backed by well-organized public relations efforts, but the real interests involved were often very limited and most European statesmen were well aware of this. Leaders such as Bismarck and Salisbury viewed the claims of the colonial lobby with great scepticism. European parliaments were willing to approve colonies as long as they did not cost anything. Colonies were forced to pay their own way, but the revenue that could be extracted from most areas being colonized was limited. Thus, European armies were small and made up primarily of soldiers recruited in the colonies. Booty, particularly human booty, attracted allies. In addition, European generals were often anxious to prevent their enemies from uniting. It was therefore important not to undermine the existing social order, which depended on slaves. The practice was often to free the slaves of enemies but to reinforce the control of allies and those who submitted willingly over their slaves. . . .

The attack on slavery took place while slavery was still profitable. Abolition was successful well before the demand for unskilled labour in the tropics could be met by an international free labour market. The most important problem was the production of sugar. The intensity of labour on the sugar plantation and the distasteful nature of the work was such that it was difficult to recruit labour without coercion. When the slave trade was abolished, the continuing decline of local population created a labour shortage. In the West Indies, this was intensified with the ending of slavery; many former slaves, particularly women, withdrew from the onerous labour of the plantation. Indentured labour systems designed primarily to provide labour for expanding sugar production in Guyana, Trinidad, Natal and Cuba were also important in older areas like Jamaica and were used to get labour for other labour short areas. Indenture systems based in Africa looked very much like the slave trade they were supposedly replacing. Within Africa, slave caravans continued to move down to the coast, and the use of pawns increased because it was difficult to recruit other forms of labour for expanding commodity production.

Unfree labour was recruited on a large scale in India, China and, to a lesser degree, Java and Japan, where poverty and landlessness created a pool of willing migrants. While the Chinese "coolie" trade involved people purchased and sold, the Indian indentured system was essentially a voluntary migration, though there was some coercion and strong economic pressures on the migrants. Emmer argues that the Indian trade tapped into existing migrating patterns within India and to areas like Ceylon and the Straits Settlements. The system provided labour not only for sugar plantations but also for tea in Ceylon, rubber in Malaya, railroads in North America and gold mines in South Africa. Watched by abolitionist interests, the British imposed controls on recruitment, which gradually became effective. The other powers were less conscientious. The French indenture system remained a disguised slave trade until 1862 and slaves were provided to Europeans from East Africa for a generation more. The Portuguese abolished slavery in 1878 but continued what amounted to a slave trade until 1910. . . .

While European enterprise used new forms of coerced labour, slavery, slave use and slave raiding were expanding in many areas outside European control. In West Africa, the end of the Atlantic trade and the decline in the Saharan trade hardly affected the price of slaves because demand within Africa was so high. Slaves were used in West Africa to produce palm oil and peanuts for European markets, grain and cloth for Saharan markets, and soldiers for the slaving armies. . . .

In Africa, serious abolition also came late. Slaves were freed at the Cape in 1833 by the same measure that freed slaves in the West Indies, but this only drove Afrikaner farmers into the interior, where they were less restrained in their efforts to coerce the labour of others. The legal status of slavery was abolished on the Gold Coast in 1874. In 1901 the British "freed" the slaves in Southern Nigeria, and then immediately forbade them to leave their masters. In spite of Freetown's historic role in the anti-slavery struggle, slavery was not abolished in the interior of Sierra Leone until 1926. In 1848 the French were reluctant to apply an emancipation law which threatened the colony's relations with its neighbours. The major concern of colonial administrations was often to limit the damage which these islands of liberty did to their relations with African states. Africa was largely conquered with armies recruited from slaves. Many of these armies, like the French, rewarded their troops and allies with slave booty.

Conquest was usually followed by a ban on slave-trading and slave-raiding, but some laws were clearly written for outside consumption and local administrators were often reluctant to enforce anti-slavery legislation. As in Asia, colonial administrators distinguished slaving from slavery and argued that slavery was benign. Furthermore, they believed that compulsion was necessary to maintain production, and they tended to identify their own interests with those of slave-owning intermediaries. Invariably, slaves were seen as lazy workers who had to be coerced. Even when forced to abolish slavery, colonial administrators tried to reinforce the control of former masters over their ex-slaves or secure other forms of labour. This was particularly true in areas that were economically important or strategic. Thus, in East Africa, the British allowed slavery to die on the coast and killed it on Zanzibar, but tried other ways to guarantee labour supplies to the Zanzibar slave plantations. In West Africa, the French recognized the property rights of the former masters in the fertile inner delta of the Niger, and former masters were able to use control over land to maintain control over labour. In Northern Nigeria, masters continued to exercise control over supposedly free persons. The legal status of slavery for all people was abolished only in 1936. In the Sudan, a British administration tolerated both slavery and slave trade until about 1930. . . .

While slavery persisted in Africa, though often in fossilized forms, in the Americas new forms of labour coercion developed. Former slaves often dreamed of "40 acres and a mule," but usually found themselves landless and dependent. In Jamaica, Guyana and Brazil slaves were able to withdraw from plantation economies onto less commercial land. In Barbados, in the American South, and in Cuba, control of land gave the former slave-owners the whip hand in the struggle to control the labour of their former slaves, who were tied by debt and landlessness to peonage and share-cropping arrangements. Increasingly plantations turned to hired labour or gave way to share-cropping arrangements. . . .

Those who abolished slavery were often concerned to maintain the social order and, in many cases, to confirm the authority of masters over those supposedly emancipated. Slaves, however, often refused to do what was expected of them. In the Americas, they rejected apprenticeship and withdrew their labour from the plantations, often retreating into upland areas. In Africa, slaves left their masters, usually to go home, but often to seek other opportunities elsewhere. Many, moreover, were born in slavery or had spent long years in slavery. . . .

In general, there was a complex process of negotiating new relationships. Thus, in many parts of the American South freed slaves forced masters to bid for their labour and in the process, asserted their social autonomy. Eventually, however, the plantation owners were able to use land ownership, control over credit and the coercive power of the state to force former slaves into dependent relationships, most often involving sharecropping. The same thing was true in the more densely populated areas of Asia, Africa and the Americas. Shortage of land restricted the freedom of the bonded. State and master struggled to develop new ways of expropriating the labour of their former dependants, while slave and bondsman sought to circumscribe their ability to do so or to extract in exchange greater security. Even where masters were not successful in maintaining control of labour, they generally maintained their social ascendancy and, as a result, the stigma of slave origins has persisted to the present.

Most slave systems were functioning well when slavery came under attack. While there are a few cases where slave labour was ceasing to be competitive or where masters acquiesced in emancipation because they had other ways of obtaining labour, this author knows of no case where slave owners as a class voluntarily rejected the institution. Emancipation came at a time when an expanding capitalism was still hungry for labour, and free labour migration was not capable of meeting that demand. Within Africa and parts of South-East Asia, this was largely because slavery tied up so much of the population. There was simply no pool of free labour available. Only in the twentieth century has free labour migration been capable of meeting the demand for labour in diverse parts of the world.

The attack on slavery involved a change in European consciousness. In the context of European history, it is impossible to argue that society became more humane, but people certainly began to regard certain kinds of exploitation as immoral. Slavery eventually became redundant, an inefficient way of getting labour, but emancipation took place long before that happened. Abolition was often forced on the periphery by a centre committed to a free labour ideology and convinced that free labour was essential to the dramatic growth and transformation of the capitalist world. This ideology was given its loftiest expression by the abolition movement spawned by and consistently supported by Christian churches. It was also powerful enough that those non-Western elites who sought to understand Europe's ascendancy invariably saw free labour as a crucial part of that ascendancy. It is only these ideological agendas that can explain why Europe turned against slavery when it was still profitable. Ironically, that ideology was resisted vigorously by colonial administrations willing to protect and exploit different kinds of servitude. To be sure, the freeing of labour from traditional restraints was often part of the colonial agenda, but it was usually put off into the distant future. Dependent on democratically elected European parliaments for their budgets, colonial administrations were vulnerable to the pressures of abolitionist groups and increasingly had difficulty controlling the flow of information about their policies. The timing of action against slavery was often motivated more by political pragmatism than by abolitionist principle. This also often shaped the way emancipation policies were carried out.

What Does Gender Have to Do with Emancipation?

DIANA PATON AND PAMELA SCULLY

From Brazil to Cuba to the U.S. South, from Jamaica to the British Cape Colony, from Martinique and Haiti to French West Africa, gender was central to slave emancipation and to the making of the nineteenth-century Atlantic world. For many participants in emancipation, including abolitionists, state authorities, and freedpeople themselves, the transformation and restabilization of gender relations and identities was a key component of the process. Ideas of masculinity and femininity shaped slaves' and abolitionists' understanding of the wrongs of slavery, consolidated notions of contract and liberalism, contributed to the organization of postemancipation wage labor and political economies, and influenced freedpeoples' dreams of freedom and family in racially charged postemancipation landscapes.

A gendered approach to the study of emancipation helps to answer more fully many of the questions about labor, contract, and formal politics that have traditionally been at the heart of comparative emancipation studies. It also raises important new questions. Women and men accessed and experienced citizenship, labor, and bodily freedom in different ways in postemancipation societies. We would argue that the transition from slavery to regimes more compatible with free wage labor ideologies was crucially dependent on the gendered organization of "free" labor which made women's work invisible. As we shall see, the claims to masculine entitlement forged through revolutionary struggles to end slavery, as in Haiti, as well as abolitionist and liberal assumptions that the individual freed from slavery was male, ensured the persistence of gender inequality in postslave societies.

Recognizing how gender shaped slave emancipation requires that we rethink narratives that have dominated the scholarship in this area. A gendered reading of emancipation that makes false claims to universality may itself drive the centrality of particular topics, such as labor and politics, to emancipation studies. For example, for women the ending of slavery may have involved a challenge to a particular patriarchal order in which they often had been sexually abused as much as a transition to a new form of labor. Reflecting on emancipation from the point of view of women, and on how emancipation confirmed or disrupted existing gender relations, places issues such as violence, sexuality, and the gendered politics of public space at the heart of emancipation studies. Slave emancipation was not only experienced differently by men and women, it also served to reconstruct the very categories "man" and "woman." . . .

The process of emancipation in Haiti demonstrates many of the key characteristics of the gendering of emancipation in other parts of the Atlantic world. Haitians achieved emancipation through an anticolonial struggle that made powerful connections among military service, citizenship, and the nation. Similar connections were made in other places where the ending of slavery was tied to attacks on colonial rule. Saint-Domingue had been the jewel in the French imperial crown, the annual importer of thirty thousand African slaves, and the producer of two-fifths of the world's sugar and more than half the world's coffee in the 1780s. This society, founded on massive violence and exploitation, began to unravel as its members participated in the upheavals precipitated by the French Revolution. The slave uprising of 1791 put the complete abolition of slavery on the agenda; the actions of the French Jacobin Léger Félicité Sonthonax and the Haitian revolutionary general and former slave Toussaint Louverture formalized abolition. Toussaint's revolutionary army defeated the imperial armies of Napoleon (who aimed to restore slavery), Britain, and Spain, creating a new nation whose achievements were, in Michel-Rolph Trouillot's words, "unthinkable history."

While the revolution swept away white privilege, it reinscribed gender inequality. All Haitian citizens were defined as black, but not all black Haitians were citizens. The 1805 constitution reserved voting, for instance, for men. The founding fathers of the Haitian nation, Toussaint, Jean-Jacques Dessalines, Henri Christophe, and Alexandre Pétion, all contributed to the construction of a masculinist and patriarchal nationalism. Haiti here showed its ideological links to the Enlightenment and to the French Revolution, which made the same connection between revolutionary citizenship and masculinity.

Part of the reason for this association in Haiti was the deep connection among military participation, masculinity, and nationalism. The revolutionary army conscripted men in massive numbers, both during the revolution and in independent Haiti, maintaining a large standing army in case of renewed French attempts to retake the former colony. Soldiers were seen as the founders of Haitian freedom. The 1805 constitution declared that "no one is worthy of being a Haitian if he is not a good father, a good son, a good husband, and above all a good soldier." But women could not be soldiers, and this had more than symbolic consequences. Under Dessalines and Christophe, the non-militarized sector of the population, of which women formed a substantial majority, had to undertake compulsory fieldwork on the plantations, many of which were now owned by the state. Pétion embarked on a policy of land distribution in 1809, in which each soldier received fifteen acres from state lands. As a result, women received no land in this founding act in the formation of the Haitian peasantry. In addition, the heavily militarized politics of nineteenth-century Haiti left little space for women to participate in government.

Other societies where slavery ended as part of an assault on colonialism similarly linked citizenship, military participation, and national identity. Thus in mainland Latin America, Simón Bolívar's republican army included many conscripted male slaves. Those who survived the military campaign were freed. Conscription and manumission of male slaves was also a significant part of the emancipation process in the rest of Spanish South America. According to Robin Blackburn, after independence the coastal haciendas of Peru "were left with slave crews containing disproportionate numbers of women, children, and old people." In Cuba, male slaves participated extensively in the Ten Years' War and the Guerra Chiquita. . . . [T]he participation of black men in the revolutionary army became a crucial sign of their citizenship. The discourse of the independence movement constructed Spain as decadent and feminized and the insurgent forces as manly and virile. The inclusion of black men within this concept of manliness defined the nation as antiracist, but at the cost of excluding women from the national story. Similarly, in French West Africa, military participation was a long-standing route to emancipation for men but one that was denied to women.

Societies where slave emancipation occurred through military campaigns and/or revolutionary violence articulated the linkages between masculinity and citizenship very explicitly. But the connection of citizenship to masculinity was germane to all postemancipation societies, as we shall see later in our discussion of contract theory and citizenship in the postemancipation Atlantic world.

In Haiti, and in most places where emancipation took place as a result of an acute political crisis, the precise way slavery would end was obviously not planned in advance. In contrast, other emancipations, of which those in the British Empire and Brazil are the most notable, were relatively managed. Of course, these emancipations emerged out of complex struggles among different contending groups; they were not top-down processes. In the British Empire even the precise terms of emancipation—for example, the timing of the ending of apprenticeship—emerged from former slaves' actions. In Brazil, emancipation was proclaimed through the "Golden Law" of 1888, but only after thousands of slaves had taken their freedom, making slavery unsustainable. Nevertheless, in contrast to the anticolonial and revolutionary contexts of emancipations in Haiti and Cuba, for instance, the British and Brazilian ruling classes were able to seize the day: to present emancipation as a gift bestowed from above.

In both the British Empire and Brazil, slave emancipation came at a point when gender relations were in flux due to the changes resulting from the development of capitalism, and when they were the subject of much anxiety and debate. As a result, the ending of slavery in the British Empire was explicitly ideological in its approach to gender relations. A central goal of British imperial emancipation was to transform colonial gender relations. Slaves, imperial officials and others believed, had been degendered by their enslavement. Emancipation, then, should make them properly into men and women.

British imperial visions of freedom had been heavily gendered long before the passage of the Emancipation Act in 1833. As Moira Ferguson has shown, the practice of criticizing slavery by attacking its impact on gender relations reached back to the seventeenth century. In the nineteenth century this critique was written into colonial policy. Gendered assumptions were evident in British policy toward "liberated Africans"—those rescued from illegal slave-trading ships—in the 1810s and 1820s. These individuals were subject to work regimes that countered their expectations of how labor should be organized by gender. The British imperial authorities barred women from most agricultural labor. Brazilian debates about slavery also frequently invoked gender. In 1871, for instance, debates around slavery focused in particular on the prostitution of enslaved women as a symbol of the corrupt relationship between slave owner and slave.

The moment of full emancipation in the British Empire in 1838 saw a widespread effort by both missionaries and colonial officials to persuade freedpeople to organize their family lives around monogamous Christian marriage and domesticity. Characteristic of this effort was a newspaper article published in the Cape Colony, praising emancipation in the following terms: "Freedom . . . offers something in addition to personal enjoyments. The Freeman becomes the Head of a Family. . . . The Father, however poor, however overlooked or despised by the world, is now an object, in one place at least, not only of love but reverence. There is now a circle where, if he chooses, he may reign as a King." This vision of emancipation conceptualized the meaning of freedom as patriarchal authority for freedmen. Women were to be released from slavery, but into a new kind of subordination and dependence.

In postemancipation Brazil, similar goals were expressed in a more authoritarian way. Elites' concern to "civilize" racially mixed urban populations led to police crackdowns on prostitutes and to campaigns to persuade the urban poor to marry and to adopt bourgeois gender norms. The authorities suspected poor women of immorality and prostitution when they did not adhere to the new standards of "civilization" but instead remained present in public space. While such campaigns were directed at the lower orders as a whole, regardless of their status prior to abolition, in practice many of the targets were freedpeople, including those who had migrated to the cities in the wake of emancipation.

Throughout the Atlantic world, state officials and reformers encouraged freedpeople to adopt monogamous patriarchal marriage and female domesticity as a mark of their civilization. Like Brazil, postemancipation Puerto Rico saw campaigns to "moralize" and "civilize" the poor, including attacks on prostitutes and consensual unions. In Martinique the Société des Femmes Schoelcheristes, named after the French abolitionist Victor Schoelcher, was founded in 1849, one year after emancipation. It aimed to promote religiosity and marriage among the freed population, and in doing so it particularly directed its attention to those women engaged in "concubinage" with white men. In the United States, the Freedmen's Bureau circulated a book titled *John Freeman and His Family*, which was intended to teach freedpeople how to adapt to their new situation. In the book, the former slave John Freeman took a new name and made a contract for his labor. His wife, Mrs. Freeman, had to learn to keep a clean house. The similarly of efforts to establish patriarchal families and attempts to curtail women's independence across a range of societies suggests a deeply embedded conception of gender within the liberal idea of freedom. . . .

Emancipation created spaces for struggle to define the meaning of freedom in ways that rarely perfectly matched the visions of liberty participants brought to the experience. Nevertheless, freedwomen and freedmen could order their lives with greater autonomy than they had been able to as slaves. The extent of this change, of course, depended on where they lived. Where the plantation system and the planter class remained strong, as in the Cape Colony, Barbados, Southeast Brazil, and parts of the United States and French West Africa, states subjected freedpeople to harsh controls intended primarily to enforce their participation in "free" wage labor, and to prevent their becoming "dependent" on state support. Such controls assumed and thus sought to impose a particular construction of gender. For instance, vagrancy, poor relief, and bastardy legislation all worked toward the goal that men should act as heads of households and provide for their families.

Planter classes were less successful in imposing gendered class legislation when freedpeople had wider opportunities. For instance, in societies such as Jamaica and Dominica where freedpeople managed to secure some land for themselves and engage in peasant farming, they were less subject to, although not completely free from, colonial or plantocratic intervention. In this sense, state and ruling-class control of gender is one aspect of a wider set of questions about the degree to which freedpeople were able to control their own lives.

Former slaves constructed postemancipation communities that drew powerfully on visions of extended and fictive families. Men and women's connections to and roles within these families sometimes confirmed and sometimes were in tension with the visions of male authority and female domesticity contained in official blueprints for emancipation. Child rearing was probably universally allocated to women, but much else seems to have been variable. The precise content of these gendered ideologies is only just beginning to be unpacked, but . . . marriage, politics, land, and family are emerging as central areas for examination and comparison. At least as substantial as the overlaps were the ways in which the gender conventions of former slaves differed from those that were imposed upon them. Substantial evidence demonstrates freedwomen's active engagement in the politics of their communities, including efforts to control their men's votes. Laura Edwards has shown that in North Carolina, for instance, freedpeople had distinctive understandings of the meaning, rights, and obligations associated with marriage and other sexual relationships. Similarly, the work of Jean Besson on the pan-Caribbean institution of family land—that is, land that is passed down to all descendants, male and female, of an original ancestor, who may also be male or female—demonstrates a very different idea of property to those embedded in legal inheritance practices. The challenge for research is to investigate the gender norms in play in situations where they did not match the norms of white observers.

The similarities and differences between the gendered conventions of freedpeople and the ruling classes they confronted are not, however, the only issues that need discussion. Such an analysis of the gendering of emancipation risks understanding gender as merely an aspect of class and/or race formation and relations, rather than a contradiction and power relation in its own right. We cannot assume the existence of a coherent and conflict-free set of gender norms within each class group, in which ruling classes seek to impose one set while former slaves adhere to another. Both feminist theory and empirical evidence point to the conclusion that relations between men and women of the same "race" and/or class involve power and conflict. For instance, a number of scholars have documented cases in which freedwomen experienced and resisted domestic violence and other forms of abuse from their husbands and partners.

Yet freedmen's power over freedwomen was limited. The widespread African diasporic pattern of separate and autonomous control of property by men and women, along with the prominence of female-headed households throughout the diaspora, meant that relatively few freedmen were in a position to use economic power to dominate freedwomen. The model of domesticity assumed that men would be able to provide for their wives and children, but this was rarely even a realistic possibility in most of the postslave societies discussed here. In many areas, most significantly Barbados and small islands in the Eastern Caribbean, lack of jobs led to male migration, leaving behind a predominantly female population. In other areas it simply meant that women had to perform some kind of income-generating work, whether that was waged work, household manufacture, or peasant farming. As a result, even had they wanted to do so, it was impossible for all but a few of the most economically successful former slaves to adopt in full the ideology that was supposed to mark their transition to freedom and civilization. This had obvious costs in terms of impoverishment, but it also prevented the consolidation of a family-wage or peasant-based patriarchy among former slaves.

Throughout the Atlantic world, the late eighteenth and nineteenth centuries witnessed the consolidation of liberal political economy as the dominant model of social and economic organization. Liberalism was inflected differently in its French, Anglophone, Hispanic, and Lusophone iterations, but it always countered the image of slave society with the ideal of a society in which each person was an autonomous individual able to make contracts. As David Brion Davis has demonstrated, the processes that led to slave emancipation in the Atlantic world involved the intellectual and moral rejection of human bondage in favor of an ideology of free waged labor that stressed the value of the contract.

Liberalism was, of course, a contradictory and protean ideology. Liberals' commitment to formal equality and to contract-making everywhere coexisted with hierarchies and exclusions based on race and class. Such exclusions were particularly marked in postslave societies, where a wide range of unfree and semifree labor systems prevented ex-slaves and other workers from acting as the contract makers of liberal theory. Many of these systems, which included sharecropping, *métayage*, convict labor, indenture, debt bondage, and coercive vagrancy legislation, were intrinsically connected to gender hierarchies within familial relationships. Meanwhile, varying combinations of racial violence, racist laws, and poverty prevented freedpeople from exercising political rights.

These race- and class-based exclusions were integrated with liberalism's gendered premise. As Carol Pateman has shown, the model of liberal individualism implicitly assumed that the individual making contracts was a man whose right and ability to do so arose from his status as head of a family of dependents. It was the marriage contract that rendered men and women's relationship to the family so different. Marriage made a man head of a family or potential family. It defined him as having the independent status required of a contract-making individual. In contrast, marriage rendered a women permanently the subordinate of her husband. Through marriage, women became minors. The father's right to make contracts on behalf of his daughter was in essence transferred to the husband.

Married women's position in contract theory was, of course, echoed by the legal position of slaves. Slaves were also legally unable to make contracts. In the transition to emancipation, then, the acquisition of the right to make contracts was symbolically crucial. Emancipation's propagandists always stressed this point, even when the actual social relations created by emancipation allowed former slaves little space to make contracts. For freedwomen, the ability to contract was even more tenuous than it was for their male peers. If they married, as moralists and missionaries wanted them to do, they were in danger of losing a capacity that was represented to them as the essence of their freedom. No wonder women did not always show great enthusiasm for married life.

The promise of emancipation was, to some extent, a gendered one: that is, men were promised the entitlement of masculinity, of being head of a household. Women, in contrast, were liberated into dependence. What was to change for women was that they would be dependents of the right person, their husband or father, rather than the wrong one, their master.

Visions of patriarchal authority vested in the family thus girded many plans for emancipation. Male dominance was legally enshrined throughout many ex-slaveholding societies. For instance, in many places, freedmen gained suffrage at or soon after emancipation. Casting a vote became freighted as a symbol of freedom and citizenship in the United States, the French colonies, and many of the British colonies (where it was somewhat less significant because of property qualifications, but still important). No postemancipation state allowed freedwomen to vote. To have done so would have been an extraordinarily radical step, given that women did not vote anywhere in the Atlantic world at this time. Nevertheless, the explicitness with which the vote was allowed to men and not to women was a significant state-ment about who was a citizen and who a dependent in these new societies. Even in places like Brazil which excluded most freedmen along with all freedwomen from citizenship—the Brazilian republican constitution of 1891 limited "active citizen-ship" to literate males aged twenty-one and over—women's exclusion *because they were women* emphasized the postemancipation state's deep commitment to gender hierarchy. . . .

A fully gendered comparative history of slave emancipation would uncover the in-volvement of gender in many of the struggles during and after emancipation, includ-ing those that have traditionally been interpreted as primarily about race and/or class. This would include, for example, recognition of the ways that struggles among competing ruling groups to achieve hegemony in postemancipation society involved contested gender conventions. Examples would include the challenge to the domi-nant hard-drinking, sexually promiscuous masculinity of Caribbean planters by more "polite," bourgeois metropolitan masculinities, as well as the important gendered dynamic of struggles over freedpeople's labor, at the heart of which was the issue of whether women would or would not become plantation wage workers in the new society. A gendered comparative history of emancipation would recognize that, while all freedpeople faced the enormous difficulties of attempting to make new lives as unpropertied people in a capitalist world, postemancipation societies were struc-tured in certain legal, institutional, political, and economic ways that made these difficulties more severe for freedwomen than for freedmen. It would need, how-ever, to explain not only the subordination of women but also the relationship of that subordination to the specific targeting of freedmen *as men* for hostility and vio-lent attack in some societies, seen most notably in the history of lynching in the postemancipation United States.

Such a history would have to come to terms with freedwomen's contradictory experience of the doubleness of gender, as both symbol of freedom and source of oppression. Because slavery had denied all enslaved people the autonomy to organize gender according to their own understandings, both freedmen and freedwomen had reasons to support the maintenance and even strengthening of gender divisions among them. And yet for freedwomen emphasizing differences between men and women was problematic, because their position as women also served as a site of oppression, experienced through, for example, wage discrimination, lack of access to citizenship, sexual violence, and disproportionate responsibility for reproductive labor.

A gendered history of emancipation would reveal difference as well as similarity in societies across the Atlantic world. Probably the biggest differences would be found between the experience of the Americas and the Cape Colony on the one hand, and the rest of Africa on the other. European bourgeois gender conventions did not dominate among the rulers of African societies as they did, to varying degrees, in other parts of the Atlantic world. The end of slavery in the Americas and the Cape led to reconstructions of racial hierarchy, often linked to debates about "miscegenation" and/or "whitening," which were always in part about sexuality. In contrast, in much of the rest of Africa "race" was connected to emancipation primarily because the latter was imposed on African societies by European colonial regimes, which construed African slavery as evidence of African barbarism. The consolidation of plantation slavery in parts of West Africa and East Africa in the nineteenth century also helped affirm and create racial and religious difference, as Muslim Africans used religious difference to justify their enslavement of Africans who practiced indigenous religions.

Nevertheless, the gender dynamics of emancipation in American societies should not be homogenized. As we suggested above, the means by which emancipation was achieved had major implications for gendered claims to citizenship and gendered understandings of the nation. Other important differences could, we suspect, be traced between societies in which postemancipation ruling classes brought in large numbers of predominantly male laborers to maintain plantation production, and those where this did not occur; between urban and rural spaces; between plantation and nonplantation societies, and so on.

Throughout Atlantic societies, slave emancipation involved, and to some extent ignited, struggles over access to land, resources, and political power, as well as over definitions of freedom, labor, and culture. Gender was always at stake in these battles. Individuals entered the postemancipation world already gendered and with understandings of masculine and feminine personhood already in place. . . . [T]he battles and conflictual processes that shaped the world of freedom provide a moment in which such understandings about gender and their connection to race and class were made transparent. Emancipation both drew on existing ideas about the meaning of manhood and womanhood, about the content of the categories "man" and "woman," and contributed to new ideologies and practices of gender.

◁ *F U R T H E R   R E A D I N G*

Berlin, Ira, et al. *Slaves No More: Three Essays on Emancipation and the Civil War.* New York: Cambridge University Press, 1992.

Blackburn, Robin. *The Overthrow of Colonial Slavery, 1776–1848.* New York: Verso, 1988.

Brown, Christopher Leslie. *Moral Capital: Foundations of British Abolitionism.* Chapel Hill: Published for the Omohundro Institute of Early American History and Culture, Williamsburg, Virginia, by the University of North Carolina Press, 2006.

Burin, Eric. *Slavery and the Peculiar Solution: A History of the American Colonization Society.* Gainesville: University Press of Florida, 2005.

Conrad, Robert Edgar. *The Destruction of Brazilian Slavery, 1850–1888.* Berkeley: University of California Press, 1972.

Davis, David Brion. *Slavery and Human Progress.* New York: Oxford University Press, 1984.

Eltis, David. *Economic Growth and the Ending of the Transatlantic Slave Trade.* New York: Oxford University Press, 1987.

Foner, Eric. *Forever Free: The Story of Emancipation and Reconstruction.* Illustrations, edited, and with commentary by Joshua Brown. New York: Knopf, 2005.

———. *Nothing but Freedom: Emancipation and Its Legacy.* Baton Rouge: Louisiana State University Press, 1983.

Getz, Trevor R. *Slavery and Reform in West Africa: Toward Emancipation in Nineteenth-Century Senegal and the Gold Coast.* Athens: Ohio University Press, 2004.

Hochschild, Adam. *Bury the Chains: Prophets and Rebels in the Fight to Free an Empire's Slaves.* Boston: Houghton Mifflin, 2005.

Holt, Thomas C. *The Problems of Freedom: Race, Labor, and Politics in Jamaica and Britain, 1832–1938.* Baltimore: The Johns Hopkins University Press, 1992.

Karasch, Mary C. *Slave Life in Rio de Janeiro, 1808–1850.* Princeton, NJ: Princeton University Press, 1987.

Klein, Martin A. *Slavery and Colonial Rule in French West Africa.* New York: Cambridge University Press, 1998.

Lovejoy, Paul E., and Jan S. Hogendorn. *Slow Death for Slavery: The Course of Abolition in Northern Nigeria, 1897–1936.* New York: Cambridge University Press, 1993.

Mason, John Edwin. *Social Death and Resurrection: Slavery and Emancipation in South Africa.* Charlottesville: University of Virginia Press, 2003.

Miers, Suzanne, and Richard Roberts, eds. *The End of Slavery in Africa.* Madison: University of Wisconsin Press, 1988.

Sanneh, Lamin O. *Abolitionists Abroad: American Blacks and the Making of Modern West Africa.* Cambridge, MA: Harvard University Press, 1999.

Schmidt-Nowara, Christopher. *Empire and Antislavery: Spain, Cuba, and Puerto Rico, 1833–1874.* Pittsburgh: University of Pittsburgh Press, 1999.

Scott, Rebecca J. *Slave Emancipation in Cuba: The Transition to Free Labor, 1860–1899.* Princeton, NJ: Princeton University Press, 1985.

Stewart, James Brewer. *Holy Warriors: The Abolitionists and American Slavery.* New York: Hill and Wang, 1976.

An Age of "Free" Migration

The patterns of Atlantic migration changed considerably in the nineteenth century. European migrants began to outnumber enslaved Africans as the transatlantic slave trade slowly came to a close. The total volume of migration increased sub-stantially. From 1821 to 1845, 1,376,100 Europeans migrated to the Americas, pre-dominantly from northern Europe, and primarily bound for North America. In the next 75 years, however, some 45 million Europeans traveled across the Atlantic, including large numbers from southern and eastern Europe. Although most were bound for the United States, Argentina received the largest number of immigrants in proportion to its population, followed by Canada. Migration was no longer a one-way trip. As many as 53% of migrants to Argentina and 30% of migrants to the United States might have returned to their home countries. Laborers arrived from outside the Atlantic world, too—primarily migrants from Asia who traveled to sugar-cultivating regions to replace and sometimes join enslaved laborers. For example, some 27,000 Chinese workers went to the British colonies of Jamaica, Trinidad, and Guiana, while 125,000 went to Cuba. Recruited as contract workers in a global labor market, the new Atlantic migrants further diversified an already-complex and heterogeneous world. It was also in this era that people of African descent reversed the middle passage, traveling from the Americas to settle in Africa, bound for the British colony of Sierra Leone, the American Colonization Society's experiment at Liberia, and the Bight of Benin. Some were missionaries who sought to "civilize" Africa, whereas others were exiles, deported in the wake of slave rebellions or dis-illusioned by the unfulfilled promise of emancipation. The documents and essays in this chapter trace these new patterns of migration, explore the continuing challenges of cultural interaction and assimilation, and question whether the new transatlantic migrants were truly free.

D O C U M E N T S

The documents in this chapter explore migration from a variety of perspectives, con-sidering the push factors that encouraged migrants to move, the lure of new lands, the challenges of assimilation, and the economic, political, religious, and cultural constraints that guided individual decisions and aspirations.

Discrimination and hardship compelled some free black people in the United States to leave the country. Document 1 reveals controversy over emigration to Haiti. The first excerpt offers a critical assessment of black migration to Haiti, while Jean Pierre Boyer's circular describes how migrants were attracted to Haiti with the promise of land: L. D. Dewey notes the preference potential migrants had for Haiti over the American Colonization Society's settlement in Liberia. The final excerpt reports on the way Philadelphia's African Methodist Episcopal Church greeted the possibility of emigration. One African-American woman who did leave the United States was Matilda Skipwith. After being emancipated by the southern planter John Hartwell Cocke in 1833, Skipwith emigrated to Liberia with her family. Document 2 includes four of her letters from the late 1840s and 1850s, which bear witness to her ordeal in Africa.

Documents 4 and 6 illustrate the acceleration of transatlantic travel and communication in the nineteenth century. Document 4, an article from *Littell's Living Age* in September 1850, describes the tumultuous departure of an emigrant ship from Liverpool's Waterloo Dock: the crowded conditions, the destitution of the mostly Irish emigrants, the confusion of steerage, the problem of stowaways, and emigrants' vague and partial knowledge of their destination in America. Cyrus Field's completion of the transatlantic cable from Ireland to Newfoundland on July 30, 1866, was one of the great feats of the era. The newspaper articles excerpted in Document 6 foresee major changes in the conduct of transatlantic business, and the *Times* of London predicts a closer connection between America and Europe as a consequence of the new technology.

Documents 3 and 5 illustrate two new migration flows. In the middle of the nineteenth century, as the British aggressively promoted settlement in their colony in South Africa, Thomas Phipson sailed to Durban with his family in 1849. Written only two months after his arrival in Durban, his letter home is a classic of its genre. He urges others to follow him, yet cautions immigrants about the challenges of life in Natal while making disparaging remarks about the abilities of Africans. Racism continued to shape new and expanding European settlements. Document 5 includes an 1862 template for the labor contract of a Chinese worker, and a second document that grants a Chinese woman the right of residence in British Guyana. Although these Asian workers came from new regions, their status as indentured laborers recalled earlier modes of coercion in the Atlantic world.

Documents 7 and 8 illustrate the challenges of assimilation that newcomers confronted. In the early 1890s, "Brazil fever" swept Poland, and tens of thousands of Poles emigrated to Brazil. Immigrants arriving in Brazil sent letters home describing the arduous voyage, the process of acquiring land from the Brazilian government, and their adjustment to life in a new country, often with a view toward enticing family members to emigrate. Brazil offered the double incentive of economic opportunity and a Catholic tradition, although one of the letters suggests that Brazilian and Polish Catholicism were quite different. In another letter, a Polish immigrant in Pennsylvania urges his brother-in-law to come to the United States instead of Brazil. It's worth noting that these letters were confiscated by Tsarist authorities and never reached their intended destinations, revealing some of the difficulties of transatlantic communication even in the late nineteenth century. In Document 8, a short story by the preeminent Jewish Argentinean writer Alberto Gerchunoff (1883–1949), published in 1910, a community of Russian Jews in Argentina celebrates the country's Independence Day. In Gerchunoff's humorous account, the Jews know little of Argentina's national history or culture, so they fit the holiday into their own sacred history of exodus from slavery and escape from persecution.

1. President Boyer of Haiti Appeals to Free Blacks in the United States, 1821–1824

Reported in The Columbian Centinel, *1821*

The Island of Hayti, to which we are sorry to perceive means are in activity to entice our free people of colour, will most probably become a renewed scene of carnage and proscription. The African race can never be reconciled with that which is mixed with the white. Of this the recent plot affords an example, in addition to those, which so many massacres have attested, in the Island.—Whilst it remained divided between the black and yellow chiefs, it enjoyed, for a number of years, a degree of tranquility which is now probably about to disappear. Why therefore are our emancipated natives to be precipitated into such an effervescing vortex? We can foresee no middle state for them, after arriving, but to assist in these exterminating scenes, or to become the passive victims of them. In the former case by becoming barbarians, and ceasing to be christians, it may be painfully experienced, that their annoyance will be much more inconvenient, at Hayti, than at home. The least consideration must, we think, convince every man, that the proposed emigration will be more destructive to their welfare, and pernicious to our interests, than almost any plan that could be adopted.—*Federal Republican.*

Jean Pierre Boyer's Invitation, 1823, with a Response

[TRANSLATION.]
CIRCULAR.

Port-au-Prince, 24th December, 1823.

Jean Pierre Boyer, President of Hayti, to the Commandants of the Districts.

Desirous to increase in the country the number of agriculturalists, and thus augment its population, I have decided, my dear General, that emigrants of colour to Hayti, who may wish to establish themselves in the mountains or vallies to cultivate with their own hands the public lands, shall be authorized to cultivate the same for their own profit. These lands, after payment of the taxes established by the authority of the place, shall be ceded in fee simple, to those who open them and enhance their value, dividing them into suitable plantations for the produce of coffee and other productions which may yield a revenue to the state. You are therefore charged so far as your authority extends, to settle the people of colour who may arrive, or who may wish to disembark and establish themselves in the district which you command, and to send me a list of the names of all such persons, and a description of the land given them.

Source: *The Columbian Centinel*, February 28, 1821; *Correspondence Relative to the Emigration to Haiti, of the Free People of Color in the United States* (New York, 1824), pp. 2, 12; *The Wilmingtonian and Delaware Register*, July 22, 1824.

It is understood, that this measure is not to change that prescribed by my circular of 2d December, 1822, in favour of the persons, who, anterior to the first of last January, should be established without title upon the state lands. Signed,

BOYER.

NOTICE.

In prosecuting an agency in behalf of the noble objects of the American Colonization Society, I found the public feeling generally was very favourable to the Emigration of the Coloured People to Hayti. Among the Coloured People themselves, a preference of Hayti over Africa was frequently expressed, and among the whites, there was not only an opposition to colonization in Africa manifested by many, but an assurance given of their ready aid to promote emigration to Hayti. The present peaceful state of the island, and the fair prospects before the Haytiens, of having their Independence acknowledged by other nations, indicated that the great obstacles in the way of emigration there, which had hitherto existed, were removed, and that the time had now come to aid our coloured population to plant themselves under the mild climate of that Island, were it encouraged by the Haytien government. On inquiry, I found very little was known definitely in this country, what the views of that government were, on this subject. There were some favourable reports brought by persons by colour who had been to Hayti; others gave discouraging accounts. Except some liberal offers, by the Secretary Inginac, which I had seen, the information obtained, was limited and uncertain. Under these circumstances, the letter with which the Correspondence commences, was addressed through the Secretary General, B. Inginac, to the President of Hayti. The generous reply of the President, together with the arrival in this country, of his agent, Citizen J. GRANVILLE, with ample means to carry into effect, the philanthropic overtures of President Boyer, shows what great good may now be hoped for our unhappy countrymen, who are the objects of his generosity. . . .

L. D. DEWEY.

New-York, June 15, 1824.

Reported in The Wilmingtonian and Delaware Register, *1824*

EMIGRATION TO HAYTI.—A large number of the coloured people of Philadelphia assembled at Bethel Church in that city on the 6th instant and passed unanimously the following resolutions, the Rev. R[ichard] Allen being in the Chair.—

Resolved, That we do approve of the proposals of President Boyer: also, heartily concur with him in the belief that the emigration to the Island of Hayti will be more advantageous to us than to the Colony in Africa [Liberia]. . .

Resolved, That a Committee of twenty be appointed to devise and adopt, such measures as shall or may be deemed most expedient for the promotion of the above object, which accordingly was done.

2. Matilda Skipwith Meets with Sorrow
in Liberia, 1848–1858

To Miss S[ally] F. Cocks   Monrovia, July 4th, 1848

Dear Miss: I now avale myself of the favourable oppertunity of addressing you with a fiew lines to inform you that I am well, and hope this may finde you and all the family in the enjoyment of the same.

Dear Miss, I hope that from our long Silence you have not been induced to think that we have withdrawn our Communications from you. If such have been your thoughts let me beseech you to do away with it as I am aware that I have not written you as often as I ought, but such shall not be the case again, that is whenever an oppertunity affords. I hope you will not fail to write me by the first affording oppertunity as I am very desireous to hear something from you all.

You requested of me in your last to say something about my marriage. I was wedlocked to a Young man by the name of Samuel B. Lomax. He is a Young man who masters one or two trades, firstly a Cooper, 2dly Printer, 3dly Sea Captain and Clerk. The latter he now turns his attention to principly as his health has been quite bad for the past Six or Seven months, and Liberia is a Country where it behooves every man to be up and doing something for his future prosperity.

I suppose you have long since heard of the Congoes that was landed in Monrovia from on board of the Am. Barque "Pons." Numbers of them died from the fatigue of the Cruel Imprisenment on board of the ship before Captured. The surviveing ons are as healthy a set of people as ever a person would wish to see. Several of which has embraced the religion of our Saviour and making rapid improvements in Education, Tho I must say of a truth that they are the most Savage, & blud thirsty people I ever saw or ever wishes to see. My Father's love to your father and You. He would of written but is not in Town. He desires that you[r] fathe[r] would be so kind as to send his Bro. on, also that he would send him a Set of Mason's Tools. Please send me on something for my Children as I have been the mother of 3 since my Marriage one of which I have lost. The other two which is girls yet servives. Theire names are as Foulers: Eliza Adala & Lydia Ann Lomax. I must now close as I wishes by indulgence from You to say afiu words at the bottom to my dear Grd Mother. I am with Respects Yours,

Matilda R. Lomax

Monrovia, R. P. [Republic] Liberia, November 23d, 49

Dear General J. F. C—:   As the Liberia Packet sails from this Port for the US on the 24th Inst I hasten with a heart over burdened with grief to write you a letter in answer to the one by the packet to my Father, which was duly received, affoarding us all much pleasure in hearing from you and all. I shall now give you the sad and mellancholly news of the death of Father who parted this life October 14th. His end

Source: Bell I. Wiley, ed., *Slaves No More: Letters from Liberia 1833–1869* (Lexington: University Press of Kentucky, 1980), 66–67, 69–70, 71–72, 90–91.

was peace. He did not live more than two weeks after the arrival of the "Packet." His complaint was that of the head and breast. He was taken sick on wednesday and expired on Sunday; he was perfectly sencible of his death. Mr. [Hilary] Teage visited him regularly during his illness and questioned him from time to time concerning of his Sole's Salvation, whether his way was clear from earth to glory or not, which he would always answer in words like these if not the same: death is no dread to me, my hope is anchored in Christ Jesus. A fiew days previous to his being taken Sick, he was remarking to us what a Kind and Effectunate letter he intended writing you and his mother, but before the "Packet" returned from Cape Palmas he fell to sleep in Jesus' Arms never more to have earthly communication with you all, but trusting to strike hands with you all in the *Fathers Kingdom* where parting shall be no more, and where we do all trust to drink of that stream that maketh glad the City of the New Jurusalem. You requested in your last to Know of Father to whome he was married to, also whether his wife belonged to any denomination or no. She was a widdow before he married her, with two Children, also a Member of the M. E. Church in Monrovia. As regards his yearly income that I can give no statement of. I can mearly say that it was derived entirely from his trade during his life. Jack Faulcon I shall say nothing about as he has written you himself. Bro. Nash has also written to you. He is not married and still carries on the Masons trade. He is capable of taking under his charge fathers apprentice boys and carry on the same as when father was liveing. Cousin Leander is not home. He has joind the [United] States Navy as Stewart. Consequently I can not give you a correct account of his health, tho he was well when last I saw him. His Children are all well. Cousin Julia and Peter is both dead, and has been for more than two years. Father had acquired ten acres of farm land & five town lots. He had just entered in a good way of farming before his death. We in generally raised on our Farms Corn, Potatoes, Cassado & rice. Of the latter father had not entered or commenced its cultivation befor his death.

Labourers can be hired in Liberia for 25 cents per day and at the outside from 3 to 4$ per month. A person may hire good common labourers to work the ground to make it productive as that in the States comparitively speaking. My husband Mr. Saml B. Lomax who writes this begs that you would receive his kindest regard and attends his respects to you and all the family trusting that you would keep up a regular corrispondance as ever, which he shall endeavour to give you every particular relating to Public as well as private affairs, taking great delight in so doing. I now close by begging of you to pardon all Grammatical and other errors &c &c. Yours with much Esteem,

Matilda R. Lomax

NB Should it meet your approbation to send us on any thing please direct to Care Rev H. Teage.

To Honorable John H. Cocke   Monrovia, Sept. 30th, 1850

Dear Sir: I lift my Pen to Embrace this opportunity to inform you that I am well, and Hope that These few lines may find you and all the families well as they leaves me and mine. This letter will inform you of the sad, the Heart broken intelligence of the death of my Dear Husband. He was Drowned about 90 miles from this Place, attempting to go on shore, when the Seas was runing mountain High. This took Place on the 23 of July Last, leaving me with three small children to provid for, in this New Country Where Every thinge is hard for a widow without sufficient means to take care of them. The Youngest child is at the Breast. I Hope that you will give me some little aid by the next vessel coming to Liberia, for if I Ever in all my life needed Help, it is now. For my father who, were he a live, I might make out beter, but he is also gone the Way of the Earth leaving behind small children who are Depending upon me to provid for them. Also, my youngest and only bro., Nash, sends his love to you. Leander is in the U.S.S. Yorktown, and has been for the Last 10 or 12 months. All of his Children is well. You will be [so] Kind as to write to my Uncle and inform him of the death of his Brother. Tell him he Departed this life on October Last—I mean his Brother George. I now write these few lines to Miss Salley F. Cocke. Tell her I Received her letter by the Packet before this, but did not get the things her agent sent. I heard from them, and that was all. If She Should here after send me any Thing Please Tell her to Direct them to the Care of Col. Jas B. McGill, Monrovia, and I will be Sure to get them. Please Remember me very kindly to my Dear Old Grand Mother. Tell her I am well in Body, but are Buried in sorrow in consequence of my Great losses, of Husband and father. Also Give my love to my other Grand Mother, Betsey, and all of my relations & friends Both White & Colored. I have nothing more to say at Present, only Remain yours &c.,

Matilda Lomax

Monrovia, Africa, July the 24th, 1858

Mrs. Sally F. Brent: I am glad that an opportunity is afforded to hand you a few lines which leave me and mine in good health and I hope may find you enjoying the Blessings of a favorable Providence. I were glad to here from you and the servents By Solmon letter for I ashore you that I am glad to here from you at any time and Beg that you would write to me By evry opportunity as it is a great treat to me to resive a letter from your hands. I am getteing on as well as I can expect But not as well as I should like to do. But I still look forde for a Better times and hope that time is not far of. I hope to live to see the day when Africa this our dark Country shall rise Bud and Blossom as the rose of the Garden of life. Thir is nothing New at this time that is worth writing. My 3 children are well and gose to school and are lurning very fast to Read and write. Leander children are well and send love to you and all the Family. Leander is not heir. He is on Board of a manofwar with Mr. John Barroad. We look for them every day. Cousin James is living with me. He is over the fever an is well please with Liberia an wish to be Rememberd to white and colored. Solmon wish to Be Remberd also to all the Friends. Jack and his Mother are well and send love to all the Freinds. This is the rany seons [season] with us now and it is very dull at this time with us in Africa. It is true that I have Been to this Country 20 years an is true I have not got a Brick House. But what is the case if my father Esate [Estate] had not Been robed, I chould have had a Plenty to live no [on] an to live well all my days. But after my Father death I had no one to see to his Estate thirfore I got nothing from his Esate But 3 or 4 lots in town which is not worth nothing if tha ware sould. Please to Remember me to all the Family. Tell aunt Lavinia that I often think of her and tell her that she must write to me By the returne of the Packet. And if we never meet in this world agane I hope to meet you on the other side of Jordan where we shall Be ever Present with the Lord and ware we shall pluck new lives from the tree of life and where Congregations never Break up and sabbaths have no end. I would like to say agreadel more But time will not atmit Just now. I must now come to a close. Yours in the Bounds of Christen love. Please to give my love [to] evry Body.

Matilda Richardson

3. Thomas Phipson Asks for Migrants, Labor, and Hedges in Natal, 1849

An Emigrant's Letters Home No 6   *Natal Witness* 6 July 1849

My dear Friends in England,

Among the most obvious deficiencies that strike a newly arrived spectator in this part of the world, is the scarcity of two prime requisites in rural economy, of which you in England have more than enough—I mean men and hedges. While your poor law officers are devising means for reducing the number of able-bodied paupers, and your farmers are thinking of grubbing up the ancient boundaries of their elms, grudging the narrow space in which stand their venerable roots, we here would fain not only take the half-starved wretch from his heap of stones under a hedge, but also (were it possible) bring with him the hedge too. Oh, how would our eyes rejoice to see here the thick rows of goodly thorn, and the heavily shod rustics wending their way between them, where now the barefoot native wanders at will over a wide range of grass unbroken by a furrow or a fence.

Lack of Hedges

Unfortunately, however, the hedgerow is not a very convenient freight for a two months' voyage, nor do the bipeds appear to be much less firmly rooted to the soil. In the meantime we are obliged to be contented with fences of figs or quince, which, whatever their intrinsic merits or romantic associations in your chilly clime, do not present a much firmer front to the assaults of the ox, calf, goat, or pig, than a regiment of drawing-room beaux would have shown to the charge of the French cuirassiers at Waterloo. In expectation, or in aid of these feeble auxiliaries, ramparts of earth, rows of posts and rails, and, in some situations, wide ditches, are called into requisition to keep out intruders; and too often in vain. Advancing as the place now is from the pastoral to the agricultural state of society, the trespassing of stock, though stringently forbidden by municipal regulations, is of frequent occurrence in the neighbourhood of the town; while the strict application of legal remedies is necessarily an invidious and difficult task. But at a little distance in the country fences are little used or needed; the cattle being simply watched during the day so far as to keep them from the crops, and at night they are shut up in a kraal or enclosure. Hereafter it is to be hoped that some thorny bush may be found among those indigenous in these regions, suitable for hedges; the ground rent of which will not be grudged here for many centuries to come.

Source: Thomas Phipson to friends in England, 26 June 1849, published in the *Natal Witness*, 6 July 1849 in R.N. Currey, ed., *Letters and Other Writings of a Natal Sheriff Thomas Phipson 1815–1876* (Cape Town: Oxford University Press, 1968), pp. 17–20.

Native Labour

Land, however, can neither be fenced nor cultivated without labour; and this must be either native or imported. Athletic as the natives are in body, they are mere children in mind; and have a great aversion to continuous exertion, or steady effort. Having few wants, where they can live for a week on a shilling's worth of maize, where clothing is a matter of mere luxury or caprice, and where they pay no taxes, they have no stimulus to urge them to industry; and while they use a rude kind of cultivation on their own land, their assistance in practical labour cannot be depended on. Any kind of compulsion is contrary to the genius of the British government and to the spirit of the times, and while the force of circumstances compels the "free" Dorsetshire labourer, whom Mr. Barker has the honour to represent, to toil ten or twelve hours a day for a scanty subsistence, and with the union-house in perspective, our Zoolah friends here can claim the dignity and advantages of British subjects, and yet be uncontrolled as the air they breathe, and as untaxed as the wild buck that roams over the hills.

Imported Labour

To the importation of labourers from Britain various obstacles are opposed. Legally considered, no bond of agreement made in England is obligatory in the colonies, unless voluntarily renewed after landing. Consequently employers have no assurance of being repaid for their expenses in transporting servants across the sea. On the contrary, I believe the master is liable to pay their expenses back to England should they wish to return. And even if the legal obstacles were removed, yet a reluctant workman can find so many ways of rendering his company undesirable, that practically it is impossible for private parties to introduce their own hinds.

Government has found a method of servile colonisation at the expense of the fund formed by the purchase of land; but that fund here is at present too small to be available for such a purpose; and should it become so, yet one man to one or two hundred acres of land would be but a scanty supply. Slavery being now happily among the things that were, the only kind of compulsory labour that the state can offer is that of convicts, to which the good people both of this and the Cape colony entertain very strong and decided objections; thus exhibiting a sacrifice of pecuniary interest to moral considerations rarely hitherto met in the political history of states young or old.

Type of Colonist Wanted

Under these circumstances if any man thinks of coming hither, let him consider well his own hands and arms, and those of his family, and let him not depend on any supply of labour which these cannot supply. With this proviso, be he farmer, gardener, tailor, smith, carpenter, or in any business ministering to the necessities rather than the luxuries of life, he may depend on obtaining a comfortable maintenance; but persons whose only ideas of comfort or prosperity are derived from and dependent upon the advanced state of civilisation prevalent in towns or cities, will (while not perhaps in any danger of destitution) encounter privations and inconveniences of a character which may disgust them with the Colony, and make them wish they had remained in their native land. But while an urban population are only partially adapted for emigration and are likely to encounter discomfort and discouragement at first, yet even these, if possessed of energy and perseverence, will ultimately do well; while the rustic labourer, the small farmer, and the industrious mechanic, are in a more speedy and certain way to ease and even to affluence.

I am, dear Friends,
Very faithfully yours,
Thomas Phipson
Pietermaritzburg, June 26th 1849

4. A Journalist Describes an Immigrant Vessel, 1849–1850

The Waterloo Dock is the principal station of the American liners in the port of Liverpool. A description of the departure of one or two of these vessels, and of the scenes on board, both in the Dock and in the Mersey, as well as an account of conversations held at various times with all classes of emigrants, may serve to convey an idea of that busy and interesting scene, the departure of a large emigrant ship with a full complement of passengers. It was a beautiful morning when I proceeded to witness the departure of the Star of the West, Captain Lowber commander, a fine new ship, then on her first voyage, and registering 1,200 tons. The scene in the dock at half-past eight in the morning was busy and animated in the extreme. All the cargo was on board, consisting principally of iron rails, the exportation of which to America is very largely on the increase. The greater part of the passengers was also on board; but every minute until half-past nine there was a fresh arrival of emigrants and their luggage. In consequence of the regulations, both of the British and American governments, it was to be presumed that the living freight of the Star of the West was in good condition, and duly certified to be unlikely to become chargeable to our Transatlantic brethren of New York. It must be confessed, however, that they did not present a very favorable specimen of the genus man. Destitution and suffering, long-continued, possibly for generations, had done their work upon the greater number of them. It was not alone their personal uncleanliness and their wretched attire, but the haggard, sallow, and prematurely aged expression of their faces, that conveyed the idea of degradation and deterioration. . . . There were many such Irish people as these on board the Star of the West, on the morning of her departure; and the general appearance of the majority to whom such a description would not apply, was weakly and care-worn, bespeaking extreme poverty, neglect and apathy. There was one family of Germans on board—a father and mother, and four grown-up and two younger children—whose appearance was in striking contrast with that of the Irish. The man was from Bavaria,—a tall, well-formed, strapping "kerl," full fed and ruddy, and looking as if he could do no ordinary duty in felling the primeval forests of the far west, and converting the wilderness into a garden. There were also two or three English families on board—the men easily recognizable by the smock-frock of the English peasantry, and the women by their superior neatness of attire. With

---

Source: "Departure of Emigrant Vessels," *Littell's Living Age*, September 14, 1850.

these few exceptions the passengers were all Irish. The whole number of passengers was 385, of whom about 300 were Irish. . . .

Until the very last moment, they kept arriving by twos and threes, with their luggage on their backs. Here might be seen a strong fellow carrying a chest, or a barrel, and a whole assemblage of tin cans and cooking utensils; and there a woman with a child in one arm and her goods and chattels in the other. When the planks and gangways were removed, at least fifty of our emigrants had not arrived, and many of them had to toss their luggage on board from the quay, and to clamber on to the ship by the rigging, as she passed through the dock-gates. The men contrived to jump on board with comparative case; but by the belated women, of whom there were nearly a score, the feat was not accomplished without much screaming and hesitation. One valiant fellow, who had been drinking overmuch with his friends on shore, made an attempt to leap aboard as the vessel was clearing the dock-gates, but, miscalculating the distance, he fell into the water. There was a general rush of people to the side of the ship, and a screaming among the women, but fortunately there was a boat along-side which rescued the man in less than a minute, and placed him on deck dripping wet, and considerably more sober than when he fell into the water. . . .

The steerage was somewhat dark, but in the uncertain light a picture presented itself full of strange "effects." The floor was strewed with luggage, rendering it a matter of difficulty to walk—bundles, trunks, cases, chests, barrels, loaves of bread, sides of bacon, and tin cooking utensils, seemed to be piled together in hopeless and inextricable confusion, while amidst them all scrambled or crawled a perfect multitude of young children. All the berths were occupied. Some of the passengers seemed as if they had resolved to go to sleep even at that early period of the voyage. Some were eating their breakfasts in their berths, and some were making use of barrel-heads and trunks for tables and chairs, and regaling themselves with bread and coffee. Here and there a man might be seen shaving himself in the dim and uncertain light; while, at other parts of the ample steerage, families were busily looking after their worldly goods, and establishing a demarcation between their own property and that of their neighbors. In some of the berths women were sitting up conversing; and in others, children were singing, hallooing, and shouting, as if the excitement of the scene were to them a joy indeed. There was a constant rushing to and fro, a frequent stumbling over chests and barrels, and a perfect Babel of tongues. All was life, bustle, and confusion; but, what seemed most singular, there was nothing like sorrow or regret at leaving England. There was not a wet eye on board—there had been no fond leave-takings, no farewells to England, no pangs of parting. Possibly there was no necessity for any. To ninety-nine out of every hundred of these emigrants the old country had been in all probability an unkind mother, a country of sorrow and distress, associated only with remembrances of poverty and suffering. . . .

In conversation with the passengers [of another vessel . . .], I found that very many of them were going out to join friends and relatives in the United States who had preceded them years before, and who had, forwarded them money to pay their passage. Some few were going to remain in the state of New York; but by far the greater proportion were bound for Ohio, Illinois, Wisconsin, and Missouri. Very few of them seemed to know whether Canada was, or was not, a British possession; and not one of the Irish to whom I put the question had ever heard of Nova Scotia, New-foundland, or New Brunswick. One respectable looking lad, of about twenty, said he had five pounds in his pocket. He knew no person in America, but as he had heard of the state of Ohio, and that land was cheap, and labor well paid, he was going thither to try his fortune. He was not, he said, afraid of hard work, and had no fear but that he should get on. The English emigrants in the second class cabins knew all about Canada and the British North American possessions, but thought the United States preferable to either of them. "Besides," said one sturdy man from Lincolnshire, "we don't know what's to happen in Canada. It won't always belong to England, and there may be a 'rumpus.' It's all right in the States, and that's the place for my money." This man and his family were bound for Wisconsin. In conversation with him upon the generally respectable appearance of the English, the squalid appearance of the Irish emigrants, and the probability that a few years' residence in the New World would much improve the latter, both physically and morally, he showed me a passage in a cheap tract, just published, entitled, "Nine Years in America. By Thomas Mooney; in a Series of Letters to his Cousin, Patrick Mooney, a farmer in Ireland," which bore upon the subject of our discourse. I reproduce the passage. "I have seen a thousand times," says Mr. Mooney, "the two growths of children from the same Irish parentage present a remarkable difference. Those born in America were brave, beautiful, and intellectual-looking—high foreheads, brights eyes, quick and intelligent. Those of the *same* parents, born before they left Ireland, wearing still the stamp of sorrow on their brow, and the stoop of suffering in their gait."

5. The British Empire Welcomes Chinese Workers, 1862–1864

Chinese Contract of Indenture (1862 version)

Articles of Agreement, made this third day of April in the year of the Christian era 1862, being the fifth day of the third month of the first year of the reign of Jeungtey, according to the Chinese Imperial Calendar, between _____, native of China, of the one or first part, and J. Gardiner Austin, Esq., Special Agent of the British Government for the regulating and encouragement of emigration from China to the British West Indies, of the other or second part, as follows:—

The said party of the first part in consideration of the covenants, agreements, and stipulations hereinafter entered into by the said party of the second part, doth hereby promise and agree to and with the said party of the second part in manner and form following, that is to say:—

1. That he the said party of the first part shall and will, so soon as he shall be required by the said party of the second part, embark on board the British ship _____, now lying at anchor in the harbour of Hong Kong, and bound for the colony of _____, and remain on board the said ship henceforward until she proceeds to sea, and shall then proceed as a passenger on board the said ship, to _____ aforesaid, for

Source: "Chinese Contract of Indenture (1862 version)" and "Contract of Residence of Chinese Female Emigrant," in Walter Look Lai, *Indentured Labor, Caribbean Sugar: Chinese and Indian Migrants to the British West Indies, 1838–1918* (Baltimore: The Johns Hopkins University Press, 1993), pp. 314–317.

the purpose of carrying out the stipulations hereinafter contained on the part of the said party of the first part.

2. That the said party of the first part shall and will from time to time, and at all times during the term of five years, to be computed from the day of the arrival of the said ship _____ in the said colony of _____, serve such persons, his heirs, executors, administrators or assigns, and on such plantation in _____ as the Governor may appoint, in the growing or manufacturing of articles, the produce of such plantation, according to the provisions hereinafter contained.

3. That the said party of the first part shall and will work as such labourer as aforesaid, for the space of seven hours and a half of each day during the aforesaid term of five years, and on such plantation as aforesaid, with a reservation of not less than five days to be set apart during each year as holidays at the China New Year by the said Governor, and of every Sabbath day. And in consideration of the agreement herein contained on the part of the said party of the first part, the said party of the second part hereby promises and agrees to and with the said party of the first part in manner following, that is to say:—

4. That the said party of the second part shall provide the said party of the first part with a free passage to the said colony of _____, and shall supply him gratuitously with such food and clothing as may be necessary for the voyage.

5. That so long as the said party of the first part shall continue and be employed as such labourer, as aforesaid, and perform the agreements on his part hereinbefore contained, he the said party of the second part shall cause to be paid weekly to the said party of the first part the same rate of wages for the same proportionate quantity of work as may from time to time be paid to unindentured labourers working on the same plantation, and shall cause to be provided for the said party of the first part during the same service, house, garden-ground and medical attendance, all free of expense to the said party of the first part.

6. That the said party of the second part shall, on demand of the said party of the first part, so soon as he shall embark on board the said ship _____ for the purpose of carrying out the terms of its agreement, make an advance on account of wages to the said party of the first part to the extent of $20, shall pay or cause to be paid monthly to the assigns or nominees of the said party of the first part in China $_____ of the wages to be earned by the said party of the first part in the said colony of _____, the first payment to be made on the day of the date of embarkation of the said party of the first part on board the said ship _____, provided always, and it is hereby agreed, that any sum so advanced to the said party of the first part as aforesaid shall be stopped or deducted out of the wages to be earned by the said party of the first part, at the rate of $1 per month, and that any payments so made as aforesaid monthly to the assigns or nominees of the said party of the first part in China, shall be stopped or deducted in equal amounts monthly from the wages to be earned by the said party of the first part.

7. That the said party of the first part shall be at liberty to terminate this agreement, at the end of any one of the said five years, by paying for each year then unexpired a sum equal to one fifth of the amount paid for his introduction, namely, $75, and shall further be at liberty to change his employer at the end of the third or fourth year.

8. That the said party of the second part shall provide or cause to be provided for the said party of the first part during such period as he continues to serve under the

terms of this agreement, with the means of corresponding monthly, free of expense, with his relations in China, and of remitting money to them.

(signed)

J. G. Austin.

This done in duplicate, each of the parties aforesaid retaining one copy, at _____, on the 3rd day of April, in the year of our Lord 1862, in the presence of the undersigned, who declares that this contract has been signed willingly, and with full knowledge of its contents, by the said _____.

G. W. Caine,
Acting Emigration Officer.

Received an advance of $20 on account of wages, and a gratuity of $_____ for wife and _____ children.

I agree to employ _____ upon the terms stated above. (_____)

I certify that the labourer whose name appears above has been allotted by His Excellency the Governor of _____ to plantation _____; and that the signature of the employer was made in my presence.

(_____)

Immigration Agent-General of _____.

Note: Resolution of the Governor and Court of Policy of British Guiana [found only in British Guiana contracts]

"That the immigrants should be guaranteed full employment on adequate wages, paid weekly, with a house rent free, with medical attendance, medicines, food, and hospital accommodation when sick, and that it should be explained to them that a man can earn easily from two to four shillings, women from one to two shillings, and children eight pence per diem, and that a full supply of food for a man can be bought for eight pence per diem."

Contract of Residence of Chinese Female Emigrant
(*specimen authorized by British Guiana Ordinance No. 4 of 1864, section 48*).

No. _____, Ship _____.

Contract made this _____ day of _____ in the year of 186_____, between _____ as Proprietor (or Attorney of the Proprietor, or Lessee, etc.) of the Plantation _____ in the county of _____ in the colony of British Guiana, of the one or first part, and _____ Chinese female immigrant of the other or second part, witnesseth as follows:—

That the said female Chinese immigrant shall reside on the said plantation for the term of five years from date; and that the party of the first part shall supply her, free of cost, with suitable lodging and with such medicine, nourishment, and medical attendance, and hospital accommodation, as she may need when sick.

Signature of Employer.
Signature of Chinese Female Emigrant.

I hereby declare that the Female Chinese Emigrant, party to this contract, signed the same voluntarily and with a due understanding of its effect.

Immigration Agent-General.

6. The Transatlantic Cable Connects the Continents, 1866

London Times, July 30, 1866

The success of the Atlantic Cable is now complete, and the most sanguine hopes have been more than realized. The Cable has been landed in Newfoundland apparently without a flaw and without the occurrence of a single check. The communication between Ireland and Newfoundland is, we are told, rapid and complete. We have not as yet any visible result of the achievement in the shape of news from New York, but the only cause of this delay is that Newfoundland is not yet in full communication with the American Continent. The short break now intervening will soon be bridged over, and New York and London will interchange salutations. . . .

If natural science ever furnished a theme for a poet, it is to be found in this achievement. It is calculated to impress the imagination in quite a different way from the ordinary triumphs of mechanical and scientific skill. The most celebrated works of modern engineering astonish us by their visible magnitude. There is something stupendous about their very appearance, and the mind is struck by the overwhelming display of power. Here, on the contrary, the wonder might be that so slight a thing should be pregnant with such results, and be of such vast importance. It would be wonderful to construct a vast ocean bridge; we are not sure it ought not to seem more wonderful to tie two Continents together by a string. It would suggest strange thoughts if we could view that slight rope lying insignificant and perhaps almost invisible in the vast depths of the Atlantic, motionless and apparently inanimate, and then reflect that by a still more tiny wire inside the life of the New and the Old World was pulsating to and fro. . . .

This influence of great mechanical or scientific discoveries upon human life is one of the commonplaces of history, but the theme has perhaps scarcely received justice. Such simple and accidental discoveries as the mariner's compass and gunpowder have transformed the character of human enterprise. . . . At the least, this great achievement cannot fail to lead to a great advance in the development of human dominion over nature. It may be expected to prove an important step in that work of "replenishing the earth and subduing it" which remains, as it has always been, the

Source: *London Times*, 30 July 1866, and "The Atlantic Cable," *New York Times*, 30 July 1866.

great task of mankind. It provides a new eye to commerce, and stretches out a new hand to assist mutual intercourse. It must diminish risks and tempt adventures. It will enlarge our conceptions, and embolden our undertakings. The link has been supplied, the spark has passed. Who shall guess the material transformations which it will be the means of producing?

But great as must be the material and commercial results of this achievement, still greater, probably, will be its moral and political effects. England and the United States, the Old and the New World, were but lately separated by a ten days' voyage on a stormy sea, which, if any other, well deserves to be called an "*oceanus dissociabilis*." They are now, for some of the most important purposes of intelligent intercourse, as closely connected as England and France. . . .

For a long time the nations of the civilized world seemed to grow up apart and independently, only occasionally coming into collision, and obtaining false or exaggerated ideas of each other. The nerves, so to say, of their mutual intercourse have been suddenly supplied, and a quick sympathy pervades the whole of Europe. Notwithstanding our policy of non-intervention, it cannot be doubted that the English people have felt this year a closer, a deeper, and a more genuine interest in great Continental events than at any former period. We cannot help it. When we know people intimately, and hear from day to day all about their doings, we cannot but feel a lively interest in them. This influence is likely to be still more marked in the present case. The two worlds have formerly been so widely separated. The one was new and the other old. Their political connexion has been gradually sundered; their histories have been quite apart; their ways of thought distinct. Perhaps, as was natural, we took more interest in them than they in us, as a father will be more interested in the rapid progress of his son than the son in the steady success of his father. But now, if all analogies be not misleading, every feeling of isolation must be dissipated on both sides. We cannot have such constant knowledge of each other without being always in each other's thoughts. The more we know the more we want to know, and the more we shall continually know. Such evidence of close connexion impresses the imagination. A veil seems torn or a mist dissipated. We not only hear from each other; we actually touch. America cannot fail to live more in Europe and Europe in America. Nor is the effect of this close communication only to be anticipated in a keener sympathy and a closer relation; it must be seen in a quickened and more energetic life. The more men are brought together, the keener does their life become, the more vigorous, rapid, and energetic are their thoughts. Like the difference between the city and the country, so is the difference between the world when split up into divided and separate communities and when united in one living and rapid organization. For the purposes of mutual intercourse the whole world is fast becoming one vast city. It was built on two sides of a deep river, but these are now united, and the city is one. Such are some of the prospects opened to us by this great victory over nature.

The New York Times, July 30, 1866

The electric chord which is to bind America and Europe by a myriad ties has been completed, and the two continents talk together, with but a few minutes to separate them. . . .

With yesterday, then, began a new era in the history of the world. Of its nature, its disturbing force, its reorganizing tendencies, we can yet only speculate. To the general public the visible result will be little more than an addition to the stock of news available for daily consumption. By-and-by they will accustom themselves to look for dispatches from St. Petersburg, Paris or London as regularly and with as little concern as now they devour scraps of intelligence from Cincinnati or New-Orleans. They will read of a Conference at Vienna within a few minutes of its termination, and will think no more of the occurrence than now they think of the transmission of the Associated Press report from Washington. They will glance at the day's market prices at Liverpool or Bremen, with as much of the matter-of-course feeling as now they scan the trade reports from Chicago or St. Louis. And they will feel almost as deeply interested in the morning's tidings of diplomacy at Paris, and Ministerial explanations in London, as now they are the passing history of President JOHNSON's Administration. The ramified agencies that are at work to concentrate intelligence from the Old World as from the New, will hardly be thought of; and the Atlantic Cable will be esteemed a familiar friend, the exact value of whose operations it were hardly necessary to compute. . . .

To none, however, is the cable fraught with so much significance as to the maker of newspapers. The merchant or the financier has but to take one bold step, look the revolution full in the face, and go on making money more rapidly than ever. The journalist may not so easily meet the case. His foreign news arrangements are upset; appliances on which he has relied for years are superseded, and a necessity arises for revising and reconstructing on nearly every hand. European mails will be little more than waste paper. The profound discussions of the Old World Press will pass unread; for long ere their receipt, the facts on which they rest will have been made known, and later facts will render distant opinions out of date. More labor, and that of a more educated kind, will be a necessity, and the value of the newspaper will more than keep pace with the enterprise, the expenditure and the ability which are already essential to its production.

7. Polish Immigrants Describe Opportunities in Brazil, 1891

São Paulo. 28 March 1891.

Dear Parents. We inform you about our health, that we are well, which health we wish for you also with our whole heart. Now with reference to our welfare, we are getting along fine, thank God. Now I inform you that I have not received a letter from you in a long time; only that one which was together with *Pan* Pomorski's and one other. I do not know why. Are you writing an incorrect address on the letter to us or have you completely forgotten about me? Julian's parents send him many letters, and from you there are none. Whenever a letter from the Gasiorowskis arrived, I rush there with desire. I think that there is a letter from you but there is none to be

Source: Josephine Wtulich, ed., *Writing Home: Immigrants in Brazil and the United States, 1890–1891* (New York: Columbia University Press, 1986), pp. 92–94, 96–99, 488–489.

seen almost never. So please, Dear parents, write me letters more frequently; do not begrudge the few *groszy* [you have to spend on] stamps because with that you will lift the great burden which I have in my heart. When I get a letter from you and I read it over, it appears to me that I have visited with you and I have spoken with all of you. So please do not forget me because I always remember about you, for you are always in my thoughts day and night, and do not worry about me. If I should return, may I find you as healthy as I left you. It is very unpleasant for us because we do not have a priest who can speak in Polish. All of them only speak in Portuguese and we do not yet speak it well [enough], so we cannot go to confession. Now I inform you that we celebrated carnival as I have never seen. The decorations in the streets in S. Paulo alone cost more than one hundred fifty thousand *milreis*. The city arranged for that. And when Lent came, no one fasted during the whole of Lent! They consider themselves to be Catholic and in their churches they have the same [services] as we do, but they do not keep the faith as strictly as we do in our religion. They hardly observe any holy days; only a few days—Christmas, Good Friday, Easter—they keep holy, and they observe every Sunday. And during Holy Week there is this kind of custom: on Holy Thursday they cast Jesus into a basement. On Good Friday they put Jesus in a tomb. At ten in the evening, the priests, with candles and [holy] picture, carry Jesus and a procession moves around the streets from church to church and those who follow the procession laugh, talk, some even whistle. They are not like us where each one of us walks in a dignified manner and prays. They do not prepare anything for the holiday, i.e. for the blessing of food. Nor do the priests bless any baskets [of food]. We fasted only three days a week during the holy season of Lent and some Poles even ate meat on Good Friday. True, Lenten food is more expensive [here] than meat is with us [in Poland], but the Poles have become very immoral in Brazil. Now I inform you that Fruscinski died, Witkoski's small children died, Wilhelm's children died, and many of our Poles died in the (_____) *Colonia*. Fruscinska is getting married to another man from the city of Łódz, a certain Urbanowski, a carpenter. We have nothing more to inform you about but we send a very low bow to you, dear parents, also to brother Francis as well as his wife, and we wish you success on your new farm and also health and prosperity, also to our sisters, to brother-in-law Ftorkowski and his whole family, we wish health and good luck.

Julian, Stanisława and Ladislaus Gasiorowski

We send a low bow to the Andrzejewskis, to *P(an)* Malewski, *P(an)* Przyborowski, to John and to all the acquaintances.

The address is the same as it was before.

São Matheus,

22 February 1891

Dearest Parents!

. . . The Brazilian government professes the Catholic faith and speaks the Portuguese language, which I have hopes of learning quickly. There are 3 thousand of us immigrants; we drew lots and I fell under the category of newly formed places. By our measurement I have 84 *morgs* of forest land. The trees are palm, oleander, mahogany, cedar, a type of Brazilian tea bush, all of which I am letting stand, and the rest I will cut down and burn. In a year I expect to have 4 *morgs* of cleared fields. What is grown here is corn, garden peas, potatoes, spring rye, grapes, and almost everything European is grown, because one can not find richer land or a more temperate climate than it is in one of these provinces albeit in May or June. . . . In Rio de Janeiro, a mason makes 8–10 *milreis*, that is, Russian rs. (*rubles*) because it is almost equal. I, in the meantime, before they begin to build the city, will cultivate a piece of land. The house will be built by the government. They will get a priest [from abroad] for us for dispensing [the sacraments of] baptism and marriage on 10 March. Brazil is such a large country that all the Poles could fit into it and there would still be space left over. At the same time, it is a country flowing with milk and honey, of unusual freedom, so you, thief and murderer, it is better that you rot in a Russian jail than look to Brazil. It is sweet-smelling the whole year. Regarding birds, there are cock pheasants, wild chickens, doves, guinea-hens and 50 different kinds of other birds, which I do not know. Brazil does not have any birds of prey. I have enough land, may God grant me health.

Dear Parents! If you get this letter, answer me at once and tell me what new things the Muscovites are doing to our religion. In general, tell me what is happening in the old country; and at the same time, send me a parental blessing, if I have earned it, though perhaps I may not live to see it. I am going to get married with one *Panna* Rosalia Rydlewska, age 18, from the province of Płock.

Joseph Jaczyński

P.S. If the Muscovite allows this letter to pass through to you and back, then in the next letter, I will write you my plan; but I await your reply impatiently. J.J.

Plymouth [PA.] 4 February 1891.

With the very first words of my letter, Praised be Jesus Christ!

Dear *Szwagier*, I am well, thank God Almighty, which I wish from my whole heart for my *szwagier*. Dear *szwagier*, I received your letter on 20 January, which I am answering at once. You write me here that I should tell you in a letter where it is better, in America or in Brazil. I know how it is in America. In America if only one will work, then in a short time he will be able to earn a few cents; but I have not been in Brazil, so I do not know how it is there. When I was in America the first time, and then when I returned to the old country, some people were going back [to Poland] from Brazil. I heard from a man who was traveling and who was in Brazil to visit his children that in Brazil there is no work and there is poverty. He said that he even cried and cursed his children for bringing him there because they did not have anything to eat themselves. When that father was leaving, they would all have left as well, but the children could not return because they did not have the money. As the father had his own family in America who had some money in America, he wrote to them and they sent him the money for the trip and brought him back to them from Brazil. When they brought him over, they had a few dollars and were going back to the old country, so the children took the father back with them to the old country. So dear *Szwagier*, I do not know anything else about Brazil because I was never there, except what I heard the old man say. Tears came to my eyes when I heard how they treat people in Brazil. In Brazil they take you there at their expense, but as for return passage, it is only if someone has his own money; but if not, then he must remain high and dry in Brazil.

8. Jewish Immigrants Celebrate Independence Day in Argentina, 1910

During their first years in the colonies of Entre Ríos, the Jews knew very little about the new homeland. Their conception of the Argentine people and customs was a confused one. They admired the Gaucho, and feared him, and they conceived of his life as a thrilling amalgam of heroism and barbarism. They had misinterpreted most of the gaucho tales of blood and bravery and, as a result, had formed a unique conception of their Argentine countryman. To the Jews of Poland and Bessarabia, the Gaucho seemed a romantic bandit, as fierce and gallant as any hero of a Schummer novel. The factory girls in Odessa had avidly read Schummer after their hard day's work. Now, the farm girls in Entre Ríos did the same thing.

In the synagogue—constituted by one or another ranchhouse in Rajíl—the old and young men discussed their ideas about Argentina. The enthusiasm they felt for the free life here—something they'd dreamed about during the dark days in Russia—had not softened a bit. All felt a fervent love for this country, however new and unknown it seemed. The hope they felt was as fresh as the new black earth their plows turned; the new hope and the new earth made their own selves feel new, their bodies young.

On Saturdays, until midday and after, the men would stand at the door of the synagogue—not far from the corral in this instance—and recall their sufferings and exodus, as if the immigration from Imperial Russia had been the historic Exodus of the Bible. . . .

On another afternoon, a neighbor brought news of a coming festival in Villaguay. He told of the arches and flags and banners being erected in the streets of the municipality. This news was commented on everywhere and another colonist proposed that they find out the reason for the festival.

The colonists did not know a word of Spanish. The young men had quickly taken up the dress and some of the manners of the Gauchos, but they could manage only the most basic Spanish phrases in their talk with the natives. It was decided, nevertheless, that their Gaucho herdsmen, Don Gabino, a comrade of the great Crispín Velázquez and a veteran of the Paraguayan War, should be consulted about the matter. Don Gabino thought that the preparations might be for some local fiesta, or might be for a coming election, perhaps. This idea seems very logical at first, but it was later rejected. Finally, it was the Commissary for the colonies, Don Benito Palas, who cleared up the matter of the preparations for the Jews and explained to the Shochet, in eloquent yet simple form, the full significance of May 25th, Argentina's Independence Day.

The idea continued to interest the colonists of Rajíl, and in the nightly conversations and rest periods of the day they talked about the date. Each one had his own idea about the significance of what had happened on May 25th, but all felt its genuine importance. Finally, it was suggested that the colony celebrate the great anniversary.

It was Israel Kelner who first offered the idea. Israel had once gone to Jerusalem to organize the immigration sponsored by Baron Rothschild. An eminent Hebraist who had been publicly praised by the Shochets of Rajíl and Karmel, Kelner enjoyed great prestige in the colonies, and often delivered the principal address at ceremonies held in the colony. Now, he took a trip to Las Moscas and learned from Don Estanislao Benítez all the necessary details about the 25th of May.

The commemoration of the day was decided upon, and the Mayor and Shochet were designated as organizers for the festival. Jacobo, the Shochet's helper, who was the most acclimated of all the young men, put on his best pair of gaucho pantaloons and rode from house to house on his smart little pony to announce the holding of an assembly that very night in the synagogue.

At the meeting, the details of the celebration were discussed and it was decided first not to work on the holiday, of course, to bedeck the doorways of the houses with flags, and to hold a big meeting in the clearing, at which Reb Kelner would deliver an appropriate speech. It was decided, furthermore, to invite the Commissary to the festival as well as the Administrator of the colonies, Herr Bergmann, a harsh and unsocial German who had little feeling about the occasion to be commemorated.

During the preparations, a further difficulty arose. It was discovered that no one knew the colors of the Argentine flag. It was too late to do anything about it now, and so the preparations had to go on. Finally, the great day came.

The dawn found Rajíl bedecked like a ship: the doorways were covered with flags and banners of all colors. The Argentine colors were there, too, though the colonists did not realize it. A mild sun shone bright but not too warm as it lit up the flat countryside and bathed the yellowed shrubs and the white walls of the huts with its new warmth. The Commissary sent his little band, and they swept into the music of the National Anthem as soon as they arrived at the colony. The hearts of the Jews filled with joy at the sound and, though they were still confused about what this date meant, the thought of this patriotic festival they were celebrating in their new homeland filled their spirits with a new happiness.

The service in the synagogue was attended by all the men and women. Their Jerusalem tunics shone white and resplendent in the sunlit room as they listened to the Rabbi bless the Republic in the solemn prayer of *Mischa-beraj*, a special prayer in praise of the Republic.

After the reading from the Sacred Book, the Mayor spoke. He was a less learned man than the Rabbi, but he knew how to keep people enthralled. He used many gestures of the synagogue preachers, and he would often tear at his chestnut-colored beard.

"I remember," he said, "that in the city of Kishinev, after that most terrible of pogroms, we closed our synagogues. We did not want to have to bless the Czar. Here, in our new country, nobody forces us to bless anyone. That's why we bless the Republic! That's why we bless the President!" Nobody knew who the President was, but that didn't seem to matter.

Immediately after the Mayor's speech, the people left the synagogue and gathered in the clearing. The wild flowers of this season shone brilliantly on an improvised arbor near which the band stood and played the Anthem, lustily and continually. The young men of the colony were showing off their horses, and the native boys from the breakwater district stood in a group, watching silently, but keeping themselves well supplied from the trays of sweets and pastries. The demijohn of wine waited on the arrival of the Commissary for its opening.

It was growing late when Don Benoit Palas appeared with his escort, carrying the Argentine flag. The ceremony began. The Commissary drank his cup of wine and Reb Israel Kelner stood on the dais to speak. In the simple Yiddish of the people, and in the name of this colony, he saluted this country "in which there are no murders of the Jews," and illustrated his feelings with the parable of the two birds—a story that his neighbors had heard on many occasions.

"There was once a bird imprisoned in a cage of iron. He believed that all birds lived as he did, until a certain day when he saw another bird flying freely through space and flitting from tree to rooftop and back again. The imprisoned bird grew very sad; he rarely sang. He thought so much about his imprisonment that he finally got the idea of breaking out and picked at the bars of his cage until he was free."

Jacobo explained the story to Don Benito, who, being a native, could make little of the involved discourse. In his answer to Reb Kelner, Don Benito recited the stanzas of the Anthem.

The Jews could not understand their meaning, but they recognized the word "liberty," *libertad*, and remembering their history of slavery, the persecutions suffered by their brothers and themselves, they felt their hearts beat faster at the word. *Libertad*! It was here. It was theirs. Speaking from their souls, with their truest feelings, they answered the word with one voice. As they did in the synagogue, now they exclaimed together: "Amen!"

△ E S S A Y S

These essays probe the meaning of freedom for transatlantic migrants in the wake of emancipation, when Atlantic societies struggled to determine what kinds of rights and opportunities should be available to which citizens and subjects. David Northrup and Monica Schuler investigate the continued movement of laborers from Africa to the sugar plantations of the Caribbean, a flow of people that was certainly dwarfed by the migration of Europeans in the same period but whose characteristics strike at the heart of the challenges of securing laborers to perform difficult, poorly compensated work. To slake their thirst for cheap labor, sugar planters recruited workers from China and India, but they also sought to continue labor migration from Africa. Northrup suggests that we need a complex and nuanced understanding of slavery and freedom along a continuum of conditions. In this essay, he explores what Africans who were recruited to labor in the French Caribbean might have thought of their status and opportunities. Rejecting the position of many historians that contract labor was a form of slavery, Northrup insists that we consider what "free" labor meant in Africa, and not simply through the lens of those European or Euro-American writers and observers who came to condemn the entire system of indenture by the end of the nineteenth century as a cruel form of unfree labor. His essay forces us to confront the problem of perspective: whose do we adopt when we consider the meaning and value of freedom? Schuler explores efforts by British West Indian officials to recruit people from Sierra Leone to work in Jamaica. Some 8,000 West and Central Africans went to Jamaica as "free" laborers in the nineteenth century. They were "recaptives"—men, women, and children liberated from slave ships and dropped in Sierra Leone for resettlement or recruitment for new labor schemes. Schuler's view of their recruitment to Jamaica is a dismal one: she finds the children and adults targeted by Jamaican recruiters in the 1840s to have been duped into service overseas, and she identifies the years between 1843 and 1846 as an era of transition from a voluntary to an involuntary labor migration.

Freedom and Consent in the Recruitment of African Labor

DAVID NORTHRUP

As the campaigns to abolish slave trading and slavery achieved their goals in the Caribbean, two questions needed to be answered if plantation colonies were to continue prospering. Where could sufficient free labor be found to meet current and future needs? And what would "free" mean in this new context? . . .

In order to replace these lost laborers and to provide sufficient hands for expansion, the colonies needed to resume some form of large-scale labor recruitment from overseas. A portion of the new laborers were recruited in Africa, a few from China; but most came from South Asia. Nearly all were recruited under contracts of indenture that bound them to work (for wages) for a period of years in return for their passage from overseas.

Arising in the shadow of the old slave trade, these new migrations have long raised troubling issues about freedom. Nineteenth-century opponents of slavery agonized and argued over what conditions of recruitment, transport, and employment would make these new indentured labor migrations a clear alternative to the old slave trade. . . .

In examining the new indentured migrations of the nineteenth century, . . . one needs to pay attention to freedom's multiple meanings and the changing particular conditions that made labor acceptably "free." In addition to the recorded positions of western officials, one also needs to consider the perspectives of the laborers, however poorly articulated at the time. . . .

After the end of slavery in 1848, French planters considered additional Africans the obvious answer to the problem of replenishing the plantation labor force. New African recruits could be absorbed into the existing creole population that slave trade had created. However, the French had to resolve two issues involving freedom if supplies of African laborers were to be found. The first was the fact that free (that is, wage) labor was largely an alien concept in mid-nineteenth-century Africa. The second was to find a way to distinguish clearly their recruitment of Africans from the slave trade that the French government had finally ended in 1831 and had agreed not to resume under a convention signed with Britain in 1845.

As Igor Kopytoff and Suzanne Miers, the editors of the groundbreaking study *Slavery in Africa*, point out, "In most African societies, 'freedom' lay not in withdrawal into a meaningless and dangerous autonomy but in attachment to a kin group, to a patron, to power." Thus most African individuals were not "free" to sell their labor in the Western sense because they "belonged" to a kinship-based community. Even if persons wished to leave, their kinsfolk or rulers were unlikely to feel their contributions could be dispensed with. Indeed, most coastal communities in the mid-nineteenth century found themselves short of the labor needed to supply rising overseas exports. To supplement their workforce, many purchased slaves, whose cost had fallen as the transatlantic demand ended. . . .

In 1856, when the 1845 anti-slave trading convention with Britain expired, French authorities felt free to change their methods to include the redemption of slaves in Africa (*rachat préalable*), so as to supply the pressing labor needs of their larger West Indian colonies of Guadeloupe and Martinique. Under government contract, French captains purchased slaves from local African authorities, declared them free, and signed them to indentured labor contracts. This method of recruitment yielded many more migrants for the French Caribbean colonies—by 1862 nearly 20,000. To distinguish it from slave trading, every contract contained a clause giving potential recruits the right to refuse to sign the contract if they preferred to stay in Africa. Conditions of transport were precisely regulated with regard to provisioning, hygiene, medicines. . . .

The status of the recruits as legally free persons was the primary issue for both the French and the British, even if officials disagreed over how to view the freedom of Africans newly emancipated from slavery. Most of the ambiguities resided in the unsettled nature of international standards, a problem with which the British abolitionist efforts had been wrestling for most of the century. . . . From 1819, most African "recaptives" were emancipated by new international tribunals, known as Courts of Mixed Commission, made up of a British representative and a commissioner from the nation that had authorized the British navy to stop and search ships flying its flag that were suspected of dealing in slaves.

Although the French procedures for emancipation lacked the sanction of another European power, as the Minister of Foreign Affairs indicated, they did have the approval of French legal experts. Moreover, purchasing the freedom of individual slaves had a long legal pedigree. French authorities in Senegal had been using such methods to recruit labor for colonial forces in prior decades. . . .

To be sure, the ransomed slaves had little, if any, freedom of choice once they were emancipated by the French, but this too was not unusual by the standards of the day. Both British and French authorities had been redeeming slaves in Africa for military conscription and apprenticeship since early in the century. Nor was much freedom of choice offered to most Africans whom the British liberated from Atlantic slaving vessels. From 1844, British authorities in Sierra Leone refused to release newly liberated Africans from the liberation depot until they had exposed them to a hard-sell recruitment campaign for the British West Indies. No alternative to indentured emigration existed for the substantial numbers of Africans liberated on the island of St. Helena, which lacked the resources to support more than a small resident population. Thus, in offering freshly ransomed Africans no alternative to an indentured contract that would pay off the bond, French procedures departed little, if at all, from accepted British procedures. . . .

Moreover, the French handling of the African recruits after redemption gained favorable comment once the system was well established. Although a British naval officer reported that in July 1858 recruits freed by the French near the Congo River were kept in irons to prevent their escape and were guarded "in the same manner as slaves," two years later another British naval officer had no criticism of the "well-conducted" French depot at the port of Loango and, in a private journal, an American officer described recruits shipped from that depot on the *Splendid* as "well fed and contented" and "in every respect . . . better situated and cared for than the majority of passengers in emigrant ships from Europe to the United States." These remarks support the view that, despite some early problems of implementation, French treatment of Africans bound for their Caribbean colonies was far removed from the horrors of the Atlantic slave trade. . . .

It is more difficult to challenge the British charge that French recruitment promoted the slave trade within Africa. Rather than liberating "surplus" slave populations, it seems clear that French actions encouraged African slavers to bring new captives to the coast for sale. One outraged British officer in 1858 declared that it was common to see Africans dragging their slaves to the Congo coast for sale to the French depot "in twos and threes, . . . secured by ropes to the forked end of a wooden pole encircling their necks, their hands strongly bound, . . . while a third negro hastens their movements by the lash." This fact is confirmed by the testimony of African rulers who were active (or would-be) participants in French recruitment. Under close questioning by British officers, Thomas Cole, the African ruler of Manna Rock on the Liberian coast, conceded that he supplied recruits to the French exactly as he had once delivered slaves. Indeed, it later turned out, one of those Cole sold to a French recruiter was an apprentice stolen from the household of the Liberian Attorney General.

African rulers usually found it hard to sell abroad their domestic slaves (or participate in European redemption schemes that would take them away) because such established servile populations had acquired partial rights in their masters' communities. Kosoko, a ruler who had set himself up farther west on the Slave Coast after the British exiled him from Lagos for persistent slave trading, was dissuaded from selling his servile dependants to French recruiters in 1859, less because of the treaty he had signed with the British agreeing to stop selling slaves abroad, than because of the argument of his advisors that his own slaves, "having for a few years past enjoyed a great amount of personal liberty, and having had, many of them the privilege of trading for themselves, would immediately desert when they perceived he was selling them."

Additional testimony comes from an Old Calabar chief who had initially agreed to sell slaves for redemption to an abortive *British* effort to recruit West African labor in 1850. King Eyo Honesty II told a missionary: "It be all same as old slave-trade. I no have too many man for myself; I must send and buy people for them in all countries, and must charge them full price, for them man when he go away no will for come back." Though King Eyo did not say so, another reason for his not wishing to sell his own people was that Old Calabar's extensive slave population had also acquired a sense of belonging, as shown in the fact that slaves in another ward of the town arose in rebellion the next year in defense of their rights.

With most of the "free" population in coastal Africa ill disposed to give up their membership in communal societies and many of the supposedly "unfree" likely to rebel if they were sold away, Africa was a frustrating place in which to recruit. However, it should not be assumed that all those whom Europeans redeemed from slavery were displeased at the prospect or devoid of their own perspectives on freedom. From the perspective of newly ransomed Africans, the key issue was not whether they had been freed in strict accordance to law nor whether they had the right to choose among different post-emancipation fates, but whether they saw in this act a step toward greater liberation and assented to it. The evidence for assessing their states of mind is limited. Both powers generated a paper trail of signed contracts, but neither British nor French recruitment of Africans was free of coercion and deception. African recruits have left no direct testimony about their willingness to emigrate, but there is circumstantial evidence that acquiescence was general in the case of both British and French recruitment of newly liberated Africans, namely, that it was normally unnecessary to employ the constraints long practiced on slave ships to prevent rebellions.

The French recruitment record contains some exceptions to this rule. A small number of disgruntled recruits deserted in Africa before captains learned to confine "troublemakers" below deck. The one spectacular case of general discontent, the 1858 rebellion on the French vessel *Regina Coeli* off Liberia, occurred under unusual circumstances. The captain was not licensed by the French government to recruit laborers, the West African recruits were intended for service in distant Réunion, and the recruits were drawn largely from domestic slaves. The last point seems the most crucial in explaining why, after coming on board, the recruits rebelled, killing many French crew, and then escaped to the capital city Monrovia. It was not the conditions on the ship (nor perhaps the distant destination of the voyage) that drove them to rebel, but their perception that the French recruiter and their masters had conspired to sell them away from their homeland without their consent. The French suffered the effects of this action, but the rebels were equally angry at their African masters for this violation of their rights. Indeed, some expressed the wish that they had staged the revolt earlier, when their masters had been on board, so that they might have killed them too. By fleeing to Monrovia, the rebels sought to remain free of the control of their African masters.

While the *Regina Coeli* rebellion reveals the complex perspectives of recruits in an extreme case, other evidence suggests that the more usual attitude of ransomed Africans was to accept the promise of something better in the French Caribbean as an improvement on their status as newly acquired slaves in Africa. The British Consul in Martinique, who investigated the shipment of 370 Africans to French Guiana on the *Orion* in 1857, was not about to accept the word of any French official on how freely the men and women had consented to emigrate and so put the question to that vessel's African interpreter. The interpreter assured him that the African recruits were glad (indeed, very glad) for an opportunity to gain release from the ill treatment of the African chiefs who owned them, not caring what was to come. In support of his claim that this migration was voluntary, the interpreter cited the fact that there had been no attempts at revolts on this ship as would have been the case on a slave ship. The comment of another British official that the recruits on one of the last French vessels from Africa appeared "cheerful," also supports this interpretation.

The evidence just cited about African perspectives on recruitment is too limited to be conclusive, but it reinforces the view that drawing a sharp distinction between "free" and "unfree" migrations may obscure more than it reveals. Participants in these recruitment ventures interpreted the meaning of freedom according to their own self-interest without attempting to resolve all the inherent ambiguities. . . .

The fundamental point is that most indentured migrants freely consented to their servitude. Their consent does not excuse the shortcomings and the mistreatment they had to endure, but it does not make their experiences fundamentally different from those of slaves. From the migrants' perspective, migration offered an escape from the harshness of life and the many constraints on freedom in their homelands. For the Africans whom the French and the British liberated from slavery, signing an indentured labor contract may have been the only viable option, but it was one they assented to. . . .

How well did African and Indian immigrants to the French Caribbean fare? By today's standards their contracts were unconscionably long, their work hard, the risks to life and limb excessive, and their masters' powers of coercion draconian. No doubt, like many of the unindentured immigrants of their day, they were disappointed with their new lots. But, while indentured laborers' freedom was limited, it was not meaningless. Those who survived might accumulate modest savings from their hard-earned wages. They could make meaningful decisions to renew contracts, change employers, and be repatriated.

What did their choices gain them? There are many imponderables in the outcomes and the personal perspectives of the immigrants themselves are always muted. For many Africans overseas indenture was a phase on the road from enslavement to legal freedom. For all who survived, choices to stay or to return were constrained by personal, practical, and political circumstances, but the mere fact that such choices existed needs to be given careful consideration if the perspectives of immigrants are to be appreciated.

Deception and Coercion in the Recruitment of African Labor

MONICA SCHULER

The Jamaica agent, dismayed to find Sierra Leonians unresponsive to recruiting efforts for the *Glen Huntley* early in 1843, turned instead to the liberated African schools. Trinidad and two British Guianese provinces, Demerara and Berbice, followed suit, and thus began the first steps toward involuntary emigration which culminated in the forced transportation of recaptives.

The Sierra Leone government regarded the schools as a partial solution to the problem of what to do with orphans landed from slave ships. Such children under the age of thirteen, and after 1844 under the age of twelve, were entitled to from one to four years of education at institutions separate from those attended by Creole children born in the colony of liberated African parents. Children from nine to thirteen could, in 1841, be apprenticed to "respectable" families in whose service they might learn a trade or, in the case of girls, where they could be protected until they married. In 1844 the British government ordered that all children over twelve be given a choice of enlistment, emigration, or self-support in Sierra Leone, but Governor Fergusson retained the apprenticeship system as a substitute for these callous alternatives. Schools thus became way stations where children too young to be

Source: From Monica Schuler, "Alas, Alas, Kongo": *A Social History of Indentured African Immigration into Jamaica, 1841–1865*, pp. 23–26. Copyright © 1980 The Johns Hopkins University Press. Reprinted with permission of The Johns Hopkins University Press.

apprenticed could be housed and initiated into "regular habits" preparatory to service in liberated African, Maroon, settler, or European households.

No wonder emigration recruiters eagerly sought liberated African school-children. W. G. Terry, an official who had at first opposed child emigration, accurately summed up the British view of the schools when in 1844 he expressed the hope that the future would bring "a never-ceasing flow of young emigrants from these wholesome nurseries of labourers, and the great advantage of these school-farms can then be justly appreciated." Few bothered to ask whether children deemed too young for apprenticeship might not also be too young to emigrate.

The encouragement of child emigration by British authorities was not unique to Sierra Leone, for the British government permitted the transportation of British orphans to Cape Colony and Canada in the nineteenth century. It was dishonest, however, for officials to pretend that such a migration could ever be the result of choices freely made. Before his conversion to child emigration W. G. Terry understood this and drew Governor George Macdonald's attention to "the impropriety of Mr. Cathcart's conduct in endeavouring to persuade children under fourteen years of age [to emigrate] . . . who are perfectly incapable of judging what is good for themselves. . . ." Terry grasped that, given the strict regimen of liberated African schools, "the very irksomeness of their situation and the natural dislike children have to the trouble of learning, would induce them one and all to volunteer to leave the schools (their present great imaginary evil) to encounter any change regardless of future result whether good or evil." He bluntly characterized this kind of recruitment as "seduction."

Recruiters, usually the emigration agents themselves, had to apply for government authorization each time they visited the schools, and liberated African managers and schoolteachers were expected to cooperate fully with them. Although encountering some initial opposition, Cathcart eventually secured the help of John Thorpe, a Maroon schoolteacher, who agreed to emigrate to Jamaica with "several of the children." Thorpe's defection, really quite a coup, may have been responsible for Jamaica's acquisition in early 1843 of eighty-five boys, more than twice as many child emigrants as Trinidad and British Guiana together received at the outset of juvenile emigration. . . .

Cathcart's constant appeals for boy delegates suggests that recruitment in the schools did not run as smoothly as expected. At Kent school, for instance, an initially enthusiastic response from the children dried up rather quickly. One student reported that a schoolmaster had advised the boys "not to go to that bad place," and so the teachers came under scrutiny. In January 1845, while still agent general for Jamaica, Terry accused all liberated African schoolteachers and even one district manager of obstruction. Terry singled out John Thorpe, lately returned to Gloucester school from Jamaica, as having "actively engaged himself in preventing the school boys under his care from emigrating, by advice, by threats, and by actual punishment," and he accused the Mountain District manager of "harsh treatment of an intending emigrant." The governor appointed a board of enquiry to investigate Terry's charges and all irregularities connected with emigration, including a Kent boatman's countercharge that Terry's boatmen had tied up two boys who refused to emigrate. The board's findings are unknown, but Thorpe, Terry, and the Mountain District manager all retained their positions. The investigation does not appear to have bothered Thorpe, who continued to obstruct, if not actually dissuade, students from emigrating.

The quarrel over emigration from the schools became rather academic by 1845, because recruiters turned to the Liberated African Yard for emigrants and, consequently, fewer children reached the schools. Only one instance of schoolchild emigration occurred after 1845 when, because few Africans remained in the Liberated African Yard, fifty-eight students sailed on the *Conservative* to St. Kitts in April 1849.

By 1844 forced emigration of recently arrived recaptives from the Queen's Yard was an idea whose time had obviously come. In February the colonial secretary issued instructions to the Sierra Leone governor to offer recaptives the choice of emigrating to the West Indies or remaining in Sierra Leone without government assistance. An older option that had always existed for men—enlistment in the West India Regiments—remained. In reality the new dispensation meant, "emigrate, enlist, or fend for yourself." The instructions made no exceptions for children.

Newly liberated Africans had never before exhibited any interest in emigrating to the West Indies and were prone to flee to the bush when emigration recruiters approached their villages. Recruiting among the newcomers in the Queen's Yard, therefore, was not simply a matter of inviting people to travel to the West Indies; it called instead for subterfuge, duplicity and, if necessary, force. It became standard practice to isolate new arrivals from all except West India Regiment and plantation recruiters, and recaptives could be detained in the Queen's Yard for one to three months awaiting the arrival of an emigrant ship.

Despite these precautions, during the first year of forced emigration more than 50 percent of the recaptives chose to settle in Sierra Leone or enlist in the army rather than leave Africa to labor in the West Indies. . . .

Taking into account the facts that the Liberated African Department staff could sometimes be bribed to encourage emigration and that West India Regiment and emigration officials sometimes conspired to divide recaptives in order to obtain recruits, the recaptives' resistance appears all the more remarkable. In 1848, for instance, Yoruba from the slaver *Bella Miquilina* were subjected to a variety of pressures when they refused to emigrate to Jamaica. First, officials brought in John Macaulay, leader of the Sierra Leone Yoruba community, to persuade the recaptives to emigrate, but the majority resisted and formed what appeared to be combat groups. At this point the acting governor arranged a deal between the military and labor recruiters: in exchange for the use of a Jamaican emigrant transport to carry soldiers to Jamaica, the Regiment would enlist the most militant recaptives, thereby offering a second Jamaican ship the chance to recruit the rest. Fifty-five of the leaders enlisted—a choice often made in the hope of remaining together in Africa, but in this case they were headed for military service in Jamaica. The rest still did not stampede to volunteer for the plantations, and the ship's captain had to bribe the staff at the depot to get his emigrants.

Enclosure in the hold of a slave vessel pursued at sea by the British navy was such a harrowing ordeal that it is hardly surprising that those Africans who survived did not wish to sail again under European auspices. There were other reasons as well. Attachment to African was one. For another, both African sailors on the naval vessels and African employees of the Liberated African Yard warned recaptives not to go to the West Indies; there, they said, the newcomers "would get hardly paid and . . . the country was altogether bad."

◢ F U R T H E R   R E A D I N G

Baily, Samuel L. *Immigrants in the Lands of Promise: Italians in Buenos Aires and New York City, 1870–1914.* Ithaca, NY: Cornell University Press, 1999.

Blyden, Nemata Amelia. *West Indians in West Africa, 1808–1880: The African Diaspora in Reverse.* Rochester, NY: University of Rochester Press, 2000.

Clegg, Claude Andrew. *The Price of Liberty: African Americans and the Making of Liberia.* Chapel Hill: University of North Carolina Press, 2004.

Dixon, Chris. *African America and Haiti: Emigration and Black Nationalism in the Nineteenth Century.* Westport, CT: Greenwood Press, 2000.

Eltis, David, ed. *Coerced and Free Migration: Global Perspectives.* Stanford, CA: Stanford University Press, 2002.

Emmer, P. C. *Colonialism and Migration: Indentured Labour Before and After Slavery.* Dordrecht, Netherlands: Martinus Nijhoff Publishers, 1986.

Hoefte, Rosemarijn. *In Place of Slavery: A Social History of British Indian and Javanese Laborers in Suriname.* Gainesville: University Press of Florida, 1998.

Hoerder, Dirk. *Cultures in Contact: World Migrations in the Second Millennium.* Durham, NC: Duke University Press, 2002.

———. ed. *Labor Migration in the Atlantic Economies: The European and North American Working Classes During the Period of Industrialization.* Westport, CT: Greenwood Press, 1985.

Holt, Thomas. *The Problem of Freedom: Race, Labor, and Politics in Jamaica and Britain, 1832–1939.* Baltimore: The Johns Hopkins University Press, 1992.

Kale, Madhavi. *Fragments of Empire: Capital, Slavery, and Indian Indentured Labor Migration to the British Caribbean.* Philadelphia: University of Pennsylvania Press, 1998.

Lai, Walter Look. *Indentured Labor, Caribbean Sugar: Chinese and Indian Migrants to the British West Indies, 1838–1918.* Baltimore: The Johns Hopkins University Press, 1993.

Mann, Kristin, and Edna G. Bay. *Rethinking the African Diaspora: The Making of a Black Atlantic World in the Bight of Benin and Brazil.* London: Frank Cass, 2001.

Miller, Floyd J. *The Search for a Black Nationality: Black Emigration and Colonization, 1787–1863.* Urbana: University of Illinois Press, 1975.

Moya, Jose C. *Cousins and Strangers: Spanish Immigrants in Buenos Aires, 1850–1930.* Berkeley: University of California Press, 1998.

Northrup, David. *Indentured Labor in the Age of Imperialism, 1834–1922.* New York: Cambridge University Press, 1995.

Nugent, Walter T. K. *Crossings: The Great Transatlantic Migrations, 1870–1914.* Bloomington: Indiana University Press, 1992.

Schuler, Monica. *"Alas, Alas, Kongo": A Social History of Indentured African Immigration into Jamaica, 1841–1865.* Baltimore: The Johns Hopkins University Press, 1980.

Vecoli, Rudolph J., and Suzanne M. Sinke, eds. *A Century of European Migrations, 1830–1930.* Urbana and Chicago: University of Illinois Press, 1991.

CHAPTER
15

Legacies

Today we grapple with the legacies of Atlantic history. The themes of explora-
tion, encounter, revolution, and migration resonate into our own time. "Atlantic
studies" gains traction among scholars. Atlantic history inspires novelists and
filmmakers. Museum curators display artifacts from around the Atlantic world.
Genealogists trace American family trees back to Europe and, increasingly, Africa.
Monuments of Atlantic history become tourist attractions. Yet the urge to remember
and commemorate can be unsettling because the past contains traumatic elements
that many would prefer to forget or suppress. The question, "How should we think
about the past?" quickly turns into the question, "How should we think about each
other?" This volume concludes with documents and essays pertaining to two con-
troversies that reveal some of the difficult moral questions provoked by Atlantic
history. The first controversy involves the public memory of Christopher Columbus,
whose transatlantic voyages first joined Europe and Africa to the Americas. Should
Columbus be regarded as a hero for his daring feats of navigation, or as a villain for
inaugurating the downfall of native people, or as neither? A second controversy
involves the haunting issue of slavery. A growing chorus of activists contends that
society owes compensation to the descendants of enslaved people for the suffering
of their ancestors. Opponents of reparations deny that today's generations should
be required to atone for yesterday's sins. Which side are you on? These controversies
reveal the politically charged ways that Atlantic history is remembered, represented,
and used in contemporary life. As William Faulkner once wrote, "The past is never
dead. It's not even past."

DOCUMENTS

These documents focus on two legacies of Atlantic history. They explore the changing
understanding of Columbus's voyage in 1492 and the consequences of that voyage for
the indigenous people of the Americas, and they consider the impact of slavery on
Africa and on people of African descent around the world.

Nations on both sides of the Atlantic celebrated the four hundredth anniversary
of Columbus's voyage in 1892. The Columbian Historical Exposition at Madrid show-
cased the cultures of Europe and the Americas at the time of contact, while the World's

Columbian Exposition in Chicago celebrated "American progress" and exhibited living Indians. Document 1 contains excerpts from the U.S. government report on the Madrid exposition and from the Official Guide to the Columbian Exposition in Chicago. One hundred years later, the Columbian quincentennial inspired considerably greater dissent, as Document 4 indicates. The 1990 Declaration of Quito, issued by Indian delegates from 120 different Indian groups and 20 different countries, asserted a common Indian identity and demanded legal, cultural, religious, and economic autonomy.

Today indigenous Americans live in many different legal jurisdictions, where they enjoy greater or lesser recognition of their rights. Canada has been a leader in the recognition of aboriginal rights. Document 3, the "Rights of the Aboriginal People of Canada," which comes from the 1982 Canadian Constitution Act, has been an important source of legal authority for First Nations activists. Yet legal recognition has not brought economic equality and self-sufficiency. Cree political activist Matthew Coon Come achieved international recognition in his struggle against Quebec's massive hydroelectric plant at James Bay, which claimed land long used by the Cree nation for traditional subsistence activities and held by them under treaties. In 2001, he received an honorary Doctor of Laws degree from the University of Toronto, and in his address, excerpted in Document 7, he links the modern legal and economic challenges confronting Canada's indigenous people to the historical and on-going impact of conquest and betrayal.

Documents 5, 6, 8, and 9 explore the legacy of the slave trade. Document 5 contains the proclamation of a gathering of representatives from around the African diaspora in Abuja, Nigeria, in 1993. The delegates argue that the slave trade harmed Africa, and those outside of Africa who benefited from it should pay reparations. In March 1996 the British House of Lords debated the question of reparations for Britain's role in the slave trade, a discussion excerpted in Document 6. Great Britain had been the leading slave-trading nation in the eighteenth century and then led the fight against the transatlantic slave trade in the nineteenth century.

Document 8 puts a human face on these discussions about the legacies of slavery, the slave trade, and the racism that accompanied it. In 1810, a Khoisan woman called Sarah Baartmann left Cape Town for Europe with an English surgeon eager to display her body's enlarged buttocks. Exhibited naked in a cage (for an extra fee, viewers could touch her body), Baartmann rejected the efforts of abolitionists to end her display, explaining that she shared in the profits of her performance. She was sold to a French entrepreneur and died in France in 1815. After her death, her body was dismembered, her genitalia cast in wax and deployed as "evidence" by European scientists of the sexual appetite of African women. Baartmann's body was on display in Paris until the 1970s. In 2002, Baartmann's remains were repatriated to South Africa, and the nation's president, Thabo Mbeki, delivered her eulogy, excerpted in Document 8.

United States President George Bush has also publicly recognized the history of slavery. In July 2003, Bush visited Gorée Island in Senegal, the site of a notorious if minor West African slave depot, which is now a UNESCO World Heritage site and tourist attraction. In his speech, included as Document 9, President Bush spoke eloquently about the horrors of slavery and the efforts of African Americans to win freedom and equality in the United States, and he expressed support for Africans' ongoing struggle for political freedom and economic prosperity, but he did not offer a formal apology for slavery. Gorée itself has become a controversial place in the politics of remembering the slave trade. Historians charge that the island's promoters have exaggerated its importance to attract tourists, while others defend Gorée as a valuable contemporary site for the commemoration of a historical atrocity.

1. Spain and the United States Celebrate Columbus, 1892–1893

The Columbian Historical Exposition, Madrid

The Spanish Government, in pursuance of a royal decree under date of January 9, 1891, provided for a series of international celebrations, prominent among which were the two joint historical expositions held in Madrid—one the Exposición Historico-Americana, the other the Exposición Historico-Europea. This report deals with the former only.

The Historic American Exposition was intended to illustrate the state of civilization of the New World in the precolumbian, Columbian, and postcolumbian periods; while in the Historic European Exposition was exhibited the evidences of the civilization of Europe, or, more particularly, that of the Iberian Peninsula, at the time when the New World was discovered and colonized. It was expected that, by the aid of these exhibitions, students and visitors generally would be enabled to understand the state of artistic and industrial civilization in Europe and in America during this important epoch, and to realize the influence which the one may have exercised upon the other.

The period which the distinguished scholars in charge of the Historic European Exposition desired especially to illustrate was that during which American history was most closely identified with that of Europe. This, it was assumed, extends from 1492, when the Spanish caravels first reached the Antilles, to 1620, when the *Mayflower*, setting forth from a Dutch seaport, brought the English Puritans to what is now known as New England.

"The Columbian Epoch," extending from the end of the fifteenth century through the first third of the seventeenth, includes most of the principal initial efforts for the exploration and colonization of the new continent by Europeans. By bringing together, in a retrospective exhibition, what remains to illustrate the arts and industries of Europe at this time, it was the aim of the Spanish authorities, to quote their own language, "to teach the people of to-day what were the elements of civilization with which, on the side of the arts, Europe was then equipped for the task of educating a daughter, courageous and untamed, but vigorous and beautiful, who had risen from the bosom of the seas, and who, in the course of a very few centuries, was to be transformed from a daughter into a sister—a sister proud in aspiration and in power."

This great and laudable design, it may be briefly stated here, was well carried out, and the success of the enterprise fully justified the hopes of the projectors.

The World's Columbian Exposition, Chicago

1492–1893.
WHY AMERICANS MAY CELEBRATE.

While the Columbian Exposition of 1893 is intended to celebrate the four-hundredth anniversary of the discovery of America, and primarily to illustrate American progress, the United States appropriately extends the hand of fellowship and hospitality

Source: *Report of the United States Commission to the Columbian Historical Exposition at Madrid* (Washington: Government Printing Office, 1895), pp. 8–9; John J. Flinn, *Official Guide to the World's Columbian Exposition* (Chicago, 1893), 7–9, 40–41.

to all other nations already represented on her soil. It will be a universal congress, which is no respecter of geographical boundary, race, color, party or sex. All the nations of Europe are bound to cosmopolitan America by invisible but indissoluble ties. England by the force of maternal kinship, and our assimilation of her language, her literature and her jurisprudence; Germany by the preponderating influence of the Germanic element engrafted upon our native stock; France by her affection for our republican form of government; Spain by her brilliant Columbian history; Russia, Austria, Hungary, Sweden and Norway, Belgium and Holland, Italy, and all the smaller European states, by their many thousands of sons and daughters in the New World; Japan by her awakened national energies; China and India by sympathy of age for youth; Australia by connection of parallel development; Mexico by the impulse of her new national life and the South American republics by close national relationship tending towards a fraternity of interests and a common political destiny. The Columbian Exposition is a tender to the Old World of the hospitalities of the New— a commingling of the Asiatic and European nations with the seventeen republics of the Western Hemisphere. . . .

Department of Ethnology (in Anthropological Building).

In the Department of Ethnology the customs of the native American tribes from the earliest times to the present are illustrated. The handiwork of the natives and photographs of themselves and habitations are sold to visitors as souvenirs. There are canoes in plenty, and at various points through the lagoons the curious visitor may occasionally see a stray Indian, in aboriginal costume, paddling among the electric launches and gondolas.

Beginning with the Eskimo, from the extreme North, the groups by latitudes descend as follows: The Cree family, from the Canadian Northwest; Haida and Fort Rupert tribes, from British Columbia; Iroquois, from the Eastern States; Chippewas, Sioux, Menominees and Winnebago tribes, from the Middle and Northwestern States; Choctaws, from Louisiana; Apaches and Navajos, from New Mexico and Arizona; Coahuilas, from Southern California, and the Papagos and Yakuis from the extreme southern border of the United States and Mexico.

South of the United States the Ethnological specimens include mementos of the time of Cortez, which were collected in Europe by Mrs. Zelia Nuttall. These objects were taken to Europe at the time of the Spanish conquest, and include a series of Mexican shields. From the South Sea Islands there is a unique collection made directly from the natives by Otto Finsch, of Germany, during several years residence on the Island, which includes objects showing the methods of life, customs and dress used by the natives long before the adoption of civilization. From Egypt and Palestine there is an interesting collection, and from Africa there is enough to indicate the habits and customs of the nations of the Dark Continent.

Living American Indians.—The popular features of the Ethnological exhibit are those which illustrate by living example the principal families of native American Indians, who have made their temporary home on the Fair grounds, living in the exact way their forefathers lived before the white man invaded their hunting grounds. This out-door exhibit is on the bank of the South Pond, in the southeastern portion of the grounds. Here may be found the native Indians with canoes, fishing and hunting tackle, costumes and all the appurtenances of Indian life. They cook, make trinkets, hold their counsels and go through the ordinary routine with which their tribes have been familiar from time immemorial.

One of the curious things connected with this department is the Parliament or Long House of the Six Nations of the Iroquois, transported from its home within a short distance of Albany, New York. It contains many relics of Indian warfare, and in connection with the Iroquois encampment is manned with the lineal descendants of the chiefs of the Six Nations. Prior to the landing of Columbus the Iroquois held sway from the Atlantic Ocean to the Mississippi River. . . .

2. Canada Recognizes Aboriginal Rights, 1982

PART II
RIGHTS OF THE ABORIGINAL PEOPLES OF CANADA

Recognition of existing aboriginal and treaty rights	**35.** (1)	The existing aboriginal and treaty rights of the aboriginal peoples of Canada are hereby recognized and affirmed.
Definition of "aboriginal peoples of Canada"	(2)	In this Act, "aboriginal peoples of Canada" includes the Indian, Inuit and Métis peoples of Canada.
Land claims agreements	(3)	For greater certainty, in subsection (1) "treaty rights" includes rights that now exist by way of land claims agreements or may be so acquired.
Aboriginal and treaty rights are guaranteed equally to both sexes	(4)	Notwithstanding any other provision of this Act, the aboriginal and treaty rights referred to in subsection (1) are guaranteed equally to male and female persons.
Commitment to participation in constitutional conference	**35.1**	The government of Canada and the provincial governments are committed to the principle that, before any amendment is made to Class 24 of section 91 of the *"Constitution Act, 1867,"* to section 25 of this Act or to this Part,

> (*a*) a constitutional conference that includes in its agenda an item relating to the proposed amendment, composed of the Prime Minister of Canada and the first ministers of the provinces, will be convened by the Prime Minister of Canada; and
>
> (*b*) the Prime Minister of Canada will invite representatives of the aboriginal peoples of Canada to participate in the discussions on that item.

Source: Canadian Constitution Act, 1982, Part II: "Rights of the Aboriginal Peoples of Canada" http://lois .justice.gc.ca/en/const/annex_e.html#II

3. American Indians Respond to the Columbian Quincentennial, 1990

We Indians of America have never abandoned our constant struggle against the conditions of oppression, discrimination and exploitation which were imposed upon us as a result of the European invasion of our ancestral territories.

Our struggle is not a mere conjunctural reflection of the memory of 500 years of oppression which the invaders, in complicity with the "democratic" governments of our countries, want to turn into events of jubilation and celebration. Our struggle as Indian People, Nations and Nationalities is based on our identity, which shall lead us to true liberation. We are responding aggressively, and commit ourselves to reject this "celebration."

The struggle of our People has acquired a new quality in recent times. This struggle is less isolated and more organized. We are now completely conscious that our total liberation can only be expressed through the complete exercise of our self-determination. Our unity is based on this fundamental right. Our self-determination is not just a simple declaration.

We must guarantee the necessary conditions that permit complete exercise of our self-determination; and this, in turn must be expressed as complete autonomy for our Peoples. Without Indian self-government and without control of our territories, there can be no autonomy.

The achievement of this objective is a principal task for Indian Peoples. However, through our struggles we have learned that our problems are not different, in many respects, from those of other popular sectors. We are convinced that we must march alongside the peasants, the workers, the marginalized sectors, together with intellectuals committed to our cause, in order to destroy the dominant system of oppression and construct a new society, pluralistic, democratic and humane, in which peace is guaranteed.

The existing nation states of the Americas, their constitutions and fundamental laws, are judicial/political expressions that negate our socio-economic, cultural and political rights.

At this point in our struggle, one of our priorities is to demand a complete structural change which allows for the recognition of Indian People's rights to self-determination, and the control of our territories through our own governments.

Our problems will not be resolved through the self-serving politics of governmental entities which seek integration and ethno-development. It is necessary to have an integral transformation at the level of the state and national society; that is to say, the creation of a new nation.

In this Gathering it has been clear that territorial rights are a fundamental demand of the Indigenous Peoples of the Americas. Based on these aforementioned reflections, the organizations united in the First Continental Gathering of Indigenous Peoples reaffirm:

Source: "The Declaration of Quito, 1990," from the Continental Gathering, "500 Years of Indian Resistance," in John Yewell, Chris Dodge, and Jan DeSirey, eds., *Confronting Columbus* (Jefferson, NC: McFarland and Company, 1992), appendix A, pp. 187–188.

1. Our emphatic rejection of the Quincentennial celebration, and the firm promise that we will turn that date into an occasion to strengthen our process of continental unity and struggle towards our liberation.

2. Ratify our resolute political project of self-determination and our autonomy, in the framework of nation states, under a new popular order, with respect for whatever forms of organization each Nation determines appropriate for their situation.

3. Affirm our decision to defend our culture, education, and religion as fundamental to our identity as Peoples, reclaiming and maintaining our own forms of spiritual life and communal coexistence, in an intimate relationship with our Mother Earth.

4. We reject the manipulation of organizations which are linked to the dominant sectors of society and have no Indigenous representation, who usurp our name for (their own) imperialist interests. At the same time, we affirm our choice to strengthen our own organizations, without excluding or isolating ourselves from other popular struggles.

5. We recognize the important role that Indigenous women play in the struggles of our Peoples. We understand the necessity to expand women's participation in our organizations and we reaffirm that it is one struggle, men and women together, in our liberation process, and a key question in our political practices.

6. We Indian Peoples consider it vital to defend and conserve our natural resources, which right now are being attacked by transnational corporations. We are convinced that this defense will be realized if it is Indian People who administer and control the territories where we live, according to our own principles of organization and communal life.

7. We oppose national judicial structures which are the result of the process of colonization and neo-colonization. We seek a New Social Order that embraces our traditional exercise of Common Law, an expression of our culture and forms of organization. We demand that we be recognized as Peoples under International Law, and that this recognition be incorporated into the respective Nation States.

8. We denounce the victimization of Indian People through violence and persecution, which constitutes a flagrant violation of human rights. We demand respect for our right to life, to land, to free organization and expression of our culture. At the same time we demand the release of our leaders who are held as political prisoners, an end to repression, and restitution for the harms caused us.

4. Pan-African Activists Demand Reparations for Slavery, 1993

The Abuja Proclamation

A declaration of the first Abuja Pan-African Conference on Reparations for African Enslavement, Colonization and Neo-Colonization, sponsored by the Organization of African Unity and its Reparations Commission April 27–29, 1993, Abuja, Nigeria

This First Pan-African Conference on Reparations held in Abuja, Nigeria, April 27–29, 1993, sponsored by the Group of Eminent Persons (GEP) and the Commission

Source: Abuja Pan-African Conference on Reparations for African Enslavement, Colonisation and Neo-Colonisation, sponsored by The Organisation of African Unity and its Reparations Commission April 27–29, 1993, Abuja, Nigeria. www.ncobra.org

for Reparations of the Organization of African Unity, and the Federal Government of the Republic of Nigeria.

Recalling the Organization of African Unity's establishment of a machinery the Group of Eminent Persons for appraising the issue of reparations in relation to the damage done to Africa and its Diaspora by enslavement, colonization, and neo-colonialism.

Convinced that the issue of reparations is an important question requiring the united action of Africa and its Diaspora and worthy of the active support of the rest of the international community.

Fully persuaded that the damage sustained by the African peoples is not a "thing of the past" but is Painfully manifest in the damaged lives of contemporary Africans from Harlem to Harare, in the damaged economies of the Black World from Guinea to Guyana, from Somalia to Surinam.

Respectfully aware of historical precedents in reparations, ranging from German Payment of restitution to the Jews for the enormous tragedy of the Nazi Holocaust to the question of compensating Japanese-Americans for injustice of internment by Roosevelt Administration in the United States during the World War II.

Cognizant of the fact that compensation for injustice need not necessarily be paid only in capital transfer but could include service to the victims or other forms of restitution and readjustment of the relationship agreeable to both parties.

Emphatically convinced that what matters is not the guilt but the responsibility of those states and nations whose economic evolution once depended on slave labor and colonialism, and whose forebears participated either in selling and buying Africans, or in owning them, or in colonizing them.

Convinced that the pursuit of reparations by the African peoples in the continent and in the Diaspora will itself be a learning experience in self-discovery and in uniting experience politically and psychologically. Convinced that numerous looting, theft and larceny have been committed on the African People calls upon those in Possession of their stolen goods artifacts and other traditional treasuries to restore them to their rightful owners the African People.

Calls upon the international community to recognize that there is a unique and unprecedented moral debt owed to the African peoples which has Yet to be paid—the debt of compensation to the Africans as the most humiliated and exploited people of the last four centuries of modern history.

Calls upon Heads of States and Governments in Africa and the Diaspora itself to set up National Committees for the purpose of studying the damaged Black experience, disseminating information and encouraging educational courses on the impact of Enslavement, colonization and neo-colonialism on present-day Africa and its Diaspora.

Urges the Organization of African Unity to grant observer status to select organizations from the African Diaspora in order to facilitate consultations between Africa and its Diaspora on reparations and related issues.

Further urges the OAU to call for full monetary payment of repayments through capital transfer and debt cancellation.

Convinced that the claim for reparations is well grounded in International Law.

Urges on the OAU to establish a legal Committee on the issue of Reparations.

Also calls upon African and Diaspora groups already working on reparations to communicate with the Organization of African Unity and establish continuing liaison;

Encourages such groups to send this declaration to various countries to obtain their official support for the movement.

Serves notice on all states in Europe and the Americas which had participated in the enslavement and colonization of the African peoples, and which may still be engaged in racism and neo-colonialism, to desist from any further damage and start building bridges of conciliation, cooperation, and through reparation.

Exhorts all African states to grant entrance as of right to all persons of African descent and right to obtain residence in those African states, if there is no disqualifying element on the African claiming the "right to return" to his ancestral home, Africa.

Urges those countries which were enriched by slavery and the slave trade to give total relief from Foreign Debt, and allow the debtor countries of the Diaspora to become free for self-development and from immediate and direct economic domination.

Calls upon the countries largely characterized as profiteers from the slave trade to support proper and reasonable representation of African peoples in the Political and economic areas of the highest decision-making bodies.

Requests the OAU to intensify its efforts in restructuring the international system in pursuit of justice with special reference to a permanent African seat on the Security Council of the U.N.

5. The British House of Lords Debates Reparations for Slavery, 1996

Lord Gifford rose to ask Her Majesty's Government whether they will make appropriate reparation to African nations and to the descendants of Africans for the damage caused by the slave trade and the practice of slavery.

The noble Lord said: My Lords, the Question raises an issue which is being debated with increasing vigour and intensity by African people around the world; and by African people I mean people of African descent, wherever they live, whether in Africa itself, in the United States, in Great Britain or in the Caribbean, where I now live and practise law.

The issue is this. The under-development and poverty which affect the majority of countries in Africa and in the Caribbean, as well as the ghetto conditions in which many black people live in the United States and elsewhere, are not, speaking in general terms, the result of laziness, incompetence or corruption of African people or their governments. They are in a very large measure the consequences—the legacy— of one of the most massive and terrible criminal enterprises in recorded human history; that is, the transatlantic slave trade and the institution of slavery.

The thesis that I advance tonight is that in accordance with international law and with basic human morality, measures of atonement and reparation are due from the successors of those who instigated and carried out the trade and who profited massively from it, to the descendants of the victims of the criminal enterprise who still suffer in many different ways from the effects of the crime.

Source: House of Lords Hansard (Cambridge, England: Chadwyck-Healey, 1997), vol. 570, part 62, columns 1041–1044, 1056–1059. Online at http://www.publications.parliament.uk.

The horrendous nature of the enterprise of African slavery is well known and documented. Around 20 million young people were kidnapped, taken in chains across the Atlantic and sold into slavery in the plantations of the New World. Millions more died in transit in the dungeons of the castles such as Goree, Elmina and Cape Coast, or in the hell holes under the decks of the slave ships. It was without doubt, in the fullest sense of the term, a crime against humanity.

A vast proportion of sub-Saharan Africa from Senegal right round to Angola and on the other side from Mozambique into Malawi and Tanzania was depopulated. Its young men and women were taken away. . . .

African governments today, who have tried to rectify the under-development which they have inherited from history, have borrowed from the financial institutions of the West and are now in a virtually uncontrollable spiral of debt. In reality—and in morality—I suggest that it is the West which is in debt to Africa, not Africa which is in debt to the West.

On the other side of the Atlantic, the African captives were cut off from their families, their land and their language. They were forced to be owned as chattels and to work as beasts of burden. When, finally, emancipation day came—in the British colonies, in 1838—the ex-slaves received nothing. It was the ex-slave owners who were compensated for the loss of their property.

The slavery experience has left a bitter legacy which endures to this day in terms of family breakdown, landlessness, under-development and a longing among many to return to the motherland from which their ancestors were taken. Once again, in the Caribbean the need to finance development programmes has bound Caribbean governments and peoples in fresh shackles, the shackles of debt. . . .

As well as the consequences in Africa and the Caribbean, there is a further element in the legacy of the slave trade, which is the damage done with in Britain, within the United States and other Western societies. The inhuman philosophy of white supremacy and black inferiority was inculcated into European peoples to justify the atrocities which were being committed by a Christian people upon fellow human beings. That philosophy continues to poison our society today. . . .

The concept that reparations are payable where a crime against humanity has been committed by one people against another is well established in international law and practice. Germany paid reparations to Israel for the crimes of the Nazi Holocaust. Indeed, the very creation of the State of Israel can be seen as a massive act of reparation for centuries of dispossession and persecution directed against Jews. . . .

African people, too, have a massive and long-standing grievance. It is no use saying that it all happened a long time ago, and we should just forget about it. The period of colonialism which succeeded the period of slavery, continued the exploitation of Africa and the Caribbean in new ways. Further acts of brutality were committed, and the peoples of those regions, until recently, were denied the status of sovereignty and independence with which alone they could themselves demand the redress of the wrongs which were done.

But the wrongs have not been forgotten. The peoples of Africa and the Caribbean live with their consequences still. A group of eminent Africans under the auspices of the Organisation of African Unity is beginning to articulate the claim for reparation.

What is meant by the claim for reparations? The details of a reparations settlement would have to be negotiated with an appropriate body of representatives of African people around the world. I would anticipate that some of the elements of an appropriate package would be, first, as with other precedents, an apology at the highest level for the criminal acts committed against millions of Africans over the centuries of the slave trade. His Holiness the Pope set the example when he visited the slave dungeons of Goree in Senegal in February 1992 when he said:

"From this African sanctuary of black pain, we implore forgiveness from Heaven."

Secondly, there would be the cancellation of the intolerable burden of debt, which has overloaded the economies of Africa and the Caribbean. There are powerful economic and social arguments for debt cancellation which were most recently deployed by former President Kaunda of Zambia during a visit to Scotland in February 1996. He said of the present state of Africa:

"It is a human tragedy. People are dying by their thousands every day, children are dying. These things bring social disorder to countries."

Thirdly, there would be the return of treasures and works of art which come from the African continent, many of which are to be found in Britain's museums as a result of acts of theft and robbery. I refer, for instance, to the Benin Bronzes in the Museum of Mankind.

Fourthly, there would be measures to facilitate the repatriation and resettlement of those who wish to return to Africa. The word "repatriation" has an ugly ring in the mouth of racists who want to drive black people out of Britain. However, it expresses, too, a yearning among many descendants of Africans which is as powerful as was the yearning of the Jewish people for the Promised Land.

Fifthly, there would be a reparations settlement which would involve programmes of development, without strings attached, in Africa, the Caribbean, Brazil and elsewhere, including programmes to promote equal rights and justice within the countries of the West. . . .

Lord Chesham: My Lords, we all agree that slavery was shameful. Indeed, my right honourable friend the Prime Minister, speaking in Cape Town in September 1994, described slavery as a moral outrage. No one can feel proud about the traffic in human beings, a traffic which is still taking place today, as many noble Lords have said, in various parts of the world, including Africa. Indeed, one of the worst aspects of the slavery of which we read today is the encompassment of child prostitution with it. The Government totally deplore that slavery. I can assure the noble and learned Lord, Lord Wilberforce, and my noble friend Lord Gisborough that the Government are doing whatever they can to see that it is stopped wherever it occurs.

I turn now to the Atlantic slave trade. Attributing responsibility for that is difficult; it is not straightforward. Slavery existed in Africa for centuries before outsiders began to engage in the trade, and continued after they had stopped. Far more people were enslaved internally in Africa than were ever exported across the Atlantic. The first outside slave traders were in fact North African Arabs, plying across the Sahara. That took place at least some seven or eight centuries before the first Europeans began to practise the trade. The Atlantic trade first began by tapping that long-standing trans-Saharan slave trade to North Africa. In East Africa, the trade was almost entirely in the hands of Arabs from Oman and the Gulf. Nor, as has been mentioned, is slavery a monopoly of Africa: it existed in the Greek and Roman empires, and in many other parts of the world.

At the height of the transatlantic slave trade, considerable numbers of African slavers and middlemen were involved. African rulers could open and close the market at will, at a time when European penetration of Africa was limited. Traders made their own arrangements with African rulers for slaves, supplied by fellow Africans, and had to pay gifts and taxes to various African rulers along the West African coast. African societies often had control of the slaves until they were loaded on to European ships. That is supported by a large body of academic research.

To claim that the Atlantic slave trade was imposed by Western nations on powerless African communities is to deny Africa's political history. African leaders were themselves active participants with the capacity to determine how trade with Europe developed. Many of the highly impressive African kingdoms and empires in West Africa were built on the foundations of slavery, such as the Asante kingdom in present-day Ghana.

Africans, Arabs and Europeans participated in the slave trade. Responsibility for British involvement in the transatlantic slave trade does not rest on the shoulders of the British Government. British participation in the trade was not conducted by the Government but by individual traders and companies. After the abolition of the slave trade in 1807, the Royal Navy played an honourable part in suppressing the transatlantic slave trade by maintaining naval patrols off the West African coast. British also drew up anti-slavery treaties with African leaders in an attempt to suppress the slave trade. As was written in the Chronicle of Abuju, written in Hausa by the two brothers of the Emir of Abuja in 1945,

> "when the British came, those men who had been earning a rich living by this trade saw their prosperity vanish, and they became poor men."

The case for reparations for slavery rests on the premise that the effects of slavery are still being felt on Africans now living in Africa and the Diaspora. There is no evidence of that. Current historical research has revised the thinking on the numbers involved in the Atlantic trade and its effects on demography and depopulation. The main areas of slaving, for example, in the Niger delta and Benin, are now among the most densely populated parts of Africa. The majority of slaves exported were male and not female, and this has less impact on demography due to the widespread practice of polygamy. . . .

Mention has been made of the growing support for the campaign for reparations for slavery. However, African leaders increasingly accept that many of the economic problems have arisen from policies pursued since independence. As former Nigerian head of state General Obasanjo said in 1991 at the Africa Leadership Forum Conference in Nigeria:

> "the major responsibility of our present impasse must be placed squarely on the shoulders of our leaders."

General Obasanjo is currently detained in Nigeria.

Many noble Lords have mentioned the problem of racism, which is an un-doubted evil. No one condones it. Any manifestation needs to be fought. To attribute racism to slavery is too simplistic. Racism occurs not just between black and white, but between different ethnic groups all over the world. It is not just a pure black and white problem.

Much has been said about debt relief. We see no linkage between the debts owed by African countries and the legacy of the slave trade. Any practical claim for reparations may serve to undermine the good and widely recognised arguments for reducing Africa's debt burden. The British Government have been active in promoting debt relief for African countries, because such debts constitute a serious obstacle to development. . . .

I touched earlier on the responsibility for slavery. I wish to return to that. Arabs, Europeans, Americans and Africans were all directly involved in the trade, but even if it could be decided to whom the bill should be sent, to whom should any proceeds go? Which Africans would benefit and how? Which descendants of slaves living in America, the Caribbean, or the UK should benefit? To whom, incidentally, should the UK send the bill for the naval squadrons that patrolled the waters of West Africa for half a century to prevent the Spaniards, Brazilians and others from slaving long after we had abolished it? We should remember also the large percentage of slaves who were prisoners of war in ethnic clashes who would otherwise just have been killed. . . .

Comment has been made about international precedents. In May 1991 in Lagos Chief Anyaoku, Secretary General of the Commonwealth, devoted an entire speech to the legacy of slavery. However, he stated that, although the moral case was strong, there was no precedent for reparations outside the post-war settlement. The fact that reparations for war crimes have been paid in this century—for example, Germany, Japan and Iraq—is a red herring. It provides no historic parallel. They were among the terms for peace imposed at once by victors in the wars upon vanquished governments and could be precisely catalogued.

6. Matthew Coon Come Condemns the Economic Status of First Nations People, 2001

The following is an excerpt of an address Thursday by Matthew Coon Come at the University of Toronto.

I am deeply honoured to be granted the degree of Doctor of Laws Honoris Causa from this great institution, the University of Toronto. I accept this degree as a recognition of the deep courage, the restraint, the forbearance, and the long-suffering in the face of enduring discrimination and dispossession, of all First Nations peoples in Canada.

I have been told that I may have six minutes today, for which I am very grateful. Mr. Chancellor and distinguished colleagues, please forgive me, what I have to say

Source: "We Are Economic Prisoners," by Matthew Coon Come, *Ottawa Citizen*, 16 June 2001, p. B8. Reprinted with permission of Matthew Coon Come.

is fundamentally important for aboriginal peoples across Canada, and I may take two or three additional minutes of your time.

I have just returned from a First Nation reserve in the Ontario riding of the Minister of Northern Affairs (Robert Nault). In (the riding of Kenora-Rainy River), as in hundreds of others like it across Canada, ill health, mass poverty and mass unemployment are endemic. Housing is overcrowded, basic community infrastructure is inferior or lacking, sanitation is inadequate, and clean water is unknown except in Evian bottles. Bi-weekly suicides and suicide attempts are a way of life.

The great majority of the homeless on the streets of this golden city are aboriginal men, women and children. In Manitoba and Saskatchewan, our people are not only the majority of the homeless, they constitute three-quarters of the prison population even though they only represent one-tenth of the general populace. They and we are not deviants and criminals, we are social, economic and political prisoners. They and we are forced into internal exile from our families and our traditional lands because of the conditions we face on reserve.

In the most recent issue of the *Canadian Bar Review*, Professor Lorraine Weinrib of the Faculty of Law at this University declares: "We live in the age of rights." Ladies and gentlemen, I agree and disagree. This may well be an age of constitutional and human rights. These are rights that most people in Canada take for granted, or at worst they are rights to which they can reasonably aspire.

However . . . there are gross disparities in the enjoyment of those constitutional and human rights.

First Nations peoples live in an ironic age of the denial and neglect of rights. I suggest that when our young choose death and by their own hands in disproportionate numbers, it is because they have concluded, empirically, that aspiring to anything is futile.

At Burnt Church, unemployment is 90 per cent. In the Acadian and anglophone communities to either side of the reserve, unemployment is 25 per cent. This rate is rightly regarded as high, but it would be heaven for the Indians. The two non-native communities have federal fishing wharves. The Indians do not. Over the last few decades, the fishing licences have almost all been assigned by the federal government to the non-natives. A treaty from 1779, signed by the Crown, assured the Mi'kmaq that in return for not siding with the American rebels, they can fish unmolested and engage in trade and commerce. The Mi'kmaq kept their side of the deal, but the Crown did not. No wonder there is conflict.

My own people, the James Bay Crees, live in the middle of a vibrant economic zone of eastern James Bay region of northern Quebec. Many billion dollars of revenue are extracted by governments and multinationals each year in the hydroelectric, forestry and mining sectors. Even though we Crees represent the majority of the population in our traditional territory, we have fewer than three per cent of the jobs. Of the 1,400 or so jobs in the forestry sector, Crees have only three per cent. Of the 1,400 mining jobs, eight per cent, are Cree jobs. In Hydro-Quebec, we have just seven positions, or one per cent of the jobs. In the middle of this economic well-being, mass unemployment, and the poverty, ill health and hopelessness it causes, are endemic among my people.

We James Bay Crees have a 1975 treaty right to affirmative involvement in employment, contracts, and the necessary training to bring us into the wage and enterprise economy of the region. We kept our side of the "bargain" when our lands were flooded and taken from us in the 1970s, to make this country rich. Canada and Quebec did not. The government of Canada alone earns more on GST from Hydro sales than it spends on all of our James Bay Cree social and municipal needs.

Many other First Nations right across this country have Treaty rights to a means of subsistence, economic inclusion, and education and training to make this inclusion possible. These rights are being ignored and violated, and they stand dispossessed. Where there are no treaties, such as in British Columbia, governments now threaten referendums, meaning that a majoritarian dictatorship of a colonial majority will now likely refuse to enter into honourable treaties with First Nations Peoples. Predictably, there will be more conflict.

The United Nations Human Rights Committee recently re-assessed Canada's compliance with its international human rights obligations. It declared that the situation facing aboriginal peoples in Canada is the most serious human rights challenge facing this country. This challenge involves the violation of the most fundamental human right, our right as peoples to self determination. As Canada was reminded by the UN, this right includes the right to determine our own political future, to enjoy our natural wealth and resources, and never to be deprived of our own means of subsistence.

For First Nations Peoples, respect for our right of self determination would mean political, economic and cultural survival rather than extinction. For Canadians, it would simply mean sharing the wealth, or in the words of the Royal Commission on Aboriginal Peoples, a redistribution of lands and resources to remedy a gross disparity. It would also mean beginning to examine how to use the wealth and resources of this land in a truly sustainable and equitable manner.

The minister of Indian Affairs has just commenced a nationwide direct consultation with First Nations people . . . as part of yet another initiative to "reform" the Indian Act. I have been widely criticized for refusing to participate in this sham. The minister says that his reforms are about "accountability" and "democracy." Actually, his reforms are only about tinkering with a racist, colonial and oppressive piece of legislation. . . .

For many years, the Canadian Human Rights Commission has noted that the Indian Act is exempt from scrutiny under the Canadian Human Rights Act. The Human Rights Commission and the United Nations have called for the immediate removal of this exemption. I challenge the minister to undertake the single most effective reform he could make to the Indian Act, namely to amend the Canadian Human Rights Act to remove this exemption. It would result in the collapse of much of the oppressive power of his department over First Nations people that keeps Indians excluded from the restitution, retention, and enjoyment of their lands and resources.

Ladies and gentlemen . . . this continuing injustice may be widespread, but it is not intractable. Canada is a G8 country with an economy large enough to do the job. . . .

I challenge you, and through you the country, to join me in a principled discussion, and then in acting on this unfinished national business, and then to continue and not stop until we can rest and say, "Halleluyah, the job is done. The rights we Canadians take for granted, are now assured to and enjoyed by all peoples in Canada, including First Nations peoples." Thank you, merci, miigwetch.

7. Sarah Baartmann Goes Home, 2002

Speech at the Funeral of Sarah Baartmann, 9 August 2002

Fellow South Africans:

The day should be a day of celebration and joy. After all, today is National Women's Day as well as the historic day when we return the remains of Sarah Baartmann to the land she walked as a child and a young woman.

Difficult as it may be, we must still celebrate. But we could not be human and not be deeply saddened and weighted down with grief as we reflect on the short life of Sarah Baartmann who has, at last, returned to her people.

This occasion can never be a solemn ceremony in which we bury her remains and bury the truth about the painful circumstances of her death as well.

To this day, 186 years after she died, we feel the pain of her intolerable misery because she was of us and we, of her. When we turn away from this grave of a simple African woman, a particle of each one of us will stay with the remains of Sarah Baartmann.

We cannot undo the damage that was done to her. But at least we can summon the courage to speak the naked but healing truth that must comfort her wherever she may be.

I speak of courage because there are many in our country would urge constantly that we should not speak of the past. They pour scorn on those who speak about who we are and where we come from and why we are where we are today. They make bold to say the past is no longer, and all that remains is a future that will be.

But, today, the gods would be angry with us if we did not, on the banks of the Gamtoos River, at the grave of Sarah Baartmann, call out for the restoration of the dignity of Sarah Baartmann, of the Khoi-San, of the millions of Africans who have known centuries of wretchedness.

Sarah Baartmann should never have been transported to Europe.

Sarah Baartmann should never have been robbed of her name and relabeled Sarah Baartmann. Sarah Baartmann should never have been stripped of her native, Khoi-San and African identity and paraded in Europe as a savage monstrosity.

As the French Parliament debated the matter of the return of the remains of our Sarah to her native land, the then Minister of Research, Roger-Gerard Scwartzenberg said: "This young woman was treated as if she was something monstrous. But where in this affair is the monstrosity?"

Indeed, where did the monstrosity lie in the matter of the gross abuse of a defenceless African woman in England and France! It was not the abused human being who was monstrous but those who abused her. It was not the lonely African woman in Europe, alienated from her identity and her motherland who was the barbarian, but those who treated her with barbaric brutality.

Among the truly monstrous were the leading scientists of the day, who sought to feed a rabid racism, such as the distinguished anatomist, Baron Georges Cuvier,

Source: Thabo Mbeki's Speech at the Funeral of Sarah Baartmann, 9 August 2002, on Republic of South Africa Department of Foreign Affairs website (http://www.dfa.gov.za/docs/speeches/2002/mbek0809.htm)

who dissected Sarah's body after her death. It is Cuvier who said after he had dismembered her:

"The Negro race . . . is marked by black complexion, crisped of woolly hair, compressed cranium and a flat nose. The projection of the lower parts of the face, and the thick lips, evidently approximate it to the monkey tribe: the hordes of which it consists have always remained in the most complete state of barbarism. . . . These races with depressed and compressed skulls are condemned to a never-ending inferiority . . . Her moves had something that reminded one of the monkey and her external genitalia recalled those of the orang-utang." . . .

Today we celebrate our National Women's Day. We therefore convey our congratulations and best wishes to all the women of our country. We also mark this day fully conscious of the responsibility that falls on us to ensure that we move with greater speed towards the accomplishment of the goal of the creation of a non-sexist society.

Our work in this regard must be driven by the knowledge that the women of our country have borne the brunt of the oppressive and exploitative system of colonial and apartheid domination. Even today, the women of our country carry the burden of poverty and continue to be exposed to unacceptable violence and abuse. It will never be possible for us to claim that we are making significant progress to create a new South Africa if we do not make significant progress towards gender equality and the emancipation of women.

The gravity and urgency of this task is emphasised by the particular place attributed to African women by those who gave themselves the responsibility of a civilising mission as "man par excellence." They, more than the African male, were presented as the very representation of what was savage and barbaric about all our people. . . .

The story of Sarah Baartmann is the story of the African people of our country in all their echelons. It is a story of the loss of our ancient freedom. It is a story of our dispossession of the land and the means that gave us an independent livelihood.

It is a story of our reduction to the status of objects that could be owned, used and disposed of by others, who claimed for themselves a manifest destiny "to run the empire of the globe."

It is an account of how it came about that we ended up being defined as a people without a past, except a past of barbarism, who had no capacity to think, who had no culture, no value system to speak of, and nothing to contribute to human civilisation—people with no names and no identity, who had to be defined by he who was "man par excellence," and described by another French thinker, Diderot, as "always vicious . . . mostly inclined to lasciviousness, vengeance, theft and lies."

We are South Africans. To understand the meaning of all these things, we do not have to refer to England, Germany, France or elsewhere in Europe. We do not have to recall a European history that extends to the 19th, the 18th earlier and later centuries.

To understand the meaning of all these things, we need only start here, on the banks of the Gamtoos River and advance to the rest of our country. We need to cast our eyes back to a period less than ten years ago. Then the state ideology, whatever the garments in which it was clothed, was firmly based on the criminal notion that some had been called upon to enlighten and tame the hordes of barbarians, as Sarah Baartmann was enlightened and tamed.

The legacy of those centuries remains with us, both in the way in which our society is structured and in the ideas that many in our country continue to carry in their heads, which inform their reaction their action on important matters.

This means that we still have an important task ahead of us—to carry out the historic mission of restoring the human dignity of Sarah Baartmann, of transforming ours into a truly non-racial, non-sexist and prosperous country, providing a better life for all our people.

A troubled and painful history has presented us with the challenge and possibility to translate into reality the noble vision that South Africa belongs to all who live in it, black and white. When that is done, then will it be possible for us to say that Sarah Baartmann has truly come home.

8. An American President Commemorates the Slave Trade, 2003

Mr. President and Madam First Lady, distinguished guests and residents of Gorée Island, citizens of Senegal, I'm honored to begin my visit to Africa in your beautiful country.

For hundreds of years on this island peoples of different continents met in fear and cruelty. Today we gather in respect and friendship, mindful of past wrongs and dedicated to the advance of human liberty.

At this place, liberty and life were stolen and sold. Human beings were delivered and sorted, and weighed, and branded with the marks of commercial enterprises, and loaded as cargo on a voyage without return. One of the largest migrations of history was also one of the greatest crimes of history.

Below the decks, the middle passage was a hot, narrow, sunless nightmare; weeks and months of confinement and abuse and confusion on a strange and lonely sea. Some refused to eat, preferring death to any future their captors might prepare for them. Some who were sick were thrown over the side. Some rose up in violent rebellion, delivering the closest thing to justice on a slave ship. Many acts of defiance and bravery are recorded. Countless others, we will never know.

Those who lived to see land again were displayed, examined, and sold at auctions across nations in the Western Hemisphere. They entered societies indifferent to their anguish and made prosperous by their unpaid labor. There was a time in my country's history when one in every seven human beings was the property of another. In law, they were regarded only as articles of commerce, having no right to travel, or to marry, or to own possessions. Because families were often separated, many denied even the comfort of suffering together.

For 250 years the captives endured an assault on their culture and their dignity. The spirit of Africans in America did not break. Yet the spirit of their captors was corrupted. Small men took on the powers and airs of tyrants and masters. Years of unpunished brutality and bullying and rape produced a dullness and hardness of conscience. Christian men and women became blind to the clearest commands of their

Source: "President Bush Speaks at Gorée Island in Senegal," July 8, 2003. [http://www.whitehouse.gov/news/releases/2003/07/20030708-1.html]

faith and added hypocrisy to injustice. A republic founded on equality for all became a prison for millions. And yet in the words of the African proverb, "no fist is big enough to hide the sky." All the generations of oppression under the laws of man could not crush the hope of freedom and defeat the purposes of God.

In America, enslaved Africans learned the story of the exodus from Egypt and set their own hearts on a promised land of freedom. Enslaved Africans discovered a suffering Savior and found he was more like themselves than their masters. Enslaved Africans heard the ringing promises of the Declaration of Independence and asked the self-evident question, then why not me?

In the year of America's founding, a man named Olaudah Equiano was taken in bondage to the New World. He witnessed all of slavery's cruelties, the ruthless and the petty. He also saw beyond the slave-holding piety of the time to a higher standard of humanity. "God tells us," wrote Equiano, "that the oppressor and the oppressed are both in His hands. And if these are not the poor, the broken-hearted, the blind, the captive, the bruised which our Savior speaks of, who are they?"

Down through the years, African Americans have upheld the ideals of America by exposing laws and habits contradicting those ideals. The rights of African Americans were not the gift of those in authority. Those rights were granted by the Author of Life, and regained by the persistence and courage of African Americans, themselves.

Among those Americans was Phyllis Wheatley, who was dragged from her home here in West Africa in 1761, at the age of seven. In my country, she became a poet, and the first noted black author in our nation's history. Phyllis Wheatley said, "In every human breast, God has implanted a principle which we call love of freedom. It is impatient of oppression and pants for deliverance."

That deliverance was demanded by escaped slaves named Frederick Douglass and Sojourner Truth, educators named Booker T. Washington and W. E. B. DuBois, and ministers of the Gospel named Leon Sullivan and Martin Luther King, Jr. At every turn, the struggle for equality was resisted by many of the powerful. And some have said we should not judge their failures by the standards of a later time. Yet, in every time, there were men and women who clearly saw this sin and called it by name.

We can fairly judge the past by the standards of President John Adams, who called slavery "an evil of callosal magnitude." We can discern eternal standards in the deeds of William Wilberforce and John Quincy Adams, and Harriet Beecher Stowe, and Abraham Lincoln. These men and women, black and white, burned with a zeal for freedom, and they left behind a different and better nation. Their moral vision caused Americans to examine our hearts, to correct our Constitution, and to teach our children the dignity and equality of every person of every race. By a plan known only to Providence, the stolen sons and daughters of Africa helped to awaken the conscience of America. The very people traded into slavery helped to set America free.

My nation's journey toward justice has not been easy and it is not over. The racial bigotry fed by slavery did not end with slavery or with segregation. And many of the issues that still trouble America have roots in the bitter experience of other times. But however long the journey, our destination is set: liberty and justice for all.

In the struggle of the centuries, America learned that freedom is not the possession of one race. We know with equal certainty that freedom is not the possession of one nation. This belief in the natural rights of man, this conviction that justice should reach wherever the sun passes leads America into the world.

With the power and resources given to us, the United States seeks to bring peace where there is conflict, hope where there is suffering, and liberty where there is tyranny. And these commitments bring me and other distinguished leaders of my government across the Atlantic to Africa.

African peoples are now writing your own story of liberty. Africans have overcome the arrogance of colonial powers, overturned the cruelties of apartheid, and made it clear that dictatorship is not the future of any nation on this continent. In the process, Africa has produced heroes of liberation—leaders like Mandela, Senghor, Nkrumah, Kenyatta, Selassie and Sadat. And many visionary African leaders, such as my friend, have grasped the power of economic and political freedom to lift whole nations and put forth bold plans for Africa's development.

Because Africans and Americans share a belief in the values of liberty and dignity, we must share in the labor of advancing those values. In a time of growing commerce across the globe, we will ensure that the nations of Africa are full partners in the trade and prosperity of the world. Against the waste and violence of civil war, we will stand together for peace. Against the merciless terrorists who threaten every nation, we will wage an unrelenting campaign of justice. Confronted with desperate hunger, we will answer with human compassion and the tools of human technology. In the face of spreading disease, we will join with you in turning the tide against AIDS in Africa.

We know that these challenges can be overcome, because history moves in the direction of justice. The evils of slavery were accepted and unchanged for centuries. Yet, eventually, the human heart would not abide them. There is a voice of conscience and hope in every man and woman that will not be silenced—what Martin Luther King called a certain kind of fire that no water could put out. That flame could not be extinguished at the Birmingham jail. It could not be stamped out at Robben Island Prison. It was seen in the darkness here at Goree Island, where no chain could bind the soul. This untamed fire of justice continues to burn in the affairs of man, and it lights the way before us.

May God bless you all.

◁ E S S A Y S

The essays in this chapter approach the question of moral responsibility for historical evils from different angles. As the world prepared for the 500th anniversary of Columbus's discovery of America, protests erupted against the celebration of Columbus and his legacy. Hearing these protests, James Axtell, a preeminent historian of American Indians, criticized the idea that Europeans committed "genocide" against American Indians. He argues that the term "genocide" has a specific meaning that does not fit what happened to the indigenous people of the Americas, and that Europeans in general should not be held morally accountable for the misdeeds of a small number of people, nor should the current generation be held morally or legally accountable for the crimes of their ancestors. For Axtell, the debate over Columbus and the fate of the Indians raises important questions about historians' own moral and professional responsibilities. What does it mean to do justice to history when history itself is full of injustices?

Whereas criticism of Columbus is relatively recent, the movement for reparations for former slaves and their descendants has a long history going back to the nineteenth century, when newly freed people in the United States called for "forty acres and a mule." African-American radicals sustained the call for reparations throughout the twentieth century, and as Martha Biondi shows, the reparations movement has recently become international. Inspired by precedents for the compensation of Jewish victims of the Holocaust and Japanese-American internees during World War Two, activists in the Caribbean and Africa have joined those in the United States in demanding reparations as atonement for the crimes of slavery and colonialism, and to assist Africans and people of African descent elsewhere to overcome the burdens of racist discrimination and exploitation. Calls for reparations are highly controversial and may never come to fruition, but they do illuminate one way that Atlantic history casts a shadow over our own times.

Did Europeans Commit Genocide in the Americas?

JAMES AXTELL

Many scholars who have endeavored to put native peoples on America's historical map and to get them a fair hearing at the bar of both justice and history have been struck by the frequency of the use of the word "genocide" to characterize European treatment of the natives in the colonial period. In the counter-Columbus, counter-celebratory literature, genocide has become the dominant abbreviation or code word to describe Columbus and his successors' relations with the Indians.

For example, an ad hoc group of "progressive" educators, ecologists, and community activists who formed "The Columbus in Context Clearing-house," proposed to "celebrate the resistance of Native Americans to 500 years of genocide."

Jan Elliott, the editor of *Indigenous Thought*, a Florida-based anti-Columbus newspaper, described the loss of American Indian life as "the biggest holocaust in history" and called Columbus a "mass murderer." Elliott wrote in the first issue that "Celebrating Columbus' 'discovery' of America is analogous to celebrating Hitler's holocaust." Indian activist Russell Means further raised the moral ante. When he protested an exhibition on Spanish-Indian encounters at the Florida State Museum, he told the press that "Columbus makes Hitler look like a juvenile delinquent." The governing board of the National Council of Churches of Christ declared that after Columbus, America was the scene of "invasion, genocide, slavery, 'ecocide,'" and the "rape of mineral as well as natural resources." Genocide appeared nine times in their five-page statement.

How should historians, teachers, and students of history respond to this characterization? . . .

First, in the protest literature, "genocide" is never defined, perhaps on the assumption that we all know what it means. But do we? The word was coined in 1944 to describe the infamous Nazi attempts to annihilate the Jews, a group they chose to characterize as a biological subspecies or race. Webster's definition of genocide is not

Source: James Axtell, "The Moral Dimensions of 1492," *The Historian*, 1993, 56(1): 17–22, 24–25, 27–28. Reprinted with permission of Blackwell Publishing.

much help: the use "of deliberate, systematic measures toward the extermination of a racial, political, or cultural group." One of the best and most comprehensive definitions in the large literature of genocide is that of Frank Chalk and Kurt Jonassohn: "Genocide is a form of one-sided *mass* killing in which a *state* or other authority *intends* to destroy a group, as that group and membership in it are defined by the *perpetrator*." Such a definition excludes from consideration victims—civilian or military—of two-sided war, of any natural or unintended disaster, and of any individuals or "loose cannons" acting outside the orders of the state or political authority. The last are, more precisely, homicidal maniacs or mass murderers who massacre innocent people.

The examples most frequently adduced to support the charge of genocide are the Spaniards' wanton killing of Taínos in the gold-bearing interior of Hispaniola during Columbus' inept governorship in 1494–95, the high body counts of Indian warriors during the conquests of Peru and Mexico, and the precipitous decline of native populations in subsequent decades. These examples do not amount to relevant or unambiguous evidence of genocide. The conquest phases of the various European invasions of the Americas were dedicated to the achievement of military, political, economic, and religious hegemony over the native peoples, not their mass destruction, and they were aimed at temporary and numerically superior political and military opponents. In Central and South America, resistant native armies were targeted for defeat or destruction, but native populations per se were largely protected by Spanish law and colonial self-interest so as later to provide labor or tribute to the *encomenderos*. Crown officials were entrusted with their spiritual and, to some extent, physical well-being. In North America, native populations were equally vital to the military and economic needs of the European colonies, as allies against colonial rivals, as fur trappers and hunters, and as food producers.

The evidence for genocide from Indian population decline is ambiguous because newly imported epidemic diseases killed the vast majority of native Americans after contact. Gross demographical statistics—conjured from fragmentary figures and social-scientific assumptions and often inflated for moral or political reasons rather than historical necessity—are impossible to interpret clearly because they include the victims of intertribal warfare, migration and dislocation, and uncontrollable natural disasters, as well as overwork and other forms of colonial oppression.

Even enslavement and forced relocation of the natives of the Bahamas and other Caribbean islands do not constitute genocide because the intent of the Spanish slavers was not to annihilate the natives physically; on the contrary, it was to ensure their physical viability so they could provide free labor wherever they were needed by colonial entrepreneurs. There is no need to resort willy-nilly to inflated indictments of genocide when man-stealing, kidnapping, enslavement, and other accurate terms are available. If genocide is to retain any meaning or moral impact at all, it must not be applied wholesale to every Indian death in the colonial period. To do so is to dilute the meaning of the word to insipidity and to squander its intellectual and moral force.

This is not to say that bona fide cases of genocide cannot be found in colonial America. Although no European colonial government ever tried to exterminate all of the Indians as a race, there are at least five authorized colonial attempts to annihilate single tribes—men, women, and children. The Puritans of Massachusetts and Connecticut tried unsuccessfully to obliterate the Pequots of Connecticut in 1636–37. The French, who in Canada come off smelling like a moral rose in the textbooks, had better success in exterminating the Mississippi River Natchez and the Wisconsin Foxes in the 1730s. The English assaults on the Powhatan chiefdom in Virginia might be included, but these took place only after the sudden native uprising of 1622, which then gave the outnumbered settlers reason to believe they were repulsing a military attack and acting in justifiable self-defense.

Perhaps the most heinous act of genocide—from the vantage point of the "Age of AIDS"—was the calculated use of germ warfare, which was not resorted to, we should emphasize, for more than two-and-a-half centuries after Columbus' landing and then by only one European power that we know of. In 1752 the acting governor of Canada told his French superior in Paris that "twere desirable that [smallpox] should break out and spread, generally, through the localities inhabited by our rebels." By this he meant the Ohio Valley and Great Lakes tribesmen who were asserting their independence or switching their allegiance to the English. "It would be fully as good as an army," he concluded, with callous disregard for native women and children.

The French governor was only indulging in wishful thinking. The English commander for the same area put the thought into action eleven years later, during Pontiac's (so-called) Rebellion. In June 1763 Sir Jeffrey Amherst conspired with his field commander, Colonel Henry Bouquet, to send two blankets and two handkerchiefs from a smallpox hospital among the "rebellious" Delawares, Shawnees, and Ohio Senecas. By the following autumn it was reported that "The poor Rascals are Dieing very fast with the small pox; they can make but Lettle Resistance and when Routed from their settlements must parish in great Numbers by the Disorders." . . .

Granting that at least some Indian groups were the victims of colonial genocide, who is, or was, to blame specifically? The protestors blackwash with a broad brush. Sometimes Columbus is the archfiend. At other times, conquistadors, the Spanish, Europeans, white males, capitalists, and Christians, as well as a generalized, modern "we" are condemned to share the admiral's guilt. Such charges are neither responsible history nor acceptable morality. The major problem with genocide as a description of, or even analogy to, the post-Columbian loss of life is that the moral onus it tries to place on the European colonists—equating them with Heinrich Himmler and the Nazi S.S.—is misdirected and inappropriate. As Edmund Burke warned in the late eighteenth century and as we have come to realize in the twentieth, "you cannot"—or rather, *should* not—"indict a whole nation" for the misdeeds and crimes of a few. The colonists were personally and directly guilty for only a small fraction of the Indians who died in the three centuries after contact. Disease, not the Spanish, was responsible for most of the native deaths in Latin America. Genocide, as distinguished from other forms of cruelty, oppression, and death, played a very small role in the European conquest of the New World. . . .

None of these criticisms should be construed as an argument against the legitimacy and utility of judging the past. Historians do it all the time, we are incapable of not doing it, and we should do it. But we should do it well and we should do it for valid reasons, not because our knees or trigger fingers twitch every time we open a history book.

We judge the past for at least three important reasons. The first is to appraise action, an intrinsic part of historical thinking. Not to make such judgments is to abandon the past to itself, rendering it unintelligible and untranslatable to the present. The second reason is to do justice to it, although making judgment is not the same as passing sentence. As historians, we are too involved in both the prosecution and the defense since the words and reputations of the dead on all sides are in our hands. History's goal is not to punish or rehabilitate historical malefactors, who are morally incorrigible in any event, but to set the record straight for future appeals to precedent. The third reason for judging the past is to advance our own moral education, to learn from and, in effect, to be judged by the past. Since we think and speak historically for our own generation, we can have judgmental effect only on ourselves. Consequently, history becomes, in Lord Bolingbroke's famous phrase, "philosophy teaching by example," a "preceptor of prudence, not of principles." After bearing witness to the past with all the disinterestedness and human empathy we can muster, we should let ourselves be judged by the past as much as, or more than, we judge it. The past is filled with the lives and struggles of countless "others," from whom we may learn to extend the possibilities of our own limited humanity. As we learn about what it is like to be other than ourselves, we are better able to do justice to the past.

The relationship between the past and the present is always troubled and troubling. Historians cannot help but draw on the past for materials, methods, and models. Our self-images and social foundations are fabricated from historical elements, all inherited but reshaped by our current needs and biases, and then rewoven by our flawed and fluid memories. We need the past to give us bearings, but we often construct pasts that are merely useful and undemanding, more wishful than true. This leads to serious problems for historians because we cannot cure inherited social ills or make moral amends for past wrongs unless we know how the past actually was. It is perhaps the profession's most important task to ensure that our image of the past is as nearly full, complex, and true as the past itself was, lest we lose our bearings in fantasy and waste our resources and moral energies on false trails. . . .

Historians are particularly well qualified to take additional steps to prevent present and future generations from perpetuating unthinkingly attitudes and actions that have damaged people in the past. We can inspire and teach students to read enough history to realize that our current fortunes and misfortunes are the product of complicated, interlocking, ongoing human stories whose next chapters do not have to be written the same way. We can work to include slighted peoples in the mainstream, not the mere eddies, of our national or continental history. In the process, of course, we must strive to fashion a new synthesis that does justice to our checkered and polychromatic past, with narratives that resemble intelligible mosaics rather than jumbled grab-bags of shreds and tatters. Finally, we can work conscientiously to destroy maleficent myths without erecting politically correct or convenient new myths in their place. Myths of any kind commit the most basic kind of injustice against the past and hobble us and our successors. Only by learning and teaching history that is palpably real, scrupulously fair, and recognizable to all the participants of the past, not merely their interested descendants in the present, will we fulfill our most important social obligation and render the past the highest form of justice.

How the Movement for Slave Reparations Has Gone Global

MARTHA BIONDI

Reparations—for the transatlantic slave trade, slavery, sexual slavery, genocide, colonialism, apartheid, disfranchisement, and the multiple other forms of racial discrimination and exploitation—has surged to the forefront of antiracist advocacy in the black world, particularly in the United States. It offers an innovative and compelling way to move beyond inadequate and besieged civil rights discourses, to revive black-led global anticapitalist and anti-imperialist projects, and to radically intervene in the discourse of globalization. Indeed, in light of the expansion of international juridical forums and precedents, the recent rise of reparations is inseparable from the rise of globalization. The philosophical and tactical brilliance of reparations lies in its synthesis of moral principles and political economy. If the crimes and depredations inflicted on African nations and African descendants over centuries have relied on strategies of dehumanization in the service of power, profit, and conquest, then the efforts to identify, halt, and redress them must insist on explicit acknowledgment and repudiation of such strategies, alongside comprehensive material efforts to indemnify them. Rather than a retreat into narrow nationalism, as many have cast(igated) it, reparations represents the culmination of a long African American human rights struggle.

The biggest achievement in the rapidly growing reparations movement was the 2001 (finalized in 2002) declaration of the United Nations World Conference against Racism, Racial Discrimination, Xenophobia, and Related Intolerance that "slavery and the transatlantic slave trade are a crime against humanity." This document vindicates the long labors of Ida B. Wells, W. E. B. Du Bois, Monroe Trotter, Marcus Garvey, Paul Robeson, Mary McLeod Bethune, William Patterson, Audley Moore, Malcolm X, Huey Newton, and Imari Obadele to use international bodies and the collective power of African and Asian nations to force the West to confront its own history. In the United States, the World Conference against Racism has drawn heightened attention to reparations initiatives already underway. The Reparations Coordinating Committee (RCC) and the National Coalition of Blacks for Reparations in America (N'COBRA), working on behalf of 35 million American descendants of enslaved Africans, is preparing to file class action lawsuits against agencies of the federal and state governments. Reparations litigation against private corporations alleged to have profited from slavery has already begun. On March 25, 2002, in a U.S. district court in Brooklyn, Deadria Farmer-Paellmann and other plaintiffs filed suit against Aetna Life Insurance Corporation, FleetBoston Financial Services, and CSX Incorporated, a railroad giant, on the grounds that they "knowingly benefited from a system that enslaved, tortured, starved and exploited human beings."

Still, reparations is not a new demand in African American advocacy. In the nineteenth century, many former slaves expressed the view that the slave system

Source: From Martha Biondi, "The Rise of the Reparations Movement [excerpts]," *Radical History Review*, Volume 87, pp. 5–9, 13–17. Copyright © 2003, MARHO: The Radical Historians Organization, Inc. Used by permission of the publisher.

constituted a theft of labor, life, and liberty that demanded an accounting. After the Civil War, landownership constituted a major goal of the former slaves who strongly supported the confiscation, division, and redistribution of large plantations. There were several federal attempts to do this, the most famous being General Sherman's Field Order #15, which divided plantations along the Atlantic Coast into forty-acre parcels to be distributed to 40,000 emancipated workers. However, these efforts to construct a foundation for a free labor system in the South—which were not necessarily motivated by a desire to compensate the former slaves for expropriated labor— were later reversed or defeated. In contrast, many slaveholders received compensation for the loss of their slave "property." The U.S. government compensated slave owners on the abolition of slavery in the District of Columbia, and Haiti was forced to pay $150 million in compensation to the French after it achieved independence.

The federal government's betrayal of a promise to transfer land to the former slaves became a foundational story in the oral history of Reconstruction passed down in black families and communities into the twentieth century. Deadria Farmer-Paellmann—the lead plaintiff in the class action lawsuit against Aetna and the researcher who discovered that the company had written life insurance policies on human property—said, "My grandfather always talked about the forty acres and a mule which we were never given." In his 1960s song "Forty Acres and a Mule," Oscar Brown Jr. reminded his listeners that "ain't nobody paid for slavery yet, we had a promise that was taken back."

With northern migration and urbanization, land receded as a primary demand, but the belief that the United States owed a debt to the descendants of enslaved Africans animated twentieth-century black protest and was a much more visible theme in the civil rights/black liberation movement than historical accounts generally acknowledge. In 1955, Audley Moore, a Harlem activist originally from Louisiana, founded the Reparations Committee of Descendants of United States Slaves. "Queen Mother" Moore pioneered grassroots education on reparations and for the next three decades dedicated herself to spreading the message among black activists and intellectuals. She planted the seed in a young Charles Ogletree Jr. when he was seated next to her on a flight to Tanzania. Currently a professor at Harvard Law School, Ogletree cochairs the RCC with Adjoa Aiyetoro and Randall Robinson. In his 1963 book, *Why We Can't Wait*, Martin Luther King Jr. argued that the United States owed social and economic compensation to black America for the wrongs of slavery and segregation and vowed to make this the next goal of the black freedom struggle. The A. Philip Randolph Institute lobbied Congress for what it called a Freedom Budget, and the National Urban League advocated a "Marshall Plan for Black America," remedies that embodied the spirit of reparations by insisting on the government's obligation to financially repair the group harm caused by institutionalized racism. The 1969 "Black Manifesto" by James Forman, a leader of the Student Non-Violent Coordinating Committee, demanded reparations in the form of a southern land bank, publishing houses, television networks, universities, and skills training centers. Forman envisioned reparations as an opportunity to reverse the consequences of racial capitalism and promote thoroughgoing social and economic development in black America.

Reparations has long been a goal for a range of U.S. black nationalist groups, usually in concert with the quest for territory and political self-determination. In the late nineteenth century, Henry McNeal Turner, a prominent AME Bishop, critic of U.S. imperialism, and advocate of African American emigration to Africa, called for $40 billion in reparations for slavery. Beginning in the 1940s, the Nation of Islam urged reparations for slavery and called on the federal government to cede several southern states to become the territory of an African American nation. In 1968, the Republic of New Africa called for reparations in tandem with its insistence that neither the former slaves nor their descendants had ever been given the option of imagining themselves as an independent nation. The Black Panther Party shared this view and put its own call for reparations alongside a demand for a U.N.-sponsored plebiscite in which black people could express a position on their national aspirations. Personifying the links between past and present reparations advocacy, Imari Obadele, one of the founders of the Republic of New Africa, also cofounded N'COBRA in 1988, currently the largest grassroots reparations organization in the United States.

The contemporary reparations struggle also builds on two hallmarks of the black radical tradition: an economic analysis of white supremacy and the use of global solidarity networks and international forums to define national racisms as a violation of international human rights protocols. Black farmers, who filed a class action lawsuit in 1999 against the U.S. Department of Agriculture for discriminatory lending that caused the loss of their land, call their struggle "economic human rights," a phrase that captures the essence of the reparations struggle as well. In the last few years of his life, King came to emphasize what W. E. B. Du Bois had underscored earlier, namely, that legal and political rights would not bring racial equality unless they were accompanied by a confrontation with the economic dimension of white supremacy past and present. Each argued that the fruits of slave labor and subsequent black labor exploitation nurtured American capitalism, which remained hostile to black economic development. Like some other African American antiracist activists who started out as integrationists, they each came to argue that the U.S. political economy needed a fundamental transformation in order to value black humanity and create the conditions for black economic empowerment.

Similarly, reparations builds on a long tradition of black internationalism and pan-Africanist organizing. After World War I, W. E. B. Du Bois organized a pan-African congress in Paris to exert influence on the Paris peace talks. Since World War II, several African American rights groups have filed petitions seeking U.N. intervention in the United States to halt the systematic violation of the human rights of black people. Malcolm X's preference for "human rights" over "civil rights" reflected his efforts to politically connect black Americans to a global history of slavery and slave trading and guided his attempts to gain the solidarity of African nations for a petition to the United Nations. Reparations, in short, is neither foreign nor marginal to African American political advocacy. It has been championed most visibly and consistently by black nationalists, yet liberals and leftists, too, have supported remedies and analyses that embody the spirit of reparations.

Still, the reparations movement has never enjoyed greater popularity among African Americans or mainstream black leadership than now, 138 years after the official end of slavery. A variety of developments account for its growing appeal. An important context for the rise of the reparations movement is the growing number of national and international settlements in which governments or corporations have been made to atone for and/or compensate a group they knowingly victimized, murdered, deprived of liberty or property, or otherwise wronged. In 1988, Congress granted an apology and compensation to the survivors and relatives of Japanese Americans imprisoned in concentration camps during the Second World War. This had a significant impact on African American organizing, sparking the formation of N'COBRA. A year after the Japanese American settlement, John Conyers, a U.S. representative from Michigan, introduced H.R. 40, a bill calling for the federal government to study the impact of slavery and make recommendations for reparations to the 35 million American descendants. In 1994, the state of Florida agreed to pay reparations to the survivors of the 1923 Rosewood massacre, and in 1993, Congress formally apologized for the U.S. conquest of Hawaii and the deprivation of sovereignty. These cases indicate the government's willingness to financially repair past injustices motivated by racial hatred, although the Rosewood and Japanese internment cases differ from the slavery case because they grant compensation to individual victims with a demonstrated link to the injustice.

Internationally, many precedents for reparations exist. The German government and private corporations have paid $65.2 billion to survivors of the death camps and forced laborers during the Holocaust. Germany has also paid reparations to the state of Israel, a redress that resembles the African American case somewhat, since the reparation is not made to actual victims of the Holocaust but to Jews collectively through the state of Israel. More recent cases against corporations for using slave laborers in wartime Germany won large settlements and have inspired similar litigation in the United States. In recent years, several countries including Argentina and South Africa have established commissions to investigate the injury and harms inflicted during apartheid or periods of military dictatorship. In contrast, the United States has never authorized an examination of this nation's participation in the enslavement of Africans and the segregation and labor exploitation of their descendants. There is neither a national slavery museum nor a memorial to the millions who perished in the transatlantic slave trade. . . .

The United Nations has emerged as an extraordinary stage for the reparations movement. Over a decade of advocacy and organizing at the U.N. Human Rights Commission by (among other African American groups) the December 12th Movement, led the United Nations to convene the World Conference against Racism, Racial Discrimination, Xenophobia, and Related Intolerance in Durban, South Africa, in September 2001. There had been other U.N. world conferences, including one on human rights in Vienna in 1993 and on the status of women in Beijing in 1996. In 1997, the lobbying of several African, Asia, Latin American, and Caribbean nations secured a commitment by the U.N. for a world conference against racism. In planning meetings, the African Descendants Caucus brought together reparations activists from across the diaspora, including representatives from many U.S. groups: The December 12th Movement, N'COBRA, All for Reparations and Emancipation—a group associated with the Lost/Found Nation of Islam—the Black Radical Congress, and the National Black United Front (NBUF). They formulated an agenda for Durban that stressed three goals: to characterize the institution of slavery and the transatlantic slave trade as crimes against humanity (crimes against humanity have no statute of limitations in international law); to assert the economic motive of white supremacy; and to call for reparations. From the earliest preparatory stages, the

United States and the European Union worked aggressively to contain the political reach of the World Conference against Racism—indeed, the words "xenophobia and related intolerance" were added as a concession to the West; the conference was originally intended to have an exclusive focus on Africa and African descendants.

The December 12th Movement and NBUF helped to organize the African American NGOs contingent to the World Conference against Racism, which became known as the Durban 400. Fully cognizant of U.S. and E.U. opposition to their agenda, the Durban 400 aggressively lobbied African, Asian, and Latin American nations to support it. When it became clear that getting a call for reparations into the document was unlikely, the Durban 400 focused on having slavery and the transatlantic slave trade declared as crimes against humanity. Gaining the support of the forty-five African nations present proved decisive. Some nations, like Senegal and Zimbabwe, were very supportive from the beginning, but Nigeria and South Africa proved harder to persuade, although they ultimately endorsed it. Evidently, South Africa, whose economic development strategy relies heavily on Western investment, feared alienating the United States.

Representatives of the U.S. government opposed the designation of transatlantic slavery as "a crime against humanity" as well as the effort to include a call for reparations in the final document. The United States threatened to boycott Durban and ultimately only sent lower-level officials, who subsequently engaged in a highly publicized walkout. The United States and Israel had also protested efforts by Middle Eastern nations to characterize the Israeli treatment of Palestinians as akin to colonial conquest and occupation. The mainstream media coverage of the U.S. walkout tended to characterize it as a principled pro-Israeli act, rather than as a cowardly retreat from confronting the history and legacy of slavery.

In the end, the Durban Declaration and Programme of Action signed by 168 nations declared that slavery and the transatlantic slave trade "are crimes against humanity," a determination that reparations advocates hope will make the United States more vulnerable in legal action. One caveat is that the document modifies this assertion with the clause, "and should always have been so, especially the transatlantic slave trade." This constitutes an apparent concession to those who argue that slavery was widespread and "lawful" in many parts of the world and is seen as a crime against humanity only in retrospect. Even though the Programme of Action failed to include advocacy of reparations, activists still view it as an extremely important achievement. Despite the U.S. walkout, and the country's failure to sign the document, the World Conference against Racism pushed the issue of reparations irrevocably into international political and media discourse. Moreover, reparations remains a hot-button issue for the body created by the United Nations to implement the results of the conference: the Working Group of Experts on People of African Descent living in the Diaspora. This working group, whose stature and seriousness remains unclear, is charged with considering the means to eliminate racial discrimination.

Reparations advocates hope to develop and institutionalize the transnational organizing and solidarity that proved so effective at the World Conference against Racism. Toward this end, the African and African Descendant NGO Follow-Up Conference convened in October 2002 in Bridgetown, Barbados, drawing six hundred people. The conference began on a note of controversy when a delegation from the United Kingdom offered a resolution to expel the twenty or so non-African descendants in attendance—reportedly a diverse group which included a Euro- and Asian American couple making a documentary on reparations, a Lebanese activist who came to offer solidarity from the Palestinian struggle, and several white Barbadians working as official translators. After a long debate, conferees passed the resolution, but a few delegations walked out in protest, including the one from Cuba. The varying perspectives on the expulsion shed light on the strains that can arise in a movement that includes a variety of ideological tendencies. Some activists expressed concern that the expulsion would stigmatize the reparations movement as "hypernationalist." They emphasized the urgency of repairing the rifts, particularly with the Cubans, who have a long record of support for African American and African liberation struggles. Yet others have argued that the attention to this issue has been excessive and have defended the expulsion on the grounds that only Africans and African descendants had been invited. The conference generated the Bridgetown Protocols, and the creation of a new organization, the Global Afrikan Congress, whose mission is to implement them.

The movement for reparations in other nations has also grown in recent years, although not quite as quickly or as broadly as it has in the United States. A major turning point in the development of support for reparations by African nations was the 1993 Abuja Proclamation sponsored by the Organization of African Unity's Reparations Commission. Many activists in Africa identify debt cancellation as an essential first step in reparations. The U.S. human rights organization, Africa Action, has condemned the "illegitimate, immoral and crippling foreign debt that African countries owe to the wealthy white countries and the international institutions that represent their economic interests." Every year, forty-eight countries in sub-Saharan Africa pay $13.5 billion to "rich foreign creditors for past loans of questionable legitimacy."

As in the United States, activists in other nations are using litigation against both corporations and nation-states to redress colonialism, slavery, and the slave trade. In Jamaica, attorneys have begun filing what will be a series of lawsuits against European nations in order to recover wealth acquired through the slave trade. They recently filed a case against the British monarchy and served a writ on the Queen of England when she visited Jamaica this past year. Litigation will follow against France, Germany, and Belgium, and later against Spain and Portugal. In Namibia, the Herrero ethnic group filed a lawsuit against three German corporations for genocide committed against their ancestors during German colonial rule. The Democratic Republic of Congo has charged Belgium with genocide for the slaughter of millions during a ruthless colonial regime as well as for the assassination of independence leader Patrice Lumumba.

The strategy of corporate litigation has taken off in South Africa, much to the concern of the government, which worries about alienating Western investors. Ed Fagan, an attorney who won a settlement from Swiss banks for victims of the Jewish Holocaust, has filed suit against a variety of corporations on behalf of victims of apartheid. Additionally, in November 2002, two activist groups in South Africa filed suit in a U.S. federal court against twenty global corporations for allegedly encouraging human rights abuses by doing business in apartheid South Africa. The companies ignored a boycott of Pretoria called by the United Nations and supplied the apartheid regime with loans and markets. The litigation, which seeks billions from oil companies, automakers, and banks, reflects, in part, the slowness of the Truth and Reconciliation Commission in awarding their extremely small pledges of reparations. Reflecting the clash between postapartheid social justice aspirations and the triumph of a market-oriented regime, the South African justice minister Penuell Maduna said, "We are not supporting the claims for individual reparations. We are talking to those very same companies named in the lawsuits about investing in post-apartheid South Africa." The government, however, is not taking a formal position on the litigation.

As the reparations movement stands poised to intensify with the imminent federal litigation, some progressives have raised concerns about the movement's progress toward achieving its post-Durban aim of creating a "critical mass demand for reparations" and expanding the movement's base to reach all sectors of the African American community. The high profile participation of attorneys new to the reparations movement has alienated some veteran activists. One journalist quipped that the Millions for Reparations Rally in Washington, DC, in August 2002 constituted an effort by nationalists to recapture leadership of the movement. Perhaps, inevitably, some ideological strains have accompanied the expansion of the movement. Unity and coordination, however, will prove urgent for organizing successful mass demonstrations or other grassroots mobilizations. Finally, the particular exploitation of black women has remained undertheorized and underdiscussed in the movement, although this can be overcome. Will, for example, the pending litigation address sexual slavery or the abuses of the reproductive liberty of African American women since emancipation? According to reparations activists, the primary challenge for the movement lies less in finding the foolproof legal argument or locating the best jurisdiction, but in building grassroots support for reparations, both in the United States and around the world.

FURTHER READING

Bailey, Anne C. *African Voices of the Atlantic Slave Trade: Beyond the Silence and the Shame.* Boston: Beacon Press, 2005.

Barkan, Elazar, and Alexander Karn, eds. *Taking Wrongs Seriously: Apologies and Reconciliation.* Stanford, CA: Stanford University Press, 2006.

Berry, Mary Frances. *My Face Is Black Is True: Callie House and the Struggle for Ex-Slave Reparations.* New York: Alfred A. Knopf, 2005.

Braxton, Joanne M., and Maria I. Diedrich, eds. *Monuments of the Black Atlantic: Slavery and Memory.* Münster: LIT; Distributed in North America by Transaction Publishers, 2004.

Gould, Stephen Jay. "The Hottentot Venus." In *The Flamingo's Smile*, 291–305. New York: W. W. Norton and Company, 1985.

Holmes, Rachel. *African Queen: The Real Life of the Hottentot Venus.* New York: Random House, 2007.

Karp, Ivan, and Steven Lavine, eds. *Exhibiting Cultures.* Washington and London: Smithsonian Institution Press, 1991.

Kowaleski Wallace, Elizabeth. *The British Slave Trade and Public Memory.* New York: Columbia University Press, 2006.

Osagie, Iyunolu Folayan. *The Amistad Revolt: Memory, Slavery, and the Politics of Identity in the United States and Sierra Leone.* Athens: University of Georgia Press, 2000.

Reinhardt, Catherine A. *Claims to Memory: Beyond Slavery and Emancipation in the French Caribbean.* New York: Berghahn Books, 2006.

Robinson, Randall. *The Debt: What America Owes to Blacks*. New York: Dutton, 2000.

Royal, Robert. *1492 and All That: Political Manipulations of History*. Washington, DC: Ethics and Public Policy Center, 1992.

Sale, Kirkpatrick. *The Conquest of Paradise: Christopher Columbus and the Columbian Legacy*. New York: Knopf, 1990.

Summerhill, Stephen J., and John Alexander Williams. *Sinking Columbus: Contested History, Cultural Politics, and Mythmaking During the Quincentenary*. Gainesville: University Press of Florida, 2000.

Torpey, John, ed. *Politics and the Past: On Repairing Historical Injustices*. Lanham, MD: Rowman & Littlefield, 2003.

Winbush, Raymond A. *Should America Pay?: Slavery and the Raging Debate over Reparations*. New York: Amistad, 2003.

Yewell, John, Chris Dodge, and Jan DeSirey, eds. *Confronting Columbus: An Anthology*. Jefferson, NC: McFarland and Company, 1992.